NP 54

NORTH SEA (WEST) PILOT

**East coasts of Scotland and England
from Rattray Head to Southwold**

**FIFTH EDITION
2000**

PUBLISHED BY THE HYDROGRAPHER OF THE NAVY

To be obtained from Agents
for the sale of Admiralty Charts and Publications

Area formerly covered by part of the following previous editions:

North Sea Pilot Volume. II

First Published 1857
2nd Edition 1868
3rd Edition 1875
4th Edition 1885
5th Edition 1895
6th Edition 1905
7th Edition 1914
8th Edition 1923
9th Edition 1935
10th Edition 1949
11th Edition 1959
12th Edition 1960

North Sea Pilot Volume. III

First Published 1858
2nd Edition 1869
3rd Edition 1874
4th Edition 1882
5th Edition 1889
6th Edition 1897
7th Edition 1905
8th Edition 1914
9th Edition 1922
10th Edition 1933
11th Edition 1948

North Sea (West) Pilot

First Published 1973
2nd Edition 1991
3rd Edition 1995
4th Edition 1997

PREFACE

The Fifth Edition of the North Sea (West) Pilot has been prepared by Lieutenant Commander J.E.J. Marshall, Royal Navy, and contains the latest information received in the United Kingdom Hydrographic Office to the date given below.

This edition supersedes the Fourth Edition (1997), which is cancelled.

Information on climate and currents has been based on data provided by the Meteorological Office, Bracknell.

The following sources of information, other than UKHO Publications and Ministry of Defence papers, have been consulted:

Local Port Authorities
Port Handbooks produced by Port Authorities
Directory of Harbours (Aberdeenshire Council) 1999
Fairplay World Ports Directory 1999–2000
Lloyds Ports of the World 1999
Lloyds Maritime Guide 1999–2000
Ports of Scotland (Graham Ogilvie) (1999/2000)
Coastguard Address List CG40 (1999)
RNLI Directory
Whitaker's Almanack 2000

J.P. Clarke CB LVO MBE
Rear Admiral
Hydrographer of the Navy

The United Kingdom Hydrographic Office
Admiralty Way
Taunton
Somerset TA1 2DN
England
20th July 2000

PREFACE
to the Third Edition (1995)

The Third Edition of the North Sea (West) Pilot has been compiled by Captain J. H. Gomersall, Master Mariner, and contains the latest information received by the Hydrographic Office to the date given below.

This edition supersedes the Second Edition (1991) which is cancelled.

Information on climate and currents has been based on data provided by the Meteorological Office, Bracknell.

The following sources of information, other than Hydrographic Office Publications and Ministry of Defence papers, have been consulted:

Guide to Port Entry 1992/93
Ports of the World 1993
Lloyds Maritime Guide 1990
Lloyds List
Royal Northumberland Yacht Club Sailing Directions 1990
United Kingdom Census 1981
Port Handbooks produced by Port Authorities

N. R. ESSENHIGH
Rear Admiral
Hydrographer of the Navy

Hydrographic Office
Ministry of Defence
Taunton
Somerset
England
21st January 1995

CONTENTS

Pages

Preface iii

Preface to the Third Edition (1995) iv

Contents v

Explanatory notes vii

Abbreviations ix

Index chartlet .... *facing 1*

CHAPTER 1

Navigation and regulations

    Limits of the book (1.1) 1

    Navigational dangers and hazards (1.2) 1

    Traffic and operations (1.8) 2

    Charts (1.25) 3

    Navigational aids (1.27) 4

    Pilotage (1.28) 4

    Radio facilities (1.32) 4

    Regulations (1.36) 4

    Signals (1.50) 7

    Distress and rescue (1.51) 7

Countries and ports

    United Kingdom (1.64) 10

    Principal ports, harbours and anchorages (1.75) 11

    Port services — summary (1.76) 12

Natural conditions

    Maritime topography (1.82) 14

    Currents, tidal streams and flow (1.83) 14

    Sea level and tides (1.88) 14

    Sea and swell (1.94) 15

    Sea water characteristics (1.97) 20

    Climate and weather (1.101) 20

    Climatic tables (1.129) 31

    Meteorological conversion table and scales (1.139) 41

CHAPTER 2

The Western Part of the North Sea 43

CHAPTER 3

Rattray Head to Isle of May 49

CHAPTER 4

Firth of Forth and River Forth 81

CHAPTER 5

Isle of May to River Tyne 109

CHAPTER 6

River Tyne to River Humber 139

CHAPTER 7

River Humber 165

CHAPTER 8

River Humber to Cromer including The Wash 185

CHAPTER 9

Cromer to Southwold 201

APPENDICES AND INDEX

Appendix I — Regulations for the Dockyard Port of Rosyth 218

Appendix II — Extracts from Forth Byelaws and General Directions for Navigation 222

Appendix III — The Territorial Waters Order in Council 226

Index 232

EXPLANATORY NOTES

Admiralty Sailing Directions are intended for use by vessels of 12 m or more in length. They amplify charted detail and contain information needed for safe navigation which is not available from Admiralty charts, or other hydrographic publications. They are intended to be read in conjunction with the charts quoted in the text.

This volume of the Sailing Directions will be kept up-to-date by the issue of a new edition at intervals of approximately 3 years, without the use of supplements. In addition important corrections which cannot await the new edition are published in Section IV of the weekly editions of *Admiralty Notices to Mariners*. A list of such corrections and notices in force is published in the last weekly edition for each month. Those still in force at the end of the year are reprinted in the *Annual Summary of Admiralty Notices to Mariners*.

This volume should not be used without reference to Section IV of the weekly editions of Admiralty Notices to Mariners.

References to hydrographic and other publications

The Mariner's Handbook gives general information affecting navigation and is complementary to this volume.

Ocean Passages for the World and *Routeing Charts* contain ocean routeing information and should be consulted for other than coastal passages.

Admiralty List of Lights should be consulted for details of lights, lanbys and fog signals, as these are not fully described in this volume.

Admiralty List of Radio Signals should be consulted for information relating to coast and port radio stations, radio details of pilotage services, radiobeacons and direction finding stations, meteorological services, radio navigational aids, Global Maritime Distress and Safety System (GMDSS) and Differential Global Positioning System (DGPS) stations, as these are only briefly referred to in this volume.

Annual Summary of Admiralty Notices to Mariners contains in addition to the temporary and preliminary notices, and corrections and notices affecting Sailing Directions, a number of notices giving information of a permanent nature covering radio messages and navigational warnings, distress and rescue at sea and exercise areas.

The International Code of Signals should be consulted for details of distress and life-saving signals, international ice-breaker signals as well as international flag signals.

Remarks on subject matter

Buoys are generally described in detail only when they have special navigational significance, or where the scale of the chart is too small to show all the details clearly.

Chart Index Diagrams in this volume show only those Admiralty charts of a suitable scale to give good coverage of the area. Mariners should consult NP 131 *Catalogue of Admiralty Charts and Publications* for details of larger scale charts.

Chart references in the text normally refer to the largest scale Admiralty chart but occasionally a smaller scale chart may be quoted where its use is more appropriate.

Firing, practice and exercise areas. Except for submarine exercise areas, details of firing, practice and exercise areas are not mentioned in Sailing Directions, but signals and buoys used in connection with these areas are sometimes mentioned if significant for navigation. Attention is invited to the Annual Notice to Mariners on this subject.

Names have been taken from the most authoritative source. When an obsolete name still appears on the chart, it is given in brackets following the proper name at the principal description of the feature in the text and where the name is first mentioned.

Tidal information relating the daily vertical movements of the water is not given; for this *Admiralty Tide Tables* should be consulted. Changes in water level of an abnormal nature are mentioned.
Time difference used in the text when applied to the time of High Water found from the *Admiralty Tide Tables*, gives the time of the event being described in the Standard Time kept in the area of that event. Due allowance must be made for any seasonal daylight saving time which may be kept.

Wreck information is included where drying or below-water wrecks are relatively permanent features having significance for navigation or anchoring.

Units and terminology used in this volume

Latitude and Longitude given in brackets are approximate and are taken from the chart quoted.

Bearings and directions are referred to the true compass and when given in degrees are reckoned clockwise from 000° (North) to 359°
Bearings used for positioning are given from the reference object.
Bearings of objects, alignments and light sectors are given as seen from the vessel.
Courses always refer to the course to be made good over the ground.

Winds are described by the direction from which they blow.

Tidal streams and currents are described by the direction towards which they flow.

Distances are expressed in sea miles of 60 to a degree of latitude and sub-divided into cables of one tenth of a sea mile.

Depths are given below chart datum, except where otherwise stated.

Heights of objects refer to the height of the structure above the ground and are invariably expressed as "... m in height".

Elevations, as distinct from heights, are given above Mean High Water Springs or Mean Higher High Water whichever is quoted in *Admiralty Tide Tables*, and expressed as, "an elevation of ... m". However the elevation of natural features such as hills may alternatively be expressed as "... m high" since in this case there can be no confusion between elevation and height.

Metric units are used for all measurements of depths, heights and short distances, but where feet/fathoms charts are referred to, these latter units are given in brackets after the metric values for depths and heights shown on the chart.

Time is expressed in the four-figure notation beginning at midnight and is given in local time unless otherwise stated. Details of local time kept will be found in the relevant *Admiralty List of Radio Signals*.

Bands is the word used to indicate horizontal marking.

Stripes is the word used to indicate markings which are vertical, unless stated to be diagonal.

Conspicuous objects are natural and artificial marks which are outstanding, easily identifiable and clearly visible to the mariner over a large area of sea in varying conditions of light. If the scale is large enough they will normally be shown on the chart in bold capitals and may be marked "conspic".

Prominent objects are those which are easily identifiable, but do not justify being classified as conspicuous.

ABBREVIATIONS

The following abbreviations are used in the text.

Directions

N	north (northerly, northward, northern, northernmost)		S	south
NNE	north-north-east		SSW	south-south-west
NE	north-east		SW	south-west
ENE	east-north-east		WSW	west-south-west
E	east		W	west
ESE	east-south-east		WNW	west-north-west
SE	south-east		NW	north-west
SSE	south-south-east		NNW	north-north-west

Navigation

DGPS	Differential Global Positioning System		Satnav	Satellite navigation
GPS	Global Positioning System		TSS	Traffic Separation Scheme
Lanby	Large automatic navigation buoy		VTS	Vessel Traffic Services
ODAS	Ocean Data Acquisition System		VTMS	Vessel Traffic Management System

Offshore Operations

ALC	Articulated loading column		FSO	Floating storage and offloading vessel
ALP	Articulated loading platform		SALM	Single anchor leg mooring system
CALM	Catenary anchor leg mooring		SALS	Single anchored leg storage system
ELSBM	Exposed location single buoy mooring		SBM	Single buoy mooring
FPSO	Floating Production Storage and Offloading vessel		SPM	Single point mooring

Organizations

IALA	International Association of Lighthouse Authorities		IMO	International Maritime Organization
			NATO	North Atlantic Treaty Organization
IHO	International Hydrographic Organization		RN	Royal Navy

Radio

DF	direction finding		RT	radio telephony
HF	high frequency		UHF	ultra high frequency
LF	low frequency		VHF	very high frequency
MF	medium frequency		WT	radio (wireless) telegraphy
Navtex	Navigational Telex System			

Rescue and distress

AMVER	Automated Mutual Assistance Vessel Rescue System		MRCC	Maritime Rescue Co-ordination Centre
			MRSC	Maritime Rescue Sub-Centre
EPIRB	Emergency Position Indicating Radio Beacon		SAR	Search and Rescue
GMDSS	Global Maritime Distress and Safety System			

Tides

HAT	Highest Astronomical Tide		MHWS	Mean High Water Springs
HW	High Water		MLHW	Mean Lower High Water
LAT	Lowest Astronomical Tide		MLLW	Mean Lower Low Water
LW	Low Water		MLW	Mean Low Water
MHHW	Mean Higher High Water		MLWN	Mean Low Water Neaps
MHLW	Mean Higher Low Water		MLWS	Mean Low Water Springs
MHW	Mean High Water		MSL	Mean Sea Level
MHWN	Mean High Water Neaps			

Times

ETA	estimated time of arrival		UT	Universal Time
ETD	estimated time of departure		UTC	Co-ordinated Universal Time

Units and Miscellaneous

°C	degrees Celsius	km	kilometre(s)
dwt	deadweight tonnage	kn	knot(s)
feu	forty foot equivalent unit	kw	kilowatt(s)
fm	fathom(s)	m	metre(s)
ft	foot(feet)	mb	millibar(s)
g/cm^3	gram per cubic centimetre	MHz	megahertz
GRP	glass reinforced plastic	mm	millimetre(s)
grt	gross register tonnage	MW	megawatt(s)
gt	gross tonnage	No	number
hp	horse power	nrt	nett register tonnage
hPa	hectopascal	teu	twenty foot equivalent unit
kHz	kilohertz		

Vessels and cargo

HMS	Her (His) Majesty's Ship	POL	Petrol, Oil & Lubricants
LASH	Lighter Aboard Ship	RMS	Royal Mail Ship
LNG	Liquefied Natural Gas	Ro-Ro	Roll-on, Roll-off
LOA	Length overall	SS	Steamship
LPG	Liquefied Petroleum Gas	ULCC	Ultra Large Crude Carrier
MV	Motor Vessel	VLCC	Very Large Crude Carrier
MY	Motor Yacht		

NOTES

Chapter Index Diagram

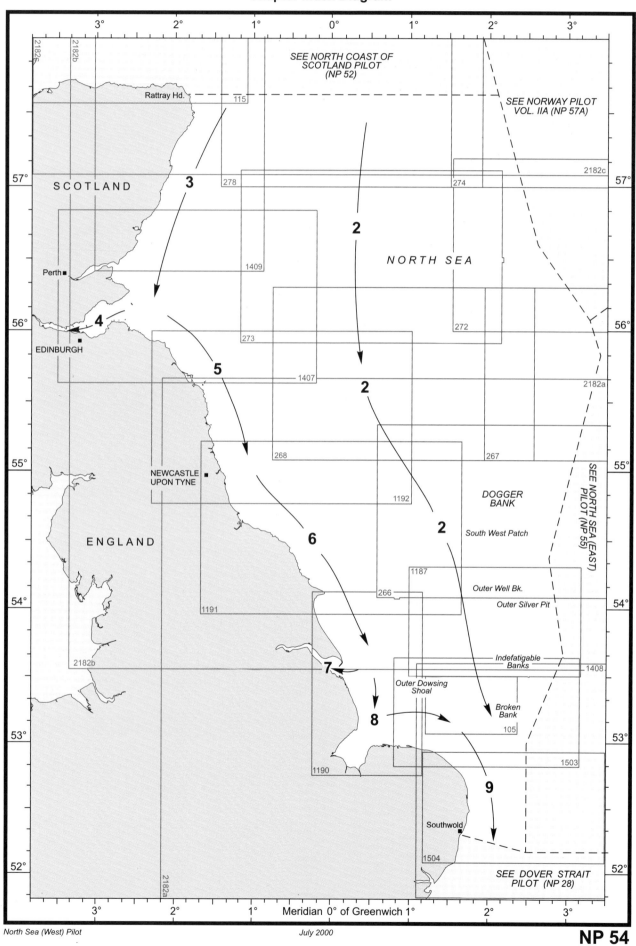

NORTH SEA (WEST) PILOT

CHAPTER 1

NAVIGATION AND REGULATIONS
COUNTRIES AND PORTS
NATURAL CONDITIONS

NAVIGATION AND REGULATIONS

LIMITS OF THE BOOK

Charts 2182A, 2182B

1.1

1   **Area covered.** This volume contains Sailing Directions for the coastal waters off the E coasts of Scotland and England from Rattray Head to Southwold, including the River Tay to Perth, the Firth of Forth and River Forth to Stirling, the River Tees to Stockton-on-Tees, the River Humber to its head, the River Trent to Gainsborough, the River Ouse to Goole, The Wash and for the sea area within the limits defined below:

	Lat N	Long E
2 Rattray Head (57°37′N, 1°49′W) E to	57°37′	2°06′
S along the UK Continental Shelf boundary, shown on the charts, to	53°40′·1	2°57′·4
SSW to	53°00′	2°30′
S to	52°10′	2°30′
WNW to a position close S of Southwold	52°18′	1°38′

NAVIGATIONAL DANGERS AND HAZARDS

Coastal conditions

General

1.2

1   In the N, prominent coastal topography permits reasonable positioning for navigation. In the S, numerous sandbanks, strong tidal streams, frequent poor visibility and a low coastline, which is rarely distinguishable at distances greater than 10 to 12 miles even in good weather, make navigation more hazardous.

2   In poor visibility, if at all doubtful of the vessel's position, it is safer to anchor until visibility is of the order of 2 to 3 miles rather than risk running aground on a sandbank, always providing there are no pipelines in the vicinity (see 1.37). It should be borne in mind that the tidal stream often sets across the banks, and the stream, especially at springs, is much stronger over the ridges than in the channels between. In these circumstances a vessel grounding during the flood is liable to be set further onto the bank as the tide rises.

3   South of the line Flamborough Head to the Texel, several large rivers enter the North Sea, including the Humber, Thames, Maas and Schelde. The approaches to these rivers are encumbered with sandbanks, making navigation difficult and even impracticable for deep draught vessels, without the assistance of working electronic navigation aids.

Rattray Head to Firth of Forth

1.3

1   The coast is mainly rocky and steep-to with no off-lying dangers except Bell Rock and the hazards off the entrance to the River Tay.

Firth of Forth to River Humber

1.4

1   The Farne Islands and other dangers extend up to 5 miles offshore. South of North Sunderland the dangers are limited to within 2 miles of the shore except in Bridlington Bay.

River Humber to Southwold
1.5

1   There are numerous sandbanks forming a series of ridges running parallel to the coast, and comparatively deep channels between them. The banks extend 45 miles NE of the Norfolk coast. The main navigable channels are buoyed and in reasonable visibility navigation through them is not too difficult.

2   Depths in the channels are such as to allow vessels to anchor almost anywhere, providing there are no pipelines in the vicinity. With offshore gales anchorage is usually safe especially close inshore or in the lee of the banks. The dangerous banks are marked by breakers during onshore gales, particularly when the tidal stream sets against the wind, and it is possible given adequate sounding to keep a safe distance on the lee side of the breakers and obtain some shelter.

Safe harbours and anchorage
1.6

1   Between the Firth of Forth and the River Humber, 200 miles to the S, there is no port that can be entered in all circumstances of wind and weather, except the Port of Tyne. The only safe harbour between the Rivers Humber and Thames is Harwich, see *Dover Strait Pilot*. Between these points therefore nothing is to be gained by staying close inshore during onshore winds.

2   Off Great Yarmouth there is a safe anchorage in the roads in most conditions, with excellent holding ground (9.50).

Ice
1.7

1   As a general rule ice does not form in any of the salt-water harbours covered by this volume.

TRAFFIC AND OPERATIONS

Traffic
1.8

1   There is regular traffic, including ferries, between the ports on the E coast of England and Scotland with those bordering the E side of the North Sea and in the Baltic. There is also considerable traffic between the E coast ports and North Sea oil and gas fields. Vessels coasting may therefore expect to meet others crossing their tracks. See diagram 2.17.

2   Many of the smaller ports have marinas and other facilities for recreational craft. Concentrations of these craft around such ports is common in the summer, particularly at weekends.

    High Speed Ferries operate in the area covered by this volume. Mariners are advised to keep a good lookout for such vessels.

Refuse burning at sea
1.9

1   Incinerator vessels burn chemical waste in the North Sea, often giving the appearance of a ship on fire. They may be at anchor or under way. In the latter case they may be restricted in their ability to manoeuvre in order to prevent smoke entering their own ship and they show the signals in Rule 27(b) of the *International Regulations for Preventing Collisions at Sea (1972)*.

2   Areas and times when incinerator vessels operate are broadcast in Radio Navigational Warnings. Vessels should pass to windward of incinerator vessels, or if passing to leeward, well clear of the smoke.

Fishing

General
1.10

1   **General.** The whole area covered by this volume, which lies within British fishery limits, is fished extensively and fishing vessels of many nationalities may be encountered. Exclusive fishing limits extend to 6 miles from the baselines of Territorial Waters and for the next 6 miles fishing is limited to countries with established rights.

2   Fishing vessels are often hampered and may need to make immediate and unannounced manoeuvres; other vessels are advised to keep well clear of them.

Methods of fishing employed
1.11

1   **Trawling** is undertaken by vessels of all sizes throughout the year over the entire area. The trawl, a funnel shaped net, may be set to fish at any level from the surface to the seabed, and may be towed by two vessels (pair trawling). Trawlers should be passed at least a cable clear by other vessels, noting that trawler speeds vary depending on the type of fish being sought.

2   Off the E coast of Scotland trawlers of all sizes operate from the Isle of May (56°11′N, 2°33′W) northward and eastward. Other grounds fished include a small area from 6 to 18 miles ESE of Saint Abb's Head (55°55′N, 2°08′W) and, in the late autumn, Great Fisher Bank (57°N, 4°E). Light trawlers fish throughout the year off Bell Rock (56°26′N, 2°23′W), Wee Bankie (56°12′N, 2°04′E), Saint Abb's Head, Longstone (55°39′N, 1°36′W) and the River Tyne. Nephrop trawling, from vessels restricted to less than 17 m in length, takes place in the Firth of Forth, as well as an area 12 miles E of the Isle of May and off North Carr Light-buoy (56°18′N, 2°33′W). Pair trawling for sprats is carried out from November to March in the Firth of Forth, off Longstone and North Shields (55°01′N, 1°26′W). There are no seasonal concentrations of trawlers.
1.12

1   **Seining** may be encountered over a wide area of the North Sea from 58°N to 61°N, between longitudes 0° to 3°E. Seine nets may extend up to 1½ miles from the seine net vessel. Smaller vessel operate the year round E of the Isle of May and off North Carr Light-buoy, through Wee Bankie to an area off the River Tyne. Seine net fishing by vessels restricted to less than 17 m in length may also be encountered in the Firth of Forth.
1.13

1   **Drifting**, although not common, is used over the whole area. Drifters shoot a long vertical wall of nets, suspended from the surface by floats or corks, to windward and then lie head to wind to leeward of their nets. Nets are set at varying depths depending on the fish being sought and may extend up to 1½ miles from the parent vessel; they are usually set at night.

2   From Berwick to Whitby numerous small drifters net salmon between April and August up to 6 miles offshore. They are prohibited from operating at weekends or between 2000 and 0400. Marker floats are not used but the vessels concerned are in close attendance. Inshore drifters operate off East Anglia, within 3 miles of the coast, between September and December.

3   Concentrations of drift-netting vessels should be given a wide berth, passing if possible to leeward away from the nets. If forced to do so, vessels should cross a line of nets at right angles midway between two floats, with propellers stopped.

1.14

1   **Potting** may be encountered off the coast anywhere in the area where conditions are suitable. The pots are often poorly marked by flags and do not carry lights.

1.15

1   **Long-line** fishing is carried out between latitudes 57°N and 59°N and longitudes 2°E and 3°E from April to September and in later summer on the Great Fisher Bank (57°N, 4°E).

2   There is also long-line fishing from small boats within 12 miles of the coast between the latitudes of 54°40′N and 53°40′N from October to March. The method involves anchoring gear to the seabed, marking by dan buoys, which are sometimes unlit, but this is not a hazard. Similar methods are employed by these boats when shell-fishing from April to September.

3   Small and hand line fishing is conducted by small craft working close to the minor ports which lie along the E coast.

1.16

1   **Cod net** fishing by means of anchored ground nets is used extensively the whole year on rough ground and in the vicinity of wrecks, between the latitudes of 55°45′N and 53°40′E. Nets, 600 m in length, are marked each end by a dan buoy and flag. They are supported by submerged floats and may be linked together to form a curtain. The method is occasionally used off the E coast of Scotland. The nets are only a few metres above the seabed and rarely a hazard.

1.17

1   **Creels**, which are crab and lobster traps, are set mainly in the summer months inshore on rocky ground. The fishing extends the whole length of the E Scottish coast, but is most intensive between Aberdeen and Berwick.

1.18

1   **Shrimping** is undertaken in The Wash by small vessels near the main channels. Minimum signals are shown by the vessels which sail on the out-going tide as far as Burnham Ridge and in the opposite direction on the in-going tide.

   Prawn fishing is undertaken by small vessels in an area off Tees Bay to the N of Ekofisk Oil Pipeline.

1.19

1   **Fish farms**, associated with fixed or floating structures, are charted approximately. They are marked by yellow beacons or buoys, which may be lit by yellow flashing lights.

Submarine and Gunnery Exercise Areas — Subfacts and Gunfacts

Naval exercises and firing practices

1.20

1   Practice exercise area (PEXA) charts Q6401 and Q6405 give details of British exercise areas covered by this volume. Details of the warning signals, naval exercises and firing practices for all British warships and submarines are given in the *Annual Summary of Admiralty Notices to Mariners* for the current year.

   For vessels requiring special consideration see *The Mariner's Handbook*.

2   **Subfacts.** Information relating to the activity of both surfaced and dived submarines off the S coast of England (see *Channel Pilot*) is broadcast by Brixham Coastguard and Falmouth Coastguard (Subfacts - South Coast). Information relating to the activity of submarines off the W coast of Scotland (see *West Coast of Scotland Pilot*) is broadcast by Belfast Coastguard, Clyde Coastguard and Stornoway Coastguard (Subfacts - Clyde). See the relevant *Admiralty List of Radio Signals* for details.

3   **Gunfacts.** Information relating to gunnery and missile firings of 20 mm calibre and above, and controlled underwater explosions in the South Coast Exercise Areas (see *Channel Pilot*), is broadcast by Brixham Coastguard and Falmouth Coastguard (Gunfacts - South Coast). Details of planned or known activity in the Scottish Exercise Areas is broadcast by Belfast Coastguard, Clyde Coastguard and Stornoway Coastguard (Gunfacts - Clyde). In all other areas, whenever firings are due to take place, warning broadcasts are made on VHF by a "Duty Broadcast Ship". See the relevant *Admiralty List of Radio Signals* for details.

Marine exploitation

General

1.21

1   Continental Shelf Boundaries, agreed between states bordering the North Sea and shown on the relevant charts, define the area in which states may exploit the natural resources of the seabed and its sub-soil. The area described in this volume lies entirely within the British Sector.

2   As conditions change from the shallower, relatively sheltered S of the North Sea to the deeper and more exposed N part, so various types of vessels and fixed structures are used in the development of oil and gas fields. Methods of search and production are described in *The Mariner's Handbook*.

Surveys

1.22

1   Seismic and other survey vessels surveying in connection with oil and gas fields are liable to be encountered throughout the North Sea. Seismic survey methods are outlined in *The Mariner's Handbook*.

Oil and gas fields

1.23

1   Drilling rigs and production platforms for the recovery of oil and gas are situated throughout the North Sea. Those in the S part of the area are usually associated with gas fields and those further N with oil fields. All structures are protected by safety zones extending to 500 m around them. A full description of these structures, safety zones, their identification markings, visual signals in use and other equipment associated with them is given in *The Mariner's Handbook*. A list of the oil and gas fields which lie within the limits of this volume is given at 2.17.

2   Many of these structures are interconnected and connected to shore by pipelines. See 1.36 and 1.37.

Dredging

1.24

1   Dredging for sand and gravel is carried out in the River Tay, off the Humber estuary, and on the shallow banks in the S part of the North Sea.

CHARTS

Admiralty Charts

1.25

1   **Source data.** The majority of charts are based on modern surveys, although some of the information used is still dependent on early lead and line work. Individual source data diagrams should be examined to ascertain the date and scale of the original surveys.

In some areas of frequent change periodic re-surveys are carried out.

1.26

1 **Horizontal datum.** Coastal charts are referred to the Ordnance Survey of Great Britain (1936) Datum and offshore charts normally to the European Datum (1950). Satellite derived positions are normally referred to World Geodetic System 1984 (WGS 84), and the difference between this and the horizontal datum of the published chart is given on the chart. In January 2000, the United Kingdom Hydrographic Office began converting British Admiralty charts of Great Britain to a WGS 84 compatible datum. This programme will take approximately three years to complete, after which British Admiralty charts of Ireland and the Channel Islands will be converted.

2 **Vertical datum** used for the reduction of soundings equates approximately to the lowest astronomical tide. When predicting offshore tidal heights reference should be made to the Co-Tidal Charts.

NAVIGATIONAL AIDS

Buoys
1.27

1 The IALA Maritime System (Region A) is in force throughout the area. *The Mariner's Handbook* should be consulted for details of the system.

Some of the coastal areas covered in this volume are subject to rapid and frequent change and buoys may be moved before notice of the move has been promulgated. Areas where this occurs are mentioned in the directions.

Radar reflectors are not mentioned in the directions as they are fitted to the great majority of the important buoys.

PILOTAGE

General
1.28

1 Every port of consequence covered by this volume is designated a Competent Harbour Authority under the Pilotage Act 1987. It is their duty to provide licensed pilots if required and decide whether pilotage should be compulsory.

Information relevant to entry is given under the port concerned. See the relevant *Admiralty List of Radio Signals* for full details.

Signals
1.29

1 The usual signals to be made by a vessel requiring a pilot are laid down in the International Code of Signals:
By day Flag G and by night Morse letter G ($- - \cdot$) by light.
In low visibility Morse letter P ($\cdot - - \cdot$) by sound.

Pilot vessels
1.30

1 Most British pilot vessels are black-hulled with the letter "P" or PILOT painted on the bow or side. A pilot flag is flown when pilots are embarked. In low visibility pilot vessels may sound Morse letter H ($\cdot \cdot \cdot \cdot$).

Deep Sea Pilots
1.31

1 The services of a licensed deep sea pilot may be obtained from a number of pilotage authorities bordering the North Sea. See 2.5 for details.

RADIO FACILITIES

Electronic position fixing systems
1.32

1 Full details of the electronic position fixing systems are given in the relevant *Admiralty List of Radio Signals*, those with a limited applicability are described below.

Loran C. The Ejde and Sylt chains provide ground wave coverage in the area covered by this volume, but see the note on the Sylt chain in the relevant *Admiralty List of Radio Signals*.

Radio navigational aids
1.33

1 Full details of the radio navigational aids outlined below are given in the relevant *Admiralty List of Radio Signals*.

DGPS. Beacons transmitting corrections for differential GPS operate throughout the area.

Racons are fitted to many lighthouses, light-floats and buoys.

VHF direction finding service for emergency use only is operated HM Coastguard; see 1.59.

Radio navigational warnings
1.34

1 Long range Navigational Warnings for NAVAREA 1, which includes the whole of the North Sea, are broadcast by Portishead. NAVTEX, a navigational telex service broadcasting safety messages is also available in the area. Messages concerning the W half of the North Sea are broadcast from Cullercoats.

2 Coastal navigation warnings are broadcast at scheduled times by coast radio stations; see the relevant *Admiralty List of Radio Signals* for details.

Radio weather reports
1.35

1 Details of radio weather reports are given in the relevant *Admiralty List of Radio Signals*.

REGULATIONS

Submarine pipelines and cables

Submarine pipelines
1.36

1 The area is crossed by a large number of submarine pipelines linking the offshore oil and gas fields with the shore, which are shown on the chart with the appropriate legend (oil or gas). See *The Mariner's Handbook* for a full description of pipelines.

1.37

1 **Caution.** Mariners are advised not to anchor or trawl in the vicinity of pipelines. Gas from a damaged oil or gas pipeline could cause an explosion, loss of a vessel's buoyancy or other serious hazard. Pipelines are not always buried and may effectively reduce the charted depth by up to 2 m. They may also span seabed undulations and cause fishing gear to become irrecoverably snagged, putting a vessel in severe danger. See Annual Notice to Mariners No 24 and *The Mariner's Handbook*.

Submarine cables
1.38

1 See *The Mariner's Handbook* for information on the International Convention for the Protection of Submarine cables.

Pollution of the sea

General
1.39

1   In the area covered by this volume pollution of the sea by oil is forbidden. See *The Mariner's Handbook* for information on the International Convention for the Prevention of Pollution from Ships 1973 (MARPOL 1973) and the 1978 Protocol to MARPOL 1973.

2   Within the North Sea there is a regional agreement for cooperation in combating oil pollution in an emergency. Participants to this agreement are Belgium, France, Germany, Netherlands, Norway, Sweden and the United Kingdom.

    See also the relevant *Admiralty List of Radio Signals* for pollution reports by radio within the waters of the United Kingdom.

Regulations for ships carrying Dangerous and Polluting Goods
1.40

1   **Application of the regulations.** Regulations came into force on 31st October 1995 relating to vessels bound for or leaving European Community ports carrying dangerous and polluting goods. This includes oil tankers, chemical tankers, gas carriers and all ships carrying dangerous or polluting packaged cargo.

2   These regulations define the minimum reporting requirements to be provided by:

      (a) the Operator of the vessel (defined as the owner, charterer, manager or agent).

      (b) the Master of the vessel.

    The Master of the vessel must submit a check list to the Pilot and the Harbour Authorities giving the following information:

3   Details and classification of the vessel.

    Brief description of the type of cargo and quantity in tonnes.

    State of machinery, anchor, fire-fighting, navigational and radio equipment.

    State of safety certificates and other documents.

    Details of officers' certificates of competence.

4   Individual member States of the European Community will make separate arrangements for implementing the regulations. For further details see the relevant *Admiralty List of Radio Signals*.

The Dangerous Substances in Harbour Areas Regulations
1.41

1   The regulations concern the marking, movements and berthing of vessels with Dangerous Substances embarked. They define the various substances and require that the Harbour Master be given notice of the entry of such substances into the Harbour Area. The Harbour Master is empowered to prohibit or remove any Dangerous Substance, which in his opinion is a risk to health or safety. Copies of these regulations may be obtained from HM Stationery Office.

Closure of ports
1.42

1   **Signals.** Should it become necessary to control the entrance of ships into, and the movement of ships within, certain ports under the control of the Ministry of Defence in the United Kingdom, the signals described below will be displayed. They will be shown from some conspicuous position in or near the approaches to the ports concerned and may also be displayed by an Examination or Traffic Control Vessel (1.44) operating in the approaches.

    The signals and their meanings are:

2   **Entrance to port prohibited:**

    By day. Three red balls disposed vertically.

    By night. Three red flashing lights disposed vertically and visible all round the horizon.

    Entrance to port permitted:

    By day. No signal.

    By night. Three green lights disposed vertically and visible all round the horizon.

3   **Movement of shipping** within the port or anchorage prohibited:

    By day. A blue flag.

    By night. Three lights red, green, red disposed vertically and visible all round the horizon.

    These lights, when exhibited by Examination vessels will be carried in addition to their ordinary navigation lights.

1.43

1   **Dangerous areas.** Masters of vessels are warned that should they approach the entrance to a port being controlled by the Ministry of Defence, they should not enter a declared "Dangerous Area", or close boom defences, without permission, nor anchor or stop in a "Dangerous Area" or prohibited anchorage unless instructed to do so. Masters are advised therefore to communicate with any Government or Port Authority vessel found patrolling in the offing to ascertain the recommended approach route to the port.

1.44

1   **Examination Service.** In certain circumstances it may be necessary to take special measures to examine or establish the identity of individual vessels desiring to enter ports and to control their entry. This is the function of the Examination Service, whose officers will be afloat in Examination Vessels or Traffic Control Vessels. These vessels will wear the distinguishing flag of the Examination Service, as illustrated, together with a Blue Ensign, or exceptionally a White Ensign.

Examination Service special flag

2   If ordered to anchor in an Examination anchorage, Masters are warned that it is forbidden, except for the purposes of avoiding an accident, to do any of the following without the prior permission of the Examination Officer:

    Lower any boat.

    Communicate with the shore or any other vessel.

    Work cables.

    Allow any person or thing to leave the ship.

3   The permission of the Immigration Officer must be obtained before any passenger or member of the crew, who has embarked outside the United Kingdom, is allowed to land.

    Nothing in the above paragraphs is to be taken as overruling any regulations issued by local authorities at particular ports or by routeing authorities.

Quarantine

Quarantine and Customs Regulations
1.45

1   Vessels arriving at any ports or harbours in the United Kingdom are subject to British Quarantine and Customs Regulations.

In British Territorial Waters no person is permitted to leave a vessel coming from a foreign place, except in the case of an emergency, until pratique has been granted by the local authority.

2   The Master of a foreign-going vessel is required to inform the Port Health Authority by radio if any person onboard is suffering from an infectious disease or has symptoms which may be indicative of an infectious disease, or if there are any circumstances requiring the attention of the Port Medical Officer. This message should be made not more than 12 hours and not less than 4 hours before arrival. See the relevant *Admiralty List of Radio Signals*.

Regulations to prevent the spread of Rabies
1.46

1   Stringent regulations are in force to prevent the spread of Rabies into the British Islands.

The following is an extract from Article 12 of *The Rabies (Importation of Dogs, Cats and Other Mammals) Order 1974* (as amended 1977). This extract is applicable to any animal which has, within the preceding 6 months, been in a place outside Great Britain, Northern Ireland, the Republic of Ireland, the Channel Islands and the Isle of Man, except one for which an import licence has been issued–

2   "It shall be the duty of a person having charge or control of a vessel in harbour in Great Britain to ensure that an animal which is onboard that vessel:

(a) is at all times restrained, and kept securely confined within a totally enclosed part of the vessel from which it cannot escape;

(b) does not come into contact with any other animal or any contact animal (other than an animal or contact animal with which it has been transported to Great Britain); and

(c) is in no circumstances permitted to land."

3   If an animal to which the above extract applies is lost from a vessel in harbour, the person having charge or control of that vessel must immediately inform an Inspector of the Ministry of Agriculture, Fisheries and Food, or the Police, or an officer of H.M. Customs and Excise.

4   No native animals or contact animals are permitted to go on board the vessel on which there is an animal from abroad. This does not apply to dogs belonging to the Police, H.M. Customs or the Armed Forces and under the constant control of a trained handler. or to animals being loaded for export.

5   A contact animal is any one of 25 species, listed in an Appendix to the Order, which is not normally subject to quarantine for Rabies unless it has been in contact with an animal which is subject to quarantine; for example, a horse, listed as a "contact animal", could become subject to quarantine if it came into contact with a dog or other animal which is subject to quarantine.

6   Other than in exceptional circumstances, only certain ports are authorised for the landing of animals for which an import licence has been issued; within the limits of this volume the only such port is Kingston-upon-Hull.

Protected wrecks
1.47

1   To prevent the disturbance of the dead, certain wrecks, post 1900, are protected from interference by the *Protection of Military Remains Act 1986*.

Protection of wildlife

General information
1.48

1   Until 1991 the main government body responsible for nature conservation was the Nature Conservancy Council (NCC). Since 1992 the NCC has been replaced by three separate Councils; in England by English Nature, whose headquarters are at Northminster House, Peterborough PE1 1VA; in Scotland by Scottish Natural Heritage, 12 Hope Terrace, Edinburgh EH9 2AS, and in Wales by the Countryside Council for Wales, Ffordd Penrhos, Plas Penrhos, Bangor LL57 2LQ.

2   These conservation bodies give advice on nature conservation to government and to all those whose activities affect wildlife and wild places. They are also responsible for establishing, maintaining and managing a series of National Nature Reserves and Marine Reserves and identifying and notifying Sites of Special Scientific Interest. The work is based on detailed ecological research and survey.

3   Information concerning bye-laws, codes of conduct, descriptions and positions of nature reserves and sites of special scientific interest can be obtained from the Councils whose addresses are given above.

4   **National Nature Reserves.** In 2000 there were nearly 300 National Nature Reserves in the United Kingdom; only those which can be found on or near the coastlines and river estuaries contained in this volume which may be of direct interest to the mariner are mentioned in the text; reserves are shown on certain charts of the British Isles.

5   **Marine Nature Reserves** provide protection for marine flora and fauna and geological and physiographical features on land covered by tidal waters up to and including the limit of territorial waters; they are shown on the chart. They also provide opportunities for study and research.

6   **Local Nature Reserves.** Local authorities in England and Wales and district councils in Scotland are able to acquire and manage local nature reserves in consultation with the conservation councils.

Conservation Trusts can also own and manage non-statutory local nature reserves; where necessary, the appropriate Trust name is given within the text of this volume.

1.49

1   **Royal Society for the Protection of Birds (RSPB),** is an organisation whose primary interest lies in the preservation of the many species of wild birds seen in Britain. For the purposes of this volume, only important bird reserves lying in and around the coastal areas which may be of direct interest to the mariner are mentioned.

Visiting a reserve in many cases is not encouraged, and often not permitted, whilst at others it is permitted but under arrangement and strict control.

2   Lists of important bird reserves can be found within the text to which reference is given as to whether visiting is permitted or not; reserves are shown on certain charts of the British Isles.

Further details can be obtained from: Head of Reserve Management, Royal Society for the Protection of Birds, The Lodge, Sandy, Bedfordshire SG19 2DL.

SIGNALS

Wreck marking vessel signals
1.50

1   Consequent upon instances when vessels have passed perilously close to Trinity House vessels engaged in marking wrecks, mariners are advised that:

2   (1) Trinity House vessels when engaged in wreck searching or surveying, during which time they may be proceeding at slow speeds on various headings, or marking wrecks prior to laying buoy(s), exhibit the lights/shapes prescribed under rule 27(b) of the International Regulations for Preventing Collisions at Sea (1972) for vessels restricted in their ability to manoeuvre. Additionally, when wreck marking, Trinity House vessels will exhibit the lights/shapes prescribed under rule 27(d) of the Regulations for a vessel engaged in underwater operations to indicate the side on which the obstruction exists and the side on which another vessel may pass.

3   (2) Trinity House vessels when marking new wrecks may also exhibit a radar beacon (morse code D). This will be in addition to the signals displayed under rule 27.

4   (3) In addition to the foregoing lights/shapes, when a Trinity House vessel on wreck marking duty wishes to draw the urgent attention of an approaching vessel which is standing dangerously close to either the marking vessel or the wreck, the Trinity House vessel will fire detonating signals and reporting procedures may be put in hand against the offending vessel.

5   (4) Mariners should both respect the efforts of the marking vessel and safeguard their own vessel by reducing speed, and by giving the area a wide berth on the clear side of the wreck marking vessel.

DISTRESS AND RESCUE

General information
1.51

1   Full details of the Global Maritime Distress and Safety System (GMDSS) and the general arrangements for Search and Rescue (SAR) are given in the relevant *Admiralty List of Radio Signals.*
1.52

1   The radio watch on the international distress frequencies which certain classes of ship are required to keep when at sea is one of the most important factors in the arrangements for the rescue of people in distress at sea. For details see the relevant *Admiralty List of Radio Signals.*

HM COASTGUARD

General information
1.53

1   The primary role of the Coastguard service is the initiation and co-ordination of civil maritime search and rescue within the United Kingdom Search and Rescue Region (UK SRR). This includes the mobilisation, organisation and tasking of adequate resources to respond to people either in distress at sea, or at risk of injury or death on the cliffs or shoreline of the United Kingdom.

2   In a maritime emergency the Coastguard Service calls on and co-ordinates the appropriate facilities, such as RNLI lifeboats, RN and RAF rotary and fixed wing aircraft and RN ships, as well as merchant ships and commercial aircraft.

It maintains Auxiliary Coastguard Rescue Teams at strategic locations around the coast and a fleet of inflatable craft for inshore patrols. For full details see the relevant *Admiralty List of Radio Signals.*

Coastguard network
1.54

1   The UK SRR is bounded by Latitudes 45°N and 61°N, by Longitude 30°W and to the E by the adjacent European Search and Rescue Regions, with whom HM Coastguard maintains a close liaison.

2   The UK SRR is divided into six Regions, with operational control of each exercised from a Maritime Rescue Co-ordination Centre (MRCC). Each region is sub-divided into 2 or 3 districts, each with a Maritime Rescue Sub-Centre (MRSC).

3   Within each district there are a number of Coastguard Sector Bases situated at strategic locations and manned by a regular Coastguard officer; within each Sector there are a number of Auxiliary Coastguard Rescue Teams trained and equipped for cliff rescue, coastal searches and patrols.

Coastguard Rescue Teams
1.55

1   In the list below coast rescue equipment is kept at all locations.

North and East Scotland Region

Buchan Sector Base
2   Fraserburgh
Peterhead
Cruden Bay
Collieston
Newburgh
Aberdeen
Portlethen

Montrose Sector Base
3   Gourdon
Montrose
Arbroath
Stonehaven

Saint Andrew's Sector Base
4   Carnoustie
Saint Andrew's
Crail
Leven

Granton Sector Base
5   Kinghorn
Rosyth
Fisherrow
South Queensferry
Granton

Eyemouth Sector Base
6   Gullane
North Berwick
Cockburnspath
Dunbar
Saint Abb's Head
Eyemouth

Eastern Search and Rescue Region

Amble Sector Base
7   Berwick-upon-Tweed
Cheswick
Holy Island
Seahouses
Newton

Craster
Boulmer
Amble
Newbiggin

Hartlepool Sector Base

8 Blyth
Sunderland
Seaham Harbour
Hartlepool
Redcar

Whitby Sector Base

9 Skinningrove
Staithes
Kettle Ness
Whitby
Robin Hood's Bay
Ravenscar

Scarborough Sector Base

10 Burniston
Scarborough
Filey
Speeton
Flamborough
Bridlington

Hull Sector Base

11 Hornsea
Withernsea
Easington
Hull
Cleethorpes

Lincolnshire Sector Base

12 Donna Nook
Mablethorpe
Chapel Saint Leonards
Skegness
Wrangle

North Norfolk Sector Base

13 Sutton Bridge
Hunstanton
Wells
Cley
Sheringham
Cromer
Mundesley

Yarmouth Sector Base

14 Happisburgh
Winterton
Gorleston
Lowestoft
Southwold

Coastguard communications
1.56

1 HM Coastguard MRCCs and MRSCs maintain continuous watch on 2182 kHz and VHF Channel 16 for distress, urgency and safety calls, covering UK waters. A number of MRCCs and MRSCs also maintain a continuous watch on 2187·5 kHz Digital Selective Calling (DSC) in accordance with GMDSS. 2182 kHz and VHF Channel 16 watch is maintained at some Coast Radio Stations operating a RT (MF)/VHF service, but the primary responsibility for keeping distress watch on these frequencies rests with HM Coastguard.

2 For details of Coast Radio Stations and Coastguard MRCCs and MRSCs available within the area covered by this volume see the relevant *Admiralty List of Radio Signals*.

1.57

1 **Medical aid procedure.** PAN MEDICO calls should be directed to the nearest, or any, Coastguard Rescue Centre, who will instigate the following procedure:
1. Transfer the call to Channel 67.
2. Contact a Coast Radio Station to secure a priority channel.
3. Call the Coast Radio Station on the allocated channel.
4. If the advice is to evacuate the patient the Coastguard should be called and requested to make the necessary arrangements.

2 For further details see the relevant *Admiralty List of Radio Signals*.

1.58

1 **Yacht and Boat Safety Scheme.** Small craft owners can join the Yacht and Boat Safety Scheme which, with the assistance of the Coastguard Service, aims to provide the nearest Rescue Centre with the information needed to effect a rescue of their boat.

Direction-finding Stations for use in emergency
1.59

1 The Coastguard operate a VHF direction-finding (D/F) service for SAR purposes at over 40 stations (RG) around the United Kingdom. Within the scope of this volume there are 12 such stations situated as follows:

Station	Position	MRSC
Inverbervie	56°51′N, 2°16′W	Aberdeen
Fife Ness	56°17′N, 2°35′W	Forth
Crosslaw	55°55′N, 2°12′W	Forth
Newton	55°31′N, 1°37′W	Tyne/Tees
Tynemouth	55°01′N, 1°25′W	Tyne/Tees
Hartlepool	54°42′N, 1°11′W	Tyne Tees
Whitby	54°29′N, 0°36′W	Humber
Flamborough	54°07′N, 0°05′W	Humber
Easington	53°39′N, 0°06′E	Humber
Hunstanton	52°57′N, 0°30′E	Yarmouth
Trimingham	52°55′N, 1°21′E	Yarmouth
Caister	52°40′N, 1°43′E	Yarmouth

2 For further details see the relevant *Admiralty List of Radio Signals*.

Royal National Lifeboat Institution

General information
1.60

1 The Royal National Lifeboat Institution maintains a fleet of over 250 lifeboats of various types at stations round the coast of the United Kingdom. It is a privately run organisation supported entirely by voluntary contributions.

2 There are over 200 lifeboat stations around the coasts of the United Kingdom and the Republic of Ireland. Many operate all-weather lifeboats, others have inshore lifeboats only; some stations operate both types. The majority of the inshore lifeboats are permanently on station, while the remainder are on station only during the summer months.

Lifeboat characteristics

1.61

1 All-weather lifeboats have the following characteristics:
Length between 10 and 17 m.
Speed 16 kn or more.
Radius of action of about 140–250 miles.
Equipment: radar; D/F on 2182 kHz and VHF; communications on MF (2182 kHz) and VHF(FM) multi-channel R/T.
Blue quick flashing light exhibited at night when on service.

1.62

1 Inshore lifeboats have the following characteristics:
Inflatable or rigid inflatable construction.
Outboard motor(s).
Speed 20 to 30 kn.
VHF (FM) multi-channel R/T.

Lifeboat stations

1.63

1 **All-weather lifeboats** are stationed as follows:
Peterhead.
Aberdeen.
Montrose.
Arbroath.
Broughty Ferry.
2 Anstruther.
Dunbar.
Eyemouth.
Berwick-upon-Tweed.
North Sunderland.
3 Amble.
Blyth.
Tynemouth.
Sunderland.
Hartlepool.
Teesmouth.
4 Whitby.
Scarborough.
Filey.
Bridlington.
Humber (Spurn Head).
Skegness.
5 Wells.
Cromer.

Caister.*
Great Yarmouth and Gorleston.
Lowestoft.

6 **Inshore lifeboats** are stationed as follows:
Aberdeen.
Montrose.
Arbroath.
Broughty Ferry.
7 Kinghorn.
Queensferry.
North Berwick.
Dunbar.
Saint Abb's.
Berwick-upon-Tweed.
8 Seahouses.
Craster.
Amble.
Newbiggin.
9 Blyth.
Cullercoats.
Tynemouth.
Sunderland
Hartlepool.
10 Redcar (2).
Staithes and Runswick.
Whitby.
Scarborough.
Filey.
11 Flamborough.
Bridlington.
Withernsea.
Cleethorpes.
Mablethorpe.
12 Skegness.
Hunstanton.
Wells.
Sheringham.
Cromer.
13 Happisburgh.
Caister.*
Great Yarmouth and Gorleston.
Southwold.

* Lifeboats operated by Caister Volunteer Rescue Service.

COUNTRY AND PORTS

UNITED KINGDOM

General information
1.64

1   The United Kingdom of Great Britain and Northern Ireland is a constitutional monarchy comprising England, Scotland, Wales and Northern Ireland, but does not include the Isle of Man or Channel Islands, which are Dependencies of the Crown. The Sovereign is also Head of the Commonwealth.

2   The population (1991 Census) of the United Kingdom is as follows:

Country	Population
England & Wales	49 890 000
Scotland	4 999 000
Northern Ireland	1 578 000

Definitions
1.65

1   **Great Britain:**
>England, including the Isles of Scilly, Wales and Scotland; the Shetland and Orkney Islands are part of Scotland.

   The United Kingdom of Great Britain and Northern Ireland:
>Great Britain, as above, and Northern Ireland.

2   **British Isles:**
>Great Britain, The Isle of Man and Ireland (both the Republic and the North).

   British Islands:
>British Isles, as above, and Channel Islands.

National limits
1.66

1   **Territorial waters.** The breadth of the Territorial Sea adjacent to the United Kingdom and the Isle of Man extends for a distance of 12 nautical miles as defined by the Territorial Sea Act 1987 given in Appendix III, and the Territorial Sea Act 1987 (Isle of Man) Order 1991. The breadth of the Territorial Sea adjacent to the Channel Islands is 3 nautical miles.

2   Baselines to be used for measuring the breadth of the territorial waters adjacent to the United Kingdom, the Channel Islands and the Isle of Man are defined in the Territorial Waters Order in Council 1964 as amended by the Territorial Sea (Amendment) Order 1996, given in Appendix III. This 12 nautical mile Territorial Sea limit is depicted on selected Admiralty charts.

   See also *Annual Summary of Admiralty Notices to Mariners.*

1.67

1   **Fishery limits.** The exclusive fishing limits of the United Kingdom extend up to 6 nautical miles from the baselines of the Territorial Sea and for the next 6 nautical miles fishing is limited to countries with established rights in accordance with the European Union's Common Fisheries Policy. These 6 nautical mile and 12 nautical mile limits are depicted on selected Admiralty charts. Foreign fishing rights in these waters are depicted on Admiralty chart Q6385. The Fishery Limits Act 1976 extended British fishery limits to 200 nautical miles measured from the baselines of the Territorial Sea, or to such limits as may be specified. This limit is depicted on Admiralty chart Q6353 and is administered in accordance with the European Union's Common Fisheries Policy.

History
1.68

1   During the first four centuries AD, Britain was a province of the Roman Empire, which withdrew its protection in 429. The country then fell into the power of the Saxon invaders from the continent of Europe. There followed a period of rivalry for leadership between various Anglo-Saxon kings and invasion by the Vikings from Scandinavia. The various kingdoms were joined into one in the early tenth century and ruled by Saxon kings until the land was conquered by the Danes in 1016. The Saxon house was restored 26 years later.

2   Meanwhile in Europe in the tenth century, a Viking settlement in Normandy, was becoming a feudatory in France. It was from this Duchy that the future rulers of England were to come. In 1066, Duke William of Normandy laid claim to the English throne, invaded and conquered the country, and founded the Norman dynasty. The monarchial system of rulers continued by descent, though not without dispute, for nearly 600 years until 1649 when it was overthrown by Oliver Cromwell, who created the Protectorate. With his death in 1658, a reaction against the Protectorate and strife over his successor resulted in the restoration of the monarchy in 1660, which has continued uninterrupted to the present day.

3   The eighteenth century was marked by the gradual increase in the power of Parliament, rise of political parties, advances in colonisation and trade, and progress of Britain as a sea power.

   In the twentieth century self-government was handed over to the majority of the former colonies, most of which joined the British Commonwealth of Nations as independent sovereign states.

   In 1973 Great Britain joined the European Economic Community, now the European Union.

History of Scotland and the northern isles
1.69

1   Unlike England, Scotland was never a province of the Roman Empire from which it was separated by a fortified wall, 75 miles long, built by the Emperor Hadrian in AD 122 to 128 to secure the N frontier of the Roman province of Britannia, present day England.

2   Following the withdrawal of the Roman Legions from England in 410 AD, invading Saxons from NW Europe gradually, in the fifth and sixth centuries, drove some of the remaining Britons and Angles N of Hadrian's Wall. At about the same time there was a large incursion of Scots from Ireland into the W part of the territory N of the wall and in the incessant tribal warfare of the next four centuries the Scots gradually achieved a unifying supremacy over the other tribes. In 1034 AD they established an effective Kingdom of Scotland in the central and S parts of the territories N of Hadrian's Wall. However the Hebrides did not become part of the Kingdom of Scotland until 1266, when they were ceded to Alexander III by Magnus of Norway.

3   Meanwhile Vikings, or Norsemen, from Scandinavia carried out repeated invasions of Britain during the eighth, ninth and tenth centuries and overran part of France now known as Normandy. They also occupied Orkney and Shetland Islands which remained Danish until 1472 when they were ceded to Scotland as part of the dowry of Margaret of Denmark who became the wife of King James III of Scotland. Strong traces of Scandinavian culture remain to the present day in both Orkney and Shetland Islands.

4 In 1066 William, Duke of Normandy, overcame the resistance of the Saxons in Britain at the Battle of Hastings. During the next 250 years the English crown, with a far more populated kingdom, made a number of attempts to overrun and annex the Scottish Kingdom but after a crushing defeat by the Scots, led by King Robert the Bruce, at the Battle of Bannockburn in 1314, the English finally and formally recognised the independence of Scotland as a sovereign state in 1328.

5 In 1603 the crowns of England and Scotland were united by the accession, through inheritance, of King James VI of Scotland as King James I of England and Scotland.

Final legislative union of the parliaments of the two countries was enacted by The Act of Union of 1707. The Scottish Parliament was revived in 1999 as a result of the government's policy of devolution.

Government
1.70

1 The supreme legislative power is vested in Parliament, which is divided into two Houses of Legislature, the House of Lords and the House of Commons, and in its present form dates from the middle of the fourteenth century, although in 1999 the House of Lords was reformed to exclude the majority of hereditary peers and peeresses.

2 The House of Lords is non-elected and consists of life peers and peeresses, Law Lords, two archbishops and twenty four bishops of the established Church of England, and, as an interim measure, 92 hereditary peers and peeresses. The House of Lords has judicial powers as the ultimate Court of Appeal for courts in Great Britain and Northern Ireland, except for criminal cases in Scotland.

3 The House of Commons consists of members representing county and borough constituencies. Every constituency returns a single member. In 2000 there was a total of 659 members, 529 from England, 72 from Scotland, 40 from Wales and 18 from Northern Ireland. Suffrage is limited to men and women aged 18 years and above.

4 Executive government is vested nominally in the Crown, but is exercised in practice by the Cabinet, a committee of ministers, which is dependent on the support of the majority in the House of Commons. The Prime Minister presides over the Cabinet and dispenses the greater portion of the patronage of the Crown.

5 Parliament can be dissolved by the will of the Sovereign, or by proclamation during its recess or by lapse of the statutory duration of five years.

In Scotland, where the judiciary and certain other areas of government still differ significantly from those of the remainder of the United Kingdom, the Scottish Parliament, first elected in 1999, has legislative power over all matters not reserved to the United Kingdom Parliament in Westminster, or otherwise outside its powers.

International relations
1.71

1 The United Kingdom is a permanent member of The Security Council of The United Nations, and a member of the Commonwealth, the European Union, the Western European Union, the Council of Europe, the Organisation for Economic Co-operation and Development and the North Atlantic Treaty Organisation.

Coastal features and rivers
1.72

1 From Rattray Head to the Firth of Forth the E coast of Scotland is mainly rocky and steep-to. The coast is similar to the S as far as Flamborough Head, where the it becomes low-lying with extensive offshore sandbanks, which form a series of shallow ridges lying parallel to the coast.

2 Several large rivers flow into the sea on the E coast and apart from Aberdeen all the major ports in this volume are estuarial ports, sometimes situated some distance up river. From the N these rivers are the Tay, Forth, Tyne, Tees and Humber. The deep bight of The Wash to the S of the Humber acts as the outlet for a number of rivers all of which give access to smaller ports.

Industry and trade
1.73

1 Britain is more dependent than most countries on its industries, and trades world-wide.

2 Major industries are iron and steel, heavy engineering, and the processing of imported goods such as wool, cotton and tobacco. In recent years with the decline of some of the traditional industries, Britain has had to rely on technical skill and inventiveness and a new range of industries has developed including motor vehicles, aircraft, nuclear power equipment, instruments, man made fibres and chemical products as well as electrical goods and machines. Considerable quantities of crude oil are imported to be refined into petroleum products.

3 The production of oil and gas from offshore fields plays an important part in the country's industry and technology.

The country is intensively farmed, mainly for home consumption but an important export trade in agricultural products has been established. A considerable fishing fleet is maintained.

1.74

1 **Scotland** has the largest share of the United Kingdom's offshore oil production industry, including rig fabrication and repair, the support of offshore installations, and the export of products from the offshore fields. A substantial part of the offshore gas industry is also Scottish based. Highly technical industries, including advanced electronics, are concentrated in the Forth/Clyde valley. Other important industries include traditional agriculture, tourism, and fishing; the farming of salmon and other marine species has become a major industry, particularly in Orkney and Shetland Islands, and development is continuing.

PRINCIPAL PORTS, HARBOURS AND ANCHORAGES
1.75

Place and Position	Remarks
1 Peterhead:	
Harbour (3.31) (57°30′N, 1°47′W)	Small commercial and fishing port.
Bay (3.31) (57°29′N, 1°47′W)	Supply base for N Sea oilfields. Tanker jetty.
Aberdeen (3.57) (57°09′N, 2°04′W)	Large commercial and fishing port. Main supply base for N Sea oilfields.
2 Montrose (3.128) (56°42′N, 2°28′W)	Small commercial and fishing port. Supply base for N Sea oilfields.
Dundee (3.198)	Commercial port. Supply base for N Sea oilfields.

Firth of Forth:

	Methil (4.24) (56°11′N, 3°00′W)	Small commercial port.
3	Burntisland (4.106) (56°03′N, 3°14′W)	Small commercial port.
	Hound Point (4.174) (56°00′N, 3°22′W)	Terminal handling crude oil from N Sea oilfields.
	Braefoot Bay (4.136) (56°02′N, 3°19′W)	Terminal for petro-chemical complex.
	Leith (4.52) (55°59′N, 3°10′W)	Large commercial port. Supply base for N Sea oilfields.
	Rosyth (4.195) (56°01′N, 3°27′W)	Former Naval Base.
4	Grangemouth (4.234) (56°02′N, 3°41′W)	Large commercial port. Terminal for petro-chemical complex.
	Berwick-upon-Tweed (5.59) (55°46′N, 2°00′W)	Small commercial and fishing port.
	Blyth (5.183) (55°07′N, 1°29′W)	Commercial port.

5 River Tyne:

	Port of Tyne (5.215) (55°01′N, 1°25′W)	Large commercial port. Shipbuilding and repairs.
	Newcastle upon Tyne (5.245) (54°58′N, 1°36′W)	Large commercial port.
	Sunderland (6.17) (54°55′N, 1°22′W)	Commercial port.
6	Seaham (6.52) (54°50′N, 1°19′W)	Commercial port.
	Hartlepool (6.70) (54°42′N, 1°12′W)	Commercial port.

River Tees:

	Teesport (6.98) (54°37′N, 1°10′W)	Large commercial port. Terminal for petro-chemical complex.
7	Whitby (6.139) (54°29′N, 0°37′W)	Small commercial and fishing port.
	Scarborough (6.174) (54°17′N, 0°23′W)	Fishing port. Yachting centre.
	Bridlington Bay (6.204) (54°06′N, 0°06′W)	Anchorage.

8 River Humber:

	Grimsby (7.34) (53°35′N, 0°04′W)	Commercial and large fishing port.
	Immingham (7.71) (53°38′N, 0°11′W)	Commercial port, bulk, oil and gas terminals.
	Salt End (7.103) (53°44′N, 0°15′W)	Oil terminal.
9	Kingston upon Hull (7.108) (53°45′N, 0°18′W)	Large commercial port.
	New Holland (7.137) (53°42′N, 0°21′W)	Small commercial port.

River Ouse:

	Goole (7.145) (53°42′N, 0°52′W)	Small commercial port.
	Howden Dyke (7.157) (53°45′N, 0°52′W)	Small commercial port.
10	Selby (7.159) (53°47′N, 1°04′W)	Small commercial port.

River Trent:

	Riverside wharves (7.165) between 53°39′N and 53°35′N	Six wharves capable of taking vessels up to 3000 dwt.

The Wash:

	Boston (8.56) (52°59′N, 0°01′W)	Small commercial port.
11	Wisbech (8.85) (52°41′N, 0°10′E)	Small commercial port.
	Port Sutton Bridge (8.100) (52°46′N, 0°12′E)	Small commercial port.
	King's Lynn (8.101) (52°45′N, 0°24′E)	Small commercial port.
12	Great Yarmouth (9.51) (52°36′N, 1°44′E)	Commercial and fishing port. Supply base for N Sea oil and gas fields.
	Lowestoft (9.92) (52°58′N, 1°45′E)	Large fishing and commercial port. Supply base for N Sea oil and gas fields.

PORT SERVICES — SUMMARY

Docking facilities

1.76

1 The summary below lists ports with docking facilities and where available the dimensions of the largest vessel that can be accommodated. Details of dock sizes are given at the reference.

Peterhead. Dry dock; length 53 m; beam 10·2 m; draught 4·4 m; (3.39). Patent slip; length 30·5 m; beam 7·39 m; draught 6·1 m.

Aberdeen. Dry dock; length 110 m; beam 20·0 m; draught 6·0 m (3.81).

2 Arbroath. Patent slip; length 30·5 m; beam 7·3 m; draught 3·6 m (3.175).

Leith. Three dry docks; largest can accommodate length 160 m; beam 21 m; draught 7·3 m (4.71).

Rosyth. Three dry docks. Mechanical lift dock; lifting capacity 1500 tonnes (4.212).

Grangemouth. Dry dock; length 105·4 m; beam 16·1 m; draught 5·6 m (4.249).

Port of Tyne. Ten dry docks; largest can accommodate length 259 m; beam 43 m; draught 10·5 m (5.246).

3 Sunderland. Dry dock (6.40).

River Tees. Three dry docks. One slipway; length 65 m; beam 24 m; draught 3·5 m (6.124).

Whitby. Floating dock; lifting capacity 500 tonnes (6.157).

Grimsby. Three slipways; largest 63·5 m LOA, 10·3 m beam, 1200 dwt (7.51).

4   Kingston upon Hull. Several dry docks; largest can accommodate length 153 m; beam 18·4 m; draught 6·2 m (7.123).

New Holland. Slip; 800 dwt (7.137).

Goole. Two dry docks; largest can accommodate length 92·5 m; beam 14·9 m; draught 4·6 m (7.155).

Lowestoft. Dry dock; draught 4·9 m; 900 dwt (9.118).

Other facilities

Salvage services

1.77

1   Immingham (7.71).

Hull (7.108).

Lowestoft (9.92).

Compass adjustment

1.78

1   Leith (4.52).

Grangemouth (4.234).

Blyth (5.183).

Port of Tyne (5.215).

Grimsby (7.34).

Kingston upon Hull (7.108).

Deratting

1.79

1   Deratting can be carried out and exemption certificates issued at the following ports:

Aberdeen (3.57).

Dundee (3.198).

Leith (4.52).

Braefoot Marine Terminal (4.136).

Rosyth (4.195).

2   Grangemouth (4.234).

Blyth (5.183).

Port of Tyne (5.215).

Hartlepool (6.70).

Middlesbrough (6.99).

Grimsby (7.34).

3   Immingham (7.71).

Kingston upon Hull (7.108).

Goole (7.145).

Wisbech (8.85).

King's Lynn (8.101).

Great Yarmouth (9.51).

Lowestoft (9.92).

4   Exemption only can be issued at the following ports:

Peterhead (3.18).

Montrose (3.128).

Methil (4.24).

Burntisland (4.106).

Berwick-upon-Tweed (5.59).

Sunderland (6.17).

Boston (8.56).

Measured distances

1.80

1   Close W of Saint Abb's Head (55°55′N, 2°08′W) (5.8).

Off Newbiggin Point (55°11′N, 1°30′W) (5.172).

Coquet Island (55°20′N, 1°32′W) to Saint Mary's Lighthouse (5.173).

River Humber (53°38′N, 0°03′W) for small craft (7.62).

River Waveney above Oulton Broad (52°29′N, 1°42′E) (9.123).

Airfields

1.81

1   There are many airfields throughout the area, ranging from large civil airfields to emergency landing grounds. The following list is comprises those of direct interest to the mariner, emergency landing grounds are omitted. They are mentioned in the text when appropriate.

	Name	*Position*		*Remarks*
2	Peterhead	57°31′N,	1°52′W	Heliport
	Aberdeen	57°12′N,	2°12′W	Civil airport
	Arbroath	56°35′N,	2°37′W	Heliport
	Leuchars	56°22′N,	2°52′W	SAR helicopters
	Edinburgh	55°57′N,	3°22′W	Civil airport
	Boulmer	55°25′N,	1°36′W	SAR helicopters
	Newcastle	55°02′N,	1°41′W	Civil airport
3	Leconfield	53°52′N,	0°27′W	SAR helicopters
	Brough	53°43′N,	0°34′W	Civil airport
	Easington	53°39′N,	0°07′E	Heliport
	Humberside	53°35′N,	0°21′W	Civil airport
	Bacton	52°52′N,	1°27′E	Heliport
	Coltishall	52°45′N,	1°22′E	SAR helicopters
	Norwich	52°41′N,	1°17′E	Civil airport

NATURAL CONDITIONS

MARITIME TOPOGRAPHY

Seabed
1.82

1   The North Sea is a largely enclosed basin lying entirely within the Continental Shelf.

2   To the N of Flamborough Head (54°07′N, 0°05′W) and Dogger Bank (54°50′N, 2°00′E) depths vary between 50 and 80 m, within which a few isolated deeps are interspersed, some of which have depths greater than 200 m, eg Devil's Hole (56°34′N, 0°40′E). Between Flamborough Head and Rattray Head (57°37′N, 1°49′W) the 50 m depth contour lies approximately 5 miles offshore, except in the approaches to the Firth of Forth and the River Tay where offshore banks, with depths between 30 and 50 m, extend up to 35 miles off Fife Ness (56°17′N, 2°35′W).

3   From Dogger Bank and Flamborough Head S depths vary generally between 10 and 40 m. Within these depths are several narrow deeps, by far the largest of which is Outer Silver Pit (54°05′N, 2°00′E), which runs E/W about 80 miles and contains depths of more than 80 m. The other deeps have a similar maximum depth, but are much shorter in extent and narrower. They are Silver Pit (53°31′N, 0°42′E), Sole Pit (53°40′N, 1°33′E), Well Hole (53°43′N, 1°51′E) and Markhams Hole (53°50′N, 2°37′E).

4   Outer Silver Pit separates Dogger Bank, with depths between 11 m and 20 m over large areas, from the equally shallow waters to its South. Most of the shoal patches within the S North Sea, which include isolated depths of less than 10 m, consist of sand banks and sandwaves. Sandwaves are formed where the water moves rapidly over an area of unconsolidated seabed sediment; they are analogous to sand dunes formed on land by the wind. Investigations have shown they reach their maximum height, and hence their most dangerous navigational state, after periods of relatively calm weather or neap tides. For further information see *The Mariner's Handbook.*

5   The sea bottom consists of sand and gravel with sand predominant over most of the area. Gravel features to a greater extent between Rattray Ness and Fife Ness, off the Farne Islands (55°38′N, 1°37′W) and in the outer approaches to the River Humber and The Wash, to the SW of a line drawn between Flamborough Head, West Sole (53°40′N, 1°15′E) and Happisburgh (52°49′N, 1°33′E).

CURRENTS, TIDAL STREAMS AND FLOW

Currents

General remarks
1.83

1   The horizontal movement of the water over the North Sea is chiefly controlled by tidal influence. Underlying the oscillatory and rotary tidal streams there is a weak and complex counter-clockwise circulation within the North Sea which gives rise to S and SE sets over the area covered by this volume (See *Dover Strait Pilot* for currents in the S part of the North Sea). These sets are very weak when compared with the tidal spring rates and are therefore of little importance to the navigation of even low-powered vessels.

Conditions that affect currents
1.84

1   On occasions of persistent strong winds, the wind-drift currents induced may approach, or even exceed, the rate of tidal streams. For further information see *The Mariner's Handbook* where the subject is treated in detail.

2   Strong currents also occur during and after positive and negative surges, which may greatly increase tidal streams or tend to cancel them out. Accurate current observations are clearly not possible during storm surges, but currents running at several knots may occur. See 1.89.

Tidal streams

General remarks
1.85

1   For waters covered by this volume, excluding The Wash, the direction of the main flood stream is deemed to be that flowing towards the Thames Estuary. See *Admiralty Tide Tables Volume 1* for a diagram showing the direction of the main flood stream.

2   Tidal stream predictions should be obtained from the *Admiralty Tidal Stream Atlas: North Sea, Northwestern Part* and *Admiralty Tidal Stream Atlas: North Sea, Southern Part.*

3   The tidal streams are referred to according to the direction toward which they are running, but are in-going and out-going in the firths and rivers.

Conditions that affect tidal streams
1.86

1   The tidal stream may be affected by both wind-drift currents (1.84) and storm surges (1.89).

Flow
1.87

1   The main component of the flow in the North Sea is the tidal stream (see 1.83). Throughout the North Sea the offshore streams are more or less rotary, but when at their greatest strength run generally S or N parallel to the coast. As land is approached they become more rectilinear.

2   Off Rattray Head the spring rate is about 2 kn and this rate is not exceeded anywhere, except off salient points and off the coast S of Winterton Ness; off Great Yarmouth the spring rate is about 3½ kn. Tidal streams are weak in the outer part of the Firth of Forth.

SEA LEVEL AND TIDES

Sea level

General remarks
1.88

1   Observed tidal levels rarely coincide exactly with those published in Tide Tables. Differences, which are usually very small, result from the effect of wind and/or variations in the barometric pressure. Significant events, in the United Kingdom where variations exceed 0·6 m, are termed storm surges (1.89). Strong winds may also cause differences between predicted and actual times of HW and LW. Ports where the effect of strong winds on the tides is common, are mentioned in the text. Tidal streams and currents are also markedly affected by strong winds (see also *Admiralty Tide Tables* and *The Mariner's Handbook*).

Storm surges
1.89

1   Strong winds associated with an intense depression tracking E to the N of Scotland, or across the N part of the

North Sea, may drive water into the North Sea raising sea level. The storm surge travels S in the form of a wave and can result in a sea level rise of 1·2 m at Aberdeen and 3·0 m in the Thames Estuary. If the peak of the surge is close to HW, severe flooding can result, as happened in the Thames Estuary and on the Netherlands coast on 31st January 1953, when the most severe surge of modern times occurred in this area. Advance warnings of storm surges are given to the emergency services around the coast of the United Kingdom.

Negative surges
1.90

1   Negative surges are important to the mariner as they result in reduced under-keel clearances. They occur and in the S part of the North Sea as the result of local winds from the S or SW and are most frequent in December or January but rare in summer. The Thames Estuary is the area most affected by these surges. The largest recorded negative surge occurred at Sheerness on the 19th December 1982, with a level 2·25 m below that predicted, which remained 1 m or more below predictions for over 12 hours. Further N the effect decreased, with a maximum negative surge of 1 m at the Tyne. In February 1968 the level in the Thames Estuary was 0·6 m below predictions for 24 hours, the lowest level being 1·8 m below prediction.

2   High pressure, mainly in the spring through to the autumn, may reduce levels by up to 0·3 m.

The United Kingdom Meteorological Office operates a warning service annually between the months of September and April (see *Annual Summary of Admiralty Notices to Mariners*).

Tides

Time differences
1.91

1   The tide is predominantly semi-diurnal off the E coasts of England and Scotland and progresses from N to S along the coast. HW is about 10 hours earlier off Peterhead (57°30′N, 1°47′W) than off Southwold (52°20′N, 1°41′E).

2   The times at which the offshore streams begin become progressively later from N to S, but though the relationship between local HW and the stream is nearly constant off the greater part of the coast, it changes considerably between Winterton Ness (52°44′N, 1°41′E) and the Thames Estuary. Off Winterton Ness the S-going stream begins 3½ hours before local HW, but off the Thames Estuary the S-going stream begins 5¾ hours after local HW.

3   The changes in the actual times at which the streams begin, or in relation between the stream and HW Dover, agree fairly closely with the changes in the times of HW along the coast, as follows:

Seaward of	S-going stream begins relative to HW Dover
Rattray Head	−2½ hours
Montrose	−¾ hour
Berwick-upon-Tweed	+¾ hour
Flamborough Head	+2¼ hours
Winterton Ness	+6 hours
Thames Estuary	−6 hours, or 9 hours later than off Rattray Head.

4   The times at which the coastal streams begin may differ considerably from those of the offshore streams, and in the large indentations of the coasts the times may differ considerably from those of the coastal streams.

Tidal ranges
1.92

1   Three tidal nodal points exist in the North Sea. One is off Norway, approximately 58°10′N, 5°10′E, the second E of Dogger Bank, approximately 55°30′N, 5°10′E and the third mid-way between Lowestoft and Ijmuiden, approximately 52°30′N, 3°00′E. From the shores of the North Sea the range of tide decreases progressively as these nodal points are approached. The slope of the co-range lines surrounding these points and the co-tidal lines emanating from them are best seen on Charts 5058 and 5059.

1.93

1   The mean spring range off the open coast varies little between Arbroath and Sunderland, ranging from 4 to 4·5 m. North of Arbroath it decreases to 3·3 m off Peterhead; S of Sunderland it increases to about 6 m off the entrance to The Wash, after which it decreases to 2 m off Lowestoft, before again increasing as the Thames Estuary is approached. See also charts 5058 and 5059 and *Admiralty Tide Tables*.

SEA AND SWELL
1.94

1   For the definitions of sea and swell, and the terminology used in describing their characteristics, see *The Mariner's Handbook*.

Sea conditions
1.95

1   Rough seas are common from October to March. Gales from the SE to NE sometimes blow with much violence causing heavy seas to roll up on the E coast of Britain. The Firth of Forth and Great Yarmouth are particularly exposed to E gales; rough conditions occur in the Tyne and Tees estuaries with strong NE winds while the River Humber is worst affected by SE gales.

2   Strongest winds and roughest seas are usually found in the mid North Sea to the E of Scotland where between 20% and 30% of the observations record sea waves of 4 m or more in autumn and winter. In extreme conditions very high waves, or on extremely rare occasions phenomenal seas can be experienced with long periods in the N of this region. Further S seas are generally rather less severe but waves of 4 m or more account for about 15% of the observations in the S of the region during autumn and winter.

3   In summer average sea states are more agreeable and waves generally only exceed 4 m on or about 4% of occasions in the N and 2% in the S.

Swell conditions
1.96

1   Diagrams 1.96.1 to 1.96.4 give swell roses for several areas for January, April, July and October. The roses show the percentage of observations recording swell waves for each sector and for several ranges of wave height.

2   The North Sea is particularly exposed to swell from the NW to NE and there is a high incidence of waves from this sector in spring and summer. The swell from SW to SE increases in frequency in autumn and winter. Over the open sea a heavy swell may arrive from any direction, particularly in winter, but waves between W and S are likely to be of shorter periods than from other directions especially in the S of the region.

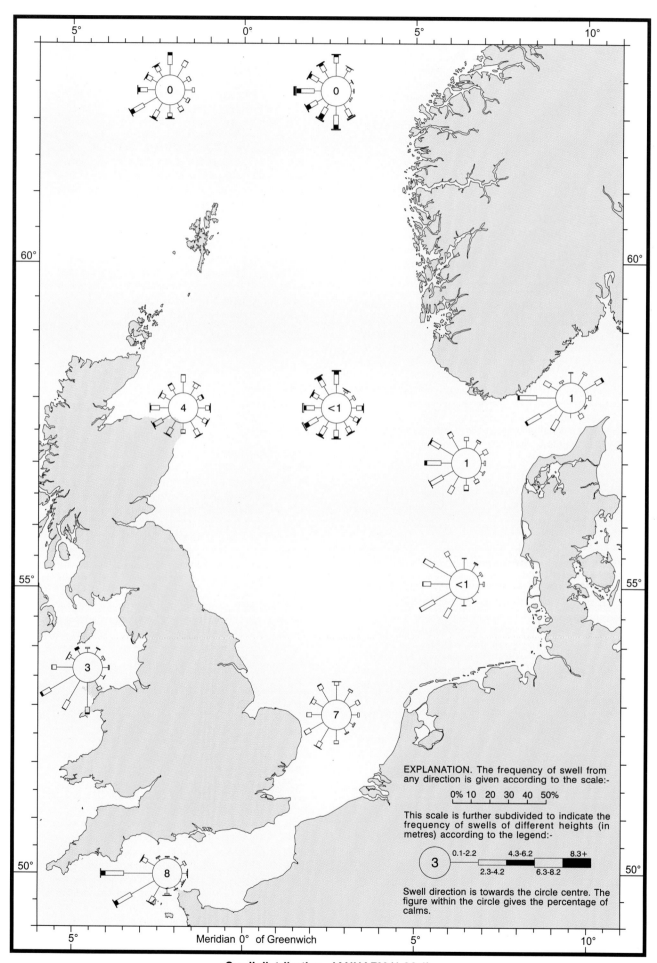

EXPLANATION. The frequency of swell from any direction is given according to the scale:-

0% 10 20 30 40 50%

This scale is further subdivided to indicate the frequency of swells of different heights (in metres) according to the legend:-

3   0.1-2.2   4.3-6.2   8.3+
         2.3-4.2   6.3-8.2

Swell direction is towards the circle centre. The figure within the circle gives the percentage of calms.

Meridian 0° of Greenwich

Swell distribution JANUARY (1.96.1)

16

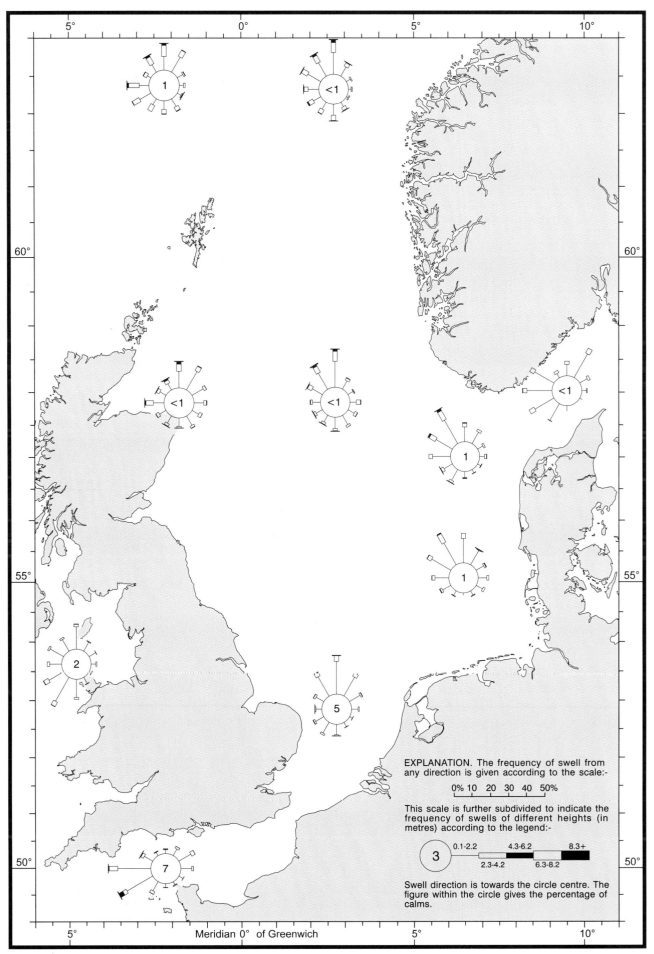

EXPLANATION. The frequency of swell from any direction is given according to the scale:-

0% 10   20   30   40   50%

This scale is further subdivided to indicate the frequency of swells of different heights (in metres) according to the legend:-

3   0.1-2.2   4.3-6.2   8.3+
        2.3-4.2   6.3-8.2

Swell direction is towards the circle centre. The figure within the circle gives the percentage of calms.

Swell distribution APRIL (1.96.2)

17

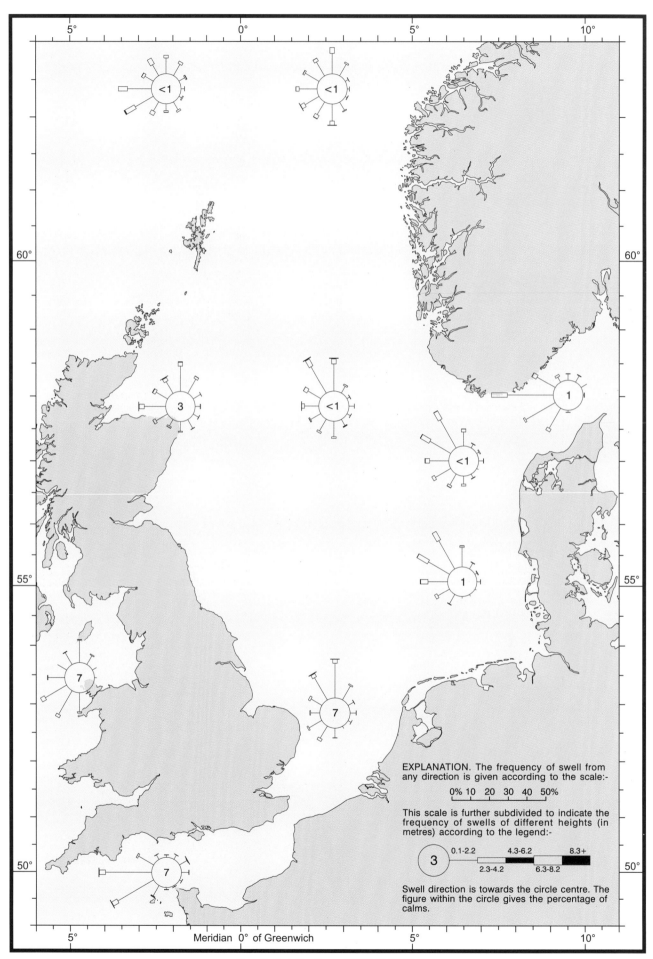

EXPLANATION. The frequency of swell from any direction is given according to the scale:-

0% 10 20 30 40 50%

This scale is further subdivided to indicate the frequency of swells of different heights (in metres) according to the legend:-

3   0.1-2.2   4.3-6.2   8.3+
     2.3-4.2   6.3-8.2

Swell direction is towards the circle centre. The figure within the circle gives the percentage of calms.

Meridian 0° of Greenwich

Swell distribution JULY (1.96.3)

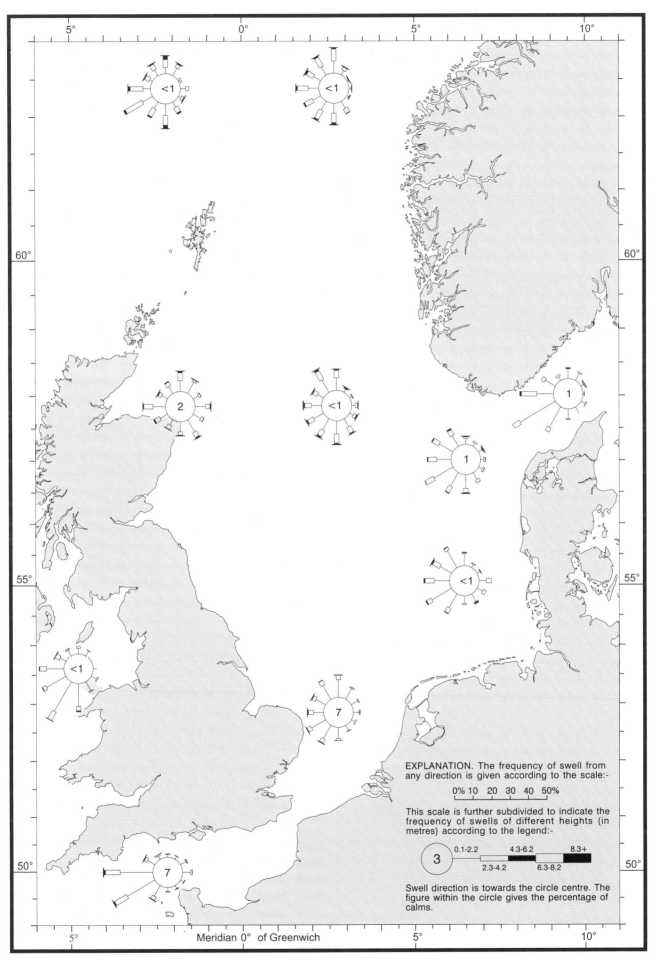

EXPLANATION. The frequency of swell from any direction is given according to the scale:-

0% 10 20 30 40 50%

This scale is further subdivided to indicate the frequency of swells of different heights (in metres) according to the legend:-

0.1-2.2   4.3-6.2   8.3+
3   2.3-4.2   6.3-8.2

Swell direction is towards the circle centre. The figure within the circle gives the percentage of calms.

Swell distribution OCTOBER (1.96.4)

SEA WATER CHARACTERISTICS

Density
1.97

1 Typical summer values are 1·027 g/cm³ and winter values are 1·025 g/cm³.

Sea surface salinity distribution
1.98

1 Summer surface salinity distribution varies from 34·50‰ around much of the coast to 34·75‰ towards the N of the region. During the winter lower salinity values of less than 34·00‰ are observed off the Firth of Forth and the coast between latitudes 52°N and 53°N, reflecting high fresh water input from river run-off. Generally much of the coastal region has typical winter surface salinity values of 34·25‰. Winter and summer bottom salinities reflect the uniform nature of the water column.

Sea surface temperature
1.99

1 The diagrams in 1.99 show the mean sea surface temperature of the waters surrounding the British Isles for February, May, August and November.

2 In winter the sea surface temperature is governed by the influx of the warm water associated with the North Atlantic Current. The limit of this warm water is usually delineated by the 6°C isotherm. Minimum sea surface temperatures are normally recorded in February or early March when values average about 5°C to 6°C along the whole of the E coast. Temperatures are generally lower in the S than in the N, with the waters between 52°30′N and 54°00′N, being the coldest around the British coastline.

3 In spring and summer, the seas warm up much more rapidly in the S of the region than in the N. Generally the seas off the E coast of Britain are warmest in August with a mean sea surface temperature of around 16 to 17°C in the extreme S of the region and 13 to 14°C off the E coast of Scotland.

Variability
1.100

1 In the warmest summers, the coastal sea temperatures can reach 20°C in the S and 17°C in the N, whilst in the coldest of winters extreme temperatures of 1°C have been recorded in the S and 2°C to 3°C in the N.

CLIMATE AND WEATHER

General information
1.101

1 The following information should be read in conjunction with the relevant chapters of *The Mariner's Handbook*.

Weather reports and forecasts which cover the area are regularly broadcast in a number of languages; see the relevant *Admiralty List of Radio Signals*.

2 **Ice accumulation.** In certain weather conditions, ice accumulation on hulls and superstructures of ships can be a serious danger. This hazard occasionally occurs in the N part of the area covered by this book. See *The Mariner's Handbook* for details on the causes of ice accumulation and the recommended course of action.

General conditions
1.102

1 The climate is in general mild for the latitude with winds most usually from between S and NW. In winter, strong to gale force winds, cloudy to overcast skies and rain/snow are common, although precipitation amounts are not large. On occasions E winds can bring exceptionally cold weather to the region. Winter temperatures are broadly similar on the E coasts of both England and Scotland, but in the N the winter is longer, spring is later and cooler and summer and autumn a few degrees cooler than in the S.

2 In summer, gales become less frequent than in winter although winds are often fresh or strong. There is little seasonal variation in the rainfall and the summer months are often cloudy and cool. However there are occasional spells of hot dry weather when temperatures can exceed 30°C.

3 Fog occasionally affects the E coast, particularly in the N. Over the open sea fog is not especially frequent; in winter it is more likely in the S than in the N, but in the summer the N has the higher incidence.

Pressure

Mean pressure fields
1.103

1 The distribution of the mean atmospheric pressure over the area is shown in diagrams 1.103. In general, pressure increases from NW to SE across the area with the lowest pressure in the NW in autumn and winter and the highest in the SE in spring and summer..

2 It is emphasised that these mean pressure fields are the average of dissimilar and often rapidly changing day to day situations, indeed an important characteristic of the North Sea region is the mobility and irregularity of the pressure systems affecting it and the variable nature of the weather associated with them.

Variability
1.104

1 Extreme pressure values may vary between 1050 hPa (mb) and 950 hPa due to the movement of depressions and anticyclones. During disturbed weather large variations can occur with, on occasions, pressure changes of 40 hPa in a period of 24 hours, especially in winter.

Anticyclones

The Azores anticyclone
1.105

1 The weather of the region is much influenced by this anticyclone. It is usually centred at around 35°N but recedes to the S in winter. It is usually the source of the mild damp W to SW airstreams which often affect the British Isles and the North Sea. In summer a ridge of high pressure often extends ENE to Europe displacing the E-moving mobile depressions further N and bringing attendant settled weather.

2 Mobile anticyclones, frequently originating as offshoots from the Azores anticyclone, often drift ENE across England and the North Sea. These anticyclones can, in winter when the sea is cold, result in persistent cloud and poor visibility.

The Scandinavian anticyclone
1.106

1 Occasionally and especially in winter, a mobile anticyclone becomes slow moving or stationary over Scandinavia. Alternatively a ridge of high pressure may extend W from the winter anticyclone over Asia and develop a separate centre over NE Europe. These anticyclones can last for 4 to 5 days and exceptionally for several weeks. They might bring very cold NE to SE winds which might reach gale force over the North Sea.

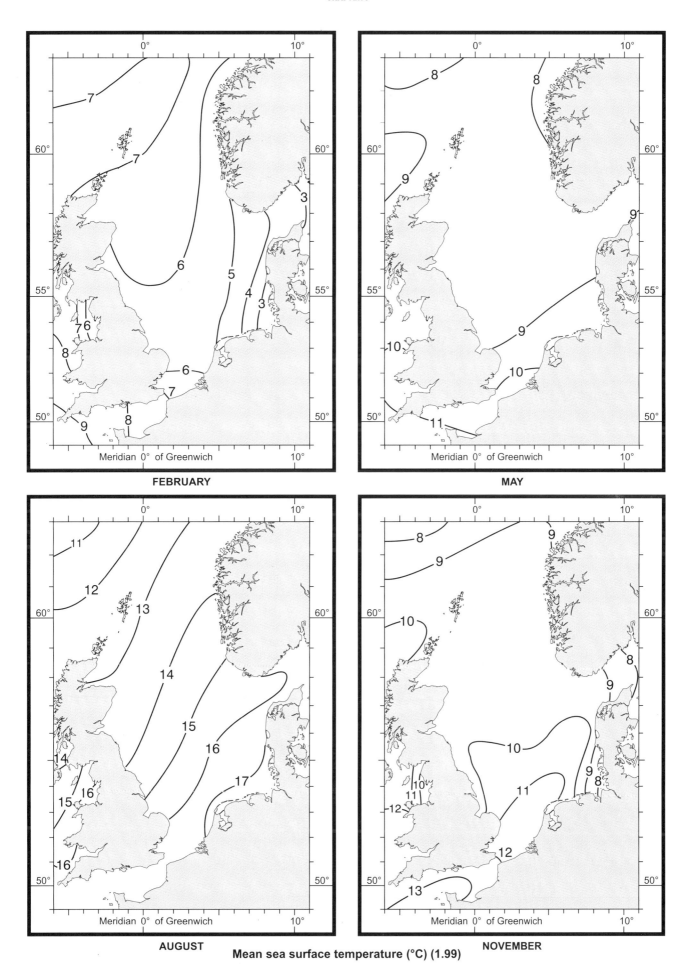

FEBRUARY

MAY

AUGUST

NOVEMBER

Mean sea surface temperature (°C) (1.99)

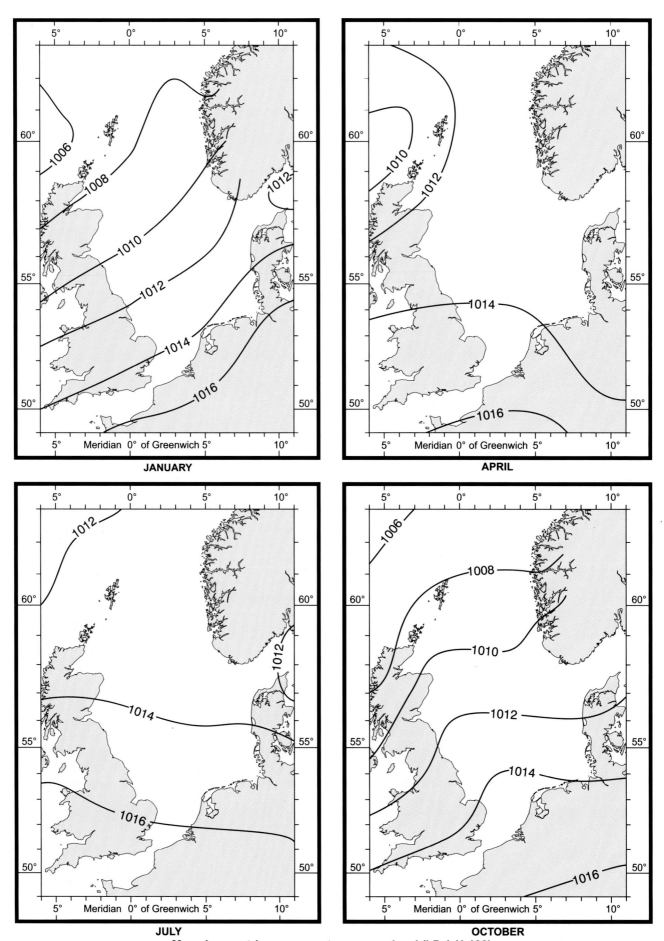

JANUARY

APRIL

JULY

OCTOBER

Mean barometric pressure at mean sea level (hPa) (1.103)

2　　The onset of strong E winds might be preceded and accompanied by a rising barometer. Sometimes the weather is crisp and clear but showers, frequently of snow in winter, might develop and become frequent on the E coast of Britain.

Depressions

Atlantic depressions
1.107

1　　Most of the major N Atlantic depressions pass N of this region, but frontal troughs on the S side of the circulations often sweep across the North Sea. The depressions which most commonly affect the North Sea are secondary lows that develop in the circulations of the major depressions. Usually originating as a "wave" on a cold front, they intensify as they move E or NE to cross the British Isles to the North Sea and the Baltic. These depressions are often fast moving, typically around 20 to 30 kn, and can develop quickly to become vigorous systems, in particular when moving E into the North Sea. They are the prime cause of the variable weather of the region and usually give rise to mild damp SW winds on their S flanks, but often leave cold strong to gale force NW or N winds with showers after passing through.

2　　Most depressions move E or NE although occasionally a system may behave erratically. When an anticyclone becomes established over Scandinavia, depressions approaching from the Atlantic are deflected N or S of their normal track. More depressions cross the N part of the North Sea than the S in all seasons and are most numerous in the N during summer, when the main track lies across or to the N of Scotland and thence to the Skagerrak. Summer depressions are usually shallower and less intense than those which develop in the winter and spring. Depressions tend to occur in groups of 3 or 4 with similar tracks at intervals of 1 to 2 days. See *The Mariner's Handbook* for a description of the sequence of weather to be expected with the passage of a depression.

Polar depressions
1.108

1　　Another distinct type of depression which might reach the region from the Norwegian Sea area is termed the polar depression. They are characterised by relatively small circulations of intense showers which frequently bring outbreaks of snow to the region in winter and spring.

Fronts

Polar front
1.109

1　　Most of the depressions which affect the North Sea have warm and cold fronts associated with them. These fronts represent the boundary between the cool unstable polar air of N origin and mild stable air of sub-tropical origin to the S. In some cases the fronts might have occluded (ie the cold front has overtaken the warm front) by the time the system reaches the North Sea, and on these occasions the contrast between conditions on either side of the front might be less marked.

2　　The E progress of warm fronts is often retarded or halted by the high ground of N Britain and the fronts rapidly become occluded. Warm air from the SW may reach the E coast from the N and S in the lee of the mountains or via the gaps in the hills such as the Forth Clyde valley, and the fronts might produce little more than patchy light rain. However, when a depression moves across Scotland or the N of England to the North Sea, and the winds ahead and to the N of the system back from SE to NE, appreciable and continuous rain on the E coast of Britain often results.

3　　Cold fronts affect the region throughout the year and in winter they frequently herald an outbreak of cold air from the Arctic with strong N winds, snow, hail and occasionally thunder. These fronts can, on occasions, give rise to violent squalls particularly in the lee of high ground.

Winds

Average distribution
1.110

1　　The wind roses in diagrams 1.110.1 to 1.110.4 show the percentage frequency of winds from various directions and the Beaufort Force.

Variability
1.111

1　　Great variability in both direction and strength is the principal characteristic of the winds over the North Sea due to the numerous mobile depressions which cross the area and the topography of the E coast of Britain, which introduces many local variations.

Open sea
1.112

1　　Over the open sea winds may blow from any direction in all seasons. Winds from between S and NW are the most common in all seasons. However, in the spring there is a marked increase in the frequency of winds from between N and E.

2　　The windiest time of the year is winter. In the S winds may reach or exceed force 7 on around 6 to 9 days a month, but the incidence increases further N, and over the waters to the E of Scotland the figure may be as much as 12 to 16 days a month. The quietest season is May to August when winds of force 7 and above are experienced on about 1 to 3 days a month in the S and 4 to 5 days a month in the N.

3　　See diagrams 1.112 for the percentage frequency of winds of force 7 or more.

Coastal areas
1.113

1　　Seasonal variability of winds in coastal waters is similar to the open sea but topography can cause local anomalies, which may extend to around 20 miles offshore. Winds from a W point are generally weaker than over the open sea to the E, but are prone to gusts and in the lee of high ground squalls may be experienced. W winds tend to be funnelled down river estuaries, such as the Firth of Forth and the River Tay, giving local increases in winds offshore. Winds blowing parallel to the coastline increase around headlands, especially where there are cliffs or high ground close inshore.

Land and sea breezes
1.114

1　　North Sea coastal waters are affected by land and sea breezes from late spring to early autumn. In otherwise calm or light wind conditions a sea breeze sets in as an onshore wind about noon, but can be delayed when opposed by a W prevailing wind, and dies around sunset.

2　　Land breezes are usually weaker than sea breezes. They arise as an offshore wind towards midnight and fade soon after dawn. They can be enhanced by a katabatic or down slope breeze. As with the sea breeze they might modify or strengthen the prevailing wind.

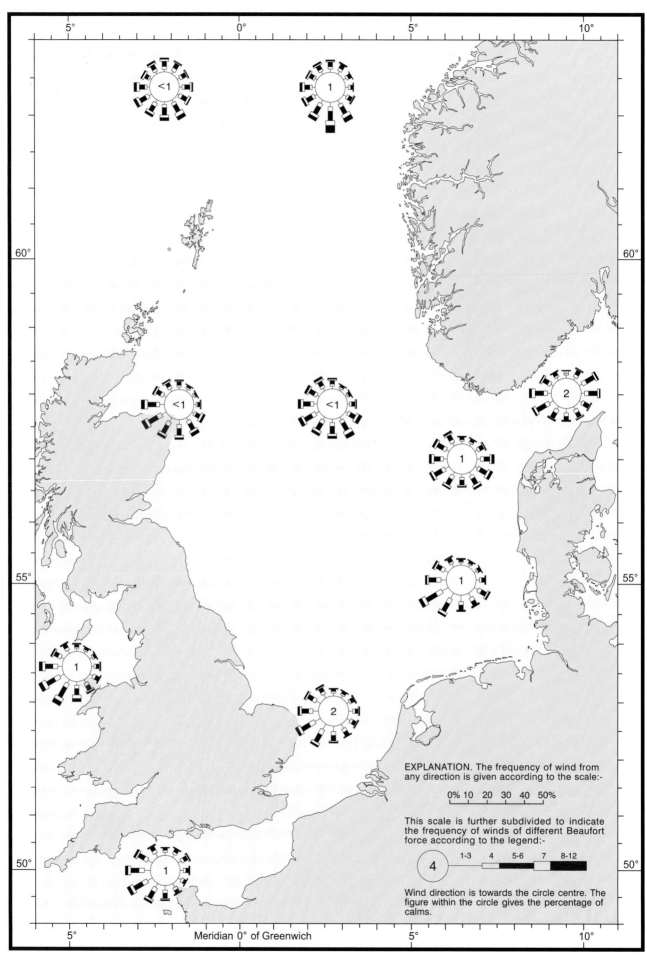

EXPLANATION. The frequency of wind from any direction is given according to the scale:-

0% 10   20   30   40   50%

This scale is further subdivided to indicate the frequency of winds of different Beaufort force according to the legend:-

1-3   4   5-6   7   8-12

Wind direction is towards the circle centre. The figure within the circle gives the percentage of calms.

Meridian 0° of Greenwich

Wind distribution JANUARY (1.110.1)

24

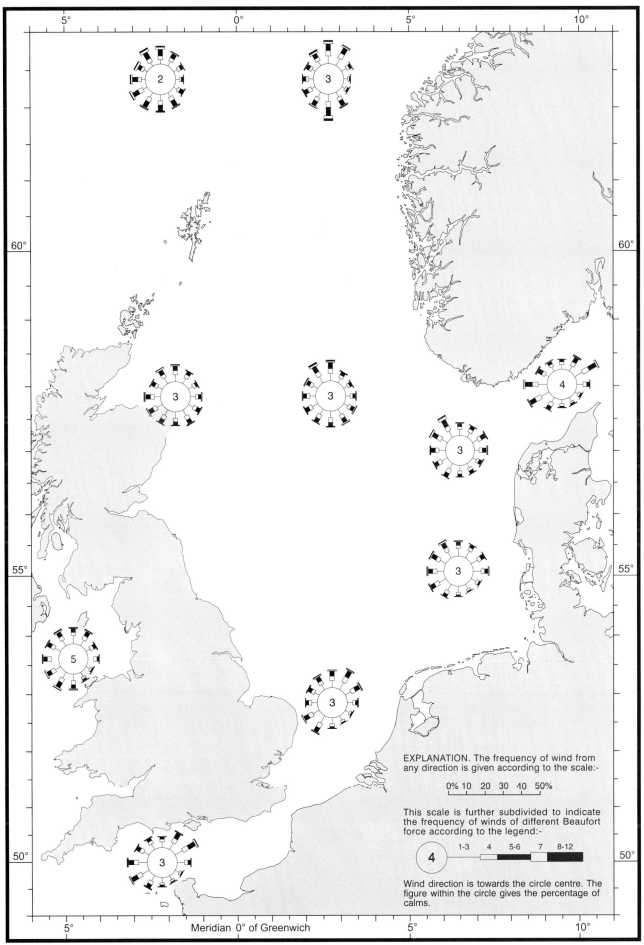

EXPLANATION. The frequency of wind from any direction is given according to the scale:-

0% 10 20 30 40 50%

This scale is further subdivided to indicate the frequency of winds of different Beaufort force according to the legend:-

4   1-3   4   5-6   7   8-12

Wind direction is towards the circle centre. The figure within the circle gives the percentage of calms.

Meridian 0° of Greenwich

Wind distribution APRIL (1.110.2)

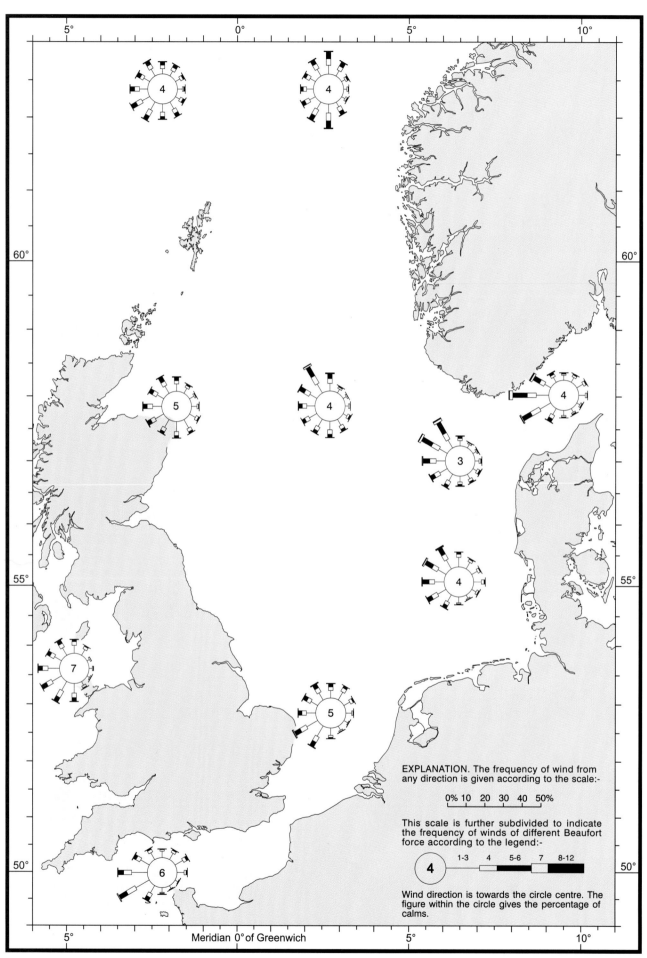

EXPLANATION. The frequency of wind from any direction is given according to the scale:-

0% 10 20 30 40 50%

This scale is further subdivided to indicate the frequency of winds of different Beaufort force according to the legend:-

1-3 4 5-6 7 8-12

Wind direction is towards the circle centre. The figure within the circle gives the percentage of calms.

Meridian 0° of Greenwich

Wind distribution JULY (1.110.3)

26

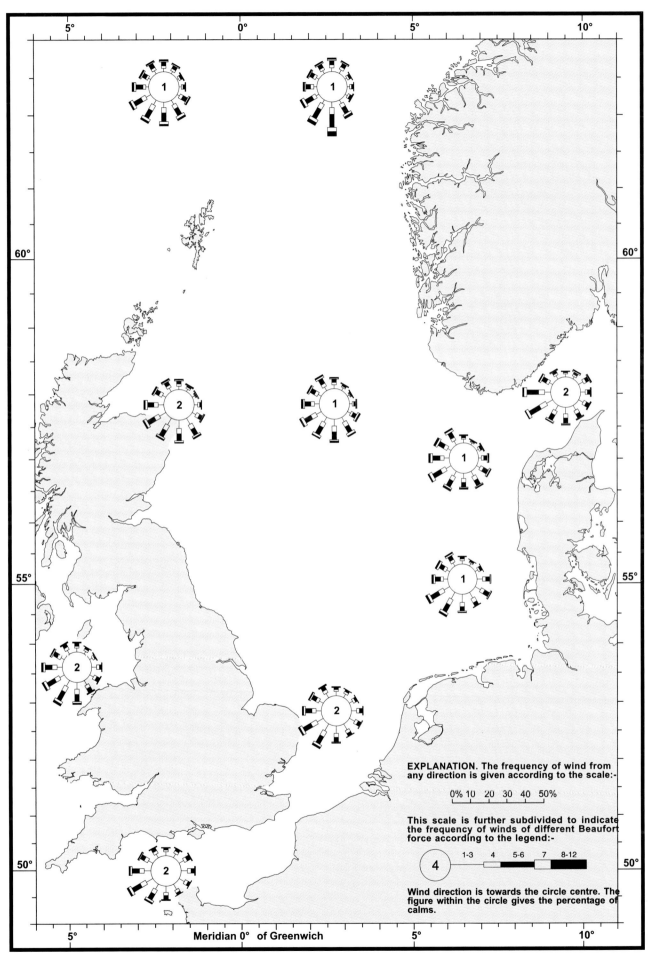

EXPLANATION. The frequency of wind from any direction is given according to the scale:-

0% 10 20 30 40 50%

This scale is further subdivided to indicate the frequency of winds of different Beaufort force according to the legend:-

4 | 1-3 | 4 | 5-6 | 7 | 8-12

Wind direction is towards the circle centre. The figure within the circle gives the percentage of calms.

Wind distribution OCTOBER (1.110.4)

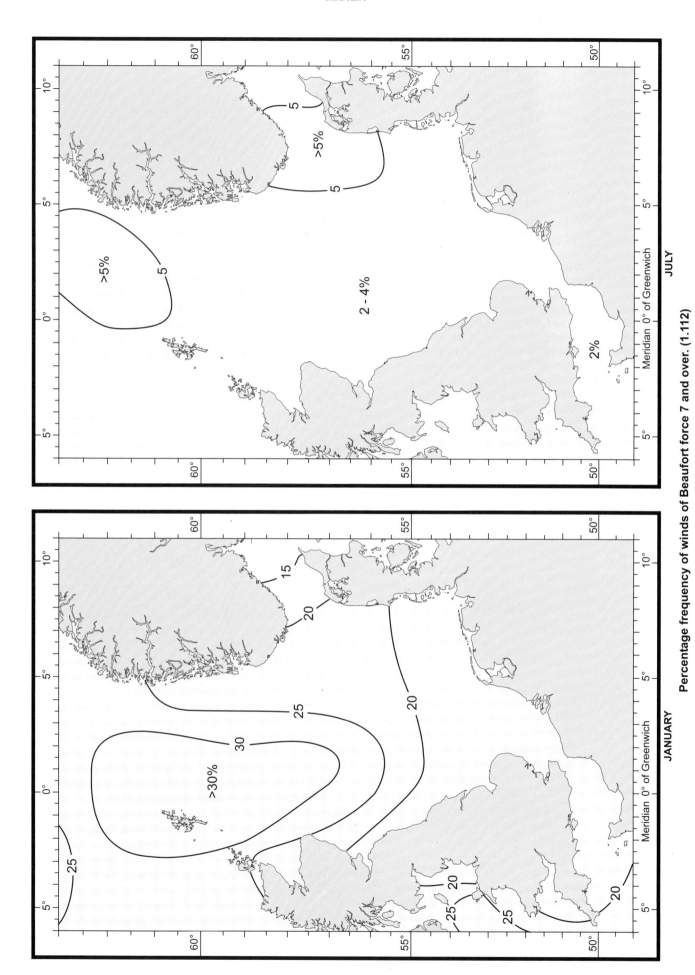

Percentage frequency of winds of Beaufort force 7 and over. (1.112)

JULY

JANUARY

Gales
1.115

1 The N of the area covered by this volume is a stormy place in winter when winds of gale force 8 or more can be expected on 8 to 12 days a month. Storm force winds are not uncommon and hurricane force 12 is recorded on occasions each winter. Farther S gale frequency is much lower and in the extreme S of the area the winter incidence of gales is about 3 to 4 days a month. Frequencies decrease throughout spring and in summer gales are to be expected on fewer than 2 days a month over the whole of the area. Autumn generally sees a rapid increase in the frequency of gales, especially in the N. Gales may blow from any direction but with fewer gales from between E and NE.

2 The Climatic Tables give the number of days with gales for each month for a number of coastal stations in the area. Gale frequencies in coastal waters are about half those for the open sea. The E coast of Britain is to some extent sheltered from W gales but these winds can raise unpleasant conditions in some river estuaries due to funnelling. The E coast of Scotland is very exposed to gales from between SE and NE. Further S on the coast of England the most dangerous gales are from between N and E.

Gusts
1.116

1 On the E coast of Britain gusts are a notable feature of winds, particularly when strong or gale force winds blow offshore. The strongest gusts have been recorded on the E coast of Scotland, with speeds reaching 90 to 95 kn. Farther S in the vicinity of latitudes 52°N to 53°N maximum gusts of 70 to 80 kn have been recorded.

2 Gusts are essentially short-lived and transient. The duration of a gust is of the order of 3 seconds, but wind speeds may be double the average speed.

Squalls
1.117

1 Distinct from gusts, squalls are of much longer duration, being sudden drastic increases in wind that last for at least a minute. They are also a well known feature of the region.

2 In the North Sea squalls associated with cold fronts may occur at any time of the year. The showers of hail, sleet or snow, common with N or NW winds in winter or spring often give rise to sudden changes in wind speed and direction.

3 Off the E coast of Scotland sudden and violent mountain squalls can sweep down to affect coastal waters and cause considerable hazard to smaller vessels. Between May and September occasional squalls drift off shore, generally appearing between noon and midnight. While they are not a frequent feature in any particular place, one or two destructive squalls of force 8 or more are reported on some part of this coast every year.

Cloud
1.118

1 The area covered by this volume is generally cloudy with an average of 5 to 6 oktas of cloud for the greater part of the year, but with winter marginally cloudier than spring or summer.

2 When W or SW airstreams blow over Britain, cloud is often well broken on the leeward E coast, especially where there is high ground to the W. In E Scotland the sheltering high ground can on occasions give rise to abnormally fine weather with only small amounts of cloud over the coastal strip between Arbroath and Aberdeen, but this fine weather only extends a few miles out to sea.

3 When transitting depressions give winds from an E point, widespread overcast conditions can result with extensive rain cloud on the coast. On the other hand, E winds associated with a high barometric pressure can give spells of fine weather in both winter and summer as dry air is brought from the continent. However, in late winter and early spring low cloud and fog is more common due to the low sea temperature.

Precipitation
1.119

1 The Climatic Tables give the average amounts of precipitation for each month at several coastal stations and the mean number of days in each month when significant precipitation is recorded.

Rain
1.120

1 Moist SW airstreams deposit much of their rain over the high ground to the W, thereby making the E coast one of the driest parts Britain.

2 South of the Firth of Forth average annual rainfall amounts are around 500 to 700 mm. Further N the coastal area is slightly wetter with annual falls of 700 to 900 mm. Seasonal variability is small with the driest conditions generally from February to April and the wettest from October to December.

Snow
1.121

1 Snow is recorded most frequently between December and April. In the S it might occur as early as November and in the N from October and as late as May. During the months of January and February, snow or sleet can be expected on an average of about 10 to 12 days a month in the extreme N of the area and on 5 to 7 days a month in the S. Snow is generally of short duration in coastal areas and rarely lies on low ground before November or after March.

Thunderstorms and hail
1.122

1 Thunderstorms can occur at any time of the year, but are most frequent between May and September and rare between October and March. Between May and September there are generally only 1 or 2 a month in most areas except for the extreme S where there might be 3 or 4 a month on occasions.

2 Hail occasionally occurs in winter but is more common in April.

Fog and visibility

Open ocean
1.123

1 Fog is not especially common over the open sea, but good visibility in excess of 10 miles is also rather infrequent. Fog is most often associated with warm moist air blowing over a relatively cold sea with winds between SE and SW.

2 Diagrams 1.123 show the average incidence of fog (visibility less than 1 km) for the months of January and July.

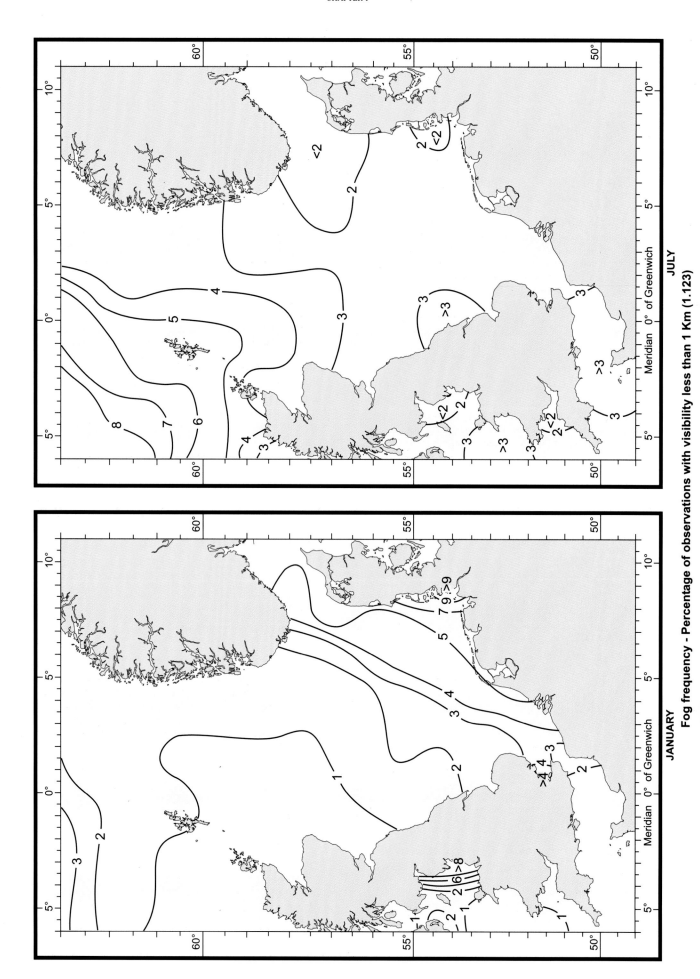

JANUARY

JULY

Meridian 0° of Greenwich

Fog frequency - Percentage of observations with visibility less than 1 Km (1.123)

2　In winter fog is most likely to be encountered in the extreme S of the area covered by this volume, where it is recorded in 3% to 4% of observations. Further N the frequency decreases to less than 1%. In summer the distribution is reversed, with fog recorded on about 2% of occasions in the S and between 3% and 4% in the extreme N.

Coastal areas
1.124
1　A characteristic of the E coast of Scotland is good visibility, but it is also liable to be affected by sea fog as indeed are all parts of the E coast of Britain throughout the year. The coast N of the River Humber is especially subject to fog, which is most commonly a hazard in spring and summer, sometimes persisting for several days. It is known locally as "haar" and the incidence is highest on the E coast of Scotland. The conditions most favourable for haar formation are winds from between E and SE that bring warm moist air to cold coastal waters. Haar is particularly troublesome after exceptionally cold winters.

2　In exceptional years fog has been recorded on the coast N of 57°N on up to 14 days a month. The coast is most affected by haar at night with a tendency for the fog to disperse or lift to low stratus over the land during the day. It is however likely to reappear towards dusk, especially when fog has persisted all day over the sea. Haar might be brought inshore very suddenly after the onset of a sea breeze and may be preceded by a very rapid fall in temperature of several degrees. The state of the tide might also have an effect with a rising tide favouring the advance of fog towards the coast.

3　Radiation fog (see *Mariner's Handbook* for a full description of the different types of fog) forms, between October and April, on about 3 to 6 days a month in the S of the area and on 2 to 4 days a month in the N. This type of fog tends to disperse soon after sunrise, especially in summer, but is often slow to clear in winter and can, on occasions, persist all day.

Air temperature

General information
1.125
1　In general the coldest months are January and February and the warmest July and August. The air temperature can be extremely variable from one day to the next due to the extremely unsettled conditions which can affect the area.

Open sea
1.126
1　The mean air temperature over the open sea in January is between 4°C and 6°C and in July it increases to about 13°C in the N of the area and around 16°C in the S. Air temperature rarely falls below 0°C or rises above 19°C, but extreme cases can occur with persistent E winds. In these circumstances very low temperatures might occur in winter and exceptionally high values in summer.

Coastal areas
1.127
1　The climatic tables at the end of this chapter include statistical information on air temperature for a number of coastal stations in the area.

2　Maximum temperatures are reached in July and August when mean daily maximum values are around 17°C to 18°C in the N and 1°C or 2°C higher in the S. During exceptionally warm spells temperature may rise to around 30°C. Lowest temperatures are usually recorded in January and February when on average they fall to between 0°C and 2°C. In extreme conditions temperatures of –6°C in the S and –11°C in the N have been recorded.

Humidity
1.128
1　Over the open sea the mean humidity is about 82% in winter and 84% in summer. In coastal areas it is more variable reaching a maximum of about 88% around dawn on most nights and falling to about 75% on summer afternoons. Very low humidities are sometimes recorded on the E coast of N England and Scotland with W winds and, on rare occasions, humidities of 20% have been recorded in the afternoon.

CLIMATIC TABLES
1.129
1　The tables which follow give data for a number of coastal stations in the area covered by this volume. It is emphasised that the data are average conditions and refer to the specific location of the observing station and therefore may not be representative of the conditions to be expected over the open sea or in the approaches to ports in their vicinity. The following notes indicate ways in which conditions over the open sea might be different from those at the nearest reporting station (see *The Mariner's Handbook* for further details).

2　Wind speeds tend to be higher at sea with more frequent gales than over the land, although funnelling in narrow inlets can result in an increase in wind strength.

Topography has a marked effect on local conditions.

Air temperature over the sea is less variable than over the land. In winter the temperature is usually higher over the sea, especially at night, and in summer it is usually cooler than over the land, especially during the day.

1.130

WMO No 03092

PETERHEAD (57° 50′ N, 1° 46′ W) Height above MSL – 15 m

Climatic Table compiled from 9 to years observations, to 1993

Month	Average pressure at MSL (mb)	Temperatures				Average humidity		Average cloud cover		Precipitation		Wind distribution – Percentage of observations from 0900									Wind distribution – Percentage of observations from 1500									Mean wind speed		Number of days with		
		Mean daily max. (°C)	Mean daily min. (°C)	Mean highest in each month (°C)	Mean lowest in each month (°C)	0900 (%)	1500 (%)	0900 (Oktas)	1500 (Oktas)	Average fall (mm)	No. of days with 1 mm or more	N	NE	E	SE	S	SW	W	NW	Calm	N	NE	E	SE	S	SW	W	NW	Calm	0900 (Knots)	1500 (Knots)	Gale	Fog	Thunder
January	1011					82	80	6	6			6	4	6	3	28	24	20	7	3	5	4	7	4	28	21	19	8	4	12	13	1	⊕	⊕
February	1010					84	78	6	6			5	4	5	5	27	20	25	6	4	7	5	5	8	29	14	22	8	2	12	12	1	1	0
March	1008					85	76	6	6			5	2	4	9	29	17	20	8	6	4	4	5	8	33	14	19	10	3	11	12	1	1	0
April	1012					84	76	6	6			16	8	6	8	24	11	13	8	5	22	10	7	9	27	7	10	7	2	10	11	⊕	2	0
May	1017					87	78	6	6			23	2	8	11	19	9	11	9	7	24	7	9	12	24	4	7	12	2	9	10	⊕	5	⊕
June	1015					88	80	6	6			25	6	6	13	14	4	12	13	8	24	6	6	14	27	2	1	16	5	8	8	0	4	⊕
July	1014					89	80	7	6			13	4	4	11	27	9	16	11	5	14	7	10	15	27	4	7	12	3	8	9	⊕	6	⊕
August	1010					88	78	6	6			10	2	2	9	31	14	17	11	5	14	5	3	15	29	7	9	14	5	9	9	⊕	2	0
September	1013					86	76	6	6			9	3	2	8	22	19	24	10	3	14	2	4	8	25	14	16	14	3	10	11	⊕	2	⊕
October	1010					84	79	6	6			4	4	7	11	28	17	20	4	4	8	5	3	13	31	14	12	10	4	11	11	1	1	0
November	1009					83	79	6	6			7	3	3	3	24	20	29	9	3	10	2	3	5	25	20	19	13	3	12	12	1	1	0
December	1011					82	81	6	6			5	4	3	4	24	24	23	7	4	5	4	4	5	24	22	26	7	5	11	11	1	1	0
Means	1012	–	–	– *	– §	85	78	6	6	–	–	11	4	5	8	25	16	19	9	5	13	5	6	10	27	12	14	11	3	10	11	–	–	–
Totals										–	–																					7	26	2
Extreme values	–	–	–	– †	– ‡	–	–			–	–																					–	–	–
No. of years observations	9						9		9									9									9				9		9	9

* Mean of highest each year
§ Mean of lowest each year
† Highest recorded temperature
‡ Lowest recorded temperature
⊕ Rare
⊕ All observations

1.131

WMO No 03091

ABERDEEN (DYCE) (57° 12' N, 2° 12' W) Height above MSL – 65 m
Climatic Table compiled from 21 to 62 years observations, 1931 to 1993

Month	Average pressure at MSL	Temperatures				Average humidity		Average cloud cover		Precipitation		Wind distribution – Percentage of observations from																		Mean wind speed		Number of days with			
		Mean daily max	Mean daily min	Mean highest in each month	Mean lowest in each month	0600	1500	0900	1500	Average fall	No. of days with 1 mm or more	0900										1500									0900	1500	Gale	Fog	Thunder	Sleet/Snow
												N	NE	E	SE	S	SW	W	NW	Calm	N	NE	E	SE	S	SW	W	NW	Calm						
	mb	°C	°C	°C	°C	%	%	Oktas	Oktas	mm																				Knots	Knots				
January	1009	6	0	11	-8	85	81	6	6	80	13	7	3	5	9	23	17	15	12	10	6	2	4	10	25	17	15	15	6	10	11	1	1	⊕	11
February	1012	6	0	12	-7	86	77	6	6	54	10	8	3	5	13	24	13	14	11	10	4	4	6	15	28	14	15	13	1	9	11	1	2	0	10
March	1012	8	1	14	-5	86	72	6	6	56	12	8	3	6	11	22	14	15	16	6	8	4	8	14	22	13	14	15	1	10	13	1	2	0	9
April	1013	10	3	17	-3	87	69	6	6	52	11	18	7	7	8	14	10	11	22	3	16	7	12	18	15	7	9	15	1	10	12	1	2	⊕	5
May	1015	13	5	20	-1	88	70	6	6	60	10	14	6	9	16	17	9	7	20	3	14	4	16	26	17	6	4	13	⊕	10	12	⊕	2	1	1
June	1014	16	8	23	2	87	70	7	6	54	9	18	6	7	11	15	9	9	22	3	13	5	16	20	18	6	4	17	1	9	11	⊕	2	1	⊕
July	1013	18	10	24	4	88	71	6	6	75	11	11	5	7	10	19	11	11	23	3	11	3	15	20	19	8	6	17	1	9	10	⊕	2	1	0
August	1013	18	10	23	4	90	71	6	6	76	11	10	3	6	9	23	14	11	21	3	7	3	12	21	24	9	8	16	⊕	9	10	⊕	3	1	0
September	1012	16	8	21	1	88	72	6	6	66	11	8	3	4	10	20	17	15	20	3	10	3	6	15	20	14	14	19	1	10	11	1	1	1	0
October	1011	12	6	18	-1	88	77	6	6	82	12	8	3	5	12	22	15	15	13	8	6	3	5	15	26	13	14	16	2	9	11	1	2	⊕	1
November	1009	8	2	14	-5	88	80	6	6	80	13	7	2	3	5	23	18	20	15	8	5	1	3	6	25	17	21	19	3	10	11	1	1	⊕	5
December	1009	6	0	12	-7	85	82	6	6	76	13	6	3	4	11	18	21	16	14	8	5	2	5	10	22	17	18	15	5	10	12	1	1	⊕	8
Means	1012	11	4	25*	-11§	87	74	6	6	–	–	10	4	6	10	20	14	13	17	6	9	4	9	16	22	12	12	16	2	10	11	–	–	–	–
Totals										811	136																					8	21	5	50
Extreme values	–	–	–	28†	-19‡	–	–	–	–	–	–																			–	–	–	–	–	–
No. of years observations	62	35				30		40		62/36		21									21									21		56	21	36	36

* Mean of highest each year
§ Mean of lowest each year
† Highest recorded temperature
‡ Lowest recorded temperature
⊕ Rare
⊕ All observations

1.132

WMO No 03396

FIFE NESS (56° 18′ N, 2° 35′ W) Height above MSL – 12 m

Climatic Table compiled from 8 to 10 years observations, 1984 to 1993

Month	Average pressure at MSL (mb)	Temp Mean daily max (°C)	Temp Mean daily min (°C)	Temp Mean highest in each month (°C)	Temp Mean lowest in each month (°C)	Humidity 0900 (%)	Humidity 1500 (%)	Cloud 0900 (Oktas)	Cloud 1500 (Oktas)	Precip Average fall (mm)	Precip No. of days with 1 mm or more	Wind 0900 N	NE	E	SE	S	SW	W	NW	Calm	Wind 1500 N	NE	E	SE	S	SW	W	NW	Calm	Wind speed 0900 (Knots)	Wind speed 1500	Gale	Fog	Thunder	Sleet/Snow
January	1012	7	2	11	-2	87	84	6	6	50	11	4	3	4	9	15	44	7	10	5	2	3	1	12	12	43	12	9	5	16	15	3	1	0	3
February	1010	7	2	12	-2	84	78	6	6	32	8	4	3	6	10	12	36	13	13	5	5	4	10	14	8	27	17	12	4	16	16	3	1	⊕	5
March	1009	8	3	13	-2	87	75	6	7	46	9	2	3	3	14	13	32	14	14	5	4	3	4	14	16	29	13	14	3	15	16	2	1	0	2
April	1012	10	4	16	0	87	76	7	6	41	9	9	11	7	12	14	19	7	14	8	12	13	10	16	13	16	8	7	5	14	14	1	3	0	2
May	1018	12	7	18	3	88	77	6	6	44	8	14	10	6	9	10	16	7	13	14	10	10	15	24	11	15	8	4	4	11	12	⊕	4	1	0
June	1015	15	9	21	5	88	79	6	6	49	9	15	14	5	12	11	12	6	12	12	6	11	14	28	11	13	4	5	8	9	11	⊕	3	1	0
July	1014	17	11	23	8	90	78	6	6	47	9	9	9	4	12	13	23	10	9	10	5	8	15	21	12	22	9	4	5	11	12	⊕	4	⊕	0
August	1011	18	11	22	7	90	76	6	6	68	12	5	2	3	13	20	27	10	13	8	5	4	7	24	18	25	9	7	2	12	13	⊕	1	⊕	0
September	1014	15	9	19	4	87	76	6	6	48	9	5	3	2	10	11	36	13	15	6	4	6	9	10	15	28	11	10	6	13	13	1	2	1	0
October	1009	12	7	16	2	87	79	6	6	52	10	4	5	7	16	13	34	8	10	4	4	4	9	20	11	27	9	10	5	14	15	1	2	⊕	⊕
November	1010	9	4	14	-1	84	79	6	6	39	9	6	2	4	9	11	37	10	16	5	5	3	4	12	13	29	18	12	5	15	14	1	⊕	0	1
December	1013	8	3	12	-2	86	83	6	6	44	9	5	1	4	10	11	41	11	11	6	4	1	4	8	12	40	12	9	10	14	13	2	1	⊕	1
Means	1012	12	6	24*	-3§	87	78	6	6	–	–	7	5	5	12	13	30	10	12	7	6	6	8	17	13	26	11	9	5	13	14	–	–	–	–
Totals										560	112																					16	24	3	14
Extreme values				26†	-5‡																														–
No. of years observations	8	8				8		8		8		8																		8		10	10	10	10

* Mean of highest each year
§ Mean of lowest each year

† Highest recorded temperature
‡ Lowest recorded temperature

⊕ Rare
① All observations

1.133

WMO No 03240

BOULMER (55° 25' N, 1° 36' W) Height above MSL - 23 m

Climatic Table compiled from 17 to 18 years observations, 1976 to 1993

Month	Average pressure at MSL	Temperatures				Average humidity		Average cloud cover		Precipitation		Wind distribution – Percentage of observations from 0900									Wind distribution – Percentage of observations from 1500									Mean wind speed		Number of days with			
		Mean daily max.	Mean daily min.	Mean highest in each month	Mean lowest in each month	0900	1500	0900	1500	Average fall	No. of days with 1 mm or more	N	NE	E	SE	S	SW	W	NW	Calm	N	NE	E	SE	S	SW	W	NW	Calm	0900	1500	Gale	Fog	Thunder	Sleet/Snow
	mb	°C	°C	°C	°C	%	%	Oktas	Oktas	mm																					Knots	Knots				
January	1012	6	1	12	-5	85	80	6	6	56	11	4	3	5	5	22	23	28	10	1	5	3	5	7	19	23	24	13	2	12	12	2	1	⊕	9
February	1014	6	1	11	-4	85	78	6	6	45	9	5	6	8	11	20	16	24	10	2	7	8	9	15	19	18	16	8	1	11	12	1	2	⊕	8
March	1010	8	3	14	-3	87	74	6	6	55	11	8	4	4	9	22	15	24	14	⊕	12	6	6	17	15	17	19	8	⊕	12	13	1	1	0	5
April	1014	10	4	16	-1	87	75	6	6	43	9	17	9	8	10	11	13	15	16	2	20	15	9	18	9	12	11	5	0	10	12	⊕	2	⊕	4
May	1016	12	6	18	1	89	78	6	6	46	9	24	12	8	18	9	11	10	9	0	19	14	13	24	9	11	7	3	⊕	9	10	⊕	3	1	⊕
June	1015	15	9	22	4	89	76	6	6	51	9	20	14	8	15	8	12	13	9	⊕	18	16	12	22	6	14	9	3	0	9	10	0	2	2	0
July	1015	18	11	23	7	89	76	6	6	48	8	14	9	7	16	9	14	18	13	1	13	13	13	21	8	15	15	3	⊕	8	10	0	3	1	0
August	1014	18	11	23	6	91	76	6	6	62	10	13	6	5	15	12	17	16	15	1	13	11	11	20	8	19	14	5	1	9	10	⊕	2	1	0
September	1013	16	9	21	4	89	74	6	6	54	9	9	3	3	8	16	22	24	14	1	9	7	6	14	10	23	20	7	1	10	12	⊕	2	1	0
October	1010	13	7	18	1	89	79	6	6	64	11	4	5	5	10	24	19	23	10	1	7	6	6	18	14	21	19	10	⊕	11	11	⊕	2	⊕	⊕
November	1011	9	4	15	-1	86	79	6	6	62	12	5	4	3	4	19	25	28	11	1	7	5	3	6	18	26	20	14	1	11	11	1	1	⊕	2
December	1011	7	3	12	-4	86	83	6	6	68	11	3	4	7	6	21	20	26	12	1	4	3	6	6	18	23	25	13	2	11	11	1	1	⊕	5
Means	1013	12	6	25 *	-7§	88	77	6	6			11	7	6	11	16	17	21	12	1	11	9	8	16	13	18	17	8	1	10	11				
Totals										654	119																						6	22	7	34
Extreme values				28†	-12‡																															
No. of years observations	18	18				18		18		17		18									18										18		18	18	17	17

* Mean of highest each year
§ Mean of lowest each year

† Highest recorded temperature
‡ Lowest recorded temperature

⊕ Rare
⊖ All observations

1.134

WMO No 03262

TYNEMOUTH (55° 01' N, 1° 25' W) Height above MSL – 29 m
Climatic Table compiled from 36 to 66 years observations, 1912 to 1993

Month	Average pressure at MSL (mb)	Temp Mean daily max (°C)	Temp Mean daily min (°C)	Temp Mean highest in each month (°C)	Temp Mean lowest in each month (°C)	Humidity 0600 (%)	Humidity 1500 (%)	Cloud cover 0900 (Oktas)	Cloud cover 1500	Precip Average fall (mm)	Precip No. of days with 1 mm or more	Wind 0900 N	NE	E	SE	S	SW	W	NW	Calm	Wind 1500 N	NE	E	SE	S	SW	W	NW	Calm	Wind speed 0900 (Knots)	Wind speed 1500	Gale	Fog	Thunder	Sleet/Snow
January	1011	6	2	11	-4	85	81	6	6	52	11	4	3	7	4	22	18	33	6	2	8	4	5	5	22	15	32	7	2	14	15	4	3	⊕	7
February	1013	6	2	11	-3	85	77	6	6	39	8	5	5	10	8	23	15	26	7	3	9	6	11	11	22	12	20	7	3	14	15	3	2	⊕	6
March	1013	8	3	14	-2	86	74	6	6	47	10	8	5	7	8	19	14	28	7	4	15	6	10	14	14	10	23	5	3	14	15	2	2	⊕	4
April	1015	10	5	16	0	87	73	6	6	40	8	22	7	7	7	12	10	22	8	6	23	11	9	18	11	7	16	3	2	13	14	1	3	1	2
May	1016	12	7	19	3	88	77	6	6	46	9	29	5	5	14	12	8	15	6	6	23	9	12	22	12	8	12	1	2	12	13	1	4	1	⊕
June	1015	16	10	22	6	87	75	6	6	49	8	24	6	5	9	11	9	22	6	8	21	9	10	18	11	8	19	1	3	11	12	1	4	2	0
July	1014	17	12	23	8	88	75	6	6	55	9	20	3	4	10	12	9	28	7	9	18	7	10	18	12	7	23	2	3	10	12	1	3	2	0
August	1014	17	12	23	8	89	76	6	6	65	10	20	3	3	5	16	12	26	7	9	17	7	9	16	15	10	22	2	3	11	12	1	3	1	0
September	1014	16	11	21	6	88	73	6	6	53	9	10	2	3	3	19	17	30	8	7	11	7	8	15	13	11	29	4	2	11	13	1	2	1	0
October	1013	13	8	18	2	88	76	6	6	51	10	5	3	4	6	24	19	28	6	5	10	4	6	13	19	13	27	4	4	12	13	2	3	⊕	0
November	1011	9	5	14	-1	86	79	6	6	57	11	5	4	5	3	21	18	32	9	3	8	5	6	5	19	12	31	11	4	13	14	2	2	⊕	2
December	1011	7	3	12	-3	85	81	6	6	54	10	4	2	6	4	20	18	35	9	2	6	3	6	4	18	17	34	9	3	14	14	3	3	⊕	4
Means	1013	11	7	25 *	-6§	87	76	6	6			13	4	6	7	17	14	27	7	5	14	6	9	13	16	11	24	5	3	12	14				
Totals										608	113																					22	35	8	25
Extreme values				32†	-11‡																														
No. of years observations	66	66				66		36		36		36										36									36		36	36	36	36

* Mean of highest each year
§ Mean of lowest each year

† Highest recorded temperature
‡ Lowest recorded temperature

⊕ Rare
① All observations

1.135

WMO No 03271

TEESMOUTH/HARTLEPOOL (54° 38' N, 1° 08' W) Height above MSL – 12 m

Climatic Table compiled from 10 to 27 years observations, 1959 to 1993

Month	Average pressure at MSL (mb)	Temperatures: Mean daily max (°C)	Mean daily min (°C)	Mean highest in each month (°C)	Mean lowest in each month (°C)	Average humidity 0900 (%)	Average humidity 1500 (%)	Average cloud cover 0900 (Oktas)	Average cloud cover 1500 (Oktas)	Precipitation Average fall (mm)	Precipitation No. of days with 1 mm or more	Wind 0900 N	NE	E	SE	S	SW	W	NW	Calm	Wind 1500 N	NE	E	SE	S	SW	W	NW	Calm	Mean wind speed 0900 (Knots)	1500 (Knots)	Gale	Fog	Thunder	Sleet/Snow
January		6	1	12	-4			6	6	51	12	2	2	7	5	11	52	15	7	0	2	4	5	5	15	38	23	8	1	17	17	6	2	+	5
February		7	2	12	-4			6	6	35	8	5	4	7	11	10	39	19	6	0	8	5	13	7	7	29	22	9	0	17	19	6	2	+	3
March		9	3	14	-2			6	6	45	10	5	5	5	8	8	41	20	11	1	11	8	9	7	10	27	23	5	0	16	18	5	2	+	3
April		11	4	17	0			6	6	39	9	13	11	11	3	6	29	15	9	2	14	15	28	4	5	18	12	4	0	14	17	2	3	+	2
May		14	7	20	3			6	6	48	9	29	14	8	4	5	22	12	6	1	19	17	30	4	5	10	12	3	0	14	15	2	3	1	+
June		17	10	24	6			6	7	52	9	25	11	11	4	4	20	14	11	1	19	14	33	4	5	13	10	3	0	12	14	1	2	1	0
July		19	12	24	8			6	6	51	8	18	6	10	2	3	28	23	8	1	13	7	30	4	1	16	25	4	0	13	16	1	2	1	0
August		19	12	24	7			6	6	56	8	8	2	7	2	8	39	22	12	1	11	7	22	3	7	21	25	5	0	14	16	2	1	1	0
September		17	10	22	5			6	6	49	9	11	4	3	3	5	39	22	12	1	10	12	11	2	4	24	27	10	0	14	17	4	2	1	0
October		14	3	19	2			6	6	53	10	4	6	7	7	8	43	16	9	1	9	9	11	7	10	25	21	8	1	13	16	3	3	+	0
November		9	4	14	-2			6	6	70	12	5	8	7	4	12	39	15	9	1	8	10	6	5	13	27	21	11	0	14	16	3	2	+	1
December		7	2	13	-4			6	6	58	12	2	3	5	7	12	45	21	6	1	5	3	7	7	8	41	21	7	0	14	15	5	2	+	2
Means		12	5	26*	-6§	–	–	6	6			11	6	7	5	8	36	18	9	1	11	9	17	5	7	24	20	6	+	14	16				
Totals										607	116																					40	26	6	16
Extreme values	–	–	–	29†	-10‡	–	–	–	–	–	–	–	–	–	–	–	–	–	–	–	–	–	–	–	–	–	–	–	–	–	–	–	–	–	–
No. of years observations	–	27				–	–	10			27						10									10				10		10	10	27	27

* Mean of highest each year
§ Mean of lowest each year
† Highest recorded temperature
‡ Lowest recorded temperature
⊕ Rare
⊙ All observations

1.136

WMO No 03292

BRIDLINGTON (54° 06′ N, 0° 10′ W) Height above MSL – 19 m
Climatic Table compiled from 6 to 13 years observations, 1981 to 1993

Month	Average pressure at MSL (mb)	Temp. Mean daily max. (°C)	Temp. Mean daily min. (°C)	Temp. Mean highest in each month (°C)	Temp. Mean lowest in each month (°C)	Avg humidity 0900 (%)	Avg humidity 1500 (%)	Avg cloud cover 0900 (Oktas)	Avg cloud cover 1500 (Oktas)	Precip. Average fall (mm)	Precip. No. of days with 1 mm or more	Wind 0900 N	NE	E	SE	S	SW	W	NW	Calm	Wind 1500 N	NE	E	SE	S	SW	W	NW	Calm	Mean wind speed 0900 (Knots)	1500 (Knots)	Days Gale	Fog	Thunder	Sleet/Snow
January	1015	6	1	11	-4	87	80	6	6	59	14	5	1	2	1	21	37	18	7	8	3	1	3	3	19	37	20	7	7	10	10	1	2	⊕	2
February	1011	6	1	11	-5	85	73	6	6	37	9	3	1	5	4	13	33	29	7	5	4	2	4	7	17	30	26	8	2	11	13	1	1	⊕	3
March	1012	8	2	14	-3	86	70	6	7	60	13	8	1	4	3	13	24	27	10	11	13	2	4	9	15	18	24	11	4	10	13	⊕	1	⊕	3
April	1013	11	4	18	-1	86	70	6	6	50	10	16	9	11	4	11	23	9	9	6	21	8	13	14	9	14	13	6	3	11	12	1	1	⊕	1
May	1019	13	6	18	2	86	75	5	5	60	11	22	10	11	5	7	12	12	9	12	25	9	24	14	3	6	11	5	3	9	11	⊕	2	1	⊕
June	1015	16	9	23	4	84	73	6	6	55	9	29	2	5	9	8	17	9	13	8	25	8	16	14	10	8	8	9	2	9	11	⊕	1	1	⊕
July	1015	19	12	25	8	87	72	6	6	47	8	14	7	7	13	15	14	16	7	7	12	7	19	19	3	15	16	7	3	9	10	⊕	1	1	0
August	1013	19	11	24	7	87	66	5	6	61	10	6	2	1	9	18	22	25	7	11	10	4	14	15	7	22	21	2	5	9	10	⊕	1	1	0
September	1015	17	9	22	4	87	71	5	6	59	8	16	5	1	3	9	20	22	12	10	23	5	10	13	10	14	21	3	1	10	11	⊕	1	⊕	0
October	1011	14	7	19	1	87	75	6	7	57	10	10	5	8	9	13	19	19	11	8	12	4	6	15	8	19	25	9	3	10	12	1	1	⊕	0
November	1012	9	4	14	-2	86	79	6	6	65	12	8	9	3	5	13	24	20	10	8	11	8	6	6	15	23	17	10	4	10	11	1	2	⊕	⊕
December	1016	8	3	14	-3	86	82	6	6	66	12	8	5	5	4	12	23	25	13	8	9	5	2	3	13	23	21	15	8	10	9	1	2	⊕	⊕
Means	1014	12	6	25 *	-6 §	86	74	6	6			12	5	5	6	13	22	19	10	9	14	5	10	11	11	19	19	8	4	10	11				
Totals										676	126																					8	16	5	10
Extreme values				28†	-10‡																														
No. of years observations	6	8	8	8		6	6	6	6	8		6										6									6		13	13	13	13

Precipitation totals: 676 mm; No. of days with 1 mm or more total: 126

* Mean of highest each year
§ Mean of lowest each year
† Highest recorded temperature
‡ Lowest recorded temperature

⊕ Rare
⊙ All observations

1.137

WMO No 03396

SPURN POINT (53° 34' N, 0° 07' E) Height above MSL - 6 m

Climatic Table compiled from 17 to 30 years observations, 1957 to 1986

Month	Average pressure at MSL (mb)	Temperatures — Mean daily max (°C)	Mean daily min (°C)	Mean highest in each month (°C)	Mean lowest in each month (°C)	Average humidity 0600 (%)	Average humidity 1500 (%)	Average cloud cover 0900 (Oktas)	Average cloud cover 1500 (Oktas)	Precipitation Average fall (mm)	No. of days with 1 mm or more	Wind 0900 N	NE	E	SE	S	SW	W	NW	Calm	Wind 1500 N	NE	E	SE	S	SW	W	NW	Calm	Mean wind speed 0900 (Knots)	1500 (Knots)	Gale	Fog	Thunder	Sleet/Snow
January	1012	6	2	10	-3	89	86	6	6	48	12	4	5	9	8	19	18	22	12	3	5	6	7	9	17	19	22	13	4	15	16	3	4	⊕	12
February	1016	6	2	10	-2	89	84	6	6	34	9	4	9	15	12	17	13	15	11	5	7	10	15	14	13	12	14	10	4	15	15	2	4	⊕	8
March	1013	8	3	13	-1	89	78	6	6	37	9	7	9	11	11	15	14	18	11	4	11	10	13	15	10	12	18	7	4	14	15	2	4	⊕	4
April	1014	10	4	16	0	89	78	6	6	45	10	18	12	8	7	9	11	17	12	6	21	16	14	14	6	9	13	4	4	13	14	1	3	1	2
May	1014	13	7	19	4	90	78	6	6	39	8	18	13	10	10	10	14	14	7	5	18	14	17	16	8	11	10	3	2	13	14	⊕	3	2	⊕
June	1016	16	10	22	6	89	77	5	6	43	8	15	12	6	8	8	13	20	9	9	15	14	15	17	5	11	16	4	4	11	13	⊕	4	2	0
July	1016	18	12	24	8	90	77	6	6	50	8	13	7	6	6	7	14	25	12	9	11	11	17	17	5	10	19	5	4	11	12	⊕	3	2	0
August	1015	18	12	23	9	91	78	6	6	56	9	12	9	6	7	12	13	23	10	8	13	15	15	15	7	12	16	4	3	11	13	⊕	3	2	0
September	1015	17	11	22	7	90	75	5	6	45	8	9	6	6	6	15	20	22	11	7	10	9	11	14	10	16	22	6	3	12	14	1	2	1	0
October	1014	13	8	18	4	90	80	6	6	45	9	4	5	5	9	19	21	20	10	6	8	5	8	12	15	18	21	7	6	13	14	1	3	⊕	0
November	1012	9	5	14	0	89	83	6	6	59	12	5	6	5	7	20	20	21	14	3	7	6	6	7	15	20	22	12	4	15	15	2	3	⊕	2
December	1011	7	3	11	-2	89	86	6	6	52	11	5	5	6	9	17	20	22	14	3	6	4	6	7	15	21	22	14	3	15	15	2	4	⊕	3
Means	1014	12	7	25*	-4§	89	80	6	6	—	—	10	8	8	8	14	16	20	11	6	11	10	12	13	11	14	18	7	4	13	14	—	—	—	—
Totals	—	—	—	—	—	—	—	—	—	553	113	—	—	—	—	—	—	—	—	—	—	—	—	—	—	—	—	—	—	—	—	14	40	10	31
Extreme values	—	—	—	27†	-6‡	—	—	—	—	—	—	—	—	—	—	—	—	—	—	—	—	—	—	—	—	—	—	—	—	—	—	—	—	—	—
No. of years observations	30	22				30		30		17		30									30									30		30	30	17	17

* Mean of highest each year
§ Mean of lowest each year
† Highest recorded temperature
‡ Lowest recorded temperature
⊕ Rare
⊘ All observations

1.138

WMO No 03496

GREAT YARMOUTH (HEMSBY) (52° 41' N, 1° 41' E) Height above MSL – 13 m

Climatic Table compiled from 14 to 17 years observations, 1976 to 1993

Month	Average pressure at MSL (mb)	Temperatures Mean daily max (°C)	Mean daily min (°C)	Mean highest in each month (°C)	Mean lowest in each month (°C)	Average humidity 0600 (%)	1500 (%)	Average cloud cover 0900 (Oktas)	1500 (Oktas)	Precipitation Average fall (mm)	No. of days with 1 mm or more	Wind 0900 N	NE	E	SE	S	SW	W	NW	Calm	Wind 1500 N	NE	E	SE	S	SW	W	NW	Calm	Mean wind speed 0900 (Knots)	1500 (Knots)	Gale	Fog	Thunder	Sleet/Snow
January	1016	6	1	12	-5	87	82	6	6	54	12	5	6	7	8	15	30	19	9	2	8	6	7	7	13	26	22	10	1	12	13	1	2	⊕	6
February	1016	6	1	12	-3	86	78	6	6	37	8	6	10	15	8	15	20	18	6	3	8	12	15	10	14	16	17	8	1	12	13	1	3	⊕	7
March	1013	9	3	15	-2	89	76	6	6	52	13	7	7	7	7	18	24	22	9	1	11	8	6	12	14	20	18	10	0	12	14	1	2	1	4
April	1014	11	4	18	-1	88	74	6	6	47	9	18	12	8	9	10	18	12	12	1	23	15	12	16	8	9	8	10	0	11	12	0	2	1	2
May	1016	14	7	21	2	89	74	5	5	45	8	18	14	12	9	11	17	9	10	1	18	17	15	17	11	9	6	7	0	11	12	⊕	2	3	⊕
June	1016	17	10	24	5	90	74	6	6	59	10	17	12	9	7	7	18	16	13	1	21	16	10	16	7	14	9	8	1	10	10	0	2	4	0
July	1017	20	12	26	8	91	72	6	6	48	8	13	9	8	8	11	19	18	13	1	18	14	13	14	7	14	12	6	1	9	10	0	2	4	0
August	1015	20	12	27	7	92	68	5	5	43	7	9	8	8	6	11	24	24	12	1	13	12	13	13	9	18	14	7	1	10	11	0	2	2	0
September	1016	18	11	24	5	91	68	5	6	45	8	9	4	4	5	14	26	27	11	1	14	6	7	12	14	19	19	8	1	10	11	⊕	2	1	0
October	1014	14	8	20	1	90	75	6	6	55	10	6	5	7	10	15	27	21	7	2	9	6	9	11	17	21	18	10	⊕	11	11	⊕	1	1	0
November	1014	10	4	15	-2	89	81	6	6	62	11	4	6	6	6	14	30	25	6	3	8	6	7	7	16	24	22	10	1	11	11	⊕	2	1	1
December	1015	8	3	13	-3	88	84	6	6	55	11	6	6	6	6	19	29	22	5	2	6	6	6	6	13	30	24	8	3	11	11	⊕	2	⊕	3
Means	1015	13	6	28*	-6§	89	76	6	6			10	8	8	7	13	23	20	9	1	13	10	10	12	12	18	16	8	1	11	12				
Totals										602	115																					4	24	18	23
Extreme values				32†	-14‡																														
No. of years observations	17	14				17		17		14		16									16									15		17	17	14	14

* Mean of highest each year
§ Mean of lowest each year
† Highest recorded temperature
‡ Lowest recorded temperature
⊕ Rare
⊙ All observations

METEOROLOGICAL CONVERSION TABLE AND SCALES

Fahrenheit to Celsius
°Fahrenheit

	0	1	2	3	4	5	6	7	8	9
°F					Degrees Celsius					
−100	−73·3	−73·9	−74·4	−75·0	−75·6	−76·1	−76·7	−77·2	−77·8	−78·3
−90	−67·8	−68·3	−68·9	−69·4	−70·0	−70·6	−71·1	−71·7	−72·2	−72·8
−80	−62·2	−62·8	−63·3	−63·9	−64·4	−65·0	−65·6	−66·1	−66·7	−67·2
−70	−56·7	−57·2	−57·8	−58·3	−58·9	−59·4	−60·0	−60·6	−61·1	−61·7
−60	−51·1	−51·7	−52·2	−52·8	−53·3	−53·9	−54·4	−55·0	−55·6	−56·1
−50	−45·6	−46·1	−46·7	−47·2	−47·8	−48·3	−48·9	−49·4	−50·0	−50·6
−40	−40·0	−40·6	−41·1	−41·7	−42·2	−42·8	−43·3	−43·9	−44·4	−45·0
−30	−34·4	−35·0	−35·6	−36·1	−36·7	−37·2	−37·8	−38·3	−38·9	−39·4
−20	−28·9	−29·4	−30·0	−30·6	−31·1	−31·7	−32·2	−32·8	−33·3	−33·9
−10	−23·3	−23·9	−24·4	−25·0	−25·6	−26·1	−26·7	−27·2	−27·8	−28·3
−0	−17·8	−18·3	−18·9	−19·4	−20·0	−20·6	−21·1	−21·7	−22·2	−22·8
+0	−17·8	−17·2	−16·7	−16·1	−15·6	−15·0	−14·4	−13·9	−13·3	−12·8
10	−12·2	−11·7	−11·1	−10·6	−10·0	−9·4	−8·9	−8·3	−7·8	−7·2
20	−6·7	−6·1	−5·6	−5·0	−4·4	−3·9	−3·3	−2·8	−2·2	−1·7
30	−1·1	−0·6	0	+0·6	+1·1	+1·7	+2·2	+2·8	+3·3	+3·9
40	+4·4	+5·0	+5·6	6·1	6·7	7·2	7·8	8·3	8·9	9·4
50	10·0	10·6	11·1	11·7	12·2	12·8	13·3	13·9	14·4	15·0
60	15·6	16·1	16·7	17·2	17·8	18·3	18·9	19·4	20·0	20·6
70	21·1	21·7	22·2	22·8	23·3	23·9	24·4	25·0	25·6	26·1
80	26·7	27·2	27·8	28·3	28·9	29·4	30·0	30·6	31·1	31·7
90	32·2	32·8	33·3	33·9	34·4	35·0	35·6	36·1	36·7	37·2
100	37·8	38·3	38·9	39·4	40·0	40·6	41·1	41·7	42·2	42·8
110	43·3	43·9	44·4	45·0	45·6	46·1	46·7	47·2	47·8	48·3
120	48·9	49·4	50·0	50·6	51·1	51·7	52·2	52·8	53·3	53·9

Celsius to Fahrenheit
°Celsius

	0	1	2	3	4	5	6	7	8	9
°C					Degrees Fahrenheit					
−70	−94·0	−95·8	−97·6	−99·4	−101·2	−103·0	−104·8	−106·6	−108·4	−110·2
−60	−76·0	−77·8	−79·6	−81·4	−83·2	−85·0	−86·8	−88·6	−90·4	−92·2
−50	−58·0	−59·8	−61·6	−63·4	−65·2	−67·0	−68·8	−70·6	−72·4	−74·2
−40	−40·0	−41·8	−43·6	−45·4	−47·2	−49·0	−50·8	−52·6	−54·4	−56·2
−30	−22·0	−23·8	−25·6	−27·4	−29·2	−31·0	−32·8	−34·6	−36·4	−38·2
−20	−4·0	−5·8	−7·6	−9·4	−11·2	−13·0	−14·8	−16·6	18·4	−20·2
−10	+14·0	+12·2	+10·4	+8·6	+6·8	+5·0	+3·2	+1·4	−0·4	−2·2
−0	32·0	30·2	28·4	26·6	24·8	23·0	21·2	19·4	+17·6	+15·8
+0	32·0	33·8	35·6	37·4	39·2	41·0	42·8	44·6	46·4	48·2
10	50·0	51·8	53·6	55·4	57·2	59·0	60·8	62·6	64·4	66·2
20	68·0	69·8	71·6	73·4	75·2	77·0	78·8	80·6	82·4	84·2
30	86·0	87·8	89·6	91·4	93·2	95·0	96·8	98·6	100·4	102·2
40	104·0	105·8	107·6	109·4	111·2	113·0	114·8	116·6	118·4	120·2
50	122·0	123·8	125·6	127·4	129·2	131·0	132·8	134·6	136·4	138·2

MILLIBARS TO INCHES

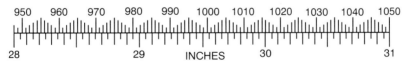

MILLIMETRES TO INCHES

(1) (for small values)

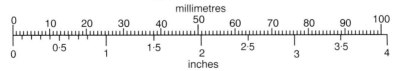

(2) (for large values)

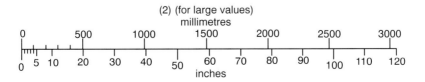

NOTES

CHAPTER 2

THE WESTERN PART OF THE NORTH SEA

GENERAL INFORMATION

Charts 2182A, 2182B
Synopsis
2.1

1 This chapter comprises a general description of the off-lying features in the W part of the North Sea, including exercise areas and a list of the oil and gas fields, to seaward of the routes adjacent to the coast, about 20 miles offshore and within the boundaries of this volume (1.1) to the latitude of Cromer (52°56′N). Regulations concerning oil and gas fields are given at 1.23 and information concerning exercise areas at 1.20.

2 Vessels proceeding on the coastal routes and S of Cromer should consult Chapters 3 to 9 as appropriate.

Hazards
2.2

1 **General.** Apart from the exploration and production rigs associated with the oil and gas fields (2.17) there are also several exercise areas (1.20). The area is also an important one for fishing, see 1.10 to 1.19.

2.3

1 **Wrecks** are numerous throughout the North Sea and some, particularly in the shallower parts may be a danger to shipping. The positions of wrecks are best seen on the charts.

Dumping grounds
2.4

1 Underwater explosives may still remain in the areas 40 miles E of Flamborough Head and 30 miles NE of Whitby, which were formerly used as dumping grounds.

Pilotage
2.5

1 Licensed Deep Sea Pilots are available for the English Channel, North Sea and other destinations in NW Europe. Because of the distance pilots have to travel to the point of embarkation, early notice, usually at least 48 hours, is required. The main boarding points are off the ports of Brixham, Cherbourg, Calais, Dover, Fishguard, Holyhead and Thurso. Pilots will also board off any port in NW Europe. *Admiralty List of Radio Signals* lists pilotage authorities bordering the North Sea who provide licensed Deep Sea Pilots.

Rescue
2.6

1 Rescue facilities are covered in chapters 3 to 9. A full description of the service maintained by the Coastguard is at 1.53.

Exercise areas
2.7

1 **General.** A range used by aircraft is centred on an offshore radio tower (53°45′N, 2°34′E), marked by a light, situated 85 miles E of Spurn Head. Five similar towers lie in a circle of 15 miles radius about the central tower. The outer towers are connected by submarine power cables to the central tower, which is also linked to shore by a submarine power cable. The range is not used for weapon firing.

2 There is a mine exercise area centred on (53°58′N, 2°56′E) in Botney Cut. See *North Sea (East) Pilot.*

A light-buoy (special) (56°20′N, 1°00′W) is used for radar training.

2.8

1 **Submarines** exercise in areas centred on 56°45′N 1°30′E, 56°10′N 0°10′W and 54°05′N 2°32′E.

Tidal streams
2.9

1 Details of tidal streams are given on the charts and in the *Admiralty Tidal Stream Atlas: North Sea, Northwestern Part* and *Southern Part.*

For details of the tidal regime see 1.83.

TOPOGRAPHY

Latitude of Rattray Head to Dogger Bank

Charts 268, 272, 273, 278
General
2.10

1 The area is open with few marked features and depths are in excess of 31 m throughout. There are a number of North Sea oil fields along the N and E boundaries of this area, see 2.17.

Banks and deeps
2.11

1 Turbot Bank (57°27′N, 0°50′W) lies in the NE corner of the area. Aberdeen Bank is 22 miles S of Turbot Bank and Marr Bank a further 48 miles SSW. There are a number of wrecks and patches with less than 50 m over them, shown on the chart, to the NE and SE of Marr Bank.

2 The Long Forties extends ENE of Marr Bank. There are several abrupt deeps on the E edge of The Long Forties of which the deepest is Devil's Hole.

Dogger Bank to Outer Silver Pit

Charts 266, 1191
General
2.12

1 The W part of this area is a continuation of the generally featureless area to the N. Dogger Bank (2.13) dominates the E half of the area. On the SW side of Dogger bank there are a few gas fields.

Banks and deeps
2.13

1 The banks mentioned below all have depths of less than 30 m, with some, in particular Dogger Bank, having depths of less than 20 m. The individual depths are best seen on the chart.

2 Dogger Bank is roughly a circle, 25 miles in radius, centred on 54°45′N, 2°15′E, with an arm extending 60 miles NE. The drab brown colour of the North Sea is largely due to stirred-up deposits of the bank held in suspension. It is a rich fishing area. South West Patch, with depths of less than 15 m over it, lies on the SW side of Dogger Bank. It is also a good fishing area but in bad weather the sea breaks heavily over it. Outer Well Bank is 15 miles S of South West Patch. South West Spit is 10 miles further W, with The Hills, a series of banks, lying to its NW.

3　　Eastermost Rough, with depths of less than 30 m, lies S of The Hills.

There are a number of dangerous wrecks, shown on the charts, on Dogger Bank and South West Patch, and an area in which unexploded ordnance has been reported (1998) (54°31′·2N, 1°53′·8E) on South West Bank.

4　　Outer Silver Pit (54°05′N, 2°25′W) separates the banks above from the large area of shoals which lie to the NE of the coast, between the River Humber (53°30′N, 0°10′E) and Great Yarmouth (52°36′N, 1°44′E). The edges of the pit are often marked by tide ripples. The W end of Outer Silver Pit is known as Skate Hole and the E end Botney Cut.

Outer Silver Pit to the latitude of Cromer

Charts 1187, 1503
General
2.14

1　　To the S of Outer Silver Pit depths decrease gradually as the banks NE of the coast are approached. Sole Pit (53°40′N, 1°33′E) with Well Hole 11 miles E and Coal Pit 6 miles SE are close N of the banks and intrude into them. The area between Sole Pit and Outer Dowsing Shoal (8.16) is typified by sandwave features (1.82) with depths of less than 20 m. Sea surface disturbance sometimes indicates the shallower areas.

2　　To the S and SW of Outer Silver Pit, and interspersed between the smaller banks which lie offshore, there is a cluster of offshore gas fields, which form the greatest concentration of production platforms in the North Sea (2.17). Most groups of production platforms are interconnected and then connected to shore by pipelines (1.36) also shown on the charts. In addition to the oil and gas fields there are a number of individual well heads, as shown on the charts.

Banks
2.15

1　　The banks mentioned below have depths of less than 20 m and some less than 5 m. The individual depths are best seen on the chart.

2　　Indefatigable Banks (NW extremity (53°35′N, 2°10′E)), two narrow ridges, lie 72 miles E of Spurn Head. They are the outermost of a series of parallel narrow banks running NW/SE which lie to the SW of the Indefatigable Banks. Swarte Bank, a sand ridge 20 miles in length, is 7 miles SW of the Indefatigable Banks. Broken Bank is similar to and 5 miles SW of Swarte Bank. Well Bank which is 28 miles long is 5 miles SW of Broken Bank with Jim Howe Bank 3 miles SE of its SE extremity. Inner Bank is 2 miles SW of Well Bank. Ower Bank is 21 miles long and is 2 miles SW of Inner Bank and 2 miles NE of Leman Bank (9.14). Depths over the banks from Swarte Bank SW are less than 10 m in places and over those furthest SW there are depths less than 5 m. The shallow areas of Ower Bank are indicated by smooth rippling when the tidal stream is strong; this rippling can be detected on radar. The sea breaks over Ower Bank in rough weather. Depths between the banks may exceed 30 m, but there are patches with depths less than 15 m.

3　　**Caution.** The banks above are unmarked and care should be taken when approaching them. The banks should not be crossed, especially in rough weather, unless the position of the vessel is accurately known.

ROUTES

Charts 2182A, 2182B
2.16

1　　There are no recognised offshore routes in the area covered by this volume. To the E of the area a deep water route runs from Shetland to Dover, joining the deep water route S from Deutsche Bucht to Dover Strait at 54°N. At its S end the E boundary of this volume abuts this deep water route, which is covered in the *North Sea (East) Pilot*.

2　　However, this route does not apply to ships sailing between ports on the E coast of the United Kingdom, including Orkney and Shetland Islands.

Vessels trading between the many ports on both sides of the North Sea generate traffic along the line of the coast and across the sea.

3　　The North Sea Oil and Gas Fields are served by a number of E coast ports, principally Peterhead (57°30′N, 1°47′W) (3.18), Aberdeen (57°09′N, 2°04′W) (3.57), Montrose (56°42′N, 2°28′W) (3.128) and Dundee (56°28′N, 2°57′W) (3.198) in the N, serving the oil fields which lie to their E and NE, and Great Yarmouth (52°36′N, 1°44′E) (9.51) and Lowestoft (52°28′N, 1°45′E) (9.92) in the S which serve the concentration of gas fields in the S part of the North Sea. In the approaches to these ports there is therefore a considerable volume of surface traffic. Helicopters, mainly engaged in ferrying personnel between shore and the platforms, follow similar routes to the North Sea support vessels. Diagram 2.17 shows the major oil and gas fields in the area covered by this volume.

OIL AND GAS FIELDS
2.17

1　　The major oil and gas fields which lie within the limits of this volume are in two main groups. Those which lie to the extreme NE are all oil fields with the exception of Lomond and Franklin Gas Fields. Those to the S are all gas fields. Most fields lie offshore, but a few gas fields in the S are mentioned in the coastal route directions as indicated in the remarks column below.

2　　All the gas fields and some of the oil fields are connected to the shore by pipelines. Those oil fields which are not so connected rely on single point moorings (see *The Mariner's Handbook*) to offload their oil direct to tankers. Auk, Clyde and Fulmar Oil Fields share one single point mooring.

3　　**Caution.** Production platforms and associated structures, including tanker moorings, storage tankers and platforms on pipelines, generally exhibit Mo (U) lights, aircraft obstruction lights, and audible fog signals. Unauthorised navigation is prohibited within 500 m of all such structures, including storage tankers, which can swing about their moorings. Tankers manoeuvring in the vicinity of platforms and moorings should be given a wide berth. For further information see *The Mariner's Handbook*.

4　　In alphabetical order the fields within the limits of this volume are:

Name	Position		Remarks
	Lat N	Long E	
5 Alison (G)	53°31′	2°09′	
Amethyst (G)	53°37′	0°44′	(8.16)
Anglia (G)	53°22′	1°43′	
Ann (G)	53°43′	2°04′	
Arbroath (O)	57°23′	1°23′	
Audrey (G)	53°34′	2°00′	

	Name	Lat	Long	Note
	Auk (O)	56°24′	2°04′	SPM
6	Banff (O)	57°00′	1°18′	Storage tanker
	Barque (G)	53°37′	1°32′	
	Bessemer (G)	53°12′	2°29′	
	Boulton (G)	54°15′	2°09′	
	Bure (G)	53°07′	2°25′	
7	Caister (G)	54°12′	2°27′	
	Camelot (G)	52°57′	2°09′	(9.14)
	Cleeton (G)	54°02′	0°44′	
	Clipper (G)	53°28′	1°44′	
	Corvette (G)	53°14′	2°37′	
	Curlew (O)	56°44′	1°18′	Storage tanker
	Clyde (O)	56°27′	2°17′	SPM
8	Della (G)	53°05′	1°54′	(9.14)
	Elgin (G)	57°00′	1°50′	
	Erskine (O)	57°02′	2°04′	
	Excalibur (G)	53°28′	1°21′	
	Fife (O)	56°01′	3°11′	Storage tanker
	Franklin (G)	56°58′	1°52′	
	Fulmar (O)	56°29′	2°09′	SPM
9	Galahad (G)	53°33′	1°22′	
	Galleon (G)	53°28′	1°55′	
	Gannet (O)	57°13′	1°12′	
	Ganymede (G)	53°19′	2°14′	
	Guinevere (G)	53°25′	1°16′	
	Hewett (G)	53°02′	1°45′	(9.14)
	Hyde (G)	53°48′	1°43′	
	Indefatigable (G)	53°20′	2°35′	
10	Janice (O)	56°24′	2°15′	
	Judy (O)	56°42′	2°21′	
	Ketch (G)	54°03′	2°29′	
	Kittiwake (O)	57°27′	0°31′	SPM
	Lancelot (G)	53°25′	1°19′	
	Leman (G)	53°05′	2°11′	(9.14)
	Lomond (G)	57°18′	2°10′	
	Malory (G)	53°33′	1°15′	
11	Marnock (O)	57°18′	1°40′	
	Markham (G)	53°51′	2°52′	
	Montrose (O)	57°27′	1°23′	
	Mungo (O)	57°23′	2°00′	
	Murdoch (G)	54°16′	2°19′	
	Neptune (G)	53°59′	0°47′	
	Norpipe (37–4–A)	55°54′	1°36′	Pumping station
	Norpipe (36–22–A)	55°18′	0°13′	Pumping station
12	North Hewett (G)	53°06′	1°46′	(9.14)
	Pierce (O)	57°10′	2°18′	Storage tanker
	Pickerill (G)	53°33′	1°08′	
	Ravenspurn N (G)	54°02′	1°06′	
	Ravenspurn S (G)	54°03′	0°54′	
13	Rough (G)	53°50′	0°28′	(6.210)
	Schooner (G)	54°04′	2°05′	
	Shearwater (O)	57°02′	1°57′	
	Sole Pit (G)	53°34′	1°38′	
	Teal & Guillemot (O)	57°15′	0°49′	Storage tanker
	Thames (G)	53°05′	2°33′	Close W of Deep Water Route
14	Trent (G)	54°18′	1°40′	
	Triton (O)	57°05′	0°54′	Storage tanker
	Tyne (G)	54°27′	2°29′	
	Valiant North (G)	53°23′	2°00′	
	Valiant South (G)	53°19′	2°06′	
	Vanguard (G)	53°23′	2°07′	
15	Victor (G)	53°20′	2°22′	
	Viking (G)	53°27′	2°20′	
	Vulcan (G)	53°15′	2°01′	
	Waveney (G)	53°21′	1°18′	
	Windermere (G)	53°50′	2°46′	
	Yare (G)	53°03′	2°35′	Close W of Deep Water Route

16 (O)=Oil Field (G)=Gas Field
SPM=Single Point Mooring

The above oil and gas fields are shown on Diagram 2.17. Some fields which lie outside the area covered by this volume are also shown on the diagram, but are not listed above.

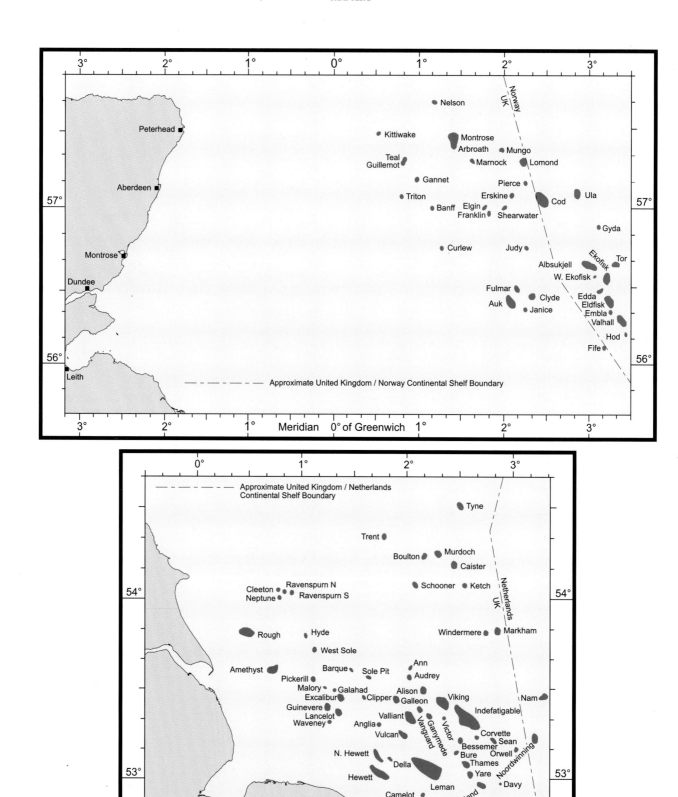

North Sea West - Major Oil and Gas Fields and Supply Bases (2.17)

NOTES

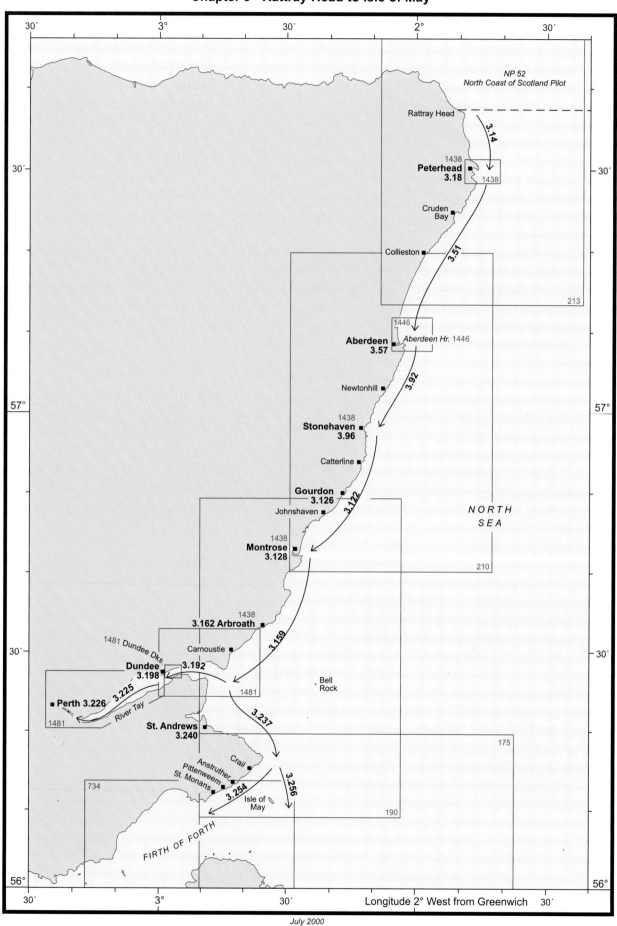

30′   3°   30′   2°   30′

NP 52
North Coast of Scotland Pilot

Rattray Head

3.14

1438
Peterhead
3.18
1438

Cruden
Bay

Collieston

3.51

213

1446
Aberdeen
3.57
Aberdeen Hr. 1446

Newtonhill

3.92

1438
Stonehaven
3.96

Catterline

Gourdon
3.126
Johnshaven

3.122

N O R T H
S E A

1438
Montrose
3.128

210

3.162 Arbroath 1438

1481 Dundee Dks.

Carnoustie

3.159

Dundee **3.192**
3.198

1481

Bell
Rock

Perth 3.226
3.225
1481
River Tay

St. Andrews
3.240

3.237

175

734

Crail

Anstruther
Pittenweem
St. Monans

3.254

Isle of
May

3.256

190

FIRTH OF FORTH

56°

30′   3°   30′   Longitude 2° West from Greenwich   30′

July 2000

CHAPTER 3

RATTRAY HEAD TO ISLE OF MAY

GENERAL INFORMATION

Charts 1409, 1407
Synopsis
3.1

1   In this chapter the coastal passage from Rattray Head (57°37′N, 1°49′W) to the Isle of May about 90 miles SSW is described, together with the ports of Peterhead (3.18), Aberdeen (3.57), Stonehaven (3.96), Montrose (3.128), Arbroath (3.162), Dundee (3.198) and Perth (3.226). For a description of features lying further offshore than 20 miles see Chapter 2.

Topography
3.2

1   From Rattray Head (57°37′N, 1°49′W) the coast runs in a generally SSW direction for 85 miles to Fife Ness. The Isle of May lies 5 miles SSE of Fife Ness, towards the centre of the approach to the Firth of Forth. The coast is mainly composed of rocky cliffs, fringed by reefs, which dry 1 to 2 cables offshore but occasionally dry 5 cables to seaward. There are several sandy stretches, from Rattray Head to Peterhead, the 12 mile stretch lying NNW of Aberdeen, the 4 miles NNW of Montrose, Lunan Bay just S of Montrose and the mouth of the River Tay.

2   The approach to the River Tay lies between Whiting Ness (56°34′N, 2°33′W) and Fife Ness 17 miles S. Bell Rock lies 9½ miles SE of Whiting Ness.

Outlying banks and deeps
3.3

1   **Buchan Deep** charted within a 100 m depth contour lies 12 to 20 miles E of Buchan Ness (57°28′N, 1°46′W) and extends 18 miles NNE/SSW.

       A deep charted within a 100 m depth contour lies 12 miles ESE of Girdle Ness (57°08′N, 2°03′W).
3.4

1   **Scalp Bank** a flat patch with a least depth of 31 m lies 17 miles E of Red Head (56°37′N, 2°29′W). Similar patches lie 5 miles S of Scalp Bank and midway between the bank and Red Head.
3.5

1   **Wee Bankie** with a least depth of 31 m over it, lies 16 miles E of the Isle of May (56°11′N, 2°33′W).

Exercise areas
3.6

1   Submarines exercise frequently in the Firth of Forth and its approaches. See also 1.20, the caution on the charts, *Annual Summary of Admiralty Notices to Mariners* and Practice and Exercise Area (PEXA) chart Q6405.

       Minesweepers and minehunters exercise in the vicinity of the Isle of May. See *Annual Summary of Admiralty Notices to Mariners* and PEXA Chart Q6405.

Tidal Stream
3.7

1   Tidal streams are given on the charts and in the *Admiralty Tidal Stream Atlas: North Sea, Northwestern Part.*

       The offshore stream runs generally N and S from Rattray Head to Bell Rock. The E-going stream from the S part of the Moray Firth sets in the direction of the coast, that is gradually SE and S round Rattray Head before joining the S-going offshore stream. The N-going offshore stream divides N of Rattray Head, part of it sets NW and W into the Moray Firth and part of it continues N.

2   The change from the S-going to the N-going stream is through W and from the N-going to the S-going stream through the E.

       South of Bell Rock, clear of the land and in the outer part of the Firth of Forth the tidal streams are weak, spring rate 1 kn, but run in various directions throughout the tidal cycle as shown in *Admiralty Tidal Stream Atlas: North Sea, Northwestern Part.*

RATTRAY HEAD TO BUCHAN NESS

General Information

Chart 213
Route
3.8

1   From Rattray Head (57°37′N, 1°49′W) the route leads S for a distance of 8½ miles to a position E of Buchan Ness, crossing the approaches to Peterhead 2 miles N of Buchan Ness.

Topography
3.9

1   The coast between Rattray Head and Buchan Ness consists of fairly low-lying sandhills as far as South Head (2 miles N of Buchan Ness), the E extremity of the promontory on which Peterhead stands. There are two bays, Peterhead Bay and Sandford Bay, between South Head and Buchan Ness.

Rescue
3.10

1   A Coastguard Rescue Team is maintained at Peterhead. See 1.53.

       An all-weather lifeboat is stationed at Peterhead. For details of lifeboat, see 1.61.

Tidal stream
3.11

1   Tidal streams for the area are shown on the charts and in the *Admiralty Tidal Stream Atlas: North Sea, Northwestern Part.*

       The spring rate in either direction is 1¾ kn.

Principal marks
3.12

1   **Landmarks:**
       Mormond Hill (57°36′N, 2°02′W) with buildings and masts on its summit.
       Radio Masts (red lights) (57°37′N, 1°53′W).
       Radio Mast (red lights) (57°36′N, 1°53′W).
       Power station chimney (lit) at Peterhead (57°29′N, 1°47′W).
       Buchan Ness Lighthouse (white tower, red bands, 35 m in height) (57°28′N, 1°46′W).
2   **Major Lights:**
       Rattray Head Light (white tower, lower part granite, upper part brick, 34 m in height) (57°37′N, 1°49′W) stands on a rock called The Ron.
       Buchan Ness Light (above).

Power Station

Buchan Ness Light   *Meikle Mackie*

Buchan Ness from SE (3.12.1)

(Original dated 2000)

(Photograph - Air Images)

Rattray Head Light from SE (3.12.2)

(Original dated 2000)

(Photograph - Air Images)

Other navigational aids

3.13

1   **Racons:**

Rattray Head Light (57°37′N, 1°49′W).
Buchan Ness Light (57°28′N, 1°46′W).

DGPS:

Girdle Ness Light (57°08′N, 2°03′W).

Directions

(Directions for passage N are given in North Coast of Scotland Pilot)

3.14

1   From a position off Rattray Head (57°37′N, 1°49′W), a sandhill partly covered by bent grass and higher than the surrounding sandy ridges, the coastal passage leads 9 miles S to a position E of Buchan Ness, passing (with positions from Rattray Head):

2   E of Rattray Hard (1½ miles ENE), an uneven rocky patch on which dangerous seas are raised during onshore gales, thence:

E of Rattray Bay (2 miles S), which lies between Rattray Hard and Scotstown Head. Submarine pipelines run to offshore oilfields from the bay,

which also has a gas terminal at Saint Fergus. Thence:

3   E of Scotstown Head (3¼ miles S) off which Scotstown Hard extends 5 cables to seaward, thence:

E of Kirton Head (4 miles S) with dangerous rocks extending 5 cables to seaward, thence:

E of The Girdle Wears (6 miles S) a patch of rocks close NE of Buchanhaven, thence:

E of North Head (6½ miles S) (chart 1438) with North Head Rock 1½ cables NE, thence:

4   E of South Head (6¾ miles S) (chart 1438) and the dangers extending ½ cable E, covered by the red sector of N Breakwater light at Peterhead, thence:

E of The Skerry (8 miles S) an isolated rock in Sandford Bay, thence:

E of Buchan Ness (8½ miles S) a rocky, rugged peninsula bordered by rocky ledges and connected to the mainland by a narrow isthmus. The lighthouse (3.12) stands in the centre of the peninsula.

3.15

1   **Clearing bearings:**

The alignment (184°) of Kirktown Spire (57°30′·3N, 1°46′·9W) (3.33) with Stirling Hill (3.52) (3 miles S) passes E of the dangers off Rattray Head, Scotstown Head and Kirton Head in depths of 22 m.

2   Buchan Ness Light (57°28′N, 1°46′W) (3.12) bearing more than 184° and open to the E of the lights of the town of Peterhead also passes E of the dangers above.

The alignment (203°) of The Skerry (3.14) with Buchan Ness Lighthouse (5½ cables SSW), passes 4 cables E of South Head.

(Directions continue for Peterhead at 3.34 and for coastal route S at 3.51)

Minor Harbour

3.16

1   **Buchanhaven** (57°31′N,1°48′W) is a small fishing village with a boat harbour among the rocks. It lies on the S side of the mouth of the River Ugie.

A jetty which extends 127 m N from the shore affords a landing for boats at all states of the tide.

Other names

3.17

1   Annachie Water (57°34′N, 1°49′W), an old canal.
Craig Ewan (57°31′N, 1°48′W), a point.
Rattray Briggs (57°37′N, 1°48′W), a detached reef.

PETERHEAD

General Information

Chart 1438 plans of Approaches to Peterhead and Peterhead Bay and Harbour

Position

3.18

1   Peterhead Bay (57°30′N, 1°47′W) is 23 miles NNE of Aberdeen on the NE coast of Scotland. Peterhead Harbour is at the N end of Peterhead Bay.

Function

3.19

1   Peterhead Harbour and Peterhead Bay Harbour are important and developing ports. The former is one of the principal fishing harbours in Scotland and also handles commercial vessels.

2   Peterhead Bay Harbour contains a supply base for the North Sea oilfields and a tanker jetty for the import of fuel oil for Peterhead power station.

The town of Peterhead, population about 20 000 (1997), lies on the N side of Peterhead Bay and to the W of the harbour.

Topography
3.20

1   Peterhead Bay is a deep indentation in the coast between Keith Inch, a promontory to the N, and Salthouse Head to the S. The bay is open to the SE but protected by breakwaters. The breakwaters afford a good measure of protection from E winds, particularly in the S of the Bay, where Peterhead Bay Harbour is situated, although seas frequently break over both breakwaters and there may be a heavy groundswell in the Bay; see also Caution at 3.34.

2   Peterhead Harbour is at the N end of the bay, protected to the E by Keith Inch.

Port limits
3.21

1   The port limits run parallel and about 2 cables to the E of the breakwaters protecting Peterhead Bay Harbour as indicated on the plan.

Approach and entry
3.22

1   Approach is from the SE and entry through the breakwaters forming Peterhead Bay Harbour.

Traffic and trade
3.23

1   A total of 104 649 tonnes of fish were landed at Peterhead Harbour in 1999. Other goods handled included grain, fertilisers, North Sea related products, coal and limestone.

In 1999, 2132 vessels totalling 5·6 million grt used Peterhead Bay Harbour; Peterhead Harbour was used by 262 vessels which landed 278 633 tonnes of cargo.

Port authority
3.24

1   Peterhead Bay Harbour: Peterhead Bay Authority, Bath House, Bath Street, Peterhead, AB42 1DX.

Peterhead Harbour: Peterhead Harbour Trustees, Harbour Office, West Pier, Peterhead, AB42 6DZ.

Limiting conditions
3.25

1   **Controlling Depths.** The approach to Peterhead Bay is in depths greater than 20 m.

Peterhead Bay Harbour is dredged (1997) to 12·5 m in its E part.

Albert Quay (3.31) has depths alongside of 8·5 m.

South Harbour (3.31) is generally less than 3 m.

2   **Deepest and longest berths.**

Peterhead Bay Harbour: Tanker berth (3.37).

Peterhead Harbour: Albert Quay (3.38).

Tidal levels: see *Admiralty Tide Tables.* Mean spring range about 3·3 m; mean neap range about 1·5 m.

3.26

1   **Maximum size of vessel:**

Peterhead Bay: length 250 m, draught 11·5 m.

Peterhead Harbour: Albert Quay length 160 m, draught 8·5 m; South Harbour length 90 m, draught 6·1 m at HW springs and 5·5 m at HW neaps;

North Harbour and Port Henry Harbour beam 10·3 m, draught 5 m.

Arrival Information

Port operations
3.27

1   **Vessel Traffic Service**, with radar surveillance is maintained for the advice of shipping, for details see the relevant *Admiralty List of Radio Signals.*

Notice of ETA
3.28

1   1 hour's notice is required. Vessels should also make contact when 2 miles from the breakwater.

Pilots and tugs
3.29

1   Pilotage is compulsory within Peterhead Bay Harbour and in Peterhead Harbours, for:

    All oil tankers.

    All vessels exceeding 3500 grt; vessels of a lesser tonnage may, due to defects or other special reasons, be required to take a pilot at the discretion of the Harbour Master or his appointed deputy.

2   All vessels carrying more than one tonne of IMO Class 1 explosives.

    All vessels carrying hazardous cargoes or dangerous goods in bulk or quantities of 100 tonnes or more.

The pilot boards 2½ cables SE of the breakwater entrance, except in bad weather when he boards within the breakwaters. The pilot vessel is equipped with VHF R/T.

Although tugs are not permanently stationed in Peterhead, they are normally available at 24 hours notice.

Regulations concerning entry
3.30

1   Vessels shall not obstruct the harbour entrance.

The harbour may be closed to either incoming or outgoing traffic.

There is a speed limit of 5 kn.

Vessels shall keep 50 m clear of other vessels working Dangerous Goods.

A navigation channel, which is the width of the harbour entrance on an axis of 314°, is deemed to exist within the harbour limits. Within the channel the following regulations apply:

2   Vessels shall not anchor or remain without permission.

    Small vessels shall not obstruct large vessels.

    Vessels shall keep to starboard. Large vessels requiring the use of the whole channel, shall only enter the channel when it is clear of other vessels.

    Vessels following one another shall keep at least 70 m apart.

    There shall be no overtaking.

Harbour

Layout
3.31

1   **Peterhead Bay Harbour** entrance faces SSE and is 198 m wide between the breakwaters. Within the bay there is a tanker jetty in the lee of South Breakwater. South Base, a quay with a maintained depth of 6·8 m, is situated on the S side of the harbour. Princess Royal Jetty extends 175 m NE from the NW end of South Base; a sectored light marks the end of this jetty.

2   Peterhead Bay Marina (3.43), enclosed by two breakwaters each with a light exhibited from its head, lies

South Base   Reform Tower

South Breakwater   *Marina*

Peterhead Bay Harbour (3.31.1)

(Original dated 2000)

(Photograph - Air Images)

W of Princess Royal Jetty. A seasonal light-buoy (starboard hand) is moored 40 m NNW of the E breakwater head.

There is a further supply base for North Sea oil fields at the N side of the bay, which uses part of North Breakwater for berths as well as berths along the S side of Keith Inch.

Peterhead Harbour consists of four interconnected tidal basins.

3   The outer basin, enclosed by Merchants Quay, West Quay and Albert Quay, is entered from Peterhead Bay. Lights are exhibited from the end of West Quay and Albert Quay. South Harbour is entered from the outer basin, and leads to North Harbour, and thence to Port Henry Harbour which is entered from the W side of North Harbour.

4   The basin walls are used for berthing together with several jetties within the basins. The inner harbours are primarily used by fishing vessels.

Tidal streams
3.32

1   The tidal stream 2 miles off the breakwater is shown on Chart 213. Closer inshore it turns up to an hour earlier. Spring rates are 1¾ kn but within the breakwaters the tidal stream is negligible.

Principal marks
3.33

1   **Landmarks:**
> North Breakwater Light (white metal tripod, 10 m in height) (57°29′·8N, 1°46′·2W).
> South Breakwater Light (white metal tower, black base, 17 m in height) (1 cable WSW of N breakwater light).
> Buchan Ness Lighthouse (57°28′N, 1°46′W) (3.12).

2   Town Hall Spire (57°30′·3N, 1°46′·6W) (illuminated clock face).

> Kirktown Spire (57°30′·3N, 1°46′·9W), 1¾ cables W of Town Hall Spire.
> Reform Tower (square) (57°29′·5N, 1°47′·8W) standing on Meet Hill.
> Power station chimney (lit) (57°28′·7N, 1°47′·3W).

Major light:
> Buchan Ness Light (above).

Directions
(Continued from 3.15)

Approaches to Peterhead Bay
3.34

1   **Kirktown Leading Lights:**
> Front light (orange mast, white top, white triangle point up) (57°30′·2N, 1°47′·1W).
> Rear light (orange mast, white top, white triangle point down) (90 m NW of front light).

The alignment (314°) of the above leading lights leads through the entrance to Peterhead Bay, passing (with positions from the front light):

2   NE of Buchan Ness (2 miles SSE) (3.14), thence:
> NE of The Skerry (1½ miles SSE) (3.14), thence:
> NE of Sandford Bay (1½ miles S), which is fringed by drying rocky ledges and has a light-buoy (special) in its centre marking the seaward end of an outfall, thence:
> To Peterhead Bay entrance (5 cables SE), lying between the breakwater heads on which stand lights (3.33).

3   **Caution.** During gales from between NE and SE, the sea to the E of the North and South Breakwaters can become extremely turbulent due to backwash from the solid walls of the breakwaters. Turbulence is greatest at close proximity to the structures.

Merchants Quay

Albert Quay   *South Breakwater Light*

Peterhead Harbour (3.31.2)

(Original dated 2000)

(Photograph - Air Images)

4   Small vessels attempting to enter Peterhead Bay in these conditions are advised to join the above leading line at a position no closer than 5 cables SE of the harbour entrance, and to remain on the leading line until inside the harbour. Similarly, if small vessels are leaving harbour in these conditions, the alignment, astern, of the leading lights should be maintained until the vessel is 5 cables SE of the entrance.

Approach to Outer Basin
3.35
1   From a position within the breakwater heads the track continues NW on the approach alignment (314°) until the light on Albert Quay (3.31) is abeam to starboard. Thence the track leads E into the outer basin.

Clearing bearings
3.36
1   The alignment (334°) of South Breakwater Light (57°29′·8N, 1°46′·4W) with Kirktown Spire (5½ cables NW) passes NE of The Skerry and the dangers N of that rock.

The alignment (251°) of South Breakwater Light with Reform Tower (8 cables WSW) passes S of South Head.

Peterhead Bay Harbour
3.37
1   **Berths** (Positions given from South Breakwater Light (3.33)):

Tanker Jetty (2½ cables SW), with a depth of 12·5 m alongside, for vessels up to 280 m in length.

North Base (2½ cables NNE): 470 m of quay giving 5 berths numbered 13 to 18, with depths of 7·0 m to 14·0 m alongside.

South Base (4 cables SW): 480 m of quay giving 12 berths numbered 1 to 12 with depths of 6·8 m to 7·8 m alongside.

2   **Anchorage.** Peterhead Bay offers an anchorage in depths up to 12·5 m. The best holding ground is under the lee of the South Breakwater consisting of fine sand over blue clay or mud with occasional boulders.

In bad weather vessels anchored in Peterhead Bay have been known to drag anchor. While at anchor vessels must maintain a good lookout and continuous VHF radio watch and have their engines ready for immediate use.

Peterhead Harbours
3.38
1   Albert Quay: 340 m of quay, depth 8 m.
West Quay: 60 m of quay each side, depth 9 m.
Merchants Quay: 130 m of quay, depth 6·2 m.
South Harbour: 350 m quay.
North Harbour: 2 jetties and 400 m of quay.
Port Henry Harbour: 1 jetty and 740 m of quay.

Port Services
3.39
1   **Repairs:** Dry dock; length overall 58 m; floor length 53 m; breadth 10·3 m; sill depth 0·5 m below Chart Datum; block depth 0·3 m at entrance reducing to nil at dock head.

There is a slipway capable of taking 4 vessels up to 30·5 m in length.

3.40

1   **Other facilities:** de-ratting exemption certificates only can be issued; oily waste disposal by road tanker; hospitals.

3.41

1   **Supplies:** marine diesel at all quays; other fuels by road tanker; water at all quays; provisions.

3.42

1   **Communications.** There is a heliport 2½ miles W of Peterhead and helicopter landing sites at Keith Inch and Boddam (2 miles S of the town).

Small craft

3.43

1   **Peterhead Bay Marina,** situated in the NW corner of Peterhead Bay Harbour, has pontoon berths and facilities for 150 small craft up to 20 m in length and 2·8 m draught.

BUCHAN NESS TO ABERDEEN

General Information

Charts 213, 210
Route
3.44

1   From a position E of Buchan Ness (57°28′N, 1°46′W) the route leads SSW for a distance of 22 miles to Fairway Light-buoy 1 mile NE of the entrance to Aberdeen Harbour.

Topography
3.45

1   The coast from Buchan Ness to the Bay of Cruden (5 miles SSW) is composed of red granite cliffs, up to 73 m in height. The Bay of Cruden is sandy and backed by sandhills. At the S extremity of the Bay is a reef, The Skares (57°25′N, 1°51′W) from which rocky cliffs continue 5 miles SSW to Hackley Head. The coast is then sandy, backed by grass-covered sandhills and curves gently SSW 12 miles to Aberdeen (57°09′N, 2°04′W) and Girdle Ness which is 1 mile E of Aberdeen.

Hazards
3.46

1   **Firing Danger Area** is situated off Blackdog Rock (57°13′N, 2°03′W) and marked by DZ buoys (special) moored 1½ miles ENE and 1 mile E of the rock. Red flags and occasionally red lights are displayed from flagstaffs on the shore when firing is taking place.

2   **Salmon Fisheries.** Numerous bag nets of considerable size and strength are placed off the coast between Newburgh (57°19′N, 2°00′W) and Aberdeen. They are obstructions to small craft navigating inshore.

Rescue
3.47

1   Aberdeen is the Maritime Rescue Coordination Centre for North and East Scotland Region, and Aberdeen District. The coastguard station is at Blaikie's Quay (3.80) in Aberdeen Harbour, and constant watch is maintained.

   There are Coastguard Rescue Teams at Cruden Bay (57°25′N, 1°51′W), Collieston (57°21′N, 1°56′W) and Newburgh (57°19′N, 2°00′W). See 1.53.

2   An all-weather lifeboat and an inshore lifeboat are stationed at Aberdeen. See 1.61 and 1.62 for details of lifeboats.

Tidal stream
3.48

1   See *Admiralty Tidal Stream Atlas: North Sea, Northwestern Part* and information on charts.

   The maximum rate in either direction is 3 kn in the N of the area, reducing to the S.

Principal marks
3.49

1   **Landmarks:**
     Buchan Ness Lighthouse (57°28′N, 1°46′W)(3.12).
     Radar aerial, charted as a structure, (57°28′N, 1°49′W).
     Oil tanks, (57°23′N, 1°53′W).

2   Silo 2 cables SW of the Hill of Strabathie, (57°13′N, 2°04′W).
     Radio mast, on the summit of Brimmond Hill, (57°10′N, 2°14′W).
     Radio mast (57°10′N, 2°09′W).

   Major lights:
     Buchan Ness Light (above).
     Girdle Ness Light (white, round tower, 37 m in height) (57°08′N, 2°03′W).

Girdle Ness Light (3.49)

(Original dated 2000)

(Photograph - Air Images)

Other navigational aids
3.50

1   **Racons:**
     Buchan Ness Light (57°28′N, 1°46′W).
     Aberdeen Fairway Light-buoy (57°09′N, 2°02′W).
   DGPS:
     Girdle Ness Light (57°08′N, 2°03′W).

Directions
(Continued from 3.15)
3.51

1   From a position off the rocky peninsula of Buchan Ness (57°28′N, 1°46′W) the coastal passage leads 22 miles SSW running parallel to the coast, to the Fairway Light-buoy off the entrance to Aberdeen Harbour, passing (positions given from Buchan Ness):
     ESE of Ward Point (4 miles SSW), the N entrance point of Bay of Cruden. Castle ruins lie close N and Slains Lodge, a large rectangular building stands 7½ cables N of the point, thence:

2   ESE of The Skares (5½ miles SSW), several patches of rock which extend 3½ cables from the S entrance point to Cruden Bay. They are marked by a light-buoy (port hand). Thence:
     ESE of Blindman Rock (8 miles SSW) which lies close off Old Slains Castle, a dark prominent

tower standing on the headland. There is a boat landing close S of the castle.

3   The route continues SSW of Hackley Head (57°20′N, 1°57′W), which marks the change along the coast from cliffs to grass covered sandhills, passing (with positions from Newburgh Bar (57°18′N, 1°59′W)):

E of the Firing Danger Area (3.46) (5½ miles SSW). Submarine cables run E through the area. The landing positions, close N of Blackdog Rock are marked by beacons. Thence:

4   ESE of the River Don Entrance Light (white tower) (8½ miles SSW). The entrance to the river is the only interruption in the sandy coast between Blackdog Rock and Aberdeen, thence:

To the vicinity of the Fairway Light-buoy (safe water) (9 miles SSW) off the entrance to Aberdeen and 1 mile NNE of Girdle Ness.

3.52

1   **Useful marks:**

Stirling Hill (57°27′·5N, 1°47′·5W), granite quarries are close by.

River Don Bridge (4 arches) (57°10·′ 5N, 2°05′·3W).

(Directions continue for Aberdeen at 3.74 and coastal passage S at 3.92)

Minor Harbours

Port Erroll
3.53

1   **General information.** Port Erroll (57°25′N, 1°51′W) is a small boat harbour at N end of Bay of Cruden. It can be entered by vessels drawing 3 m at HW Springs.

Useful mark:

Church spire (1½ miles W).

Collieston
3.54

1   **General information.** Collieston (57°21′N, 1°56′W) is a fishing village with a small harbour formed by a pier.

Useful mark:

Church (57°21′N, 1°56′W) at Kirktown of Slains.

Nature reserve. The coast between Collieston and Newburgh (3.55) is part of Sands of Forvie National Nature Reserve.

Newburgh
3.55

1   **General information.** Newburgh (57°19′N, 2°00′W) is a small harbour on the SW side of the River Ythan which is navigable by small craft for a few miles.

Directions. There is usually 3·4 m over Newburgh Bar but the channel is constantly changing and should not be attempted without local knowledge.

Useful mark. Two bare white hills mark the N side of the entrance.

Other Names
3.56

1   Bullars of Buchan (57°26′N, 1°49′W), a cauldron hollowed out by the sea.

Dunbuy Rock (57°25′·5N, 1°49′·1W).

Grey Mare (57°25′·7N, 1°48′·8W), a rock.

Pitscur Buss (57°24′·8N, 1°49′·5W), a steep-to rock.

Skelly Rock (57°13′N, 2°03′W).

ABERDEEN AND APPROACHES

General Information

Chart 1446
Position
3.57

1   Aberdeen (57°09′N, 2°04′W) lies at the S end of Aberdeen Bay on the mouth of the River Dee.

Function
3.58

1   Aberdeen, population 189 707 (1991), is one of the larger fishing ports in the UK. It is a commercial port of significance and a main supply base for the North Sea oil industry.

Port limits
3.59

1   The Port limits are defined by an arc of 2 miles radius centred on North Pier Head (57°08′·7N, 2°03′·7W). The limits extend from just N of the River Don to the latitude of Greg Ness.

Approach and entry
3.60

1   Aberdeen is approached from the NE through Aberdeen Bay and entered via the mouth of the River Dee. The entrance faces NNE and is protected to the NW by North Pier, a breakwater, 3½ cables long, running NE and parallel to the promontory on which Girdle Ness Lighthouse (3.49) stands and to the E by South Breakwater which runs 1½ cables N from the NE point of the promontory. Other jetties within the entrance serve to decrease the scend in the harbour. The approach to Aberdeen is dredged.

2   A disused explosives dumping ground lies 3 miles E of the harbour entrance.

Traffic
3.61

1   In 1999 the port was used by 1853 vessels totalling 5 152 338 dwt. Aberdeen handles about 4 million tonnes of cargo annually; there is also a considerable passenger traffic.

Port authority
3.62

1   The Aberdeen Harbour Board, 16 Regent Quay, Aberdeen, AB11 5SS.

Limiting Conditions
3.63

1   **Controlling Depths.** The entrance channel has a dredged depth of 6 m, but is subject to silting and this level may not always be maintained. The Harbour Master should be consulted for the latest depths. Within the harbour the approaches to the major berths are also dredged to 6 m.

Deepest and longest berth. Regent Quay (3.80).

Tidal levels: see *Admiralty Tide Tables.* Mean spring range about 3·7 m; mean neap range about 1·8 m.

3.64

1   **Largest vessel.** The maximum size of vessels routinely handled is length 160 m; beam 23 m; draught 9·1 m (MHWS), 8·3 m (MHWN). Vessels over length 160 m or draught 8·5 m should consult the Harbour Master prior to entry.

3.65

1   **Local weather.** Entry into the harbour is difficult in winds from the E quadrant. There is some protection from the land during gales from the N but the harbour should

not be attempted in strong NE gales when seas are heaviest. In SE gales entry is also difficult in the broadside sea.

2 **Hazard warning.** The fixed red light on each of the leading lights (3.76) is changed to green when conditions in the entrance channel are hazardous.

Arrival Information

Port operations
3.66

1 **Traffic signals** regulating entry and departure are shown from the port control tower (57°08′·5N, 2°04′·2W) at the root of North Pier as follows:

Signal (day or night)	Meaning
Green light	Entry prohibited
Red light	Departure prohibited
Red and green light	Port closed

2 At the entrance to Victoria Docks lights are shown from a lamp post near the Lifeboat Station on Telford Jetty as follows:

Signal (day or night)	Meaning
Red light	Entry/Exit prohibited
Green light	Entry/Exit permitted

Notice of ETA
3.67

1 Notice of one hour is required.

Outer anchorage
3.68

1 Aberdeen Bay is free of dangers and an anchorage can be made in any part of it. The bay has a regular sandy bottom.

Pilots and tugs
3.69

1 **Pilotage** is compulsory for vessels navigating in the Aberdeen Pilotage District except for:
   All vessels under 60 m in length.
   Vessels of 60 m in length and over, but less than 75 m, which are fitted with at least an operational bow thruster unit.
   Vessels moving within the harbour from berth to berth with permission of the Harbour Master.

2 Vessels requiring a pilot should give at least one hour's notice to Port Control. The normal boarding point is in the vicinity of Fairway Light-buoy (1 mile NE of the harbour entrance). Vessels are advised to wait to seaward of Fairway Light-buoy until cleared to enter (Traffic signals 3.66). The two pilot vessels are of MFV type and have the word PILOT displayed on the cabin. Pilots may be ordered in advance through Aberdeen Port Radio and the R/T link to the pilot station.
   Tugs are available.

Regulations concerning entry
3.70

1 The following is an extract from the Aberdeen Harbour Bye-laws:
   The master of a vessel navigating the harbour shall comply with the Collision Regulations except insofar as provisions of these bye-laws otherwise require.

2 The master of a vessel waiting within the limits of the port and harbour to enter the harbour shall so manoeuvre such vessel as to be at all times clear of the ordinary course of ships entering or leaving the harbour.

3 The master or owner of a vessel which is to enter the harbour shall, on the arrival of such vessel in Aberdeen Bay and before it approaches the harbour entrance, notify the Harbour Master of the intended entry of the vessel, giving the name of the vessel, the name of the master, the port or place from which the vessel has arrived and the draught of water of the vessel.

4 The master of a vessel shall not cause or permit such vessel to enter the navigation channel abreast of any other vessel or to overtake any other vessel in said channel, and every master shall keep his vessel at a distance of not less than 70 m behind any other vessel proceeding in the same direction ahead of his vessel in the said channel except when towing or being towed.

5 The master of a vessel shall not cause or permit such vessel to proceed in any part of the harbour at a speed in excess of 5 kn over the ground.

Harbour

Layout
3.71

1 Once clear of the dredged approach channel Aberdeen Harbour opens out to the W and NW. The S arm is the River Dee which is dredged in mid-channel to 6 m, with quays on both sides for a distance of 3 cables. To the NW is Tidal Harbour which splits into 2 tidal basins running W in which the main berths are situated. The N of the basins is Victoria Dock, which runs into Upper Dock, and that to the S is Albert Basin.

Tidal stream
3.72

1 The tidal stream runs SE/NW across the approach to Aberdeen, with a spring rate in each direction of 1½–2 kn, which also applies in the anchorage. Off the entrance the stream is weak. The SE-going stream commences at −0450 HW Aberdeen and the NW-going stream at +0110 HW Aberdeen.

2 Within the breakwaters the River Dee runs with considerable strength particularly during freshets and may achieve 6 kn. The strong outflow may continue even on a flood tide. In Tidal Harbour there is a weak anti-clockwise current.

Principal marks
3.73

1 **Landmarks:**
   Girdle Ness Lighthouse (57°08′N, 2°03′W) (3.49).
   Red conical roof (57°09′·3N, 2°04′·8W).
   Marischal College (tower) (57°09′·0N, 2°05′·8W).
   Pavilion (57°09′·1N, 2°04′·7W).
   Major light:
   Girdle Ness Light (above).

Directions
(continued from 3.52)

Approaches
3.74

1 The approach from the N to Fairway Light-buoy (57°09′·3N, 2°01′·9W) is clear. From S do not approach

River Dee   *Albert Basin*   *Victoria Dock*

Point Law   *Pilot Jetty*   *Round House*

Aberdeen Harbour (3.71)

(Original dated 2000)

(Photograph - Air Images)

within depths of 22 m until clear N of Girdlestone (57°08'·4N, 2°02'·6W).

3.75

1   **Clearing bearing.** The alignment (284°) of the light tower on South Breakwater with the light tower on North Pier (3.76) passes N of the Girdlestone.

Fairway Light-buoy to Aberdeen Harbour

3.76

1   **Torry Leading Lights:**
> Front light (white tower, 13 m in height) (57°08'·4N, 2°04'·5W).
> Rear mark (white tower 14 m in height) (205 m SW of front light).

2   From the vicinity of the Fairway Light-buoy the alignment (235¾°) of the above leading lights leads in the approach to Aberdeen and the dredged channel, whose limits are indicated by beacons (orange topmarks) in line standing on either side of the front leading light, passing (with positions from the front light):

3   NW of South Breakwater Light (white tower) (7 cables ENE), thence:
> SE of North Pier Light (white tower, 9 m in height) (5·8 cables NE), thence:
> NW of Old South Breakwater Light (truncated concrete pillar) (5 cables ENE), thence:
> NW of South Jetty Light (red column, square topmark, 3 m in height) (2·8 cables ENE), thence:

4   SE of Abercromby Jetty Light (green column, triangle topmark, 3 m in height) (2·5 cables NE), thence:

SE of the Pilot station and signal tower (2·3 cables NE).

Once clear of the Pilot station keep in mid-stream for passage to the berth.

5   **Cautions.** In strong ENE and NE winds the Torry Leading Lights should be brought into line 1 to 1½ miles from the harbour entrance.

If the wind is SE or S care must be taken to guard against the strong N set around North Pier Head which is particularly pronounced during freshets.

6   When entering Aberdeen in adverse weather from seaward masters should assess the effects of wind, sea and tidal stream while still to seaward of the Fairway Light-buoy, using this information to adjust the ship's position so that on entry the vessel will have been set onto the line of the leading lights at the Pierheads, or just inside the Pierheads in more severe conditions from a SE direction.

Basins and Berths

River Dee

3.77

1   North bank:
> Point Law South Berth, close E of Mearns Quay.
> Mearns Quay (oilfield supply vessels), 320 m long, 6 m alongside depth.
> South bank:
> Total Quay, with Torry Quay to W.
> River Dee Dock (Maitland Quays).
> River Berth, Repair Berth and Texaco Quay.

South Breakwater   *North Pier*

Entrance to River Dee (3.76)

(Original dated 2000)

(Photograph - Air Images)

Tidal Harbour
3.78

1   Pocra Quay, 166 m long, 6 m alongside depth.
      Pocra Base.
      Multi-berth and ship repair/dry dock facility.
      Telford Dock: Four deep water quays each capable of
         handling ships up to 20 000 dwt. Alongside depths
         9 m.

2   Matthews Quay Cross Berth.
      Point Law North (tanker terminal).

Albert Basin
3.79

1   Atlantic Wharf, 137 m long, 8·7 m alongside depth.
      Pacific Wharf, 200 m long, 9·3 m alongside depth.
      Commercial Quay and Fish market (dredged to 6 m).
      Albert Quay (dredged to 4·4 m from Jetty 2 to
         Pontoon Dock).

Victoria Dock
3.80

1   Waterloo Quay East and West, 380 m long, alongside
         depths, 6 m (E), 9·3 m (W).
      Regent Quay, 250 m long, 9·3 m alongside depth.
      Upper Dock, includes Ro-Ro berth.
      Blaikie's Quay, 635 m long, 6 m depth alongside.
      Matthews Quay.

Port Services
3.81

1   **Repairs** of all kinds can be carried out. A pontoon
dock, 65 m long with a lifting capacity of 1000 tonnes, is
operated by the Port Authority.
      A privately operated dry dock, length 112·8 m, breadth
21·33 m, depth of blocks 1·8 m below chart datum, is also
available.

3.82

1   **Other facilities:** several hospitals; Royal Infirmary at
Forrester Hill (8 cables NW of the harbour entrance) has a
helicopter landing site; reception of oily waste; fixed Ro-Ro
berth in Upper Dock and floating Ro-Ro terminal normally
situated at Commercial Quay; de-ratting and exemption
certificates issued; customs.
3.83

1   **Supplies:** furnace fuel, marine diesel (heavy and light)
at Pocra Quay, Albert Quay, Mearns Quay, Torry Quay and
Texaco berth in the River Dee; water at the quays;
provisions of all kinds. An ice factory operates at the W
end of Albert Quay.
3.84

1   **Communications.** There are ferry services to the
Orkneys, Shetland Islands and to Norwegian ports.
      There are regular shipping services to Scandinavia,
Western Europe, Portugal and the United States.
      Dyce airport (57°12′N, 2°13′W) is 5 miles from
Aberdeen.

ABERDEEN TO STONEHAVEN

General Information

Chart 210
Route
3.85

1   From a position E of Girdle Ness (57°08′N, 2°03′W) the
coastal route leads SSW to a position E of Stonehaven.

Topography
3.86

1   Nigg Bay (3.95) lies between Girdle Ness and Greg
Ness, 6 cables S. Thence the coast from Greg Ness to
Garron Point, at the N entrance to Stonehaven Bay, runs
10 miles SSW. It is composed of nearly perpendicular cliffs
of mica slate over granite, topped by grassy slopes, with
bare hills of moderate elevation in the background. The

coast is mainly steep-to with the 30 m depth contour lying parallel to the coast approximately one mile offshore. In places the cliffs are fringed by reefs and isolated rocks up to three cables to seaward. Stonehaven is at the head of Stonehaven Bay, which lies between Garron Point and Downie Point 1½ miles SSW.

Rescue
3.87

1   There are Coastguard Rescue Teams at Portlethen (3.92) and Stonehaven. See 3.47 for coastguard at Aberdeen and 1.53.

Hazards
3.88

1   **Oil rigs** are frequently anchored about 5 cables SE of Greg Ness and in Nigg Bay.

    Bag nets of considerable size and strength are placed off every point during the fishing season, and are obstructions to small craft navigating inshore.

Tidal streams
3.89

1   Tidal streams which run parallel to the coast in either direction, are shown on the charts and in the *Admiralty Tidal Stream Atlas: North Sea, Northwestern Part.*

    The spring rate close inshore in either direction is 2½ kn.

    A race forms off Girdle Ness during the S-going stream.

Principal Marks
3.90

1   Radio mast (57°07′N, 2°05′W).
    Radio mast (57°04′N, 2°09′W).
    Memorial tower on Hill of Auchlee (57°04′N, 2°11′W).
    Radio mast on summit of Cairn-mon-earn (57°01′·1, 2°21′·5W).
    TV mast, red obstruction lights (57°00′·0N, 2°23′·5W).
    Clachnaben (56°58′N, 2°38′W) (chart 1409) is a mountain about 14 miles W of Stonehaven.

2   **Major lights:**
    Girdle Ness Light (57°08′N, 2°03′W) (3.49).
    Todhead Point Light (56°53′N, 2°13′W) (3.120).

Other navigational aids
3.91

1   **Racons:**
    Aberdeen Fairway Light-buoy (57°09′N, 2°02′W).
    Girdle Ness Light (57°08′N, 2°03′W).

    DGPS:
    Girdle Ness Light — as above.

Directions
(continued from 3.52)
3.92

1   From a position E of the rocky promontory of Girdle Ness (57°08′N, 2°03′W) the coastal passage leads SSW for 12 miles to a position off Downie Point, 2 cables SE of Stonehaven Harbour, running parallel to the coast, passing (with positions from Findon Ness (57°04′·0N, 2°05′·6W)):

2   ESE of Girdlestone (4¾ miles NNE), a rocky patch 1½ cables E of Girdle Ness, with depths of less than 2 m (charted as a dangerous rock) over it, thence;

3   ESE of two rocky patches (4½ miles NNE) the S of which dries, thence;
    ESE of Greg Ness (4 miles NNE), the S entry point of Nigg Bay, thence;
    ESE of Hasman Rock (3 miles NNE), a rock which dries lying a cable offshore, thence;
    ESE of Mutton Rock (2 miles NNE), which dries and lies 1½ cables offshore of the fishing village of Cove Bay. The village is at an elevation of 61 m with a small harbour below in the rocks. Thence;

4   ESE of Findon Ness, a steep-to headland. Findon village stands on sloping ground rising to elevations of between 60 and 90 m, close W of the headland, thence;
    ESE of Portlethen (1 mile SSW) a fishing village with a landing place for boats, fronted by a drying reef. Seal Craig, lying 3 cables offshore, is the E extremity of the reef. Thence;

5   ESE of Newtonhill (3 miles SSW), a village with a boat landing over a gravel beach, thence;
    ESE of Grim Brigs (3¾ miles SSW), a small headland close E of the village of Muchalls, thence;

6   ESE of Garron Point (6 miles SSW), a high rocky promontory. It shelves 2½ cables from the summit and is steep-to terminating in Garron Rock. Skatie Shore a rocky ledge extends 1 cable to the N of the point. Boat landing can be made S of the point. Thence;

7   ESE of Stonehaven Bay (7 miles SSW), lying between Garron Point and Downie Point (11½ miles SSW).

    Caution. Depths are irregular in places and soundings give little guidance. There is no reason to stand close inshore as the coast is straight and the strength of the tidal stream does not diminish close inshore.
3.93

1   **Clearing bearings:**
    The line of bearing of more than 205° of Findon Ness and open E of Greg Ness passes clear of Girdlestone. Alternatively do not approach within depths of 22 m.

2   The line of bearing 022° of Greg Ness and well open of Findon Ness passes E of Seal Craig.
    The line of bearing 187° of Crawton Ness (56°55′N, 2°12′W) and open E of Bowdun Head (57°57′N, 2°11′W) passes E of the shoal and ledges in Stonehaven Bay.
3.94

1   **Useful marks:**
    Greg Ness Coastguard Station (57°08′N, 2°03′W).
    Glenury Viaduct (56°58′N, 2°13′W) (3.107).
    War memorial (56°57′·3N, 2°12′·0W) (3.107).
(Directions continue for Stonehaven at 3.108 and for coastal passage S at 3.122)

Anchorage

Chart 1446
Nigg Bay
3.95

1   There is temporary anchorage in offshore winds in Nigg Bay (57°08′·0N, 2°03′·0W). The bay is fringed by foul ground up to a cable offshore, thence there is a regular sandy bottom to the 9 m depth contour.

Stonehaven

Chart 1438 plan of Stonehaven Harbour
General Information
3.96

1   **Position.** Stonehaven (56°58′N, 2°12′W) stands at the mouth of the River Carron at the head of Stonehaven Bay.
3.97

1   **Function.** Formerly a fishing port, it is now mainly a holiday resort and is used only by recreational craft and a few small inshore fishing boats.

The population in 1995 was 10 000.
3.98

1   **Approach and entry.** Stonehaven is approached from the E through the S part of Stonehaven Bay. The bay has a sandy bottom but there are rocky ledges extending as far as 2 cables offshore.
3.99

1   **Port authority.** Aberdeenshire Council, Carlton House, Arduthie Road, Stonehaven AB39 2DP.

Limiting conditions
3.100

1   **Depths.** There are depths between 0·6 and 1·8 m in the Outer Harbour. The Inner Harbour dries 3·4 m sand and mud.

Tidal levels: see *Admiralty Tide Tables.* Mean spring range about 3·0 m; mean neap range about 1·9 m.

Maximum size of vessel. Length 34 m, draught 3 m.
3.101

1   **Weather.** During NE and E gales vessels cannot lie alongside in the Outer Harbour. A boom is placed across the entrance to Inner Basin in NE and E gales.

In E gales the sea breaks beyond the S entrance point to Stonehaven Bay, 1½ cables E of the harbour and even bursts over the breakwaters.

Arrival Information
3.102

1   **Pilotage** is not compulsory.
3.103

1   **An anchorage** may be obtained in Stonehaven Bay as indicated on the chart, in depths of 11 m, good holding ground, 7¾ cables E of the Bay Hotel (3.107), with the ruins of Dunnottar Castle (3.107) seen over Bowdun Head, bearing 194°.

2   Small craft may anchor closer into the shore but should keep Garron Rock (3.92) (Chart 210) open to the E of the land to the NE.

Harbour
3.104

1   **Layout.** There is an Outer Harbour, protected on its N side by a breakwater and to the S by Downie Point. Middle Basin lies W of the Outer Harbour and is protected by breakwaters on its E and S sides and by the land to the N and W. Inner Basin, also protected by breakwaters, is entered from Middle Basin.
3.105

1   **Boom signal.** When the entrance to Inner Basin is closed, a green light is exhibited from the concrete post 7 m in height, standing in the NE corner of the Inner Basin Breakwater.
3.106

1   **Tidal stream** is weak in Stonehaven Bay with a spring rate of 1 kn.

Stonehaven Harbour (3.104)

(Original dated 2000)

(Photograph – Air Images)

3.107

1 **Principal marks:**

Glenury Viaduct (56°58'N, 2°13'W), to the NW of Stonehaven.

Bay Hotel (three gables) (56°58'·0N, 2°12'·5W).

War Memorial (monument) (56°57'·3N, 2°12'·0W), standing on Black Hill.

Dunnottar Castle (56°56'·7N, 2°11'·7W), in ruins.

Directions
(continued from 3.94)

3.108

1 **Approach to Outer Harbour.** From a position about 1 mile ENE of Downie Point (3.92) the route leads WSW within the white sector (246°–268°) of the Outer Breakwater Light (post, 2 m in height), passing (with positions from the Outer Breakwater Light):

2 SSE of a 4 m shoal (3 cables ENE), thence:

About 1 cable NNW of Downie Point (1½ cables E), rocky ledges run WSW of the point, and:

SSE of Bellman's Head (1 cable NE), a ledge and rocky shoals that run to the SW of it, thence:

To a position ½ cable ENE of the Outer Breakwater Light where the track rounds to the S of the outer breakwater head into the Outer Harbour.

3.109

1 **Approach to Middle Basin.** The alignment (273°) of the leading lights at the W side of the Middle Basin leads through its entrance, from the S side of which a light (post, 7 m in height) is exhibited:

Front light (mast, 5 m in height) (56°57'·6N, 2°12'·1W).

Rear light (lantern on building, 7 m in height) (10 m W of front light).

2 **Caution.** These lights are unsuitable for use in entering the Outer Harbour.

3.110

1 Vessels exceeding 30 m in length are advised to turn before berthing. They are recommended to pass a line to the breakwater before commencing their turn to avoid drifting down on the rocky spit 46 m SW of the breakwater head.

Berths

3.111

1 There is 550 m of berthing space on the quays in the three basins. In the Outer Harbour there is a minimum depth of 1 2 m at MLWS, but the Middle and Inner Basins both dry at MLWS.

Port services

3.112

1 Hospital available at Aberdeen.

3.113

1 **Supplies:** fuel by road tanker; water at quays; fresh provisions.

Small craft

3.114

1 There are berths and facilities for recreational craft in the harbour.

Other names

Charts 210, 1438 plan of Stonehaven Harbour

3.115

1 Brachans (56°57'·9N, 2°11'·9W), a ledge.

Cowie (56°58'N, 2°12'W), a fishing village.

Craigmaroinn (57°03'N, 2°06'W), a reef.

Doonie Point (57°00'·5N, 2°09'·5W).

Hare Ness (57°05'N, 2°05'W).

Totties (56°58'·2N, 2°11'·5W), a ledge.

STONEHAVEN TO MONTROSE

General Information

Chart 210

Route

3.116

1 From a position E of Downie Point (56°57'·5N, 2°11'·5W) the coastal route leads SSW for a distance of 18 miles to a position off Scurdie Ness, the S entrance point to Montrose.

Topography

3.117

1 From Downie Point as far as Craig David, 7 miles SSW there are cliffs fringed with occasional reefs. South of Craig David the cliffs give way to grassy slopes which continue 6 miles SSW to Milton Ness (56°46'·5N, 2°22'·6W), where the coast changes yet again to sandy beaches backed by sandhills until the River South Esk, which forms the entrance to Montrose, is reached.

Rescue

3.118

1 There are Coastguard Rescue Teams at Gourdon and Montrose. See 1.53.

An all-weather lifeboat and an inshore lifeboat are stationed at Montrose. See 1.61 for details of lifeboats.

Tidal information

3.119

1 Tidal streams for the area, which run parallel to the coast, are shown on the chart and in the *Admiralty Tidal Stream Atlas: North Sea, Northwestern Part.*

Principal marks

3.120

1 **Landmarks:**

War Memorial (56°57'·3N, 2°12'·0W) (3.107).

Radio Mast on Bruxie Hill (56°55'N, 2°17'W).

Radio tower (grey mast) on Bervie Brow (3.122) (56°51'N, 2°15'W).

Todhead Point Lighthouse (white tower, 13 m in height) (56°53'N, 2°13'W).

Tower of Johnston on Hill of Garvock (56°49'N, 2°27'W).

2 **Major Lights:**

Todhead Point Light — as above.

Scurdie Ness Light (white tower, 39 m in height) (56°42'N, 2°26'W).

Other navigational aids

3.121

1 **Racon:**

Scurdie Ness Light (56°42'N, 2°26'W).

DGPS:

Girdle Ness Light (57°08'N, 2°03'W).

Directions
(continued from 3.94)

3.122

1 From a position E of Downie Point the coastal passage leads SSW to the vicinity of Scurdie Ness, passing (with positions from Gourdon (55°50'N, 2°17'W)):

ESE of Strathlethan Bay (8½ miles NNE), lying between Downie Point and Bowdun Head, thence:

ESE of Crawton Ness (5½ miles NNE), a low point with cliffs 91 m high close N, thence:

2 ESE of Todhead Point (4 miles NNE) with a lighthouse. The point ends in a cliff 15 m high, which from the S has the appearance of a double fall. Thence:

ESE of Shieldhill (3 miles NNE), a headland and overhanging cliff with a high rock close SE, thence:

3 ESE of Craig David (1½ miles NNE), with Bervie Brow, 135 m high, close W, thence:

ESE of Bervie Bay (1 mile NNE), with the small town of Inverbervie at its head, thence:

ESE of Gourdon, a fishing station (3.126), thence:

ESE of Johnshaven (2½ miles SSW), a fishing village (3.127), thence:

4 ESE of Milton Ness (4½ miles SW), a wedge shaped low grassy point bordered by rocks with a perpendicular red sandstone cliff close W, and the Heughs of St Cyrus, cliffs 73 m high 1 mile SW, which are in the vicinity of a National Nature Reserve. Thence:

5 ESE of Annat Bank and its E extremity, Tod Head (9 miles SSW), which lie on the N side of the entrance to Montrose, thence:

ESE of Scurdie Rocks (9 miles SSW) 1½ cables E of Scurdie Ness, which forms the S side of the entrance to Montrose.

Clearing bearing
3.123
1 The line of bearing 027° of Todhead Point open E of Shieldhill passes E of the rocky ledges between Johnshaven and Gourdon.

Useful marks
3.124
1 Dunnottar Castle (56°57′N, 2°12′W) (3.107).

Inverbervie Church (tower) (56°51′N, 2°17′W).

Hallgreen Castle (56°50′·5N, 2°16′·5W).

Lathallan School (56°48′N, 2°19′W) is well sheltered by trees.

Saint Cyrus Church (spire) (56°46′·5N, 2°24′·5W), standing back from the coast.

2 Radio Mast 37 m in height, surrounded by 6 framework masts each 20 m in height (56°45′N, 2°26′W).

Montrose Church (spire) (56°42′·6N, 2°28′·0W).

Grain Silo (56°42′·4N, 2°27′·6W).

(Directions for Montrose continue at 3.144 and for coastal passage South at 3.159)

Minor Harbours, anchorage and landings

Boat landings
3.125
1 Catterline village (56°54′N, 2°13′W), has a small pier 32 m long which extends into a shallow bay and is used by small fishing boats.

Bervie Water (56°51′N, 2°16′W), which flows into Bervie Bay can be used by small boats at HW.

Gourdon
3.126
1 **General information.** Gourdon (56°50′N, 2°17′W) is a fishing station 1 mile SSW of Inverbervie. There is an outer harbour formed by a pier on its W side and a breakwater to the E, which is used by recreational craft. Main Harbour, which is fitted with storm gates at its entrance, leads off W from the outer harbour and is used by fishing vessels. Both harbours dry and it is advisable to consult the Harbour Master about arrival times and access.

Gourdon (3.126)

(Original dated 2000)

(Photograph - Air Images)

2 **Harbour Authority.** Aberdeenshire Council, Carlton House, Arduthie Road, Stonehaven AB32 2DP.

Signals. The following signal is displayed:

Signal	Meaning
Front leading light shows green	Unsafe to enter harbour

3 **Directions.** The entrance channel is marked by beacons. The alignment (358°) of the leading lights leads through the harbour entrance, which lies between the W pier and the E breakwater, which each exhibit lights (metal columns, 1 m in height) from their heads:

Front light (white tower, 5 m in height) (56°49′·6N, 2°17′·1W).

Rear light (white tower, 6 m in height) (120 m N of the front light).

4 A rocky patch, which dries, lies 7 cables S of the harbour entrance.

Caution. The sea breaks heavily outside Gourdon harbour during E gales and the harbour can only be entered in moderate weather.

Johnshaven
3.127
1 **General Information.** Johnshaven (56°48′N, 2°20′W) is a fishing village 2 miles SW of Gourdon. The harbour, which dries, consists of two basins separated by a central jetty. It provides good shelter for fishing boats in all weathers but it is advisable to check access with the Harbour Master. The narrow entrance and rocky foreshore can be difficult in winds between NE and SE.

2 **Directions.** The alignment (316°) of the leading lights leads to the harbour entrance.

Front light (red structure, 2 m in height) (56°47′·6N, 2°19′·9W).

Rear light (green structure, 3 m in height) (85 m NW of the front light).

The rear light shows red when it is unsafe to enter harbour.

Johnshaven (3.127)

(Original dated 2000)

(Photograph - Air Images)

Montrose

Chart 1438 plan of Montrose Harbour

General information

3.128

1 **Position.** Montrose (56°42′N, 2°28′W) lies at the entrance of the River South Esk on its N bank.

3.129

1 **Function.** Formerly a small commercial and fishing port its commercial activity has increased in recent years. It is also an important supply base for North Sea oilfields.

The population of Montrose in 1991 was 11 440.

3.130

1 **Topography.** The town of Montrose lies at the S end of a sandy peninsula with the sea to the E and Montrose Basin to the W. The River South Esk flows from Montrose Basin to the sea. Montrose Harbour lies along the banks of the river.

3.131

1 **Harbour limits** encompass the mouth of the River South Esk and are shown on the chart.

3.132

1 **Approach and entry.** Montrose Harbour is approached from the E through a dredged channel within the mouth of the River South Esk.

3.133

1 **Traffic.** In 1999 the port was used by 336 vessels totalling 1 002 795 dwt.

3.134

1 **Port authority.** The Montrose Port Authority, Harbour Office, South Quay, Ferryden, Montrose DD10 9SL.

Limiting conditions

3.135

1 **Controlling depths.** The entrance channel and the harbour are dredged to 5·5 m, but the entrance channel is liable to silting, particularly after E winds. The channel has a minimum width of 49·8 m.

Deepest and longest berth. No 16 Berth (3.146).

Tidal levels: see *Admiralty Tide Tables*. Mean spring range about 4·1 m; mean neap range about 3·2 m.

3.136

1 **Maximum size of vessel.** Normally vessels up to 165 m long and draught 7 m are accepted by arrangement but 135 m and upwards must have a bow thruster.

3.137

1 **Local weather.** The entrance to the harbour is dangerous at all states of the tide in strong E gales. Under these conditions the best time to enter harbour, if it is essential to do so, is during the last quarter of the in-going tidal stream, since during the out-going stream breaking seas extend as far as the outer end of the dredged channel.

2 It should be remembered that even with the vessel maintaining the channel centreline it only passes 55 m N of the rocks off Scurdie Ness and 60 m S of the drying part of Annat Bank.

Arrival information

3.138

1 **Notice of ETA.** 24 hours' notice required to ship's agent, to include overall length and draught. Montrose Harbour Radio should be contacted 2 hours before arrival at the pilot station.

3.139

1 **Outer anchorages.** Anchorage is available one mile off the coast in depths of 10 metres, but this is exposed to the E. Anchorage is also available in Lunan Bay (3.179).

3.140

1 **Pilot and tugs.** Pilotage is compulsory for all merchant vessels except fishing boats. Pilots embark from a pilot launch, fitted with VHF, 8 cables to the E of Scurdie Ness Lighthouse. Pilots may be ordered in advance through Montrose Harbour Radio; see the relevant *Admiralty List of Radio Signals*.

2 **Caution.** Vessels are advised to wait to the E of the 10 m depth contour, marked by 2 light-buoys (3.144) when embarking a pilot.

One tug is available and the pilot boat also assists ships berthing.

Harbour

3.141

1 **General layout.** Within the entrance channel the River South Esk broadens to a basin 1½ cables wide running NW/SE for a distance of 4½ cables to New Bridge. The harbour lies at the E end of the basin, which has quays for 550 m on the N bank and 460 m on the S bank. At the W end of the basin there is a shingle bank, The Scaup, which dries. Beyond New Bridge and a rail bridge close W is Montrose Basin, approximately 1½ miles square. There is a vertical clearance of 3 m under the bridges at MHWS and vessels lie aground in Montrose Basin, which dries, soft mud.

Montrose Harbour from SE (3.141)

(Original dated 2000)

(Photograph - Air Images)

3.142

1   **Tidal stream.** The in-going stream sets S and the out-going N across the outer entrance to Montrose Harbour.

At the inner entrance to the harbour the in-going stream begins at −0520 HW Aberdeen and the out-going at +0055 HW Aberdeen. Both streams are reported to attain a spring rate of 7 kn.

Off the entrance, during the out-going stream, there is turbulence which even in fine weather is dangerous to boats.

2   When Annat Bank (3.144) is dry the streams run strongly through the whole length of the channel, but as the bank covers they spread out, run across it and are weaker at the outer end of the channel.

After heavy rain and melting snow, both the duration and rate of the out-going stream are increased and the in-going stream is correspondingly weaker.

3   Within the harbour the in-going stream sets along the S side of the channel and causes an out-going eddy along the E berths on the N bank. The in-going stream is not marked for the first hour, but as the tide begins to rise in Montrose basin it runs strongly. The out-going stream runs most strongly on the N side of the harbour; the duration of slack water is negligible.

3.143

1   **Landmarks:**

    Scurdie Ness Lighthouse (56°42′N, 2°26′W) (3.120).
    Montrose Parish Church Spire (56°42′·6N, 2°28′·0W).
    Grain silo (56°42′·5N, 2°27′·6W).

    Major light:

    Scurdie Ness Light (above).

Directions
(continued from 3.124)

3.144

1   **Outer approaches.** From a position E of Scurdie Ness and to seaward of Scurdie Rocks the approach is indicated by the outer leading lights.

    Front light (white twin pillars, red bands, 10 m in height) (56°42′·2N, 2°27′·3W).
    Rear light (white tower, red cupola, 19 m in height) (1½ cables W of front light).

2   The alignment (271½°) of these lights leads to the harbour entrance and through the outer part of the narrow entrance channel, passing (with positions from the front light):

    N of the light-buoy (port hand) (1¼ miles E), and:
    S of the light-buoy (starboard hand) (1¼ miles ENE), thence:

3   S of Tod Head (7 cables E), the SE extremity of Annat Bank, which lies along the N side of the entrance channel. The head is marked by Annat Light-buoy (starboard hand). The bank extends 7½ cables from the shore and its inner part dries. Runnels of deep water navigable by small craft exist over Annat Bank, but they are constantly changing and local knowledge is required for their navigation. Thence:

4   N of Scurdie Rocks (8 cables ESE) which lie on a spit extending 2 cables E of Scurdie Ness which together form the S side of the entrance channel. Conspicuous beacons stand 1½ cables and 3 cables W of Scurdie Ness, the alignment of which clears N of Scurdie Rocks. Thence:

5   N of Scurdie Ness Lighthouse (6·5 cables ESE) (3.120) and the front beacon (5 cables ESE) marking the clearing bearing for Scurdie Rocks. The coast to the W of Scurdie Ness is fringed by shingle and rocky ledges which dry up to a cable offshore.

6   **Caution.** In bad weather, with onshore winds, the outer leading light towers should be brought in line about 1 mile E of Scurdie Ness.

Spire

Scurdie Ness Light

Approaches to Montrose from ESE (3.144)

(Original dated 2000)

(Photograph - Air Images)

3.145

1   **Inner approaches.** From a position in mid-channel 4½ cables E of the outer front light, the centreline of the channel is indicated by the inner leading lights.

    Front light (framework tower, orange triangle, point up, 20 m in height) (56°42'·1N, 2°28'·1W).

    Rear light (framework tower, orange triangle, point down, 32 m in height) (1 cable W of front light).

2   The alignment (265°) of these lights leads through the inner part of the dredged channel and into the harbour, passing (with positions from the front light):

    N of the rear beacon (8 cables W), marking the clearing bearing for Scurdie Rocks, thence:

3   S of a beacon (starboard hand) (5 cables ENE). A drying bank fronting the land runs W from the beacon for 3 cables to a light-beacon (starboard hand). Three sewer outfall beacons (triangular topmarks) stand between the beacons on the drying bank. Thence:

4   N of a tide gauge (2 cables ESE). At this point the harbour broadens out to the NW and there is a direct approach to the major berths, clear of The Scaup (3.141).

Berths
3.146

1   South side of river (oilfield support base) 480 m of quays, giving six berths numbered 12 to 17. No 16 berth is 150 m long with a depth alongside of 7·3 m.

   North side of river (Port of Montrose) 560 m of quays, giving six berths numbered 6 to 11. There is a Ro-Ro berth in the knuckle between No 6 and No 7 Berths.

Port services
3.147

1   **Repairs.** Minor repairs can be executed; facilities for the reception of oily waste.

3.148

1   **Other facilities:** de-ratting certificates; two hospitals.

3.149

1   **Supplies:** fuel available by road tanker to ships on both sides of the river; water; fresh provisions and supplies.

3.150

1   **Communications.** There is a landing strip for light aircraft at Montrose.

Small craft
3.151

1   Limited facilities and berths are available for small craft for overnight stops only.

Other names

Chart 210, 1438 plan of Stonehaven Harbour
3.152

1   Castle Haven (56°56'·8N, 2°11'·5W).

   Doolie Ness (56°50'N, 2°16'W).

   Job's Craig (56°57'·1N, 2°11'·3W), a rock.

MONTROSE TO RIVER TAY ENTRANCE

General Information

Chart 190
Route
3.153

1   From a position E of Scurdie Ness (56°42'N, 2°26'W), the S entrance point to Montrose, the coastal route leads

SSW for a distance of 18 miles to the Fairway Light-buoy off the entrance to the River Tay.

Topography
3.154

1   The coast from Scurdie Ness to Whiting Ness, 9½ miles SSW is free from dangers but, with the exception of Lunan Bay, 2 miles SSW of Scurdie Ness, fronted by rocks which dry up to 1 cable offshore. Apart from Lunan Bay it is a difficult coast and should not be approached without local knowledge. The stretch of coast from Red Head, the S point of Lunan Bay, to Whiting Ness, 4 miles SSW is composed of old red sandstone cliffs broken by coves and caverns.

2   The approach to the River Tay lies between Whiting Ness and Fife Ness (56°17'N, 2°35'W). Bell Rock, a mass of red sandstone, lies in the centre of the approach 9½ miles SE of Whiting Ness.

3   The town of Arbroath lies 1 mile W of Whiting Ness on low ground fronted by rocky ledges. From Arbroath to Buddon Ness, 7½ miles SW, the N point of the mouth of the River Tay, the coast is sandy and backed by grassy slopes. Some stretches are fronted by rocky ledges extending 2 cables offshore. Abertay Sands, which dry, lie S and W of Buddon Ness and form the S point of the mouth of the River Tay.

Rescue
3.155

1   There are Coastguard Rescue Teams at Arbroath and Carnoustie. See 1.53.

   An all-weather lifeboat and an inshore lifeboat are stationed at Arbroath. See 1.61 for details of lifeboats.

Tidal stream
3.156

1   The tidal stream is shown on the charts and in *Admiralty Tidal Stream Atlas: North Sea, Northwestern Part.*

Principal marks
3.157

1   **Landmarks:**

   Silo 1¼ miles SW of Red Head (56°37'N, 2°29'W).

   Dickmontlaw (56°35'N, 2°34'W), a slight rise topped by a conspicuous clump of trees close N of Arbroath.

2   Two chimneys, 1 cable apart in the W part of Carnoustie (56°30'N, 2°44'W).

   Old Buddon High Lighthouse (56°28'N, 2°45'W) (3.190).

   Bell Rock (56°26'N, 2°23°W) (3.159).

3   **Major lights:**

   Scurdie Ness Light (56°42'N, 2°26'W) (3.120).

   Bell Rock Light (white round tower, 36 m in height) (56°26'N, 2°23'W).

   Fife Ness Light (56°17'N, 2°35'W) (3.235).

Other navigational aids
3.158

1   **Racons:**

   Scurdie Ness Light (56°42'N, 2°26'W).

   Bell Rock Light (56°26'N, 2°23'W).

   DGPS:

   Girdle Ness Light (57°08'N, 2°03'W).

Directions
(continued from 3.124)
3.159

1   From a position E of Scurdie Ness (56°42'N, 2°26'W) the coastal passage runs SSW to the vicinity of the Fairway

Bell Rock Lighthouse (3.157)

(Original dated 2000)

(Photograph - Air Images)

Light-buoy off the entrance to the River Tay, passing (with positions from Whiting Ness (56°34′N, 2°33′W)):

2   ESE of Usan Ness (8½ miles NNE), a broad point 9 m high and fringed by rocks, thence:

ESE of Boddin Point (7¼ miles NNE) which rises to 4 m at its tip, thence:

ESE of Red Head (4 miles NNE), a perpendicular cliff 79 m high. Lunan Bay lies between Boddin Point and the NE extremity of Red Head. Thence:

3   ESE of a pair of former measured distance beacons (1½ miles NNE) and a single beacon a mile further S standing on The Deil's Heid, thence:

ESE of Whiting Ness, thence:

ESE of Arbroath (1 mile WSW) (3.162), thence:

ESE of Elliot Horses (2¼ miles SW), a shoal patch with a depth of 1·9 m over it. Elliot Water, marked by a prominent chimney, reaches the sea on the coast 1 mile W of Elliot Horses. Thence:

4   WNW of Bell Rock (9½ miles SSE), a reef with a lighthouse on it (3.157). There is a shoal patch with a depth of 4·4 m over it 2 cables N and one 2¾ cables S with a depth of 2·5 m over it. Thence:

E of Carnoustie (6 miles SW), thence:

E of the Fairway Light-buoy (safe water) (5½ miles SW) and the entrance to the River Tay, lying between Buddon Ness and Tentsmuir Point. Other light-buoys marking the entrance lie to the SW of the Fairway Light-buoy.

3.160

1   **Clearing bearing.** The line of bearing 022° of the clump of trees on the summit of Dickmontlaw (3.157), and seen between the Presbyterian Church spire (3.173) and the light tower on the Harbour Pier at Arbroath (3.174) (Chart 1438) passes E of Elliot Horses in depths not less than 6 m.

Useful marks
3.161

1   Red Castle (56°39′N, 2°31′W), a ruin at the head of Lunan Bay.

Abbey ruins (56°33′·8N, 2°34′·8W) (3.173).

Church spires (56°33′·7N, 2°34′·5W and 56°33′·6N, 2°34′·8W) in Arbroath (3.173).

(Directions continue for River Tay at 3.192 for coastal passage S at 3.237)

Arbroath

Chart 1438 plan of Arbroath Harbour
General information
3.162

1   **Position.** Arbroath (56°33′N, 2°35′W), is 1 mile W of Whiting Ness.

3.163

1   **Function.** Arbroath, population 23 474 (1991), is mainly a fishing port used by medium and small sized fishing vessels.

3.164

1   **Topography.** The town of Arbroath stands on low ground either side of the mouth of Brothock Water. The coast fronting the town consists of rocky ledges which dry up to 2 cables offshore.

3.165

1   **Approach and entry.** The harbour is approached from the SE by a dredged channel leading through a gap in the reefs fronting the coast. The entrance between piers is about 33 m wide. Within the 10 m depth contour the bottom is generally rock with numerous small boulders and patches of stone, sand and mud.

3.166

1   **Port authority.** Angus Council, Roads Department, County Buildings, Market Street, Forfar DD8 3WR.

Management of the harbour is under the direction of the Harbour Master, Harbour Office, Arbroath DD11 1PD.

Limiting Conditions
3.167

1   **Controlling depths.** A channel, dredged to 2·0 m (1999), leads to the harbour entrance; thence, as far as the entrance to the Tidal Basin, the channel is dredged to 1·5 m (1999).

The Tidal Basin, which dries, bottom mud, has an entrance 15 m wide. The depth over the sill of the Wet Dock is 4·3 m at HW Springs.

2   **Tidal levels:** see *Admiralty Tide Tables.* Mean spring range about 4·3 m; mean neap range about 2·3 m.

Maximum size of vessel. Length 67 m, beam 11 m, draught 4 m.

3.168

1   **Weather.** During strong onshore winds with a heavy groundswell, there is a strong SW set across the harbour entrance. Vessels approaching in these conditions are advised to keep well to windward.

Arrival Information
3.169

1   **Pilotage** is not available.

3.170

1   **Regulations** affecting entry:

All vessels entering or being within the harbour shall be in all respects under the control of the Harbour Master, whose directions shall be implicitly obeyed in all matters within his jurisdiction.

2   No vessel shall anchor or lie within 76 m of the pierhead and no vessel shall at any time obstruct the fairway.

No vessel when entering, approaching or leaving the harbour, shall overtake or attempt to pass abreast or ahead of any other vessel so approaching, entering, or leaving.

Harbour
3.171

1   **Layout.** The harbour is open to the SE but protected by Harbour Pier to the NE and West Breakwater, which is

Signal Tower

West Breakwater   *Harbour Pier*

Arbroath Harbour (3.171)

(Original dated 2000)

(Photograph - Air Images)

detached, to the S. The harbour contains a tidal basin and a wet dock leading off the tidal basin. The gates to the latter are permanently open and vessels lie on the mud at LW in both the tidal basin and the wet dock.

3.172

1   **Traffic signal.** At night when it is unsafe to enter harbour the light on Harbour Pier (3.174) is changed to fixed red.

3.173

1   **Principal marks:**
Clump of trees (56°35′N, 2°34′W) (Chart 190) (3.157).
Abbey ruins with a circular window (56°33′·8N, 2°34′·8W).
Saint Mary's Church (spire) (56°33′·7N, 2°34′·5W).
Presbyterian Church (spire) (56°33′·6N, 2°34′·8W).

2   Signal Tower (56°33′·3N, 2°35′·1W) (disused), a white castellated structure with a flagstaff.
Reservoir Tower (56°33′·5N, 2°35′·6W), standing on Keptie Hill and resembling a castle from seaward.

The extremities of the Harbour Pier and the West Breakwater, flanking the harbour entrance (56°33′·2N, 2°34′·9W) painted white and prominent.

Directions

3.174

1   **Leading Lights:**
Front Light (white column, 4 m in height) (56°33′·3N, 2°35′·1W).
Rear Light (white column, 9 m in height) (50 m WNW of the front light).

From a position about 1 mile ESE of the harbour entrance the alignment (299¼°) of these lights leads through the dredged channel to the Harbour entrance, passing (with positions from the front light);

2   NNE of the seaward end of an outfall (6½ cables S), extending 5½ cables S from the shore and marked by a light-buoy (special), thence:

Signal tower

West Breakwater   *Leading Lights*   *Harbour Pier*

Arbroath Harbour entrance (3.174)

(Original dated 2000)

NNE of Cheek Bush and Chapel Rock (3½ cables SE and 4 cables SSE respectively), thence:

SSW of Knuckle Rock (3½ cables ESE), thence:

NNE of two rocks (2½ cables SE) which dry 0·2 m and 0·5 m respectively, thence:

3 NNE of a light-beacon (special) (2¼ cables SE) marking the seaward end of an outfall, thence:

To the harbour entrance (1 cable SE) which is about 50 m wide and lies between the heads of Harbour Pier (light: white tower, 9 m in height) and West Breakwater (light: white metal post, 2 m in height). Thence:

4 To the entrance to the Tidal Basin (150 m E), which is 15 m wide.

Alternative Leading Marks.

Saint Thomas Church (56°33'·4N, 2°35'·4W) (twin towers) bearing 298° between the harbour entrance lights, leads through the harbour entrance.

Reservoir Tower, Keptie Hill (3.173) bearing 299° and seen between the twin towers of Saint Thomas Church leads through the harbour entrance.

Port Services

3.175

1 **Repairs.** Timber, steel and mechanical repairs can be undertaken. There is a patent slip capable of handling vessels up to 250 tonnes.

3.176

1 **Other facility:** hospital.

3.177

1 **Supplies:** marine diesel and water at the quays; fresh provisions.

3.178

1 **Communications.** Direct rail services to London and Aberdeen. There is a helicopter landing site 1¾ miles NW of Arbroath and an emergency only site at Arbroath Hospital.

Anchorage

Chart 190
Lunan Bay
3.179

1 Lunan Bay (56°39'N, 2°28'W) which lies between Boddin Point and Red Head, is sandy and free from dangers, apart from the rocky ledges off the Point and Head. There is a good anchorage in the bay, indicated on the chart, 1 mile E of the ruins of Red Castle (3.161) in depths of 14 m, sand over clay.

2 Small craft can anchor in Ethie Haven which lies in the SW corner of Lunan Bay.

Other names

3.180

1 Auchmithie Bay (56°36'N, 2°31'W).
Dickmont's Den (56°34'N, 2°32'W), a cove.
East Haven (56°31'N, 2°40'W), a sandy beach.
Long Craig (56°41'N, 2°27'W), a reef.
2 Sillo Craig (56°42'N, 2°26'W) a reef.
West Haven (56°30'N, 2°41'W), a shelter for small fishing boats.

RIVER TAY ENTRANCE TO TAY ROAD BRIDGE

General Information

Chart 1481
General description
3.181

1 The River Tay flows into the sea between Buddon Ness (56°27'·8N, 2°44'·3W) and Tentsmuir Point (56°26'·7N, 2°48'·8W). Dundee Harbour is 7 miles W of Buddon Ness. Tay Road Bridge lies at the W end of the Dundee Harbour and connects Dundee with the S bank of the Tay in the vicinity of East Newport.

2 Tayport Harbour, a small tidal basin, lies on the S bank of the River Tay 5 miles W of Buddon Ness.

3 There is a bar 3 miles E of Buddon Ness. The buoyed channel across the bar and through the entrance lies between extensive drying sandbanks, Gaa Sand to the N and Elbow and Abertay Sands to the S, which are liable to change especially during heavy weather from the E. Abertay Sands and Elbow have been extending E for many years and the extension to Elbow together with the bar, has been moving NE, but depths have remained fairly constant. Within the entrance the channel is narrow with a minimum width of 450 m, and still encumbered with sandbanks as far as Broughty Ferry, 4½ miles W of Buddon Ness. The channel is wider for the final approach to Dundee.

4 A National Nature Reserve covers Abertay Sands and the sands off Tentsmuir Point.

Controlling Depths
3.182

1 The controlling depth to Dundee is at Lady Shoal (3.193) where the channel is 1½ cables wide with a least depth of 4·6 m in mid-channel. Depths in the buoyed channel across The Bar are 5 m or more providing the centreline is maintained.

2 **Tidal levels:** see *Admiralty Tide Tables*.
The Bar: mean spring range about 4·5 m; mean neap range about 2·3 m.
Dundee: mean spring range about 4·7 m; mean neap range about 2·4 m.

3 **Caution.** Depths in the channel are liable to change. The Harbour Master and pilots can advise on arrival times should draught present a problem.

Deep draught vessels should arrive at Fairway Light-buoy at least 3 hours before HW to berth on the same tide.

Exercise area
3.183

1 A military exercise area exists at Buddon Ness. Ranges fire W across Monifieth Bay and E across Carnoustie Bay. A safety zone exists between the south boundary of the firing areas and the north boundary of the buoyed channel. See *Annual Summary of Admiralty Notices to Mariners* and PEXA chart Q6405.

Pilotage
3.184

1 Pilotage is compulsory in the Dundee Pilotage District which extends to the port limits just SSW of Fairway Light-buoy, as shown on the chart.

2 Pilots board large vessels at the Outer Pilot Station which is close S of Fairway Light-buoy. In adverse conditions pilots board at the Inner Pilot Station which is SW of Buddon Ness as shown on the chart. This station is also used as the boarding point for small vessels. In rough weather the pilot boat will lead in until the pilot is able to board.

3   The pilot boat is either a 12 m semi-rigid boat with an enclosed wheelhouse, orange hull and the word "Pilots" shown on each side of the upper works; or a 15 m pilot boat with blue hull, and white upperworks with "Dundee Pilot" marked on each side. A pilot boat is only on station when a vessel is expected.

Tugs. One tug is available at Dundee; additional tugs may be obtained by prior arrangement.

Port operations
3.185
1   Radar surveillance for monitoring shipping in the estuary and River Tay is maintained at Dundee.

Notice of ETA
3.186
1   ETA should be signalled 6 hours in advance, and amendments up to 2 hours in advance, to Port Control Dundee. ETA should be confirmed on VHF with Port Control, who will pass instructions.

Prohibited anchorage
3.187
1   There is a prohibited anchorage, shown on the chart, S of Dundee Docks. Vessels are also cautioned against anchoring in the vicinity of the submarine cables crossing the river close W of Tayport High Lighthouse and the submarine gas pipeline (1.23) which runs NNE across the river from Tentsmuir Point. The landing places of the pipeline are marked by light-beacons.

Rescue
3.188
1   An all-weather and an inshore lifeboat are maintained at Broughty Ferry (5 miles W of Buddon Ness (3.192)). See 1.61 for details of lifeboats.

Natural conditions
3.189
1   **Tidal stream** in the vicinity of the entrance to the River Tay is shown on the chart. In the buoyed channel between Inner Light-buoy and Tentsmuir Point, a NW set occurs on the flood tide which is especially noticeable in the vicinity of Pool Buoy before Abertay Sands (3.193) are covered.

2   Tidal streams run strongly in the channel S of Horse Shoe (56°27'·4N, 2°50'·0W) (3.193), where the in-going stream runs in a direction towards Tayport and the out-going stream towards Green Scalp (3.193). There is usually some turbulence between Horse Shoe and Broughty Castle (3.190), especially during the E going stream with W winds.

3   Off Dundee inner docks, the in-going stream sets across the entrance to Camperdown Dock (3.211) at less strength than in the centre of the river. The stream is weak or slack from 30 minutes to 40 minutes before HW which is the best time for entry into the enclosed dock system.

4   Both the duration and rate of the out-going stream may be increased and the in-going stream correspondingly reduced, during and after heavy rain or when snow is melting.

Principal marks
3.190
1   **Landmarks:**
Old High Lighthouse on Buddon Ness (white tower, 32 m in height) (56°28'·1N, 2°44'·9W), now disused.

Broughty Castle (56°27'·8N, 2°52'·1W), a conspicuous square building.
TV mast (56°26'·7N, 2°55'·4W), close SE of Tay Road Bridge.

2   Monument (56°26'·8N, 2°55'·9W), close SE of Tay Road Bridge.
War Memorial on summit of Dundee Law (56°28'·2N, 2°59'·3W).
TV mast, 197 m in height, 40 m N of War Memorial (above).
Buildings (4 blocks of flats) (56°28'·2N, 2°58'·0W).
Saint Paul's Church Spire (56°28'N, 2°58'W) in SE part of Dundee.

3   Building, 180 m S of Church Spire (above).
Building (56°28'·5N, 2°58'·7W). Another building lies close W and a third close SE.

Major light:
Tayport High Direction Light (white tower, 23 m in height) (56°27'·2N, 2°53'·8W).

Other navigational aids
3.191
1   **Racon:**
Abertay Light-buoy (56°27'·4N, 2°40'·5W).
DGPS:
Girdle Ness Light (57°08'N, 2°03'W).

Directions
(continued from 3.161)

Fairway Light-buoy to Buddon Ness
3.192
1   From the vicinity of Fairway Light-buoy (safe water) (56°29'·2N, 2°38'·2W) the route leads SW thence W to a position in the channel S of Buddon Ness, passing (with positions from Buddon Ness):
Over The Bar (3 miles ENE), passing between Middle Light-buoys (port hand and starboard hand), which are 3½ cables apart, thence:

2   NW of Elbow (2 miles SE), a spit extending 3 miles ENE from Abertay Sands, with depths of less than 5 m, thence:
Between the Abertay Light-buoys (E cardinal and port hand) (2 miles ESE) 4 cables apart.

3   The line of bearing 269° within the white sector (268°–270°) of Tayport High Direction Light then leads in the channel, passing (with positions from Buddon Ness):
S of Gaa Sand and Gaa Spit, which extend 2 miles E of Buddon Ness. Gaa Sand dries up to 1½ miles E of Buddon Ness, thence:
S of Buddon Ness, consisting of grass covered sand dunes up to 9 m high on its E side.

4   **Cautions.** When entering the River Tay during onshore gales from the NE or SE, the tidal set must be watched carefully in order to keep in the buoyed channel. It might be dangerous to cross The Bar in these conditions, particularly during the out-going stream; depths might alter and light-buoys drag out of position. The best time to cross The Bar is from 2 hours before HW to HW.

Passage across Abertay and Gaa Sands can be highly dangerous and should not be attempted.

Buddon Ness to Tayport High Lighthouse
3.193
1   From a position in the channel S of Buddon Ness the route leads W, remaining in the white sector of Tayport High Direction Light as far as Horse Shoe Light-buoy, thence WNW until Tayport High Lighthouse is abeam, passing (positions given from Tayport High Lighthouse):

2   N of Abertay Sands (4½ miles E), which dry and extend E of Tentsmuir Point (below) and lie to the S of the channel for a distance of 2 miles. Inner Light-buoy (port hand) is moored close N of the sands. Thence:

N of Lady Shoal (4 miles E), an extension N of Abertay Sands, which almost forms an inner bar, thence:

3   Between North Lady and South Lady Light-buoys (starboard hand and port hand respectively) (4 miles E), which lie close to the limits of the white sector (268°–270°) of Tayport High Direction Light. North Lady Light-buoy marks the S limit of Lady Bank which fills the greater part of the bay lying between Buddon Ness and Broughty Castle. Thence:

4   N of Pool Light-buoy (3 miles E) (port hand), thence:

N of Tentsmuir Point (2½ miles ESE), which is low and sandy and fronted by Green Scalp, a bank of sand and gravel which dries, thence:

5   S of Horse Shoe (2 miles E), a patch of foul ground to the W of Lady Bank, marked on its S side by Horse Shoe Light-buoy (S cardinal). A light-buoy (special) marking the seaward end of Dighty outfall lies 2½ cables NE of Horse Shoe Light-buoy. The channel is only 2 cables wide at this point and shoal patches, with depths of less than 3 m lie close S of the white sector of Tayport High Direction Light. Thence:

6   N of Lucky Scalp (2 miles E), with Larick Scalp to its W. These drying banks of sand and gravel lie W of Green Scalp and fill the bay between Tentsmuir Point and Tayport (3.195). Scalp Light-buoy (port hand) is moored close N of Larick Scalp. Thence:

7   SSW of Broughty Castle (1 mile NE) (3.190). The S extremity of Broughty Castle in transit with Old High Lighthouse bears 084½° and provides a useful compass check for vessels leaving Dundee. And:

Broughty Castle (3.193)

(Original dated 2000)

(Photograph - Air Images)

8   NNE of Tayport (6 cables E). The ruins of Larick Beacon lie 3 cables ENE of the harbour entrance; an outfall extends from Tayport to a position ¾ cable WNW of Larick Beacon. Thence:

NNE of Craig Light-buoy (port hand) (6 cables NE) and Tayport High Lighthouse.

Tayport High Lighthouse to Tay Road Bridge
3.194

1   From a position in the channel NNE of Tayport High Lighthouse the route leads W for 1 mile then SW for a further mile to the navigation spans under the Tay Road Bridge (56°27'·2N, 2°56'·8W), passing (with positions from navigation spans):

2   N of Newcome Shoal (1¾ miles ENE), marked on its NE extremity by Newcome Light-buoy (port hand), thence:

N of Tayport High Lighthouse (1½ miles E). From this point vessels can proceed to Dundee Docks 1 mile to the W or the anchorage 7 cables SW. Thence:

3   NW of West Deep Light-buoy (port hand) (2 cables NE), thence:

SE of Middle Bank (2½ cables N), which lies in the centre of the river on both sides of the road bridge, and is marked at its NW extremity by Middle Bank Light-buoy (E cardinal). Thence:

4   To the navigation spans under the road bridge. For description of Tay Road Bridge and the navigation spans see 3.222.

(Directions continue at 3.222)

Anchorage and Harbour

Tayport Harbour
3.195

1   Tayport Harbour (56°27'N, 2°53'W) is a small tidal basin which dries. The entrance is 25 m wide and marked on either pierhead by masts (white and red bands). There are depths of 1·2 m to 1·5 m at the entrance and there are 488 m of quays and pontoon berths for small craft. Vessels that use the harbour take the mud at low water.

The harbour is privately owned.

Anchorage
3.196

1   There is an anchorage in 6·1 m, 6 cables WSW of Buddon Ness, as shown on the chart.

Vessels also anchor 1¼ miles ESE of Dundee Docks.

Other names
3.197

1   Abertay Spit (56°26'·2N, 2°41'·7W).
Barry Sands (56°28'·5N, 2°47'·0W).
Beacon Rock (56°27'·5N, 2°57'·2W).
Camus Stone Law (56°31'·8N, 2°47'·3W).
Hare Law (56°26'·8N, 2°54'·2W).
Monifieth (fronted by Monifieth Sands) (56°29'·0N, 2°49'·0W).
Old Low Lighthouse (disused) (56°28'·0N, 2°44'·6W) on Buddon Ness.

DUNDEE

General Information

Chart 1481 and plan of Dundee Docks
Position
3.198

1   The City of Dundee (56°28'N, 2°57'W), spreads along the N side of the River Tay over a distance of 3 miles. The river is crossed by two bridges at Dundee, Tay Road Bridge, which runs from the centre of the City, and the rail bridge 1½ miles to the W.

Function
3.199

1   The port handles crude oil and general cargo and also undertakes the repair and servicing of offshore oil installations.

   The population of the city in 1999 was about 160 000.

Port limits
3.200

1   The E limit is close SSW of the Fairway Light-buoy (3.192). The W limit lies at Balmerino 2 miles W of the Rail Bridge. The limits are shown on Chart 1481 and plan River Tay to Perth.

Traffic
3.201

1   In 1999 Dundee was used by 431 vessels totalling 2 726 325 dwt.

Port authority
3.202

1   Port of Dundee Ltd, Harbour Chambers, Dock Street, Dundee DD1 3HW.

Limiting conditions
3.203

1   **Controlling depths.** See 3.182.
   Deepest berth. Caledon West Wharf (3.210).
   Mean tidal levels. See 3.182.
3.204

1   **Maximum size of vessel.** Vessels with a maximum length of 250 m, beam 50 m and draught up to 9·0 m can normally be accommodated at the riverside berths.

Arrival Information

Notice of ETA
3.205

1   6 hours' notice of ETA is required, with amendments up to 2 hours in advance. See 3.186.

Regulations concerning entry
3.206

1   Subject to the requirements of maintaining steerage way vessels shall not exceed 8 kn to the W of 2°53′W (vicinity

of Craig Light-buoy). Within the docks and Tidal Basin the speed limit is 3 kn.

   Small vessels under power or sail and not confined to a fairway shall not obstruct vessels which can only navigate within a fairway.

2   Vessels crossing, turning or manoeuvring in a fairway shall only do so when it is clear and not impede other vessels navigating in the fairway.

   Power driven vessels navigating against the stream shall slow or stop to allow vessels navigating with the stream to pass clear.

Harbour

Layout
3.207

1   Dundee Docks consist of a number of riverside berths which extend E from the NW end of the Tay Road Bridge. There are two docks, Camperdown Dock, entered from the River Tay and Victoria Docks entered from Camperdown Dock.

Dock signals
3.208

1   No vessel should approach Camperdown Lockway to transit it without first receiving permission from Port Control. If, after having obtained permission, a red flashing light is exhibited from the roof of the Port Control Building the approaching vessel should stand off and not approach the lockway again until it has received further permission to do so.

Directions
3.209

1   Principal marks and directions are given at 3.190 to 3.194.

Berths

Riverside berths
3.210 y

1   Queen Elizabeth Wharf, 194 m long, 7 m depth alongside. This berth is not available to commercial vessels.

   King George V Wharf, 445 m long, 8·5 m depth alongside.

Victoria Dock

Beacon Rock   *Fowler Rock Buoy*   *Camperdown Dock*

Dundee Docks (3.210)

(Original dated 2000)

(Photograph - Air Images)

Caledon West Wharf, 76 m long, 9·5 m depth alongside, is dredged W in front of King George V Wharf and E in front of Princess Alexandra Wharf to provide a berth 300 m long and 55 m wide, with 9·5 m depth alongside and is used principally for oil tankers.

2　Princess Alexandra Wharf, 256 m long, 8 m depth alongside.

Eastern Wharf, 213 m long, 8 m alongside, with a Ro-Ro linkspan at the E end.

Caledon East Wharf, 150 m long, 5·8 m depth alongside.

Prince Charles' Wharf, 114 m long, 8·0 m depth alongside.

Total length of riverside berths is 1450 m.

Docks
3.211

1　**Note.** Camperdown and Victoria docks are no longer in commercial use. They are available only to leisure craft and for limited lay-up use.

Camperdown Dock has 560 m of quays and is entered through dock gates facing S, immediately W of King George V Wharf. The entrance is 15 m wide and the nominal bottom of the dock is LAT; there are depths in the dock of 4·0 m. The dock gates may be opened on request from 1 to 2 hours before and until HW.

2　Victoria Dock has 840 m of quays and is entered from the W side of Camperdown Dock. Depths within the dock are similar to Camperdown Dock.

There is a Tidal Basin at the E end of the riverside berths, which is reserved for use by the Port Authority.

Port services
3.212

1　**Repairs** of all kinds can be carried out.
3.213

1　**Other facilities:** hospitals; helicopter landing site at Ninewells Hospital, 2 miles WNW of the NW end of Tay Road Bridge; reception of oily waste; de-ratting carried out and certificates issued; customs.
3.214

1　**Supplies:** furnace fuel oil; marine diesel (heavy and light); water; provisions of all kinds.
3.215

1　**Communications.** Dundee Airport (56°27′N, 3°01′W) is situated close W of the N end of Tay Railway Bridge.

Small craft
3.216

1　There are facilities for small craft in the West Ferry area which lies E of the port.

TAY ROAD BRIDGE TO PERTH

General information

Chart 1481
General description
3.217

1　The River Tay runs 19 miles from the Tay Road Bridge to Perth. Above the railway bridge the river broadens to 3 miles in width but gradually slims until just W of Mugdrum Island (10 miles SW of the railway bridge) it is only 2 cables wide, but continuing to narrow further upstream. For the 10 miles to Mugdrum Island the N side of the river is heavily encumbered with banks up to 2 miles wide. The S side of the river is relatively free of banks but there are a number of banks in the middle.

Controlling depths
3.218

1　Depths in the River Tay are uncertain (see 3.221), but vessels are advised to leave Dundee 2 hours before HW Dundee, to arrive at HW Perth.

Tidal levels at Perth: see *Admiralty Tide Tables.* Mean spring range about 3·5 m; mean neap range about 1·8 m.

Hazards
3.219

1　Dredging for sand and gravel takes place in the main channel, between longitudes 2°59′·6W and 3°04′·5W.

Pilotage and tugs
3.220

1　Navigation on the River Tay between Dundee and Perth is difficult and can be hazardous. Pilotage is not compulsory and is not provided under the terms of the Pilotage Act 1987, but masters are strongly advised to make use of the services of a local pilot which will be arranged by the Perth Harbour Master.

2　Local charts are available from the Tay Estuary Research Centre, Old Ferry Pier, Newport-on-Tay, Fife DD6 8EX, or from chandlers in the area.

Towage can be arranged when necessary by the agent and/or Harbour Master.

Local knowledge
3.221

1　The channel between My Lord's Bank and Birkhill Bank (3.225), and its continuation W, should not be attempted without local knowledge.

Directions
(continued from 3.194)

Tay Road Bridge
3.222

1　The Tay Road Bridge spans the river from East Newport (56°27′N, 2°56′W) NW to Dundee. There are 2 navigation spans, the N span between piers 31 and 32, and the S span between 32 and 33. The width of the spans is 76 m and the vertical clearance 22·86 m, in the centre span. Lights are exhibited on the piers and in the centre of each span, together with daymarks (cone, point down, black and white diagonal stripes). Inbound vessels proceeding from E to W must use the N span and outbound vessels the S span. Use of the 2 spans either side of the navigation spans is not permitted.

Tay Road Bridge to Tay Railway Bridge
3.223

1　From a position close W of the road bridge the route leads SW to the navigation spans of the Tay Railway Bridge, passing (positions given from the road bridge navigation spans):

2　　SE of Middle Bank (3.194), thence:
　　NW of Newport-on-Tay (5 cables S) and across a cable area running NW from Newport to Dundee as shown on the chart. Vessels are cautioned against anchoring in the area. The NE limit of the area is marked by beacons on either bank. Thence:
　　To the navigation spans of the railway bridge.

Tay Railway Bridge
3.224

1　Tay Railway Bridge (56°26′N, 2°59′W) spans the river at the W end of Dundee. The navigable channel under the bridge is between the seventh and eighth largest spans from the N, which in turn lie between piers 30 to 35. Piers 31 to 34 are marked by lights on either side. The headway under the bridge is greater than the Road Bridge in the centre span. The channel between the fourth and fifth spans from the N is obstructed by the remains of an old bridge, and must not be used for navigation.

Tay Railway Bridge to Perth
3.225

1 To the W of the railway bridge lie My Lord's Bank and Birkhill Bank. The channel between the two banks and its continuation to the W between the numerous other banks is marked by buoys.

Between the railway bridge and Perth there are power cables (56°22′N, 3°19′W) spanning the river with a vertical clearance of 26 m and a bridge, Friarton Road Bridge, (56°23′N, 3°25′W) which is marked by lights, and has a vertical clearance of 25 m.

2 Two submarine power cables cross the river at Cairnie Pier (56°21′·5N 3°18′·1W). They are each marked by a light-beacon on Cairnie Pier and by a beacon on the bank opposite with a light-beacon centrally disposed between the two.

Perth

General information
3.226

1 The Royal Burgh of Perth (56°24′N, 3°27′W) is on the W bank of the River Tay 17 miles above the Tay Railway Bridge.

The population of Perth was 41 453 in 1991.

Perth Tidal Harbour, 5 cables S of Perth is also on the W bank of the river. The small commercial port has 418 m of quays providing 6 berths and is capable of handling vessels up to 90 m in length and 4·2 m draught at HW springs.

Perth Tidal Harbour from S (3.226)

(Original dated 2000)

(Photograph - Air Images)

2 The port handles over 200 000 tonnes of cargo a year, mainly agricultural products, sand, chemicals and all forest products. In 1999 178 vessels totalling 288 618 dwt used the port.

Port authority. Perth & Kinross Council, Planning and Development Services, 2 High Street, Perth PH1 5PH. Communications should be addressed to the Harbour Master, Friarton Road, Perth PH2 8BB.

Port services
3.227

1 Small repairs can be carried out locally, major repairs at Dundee. Oily waste reception facilities using road tankers available by arrangement with vessel's agents. There is a hospital.

3.228

1 **Supplies:** marine diesel by road tanker; water at quays; provisions.

Small craft
3.229

1 There are no facilities for small craft in Perth harbour. Perth Sailing Club is based at Lairwell, about 1 mile S of Perth.

Other names
3.230

1 Craig Harbour (disused) (56°27′·4N, 2°58′·0W).
Earn, River (56°21N, 3°18′W).
Flisk Point (56°24′N, 3°07′W).
Jock's Hole (56°22′N, 3°12′W).
Newburgh (56°21′N, 3°14′W), a town.
Peat, The (56°21′N, 3°16′W).
Queen's Road (56°27′N, 2°58′W), a deep.
Seggieden (56°23′N, 3°21′W).

RIVER TAY TO FIFE NESS

General information

Chart 190
Route
3.231

1 From the vicinity of the Fairway Light-buoy (56°27′·5N, 2°37′·2W) off the entrance to the River Tay the coastal route leads SSE for a distance of 11½ miles to a position E of Fife Ness.

Topography
3.232

1 St Andrew's Bay lies between Tentsmuir Point the S entrance point of the River Tay and Fife Ness. Tentsmuir Point is at the W end of Abertay Sands (3.193) and from here the coast runs S for 6 miles to the town of St Andrew's. This part of the coast is fronted by Tentsmuir Sands and backed by sandhills. There is a nature reserve on Tentsmuir Sands. The mouth of the River Eden is 2 miles N of St Andrew's. The coast forming the S part of the bay lies between St Andrew's and Fife Ness, 8 miles ESE. It is generally rocky, with cliffs in places rising to 30 m.

Rescue
3.233

1 Fife Ness is the Maritime Rescue Sub-centre for the Forth District and maintains a continuous watch.

There is a Coastguard Rescue Team at St Andrew's.

Tidal stream
3.234

1 The tidal stream is shown on the chart and in the *Admiralty Tidal Stream Atlas: North Sea, Northwestern Part.*

Principal marks
3.235

1 **Landmarks:**
Old High Lighthouse (56°28′N, 2°45′W) (3.190).

Regulus Tower on the E side of St Andrew's (56°20′N, 2°47′W).

Silo, the position of which is approximate, 1¼ miles SSW of Kinkell Ness (56°20′N, 2°45′W).

Balcomie Tower (56°17′N, 2°36′W), square tower and outbuildings, standing close W of Fife Ness.

2   **Major lights:**

Bell Rock Light (56°26′N, 2°23′W) (3.157).

Fife Ness Light (white building, 5 m in height) (56°17′N, 2°35′W).

Isle of May Light (56°11′N, 2°33′W) (3.252).

Other navigational aids
3.236

1   **Racon:**

Bell Rock Light (56°26′N, 2°23′W).

DGPS:

Girdle Ness Light (57°08′N, 2°03′W).

Directions
(continued from 3.161)
3.237

1   From the vicinity of the Fairway Light-buoy (56°29′·2N, 2°38′·2W) off the entrance to the River Tay the coastal route is SSE to Fife Ness, passing (with positions from Fife Ness):

2   ENE of St Andrew's Bay (7 miles WNW), with the town of St Andrew's (3.240) at its head. The W coast of the bay is fronted by shoal water with depths of less than 5 m. Targets and target buoys may be moored off Tentsmuir Sands (3.232) and there are range beacons ashore. Thence:

3   ENE of North Carr Rock (1 mile NNE), which dries. The rock has a prominent beacon (red column on a stone base, globe topmark, all supported by 6 metal stays) and lies at the NE extremity of foul ground extending 1 mile NE of Fife Ness. North Carr Light-buoy (E cardinal) is moored 1 mile NE of North Carr Rock, which is also covered by the red sector (197°–217°) of Fife Ness light. Thence:

4   ENE of Fife Ness, a dark cliff, 10 m high, above a rocky foreshore.

Useful marks
3.238

1   University spire (56°20′·5N, 2°47′·6W).
Cathedral ruins (56°20′·4N, 2°47′·2W) (3.241).
Kingsbarn village church spire (56°18′N, 2°40′W).
Coastguard radio tower on Fife Ness (56°17′N, 2°35′W).

(Directions continue for coastal passage at 3.254)

Minor harbours

Guardbridge
3.239

1   **General information.** Guardbridge (56°21′N, 2°53′W) (Chart 1407) is situated about 3 miles above the bar of the River Eden, where the river is spanned by a road bridge.

Local knowledge is required for the river passage.

2   **Directions.** There is usually a depth of 5 m at HW springs at the bar. Within the bar there are depths of 3 m reducing to 2 m at Guardbridge. The bar itself is constantly changing and the channel to Guardbridge, via the River Eden, is narrow and bounded by wide sand flats.

Berths. There is a quay near the bridge and the tall chimney of a paper mill stands close N of the quay.

St Andrew's
3.240

1   **General information.** St Andrew's (56°20′N, 2°48′W), population 11 138 (1991), stands on a flat table-land 18 m high, 6 miles S of Tentsmuir Point. It has a small harbour, which dries, used by fishing boats and pleasure craft. The harbour lies on the mouth of Kiness Burn. Long Pier, 213 m long, protects the harbour and is built on The Skellies, a rocky ledge running ESE for 3 cables. Other ledges lie close S of and parallel to The Skellies.

2   **The harbour** lies S of Long Pier and there is a short pier extending NE from close S of Long Pier. It is divided into an outer and inner harbour by an entrance 8 m wide, spanned by a movable pedestrian bridge. Both the harbours are tidal. At MHWS depths of 4 m to 5 m have been reported in the approach channel and 4 m in parts of the outer harbour. These depths are liable to change.

Regulus Tower

Long Pier

St Andrew's Harbour (3.240)

(Original dated 2000)

(Photograph - Air Images)

3.241

1   **Principal marks**

Regulus Tower (56°20′·4N, 2°47′·2W) conspicuous, in the E side of the Town.

University Spire (56°20′·5N, 2°47′·6W).

2   Cathedral ruins (56°20′·4N, 2°47′·2W), close N of Regulus Tower.

Drumcarrow Craig (215 m high) (3½ miles SW of Regulus Tower) a rugged topped hill, surmounted by a mast (Chart 1407).

3.242

1   **Directions.** From a position NNE of Long Pier the approach lies close to the SE of the pierhead, about 16 m off, thence close S of Long Pier and parallel to it and to the N of the ledges on the S side of the channel.

Caution. The passage between Long Pier and the ledges is narrow. In E gales there is a considerable swell in the outer harbour.

3.243

1   **Boat Landing.** There are steps, available at half tide, within Long Pier.

3.244

1   **Facilities:** limited supplies of water; slipway for small boats only; cottage hospital.

Other names
3.245

1   Balcomie Brigs (56°17'·5N, 2°35'·5W) a reef.
Buddo Ness (56°19'·5N, 2°43'·0W).
Cambo Ness (56°18'N, 2°38'W).
Babbet Ness (56°19'N, 2°40'W).
Out Head (56°22'N, 2°49'W).

FIFE NESS TO ELIE NESS AND ISLE OF MAY

General information

Charts 175, 734
Routes
3.246

1   The routes described are those to enter the Firth of Forth from the NW, and the N part of the route across the approaches to the Firth of Forth.

2   The fishing ports of Crail (3.257), Anstruther (3.258), Pittenweem (3.259) and St Monans (3.260) are also described.

Topography
3.247

1   From Fife Ness (56°17'N, 2°35'W) the coast runs in a SW direction for 9½ miles to Elie Ness, which is considered to be the N entry point of the Firth of Forth. The coast consists of low cliffs and grassy banks above a rocky foreshore, and is mostly foul up to 2 cables offshore.

2   Isle of May is 5 miles SSE of Fife Ness. It is composed of dark grey greenstone, with an elevated grassy surface. The W side is formed by cliffs, up to 62 m high, which slope irregularly E to a rocky coast indented by deep fissures. The NW end of the island is lower and terminates in rocks offshore. The island has a bird observatory and is a National Nature Reserve.

Isle of May from S (3.247)

(Original dated 2000)

(Photograph – Air Images)

Exercise areas
3.248

1   Submarines and minesweepers exercise in the Approaches to the Firth of Forth. See 1.20 for details of exercise areas.

Dumping ground
3.249

1   There is a dumping ground for ammunition and boom gear, now disused, 2½ miles E of the Isle of May. A second disused dumping ground for ammunition is close W. Both are shown on the chart.

Rescue
3.250

1   There is a Coastguard Rescue Team at Crail (56°15'N, 2°38'W). See 1.53.

An all-weather lifeboat is stationed at Anstruther (56°13'N, 2°42'W). For details of lifeboat, see 1.61.

Tidal stream
3.251

1   Tidal streams for the area are shown on the chart and in the *Admiralty Tidal Stream Atlas: North Sea, Northwestern Part.*

The spring rate in either direction is 1 to 1½ kn off salient points.

Principal marks
3.252

1   **Landmarks:**

    West Lomond (56°15'N, 3°18'W), a sugar loaf mountain (Chart 1407).

    East Lomond (56°14'N, 3°13'W), a sugar loaf mountain (Chart 1407).

    Largo Law (56°14'N, 2°56'W), a notched summit and stone cairn (Chart 1407).

    Kellie Law (56°15'N, 2°47'W), a ridge to Largo Law (Chart 1407).

    Boatyard (56°12'·3N, 2°45'·7W), a conspicuous white building in St Monans.

2   **Major lights:**

    Fife Ness Light (56°17'N, 2°35'W) (3.235).

    Elie Ness Light (white tower 11 m high) (56°11'N, 2°49'W), on SW point of Elie Ness.

    Isle of May Light (square tower on stone dwelling 24 m high) (56°11'N, 2°33'W).

Other navigational aid
3.253

1   **DGPS:**

    Girdle Ness Light (57°08'N, 2°03'W).

Directions
(continued from 3.238)

Fife Ness to Elie Ness
3.254

1   From a position E of Fife Ness (56°17'N, 2°35'W), the coastal passage runs 11½ miles SW to a position S of Elie Ness, passing (with positions from Fife Ness):

    Depending on draught, clear of Hurst (1·6 miles SSE), a 10·8 m patch. A wreck with a depth of 15 m over it lies 8 cables E of Hurst, thence:

2   SE of Crail (2 miles SW) (3.257), a village lying in Roome Bight, 7 cables wide between Roome Ness and West Ness. The coast between Kilminning Craig (3.255) and Roome Ness is foul up to 4 cables offshore. Thence:

    SE of Caiplie Rock (3½ miles SW) with a depth of 3·8 m over it, which lies off Caiplie village. The Coves, several caverns in the face of the coastal banks, lie 8 cables N of Caiplie Rock. Thence:

3   SE of Anstruther Easter (5 miles SW) and its harbour (3.258). Anstruther Easter is the central part of a long straggling town with Cellardyke at the E end and Anstruther Wester at the W. Thence:

    SE of Pittenweem (6½ miles SW) (3.259), a fishing village standing on higher ground with a small harbour below. Shield Rock with a depth of 4·5 m over it lies 4 cables SSE of the harbour entrance. Thence:

4   SE of St Monans (St Monance) (7½ miles SE) (3.260), a fishing village and small harbour, thence:

SE of Elie Ness (9½ miles SW), a prominent low rocky headland whence Elie Ness Light (3.252) is exhibited.

3.255

1   **Useful marks:**

Kilminning Craig (56°16′N, 2°36′W), a prominent high black rock.

Pittenweem Church (clock tower and short spire) (56°13′N, 2°44′W).

2   St Monans sector light (breakwater head, elevation 5 m) (56°12′·2N, 2°45′·9W).

St Monans Church (spire) (56°12′N, 2°46′W), at W end of the village.

Newark Castle (ruins) (56°12′N, 2°47′W), 5 cables SW of St Monans Church.

Fife Ness to the Isle of May
3.256

1   From a position E of Fife Ness the route leads 5 miles S in open sea to the Isle of May, passing E of the coast between Fife Ness and Elie Ness (3.254) and the island itself.

(Directions continue for the Firth of Forth at 4.22 and for coastal passage S at 5.12).

Minor Harbours and anchorage

Crail Harbour
3.257

1   **General information.** Crail Harbour (56°15′N, 2°38′W) stands at the SW end of the village and is formed by a main pier to the S and a small jetty on the W side. The inner approach to the harbour is obstructed by rocky ledges, but vessels drawing up to 3 m may enter at HW.

Crail Harbour (3.257)

(Original dated 2000)

(Photograph - Air Images)

2   **Harbour Authority.** Fife Council, Fife House, North Street, Glenrothes, Fife KY7 5LT.

Directions. From SE of the harbour the alignment (295°) of the leading lights leads to the harbour entrance which is 7 m wide:

Front light (white stone beacon, 6 m in height) on cliff (56°15′·5N, 2°37′·7W).

Rear light (similar beacon) (30 m WNW of front beacon).

3   **Caution.** NE gales cause a heavy swell in the harbour, and it is not possible to enter in strong NE or SE winds.

Useful mark:

Crail Church (square tower surmounted by spire) (56°15′·7N, 2°37′·7W).

Facilities: limited small craft berths and facilities available; there is a slipway; hospital at St Andrew's.

Chart 734
Anstruther Harbour
3.258

1   **General information.** Anstruther Harbour (56°13′N, 2°42′W), a fishing harbour, is close SE of Anstruther Easter. There are 1170 m of quays in the harbour, with an inner basin which dries soft mud. It is formed by E and W piers (both lighted at their heads) with an entrance which faces SW and has a depth of 0·3 m. The harbour has a depth of 4·6 m at HW springs.

2   **Harbour Authority.** Fife Council, Fife House, North Street, Glenrothes, Fife KY7 5LT. The harbour authority is represented by a Harbour Master who may be contacted by telephone or VHF radio; see the relevant *Admiralty List of Radio Signals* for details.

3   **Directions.** From S of the harbour the alignment (019°) of leading lights leads to the harbour entrance:

Front light (white mast 6 m high) (56°13′·2N, 2°41′·5W).

Rear light (white mast 8 m high) (38 m NNE of front light).

4   **Caution.** Entry should not be attempted in strong winds from the E and S.

Repairs may be made. There is a slipway and a beaching area.

Supplies: marine diesel by road tanker; water; provisions.

Hospital at St Andrew's.

Small craft. The inner basin has 32 pontoon berths with water and power available; lavatories and showers adjoin the Harbour Office.

Pittenweem Harbour
3.259

1   **General information.** Pittenweem Harbour (56°13′N, 2°44′W) is a busy fishing port which can be used by vessels up to 27·5 m in length. It is formed by three piers, with an entrance 23 m wide, depth 1·5 m, facing SW. There is a small inner basin, entrance 8 m wide and depth 3 m at HW springs. The inner harbour is liable to be congested and the Harbour Master must be consulted before berthing.

2   **Harbour Authority.** Fife Council, Fife House, North Street, Glenrothes, Fife KY7 5LT. The harbour authority is represented by a Harbour Master who may be contacted by telephone or VHF radio; see the relevant *Admiralty List of Radio Signals* for details.

3   **Directions.** The W side of the approach channel is marked by a light-beacon and the E side by a sector light on the head of the breakwater. From SW of the harbour the alignment (037°) of the leading lights leads to the harbour entrance:

Front light (white column, orange stripe, 3 m high) (56°12′·7N, 2°43′·5W).

Rear light (white column, orange stripe, 10 m high).

Anstruther (3.258)

(Original dated 2000)

(Photograph - Air Images)

Church

Light-beacon

Pittenweem (3.259)

(Original dated 2000)

(Photograph - Air Images)

4   **Useful mark:**
      Church (56°13′N, 2°44′W) (3.255).
      Caution. South East gales cause a heavy scend in the harbour, making entry difficult in a beam sea. Mariners are advised not to approach the port in these conditions.
      Vessels drawing less than 3 m lie securely aground in the inner basin.

5   **Supplies:** marine diesel by road tanker; water at the quays; provisions.
      Hospital at St Andrew's.

St Monans Harbour
3.260

1   **General information.** St Monans (St Monance) Harbour (56°12′N, 2°46′W) is a small fishing port formed by piers. There are two basins protected by an angled breakwater running 1 cable SW of the outer arm of E pier. There is a light at the head of the breakwater and there are lights at the heads of both E and W piers. Vessels drawing 2 m can enter approximately 3 hours before HW and vessels drawing 3 m can enter at HW springs. The harbour dries, hard sand and mud.

Boatyard

St. Monans (3.260)

(Original dated 2000)

(Photograph - Air Images)

2   **Harbour Authority.** Fife Council, Fife House, North Street, Glenrothes, Fife KY7 5LT.

Useful marks:
>Church (spire) (56°12′N, 2°46′W) (3.255).
>Sector light (56°12′·2N, 2°45′·9W) (3.255).
>Newark Castle (56°12′N, 2°47′W) (3.255).

Caution. The approach to St Monans harbour should not be attempted in strong SE winds or when there is a NE swell.

3 **Repairs.** There is a boatyard (3.252) in the NE corner of the harbour, and a slipway and two cradles suitable for craft up to 30 m in length and 4 m draught. Engine repairs can be carried out.

Supplies: marine diesel by road tanker; water; provisions.

Hospital at St Andrew's.

Small craft berths and facilities available.

Isle of May — boat landings
3.261

1 **Altarstones** boat harbour lies on the NW side of the island and is used during E winds.

2 **Kirk Haven** boat harbour lies on the SE side of the island and is used during W winds. It is the larger of the two boat harbours, but a sunken rock lies near the entrance. Two uncharted white beacons lead towards Kirk Haven until the harbour opens, when two similar beacons at the head of the harbour become visible and lead up the harbour. There is a small quay, with a crane, at the head of the harbour.

Other names
3.262

1 >Billow Ness (56°12′·6N, 2°44′·1W).
>Lady's Folly (56°11′·1N, 2°48′·4W), a ruined round stone tower.
>Ox Rock (56°11′·2N, 2°47′·8W).
>Skinfast Haven (56°13′·5N, 2°40′·9W).

NOTES

Chapter 4 - Firth of Forth and River Forth

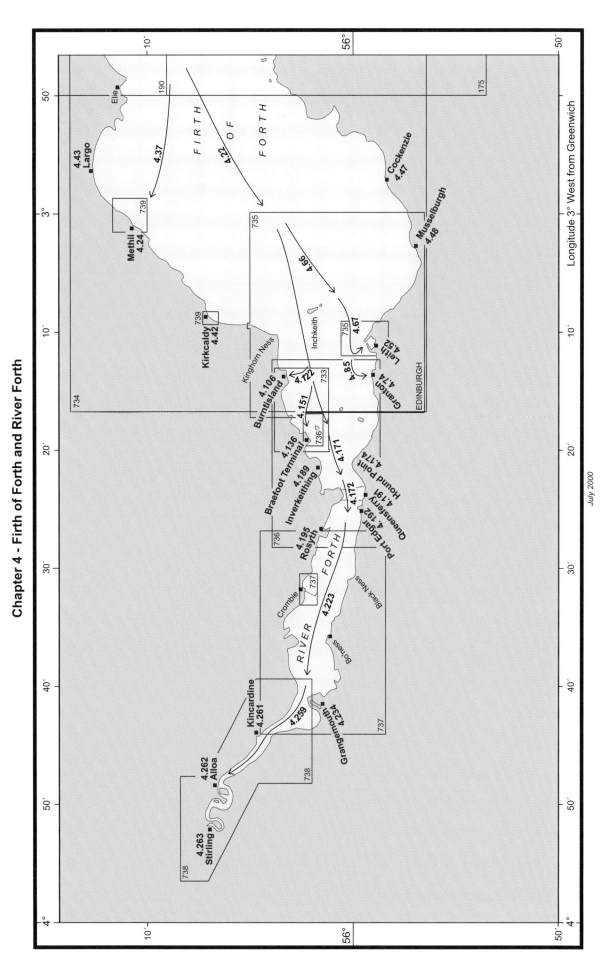

July 2000

Longitude 3° West from Greenwich

CHAPTER 4

FIRTH OF FORTH AND RIVER FORTH

GENERAL INFORMATION

Charts 734, 735, 736, 737, 739

Description
4.1

1   The entrance to the Firth of Forth lies between Elie Ness (56°11′N, 2°49′W) and Fidra, an islet 6¾ miles S. The Firth of Forth extends for 20 miles W to Queensferry at which point it is crossed by the Forth Railway and Forth Road bridges and the River Forth itself commences. Forth Deep Water Channel leads from Fairway Light-buoy (56°03′·5N, 3°00′·0W) to a position NW of Hound Point, 1 mile E of the Rail Bridge. Depths in the River Forth gradually reduce but it remains navigable for small pleasure craft as far as Stirling, 62 miles from the entrance.

2   Within the area there are the major ports of Leith (4.52), Rosyth (4.195) and Grangemouth (4.234); the oil terminal at Hound Point (4.174) and the gas terminal at Braefoot (4.136). There are close on 40 pier and tidal harbours as well as good anchorages on both sides of the bridges.

Forth Ports PLC

General
4.2

1   Forth Ports PLC, Tower Place, Leith, Edinburgh EH6 7DB.

2   Forth Ports PLC, through the powers conferred on it by the Forth Ports Authority Order Confirmation Act 1969, exercises jurisdiction over all the waters of the Firth of Forth and River Forth between a line joining North Carr Beacon (56°18′N, 2°34′W) and South Carr Beacon (14½ miles S) and the head of navigation at Stirling Bridge. The Forth Byelaws and General Directions for Navigation set out the detailed regulations for the conduct of vessels within Forth Ports PLC's area of jurisdiction. A summary of those regulations which affect vessels on entry to the Forth is at Appendix II. Forth Ports PLC is also the Local Lighthouse Authority for the estuary and river of the Firth of Forth.

3   Forth Ports PLC owns and operates the port premises at Burntisland, Grangemouth, Granton, Leith and Methil. Rosyth is owned by a consortium, Rosyth 2000, and operated by Forth Ports PLC. Forth Ports Authority (Port Premises) Byelaws 1983, containing general rules and regulations, applies to these harbours; copies may be obtained from Forth Ports PLC.

4   It also owns Hound Point Marine Terminal Jetty No 1 which is operated by BP. Hound Point Marine Terminal Jetty No 2 is owned and operated by BP. Braefoot Bay Marine Terminal is owned and operated by Shell/Exxon.

Vessel traffic and Trade
4.3

1   The Forth ports handle annually about 20 000 ship movements and over 30 million tonnes of cargo, mostly oil, petro-chemicals and liquefied gases, which pass through the port of Grangemouth and the two marine terminals at Hound Point and Braefoot, but these figures also include a very considerable trade in more general cargo and containers at Grangemouth and the other ports.

Pilotage
4.4

1   Forth Ports PLC exercises pilotage jurisdiction within its area. Pilotage is compulsory for all passenger-carrying vessels W of 3°00′·0W, and for other vessels in the Forth Deep Water Channel and its immediate vicinity and in the firth and river as a whole W of the meridian 3°15′·36W but excluding any closed dock, lock or other closed work within the limits, with the exception of the Eastern Channel lying within Grangemouth Docks. Pilotage is also compulsory for vessels over 8000 dwt bound for Leith. For details see the relevant *Admiralty List of Radio Signals.*

4.5

1   Requests for pilots should be made 24 hours in advance to Forth Ports PLC and amended or confirmed 2 hours before arrival to the Forth Pilot Station at Granton on VHF. An ETA must be made 12 hours in advance otherwise vessels could be delayed as well as being surcharged.

2   The following details are required:
        Gross register tonnage.
        Maximum draught.
        Destination and position for embarking the pilot.

4.6

1   Pilots are normally embarked or disembarked as follows:
        Inward bound vessels proceeding to Methil should arrange an embarkation position off the port.
        Inward bound vessels proceeding to Leith or Granton embark the pilot NE of the Narrow Deep Light-buoy, or in the vicinity of Leith Approach Light-buoy.

2   Inward bound vessels proceeding N of Inchkeith in the Compulsory Pilotage area embark the pilot between Fairway Light-buoy (56°03′·5N, 3°00′·0W) and No 3 Light-buoy, keeping N of the Forth Deep Water Channel.
        Vessels bound to or from Hound Point Terminal embark or disembark the pilot at Fairway Light-buoy.

3   Outward bound vessels, other than those from Hound Point Terminal, passing N of Inchkeith, disembark pilots between No 4 Light-buoy and No 2 Light-buoy keeping S of the Forth Deep Water Channel.
        Vessels at anchor in A4 or A5 anchorages, or the small vessel anchorages, embark pilots at or near the anchorage position before proceeding inbound.
    The pilot launches operate from Granton and are fitted with radar and VHF.

4.7

1   **Tankers.** Until the pilot is on board and has the conduct of the vessel, tankers proceeding from K1-K7 anchorages (4.42) to embark a pilot must not proceed S of 56°05′N, and tankers inward bound from sea or from A1-A3 anchorages (4.49) must not proceed W of 3°00′W.

Port operations
4.8

1   **Vessel Traffic Service** scheme, called the Forth Navigation Service, with full radar surveillance is maintained for the control of shipping from the Harbour Master's Office, Leith. For details and list of reporting positions, which are also shown on the charts, see the relevant *Admiralty List of Radio Signals*.

Notice of ETA
4.9

1   Ships should advise the Forth Navigation Service and Forth Pilots of their ETA at Fairway Light-buoy (56°03′·5N, 3°00′·0W) 24 hours in advance, amending the time if it becomes more than 2 hours in error (see 4.144 concerning notice for tankers bound for Braefoot Bay Marine Terminal).

Dockyard Port of Rosyth
4.10

1   The limits of the Dockyard Port of Rosyth, shown on the charts, lie within the area of jurisdiction of Forth Ports PLC. The Dockyard Port of Rosyth Order 1975, as amended by the Dockyard Port of Rosyth (Amendment) Order 1980, given at Appendix I, applies within the Dockyard Port as well as the Forth Byelaws. In the event of inconsistency between the two sets of regulations then the Dockyard Port of Rosyth Order takes precedence.

FIRTH OF FORTH ENTRANCE TO FAIRWAY LIGHT-BUOY

General information

Charts 734, 735
Route
4.11

1   From a position S of Elie Ness (56°11′N, 2°49′W) the route leads 7 miles SW to Fairway Light-buoy, which is moored at the E end of the Forth Deep Water Channel.

Topography
4.12

1   At its entrance the Firth of Forth is 7 miles wide, but opens out to a width of 10 miles until the vicinity of Inchkeith where it narrows to 5 miles. The coast to the S is generally low and sandy with the 10 m depth contour running up to 2 miles offshore. The N coast is generally well-wooded and more steep-to, with the exception of Largo Bay (56°12′N, 2°56′W), and much of it is fronted by rocky reefs.

Depths
4.13

1   Depths in the approaches to the Forth Deep Water Channel are in excess of 20 m.

Exercise areas
4.14

1   Submarines and other Naval vessels exercise in the E part of the Firth of Forth. See *Annual Summary of Admiralty Notices to Mariners* and PEXA chart Q6405.

Pilotage
4.15

1   See 4.4 to 4.6.

Traffic regulations
4.16

1   See 4.8 and 4.9.
4.17

1   **Prohibited anchorage** area lies 1 mile either side of the gas pipeline (1.37), which crosses the Firth of Forth from the N coast at the E end of Largo Bay (4.22) to the S coast just SW of Eyebroughy (4.22).

Rescue
4.18

1   There are Coastguard Rescue Teams at Leven (56°12′N, 2°59′W), Gullane (56°02′N, 2°50′W), Fisherrow (55°57′N, 3°04′W) and Granton (55°59′N, 3°13′W). See 1.53.

Tidal streams
4.19

1   At the entrance and in the outer part of the firth the streams are weak and rarely exceed a spring rate of 1 kn. See tables on charts.

Principal marks
4.20

1   **Landmarks:**
   Gullane House (56°02′N, 2°51′W).
   Hopetoun Monument (55°59′N, 2°48′W).
   Power station chimneys (55°58′N, 2°58′W), white concrete.
   Arthur's Seat (55°57′N, 3°10′W) (4.54).
2   Radio mast (shown as tower on chart) (56°11′N, 2°51′W) standing on Craig Heugh, a prominent ridge even at night.
   Power station chimney (56°11′·5N, 2°59′·8W) in Leven.
   Building (56°09′N, 3°05′W).
3   **Major Lights:**
   Isle of May Light (56°11′N, 2°33′W) (3.252).
   Fidra Light (white brick tower, 17 m high) (56°04′N, 2°47′W).
   Inchkeith Light (stone tower, 19 m high) (56°02′N, 3°08′W).
   Elie Ness Light (56°11′·0N, 2°48′·6W) (3.252).

Other navigational aids
4.21

1   **Racon:**
   Fairway Light-buoy (56°04′N, 3°00′W).
   DGPS:
   Girdle Ness Light (57°08′N, 2°03′W).

Directions
(continued from 3.256)
4.22

1   From a position S of Elie Ness (56°11′N, 2°49′W) the route leads 7 miles WSW to Fairway Light-buoy, passing (with positions from Chapel Ness (56°11′N, 2°50′W)):
   SSE of Chapel Ness, the W entrance point of Elie Bay (4.50), with three drying rocks in its vicinity, Thill Rock to the E, East Vows marked by a beacon (pyramid structure, surmounted by a cage, 12 m high) to the SE and West Vows to the W, thence:
2   SSE of Kincraig Point (1 mile WNW), backed by Craig Heugh (4.20), thence:
   NNW of Fidra (6¾ miles SSE), a dark rocky islet with a lighthouse (4.20). The S end is detached at HW and is flat-topped with a ruined chapel. The islet is a bird sanctuary, thence:
3   NNW of Eyebroughy (7 miles S), an islet connected by a reef to the mainland 2½ cables S, which is a bird sanctuary, thence:
   SSE of Largo Bay (3½ miles WNW) 5½ miles wide lying between Kincraig Point and the village of Buckhaven where the small disused harbour has silted up. Thence:
   NNW of Gullane Point (56°02′N, 2°52′W), which is black and rocky, thence:

*North Berwick
Law*

Lamb I.   *Fidra Light*

Fidra and North Berwick from WNW (4.22)

(Original dated 2000)

(Photograph - Air Images)

NNW of Craigielaw Point (56°01′N, 2°53′W), with Aberlady Bay lying between the point and Gullane Point to the NNE. The greater part of the bay is a nature reserve and it is mostly drying sands. There are several stranded wrecks in the bay. Thence:

N of Fairway Light-buoy (safe water) (56°03′·5N, 3°00′·0W) at the start of the Forth Deep Water Channel.

Useful marks

4.23

Gosford House (56°00′N, 2°53′W), with a cupola and ruins close inland.

Ruddon's Point (56°12′N, 2°53′W) close SW of a remarkable conical hill surmounted by a white mast.

Railway bridge (56°13′N, 2°56′W) of four arches, at Largo.

(Directions continue for Forth Deep Water Channel at 4.103 and for Leith Channel at 4.66)

Methil

Charts 734, 739 plan of Methil

General information

4.24

Position. Methil (56°11′N, 3°00′W) stands on the S bank of the River Leven on the W side of Largo Bay.

4.25

Function. Methil is a commercial port handling woodpulp and timber, fertiliser, stone and coal. North sea oil production platforms are constructed adjacent to the port.

The population with Buckhaven (4.22) was 17 069 in 1991.

4.26

Traffic. In 1999 the port handled 52 vessels of 109 263 dwt.

4.27

Port authority. The harbour is administered by Forth Ports PLC, Fife Ports, Exmouth Building, Rosyth, Fife KY11 2XP.

Limiting conditions

4.28

Controlling depths. The inner part of the approach was dredged to 2·3 m in 1993. To the S of the dredged area the approach is over uneven ground and within the 10 m depth contour there are patches with less than 5 m over them. The Harbour Master should be consulted for the latest information on depths.

At the sill of No 2 Dock, the outer dock, there is a depth of 7·9 m at HW springs.

Deepest and longest berth. No 2 Dock (4.38).

Tidal levels: see *Admiralty Tide Tables.* Mean spring range about 4·8 m; mean neap range about 2·4 m.

4.29

Largest vessel. The port can accommodate vessels up to 102 m in length, beam 14·6 m and draught 5·5 m.

Arrival information

4.30

Port Operations. See 4.8.

4.31

Traffic signals are shown from a staff on the E side of the entrance to No 2 Dock as follows:

Signal, day or night	Meaning
Red light over green light	Dangerous to enter, bring up in roads
Red light over white light	Clear to come into No 2 Dock
Red light	Remain in roads until another signal is made

2   The above signals are shown from 3 hours before HW until such time as the dock gates are closed.

4.32

1   **Notice of ETA.** See 4.9.

4.33

1   **Anchorages.** There are 5 anchor berths for large vessels numbered M2 to M6, which lie just to the NE of an area fouled by obstructions, shown on chart 734. Vessels are cautioned against anchoring in the foul area.

2   There is an anchorage area for small vessels close SE of the port. A spoil ground encroaches on the SE corner of this anchorage and on the NW sector of M5 anchor berth, and an outfall extends SE from the shore to a position close N of the small craft anchorage.

4.34

1   **Pilotage** is not compulsory. If required the pilot normally embarks in the roads. See 4.4 to 4.6.

Harbour

4.35

1   **Layout.** The port consists of two working docks, No 1 and No 2. The docks are protected to the E by an outer pier and entered from the S via a short channel 15 m wide into No 2 Dock through gates which are normally operated from 3 hours before HW until HW. No 1 Dock is entered from the N end of No 2 Dock through a channel 15 m wide. A disused dock, No 3, and its entry channel lie to the E of the working docks.

4.36

1   **Principal marks:**
Power station chimney (56°11′·5N, 2°59′·8W).
Two tower blocks (8½ cables SW of chimney).

Directions

4.37

1   From a position S of Elie Ness (56°11′N, 2°49′W) (3.254) the route leads WNW diverging N from the main approach route (4.22) passing S of Largo Bay (4.22), through the anchorage area (4.33) to a position S of the entrance to Methil Harbour. Thence the track rounds to the N for the harbour entrance, passing (with positions from the harbour entrance):

2   E of the wharf (190 m long) (3½ cables SW) which partly dries alongside with two wet docks at its S

Power station chimney

Methil Harbour (4.35)

(Original dated 2000)

(Photograph - Air Images)

end, associated with an oil rig construction yard, thence:

W of Outer pierhead light (white tower, 8 m in height) and the entrance to No 3 Dock, now disused, thence:

3 Into the channel which leads to No 2 Dock (1 cable NNW) formed by two piers each marked by a light (masts, 4 m in height) at their S extremities.

Caution. Vessels waiting for sufficient water to enter the docks should stay in depths greater than 13 m.

Berths
4.38
1 The total length of quays in No 1 Dock is 500 m and in No 2 Dock 340 m. A depth of 6 m is maintained in No 2 Dock.

Port services
4.39
1 **Repairs.** Limited hull and engineering repairs can be executed.
4.40
1 **Other services:** reception of oily waste; hospital.
4.41
1 **Supplies.** Marine diesel by road tanker; water at the quays; provisions and stores.

Minor harbours, anchorages and landings

Charts 734, 739 plan of Kirkcaldy
Kirkcaldy
4.42
1 **General information.** Kirkcaldy Harbour (56°07′N, 3°09′W), at the N end of the town of Kirkcaldy, is closed to commercial traffic but is still used by local fishing vessels. Pier Harbour is formed by East Pier, from which a light is exhibited, and South Pier; the harbour entrance faces S and is 46 m wide. Depths within the harbour are no longer maintained, and may be less than charted.

2 A former dock situated N of Pier Harbour is now disused and is to be filled in.

Port authority. The harbour is administered by Forth Ports PLC, Fife Ports, Exmouth Building, Rosyth, Fife KY11 2XP.

Anchorage. There are 9 anchor berths for large vessels, K1 to K7, off Kirkcaldy, shown on chart 734. K2 anchorage is not to be used by tankers proceeding to Hound Point Terminal.

3 There is also an anchorage area for small vessels SE of the harbour in Kirkcaldy Bay. At its NW corner a light-buoy (special) marks the seaward end of an outfall. The bay is generally free from dangers but the bottom is rock covered with sand and not good holding ground. The anchorage is sheltered from the W but open to the E and vessels should not lie there during onshore winds in winter. A recommended berth, in a depth of 10 m, is 7 cables ESE of the pierhead.

4 **Directions.** From a position S of Elie Ness (56°11′N, 2°49′W) (3.261) the route leads W diverging slowly to the N from the main approach route (4.20) passing S of Largo Bay (4.20), through the anchorages to a position SE of the entrance to Kirkcaldy Harbour. Thence the track leads W and then NW to the harbour entrance, passing (with positions from the harbour entrance):

5 S of the Rockheads, patches with depths of 1 to 2 m over them, thence:

S of the buoy (special) marking the seaward end of the outfall (6 cables ESE) running 6 cables SE

from the coast to the NW corner of the small vessel anchorage, thence:

6 SE of a beacon (special, yellow triangular topmark, point up) (60 m SE). The track rounds to the NW for the harbour entrance on crossing from the green sector (156°–336°) to the white sector (336°–156°) of East Pier light. Thence:

SW of East Pier light (column, 7 m in height) and close along the W side of East Pier towards the dock gates.

7 **Caution.** Kirkcaldy Harbour should not be attempted in E gales as the sea breaks in depths of 9 m to 11 m.

Chart 734
Largo Harbour
4.43
1 **General information.** Largo Harbour (56°13′N, 2°56′W) stands at the mouth of Kiel Burn with a rough stone pier on its E side and a parallel ridge of rocks, the Pier of Lundin, to the W. The approach channel is 17 m wide and the Pier of Lundin is well marked by warping posts. The approach is over a wide sand bank with patches of rock and is subject to a marked scend when the wind is in the S quadrant. There can be freshets in Kiel Burn.

2 **An anchorage** is available in Largo Bay, even in E gales, in an area shown on the chart. A recommended berth in a depth of 11 m is 3¾ miles W of Elie Ness with the Ness open S of Chapel Ness (4.22). Smaller vessels may anchor closer in. This anchorage lies close W of the prohibited anchorage associated with the gas pipeline (4.17). The holding ground in the W part of the bay is bad, and patches with depths of 3 m to 7 m over them lie up to 7 cables offshore.

3 **Berths.** The harbour is only used by local fishing boats and pleasure craft and there are 4 berths in the elbow of the pier, on a clay bottom, for vessels up to 2 m draught.

Leven Harbour
4.44
1 **General information.** Leven Harbour (56°12′N, 3°00′W) close NE of Methil Harbour and at the mouth of the River Leven is no longer used as a commercial port. The town, population 8317 (1991), can be identified by the chimney of the power station close SW (4.20), other tall chimneys and three church spires.

2 **Directions.** A bank with depths of less than 5 m extends 1 mile E of the entrance to the River Leven. The approach channel, 27 m wide, dries at its outer part and is marked by posts at the bar and thence perches on both sides. On the S side of the channel there is a light-beacon (yellow over black, triangular topmark) marking a sewer outfall and close SW of the beacon a light tower marking the intake of the power station. Within the bar there is a depth of 1·5 m in the channel. SW winds cause a considerable sea when the harbour should not be attempted.

3 **Berth.** There is a jetty on the N side of the harbour with a depth alongside of 3·6 m at HW springs. There are no services at the jetty.

Dysart
4.45
1 **General information.** Dysart (56°08′N, 3°07′W) stands on the crest of a hill just clear of the coast. There is a church, with its spire, and factories at the NE end. A small harbour, formed by piers and used by yachts, lies at its S end. The Rockheads (4.42) are 4 cables SE of Dysart.

Port Seton
4.46

1   **General information.** Port Seton (55°58′N, 2°57′W) is a small harbour used by fishing vessels up to 27 m in length. The harbour, which dries, is formed by piers and is open N. The E pierhead is marked by a light (white metal framework tower, 7 m in height).

    Port authority. The harbour is owned and operated by the Port Seton Harbour Commissioners.

2   **Repairs.** There is a small shipyard, shared with Cockenzie (4.47).

    Supplies: marine diesel; limited supplies of water; ships chandlery operated by the Cockenzie and Port Seton Fishermen's Association Limited.

Cockenzie
4.47

1   **General information.** Cockenzie Harbour lies 5 cables WSW of Port Seton and is close E of a power station (4.20). The small port is mainly used by fishing vessels. It can accommodate vessels up to 18 m in length and 2 m draught on berths of thick mud over rocks.

2   **Port authority.** The harbour is owned and operated by East Lothian Council, Council Buildings, Haddington, East Lothian EH41 3HA.

    Directions. The harbour entrance, 24 m wide, faces N and has depths of 5 m at HW springs. The approach to the entrance is on a track of 160° passing close W of Corsik Rock which lies 2 cables NNE of E pierhead.

3   **Berth.** A small jetty with a light at its head, associated with the power station, with a depth alongside of 6 m at HW springs, lies close W of Cockenzie Harbour.

    Supplies: marine diesel by road tanker; limited supplies of water.

    Small craft. There are limited facilities for yachts, but priority is given to fishing vessels. Small craft can anchor in Cockenzie Roads in depths of 7 m.

Musselburgh and Fisherrow
4.48

1   **General information.** Musselburgh (55°57′N, 3°03′W), population 18 500 (1991), stands on low ground on either bank of the River Esk.

2   The River Esk flows into the sea across a broad flat, with Musselburgh Sand, mostly reclaimed, to the E and Fisherrow Sand to the W. Fisherrow Harbour, close W of Musselburgh, is the town's tidal harbour. It dries, bottom soft mud, and can accommodate vessels up to 18 m in length and draught 2 m. The harbour is mainly used by yachts.

3   **Port authority.** The harbour is owned and operated by East Lothian Council (4.47).

    Anchorage. A Small Vessel Anchorage is situated in Musselburgh Road between Fisherrow and Portobello in depths of 5 m to 6 m, as shown on the chart. Obstructions lie within an extensive area, also shown on the chart, to the NE of this anchorage.

4   **Directions.** The entrance, between two curved piers, is 19 m wide facing NW and has depths of 4 m at HW springs. There is an unmarked approach channel with depths of 3 m and a light tower on the E pierhead.

    Facilities: nearest hospital for accidents and emergencies is at Edinburgh.

5   **Supplies:** marine diesel by road tanker but no heavy goods vehicle access to the piers; water; provisions.

    Small craft. There are two launching slips for small boats as well as facilities and berths for pleasure craft plus the headquarters of the Fisherrow Yacht Club.

Anchorages
4.49

1   In addition to the anchorages already described there are anchor berths for large vessels, numbered A1 to A10, off Aberlady Bay (56°01′N, 2°52′W) (4.22). These berths are allocated by the Forth Navigation Service.

Boat landings
4.50

1   **Elie Bay** (56°11′N, 2°49′W) provides shelter for small vessels. Within the bay there is a small pier with depths of 4 m to 5m at HW springs; it is connected to the village of Elie. Local knowledge is required.

2   **Peffer Burn** runs into Aberlady Bay (56°01′N, 2°52′W) and provides shelter to vessels drawing up to 3 m, but the bed of the stream is rocky and the anchorage is considered unsafe. Local knowledge is required.

Other names
4.51

1   Ferny Ness (55°59′N, 2°54′W).
    Heckles, The (55°58′N, 3°00′W), rocky patch.
    Morrison's Haven (55°57′N, 3°00′W).
    Standing Stones of Lundin (56°13′N, 2°58′W), blocks of sandstone.

LEITH AND GRANTON

General information

Chart 735
Position
4.52

1   Leith (55°59′N, 3°10′W) stands at the mouth of Water of Leith. It has virtually merged with Edinburgh, the centre of which lies 3 km SW.

Function
4.53

1   Leith is the port of Edinburgh which had a population of 401 910 in 1991. It is also a base for North Sea oilfields and pipelines are constructed there.

    The former Royal Yacht *Britannia* is preserved at Leith.

Topography
4.54

1   To the SE of Leith the coast is low and fringed by a drying sandbank. Granton (4.74) is 1 mile W of Leith, thence the coast to the W is fronted by Drum Sands, which dry up to 1 mile offshore. The background to Leith is well wooded and rises to Arthur's Seat, a conspicuous hill 248 m high.

Approach and entry
4.55

1   Leith is approached from the ENE via Leith Channel (4.66), which runs through South Channel and Narrow Deep. Entry to the port is from NNW through a dredged channel to the harbour entrance.

Traffic and trade
4.56

1   In 1999 the port handled 539 vessels totalling 2 167 459 dwt.

Arthur's Seat from NNE (4.54)

(Original dated 2000)

(Photograph - Air Images)

Port authority
4.57

1   Forth Ports PLC, Leith Port Office, 1 Prince of Wales' Dock, Leith, Edinburgh EH6 7DX.

Limiting conditions
4.58

1   **Controlling depths.** The approach channel has a depth of 6·7 m and there is the same depth over the sill of the entrance lock at MLWS.

    Deepest berth. Cross Quay in Western Harbour (4.69).
    Longest berth. The NE face of Imperial Dock (4.70).
    Tidal levels: see *Admiralty Tide Tables*. Mean spring range about 4·8 m; mean neap range about 2·4 m.

4.59

1   **Maximum size of vessel handled.** The port can accommodate vessels up to 240 m in length, beam 30 m, draught 9·75 m and 50 000 dwt.

Arrival information

Port operations
4.60

1   See 4.8.

Traffic signals
4.61

1   Lights controlling entry and departure from the entrance lock are exhibited from both ends of the E and W walls of the lock as follows:

Signal	Meaning
Red light	Harbour is closed
Green light	Vessel may enter lock
Two green lights disposed vertically	Indicates side of lock to which vessel will be secured

Outer anchorages
4.62

1   There are three designated anchor berths, L5, L6 and L7, in Leith Road and a small vessel anchorage to the N of Granton. These anchorages are all shown on the chart.

Pilots and tugs
4.63

1   Pilotage is compulsory in Leith Channel for vessels over 8000 dwt. See 4.4 to 4.6 for details of pilotage. Apart from the boarding points listed in 4.6, pilots also board NE of Narrow Deep Light-buoy (56°01'·5N, 3°04'·5W), in Cockenzie Small Vessel Anchorage (55°59'N, 3°03'W) and in A4 and A5 anchorages (56°02'N, 3°01'W).

2   Tugs are available.

Tower blocks   *Elevator*

Leith Harbour (4.64)

(Original dated 2000)

(Photograph - Air Images)

Harbour

Layout
4.64

1 The harbour is enclosed by two large breakwaters, East and West, and is entered via a lock which lies between the heads of the breakwaters.The harbour is non-tidal and divided into Western Harbour entered direct from the lock and which is the largest and deepest area within the harbour and a somewhat smaller Outer Harbour entered from Western Harbour. The deepest part of Western Harbour is marked by buoys and has a dredged depth of 10·3 m. Outer Harbour gives access to the enclosed docks.

Principal marks
4.65

1 **Landmarks:**
Salisbury Craigs (55°56'·8N, 3°10'·4W).
Arthur's Seat (55°57'N, 3°10'W) (4.54).
Nelson's Monument (55°57'·2N, 3°10'·9W).
Edinburgh Castle (55°56'·9N, 3°11'·9W).
Saint Mary's Cathedral, three spires, (55°56'·9N, 3°12'·9W).
Grain elevator (55°59'N, 3°11'W).

2 **Major light:**
Inchkeith Light (56°02'N, 3°08'W) (4.20).

Directions
(continued from 4.23)
4.66

1 **Leith Channel** commences close S of Fairway Light-buoy (56°03'·5N, 3°00'·0W) and runs 4½ miles SW through South Channel and Narrow Deep to a position SE of Inchkeith Lighthouse, passing (with positions from Inchkeith Lighthouse):
NW of North Craig (2½ miles ESE), a rocky shoal, marked on its NW side by Narrow Deep Light-buoy (port hand), thence:

2 NW of Craig Waugh (2½ miles SE), a rocky shoal (charted as a dangerous rock), thence:
SE of Herwit (1 mile SSE), a rocky ledge which dries, with Little Herwit close NNW. A conspicuous stranded wreck lies on Herwit. Thence:
SE of Inchkeith (4.128).

4.67

1 **Inchkeith to Leith.** From a position in the channel SE of Inchkeith, the route leads 1·4 miles WSW thence 2 miles W and runs through South Channel and Leith Road to the approach to the dredged channel which leads SE to the harbour entrance, passing (with positions from the harbour entrance):

2 SSE of Briggs (2½ miles NE), a rocky ledge which dries to the SSE of Inchkeith. Foul ground extends a further cable SE of Briggs, thence:
N of the seaward end of an outfall (1·8 miles E), which is marked by a buoy (N cardinal) and extends 1½ miles N from the coast, thence:
Clear of the anchor berths off Leith (4.62), thence:
N of East Breakwater, fronted by Leith Sands, which have several rocky ledges embedded in their seaward edge, thence:

3 N and WSW of Leith Approach Light-buoy (port hand) (6 cables NW) and into the dredged approach channel (122 m wide, centreline 147°). The E limit of the approach channel is marked by the Leith Approach Light-buoy and a light dolphin

4 (5 cables SE of the approach buoy) together with a line of dolphins to the SE of the beacon. Thence:
To the harbour entrance and lock (259 m long, 33·5 m wide), which is 1½ cables inside the entrance. The lock gates can be operated at all times.
Caution. Tidal streams set across the approach channel at rates up to 1½ kn in a 080°/260° direction. Great care is required to maintain the correct approach. An eddy forms off Leith Breakwater heads during the in-going streams.

Useful mark
4.68

1 East Breakwater Light (red lantern on concrete base, 4 m high) (55°59'·5N, 3°10'·8W).

Basins and berths
Alongside berths
4.69

1 **Western Harbour:**
Ocean Terminal (Cruise Liner Terminal), 162 m long, 10·3 m alongside.
Cross Quay, 129 m long, 11·3 m alongside.
Oil Quay, 160 m long, 9·5 m alongside.

2 **Outer Harbour:**
8, 10 and 12 berths, 305 m long, 9·5 m alongside.
6 berth, 149 m long, 8 m alongside, includes Ro-Ro berth.

Docks
4.70

1 Imperial Dock, 1396 m of quayage, NE face 500 m long, depth 9·5 m, can accommodate vessels up to 30 m beam, and includes Ro-Ro berth.
Albert Dock, 844 m of quayage, depth 8 m, entrance width 18·2 m, includes Ro-Ro berth and container berth.
Edinburgh Dock, 1120 m of quayage, depth 8 m, entrance width 18·2 m, includes coal handling plant.

Port services
4.71

1 **Repairs.** Limited repairs can be carried out. There are three dry docks.
Largest dock: length 167·6 m overall, floor breadth 21·3 m, depths (below chart datum) sill 1·9 m and blocks 1·8 m.
4.72

1 **Other facilities:** hospitals; helicopter landing site at Royal Infirmary Edinburgh; reception of oily waste; de-ratting and exemption certificates issued.
4.73

1 **Supplies:** all types of fuel from the Oil berth in the NE corner of Imperial Dock or by road tanker or small coastal tanker; fresh water at working berths; stores and provisions.

Granton

General information
4.74

1 **Position.** Granton Harbour (55°59'N, 3°13'W) lies 1½ miles W of Leith (4.52).
4.75

1 **Function.** Granton, formerly a small commercial port, is now used mainly by small craft.
4.76

1 **Approach and entry.** Granton is approached through South Channel (4.66) and Leith Road (4.67) and entered from the N.

4.77

1   **Port authority.** The harbour is administered by Forth Ports PLC, Leith Port Office, 1 Prince of Wales' Dock, Leith, Edinburgh EH6 7DX.

Limiting conditions

4.78

1   **Controlling depths.** The depth in the harbour entrance is reported to be 5·1 m at MLWS. The depth alongside the head of Middle Pier is 3·1 m.

   Caution. Vessel's draught should be discussed with the Harbour Master Leith prior to arrival.

   Tidal levels: see *Admiralty Tide Tables*. Mean spring range about 4·8 m; mean neap range about 2·4 m.

Arrival information

4.79

1   **Port operations.** See 4.8.

4.80

1   **Notice of ETA** See 4.9.

4.81

1   **Anchorage.** There is an anchorage for small vessels 1 mile N of the harbour entrance. Anchoring is forbidden within 2½ cables of the harbour entrance.

4.82

1   **Pilotage.** See 4.4 to 4.6.

   Forth Pilots Watch-house is situated at Granton near Middle Pierhead.

Harbour

4.83

1   **Layout.** The harbour is formed by East Breakwater and West Pier, and divided into two by Middle Pier, which runs N/S with its head a cable inside the entrance. The entrance faces N and is 104 m wide. Much of the harbour, which dries on both sides close to the breakwaters, is being reclaimed.

Granton Harbour (4.83)

(Original dated 2000)

(Photograph - Air Images)

4.84

1   **Principal marks:**

   See 4.65 for marks in the approach channel.

   Gasholder (55°58'·8N, 3°14'·6W).

Directions

4.85

1   Vessels bound for Granton should approach through South Channel and Narrow Deep, as for Leith (4.66, 4.67), passing to the N of Leith Approach Light-buoy (port hand) and thence S of the small vessel anchorage (4.81) to a position N of the harbour entrance. Thence the route is S, passing E of the long sea outfall marked at its seaward end by a buoy (white can, X topmark), to the harbour entrance.

4.86

1   **Useful marks:**

   East Breakwater light (white square brick building, 5 m high) (55°59'·3N, 3°13'·2W).

Berths

4.87

1   There are 210 m of quay available alongside Middle Pier and an additional 122 m on the crosspiece of the pier.

Port services

4.88

1   **Repairs.** Minor repairs can be undertaken.

4.89

1   **Other facilities:** hospital at Leith.

4.90

1   **Supplies:** marine diesel by road tanker; fresh water; provisions and stores.

Small craft

4.91

1   Small craft moorings are allocated by the Royal Forth Yacht Club or the Forth Corinthian Yacht Club. There is a marina on the E side of Middle Pier with a berthing pontoon, which is lit, and a boat slip. Marina facilities are available as indicated on the chart.

Minor harbour

Newhaven Harbour

4.92

1   **General information.** Newhaven Harbour (56°58'·9N, 3°11'·7W) lies on the W side of the root of the W breakwater, Leith (4.52). The harbour dries 1 to 2 m and is used by fishing vessels and recreational craft. Small craft facilities are available as indicated on the chart.

2   A disused lighthouse, 15 m in height, is on the N side of the entrance.

   The harbour has no direct connection with Leith, but is administered by Forth Ports PLC (Leith and Granton).

FAIRWAY LIGHT-BUOY TO INCHCOLM

General information

Charts 735, 736

Route

4.93

1   From the vicinity of the Fairway Light-buoy the route leads 5 miles W following Forth Deep Water Channel to a position N of Inchkeith (56°02'N, 3°08'W), thence the route leads 6 miles WSW remaining in the channel to a position SW of Inchcolm, passing the port of Burntisland and the marine terminal at Braefoot, which lies N of Inchcolm.

Topography

4.94

1   Between Inchkeith (56°02'N, 3°08'W) and Inchcolm the Firth of Forth runs 6 miles in a WSW direction and narrows from some 5 miles wide to 2 miles at Inchcolm. Both the N coast and the S coast are wooded, apart from the towns. The N coast is somewhat irregular with a number of sandy bays separated by rocky headlands. The island of Inchcolm is 5½ miles W of Inchkeith and is separated from the N coast by Mortimer's Deep. The islands of Oxcars, Cow and Calves, Inchmickery and Cramond lie on the extensive sandbanks which front the S coast.

Controlling depth
4.95

1   There is a least depth of 18·8 m in the Forth Deep Water Channel.

Degaussing range
4.96

1   Two degaussing ranges, the N of which is marked by light-buoys (special), lie 4 cables W and 8 cables SW of Burntisland Harbour entrance (56°03′N, 3°14′W) respectively. The range area, in which fishing and anchoring are prohibited, is indicated on the charts. Use of the SW range is prohibited when tankers are manoeuvring to enter or depart from Mortimer's Deep or any of the Braefoot approaches. At all other times vessels should keep clear of vessels on the degaussing range.

Pilotage
4.97

1   See 4.4 to 4.6.

Traffic regulations
4.98

1   See 4.8.

Rescue
4.99

1   There is a Coastguard Rescue Team at Kinghorn, see 1.53. An inshore lifeboat is also stationed there; see 1.62 for details of lifeboat.

Tidal streams
4.100

1   As Inchkeith is approached the tidal streams are more or less rotary, clockwise. They change direction rapidly when weak and are strongest in the directions 235° and 055° with spring rates of ¾ kn and 1 kn respectively.

   Between Inchkeith and Inchcolm the tidal stream runs in the direction of North Channel (4.103).

2   The tides and tidal streams are greatly affected by the meteorological conditions in the North Sea and by melting snow and rain inland.

   Tidal stream information is shown on the chart.

Principal marks
4.101

1   **Landmarks:**
> Macduff's Castle (56°10′N, 3°03′W), ruins seen as two towers.
> Chimney (56°09′N, 3°04′W) at East Wemyss.
> Building (56°09′N, 3°05′W).
> Wemyss Castle (56°09′N, 3°05′W).

2   Ravenscraig Castle (56°07′N, 3°08′W), ruins on a steep slope at head of Pathead Bay.
> Radio mast (56°04′N, 3°14′W).
> Church tower (56°03′·8N, 3°13′·4W).
> Church spire (55°57′N, 3°06′W).
> Church spire (4 cables WNW of above).

3   Arthur's Seat (55°57′N, 3°10′W) (4.54).
> Nelson's Monument (55°57′·2N, 3°10′·9W).
> Edinburgh Castle (55°56′·9N, 3°11′·8W).
> Salisbury Craigs (55°56′·8N, 3°10′·4W).

   Major light:
> Inchkeith Light (56°02′N, 3°08′W) (4.20).

Other navigational aids
4.102

1   **Racon:**
> No 7 Light-buoy (56°03′N, 3°11′W).

DGPS:
> Girdle Ness Light (57°08′N, 2°03′W).

Directions
(continued from 4.23)

4.103

1   From a position N of Fairway Light-buoy (56°03′·5N, 3°00′·0W) the route leads 5 miles W, thence 6 miles WSW, following the Forth Deep Water Channel, which is marked by light-buoys and runs through North Channel, to a position 5 cables SW of Inchcolm. As an alternative, vessels drawing less than 10 m heading W towards the Forth bridges may proceed from Fairway Light-buoy S of Forth Deep Water Channel, passing 6 cables N of Inchkeith. When NW of Inchkeith they should adjust course to rejoin the deep water channel before reaching No 10 Light-buoy (port hand) moored on the N side of Oxcars Bank. The route through Forth Deep Water Channel passes (with positions from Inchkeith Light):

2   N of Inchkeith (4.128), thence:
> N of Rost Bank (1 mile NNW), which lies close S of the fairway. During spring tides or strong winds there are tide rips over the bank. Thence:
> SSE of Kinghorn Ness (2 miles NNW), fringed by a rocky bank, thence:
> SSE of Blae Rock (2 miles NW). In E gales the sea breaks heavily on the rock, thence:
> NNW of Gunnet Ledge (1½ miles WSW).

3   The route continues WSW in the deep water channel, passing (with positions from Oxcars, 5 miles W of Inchkeith):
> SSE of Lammerlaws Point (3 miles NE) close W of Burntisland (4.106) and the W entrance point to the bay which lies between the point and Kinghorn Ness. The bay is fronted by an extensive drying sand flat and includes Black Rocks (4.105). Heuchboy, a rocky ledge lies close SSE of the point. Thence:

4   NNW of Middle Bank (2 miles NE), which runs into Oxcars Bank (below) at its NW extremity. Middle Bank connects the shoals to the W of Inchkeith to the E extension of Drum Flat which lies to the E of Inchmickery. Middle Bank forms a bar between North and South Channels. No 10 Light-buoy (port hand) lies close N of the bank and vessels drawing less than 10 m, which have remained S of the deep water channel, should rejoin the channel prior to passing the light-buoy. A recommended channel leads to the NE extremity of Mortimer's Deep along the alignment of Hawkcraig Point leading lights (4.151).Thence:

5   NNW of Oxcars, a rocky islet on which stands a light (4.105). The islet lies at the W end of Oxcars Bank and has a bridge clearance gauge (4.162). Thence:

6   To a position SW of Inchcolm (7 cables NW), a rocky island. A light (4.105) stands on its SE corner. The island is hilly at either end and the ruins of an abbey (4.105) lie in the centre. The island lies at the SW corner of a bank, 1½ miles long, running ENE/WSW, which separates the main channel to the SE from Mortimer's Deep (4.138) to the NW. Meadulse Rocks, a group of drying rocks, lie on the bank to the N of Inchcolm; a ruined beacon stands near their W end, and the islet Car Craig lies at their E end,

4 cables NE of Inchcolm. There are depths of less than 5 m up to 1 mile to the NE of Inchcolm.

4.104

1   **Clearing bearing.** The alignment (250°) of the top of the centre cantilever of Forth Railway Bridge (56°00'·1N, 3°23'·2W) with Oxcars Lighthouse passes S of Blae Rock.

Useful marks
4.105

1   Saint Colm's Abbey (ruin) (56°02'N, 3°18'W), square tower with grey spire on Inchcolm.

Flagstaff (white, about 10 m in height), close E of Saint Colm's Abbey.

Black Rocks (56°03'·4N, 3°12'·5W) W of Kinghorn Ness.

2   White metal building (56°03'N, 3°17'W).

Oxcars Light (white tower, red band, 22 m in height) (56°01'N, 3°17'W).

Inchcolm Light (grey metal framework tower, 10 m in height) (56°02'N, 3°18'W).

Flagstaff (55°59'N, 3°18'W) at head of the breakwater.

(Directions continue for Forth Bridges and River Forth at 4.171)

Burntisland

Chart 733
General information
4.106

1   **Position.** Burntisland (56°03'N, 3°14'W) stands prominently at the foot of The Binn of Burntisland (chart 735), a bold steep hill, with the harbour 8 cables to the S.

4.107

1   **Function.** Burntisland, population 5951 (1991), is a small commercial port handling mainly bauxite for the nearby aluminium works, and caustic soda.

4.108

1   **Approach and entry.** There is unimpeded access from Forth Deep Water Channel, which passes 1 mile S of the port.

4.109

1   **Traffic.** In 1999, 18 vessels totalling 269 279 dwt used the port.

4.110

1   **Port authority.** The harbour is administered by Forth Ports PLC.

Limiting conditions
4.111

1   **Controlling depths.** The depth at the harbour entrance is 3·1 m.

East Dock has a depth of 8·6 m over the sill at HW springs; West Dock has a depth of 6·4 m over the sill at HW springs. For the latest information on the depths inside both docks, the Harbour Master should be consulted.

Tidal levels: see *Admiralty Tide Tables.* Mean spring range about 4·8 m; mean neap range about 2·4 m.

4.112

1   **Largest vessel.** The port can accommodate vessels up to 122 m in length, beam 16·8 m, draught 6·7 m and 8000 dwt.

Arrival information
4.113

1   **Port operations.** See 4.8.

4.114

1   **Traffic signals.**

Signal	Meaning
Green over red light	Dangerous to enter harbour; bring up in roads
Red over white light	Clear to enter E Dock
Red over two white lights	Clear to enter W Dock
Red light	Remain in roads until another signal made
Green light	Dock gates closed but come to W Dock gates or Island Jetty with caution

4.115

1   **Notice of ETA.** See 4.9.

4.116

1   **Anchorage.** There are three anchor berths in Burntisland Road for bauxite carriers discharging into barges, B2 (chart 736), B4 and B5, to the SE of the port but N of Forth Deep Water Channel. Their positions are shown on the chart.

An anchorage can also be obtained elsewhere in Burntisland Road clear of the degaussing ranges (4.96).

4.117

1   **Pilotage** is compulsory. See 4.4 to 4.6.

Tugs are available from Leith.

4.118

1   **Regulations concerning entry.** Vessels must reduce speed and keep clear of those anchored in berths B2, B4 and B5 if such vessels have barges alongside.

Harbour
4.119

1   The port consists of two wet docks leading off a tidal basin, the Outer Harbour, which is formed by two piers. The harbour entrance lies between these two piers and is 76 m wide. East Dock, entrance 18·29 m wide, is approached from the E side of Outer Harbour through a set of storm gates, which are normally opened from 3 hours before HW to HW. West Dock lies to the N of Outer Harbour and is approached from the NW corner of Outer Harbour through a passage.

4.120

1   **Degaussing range** lies close W of the harbour entrance. See 4.96.

4.121

1   **Principal marks:**

Radio mast (56°04'N, 3°14'W) (Chart 735).

Erskine church (tower surmounted by small spire) (56°03'·8N, 3°13'·4W).

Radar tower (56°03'·3N, 3°14'·0W).

Shed (56°03'·5N, 3°14'·4W).

Radio mast (56°03'·7N, 3°15'·1W).

Directions
4.122

1   From the Forth Deep Water Channel immediately S of Burntisland, the route leads N for 1·1 miles to the harbour entrance, passing (with positions from the harbour entrance):

Through the Burntisland anchorage (5 cables S) at reduced speed if required (4.118), thence:

E of the degaussing ranges (4.96), thence:

2   To the harbour entrance which lies between pierheads on which stand lights, E pierhead (pole, 5 m in

Shed

Burntisland Harbour (4.119)

(Original dated 2000)

(Photograph - Air Images)

height), W pierhead (white tower, 6 m in height). A submarine cable runs from W breakwater to E pierhead.

Vessels bound for West Dock should be under way before half-flood, and be ready to enter as soon as required, otherwise the Harbour Master must be informed.

Berths
4.123

1 The NW quay of East Dock is used by barges ferrying bauxite to discharge alongside.

The quay on the W side of West Dock is used as a fitting out berth for vessels up to 167 m in length and beam 23 m.

2 Island Jetty projects S from the entrance to East Dock and as well as being used as a temporary berth forms a boat shelter in the E corner of Outer Harbour with depths of 1·1 m.

Port services
4.124

1 **Repairs** of a limited nature can be carried out.
4.125

1 **Other facilities:** deratting exemption certificates can be issued; reception of oily waste; hospital at Kirkcaldy (4.42).
4.126

1 **Supplies:** fuel of all types by road or rail tanker; water at the quays; provisions and stores.

Small craft
4.127

1 There is a Yacht Club. Visiting small craft should berth in the Tidal Basin or East Dock.

Minor harbours, anchorage and landings
4.128

1 **Inchkeith** island (56°02′N, 3°08′W) has a central ridge up to 55 m in height, terminating in a point at its S end. Elsewhere it descends regularly to the coast, which is fringed with rocks. It is generally forbidden to land on the island. West Harbour, on the W side of the island is formed by piers and has depths of 1 to 2 m. The harbour is protected from all but the S.

2 **Inchkeith Small Vessel Anchorage**, shown on the chart, is 5 cables E of the island. The anchorage is controlled by the Forth Navigation Service; inbound vessels should request a berth before passing Fairway Buoy and outbound before passing Inchkeith.

Chart 735
4.129

1 **Pettycur** Harbour (56°04′N, 3°11′W) lies 3 cables WSW of Kinghorn Ness. The harbour, which dries 1·5 m, is formed by a curved pier.

Chart 739
4.130

1 **Carron** Harbour (56°03′·6N, 3°15′·4W) has a boat yard and a pier both of which dry.

Chart 736
4.131

1 **Aberdour** (56°03′N, 3°18′W) has a small harbour at the mouth of Dour Burn. The harbour is formed by a pier extending ESE from the W side of the burn, with a depth of 2·7 m at HW springs on its inner side. The pier extremity dries 2 m. Within the pier the bottom is soft mud and vessels are well protected from every direction.
4.132

1 **Inchcolm** (56°02′N, 3°18′W) (4.103) has a boat landing on its N side, 1 cable to the E of the ruined abbey (4.105).
4.133

1 **Inchmickery** (56°01′N, 3°16′W) (4.103) has a boat pier on its W side.
4.134

1 **Cramond** (55°58′·5N, 3°18′W) lies at the mouth of R. Almond. The harbour is approached via a winding channel leading in a SW direction from a position close W of Cramond Island (4.94). The channel, marked by stakes (starboard hand), is subject to considerable change. Craft with a draught of 1·2 m can enter about 2 hours either side of HW. Limited facilities are available at Cramond Boat Club.

Other names

Charts 735, 736
4.135

1   Barnhill Bay (56°02'·6N, 3°18'·4W).
Bellhouse Point (56°02'·8N, 3°17'·9W).
Big Bush (55°58'·9N, 3°07'·5W), a rocky patch.
Buchans, The (55°59'·9N, 3°19'·8W), rocks.
Familars Rocks (56°03'·4N, 3°14'·6W).
Hummel Rocks (56°04'·1N, 3°10'·1W).
2   Iron Craig (56°01'·6N, 3°08'·2W), a rock.
Limekiln Rock (56°04'·7N, 3°09'·3W).
Little Craigs (56°02'·8N, 3°17'·6W), a rock.
Long Craig (56°01'·5N, 3°07'·7W), a rock.
Middens (56°01'·6N, 3°18'·5W), a reef.
Ross Point (56°03'·5N, 3°14'·8W).
3   Saint Anthony's Bush (55°58'·9N, 3°08'·6W), a rocky ledge.
Seafield Vows (56°05'·2N, 3°09'·0W).
Seal Carr (56°01'·9N, 3°08'·5W), a rock.
Silversands Bay (56°03'·2N, 3°17'·0W).
Swallow Craig (56°01'·9N, 3°17'·8W), an islet.

BRAEFOOT MARINE TERMINAL

General information

Chart 733, 736
Position
4.136

1   **Braefoot Marine Terminal** (56°02'N, 3°19'W) is situated on the NW side of Mortimer's Deep 4 cables ENE of Braefoot Point.

Function
4.137

1   Braefoot is a gas tanker terminal serving the Mossmorran petro-chemical complex. The E jetty exports ethylene and the W jetty exports propane, butane and natural gasoline.

Approach and entry
4.138

1   The Braefoot Marine Terminal is approached from Forth Deep Water Channel via Mortimer's Deep, the channel between Inchcolm and the N side of the firth, which is two cables wide at its narrowest point. The deep runs approximately ENE/WSW, 5 cables to 6 cables NW of the deep draught channel. The terminal may be approached from either the E or W end of the deep.

Traffic
4.139

1   In 1999 the terminal received 304 vessels totalling 5 655 522 dwt, and handled over 2 million tonnes of cargo.

Terminal operator
4.140

1   Shell UK Exploration and Production, PO Box 16, Mossmorran, Cowdenbeath, Fife.

Limiting conditions
4.141

1   **Controlling depth** on the E approach is 9·9 m in the recommended channel (4.151). In the W approach the controlling depth is 14·7 m, as shown on the chart, in a position 2 cables E of Haystack (4.153), but the approach is narrower than from the E.
      Deepest and longest berth. W jetty (4.147).
      Mean tidal levels: see Burntisland (4.111).
4.142

1   **Maximum size of vessel.** The W jetty can accommodate tankers up to 60 000 cubic metres capacity, maximum

Braefoot Terminal

Inchcolm   *Abbey*

Mortimer's Deep from SE (4.138)

(Original dated 2000)

(Photograph - Air Images)

draught 10·8 m. The E jetty is used by tankers up to 12 000 cubic metres capacity.

Arrival information

Port operations
4.143

1   See 4.8.

Local VHF frequencies are manned 2 hours before a vessel's arrival.

Notice of ETA
4.144

1   Notice of ETA should be sent 72 hours in advance and amended for any change greater than 12 hours. ETA should be confirmed 24 hours in advance and amended for any change greater than 4 hours.

Pilots and tugs
4.145

1   See 4.4 to 4.6.

Tugs are available.

Regulations concerning entry
4.146

1   The general rules for navigation in the Forth are given in Appendix II. The following rules apply to the movement of tankers using Braefoot Bay Marine Terminal:

2   No vessel shall enter Mortimer's Deep without the express permission of the Forth Navigational Service, unless the vessel is destined for Braefoot Marine Terminal. This Byelaw shall not apply to pleasure boats not exceeding 12 m in length provided they shall reduce speed as low as possible and do not approach within 100 m of vessels berthed at each terminal.

3   Every tanker destined for the terminal shall regulate its approach so as not to arrive before the agreed berthing time.

Berthing and unberthing at the terminal will not be permitted when visibility is less than 5 cables.

Tankers of 145 m or more in length should approach Shell Jetty through the W channel of Mortimer's Deep on a flood tide or at slack water and berth port side-to, heading NE.

4   Tankers of less than 145 m in length may approach Esso Jetty through the E channel of Mortimer's Deep and berth, on an ebb tide or at slack water, heading SW. Such vessels may be required to swing, using tugs, on departure.

Tankers departing the terminal may be directed via the E or W channel.

5   No vessel shall enter Mortimer's Deep, or the channels leading to it, when the terminal is occupied or when a tanker is manoeuvring in the area, except that a second tanker may enter any berth when the first tanker is securely berthed.

6   Radio transmissions and the operation of radar are prohibited in the vicinity of the terminal, except that a vessel's normal equipment may be tested provided that a source of ignition is not present and that the Chief Harbour Master's permission has been obtained.

Terminal

Layout
4.147

1   There are two jetties, Shell Jetty to the W, which is 85 m long with a swept depth alongside of 15 m (1984) and Exxon Jetty, with a swept depth alongside of 10 m (1984), to the E. The seaward ends of both jetties are

Braefoot Marine Terminal (4.147)

(Original dated 2000)

(Photograph - Air Images)

flanked by berthing and mooring dolphins, which are marked by lights and joined by catwalks.

Traffic signal
4.148

1 An amber flashing light exhibited from the main jetty 2 hours prior to and during a tanker movement, warns other mariners that a movement is imminent or in progress.

Tidal stream
4.149

1 The tidal stream can attain rates of up to 2½ kn through Mortimer's Deep.

Principal marks
4.150

1 **Landmarks:**
Saint Colm's Abbey (56°02'N, 3°18'W) (4.105).
White metal building (56°03'N, 3°17'W), on Hawkcraig Point.

Directions

Approach from the east
4.151

1 Leading lights (only in operation when traffic is moving in the terminal):
Front light (white tower, red band, 4 m in height) (56°03'·0N, 3°17'·0W).
Rear light (white tower, red band, 8 m in height) (96 m WNW of front light).

2 From a position in Forth Deep Water Channel S of Lammerlaws Point (4.103) the alignment (292°) of these lights on Hawkcraig Point (4.152) leads through a recommended channel, 200 m wide and marked by light-buoys at its NW end, to the E end of Mortimer's Deep, passing (with positions from front leading light):

3 SSW of Burntisland Docks (1·6 miles E) and the anchor berths in Burntisland Road (4.116), thence:
Across the S extremity of the degaussing range (1 mile ESE) (4.96), thence:
To the NE end of Mortimer's Deep (6 cables ESE).

Mortimer's Deep, east
4.152

1 Leading lights (only in operation when traffic is moving in terminal):
Front light (triangle point up, white post, 2 m in height) (56°02'·2N, 3°18'·6W).
Rear light (triangle point down, white post, 2 m in height) (88 m from front light).

2 From a position on the leading line 1·6 miles ENE of the front light the alignment (247¼°) of these lights in the Bracfoot Marine Terminal leads to the marine terminal, via a channel marked by light-buoys, passing (with positions from the front light):
SSE of Hawkcraig Point (1·3 miles NE), a bold cliffy headland, thence:

3 NNW of Car Craig (8½ cables E), an islet with Meadulse Rocks lying close W, and Inchcolm to the WSW. Thence:
SSE of Craigdimas (5 cables ENE), a drying rocky ledge, marked by a beacon, now in ruins, thence:
SSE of Vault Point (2 cables NE) and to the terminal.
Leading marks. The alignment (231°) of Haystack (4.153) with the centre of the S span of the Forth Railway Bridge leads through the centre of Mortimer's Deep.

Approach from the South West
4.153

1 Channel marking lights, Inchcolm (only in operation when traffic is moving in terminal):
S front light (white tower, 2 m in height) (84 m WSW of rear light).
N front light (white tower, 2 m in height) (80 m W of rear light).
Common rear light (white tower, 2 m in height) (56°01'·8N, 3°18'·1W).

2 The S front light in line with the rear light (066°) and the N front light in line with the rear light (076¾°) mark the limits of the channel leading into Mortimer's Deep from the WSW. From a position WSW of the rear light the track leads ENE, thence NNE to the terminal, passing (with positions from rear leading light):
SSE of Dalgety Bay (1 mile WNW), which dries and lies between Braefoot Point and Downing Point, 1 mile WSW of Braefoot Point. Thence:

3 SSE of Haystack (6 cables W), a bare rock, 6 m high, and:
NNW of the W extent of the foul ground W of Inchcolm, all marked by light-buoys, thence:
To a position SSW of the marine terminal, where a direct approach to the terminal can be made, 4 cables NNE.

4 Lights in line (only in operation when traffic is moving in terminal):
Front light (pole on dolphin, triangle point up) (56°02'·1N, 3°18'·8W).
Rear light (post, triangle point down) (220 m NNE of front light).
These lights in line (017½°) mark the direct approach to the terminal. A beacon (triangle, apex up) (56°02'·1N, 3°18'·75W) in line (014½°) with the rear leading light marks the E limit of this direct approach.

Marine terminal services
4.154

1 **Facilities:** hospital at Kirkcaldy; deratting exemption certificates issued.
4.155

1 **Supplies:** marine diesel at Shell jetty only; fresh water; provisions.
4.156

1 **Regulations** are stringent with regard to loading cargo. Copies of the regulations can be obtained from the appropriate operating company.

INCHCOLM TO FORTH BRIDGES

General information

Chart 736
Route
4.157

1 From a position SW of Inchcolm the route leads 3 miles WSW initially following Forth Deep Water Channel, thence 6 cables WSW and W through the Forth Bridges, to a position close W of the bridges.

Topography
4.158

1 From Inchcolm to the head of the firth, where the River Forth commences and the two bridges span the river, is a distance of 3 miles. Both coasts are wooded, with the N coast consisting of sandy bays separated by rocky headlands and the S coast trending NW to Hound Point.

The Forth Road Bridge is 5 cables W of the rail bridge and both bridges cross the River Forth where the river narrows to 1 mile, between Queensferry and the peninsula to the N on which North Queensferry stands. Rosyth (4.195) lies 1½ miles NW of the Forth Road Bridge on the N bank of the river.

Controlling depths
4.159

1 Within the Forth Deep Water Channel, which runs 2½ miles WSW from Inchcolm to the vicinity of Hound Point Marine Terminal, there is a least depth of 18·8 m. Continuing WSW from the channel and under the bridges the depths on the recommended routes shown on the chart are in excess of 20 m.

Forth Bridges vertical clearance
4.160

1 **Rail Bridge.** The central part of each navigation span (4.172) is level for 146 m and has a vertical clearance at MHWS of 44 m below the painting and maintenance platforms, These platforms can be removed, giving an additional clearance of 1·58 m to a maximum of 45·58 m.

2 **Road Bridge.** With painting and maintenance platforms fitted there is a vertical clearance at MHWS of 45 m between the green and red lights, rising to 46 m under the central white light. If the platforms are removed the vertical clearance is increased by 2·45 m.

3 The Rail Bridge has a lesser clearance than the Road Bridge and is therefore the critical bridge for a vessel concerned with vertical clearance, provided vessels pass under the centre of the main span of the Road Bridge.

4.161

1 **Regulations.**

No vessel may pass another under the Forth Railway Bridge whether in conditions of good visibility or not. In the event of vessels approaching the bridge from opposite directions, the outward bound vessel shall have priority of passage under the bridge and the inbound vessel shall keep clear.

2 In conditions where visibility is less than 5 cables, an inward bound vessel shall not, under any circumstances, pass No 19 buoy unless she has obtained clearance to do so from the Forth Navigation Service.

Vessels must not approach within 100 m of the main piers of the Forth Road Bridge.

4.162

1 A **tide gauge** is sited on Oxcars (4.103) and gives the vertical clearance under the Rail Bridge. The gauge consists of black and white bands, 0·3 m wide.The top of the top white band indicates the 44 m clearance level below the painting and maintenance platforms, while other clearance levels are indicated by figures.

Local magnetic anomaly
4.163

1 A compass deflection of up to 11° has been observed by vessels passing under the rail bridge. Vessels steering on a magnetic compass are therefore advised to steady on a distant object before passing under the bridge.

Radar interference
4.164

1 It has been reported that vessels leaving Port Edgar (4.192) and the Rosyth Main Channel (4.209) are unlikely to be detected on radar by vessels in the river, although vessels with an aerial height of between 12 m and 24 m,

when between the bridges, should have no difficulty with radar interference.

Pilotage
4.165

1 See 4.4 to 4.6.

Traffic regulations
4.166

1 See 4.8.

4.167

1 **Protected channel.** A protected channel is established from No 13 and No 14 Light-buoys NNW of Oxcars, to the N passage under Forth Railway Bridge, thence to Rosyth.

When the protected channel is in operation details are promulgated on VHF by Forth Navigation Service; see 4.8.

Rescue
4.168

1 There are Coastguard Rescue Teams at Rosyth and South Queensferry; see 1.53.

An inshore lifeboat is permanently stationed at Queensferry; for details of lifeboats see 1.61.

Tidal streams
4.169

1 The strength of the tidal stream increases towards the head of the firth reaching 2½ kn through the channels under the bridges. There may be turbulence in North Channel off North Queensferry (4.190).

During the W-going tidal stream eddies around Beamer Rock (56°00'·3N, 3°24'·7W) (4.223) extend up to 2 cables WNW.

2 During the E-going tidal stream eddies exist between Beamer Rock and Long Craig (3 cables ENE) and at springs can extend E as far as Inch Garvie (9 cables ESE) (4.172). In addition the E-going stream sets strongly onto Inch Garvie.

Principal mark
4.170

1 Crane (56°01'·4N, 3°27'·3W).

Directions
(continued from 4.105)

Inchcolm to Hound Point
4.171

1 From a position SW of Inchcolm (56°02'N, 3°18'W) the route leads WSW in the Forth Deep Water Channel, passing (with positions from Inchcolm):

NNW of Drum Flat (1 mile S), which runs ENE and eventually to the S of Oxcars Bank (4.103). The flat, together with Drum Sand at its W extremity extends from Hound Point (below) 4¼ miles ENE. Thence:

2 SSE of Haystack (5 cables W) (4.153) which lies at the W end of Mortimer's Deep, thence:

To a position NW of Hound Point (2 miles SW) and the Marine Terminal (4.174).

The Forth Bridges
4.172

1 From a position ENE of the Forth Railway Bridge (56°00'N, 3°23'W), and 2½ cables NW of the Hound Point Marine Terminal, the route leads 7 cables WSW to the rail bridge, thence 5 cables W through the two bridges, passing:

2 NNW of Inch Garvie, following the recommended W-going track shown on the chart. Inch Garvie, on which the centre span of the rail bridge stands, is

Forth bridges from NE (4.172.1)

(Original dated 2000)

(Photograph - Air Images)

a rocky islet 12 m high. A light (black round beacon, white lantern, 10 m in height) is exhibited from its NW end. Thence:

3 Under the Forth Railway Bridge, which has two navigation spans, each 521 m wide, N and S of Inch Garvie. Lights are exhibited on each side of the bridge, at the centre of the navigation spans and near the ends of the cantilevers, so defining the N and S channels under the bridge. The bridge is floodlit. The recommended tracks, both E and W, pass under the N navigation span but vessels may also pass under the bridge to the S of Inch Garvie if required. Thence:

4 Under the Forth Road Bridge, which is a suspension bridge of three spans. The two towers supporting the centre span of the bridge lie either side of the navigable channel and are just over 1000 m apart. Lights are exhibited on both sides of the bridge at the centre, midway between the centre and the supports, and at the supports themselves.

Useful marks
4.173

1 Two radio masts (56°01'·8N, 3°24'·8W).
(Directions continue for Rosyth at 4.209 and for River Forth at 4.223)

Beamer Rock

Forth bridges from NW (4.172.2)

(Original dated 2000)

(Photograph - Air Images)

Hound Point Marine Terminal

Chart 736
General information
4.174

1   **Position.** Hound Point Marine Terminal (56°00′N, 3°22′W) is 3½ cables offshore and 4 cables NW of Hound Point itself. It lies on the W extremity of the Forth Deep Water Channel.

4.175

1   **Function.** The terminal handles crude oil from the Forties Oil Field.

4.176

1   **Approach and entry.** The terminal is approached direct from the Forth Deep Water Channel.

4.177

1   **Traffic.** The terminal handled 393 vessels totalling 38 497 925 dwt, and loaded 32 million tonnes of cargo in 1999.

4.178

1   **Terminal Operator.** The terminal is operated by British Petroleum.

Limiting conditions
4.179

1   **Controlling depths.** There is a least depth of 18·8 m in the Forth Deep Water Channel.

   Least charted depth. A 19 m patch lies 2 cables NE of the E dolphin of the terminal and a 19·2 m patch lies 1½ cables ENE of the 19 m patch.

   A minimum depth of 24 m is maintained alongside.

   Mean tidal levels for Granton: see 4.78.

4.180

1   **Maximum size of vessel.** The terminal can accommodate tankers of draught 21·64 m (springs), 20·72 m (neaps) and up to 300 000 dwt.

4.181

1   **Weather limitations.** Berthing will not be attempted if:
   The wind exceeds 20 kn on/off the berth.
   The wind exceeds 30 kn in any direction.
   The visibility is less than 1 mile.

Arrival information
4.182

1   **Port operations.** See 4.8.

4.183

1   **Pilotage** is compulsory. See 4.4 to 4.6.
   Tugs are available.

Terminal
4.184

1   The terminal consists of two berths, each with a concrete island structure flanked by berthing and mooring dolphins linked by catwalks; a central island structure connects the two berths. The line of the terminal runs ENE/WSW along the S edge of the Forth Deep Water Channel. The berths and the outer mooring dolphins are marked by lights and the W island structure displays an aero obstruction light.

Directions
4.185

1   See 4.171.

Port services
4.186

1   Three tugs are available, all of which are equipped for fire-fighting and anti-pollution operations. They are normally moored at buoys 1¼ cables SW of the terminal. There are facilities for receiving oily waste.

   No other facilities or supplies available.

4.187

1   **Regulations:**
   Vessels must reduce speed if necessary and must not approach within 100 m when passing vessels berthed at the terminal.

   Anchoring is prohibited between the terminal and the shore at Whitehouse Point, where pipelines are laid.

2   No unauthorised person is permitted to approach within 100 m of the terminal.

   There are stringent regulations concerning the state of moorings. The terminal is entitled to suspend

Barnbougle Castle   Hound Point

Hound Point Marine Terminal from NW (4.184)

(Original dated 2000)

(Photograph - Air Images)

operations and/or summon tugs in the absence of an alert and efficient deck watch or if it appears that a vessel's movement will endanger the flow arms.

Minor harbours

Saint David's Harbour
4.188

1 **General information.** Saint David's Harbour (56°02′N, 3°22′W) is on the NE side of Inverkeithing Bay. The harbour is in a poor state of preservation.

Directions. The harbour is 3 cables N of Saint David's Direction Light (4.189), but there are no other navigational marks. The entrance, 62 m wide faces W and is formed by two piers.

Berth. The S pier has depths alongside of 5·5 m at HW.

Inverkeithing Harbour
4.189

1 **General information.** Inverkeithing Harbour (56°02′N, 3°23′W), a natural basin at the NW end of Inverkeithing Bay is used for the export of scrap and stone. The bay, which is shallow with depths of under 2 m, lies between Battery Point which is the N landing point of the Forth Railway Bridge (4.172) and Middle Point, 1½ miles NE of Battery Point. In 1999 the port was used by 85 vessels totalling 197 414 dwt.

2 **Port authority.** The port is owned and operated by Port Services (Inverkeithing) Ltd, The Bay, Inverkeithing, Fife KY1 2HR.

Pilotage. See 4.4 to 4.6.

Directions. From a position S of Doig Rock (56°01′·4N, 3°21′·4W) the track leads 1·1 miles W through a channel, once dredged but now silted, to the harbour entrance, passing (with positions from the harbour entrance):

3   Clear of Saint David's Direction Light (pile, orange box) (6 cables E). The line of bearing 098° astern of the light leads to the harbour entrance. Thence:

    S of a light-buoy (starboard hand) (1¾ cables E) marking the SW extremity of the drying bank which lies N of the channel. Thence:

4   S of Prestonhill Wharf (1¼ cables ENE), a T-shaped jetty (disused), lying close E of East Ness which forms the N side of the entrance to the harbour, thence:

    To the harbour entrance which is 120 m wide and lies between two piers extending from the shore at East Ness and West Ness. A light-buoy (port hand) marks the N extremity of the drying bank close NW of the pier extending from the shore at West Ness.

5 **Limiting depth** of 1·0 m lies in the harbour entrance.

Useful mark. A conspicuous white conical mark (56°01′·75N 3°22′·6W) about 4½ cables NW of Saint David's Light.

Caution. The channel which is indicated by the direction light is subject to siltation.

6 **Berths.** Vessels up to 90 m in length (approx.) load scrap at the Deep Water Berth and No 1 Berth. Small vessels up to 70 m in length (approx.) load stone at the Quarry Berth. There is also a berth at the S end of East Ness Pier.

Services. There are no services or facilities.

North Queensferry
4.190

1 **General information.** North Queensferry (56°01′N, 3°24′W) lies between the N landings of the two bridges. Town Pier is at the E end of the town, with Railway Pier 1½ cables to the W.

Berths. Small craft moorings lie between the two piers.

Queensferry
4.191

1 **General information.** Hawes Pier (55°59′·5N, 3°23′·0W) lies close W of the rail bridge; there is a speed restriction of 4 kn within an area, marked by buoys, adjacent to the pier. There are a number of small craft moorings to the E of the rail bridge.

There is also a small harbour at Queensferry, 3 cables W of the pier, which is densely occupied with moorings managed by the Queensferry Boat Club.

Port Edgar
4.192

1 **General information.** Port Edgar (56°00′N, 3°25′W) is situated close W of the Forth Road Bridge, and accommodates a yacht marina administered by City of Edinburgh Council. Limited commercial berths are available by prior arrangement.

2 **Harbour.** The harbour is formed by two breakwaters with an entrance open N 222 m wide. East and West Piers lie within the breakwaters and extend from the shore. The marina lies between these two piers and is protected from the N by a floating breakwater.

Port Edgar (4.192)

(Original dated 2000)

(Photograph - Air Images)

3 **Directions.** The line of bearing (244°) of West Breakwater Light (white blockhouse, 4 m high) (55°59′·9N,3°24′·7W) leads to the harbour entrance.

Caution. Vessels up to 18 m in length can use the harbour at all states of the tide. On both the in-going and the out-going tides, a weak eddy opposing the main stream is set up just outside the line of the breakwater heads and vessels should guard against a sheer when entering.

4 **Berths.** The commercial berths are at a finger pier in the SW part of the harbour. The marina has accommodation for 310 craft up to 12·2 m in length and draught 2·4 m.

Small craft
4.193

1 **Donibristle Bay** (56°02′N, 3°21′W) has a boat harbour with a slip at its NE end and the headquarters of the

Dalgety Bay Sailing Club. The bay and the approach to the harbour are foul.

Other name
4.194

1   Thank Rock (56°01′·7N, 3°20′·6W).

ROSYTH

General information

Chart 736
Position and function
4.195

1   Rosyth (56°01′N, 3°27′W) is situated on the N side of the River Forth, 1½ miles WNW of the Forth Road Bridge. Formerly a naval base, Rosyth is now a commercial port handling forest products, dry and liquid bulk cargo, general cargo and cruise liners.

Port limits
4.196

1   The limits of the Dockyard Port of Rosyth stretch from close E of Oxcars (4.103) to 4 miles W of Rosyth and are shown on charts 736 and 737.

Approach and entry
4.197

1   Rosyth is approached from the E via the River Forth and thence through Main Channel.

Traffic
4.198

1   In 1999 the port was used by 108 vessels totalling 281 755 dwt.

Port authority
4.199

1   Port of Rosyth, Exmouth Building, Rosyth, Fife KY11 2XP. The port is operated by Forth Ports PLC; see 4.2.

Limiting conditions
4.200

1   **Controlling depths.** Main Channel leading to Rosyth is maintained by dredging to a depth of 8·8 m, but due to siltation depths less than the charted maintained depth are likely to exist. The Queen's Harbour Master, Rosyth should be consulted for the latest information on depth. The channel was dredged to the maintained depth in April 2000.

2   **Deepest and longest berths:** deepest berth, Main Basin (4.211); longest berth, North Wall (4.211).
    Tidal levels: see *Admiralty Tide Tables.* Mean spring range about 5 m; mean neap range about 2·5 m.
4.201

1   **Maximum size of vessel.** The port can accept vessels up to 250 m in length and with an air draught up to 44 m at MHWS.

Arrival information

Port operations
4.202

1   For Forth Navigation Service see 4.8.

Anchorages
4.203

1   See 4.229.

Pilots and tugs
4.204

1   Pilotage is compulsory for all commercial vessels, and is provided by Forth Ports PLC; see 4.4. Admiralty licensed pilots for naval and other government-owned vessels bound for Rosyth or Crombie (4.223) normally board 1 mile E of the Forth Railway Bridge.

2   Tugs are available and at least one tug will normally attend vessels berthing and unberthing.

Regulations concerning entry
4.205

1   See Appendix I.

Harbour

Layout
4.206

1   Port of Rosyth consists of tidal berths and a non tidal basin. To the E there are a number of tidal berths, which are approached direct from Main Channel. At the W end of the base there is a large basin entered via a lock from Main Channel (4.209). The lock can be used when required.

2   The basin is approximately 500 m square; 3 dry docks lie on its NE side.
    There is a direct entrance gate to Main Basin which lies just N of the main entrance lock. There is a depth of 6·6 m above chart datum at the entrance gate and its use is restricted to a rising tide, between the time the tide reaches a height of 4·25 m to ½ hour before HW. A tide gauge is situated N of the entrance gate, as shown on the chart.

Tidal stream
4.207

1   In Main Channel the in-going stream begins at about −0530 HW Rosyth and the out-going stream at −0045 HW Rosyth. Both run for about 4 hours, with maximum spring rates of 1½ kn. The in-going stream runs out through the boat channel (4.223) to rejoin the main stream in the river, conversely, a branch of the out-going stream sets through the boat channel to join the out-going stream in the Main Channel.

2   In the vicinity of North Wall and the immediate approaches to Main Basin, circular streams, with rates not exceeding ½ kn, occur on both the in-going and out-going streams. A strong SW set has been reported on the N side of Middle Jetty (4.211), one hour before HW.

Principal marks
4.208

1   **Landmarks:**
    Flagstaff (56°00′·9N, 3°24′·4W).
    Radio masts (56°01′·7N, 3°24′·8W).
    Rosyth Castle (56°01′·4N, 3°25′·8W), a ruin.
    Beamer Rock Light-tower (white tower, red top) (56°00′·3N, 3°24′·6W).

Directions
(continued from 4.173)

Main Channel, outer leg
4.209

1   From the vicinity of 56°00′·3N, 3°24′·3W, close W of the Forth Road Bridge within the white sector of Directional Light-beacon A (red square, on white post with red bands) (56°01′·2N, 3°25′·5W), the track leads 323½° through the buoyed channel, passing (with positions from Light-beacon A):

Rosyth (4.206)

(Original dated 2000)

(Photograph - Air Images)

2   NE of Beamer Rock (1 mile SE) (4.223), thence:

SW of Light-beacon C (red and white post, white triangle point down over red rectangle) (1 mile SE), thence:

SW of Beacon D (black and white post, black triangle) (6 cables SE), thence:

NE of the E end of Whale Back (4.223) (5 cables SSE).

3   An approach to the Main Channel can be made from the W, passing W of Beamer Rock, but care should be exercised when the E-going stream is running.

Main Channel, inner leg
4.210

1   From a position NE of Whale Back, at the intersection of the white sector of Directional Light-beacon A (4.209) and the white sector of Directional Light-beacon E (floodlight mast, only exhibited at night) (56°01′·3N, 3°26′·8W) the track leads 295° through Main Channel which is buoyed, passing (with positions from Light-beacon E):

2   N of Whale Back (7 cables SE) (4.223), thence:

Between No 5 Light-buoy (starboard hand) (6 cables ESE) and No 6 Light-buoy (port hand) (6 cables ESE) at the W end of the buoyed channel, from whence the entrance lock and the tidal berths can be directly approached.

Both the white sector of Directional Light-beacon C (4.209) and the alignment (115°) of Beacon D (4.209) with Light-beacon C indicate the track 295° astern.

Basins and berths
4.211

1   Tidal berths:

North Wall; 550 m long, depth alongside 8·3 m but liable to silting.

South Arm; 200 m long, depth alongside 10·5 m.

There are berths at Middle Jetty and, for smaller vessels, in Tidal Basin.

2   Main Basin:

Main Basin has berths alongside its E, W and S sides. Depth below chart datum is 6·1 m, but the water level is normally maintained above this, giving a depth of 11 m in the basin.

Port services
4.212

1   **Repairs** of all kinds can be carried out. There are 3 dry docks, and a mechanical lift dock serving 5 covered refit bays.

Largest dry dock: length overall 311·2 m; breadth 42·4 m; depth 12·4 m over sill at MHWS.
4.213

1   **Supplies:** Fresh water; electrical power (440 volts AC) at some berths.

FORTH BRIDGES TO GRANGEMOUTH

General information

Charts 736, 737
Route
4.214

1   From a position close W of the Forth Railway Bridge (56°00′N, 3°22′W) (4.172) the route leads 8 miles WNW and W following the River Forth to the dredged approach channel to Grangemouth.

Topography
4.215

1   Between the Forth Railway Bridge (56°00′N, 3°23′W) and Grangemouth the River Forth runs 8 miles WNW. To the W of the bridges the river widens to 2 miles until Grangemouth is reached. Both banks of the river dry up to several cables offshore.

Controlling depths
4.216

1   The approach channel to Grangemouth is dredged to 6·5 m but is subject to occasional silting. The Harbour

Master Grangemouth should be consulted for the latest information regarding depths.

Pilotage
4.217
1   See 4.4 to 4.6.

Traffic regulations
4.218
1   See 4.8.
4.219
1   **Prohibited area.** Crombie Jetty and Crombie Pier (56°02′N, 3°32′W) (4.223) lie within an area, shown on the chart, into which entry is prohibited.
4.220
1   **A prohibited anchorage** area lies between Charlestown (56°02′N, 3°31′W) (4.227) and Blackness (4.223), where a gas pipeline and submarine cables cross the river. Two light-beacons (special, cone topmark) indicating the line of the pipeline stand close W of Charlestown.

2   Anchoring is prohibited in an area between Bo'ness (56°01′N, 3°36′W) (4.223) NNE to Low Torry (4.223) where a crude oil pipeline crosses the river.

The pipelines above carry dangerous products. Any damage or potential damage to them should be reported to the Forth Navigation Service.

Tidal streams
4.221
1   Tidal streams in the river are subject to great changes due to astronomical and meteorological conditions. At springs there is generally a relatively short and strong in-going stream and a longer and weaker out-going stream; at neaps the streams are of nearly equal duration, with the out-going stream rather the stronger.

2   With strong and long-continued E winds both the duration and the rate of the in-going stream may be increased and the out-going stream correspondingly decreased. When snow is melting and during heavy rain, both the duration and the rate of the out-going stream will be increased, and the rate of the in-going stream correspondingly decreased; these effects increase as the river is ascended.

3   Off Bo'ness (56°01′N, 3°36′W) the tidal stream runs as follows, with a spring rate of 2 kn:

Time from HW Leith	Remarks
−0430 to −0300	In-going stream commences
+0100 to +0200	Out-going stream commences

Principal marks
4.222
1   **Landmarks:**
   Crombie Jetty (L-shaped) (56°01′·9N, 3°31′·8W).
   Chimney (56°03′·0N, 3°35′·7W).
   Chimney (56°02′·9N, 3°40′·9W) at Longannet Power Station.
   White house (turret) (55°59′·8N, 3°26′·8W).
2   Blackness Castle (56°00′·4N, 3°30′·9W) with high walls.
   Binn's Tower (55°59′·5N, 3°31′·2W), on a hill.
   Bridgeness Tower (56°01′·0N, 3°35′·0W), an old windmill.
   Church spire (56°00′·8N, 3°36′·8W) in Bo'ness.
   Oil tanks (56°02′·2N, 3°41′·4W) at entrance to Grangemouth Docks.

Directions
(continued from 4.173)

Forth Bridges to Grangemouth
4.223
1   From a position close W of the Road Bridge, on the recommended track shown on the chart, the route leads 6 miles WNW and finally 4 miles W to Grangemouth, passing (with positions from the SW corner Main Basin, Rosyth (56°01′N, 3°27′W)):
   S of Beamer Rock (1·8 miles ESE), which dries, and is marked by a light on its SE side (white tower, red band), and:
2   N of Port Edgar (2 miles SE) (4.192), thence:
   SSW of Whale Back (1 mile ESE), a shoal on the N side of the river and which divides it from Main Channel leading to Rosyth. Dhu Craig, a bank, is close W of Whale Back and fronts Rosyth. There is a boat channel, least depth 3 m, between the shoal and the bank. Thence:
   NNE of Abercorn Point (1½ miles SW) at the W end of Society Bank, which lies between the point and Port Edgar, thence:
3   NNE of Black Ness (2 miles SW) with a conspicuous castle (4.222). There are a number of anchor berths (4.229) between Dhu Craig Light-buoy (2 cables S of Dhu Craig) and Blackness Light-buoy, 1·7 miles WNW. A buoy (special) marks the head of a sewage outfall (9 cables W).
4   The route continues WNW for 2 miles, then W for 4 miles to Grangemouth, passing (with positions from Bridgeness Tower (56°01′·0N, 3°31′·2W) (4.222):
   SSW of Crombie Jetty, the outer of the two jetties at Crombie (2 miles ENE) and the prohibited area (4.219) around both Crombie Jetty and Crombie Pier. A fog signal (horn) is sounded from a building on the head of Crombie Jetty. Lights (column, 5 m in height) are exhibited from dolphins off the E and W ends of Crombie Jetty.

Crombie Jetty   *Crombie Pier*

Crombie (4.223)

(Original dated 2000)

(Photograph - Air Images)

5   Thence:
   NNE of Tancred Bank (1·3 miles NE). Torry Light-beacon (green structure, 12 m in height) (1½ miles WNW of Tancred Bank), bearing 291°, leads N of Tancred Bank. Thence:
   NNE of Dods Bank (8 cables NW), an extensive flat of sand, mud, gravel and stones which fronts the town of Bo'ness. Thence:

6   SSW of Torry Light-beacon (1½ miles N) standing on the SW side of Torry Bay, which dries, with Low Torry at its head. The W side of the bay is being reclaimed. Thence:

S of Dog Rock (1·8 miles NW), which is awash at HW and lies at the S end of Craigmore Rocks at the W entry point to Torry Bay, thence:

7   S of Hen and Chickens (2·2 miles NW), a patch of sand, mud and rocks which dry. Hen and Chickens Light-buoy is moored 1½ cables to the S of the patch on the N side of the fairway at the commencement of the dredged approach channel, which has a least width of 120 m. No 1 Light-beacon (red cylinder on pile) lies 2 cables S of the buoy and to the S side of the approach channel. Thereafter the channel is marked by light-beacons and light-buoys to the Grangemouth entrance lock (4.247) 1½ miles to the W. A diversionary channel 200 m wide, leads off the approach channel close W of Hen and Chickens Buoy, rejoining the approach channel 4 cables NE of the entrance lock.

8   **Cautions.** The stretch of water between Bo'ness and Culross (2½ miles NNW of Bo'ness) on the N bank, in the vicinity of Craigmore Rocks (above), can be dangerous for small craft during in-going tides with a strong SW wind, when a heavy sea develops.

There are a number of unlit mooring buoys shown on the chart, used by warships, between Beamer Rock and the S of Dhu Craig. Vessels at these moorings might not exhibit lights or make fog signals.

Useful mark
4.224
1   Culross church spire (56°03'·5N, 3°37'·4W), with abbey ruins close W.

(Directions continue for the entrance lock at 4.247, and for Stirling at 4.259)

Minor harbours and anchorages
4.225
1   **Brucehaven** (56°02'N, 3°29'W), 8 cables W of Rosyth, is formed by a curved pier extending SSW from Capernaum Point. Rocks, which dry, marked by a beacon at their SW extremity, lie on the E side of the entrance.
4.226
1   **Limekilns** (56°02'N, 3°29'W) has a boat harbour protected to the W by Limekilns Pier.
4.227
1   **Charlestown** Harbour (56°02'N, 3°30'W) is formed by piers and now only used as a sailing centre. It is protected from all winds and has depths of 4 m, soft mud, at HW springs.
4.228
1   **Bo'ness Harbour** (56°01'N, 3°36'W) is closed.

Anchorages
4.229
1   **Rosyth.** There are a number of anchorages for warships, R1 to R7 indicated on the chart, which lie to the S and W of Rosyth. Eddies to the W of Beamer Rock during W-going spring tides cause a vessel to sheer considerably if anchored within 7 cables W of the rock.
4.230
1   **Charlestown Road Anchorage** for merchant vessels, which also includes anchor berths R5, R6 and R7 (above),

Charlestown Harbour (4.227)

(Original dated 2000)

(Photograph - Air Images)

is indicated on the chart and lies in the fairway off Charlestown (4.227) and Limekilns (4.226).
4.231
1   **Bo'ness Anchorage.** There are six anchor berths for merchant ships, shown on the chart as Bo'ness 1 to 6, in the middle of the river off Bridgeness (7 cables E of Bo'ness).
4.232
1   **Blackness Harbour** (56°00'·3N, 3°31'·4W) consists of a stone pier surrounded by drying moorings. The pier can be approached 2 hours either side of HW. Facilities are limited.

Other names
4.233
1   Crombie Point (56°02'·7N, 3°33'·3W).
Gellet Rock (56°02'·2N, 3°29'·5W).

GRANGEMOUTH

General information

Chart 737
Position
4.234
1   Grangemouth (56°02'N, 3°41'W) is situated on the S side of the River Carron, where the latter enters the River Forth.

Function
4.235
1   Grangemouth population 18 739 (1991), the second largest port in Scotland, handles all types of cargo, tankers and liquid chemical and LPG carriers.

Topography
4.236
1   The major part of Grangemouth Docks lies on a promontory which juts NE from the S bank of the River Forth. The River Carron runs parallel to W side of the promontory, 1 cable to the W. The river is contained to its W by an embankment, marked by stone beacons. The entrance dock is at the head of the promontory and either side of the lock there are numerous oil tanks. There are bays, bottom mud, which dry, flanking the promontory. Part of the bay to the E has been reclaimed.

Approach and entry
4.237
1   Grangemouth Docks are approached from the E, via the River Forth and entered through an entrance lock. The immediate approach to the lock is dredged.

Traffic
4.238

1 In 1999, Grangemouth Docks handled 2374 vessels totalling 9 677 740 dwt.

Port authority
4.239

1 The harbour is administered by Forth Ports PLC, Dock Office, Grangemouth.

Limiting conditions
4.240

1 **Controlling depths.** The entrance channel is dredged to 6·5 m but is subject to occasional silting. The entrance lock has a depth of 11·7 m over the sill at HW springs. The Harbour Master should be consulted for the latest information on depths.

Deepest and longest berths: tanker berths, Eastern Channel (4.248); other vessels, Grange Dock (4.248).

Tidal levels: see *Admiralty Tide Tables*. Mean spring range about 4·8 m; mean neap range about 2·6 m.

4.241

1 **Maximum size of vessel.** Grangemouth Docks can accept vessels up to 32 000 dwt, length 187 m, beam 27 m and draught 10·6 m (tankers) and 7·6 m (other vessels).

Arrival information

Port operations
4.242

1 See 4.8.

Lock control office should be contacted before passing Hen and Chickens Buoy (4.223) with regard to the depth over the sill at the entrance lock. The lock operates continuously.

Anchorage
4.243

1 Apart from the Bo'ness anchor berths (4.231), there is an anchorage for small vessels in Grangemouth Roads 5 cables NE of the entrance lock.

Pilots and tugs
4.244

1 For pilotage in the River Forth see 4.4 to 4.6.

Inbound vessels requiring tugs are met S of Hen and Chickens (4.223).

Two tugs are available.

Harbour

Layout
4.245

1 There are three separate berthing areas leading one from another. They lie in a NE/SW direction over a distance of 1½ miles. The entrance lock lies SE of an old entrance now disused and sealed off, and is protected by approach jetties on either side. The lock leads into Eastern Channel, which leads to Grange Dock via East Cut. Western Channel runs W from Grange Dock and thence into Carron Dock via West Cut. Two small docks, Old Dock and Junction Dock, lie to the W of Carron Dock but are no longer in use.

Grangemouth Harbour (4.245)

(Original dated 2000)

(Photograph - Air Images)

Principal mark
4.246

1   **Landmark:**

Group of oil tanks (56°02′·2N, 3°41′·3W), 2 cables W of entrance lock.

Directions
(continued from 4.224)

4.247

1   From a position at the W end of the approach channel the track leads 3 cables SW between the protecting approach jetties and thence to the lock entrance. The lock is 238 m long, 31 m wide (29·1 m between fenders) and lies on a charted axis 062°/242°.

Basins and berths
4.248

1   Eastern Channel, 7 tanker berths, largest 210 m long, 11 m depth alongside.

Grange Dock, 2175 m of quayage, depth 7·9 m, container terminal, Ro-Ro berth.

Carron Dock, 775 m of quayage, depth 7 m.

Port services
4.249

1   **Repairs** of all kinds can be carried out.

One dry dock; length 105·4 m; floor length 104 m; breadth 16·1 m; depth over the blocks, 6·1 m at MHWS, but never less than 5·6 m.

4.250

1   **Other facilities:** reception of oily waste; de-ratting and exemption certificates issued; hospital at Falkirk.

4.251

1   **Supplies:** fuel oils of all types at oil jetties in Eastern Channel, elsewhere by road tanker; fresh water; stores and provisions.

GRANGEMOUTH TO STIRLING

General information

Chart 738

Route
4.252

1   From a position (56°02′N, 3°41′W) off the entrance lock at Grangemouth, the route follows the River Forth for a distance of 17 miles to Stirling, passing the towns of Kincardine and Alloa.

Controlling depths
4.253

1   At HW vessels of 5 m draught can proceed as far as Alloa (56°06′N, 3°48′W). Vessels of up to 3 m draught can reach Stirling at HW springs.

Bridge and overhead cable clearance
4.254

1   Kincardine Bridge (56°04′N, 3°44′W) has a vertical clearance of 9 m. There is a bridge at Upper Taylorton (56°07′N, 3°54′W) with a vertical clearance of 4·2 m and a footbridge at Cambuskenneth (7 cables W of Upper Taylorton) with a clearance of 4 m.

2   A number of power cables cross this stretch of the river. All have a vertical clearance well in excess of the bridge clearances.

Pilotage and local knowledge
4.255

1   Pilotage is compulsory as far as Kincardine Bridge. For details see 4.4 to 4.6. There are no pilots available above Kincardine Bridge. There is an embargo on commercial movements above the bridge for safety reasons and the channel is not buoyed. It is continually changing and the chart should not be relied on. Local knowledge is necessary for small craft to proceed above this bridge.

Traffic regulations
4.256

1   See 4.8.

4.257

1   **Regulations for Kincardine Bridge:**

Only one vessel at a time shall approach the bridge with the intention of passing through.

In the event of two vessels approaching the bridge from opposite directions, the vessel, or vessels from seaward shall have precedence. A vessel, or vessels outward bound from Alloa shall not pass the line 1000 m from the bridge until it is evident that no vessel is attempting the inward passage.

2   In the event of two or more vessels abreast or nearly abreast approaching the bridge from the same direction, the vessel to starboard shall have precedence, and this precedence is given in sequence from starboard to port.

There shall be an interval of at least 600 m between vessels when about to pass through the bridge.

3   Vessels are to approach the bridge at a reduced speed which must not exceed 10 knots over the ground.

No vessel of any description shall anchor within 1000 m of the bridge in the fairway.

Vessels of all descriptions are to keep out of the way of any vessel which may be approaching the bridge with the intention of passing through.

Tidal streams
4.258

1   Tidal streams run as follows:

Time from HW Leith	*Remarks*
Kincardine	
−0400 to −0330	In-going stream commences
+0300 to +0100	Out-going stream commences. Spring rate 2¾ kn.
Alloa	
−0400	In-going stream commences
+0100	Out-going stream commences. Spring rate 3 kn.

2   At Kincardine the channel contracts, causing the tide to accelerate up to 4 kn. Above and below Kincardine there is a local phenomenon, the "Leaky Tide", when the in-going/out-going stream is interrupted soon after it begins by a short period of out-going/in-going stream.

Between Alloa and Stirling the river bed rises by about 3 m reducing a 5 m tidal range at Alloa to 3 m at Stirling. This also has an effect on the time of HW at Stirling which is ½ hour later than Alloa.

Directions
(continued from 4.224)

Grangemouth to Kincardine Bridge
4.259

1 From the vicinity of 56°02'·3N, 3°40'·8W just N of the entrance lock for Grangemouth Docks the route leads 2 miles NW to Kincardine Bridge, passing (with positions from Kincardine Bridge):

2 SW of the head of a bank (2 miles SW), which lies 6 cables SSE of the Longannet Point and 1¾ cables N of the land enclosing Grangemouth Docks. The point is low and surrounded by a sea wall with a power station 5 cables to its E. A cooling water intake jetty with a T-head extends 67 m from the sea wall close S of the power station. And:

3 NE of the mouth of the River Carron (2 miles SE) (4.236) and a beacon (square topmark) marking the seaward end of an outfall 2 cables NW, thence:

NE of a bank (1 mile SE) running NW/SE for a distance of 1½ miles. The bank fronts a bight which extends to Kincardine Bridge. Between this bank and the bank off Longannet the channel is 1½ cables wide. Thence:

4 SW of Inch Brake (4 cables SE), a shoal marked by a buoy (starboard hand), thence:

To Kincardine Bridge. The bridge is 4½ cables long and was formerly a swing bridge. It has two navigation spans each 46 m wide. A timber jetty 143 m long projects either side of the centre and assists vessels to warp through if required.

No directions can be given above Kincardine Bridge due to the continually changing nature of the channel. See 4.255.

Useful marks
4.260

1 Chimney (56°02'·9N, 3°40'·8W) at Longannet Power Station.

Tower blocks (56°04'·3N, 3°42'·7W).

Church Tower (56°04'·3N, 3°42'·9W).

Town pier and pylon (56°03'·9N, 3°43'·3W).

2 Chimneys (56°04'·4N, 3°43'·5W) at Kincardine Power Station.

Clackmannan Tower (56°06'·5N, 3°45'·5W) in ruins.

Longannet Power Station chimney from E (4.260)

(Original dated 2000)

(Photograph - Air Images)

Spire (56°06'·8N, 3°47'·7W).

Chimney (56°06'·7N, 3°47'·8W).

Tower (56°06'·7N, 3°48'·1W).

Minor harbours
4.261

1 **Kincardine** (56°04'N, 3°43'W) lies 2 miles NNW of Grangemouth on the N bank of the River Forth. There are no shipping facilities but boats can land at Town Pier or Ferry Pier close above the bridge.

4.262

1 **Alloa** (56°06'N, 3°48'W), population 18 842 (1991), lies 4 miles N of Kincardine. Vessels of light draught may lie alongside Harbour Pier at their own risk. The harbour is closed and the former wet dock filled in. On the S bank of the river there are several jetties in poor state of repair. There is a hospital at Alloa.

4.263

1 **Stirling** (56°07'N, 3°56'W), population 30 515 (1991), is 62 miles from the Isle of May and may be considered the head of navigation in the River Forth. There is a disused quay, 1 cable long.

Other names
4.264

1 Alloa Inch (56°06'N, 3°49'W), an island.

Black Devon (56°06'N, 3°46'W), a river.

Tullibody Inch (56°06'·7N, 3°49'·7W), an island.

NOTES

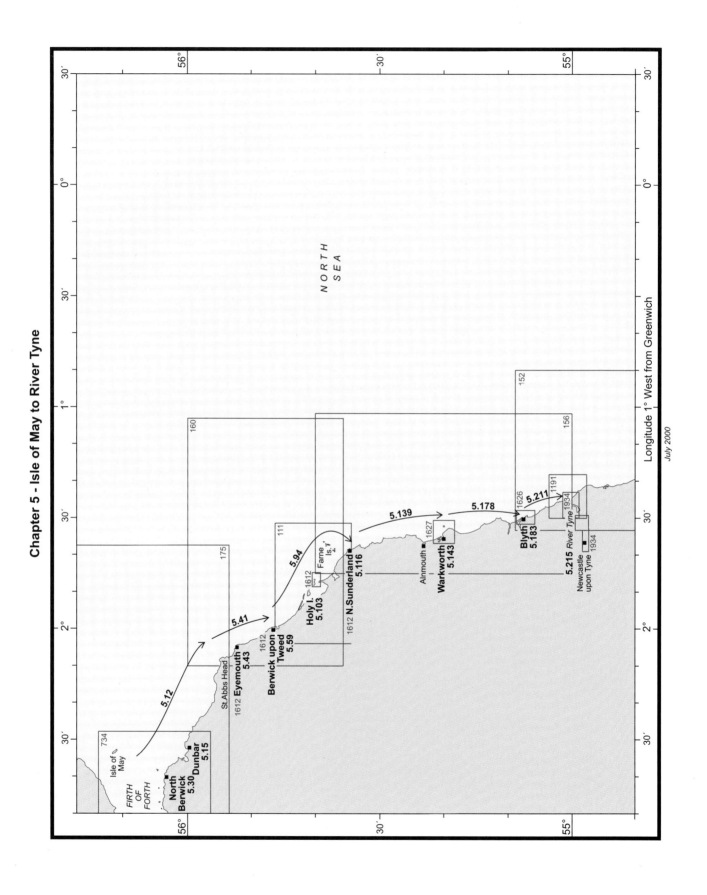

NORTH SEA

FIRTH OF FORTH

Isle of May
734

North Berwick
5.30

Dunbar
5.15

St.Abbs Head

5.12

5.41

1612 Eyemouth
5.43

1612 Berwick upon Tweed
5.59

5.94

Holy I. 1612
5.103

Farne Is.

1612 N.Sunderland
5.116

5.139

160

175

111

Alnmouth 1627

Warkworth
5.143

5.178

Blyth
5.183

1626

5.211

1191

152

156

5.215 River Tyne 1934

Newcastle upon Tyne 1934

Longitude 1° West from Greenwich

July 2000

CHAPTER 5

ISLE OF MAY TO RIVER TYNE

GENERAL INFORMATION

Charts 1407, 1192
Synopsis
5.1

1   In this chapter the coastal passage from the Isle of May (56°11'N, 2°33'W) (3.247) to the River Tyne, 80 miles SSE, is described together with the ports of Eyemouth (5.43), Warkworth (5.143), Blyth (5.183) and the Port of Tyne (5.215).

Topography
5.2

1   The Isle of May lies 10 miles NE of Fidra (56°04'N, 2°47'W) (4.22), the S point of the entrance to the Firth of Forth. From Fidra the coast continues 24 miles ESE to Saint Abb's Head, thence 60 miles SSE to the mouth of the River Tyne. The coast is a mixture of rocky cliffs fringed with reefs and sandy bays, with the exception of the area around Holy Island (55°41'N, 1°48'W) and the Farne Islands, which lie 6 miles SE of Holy Island.

2   This particular stretch of coast is dangerous. Within the 30 m depth contour, which elsewhere is less than 2 miles offshore but here lies up to 5 miles off the mainland, there are many shoals and rocks and extensive sands to the W and N of Holy Island.

Outlying banks and deeps
5.3

1   Spittal Hirst, a bank charted within the 30 m depth contour, lies 4½ miles E of Berwick-upon-Tweed (55°46'N, 2°00'W).

Dicky Shad and Newton Skere, two rocky banks charted outside the 30 m depth contour, lie respectively 1¾ miles ENE and 4½ miles E of Beadnell Point (55°33'N, 1°37'W).

2   Craster Skeres, a rocky patch close to the 50 m depth contour, lies 5 miles E of Castle Point (55°30'N, 1°35'W).

Farne Deeps, spread over an area 15 miles by 12 miles, lie E of Castle Point (55°30'N, 1°35'W) about 20 miles off the coast.

Tidal streams
5.4

1   The offshore streams are not strong with spring rates of 1 kn. They are regular and run in the direction of the coast. The tidal streams are given on the charts and in the *Admiralty Tidal Stream Atlas: North Sea, Northwestern Part.*

ISLE OF MAY TO SAINT ABB'S HEAD

General information

Charts 734, 175
Route
5.5

1   From a position midway between the Isle of May (56°11'N, 2°33'W) (3.247) and Fidra (10 miles SW) (4.22) the route leads ESE for a distance of 22 miles to a position NE of Saint Abb's Head.

Traffic recommendation. A recommendation has been adopted by IMO that laden tankers should avoid the area between Bass Rock and the coast.

Topography
5.6

1   Fidra lies 5 cables off the coast, which runs 5½ miles E to Great Car (5.12). As far as North Berwick (5.30), 2½ miles E of Fidra, the coast is low and sandy, with occasional clumps of trees and fringed by rocky ledges up to 4 cables offshore which are interrupted by sandy beaches. To the E of North Berwick, the coast is composed of cliffs and steep slopes with somewhat narrower rocky ledges offshore. Apart from Fidra there are the islets of Lamb, Craigleith and Bass Rock (5.12) lying offshore. Bass Rock is the most northerly and 1¼ miles off the coast. At Great Car the trend of the coast turns to ESE as far as Saint Abb's Head (5.12), a distance of 19 miles. Initially the coast is rocky thence sandy to Dunbar (5.15), 4½ miles ESE of Great Car. The coast to the ESE of Dunbar is backed by high ground with a flat foreground on which the railway is occasionally visible. About 5 miles short of Saint Abb's Head the coast becomes bold and rugged, backed by elevated land which is nearly bare of trees, and slopes steeply forming cliffs in places.

Rescue
5.7

1   There are Coastguard Rescue Teams at North Berwick and Cockburnspath (55°56'N, 2°22'W); see 1.53.

An all-weather lifeboat is stationed at Dunbar; inshore lifeboats are stationed at Dunbar and North Berwick. See 1.61 for details of lifeboats.

Measured distance
5.8

1   A measured distance is charted close W of Saint Abb's Head (55°55'N, 2°08'W).

Limit Marks. Two pairs of beacons, surmounted by triangles with the front triangles point down.
Distance. 1849 m.
Running track. 111°/291°.

2   Beyond 2 miles offshore the W beacons are difficult to see against the background of dark fir trees.

It is reported (1999) that the beacons are no longer maintained.

Tidal streams
5.9

1   The offshore streams are weak, with rates not exceeding 1 kn, and change regularly. Near the land the tidal stream follows the line of the coast. In the entrance to the Firth of Forth spring rates are 1½ kn but from Barns Ness (55°59'N, 2°27'W) to the S rates reduce to 1 kn. The tidal stream runs strongly round Saint Abb's Head and there is turbulence especially with opposing winds. Details of the tidal streams are given on the chart and in the *Admiralty Tidal Stream Atlas: North Sea, Northwestern Part.*

2   **Caution.** During onshore gales the sea breaks heavily over the below water rocks and ledges fronting the coast between Great Car and Saint Abb's Head. As the SE-going stream sets towards Saint Abb's Head it should be given a wide berth.

Principal marks
5.10

1   **Landmarks:**
Bass Rock (56°05'N, 2°38'W) (5.12).

North Berwick Law (56°03′N, 2°43′W), a pyramidal hill covered in grass with a plantation on its S side.

Traprain Law (55°58′N, 2°40′W), a remarkable isolated hill not to be confused with North Berwick Law.

2   Mast (55°56′N, 2°27′W) with a pylon 5 cables N. Torness Power Station (55°58′N, 2°25′W).

Major lights:

Isle of May Light (56°11′N, 2°33′W) (3.252).

Fidra Light (56°04′N, 2°47′W) (4.20).

Saint Abb's Head Light (white tower and buildings, 9 m in height) (55°55′N, 2°08′W).

Other navigational aids

5.11

1   **Racon:**

Saint Abb's Head Light (55°55′N, 2°08′W).

DGPS:

Girdle Ness Light (57°08′N, 2°03′W).

Directions
(continued from 3.256)

5.12

1   From a position midway between the Isle of May (56°11′N, 2°33′W) and Fidra (10 miles SW) the coastal route leads ESE to a position NE of Saint Abb's Head, passing (with positions from Barns Ness Light (55°59′·2N, 2°26′·6W)):

NNE of Craigleith (56°04′N, 2°43′W), a rocky islet 6 cables N of North Berwick. A similar but smaller islet, Lamb, lies 1 mile WSW of Craigleith, thence:

2   NNE of Bass Rock (8½ miles WNW), a conspicuous pyramidal rock which is precipitous on all sides, particularly the NE and NW. Its cliffs are a brilliant white from the droppings of seabirds. Bass Rock Light (white tower and dwellings, 20 m high) stands on its S side. An area in which experimental buoys, both lit and unlit, are regularly moored is centred 2½ miles NE of Bass Rock, as shown on the charts. Thence:

Light

Bass Rock from NE (5.12.1)

(Original dated 2000)

(Photograph - Air Images)

3   NNE of Satan Bush (6½ miles NW), a rocky patch. Great Car, a ledge of rocks which nearly covers at HW, lies 1 mile W of Satan Bush. South Carr Beacon (black round stone tower, surmounted by a cross) stands at the N extremity of Great Car. Thence:

4   NNE of Lady Ground (4½ miles WNW), a steep-to patch. Whitberry Point, a low dark point, with a small conical hill near its centre, lies 9 cables W of Lady Ground and at the SE end of Peffer Sands. Thence:

5   NNE of Dunbar (5.15) (2½ miles WNW). Belhaven Bay, which fronts Tyne Sands, lies between Dunbar and Whitberry Point. A buoy (special, pillar) marks the outlet of a sewage outfall 1·1 miles ESE of Whitberry Point. Thence:

6   NNE of Sicar (2 miles NW), an isolated rock on which the sea breaks heavily during onshore gales, thence:

NNE of Barns Ness, a low point fringed by rocky ledges. Barns Ness Light (white round tower, 37 m in height) stands on the point. Ruddystone, a rocky shoal with a dangerous wreck close SE, lies 5 cables N of the point. Thence:

Barns Ness Light (5.12.2)

(Original dated 2000)

(Photograph - Air Images)

7   NNE of Torness Point (2 miles ESE), from which rocky ledges extend 2½ cables offshore. Torness Power Station lies 2½ cables SW of the point. Skateraw Harbour, now unusable, is 6 cables W of the point. Thence:

Torness Power Station (5.12.3)

(Original dated 2000)

(Photograph - Air Images)

8   NNE of Cove Harbour (5.31) (4½ miles ESE) with Pease Bay 7 cables SE. The Bay lies at the mouth of a deep, well-wooded ravine, spanned by a stone viaduct with four unequal arches. Thence:

NNE of Fast Castle Head (8 miles ESE). The ruins of Fast Castle stand on the head, thence:

NNE of the measured distance (10 miles ESE) (5.8), thence:

9   NNE of Saint Abb's Head (56°55′N, 2°08′W), a bold promontory of dark rock which rises almost vertically. The face of the rock is broken by deep fissures. Parts of the cliff have become detached but the head is steep-to. Between the head and Cross Law, 2 miles W, is a valley which causes the head to appear as an island from the NW or SE. Saint Abb's Head Light (5.10) stands on the head, which is a National Nature Reserve.

Saint Abb's Head from E (5.12.4)

(Original dated 2000)

(Photograph - Air Images)

5.13

1   **Clearing bearing.** Small craft can pass S of Craigleith (5.12). For such craft the line of bearing 273° on the S extremity of Fidra (56°04′N, 2°47′W) well open N of the N extremity of Lamb, an islet 1 mile E of Fidra, passes N of Stubb Rock, 1 mile ESE of Craigleith, and the foul ground W of North Berwick. A light-buoy (special, pillar) marks the outlet of a sewage outfall 1¼ miles E of Craigleith.

Useful marks
5.14

1   Tantallon Castle (56°03′·3N, 2°38′·9W), a ruin on the edge of a cliff.

House (56°00′·2N, 2°32′·3W) of brown brick, slate roof and tall chimneys.

Doon Hill (55°58′N, 2°30′W) with a well defined NW extremity of high land.

Two chimneys (55°59′N, 2°28′W).

(Directions continue at 5.41)

Dunbar

General information
5.15

1   **Position.** Dunbar (56°00′N, 2°31′W) mostly built of dark coloured stone, stands at the E end of Tyne Sands (5.12).
5.16

1   **Function.** The harbour, called Victoria Harbour, is only used for landing fish and by recreational craft. The population was 6518 in 1991.

5.17

1   **Port authority.** Victoria Harbour is administered by East Lothian Council, Council Buildings, Haddington, East Lothian EH41 3HA.

Limiting conditions
5.18

1   **Controlling depth** is 5·6 m in the approach channel at HW springs and 4·6 m at HW neaps. Within the harbour Middle Quay has a depth alongside of 5·3 m at HW springs.

Tidal levels: see *Admiralty Tide Tables.* Mean spring range about 4·5 m; mean neap about range 2·2 m.
5.19

1   **Maximum size of vessel.** Length 50 m, draught 4 m at HW springs. Vessels lie aground on a sandy bottom at LW.
5.20

1   **Local weather.** When the wind is strong from between the WNW through N to E, the harbour is difficult to enter and the berths may be untenable due to a heavy swell in the harbour. In these conditions vessels move into Old Harbour (5.23).

Arrival information
5.21

1   **Pilotage** is not available.
5.22

1   An **anchorage**, shown on the chart, may be obtained in Dunbar Roads in depths of 13 m, 4 cables NW of the harbour entrance.

Harbour
5.23

1   **Layout.** Victoria Harbour lies at the NW end of Dunbar and has 183 m of quays. It is protected from the N by a breakwater and the entrance, cut through solid rock, lies on the W side of the harbour and faces NW. Old Harbour is close E of Victoria Harbour and is entered through a 12 m wide passage in East Quay which is spanned by a lifting bridge.

Directions
5.24

1   **Leading lights:**

Front leading light (orange column, white triangle point up, 4m in height) (56°00′·5N, 2°31′·1W).

Rear leading light (orange column, white triangle point down, 4 m in height).

2   From a position NNE of the harbour entrance, the alignment (198°) of these lights leads from NNE of the harbour entrance to a position N of the entrance then generally S to the NW of the entrance, passing (with positions from the front light):

3   ESE of Scart Rock (2¾ cables N), an above water rock, thence:

WNW of Castlefoot Rock (2¾ cables NNE), an above water rock, thence:

To a position NW of the harbour entrance whence a direct approach may be made to the entrance (5.25).
5.25

1   **Approach from the North West.** The line of bearing 132° of the harbour entrance, with the light on Middle Quay (column, 5 m in height) seen through it, leads to the harbour entrance, passing (with positions from the harbour entrance):

NE of Wallace's Head (2½ cables WNW), a rock which dries 1 m and is marked by a metal perch, thence:

Victoria Harbour　　　　　　　*Castle Rocks*

Old Harbour　　　　　　　　　　　　　　　　　　*Castlefoot Rock*

Dunbar Harbour from NNE (5.23)

(Original dated 2000)

(Photograph - Air Images)

2　　　SW of Half Ebb Rock (1¾ cables NW), which dries 2·1 m and is marked by a metal perch, thence:
To the harbour entrance.

If weather permits (5.20) it is best to enter harbour within 1 hour of HW.

Caution. There are several isolated rocks, known as The Steeples, lying E-W about the approach to Dunbar.

Port services
5.26

1　　　**Repairs.** Minor repairs can be carried out.
5.27

1　　　The nearest hospital for accidents and emergencies is at the Royal Infirmary, Edinburgh.
5.28

1　　　**Supplies:** marine diesel by road tanker; water at Middle Quay; provisions.

Small craft
5.29

1　　　There are facilities for recreational craft.

Minor harbours, anchorages and boat landings

North Berwick
5.30

1　　　**General information.** North Berwick (56°04′N, 2°43′W) stands partly within a black rocky point and partly at the foot of North Berwick Law (5.10). The harbour is mainly used by recreational craft, but a few fishing boats remain. The population in 1991 was 5687. The harbour is owned and operated by the East Lothian Council (5.17).

2　　　**Limiting conditions.** The harbour dries at LW, but has depths of 5 m at HW springs. NE gales raise heavy seas

and a scend in the harbour and in these conditions the harbour might be closed by booms so that vessels can lie safely. The harbour should not be used without local knowledge.

3　　　**The harbour** is formed by piers. The entrance is 8 m wide and faces SW. The quays are 30 m and 91 m in length.

North Berwick Harbour (5.30)

(Original dated 2000)

(Photograph - Air Images)

Principal marks:
　　North Berwick Law (56°03′N, 2°43′W) (5.10).
　　Church (spire) (56°03′·6N, 2°42′·9W).
　　Church (56°03′·5N, 2°43′·2W).

4   **Directions.** The alignment of the W slope of North Berwick Law with the stone beacon on the pierhead passes E of The Maidenfoot, a rock (beacon) 1 cable NW of the harbour entrance. A light (3 m in height) is exhibited on North Pier Head. This light is extinguished when vessels cannot enter the harbour. A second light (bracket on building) is exhibited 100 m SE of the harbour entrance.

Supplies: marine diesel by road tanker.

Small craft facilities are available.

Cove Harbour
5.31

1   **General information.** Cove Harbour (55°56′N, 2°21′W), which is privately owned, is a small fishing harbour formed by piers. The village of Cove is on top of the cliff close W of the harbour.

2   **Limiting conditions.** The entrance is 22 m wide and has a depth in it of 3·7 m at HW springs. Within the harbour there are depths of 3 m at HW springs. The bottom of the harbour is mainly sandy, but there are occasional rocky patches. Onshore gales throw a heavy sea into the harbour.

3   **Caution.** There are below water rocks 3 cables E of the entrance.

Landmark. Dunglass Mansion (55°56′·4N, 2°22′·5W) stands in a wood 8 cables W of Cove.

Anchorages
5.32

1   In addition to the anchorage off Dunbar (5.22) there are anchorages for small craft, shown on the chart, as follows:

5 cables ENE of Fidra Light (4.20) in W winds.

2   Off the W end of Craigleith (5.12), sand and clay. E of the anchorage position the bottom is foul and uneven.

In Scoughall Road, 7 cables NNW of Whitberry Point (56°01′N, 2°35′W), in depths of 9 to 11 m, clay, during offshore winds.

Boat landings
5.33

1   Available at:

Bass Rock (5.12). Moderate weather only, SW side below ruins of castle.

Redheugh (55°55′·5N, 2°16′·7W), at a position shown on the chart.

Pettico Wick (55°55′N, 2°09′W), at a position shown on the chart.

Other names
5.34

1   Bush of Blackstanes (56°00′N, 2°28′W), a rock.
Cargill Rock (55°56′N, 2°17′W).
Gin Head (56°04′N, 2°39′W).
Greenheugh Point (55°56′N, 2°19′W).
Guardy (56°00′N, 2°27′W), a shoal.
The Leithies (56°04′N, 2°42′W), a group of black rocks.
Milsey Bay (56°03′N, 2°42′W).

2   Nick Cove (55°56′N, 2°14′W).
Podlie Craig (56°04′N, 2°40′W).
Rath Grounds (56°08′N, 2°38′W), a bank.
Rodgers, The (56°03′N, 2°37′W), a ledge.
Siccar Point (55°56′N, 2°18′W).
Vaultness (56°00′N, 2°29′W), a point.
Wildfire Rocks (56°01′N, 2°34′W).
Windylaw Cove (55°55′N, 2°16′W).

SAINT ABB'S HEAD TO BERWICK-UPON-TWEED

General information

Chart 160
Route
5.35

1   From a position NE of Saint Abb's Head (55°55′N, 2°08′W) the coastal route leads 12 miles SSE to a position E of Berwick-upon-Tweed, which stands at the mouth of the River Tweed.

Topography
5.36

1   From Saint Abb's Head as far as Hare Point, 3 miles SE, the coast is rugged and bleak and backed by high land which rises boldly and has few identifiable objects. Eyemouth (5.43), close S of Hare Point stands on low ground, but to the SSE the coast climbs reaching an elevation of 93 m until Burnmouth (5.83), 2¼ miles SSE of Eyemouth is reached. Between Burnmouth and Berwick-upon-Tweed, 5 miles SSE, the coast consists of a steep bank and cliffs, about 18 m high, which decrease in height towards Berwick-upon-Tweed. Rocks fringe the coast up to 3½ cables offshore. The coast is backed by Lamberton Hill, 1½ miles SW of Burnmouth and Halidon Hill, 3½ miles S of Burnmouth, and the railway which skirts the bases of the two hills is usually in sight from seaward. Otherwise the background is generally bare and featureless. The Scotland-England border lies midway between Burnmouth and Berwick.

Rescue
5.37

1   There are Coastguard Rescue Teams at St Abb's, Eyemouth and Berwick. See 1.53.

All-weather lifeboats are stationed at Eyemouth and at Berwick; inshore lifeboats are stationed at Berwick and St Abb's. See 1.61 and 1.62 for details of lifeboats.

Tidal stream
5.38

1   The tidal stream is given on the chart and in the *Admiralty Tidal Stream Atlas: North Sea, Northwestern Part.*

Principal marks
5.39

1   **Landmarks:**
Mast (radio/TV) (55°50′N, 2°05′W).
Berwick Town Hall (spire) (55°46′·2N, 2°00′·1W).
Berwick Lighthouse (white round stone tower, red cupola and base, 13 m in height) (55°45′·9N, 1°59′·0W).
Chimney (55°45′·6N, 1°59′·5W).

2   **Major lights:**
Saint Abb's Head Light (55°55′N, 2°08′W) (5.10).
Longstone Light (55°39′N, 1°36′W) (5.92).

Other navigational aids
5.40

1   **Racon:**
Saint Abb's Head Light (55°55′N, 2°08′W).
DGPS:
Girdle Ness Light (57°08′N, 2°03′W).

Directions
(continued from 5.14)

5.41

1   From a position NE of Saint Abb's Head (55°55′N, 2°08′W) the coastal route leads 12 miles SSE to a position E of Berwick Lighthouse, passing (with positions from Berwick Lighthouse):

ENE of Gunsgreen Point (7½ miles NNW), fringed by rocky ledges, which is 3 cables ESE of Hare Point and the S entry point of the small bay with Eyemouth at its head, thence:

2   ENE of Ross Carrs (5½ miles NNW), two rocks which dry and lie 6 cables N of Burnmouth Harbour, thence:

ENE of South Carr (5 miles NNW), a rock which lies to the E of Burnmouth Harbour, thence:

3   ENE of Seal Carr (1¼ miles NNW), a below water ledge extending 2½ cables NE of Shaper's Head, thence:

ENE of Berwick Lighthouse (55°45′·9N, 1°59′·0W) (5.39).

5.42

1   **Clearing bearing.** The alignment (185°) of Borewell Chimney (55°44′·4N, 1°58′·5W) with Inlandpasture Chimney, 2½ cables S, passes E of Seal Carr and three similar ledges SSE of Seal Carr. Berwick Light is obscured over these dangers when bearing less than 201°.

(Directions continue at 5.94)

Eyemouth

Chart 1612 plan of Eyemouth Harbour

General information

5.43

1   **Position.** Eyemouth (55°52′N, 2°05′W) stands on low ground on the W side of the River Eye 3 miles SSE of Saint Abb's Head. The harbour is on the E side of the town in the SE corner of the bay which fronts the town and lies between Hare Point and Gunsgreen Point.

5.44

1   **Function.** Eyemouth Harbour is the base for a small fishing fleet and fish are also processed. Berthing for vessels other than the fishing fleet is limited. The population in 1991 was 3473.

5.45

1   **Approach and entry.** The harbour is approached from the N across the bay and thence by an entrance channel, 18 m wide and 300 m long. The entrance is protected by East and West Breakwaters.

5.46

1   **Port authority.** Eyemouth Harbour Trust, 2 Church St, Eyemouth. TD14 5DH.

Limiting conditions

5.47

1   **Controlling depths.** The harbour approaches, entrance channel and Gunsgreen Basin were dredged to 3·0 m (1998). The inner harbour is maintained to a depth of 0·9 m at LW springs and 2·4 m at LW neaps.

Tidal levels see *Admiralty Tide Tables.*

5.48

1   **Largest vessel.** Vessels up to 4·6 m draught can enter the harbour at HW springs.

5.49

1   **Local weather.** While there is some protection given from the N and E by a group of rocks, the Hurkars (5.54),

Eyemouth should not be attempted in strong winds from these directions as the bay is a mass of broken water.

Arrival information

5.50

1   An **anchorage**, shown on the chart, is available in depths of 5 m in the bay to the SW of the Hurkars.

5.51

1   **Pilotage** is not compulsory. The pilot boards from an open fishing boat. Vessels requiring a pilot should contact the Harbour Office during working hours or otherwise the Forth Coastguard on VHF R/T.

Harbour

5.52

1   **Layout.** The outer harbour consists of Gunsgreen Basin, a tidal basin for large fishing vessels, which lies on the E side of the harbour at Gunsgreen Point. The basin, 185 m long and 60 m wide, has 230 m of quayside berthing.

2   The inner harbour is a long, thin tidal basin lying NNE/SSW. The main berthing is on the W side at Saltgreens Quay, 244 m in length, with Gunsgreen Quay, 115 m in length, on the E side. The inner basin is protected against freshets by Middle Quay.

Eyemouth Harbour (5.52)

(Original dated 2000)

(Photograph - Air Images)

5.53

1   **Traffic signals.** A red light is exhibited from the E end of the promenade when it is considered unsafe to enter either the bay or the harbour.

Directions

5.54

1   **Leading lights:**

Front light (orange column, 4 m in height) (55°52′·5N, 2°05′·2W).

Rear light (orange column, 6 m in height) (55 m S of front light).

2   **Northern approach.** From a position N of Hare Point (55°52′·7N, 2°05′·4W) the alignment (174°) of these lights standing on West Breakwater leads to the harbour entrance, passing (with positions from front light):

W of a light-buoy (N cardinal) (3¼ cables N), marking the N extremity of the Hurkars, a group of dark rugged rocks which dry, extending 2 cables S of the light-buoy; thence:

| Hurkars | Luff Hard Rock | Hare Point |

Approaches to Eyemouth from N (5.54)

(Original dated 2000)

(Photograph - Air Images)

3   E of Luff Hard Rock (2½ cables N), an above water rock which lies off Hare Point, thence:

W of Hinkar (2½ cables NNE), an above water rock lying in the centre of the Hurkars, thence:

Close W of Inner Buss (2 cables N), a small underwater rock, thence:

4   To the harbour entrance channel, which is 15 m wide and lies between West and East Breakwaters, on which stand lights (West Breakwater, front leading light; East Breakwater, white mast 5 m in height). Within the breakwaters, the W side of the channel is marked by a light-beacon; on the E side is the quay forming the W side of Gunsgreen Basin. A light-beacon at the head of the quay marks the entrance to the basin.

5.55

1   **Eastern approach.** From a position ENE of Gunsgreen Point (55°52′·5N, 2°04′·9W), the route leads WSW thence S on the alignment (174°) of the leading lights (5.54), passing (with positions from front leading light):

NNW of Gunsgreen Point (1½ cables ENE) (5.41), thence:

2   SSE of the Hurkars (2½ cables NNE) (5.54), thence:

NNW and W of Hettle Scar (1 cable NE), a drying reef off the NW edge of the rocky ledges fronting Gunsgreen Point, thence:

To the harbour entrance channel (5.54) on the alignment (174°) of the leading lights.

Port services

5.56

1   **Repairs.** There is a slipway at the head of the basin and cradle for vessels up to 21 m in length and draught 2 m. Engine repairs can be carried out.

5.57

1   **Other facilities:** hospital at Berwick-upon-Tweed; ice plant.

5.58

1   **Supplies:** marine diesel at Gunsgreen Basin and by road tanker at other berths; fresh water at Gunsgreen Basin, Saltgreens Quay and Middle Quay; provisions.

Berwick-upon-Tweed

Chart 1612 plan of Berwick Harbour
General information
5.59

1   **Position.** Berwick-upon-Tweed (55°46′N, 2°00′W) stands on the N side of the mouth of the River Tweed. Tweedmouth and Spittal lie on the S side of the entrance.

5.60

1   **Function.** The harbour is a small commercial and fishing port. The population in 1991 was 13 544.

5.61

1   **Topography.** The harbour is formed by the sea reach of the River Tweed. The river has a large catchment basin and runs generally E for 96 miles. It rises at an elevation of 457 m, falling rapidly at first but at less than 0·6 m a mile for its last 8 miles. The harbour lies between a breakwater on the N side and a drying sandy spit extending from Spittal Point on the S side. The spit serves as a natural breakwater. To the N of the breakwater the coast is fringed by ledges and the ground is foul for a distance of 4 cables offshore. Between the E extremity of the sandy spit, Sandstell Point, and the head of the breakwater there is a bar composed of sand and rocky boulders.

5.62

1   **Port authority.** Berwick Harbour Commission, Harbour Master's Office, Tweed Dock, Tweedmouth, Berwick-upon-Tweed. TD15 2AB.

5.63

1   **Traffic.** In 1999 the port was used by 114 vessels totalling 157 542 dwt.

Limiting conditions
5.64
1   **Controlling depths.** The depth at the bar is 0·6 m. There are depths of between 5·8 m and 6·4 m over the sill of Tweed Dock at HW springs.

   Tidal levels: see *Admiralty Tide Tables.* Mean spring range about 4·1 m; mean neap range about 2·2 m.

   Deepest berth. Tweed Dock (5.77).
5.65
1   **Largest vessel** handled is length 115 m with a bow thruster otherwise 68 m, beam 16·5 m and draught 4·6 m at HW springs and 3·9 m at HW neaps.

Arrival information
5.66
1   **Notice of ETA** should be sent to the Harbour Office during working hours at least 1 hour in advance. Larger vessels for this port should confirm length, beam and draught prior to arrival.
5.67
1   An **anchorage** in depths of 13 to 15 m can be found on the alignment (294°) of Breakwater Lighthouse with Berwick Town Hall (5.72) spire 7 cables ESE of the lighthouse. The anchorage is indicated on the chart.

   In strong E winds it might be possible to enter Holy Island Harbour (5.103) when entry into Berwick is impracticable. In strong W winds anchoring in Berwick Bay with its better holding ground is to be preferred.
5.68
1   **Pilotage** is compulsory. If vessels are expected, the pilot boat monitors VHF from 3 hours before HW to HW, which is the only time pilotage is normally carried out. Weather permitting the pilot boards 5 cables outside the breakwater. See the relevant *Admiralty List of Radio Signals.*
5.69
1   **Local knowledge.** The sandbank off Spittal Point (5.61) is liable to much alteration and considerable shoaling may take place in the entrance to the harbour and in the Tweed Dock (5.77) area, especially after W gales. Due to these frequent changes local knowledge is essential.

Harbour
5.70
1   **Layout.** The mouth of the River Tweed, which forms the harbour, is U-shaped, leading from S through E to N before finally entering the sea on an E heading. There are riverside berths at the base of the U and at Tweed Dock (5.77) which lies 4 cables further upstream.
5.71
1   **Tidal streams** to the E of the harbour entrance are given on chart 160. Within the river the in-going stream commences HW Tyne +0515 and the out-going stream at HW Tyne −0100. Spring rates in both directions are fairly strong. During freshets the durations and rates of the out-going streams are increased and the in-going streams correspondingly reduced. The bed of the River Tweed may be strewn with large stones brought down by freshets.

2   An indraught into Berwick Bay has been reported after strong E winds.

   Caution. It is considered dangerous to enter or leave harbour during the period of the out-going stream, particularly during freshets.
5.72
1   **Principal marks:**
     Town Hall (spire) (55°46'·2N, 2°00'·1W).
     Berwick Lighthouse (55°45'·9N, 1°59'·0W) (5.39).
     Saint Mary's Church (spire (55°46'·4N, 2°00'·4W).
     Presbyterian Church (spire) (55°46'·3N, 2°00'·0W).

Directions
5.73
1   **Outer approaches.** From a position in the vicinity of 55°45'·5N, 1°56'·0W (chart 160) the track leads to the harbour entrance on the line of bearing 281° of Berwick Lighthouse.

2   **Caution.** Vessels approaching from the N are advised to keep to seaward of the 20 m depth contour until S of the line of bearing 270° of Berwick Lighthouse. For vessels approaching from the S see 5.95.

Bridges

Spittal Point

Approaches to Berwick-upon-Tweed from SE (5.73)

(Original dated 2000)

(Photograph - Air Images)

5.74

1   **Berwick Lighthouse to Crabwater Rock.** From the harbour entrance, the channel which is about 100 m wide, leads W for a distance of 2½ cables, passing (with positions from Berwick Light):

> S of Berwick Light and the breakwater itself which lies along the N side of the channel, thence:

2   > N of the drying spit which has Sandstell Point (1 cable SSW) as its E extremity. The bar (5.64) lies between Sandstell Point and the E end of the breakwater. Thence:

> S of Crabwater Rock (2·7 cables WNW), awash, lying close W of the elbow of the breakwater which is marked by a light structure.

5.75

1   **Crabwater Rock to Spittal. Leading Lights:**

> Front light (orange triangle point down, orange mast, black bands, 4 m in height) (55°45'·7N, 1°59'·7W).
> Rear light (similar structure, 12 m in height) (55m SSW of front light).

2   From a position in mid channel, SW of Crabwater Rock, the alignment (207°) of these lights leads SSW in the channel, passing (with positions from front light):

> ESE of Calot Shad (1½ cables N), a bank of sand and stones which dries, and extends from the S side of Berwick nearly across the harbour, marked on its E and S sides by two light-buoys (both starboard hand), thence:

3   > WNW of Spittal Point (1·4 cables ENE), from whence there is a clear approach to Stoneberth and Carr Rock Jetty, 1½ cables WSW.

5.76

1   **Spittal to Tweed Dock.** From a position in mid channel N of the berths at Spittal, the channel runs NNW for a distance of 2½ cables to Tweed Dock, passing (with positions from Tweed Dock entrance):

> WSW of the buoy (starboard hand) (2¼ cables SE) marking the SW corner of Calot Shad (5.75), thence:

2   > To the entrance to Tweed Dock, which is entered between a docking pier on the S side and a groyne on the N side. The entrance to the dock is 17·5 m wide. The dock is tidal. A light-buoy (special, conical) is moored on the W side of Calot Shad and marks the swinging area limit E of Tweed Dock entrance. This buoy might be moved as necessary.

Berths

5.77

1   There is a riverside berth at Spittal.

Tweed Dock has 457 m of quays available, providing 5 berths. Depths in the docks vary between 6·4 m at spring tides and 4·9 m at neap tides.

Port services

5.78

1   **Repairs:** minor repairs to the hull; major engine repairs; slip.

5.79

1   **Other facilities:** hospital; helicopter landing site close E of the coastguard station; deratting exemption certificates issued; customs; boat landing Salmon Jetty (E bank, close S of Berwick Bridge).

5.80

1   **Supplies:** marine diesel by road tanker; water at the quays; provisions.

Small craft

5.81

1   There is a slipway for launching small craft on the W side of Carr Rock Jetty (5.75), and a maintenance area with water and electricity near the Harbour Office.

Small craft harbours, anchorage and boat landing

Chart 160
Saint Abb's Boat Harbour
5.82

1   **General information.** Saint Abb's Boat Harbour (55°54'N, 2°08'W) is 1¼ miles S of Saint Abb's Head. The entrance, 6 m wide, faces N and lies between piers, which together with a central jetty form an outer and inner harbour. There are depths in places of 2 m in the outer harbour. The inner harbour dries.

2   **Directions.** From a position close E of Maw Carr (150 m NNW of the entrance), a reddish rock with vertical sides, the alignment of the leading lights within the harbour leads to harbour entrance:

> Front light (post, 2 m high, on head of jetty) (55°53'·9N, 2°07'·6W).
> Rear light (mast, 5 m high, SW corner of outer harbour). A number of rocky ledges lie to the NE and E of the harbour.

Burnmouth Harbour
5.83

1   **General information.** Burnmouth (55°50'N, 2°04'W) is a fishing village at the mouth of a deep ravine. The small harbour, which dries, is formed by a pier at the inner end of an opening in the rocks, and is well protected.

2   **Directions.** The alignment (WSW) of the leading lights on the shore close by old coastguard houses and church leads to a position NNE of the harbour, which opens up the entrance, whence the track leads SSW to the harbour:

> Front leading light (white post, 2 m in height) (55°50'·6N, 2°04'·1W).
> Rear leading light (white post, 2 m in height) (45 m from front light).

Anchorage
5.84

1   An **anchorage** at a position shown on the chart might be obtained in Coldingham Bay (55°54'N, 2°08'W) 4 cables S of Saint Abb's Boat Harbour (5.82). The bay is generally foul and the anchorage rarely used except in the summer during offshore winds.

Boat landing
5.85

1   Boat landing can be made in Marshall Meadows Bay (55°48'N, 2°02'W).

Other names

5.86

1   Ebb Carrs (55°54'N, 2°07'W), a rock.
Yellow Craig (55°53'N, 2°07'W).

BERWICK-UPON-TWEED TO NORTH SUNDERLAND, INCLUDING FARNE ISLANDS

General information

Chart 111

Route

5.87

1   The coastal route from a position ENE of Berwick-upon-Tweed (55°46′N, 2°00′W) runs 14 miles SE to a position E of Longstone, the E point of the Farne Islands, thence 4 miles SSE to a position E of North Sunderland. Alternative inshore routes either through or to the W of the Farne Islands are also described.

Topography

5.88

1   The coast between Berwick-upon-Tweed and Snook (5.94), the point 4 cables SE of the entrance to North Sunderland, is the most dangerous in NE England, N of the River Humber. Numerous dangers front this part of the coast, with the Farne Islands and associated shoals extending 4½ miles NE of Snook. These dangers, with the exception of Spittal Hirst (55°46′N, 1°51′W), lie within the 20 m depth contour.

2   Berwick Bay lies between Spittal Point (55°46′N, 1°59′W) and Snipe Point, 8 miles to the SE, the N extremity of Holy Island. Initially the coast of the bay is sandy but it is then fronted by a narrow rocky ledge extending as far as Cheswick, 3½ miles SE of Spittal Point.

The central part of this ledge is backed in by cliffs about 30 m high. SE of Cheswick there are low sand dunes fronted by sands which broaden out from the coast and eventually meet Holy Island at Snipe Point, 5 miles ESE of Cheswick, forming Goswick Sands and Sand Ridge. To the W and S of Holy Island lie extensive tracts of drying sands, Holy Island Sands and Fenham Flats. The sands are intersected at LW by rivulets which connect to the sea and are passable on foot in many places at LW. Holy Island is based on limestone rock and is a moderately elevated plain, sloping SW with scarcely a tree or shrub upon it. A causeway crosses a tract of sand 7 cables wide and connects the shore at Beal Point with The Snook, a long narrow ridge of sandhills extending W from the main part of Holy Island.

3   South of Holy Island the coast runs 7 miles SE to Snook off North Sunderland. It is generally sandy, fringed by rocks in places and in the S backed by low undulating country. Budle Bay lies between Ross Links, a sandy ridge, at the N end of this stretch of coast and Budle Point, 4 miles NW of Snook. Warnham Flats, which dry, occupy the greater part of Budle Bay.

4   The Farne Islands, a chain of rocky islets, reefs and shoals are divided by Farne Sound and Staple Sound (5.102). Farne Island (5.99) itself (55°37′N, 1°39′W), the innermost island, lies 2¼ miles E of Black Rocks Point and is separated from the mainland by Inner Sound (5.99). Due to the considerable tidal range, about 4·5 m, the islands present very different aspects at HW and LW. The islands are owned by the National Trust and are a bird sanctuary.

Steel End

Castle   *Castle Point*

Holy Island from ESE (5.88.1)

(Original dated 2000)

(Photograph - Air Images)

Farne Island Lighthouse   *E Wideopen*

Farne Islands from SW (5.88.2)

(Original dated 2000)

(Photograph - Air Images)

Rescue
5.89
1   There are Coastguard Rescue Teams at Cheswick, at Holy Island village and at Seahouses on the SW side of North Sunderland harbour; see 1.53.

An all-weather lifeboat and an inshore lifeboat are stationed at North Sunderland. See 1.61 and 1.62 for details of lifeboats.

Natural conditions
5.90
1   **Tidal streams.** Offshore streams are regular and rarely exceed 1 kn at springs. They are given on the chart and in *Admiralty Tidal Stream Atlas: North Sea, Northwestern Part.*

2   The streams are strong near the Farne Islands and at a position 1 mile NE of Longstone (5.94) spring rates are 3½ to 4 kn, decreasing seaward. There is turbulence over Knivestone and Whirl Rocks which lie to the NE of Longstone. Within Inner Sound (5.99) the spring rate in each direction is 2½ kn.
5.91
1   **Current.** A weak current runs S off the coast. Strong and continued NW and N winds increase its rate and the current may be strong enough to affect navigation. Conversely SE and S winds reduce its rate and if prolonged may reverse its direction.

Principal marks
5.92
1   **Landmarks:**
   Tower (55°42′N, 1°54′W) at Goswick Links.
   Holy Island Castle (55°40′N, 1°47′W), surmounted by a flagstaff and standing on a rocky hill.
   Bamburgh Castle (55°37′N, 1°42′W), standing on a high rock rising abruptly from a flat beach. Its principal tower is square with a turret.
2   Longstone Lighthouse (red tower, white band, 26 m in height) (55°39′N, 1°36′W).
   Tower (55°38′N, 1°37′W) on Staple Island.
   Tower (2½ cables N of Staple Island Tower) on Brownsman Islet.
   Farne Island Lighthouse (white round tower, 13 m in height) (55°37′N, 1°39′W).

Longstone Lighthouse from N (5.92)

(Original dated 2000)

(Photograph - Air Images)

3   **Major Lights:**
   Saint Abb's Head Light (55°55′N, 2°08′W) (5.10).
   Black Rocks Point Light (white building, 9 m in height) (55°37′N, 1°43′W).
   Longstone Light (above).

Other navigational aid
5.93
1   **DGPS:**
   Girdle Ness Light (57°08′N, 2°03′W).

Directions
(continued from 5.41)

Coastal Route
5.94
1   From the vicinity of 55°46′N, 1°51′W to the E of Berwick-upon-Tweed, the coastal route leads 12 miles SE to a position E of Longstone, thence 5 miles S to a position E of North Sunderland, passing (with positions from Emmanuel Head Beacon (15 m in height) (55°41′N, 1°47′W)):
2   Clear of Spittal Hirst (55°45′·7N, 1°51′·1W) (5.3), thence:
   NE of Outer Tours (3½ miles NNW), thence:
   NE of Tours and Park Dyke (2 miles NW), two rocky shoals lying within 3 cables of each other, thence:

3   NE of Emmanuel Head, a cliff 3 m high surmounted by a beacon at the NE extremity of Holy Island, thence:

Emmanuel Head Beacon (5.94)

(Original dated 2000)

(Photograph - Air Images)

4   NE of Goldstone (2 miles ESE), a rock which dries, marked by a buoy (starboard hand) on its W side. Stiel Reef extends 1¼ cables ESE of Goldstone, and Saint Nicholas Rock, on which the sea breaks heavily, lies 3 cables NW. Less water than charted has been reported (1999) to exist in the area close E of Stiel Reef. Thence:

5   NE of Whirl Rocks (55°39′N, 1°36′W), lying 6 cables NE of Longstone. The island, on which stands a lighthouse (5.92), is the outermost of the Farne Islands. At LW Longstone appears as one island, but at HW it is divided into several parts. The sea breaks over Whirl Rocks.

6   The route continues S, passing (with positions from Longstone Lighthouse (55°39′N, 1°36′W) (5.92)):

        E of Whirl Rocks, thence:

        E of Crumstone (1 mile SSE), a flat black rock 1 mile S of Longstone. Callers, a reef, extends 2½ cables WNW of Crumstone and is part of the bank surrounding the latter, thence:

7   To a position NE of Grimstone (4 miles SSW), a rock which dries lying 2 cables E of Snook. Snook is a cliff 9 m high, 5 cables SE of North Sunderland Lighthouse (5.97) and the entrance to the harbour. The point has an extensive foreshore of parallel ledges dipping S. The Falls, a continuation of the ledges to the SE of Snook and 2 cables SSE of Grimstone, are marked by a buoy (port hand) 3 cables to the E.

8   The Farne Islands and the dangers surrounding them are covered by the red sector of Farne Light (119°–280°) (5.92) and by a red sector of Black Rocks Point Light (238°–275°) (5.92).

9   **Caution.** The area E of Longstone (55°39′N, 1°36′W) is a focal point for shipping. Whirl Rocks extend to its NE and Crumstone, which is not lit, lies 1 mile SSE. Whirl Rocks are steep-to and there are depths of 45 to 55 m within a mile. In poor visibility or at night therefore vessels should not attempt to pass E of Longstone in depths of less

than 65 m which occur 3 miles E of the islet and due allowance should be made for the tidal stream.

5.95

1   **Clearing bearing.** The alignment (162°) of the beacon on Emmanuel Head (5.94) with Newton Hill summit 4½ miles SSE of the beacon passes E of Spittal Hirst and the dangers which lie SE of Spittal Hirst in Berwick Bay (5.88).

Useful mark
5.96

1   The Cheviot (55°29′N, 2°09′W), marked by a large cairn (Chart 1192).

        (Directions for North Sunderland are given at 5.113, and for coastal passage S at 5.139)

Inshore route via Inner Sound
5.97

1   From a position ENE of Park Dyke (55°43′N, 1°49′W), the alignment (162¼°) of Megstone (black rock, 5 m high) (55°38′N, 1°40′W) with North Sunderland Lighthouse (white tower, 8 m high) (2¾ miles SSE of Megstone) leads 4½ miles SSE to a position ENE of Tree o'the House and E of the dangers which lie to the E of Holy Island, passing (with positions from Megstone):

2   ENE of Saint Nicholas Rock (3½ miles NNW) (5.94), thence:

        ENE of Goldstone (3 miles NNW) (5.94), thence:

        ENE of Guzzard (2½ miles NNW), a shoal, thence:

        To a position ENE of Tree o'the House (2 miles NNW).

        The dangers above are covered by a red sector of Black Rocks Point Light (175°–191°).

5.98

1   From a position ENE of Tree o'the House the alignment (206°) of Black Rocks Point Lighthouse (5.92) with the right hand edge of a prominent clump of trees (not charted) leads 1½ miles SSW until Holy Island Castle (5.92) bears 312°, or at night Farne Island Light (5.92) shows white bearing 119°, passing:

2   WNW of Oxscar, also known as South Goldstone (4½ cables NE), a rock which dries, thence:

        WNW of Megstone (5.97), thence:

        To a position WNW of Swedman (4 cables W), a drying reef which is marked by a buoy (starboard hand) moored 4½ cables to the W.

5.99

1   The bearing 312° (astern) of Holy Island Castle leads 3½ miles SE through Inner Sound, passing:

        NE of Black Rocks Point Lighthouse (2 miles WSW) (5.92), thence:

        SW of Swedman (4 cables W) (5.98), thence:

        NE of Islestone (1¼ miles SSW) a rocky reef which dries, covered by a green sector (289°–300°) of Black Rocks Point Light, thence:

2   SW of Farne Island (1 mile SE), the SW of the inner group of islands and the highest which is covered with grass. A bold cliff of columnar basalt, 8 m high, stands on its SW side and slopes gradually to the NE. Farne Island Lighthouse (5.92) stands on the SE extremity of the island. Thence:

3   NE of Shoreston Outcars (2¼ miles SSE), a ledge of rocks which dries and is marked by a buoy (port hand) moored 3 cables to the NE of the ledge, thence:

        To a position NE of Grimstone (3¼ miles SSE) (5.94).

Goldstone Channel
5.100

1 As an alternative to the inshore route (5.97, 5.98) Goldstone Channel may be used. From a position ENE of Park Dyke (5°43′N, 1°49′W) (5.94) the alignment (171°) of Black Rocks Point Lighthouse (55°37′N, 1°43′W) (5.92) with a white house standing in front of trees (1½ miles S of the lighthouse) leads 5¼ miles through Goldstone Channel, passing (with positions from Black Rocks Point Lighthouse):

2   E of Emmanuel Head (4½ miles NNW) (5.94), thence:

    E of Outer Wingate (3¾ miles NNW) with Wingate, a group of rocks close SW. The sea breaks over Outer Wingate, thence:

    W of Saint Nicholas Rock (3½ miles N) (5.94), thence:

3   E of Plough Seat Reef (3½ miles NNW), which dries, marked on its E side by a light-buoy (port hand). Plough Rock, a drying rock 2 cables W of the reef, is marked on its W side by a buoy (W cardinal). Thence:

4   W of Goldstone (3¼ miles N) (5.94), thence:

    E of Ridge End (3¼ miles NNW), a patch of rock and stones marked by Ridge Buoy (E cardinal) at its E extremity, thence:

    W of Guzzard (2¾ miles N) (5.97), thence:

    E of Holy Island Harbour (3 miles NNW) (5.103), thence:

5   To a position W of Tree o'the House (2¼ miles N) (5.97).

A white sector (165°–175°) of Black Rocks Point Light leads through Goldstone Channel.

Caution. Goldstone Channel should only be used when the marks and lights can be seen readily, as the soundings are irregular and the tidal streams are strong.

(Directions for Holy Island Harbour are given at 5.125)

5.101

1 From a position W of Tree o'the House the bearing 324° (astern) of Emmanuel Head Beacon leads 1½ miles SE, until Holy Island Castle bears 312° or at night Farne Light shows white bearing 119°, passing:

    NE of Ross Links (3 miles WNW) (5.88), thence:

    NE of Budle Bay (2½ miles W) (5.88), whence the inshore route (5.99) is rejoined.

Staple Sound
5.102

1 **Caution.** The passage through Staple Sound, which separates the outer group of the Farne Islands from the inner group, is seldom used. The tidal stream is strong, with spring rates up to 4 kn, and there are no leading marks so that accurate fixing is essential. The track lies on the NE side of Staple Sound and not on the apparent mid-channel between Staple Island (55°38′N, 1°37′W) and the islets NE of Farne Island.

2 From the vicinity of 55°39′N, 1°40′W, the route is 5 miles SE through Staple Sound, passing (with positions from the tower on Staple Island (5.92)):

    NE of Oxscar (1½ miles W) (5.98), thence:

    NE of Glororum Shad (1 mile WNW). N of this shoal depths are irregular, thence:

    SW of North Wamses and South Wamses (5 cables NNW), two rocky islets, thence:

3   NE of Islestone Shad (7 cables E), a rocky patch over which the sea breaks in bad weather, thence:

    SW of Gun Rocks (2 cables WNW) which dry 3·6m. They lie at the extremity of the reef running NW from the S point of Staple Island, thence:

4   NE of Knocks Reef (7 cables SW), which dries and extends 6 cables ENE of Farne Island. An islet and rock lie on its SW side, thence:

    SW of Staple Island, with a conspicuous tower (5.92). The S side of the island is a bold cliff with Pinnacles, detached steep-to rocks resembling broken pillars, lying close E. The island swarms with birds. Thence:

5   NE of the Bush (8 cables SSW), a rocky ledge which dries and lies E of the islets of East Wideopen and West Wideopen, thence:

    SW of Fang (8 cables ESE), a spit extending S from Crumstone (5.94) and clear of Staple Sound, rejoining the coastal route (5.94).

Holy Island Harbour

Chart 1612 plan of Holy Island Harbour

General information
5.103

1 **Position.** Holy Island Harbour (55°40′N, 1°48′W) is on the S side of Holy Island.

5.104

1 **Function.** The harbour is small although it appears large at HW. It is secure and sheltered and has proved useful as a port of refuge. During E winds, when it is impracticable to enter Berwick Harbour (5.67), it might be possible to use Holy Island Harbour.

The population of Holy Island is about 150.

5.105

1 **Approach and Entry.** The harbour is approached from the SE of Holy Island and entered between Castle Point, fringed by rocks and fronted by off-lying dangers on the SE corner of Holy Island, and Guile Point, the N extremity of Old Law.

5.106

1 **Port authority.** The Harbour Master, Falkland House, Holy Island.

Limiting conditions
5.107

1 **Controlling depths.** The minimum depth at the Bar is 2 m. However the Nob, a stony patch with a depth of 1·6 m over it, lies close N of the white sector (262°–264°) of Old Law East Light-beacon (5.113).

Arrival information
5.108

1 An **anchorage** is available in depths of 8 m, 4½ cables E of Castle Point (5.105) or in Skate Road (chart 111) 1½ miles SE of Holy Island Castle (5.92). Both anchorages are exposed.

2 Hole Mouth (55°40′N, 1°47′W), a small opening between Castle Point and Ridge End (5.100) has depths of 2 m to 3 m in it and has been used as a haven by small craft driven too close inshore to weather Ridge End.

5.109

1 **Pilotage** is not available.

Harbour
5.110

1 **Layout.** There are no alongside berths apart from a jetty 60 m long at Steel End (55°40′·1N, 1°47′·6W), which is used to land fish. There is a slipway equipped with an electric winch 2 cables W of the jetty.

Within the harbour an anchorage may be found in depths of between 5 m and 7 m, bottom sand.

5.111

1 **Tidal streams** run strongly into and out of Holy Island Harbour as follows:

Time from HW Tyne	Remarks
+0510 Tyne	W-going stream begins
−0045 Tyne	E-going stream begins

2 The sands between the W extremity of Holy Island, Snook Point, and the nearest point of the mainland, Beal Point (5.88), are only covered for about 3 hours at springs, between −0215 and +0045 HW Tyne, and scarcely at all at neaps. Throughout this period there is a SE-going stream off the coast, but in the harbour initially there is a W-going stream and then an E-going stream. When the sands are covered the W-going stream from the harbour runs across the sands, turns E along the N coast of the island and then joins the SE-going stream off the coast. When there is an E-going stream in the harbour, the SE-going coastal stream runs across the sands and joins the E-going harbour stream.

5.112

1 **Principal marks:**

Holy Island Castle (55°40′N, 1°47′W) (5.92).

Ruined chapel (55°40′·1N, 1°48′·3W) standing on the summit of Saint Cuthbert's Islet.

Directions

(continued from 5.96)

5.113

1 From a position in mid Goldstone Channel and ESE of Castle Point the white sector (262°−264°) of Old Law East Light-beacon (stone obelisk, 21 m in height) (55°39′·5N, 1°47′·5W) leads to the harbour entrance, passing (with positions from the light):

Old Law Beacons (5.113)

(Original dated 2000)

(Photograph - Air Images)

2 S of Plough Seat Reef (1½ miles ENE) (5.100), thence:

S of Ridge Buoy (E cardinal) (9 cables ENE), marking Ridge End (5.100), thence:

S of Triton Shoal (6 cables ENE), composed of large stones covered in kelp. It is marked on its SW corner by a buoy (starboard hand) moored close NNE of the Nob (5.107), thence:

3 N of Parton Stiel (5 cables ESE), a stony patch. The Bar lies between Triton Shoal and Parton Stiel. The bottom is chiefly of stones covered with kelp and patches of sand in between.

5.114

1 **Inner leading marks:**

Heugh Light-beacon (black triangle apex up, on framework tower, 8 m in height) (55°40′·1N, 1°47′·9W) standing on Heugh Hill, a dark cliff 14 m high.

Saint Mary's Church belfry (200 m W of Heugh Beacon).

2 From a position close W of the Bar the alignment of these marks (310°), or at night, the white sector of Heugh Light-beacon (308°−311°) leads through Burrow Hole, the inner channel, to the inner anchorage (5.108), passing (with positions from Heugh Beacon):

NE of Black Law (4½ cables SSE), an islet covered in grass, and:

3 SW of Stone Ridge (5 cables ESE), composed of large stones running W from Ridge End (5.100), thence:

NE of Seal Spit (4 cables SE), the N extremity of the bank surrounding Black Law, thence:

4 SW of Wheel Shoal (3 cables ESE), the W extremity of Stone Ridge, thence:

To the inner anchorage in the deeper water SE of Heugh Hill.

Caution. The channel is narrow and it is necessary to adjust from the outer to the inner marks quickly.

Supplies

5.115

1 Limited supplies of fresh water and provisions.

North Sunderland Harbour

General information

Chart 1612 plan of North Sunderland Harbour

5.116

1 **Position.** North Sunderland Harbour (55°35′N, 1°39′W) lies 5 cables NW of Snook. Seahouses village stands on the SW side of the harbour and the town of North Sunderland is 5 cables inland.

5.117

1 **Function.** The harbour is used only for fishing vessels which can lie aground.

5.118

1 **Port authority.** North Sunderland Harbour Commissioners, Seahouses, Northumberland.

Limiting conditions

5.119

1 **Controlling depths.** The Outer Harbour is dredged to 0·7 m above chart datum.

The Inner Harbour has depths of 4·0 m at HW springs and 2·8 m at HW neaps.

Tidal levels: see *Admiralty Tide Tables*. Mean spring range about 4·1 m; mean neap range about 2·1 m.

5.120

1 **Maximum size of vessel** handled is length 30·5 m and 2·75 m draught, at HW springs. Vessels smaller in length may enter with a maximum draught of 3·7 m.

Pilotage

5.121

1 Pilotage is not compulsory.

Harbour

5.122

1 **Layout.** The small artificial harbour is protected by a low-lying rocky headland to the SE, a detached breakwater to the NE and from the NW by Outer or North West Pier.

North Sunderland Harbour, Seahouses (5.122)

(Original dated 2000)

(Photograph - Air Images)

Middle Pier divides Outer Harbour from Inner Harbour. The latter lies at the inner end of the breakwater and has an entrance 18 m wide facing E.

5.123

1 **Traffic signals.** When it is dangerous to enter harbour the following signals are shown:

Position		Signal
By day	Flagstaff on North West Pier	Red flag over blue flag
By night	The main Lighthouse	Red light over green light

5.124

1 **Principal mark:**
> North Sunderland Lighthouse (55°35′N, 1°39′W) (5.97).

Directions

5.125

1 From a position NE of the harbour the route leads SW to a position NNW of the harbour, thence SSE to the harbour, passing (with positions from North Sunderland Lighthouse):
> NE of Carr End (1·7 cables ENE), a drying rocky ledge which is steep-to and extends 1½ cables seaward of the breakwater. Southend Rock, 1 cable SE of Carr End, is the E extremity of this ledge, thence:

2
> To the harbour entrance, which is 61 m wide, facing N. The entrance lies between the heads of Outer Pier, on which stands North Sunderland Lighthouse (5.97), and the breakwater, with a light (metal tripod) at its NW extremity.

When approaching from the S the line of bearing 300° of Black Rocks Point Light (5.92), which is also the left hand limit of a green sector of the light, passes NE of Carr End and Southend Rock.

Port services

5.126

1 **Repairs** to fishing craft can be undertaken. There is a slipway but no carriage.

5.127

1 **Supplies:** marine diesel (light); lubricating oil; 10 tonne per day ice plant; limited fresh water; provisions.

Small craft

5.128

1 A marked channel leads from Outer Harbour to moorings in the SE of the harbour. There is a boatyard at the root of North West Pier and a slip onto the sandy beach close SE of the harbour.

Anchorages and boat landings

Chart 111

Anchorages

5.129

1 Apart from the anchorages associated with Holy Island (5.108) an anchorage may also be found in depths of 22 m, sand, 2 cables S of Staple Island (55°38′N, 1°37′W). This anchorage should only be used if absolutely necessary. Vessels approaching the anchorage from the NE can use the passage between Callers (55°38′N,1°36′W) (5.94) and Staple Island but only in an emergency. The alignment (242°) of Saint Cuthbert's Tower (55°37′N, 1°39′W), an old square tower on the NE side of Farne Island (5.99) with the large house in Glororum village (55°36′N, 1°44′W) leads through the passage.

2 In S winds a temporary anchorage might be obtained N of the Farne Island. However the bottom is rocky and the holding bad.

In fair weather there is an anchorage in 16 m, 3 cables SE of Farne Island (55°37′N,1°39′W) indicated on the chart.

3 There is an anchorage in favourable conditions for small craft in The Kettle (55°37′N,1°39′W), a natural basin on The N side of Farne Island. The anchorage is in 3·5 m, clean sand, good holding and is indicated on the chart. Vessels approaching this anchorage should do so on the alignment of Emmanuel Head Beacon (5.94) with the E extremity of Megstone (5.97).

Landings

5.130

1 There are landings at:
> Granary Point (55°40′N, 1°52′W) where, with local knowledge, small craft can take the ground safely.
> Warren Mill (55°36′N, 1°46′W) at the head of Warren Burn in the SW corner of Budle Bay (5.88).
> Warnham Bar, with a depth of 4 m at HW springs,

shifts occasionally and should not be attempted without local knowledge.

Farne Island (55°37′N, 1°39′W) (5.99) in the small bay at the NE end of the island.

Other Names

5.131

1   Beanstack (55°43′N, 1°51′W), a shoal.

Big Harcar (55°38′N, 1°37′W), an islet.

Blue Caps (55°38′N, 1°37′W), an islet.

Brada (55°38′N, 1°36′W), an islet.

Castlehead Rocks (55°41′N, 1°47′W).

Crafords Gut (55°38′N, 1°37′W), a passage.

2   Elbow (55°38′N, 1°40′W), a shoal.

False Emmanuel Head (55°41′N, 1°47′W).

Goswick Bay (55°43′N, 1°54′W).

Harkness Rocks (55°37′N, 1°43′W).

Inner Hirst (55°45′N, 1°52′W), a shoal.

Little Harcar (55°38′N, 1°37′W), an islet.

3   Long Batt (55°40′N, 1°48′W), a sand spit.

Minscore (55°41′N, 1°46′W), a shoal.

North Beanstack (55°43′N, 1°52′W), a shoal.

Northern Hares (55°39′N, 1°37′W), an islet.

North Tours (55°44′N, 1°51′W), a shoal.

Ross Low (55°37′N, 1°46′W), a rivulet.

South Low (55°40′N, 1°51′W), a rivulet.

NORTH SUNDERLAND TO COQUET ISLAND

General information

Chart 156

Route

5.132

1   From a position NE of North Sunderland (55°35′N, 1°39′W) the route leads 16 miles SSE to a position E of Coquet Island.

Topography

5.133

1   The coast is formed by a number of headlands with off-lying ledges and rocks extending up to 1 mile offshore. Between the headlands there are several sandy bays. The land backing the coast is generally grassy and rises to a moderate elevation with the rounded mass of The Cheviot (5.96), the highest point in the distance. Coquet Island, which is a bird reserve, owned by the Royal Society for the Protection of Birds, lies 1 mile ESE of Warkworth Harbour (5.143).

Depths

5.134

1   The 30 m depth contour runs parallel to the coast about 2½ miles offshore, but closes the land in the vicinity of Coquet Island. The island is 7 cables offshore and separated from the mainland by Coquet Channel. There are no dangers outside the 30 m depth contour but there are two off-lying rocky banks, Newton Skere and Craster Skeres (5.3), which are 6½ miles and 11 miles respectively SE of Longstone (55°39′N, 1°36′W) (5.94). The sea breaks heavily over these patches in bad weather.

Rescue

5.135

1   There are Coastguard Rescue Teams at Low Newton-by-the-Sea (55°31′N, 1°37′W), Craster (55°28′N, 1°35′W), Boulmer (55°25′N, 1°35′W) and Amble (55°20′N, 1°34′W); see 1.53.

An all-weather lifeboat is stationed at Amble; inshore lifeboats are stationed at Amble and Craster. See 1.61 and 1.62 for details of lifeboats.

Tidal streams

5.136

1   The tidal streams run in the direction of the coast and are of no great strength, except off salient points where there may be eddies. Tidal streams are given on the chart and in the *Admiralty Tidal Stream Atlas: North Sea, Northwestern Part*.

Principal marks:

5.137

1   **Landmarks:**

Hepburn Hill (55°31′N, 1°52′W) (chart 1192).

Heiferlaw (55°27′N, 1°45′W) (chart 1192).

Radar aerials (55°25′N, 1°46′W) (chart 1192).

Radio mast (55°23′N, 1°47′W), a framework tower (chart 1192).

2   Alnmouth Church (spire) (55°23′·3N, 1°35′·7W).

Warkworth Castle (55°21′N, 1°37′W), a conspicuous tower.

Coquet Lighthouse (white square tower, turreted parapet, lower half grey, 22 m in height) (55°20′N, 1°32′W).

3   **Major lights:**

Longstone Light (55°40′N, 1°37′W) (5.92).

Coquet Light (above).

Other navigational aids

5.138

1   **DGPS:**

Girdle Ness Light (57°08′N, 2°03′W).

Flamborough Head Light (54°07′N, 0°05′W).

Directions
(continued from 5.96)

5.139

1   From a position ENE of Grimstone (5.94), which lies 6 cables ENE of North Sunderland (55°35′N, 1°39′W), the coastal route leads 16 miles SSE to a position E of Coquet Island, passing (with positions from Castle Point (55°29′·5N, 1°35′·5W)):

2   ENE of Beadnell Point (3½ miles ENE), which is low and wedged shaped with strata that dips to the south. Red Brae, a dark low projecting cliff is 5 cables NW of the point.Thence:

3   ENE of Barnyard and Faggot (2½ miles N), two rocks marked by Newton Rock Buoy (port hand) lying 9½ cables NE of Snook Point. Beadnell Bay with sandy foul shores, lies between Snook Point and Beadnell Point. Thence:

ENE of Ice Carr (2 miles NNW) lying 2 cables NE of Newton Point, a rounded point, thence:

4   ENE of Castle Point, which has shelving black perpendicular pillars on its E and S sides. The ruins of Dunstanburgh Castle stand prominently on the N side of the point. Embleton Bay lies between Castle Point and a group of rocks 1¼ miles NNW of the point. The rocks run 5 cables to seaward with Fills, an extensive rocky patch, at their extremity. Thence:

5   ENE of Longhoughton Steel (4 miles S), where the coast is low and sandy, Thence:

ENE of Seaton Point (5 miles S), which is low, round and sandy. Between this point and Longhoughton

Steel to the N, the coast is fronted by a series of rocky ledges extending up to 6 cables offshore. Boulmer Stile, a rocky ledge, with Seaton Shad, a shoal extending 7 cables to its S, form the SE point of these ledges. Thence:

6 ENE of Alnmouth Bay (8 miles S). The bay lies between Seaton Point to the N and Coquet Island 4½ miles SSE of the point. Aln Harbour (5.163) lies at its N end and Warkworth Harbour (5.143) at the S end. The coast of the bay is mainly of sandhills, broken by a cliff at its midpoint at the foot of which is a rocky ledge, Birling Carrs. Thence:

7 To a position E of Coquet Island (55°20′N, 1°32′W) with a light on its SE side (5.137). Two detached shoals, Steel Bush with 1·2 m over it and North East Bush with 2·8 m over it, lie 2½ cables NNE of the island.

Light

Coquet Island from SE (5.139)

(Original dated 2000)

(Photograph - Air Images)

5.140

1 **Clearing bearings:**

The line of bearing 316° of Bamburgh Castle (5.92), open NE of Beadnell Point passes NE of Barnyard and Faggot (5.139) and the other dangers off Snook Point.

2 The alignment of Dunstanburgh Castle (5.139) with the coastguard house (55°31′N, 1°37′W) at Newton, passes NE of Boulmer Stile and Seaton Shad and the other dangers between Longhoughton Steel and Seaton Point.

3 The line of bearing 215° of Warkworth Castle, well open SE of Birling Carrs (5.139) passes SE of Boulmer Stile and Seaton Shad off Seaton Point, but inside Boulmer Stile buoy. These dangers are also covered by a red sector (163°–180°) of Coquet Light.

4 The clearing bearings for Boulmer Stile and Seaton Shad are intended for use by vessels working into Alnmouth Bay to avoid the strength of the tide. If the marks cannot be seen then vessels should keep in depths of not less than 37 m.

Chart 1627 plan of Warkworth Harbour
Coquet Channel
5.141

1 Coquet Island is separated from the mainland by Coquet Road (5.164) in the N and Coquet Channel in the S. The channel lies between Podler Ware Spit and the foul ground on the SW side of the island. It is only 1 cable wide and

has a least depth of 1·2 m. There are no navigation marks and local knowledge is required for passage through Coquet Channel.

Chart 156
Useful marks
5.142

1 Tank (55°35′N, 1°39′W).
Beadnell Church (spire) (55°33′N, 1°38′W) showing above woods W of Beadnell Point.
White house (55°20′·2N, 1°34′·2W).
Spire (55°20′N, 1°34′W).

(Directions continue for coastal passage SSE at 5.178)

Warkworth

Chart 1627, plan of Warkworth Harbour
General information
5.143

1 **Position.** Warkworth Harbour or Amble (55°20′N, 1°34′W) is situated at the mouth of the River Coquet, at the S end of Alnmouth Bay. The river is 27 miles long and after heavy rain is liable to flood, but at other times its volume is inconsiderable.

5.144

1 **Function.** Warkworth Harbour is a commercial port predominantly used by the fishing industry. There is also a marina. Warkworth village is 1½ miles NW of the port. With the exception of the name Warkworth, applied in accordance with an Act of Parliament, there is little connection with Warkworth village. Amble lies on the S bank of the entrance to the River Coquet and all business of the port is conducted there.

2 The population of Amble in 1993 was 5639.

5.145

1 **Approach and entry.** The harbour is approached from the NNE across Alnmouth Bay and entered through breakwaters which form the entrance.

5.146

1 **Port authority.** Warkworth Harbour Commissioners, Quayside, Amble. Office hours Monday to Friday VHF Channel 16 for Channel 14.

Limiting conditions
5.147

1 **Controlling depths.** The bar off the entrance to the harbour has varying depths of between 0·9 m and 1·8 m over it.

Within the harbour depths alongside the quays are just over 1 m.

Tidal levels: see *Admiralty Tide Tables*. Mean spring range about 4·2 m; mean neap range about 2·1 m.

5.148

1 **Maximum size of vessel handled.** Vessels up to 4·0 m draught can enter the harbour at HW.

5.149

1 **Local weather.** NE gales cause the most sea, when broken water extends from the harbour entrance to Coquet Island. When a swell is running a dangerous short sea builds up over Pan Bush, 4 cables ENE of the entrance. In these conditions small craft should not attempt to cross the shoal even at HW.

Arrival Information
5.150

1 **Notice of ETA.** 24 hours' notice is required for commercial vessels. Notice is not required for fishing vessels or recreational craft.

Warkworth Harbour, Amble (5.153)

(Original dated 2000)

(Photograph - Air Images)

5.151

1   **Pilotage** is available. The pilot normally boards in the anchorage (5.152), but if this is impossible due to heavy weather, or in an emergency, a vessel should enter the harbour and proceed to Broomhill Quay (5.158). Requests for pilots should be passed on VHF R/T unless previous arrangements have been made.

5.152

1   An **anchorage** with South Breakwater light bearing 200° in 9 m sand and mud, is available for vessels awaiting the tide to enter Warkworth Harbour. The anchorage position is indicated on the chart.

Harbour

5.153

1   **Layout.** The harbour is formed at the lower reach of the River Coquet by two outer breakwaters and within the breakwaters North and South Jetties which extend W into Broomhill Quay. Fish Dock lies between Broomhill Quay and Radcliffe Quay.

5.154

1   **Tidal streams** see (5.164). The S-going stream sets across the entrance.

5.155

1   **Principal marks:**

    Warkworth Castle (55°21′N, 1°37′W) (5.137).

    Coquet Lighthouse (55°20′N, 1°32′W) (5.137).

    White house (55°20′·2N, 1°34′·2W).

    Spire (55°20′N, 1°34′W).

    Water Tower (55°19′·6N,1°37′·5W) (Chart 156), which is mushroom shaped.

Directions

5.156

1   **Outer approach.** From a position in Alnmouth Bay to the NNE of the harbour entrance the line of bearing 190° of the spire (55°20′N, 1°34′W) leads to a position ENE of the entrance, passing (with positions from the spire):

2   Through the anchorage (1 mile NNE) (5.152), thence:

    W of Pan Bush (6½ cables NNE), a rocky shoal which lies at the N end of a rocky spit, thence:

    To a position close W of a wreck (4½ cables NNE).

5.157

1   **Harbour entrance.** From a position ENE of the harbour entrance and clear W of the wreck, the alignment (248°) of North Jetty with the water tower (5.155) leads through the entrance, passing (with positions from the entrance):

2   NNW of Pan Rocks (1 cable SE) extending 1½ cables NE of Pan Point, which is cliffy and lies E of South Breakwater. The rocks are marked close to their N extremity by a beacon which has toppled and is only visible from half tide. The rocks are crossed by an outfall marked at its seaward end by a light-buoy which is moored 2 cables E of the beacon. Thence:

3   To the harbour entrance, which is 68 m wide and lies between the heads of North and South Breakwaters, on which stand light towers, North (white metal framework tower, 8 m in height) and South (white round tower, red bands, white base, 8 m in height).

Berths

5.158

1   There is berthing available alongside South Jetty and Radcliffe Quay. Broomhill Quay is used by the fishing fleet. These jetties have depths alongside of 1 m. The total length of quays available is 610 m.

Port services

5.159

1   **Repairs.** Light repairs can be carried out. There is a boat building yard and a slipway.

5.160

1   **Supplies:** marine diesel; water at the berths on Broomhill Quay; provisions.

Small craft
5.161

1   Amble Marina, with pontoon berths and facilities for up to 250 boats, lies close W of Radcliffe Quay. Access to the marina is possible 4 hours either side of HW.

Amble Marina (5.161)

(Original dated 2000)

(Photograph - Air Images)

Minor harbours and anchorages

Chart 156
Craster Harbour
5.162

1   **General information.** Craster Harbour (55°28′N, 1°35′W) is formed by two piers, the N pier is 76 m long and the S pier 91 m long and marked by the base of a tower. There are depths of 4 m in the harbour at HW springs.

2   **Directions.** Little Carr and Great Carr are two drying ledges lying N and S of the harbour respectively. Little Carr is marked by a concrete beacon and the recommended track lies to the W of the beacon when entering harbour. Local knowledge is required.

Aln Harbour
5.163

1   **General information.** Aln Harbour (55°23′N, 1°37′W) is formed by the lower reach of the River Aln. It is little used except for a few fishing boats and recreational craft which lie aground at LW. Alnmouth village, with a conspicuous church spire, is on the N side of the harbour and Church Hill, 13 m high, on the S side.

   Depths at HW springs are 3·5 m both at the bar and in the harbour.

2   **Harbour.** Some protection is afforded to the harbour during N winds by the foul ground off Seaton Point (5.139), but in E gales there is a heavy sea. There is a considerable scend in the harbour but this is lessened if the sea breaks outside the bar. However the entrance is not considered as dangerous as those of some of the neighbouring harbours.

3   **Directions.** The channel is easiest after freshets, which occur in the winter, but the width of the channel and the position of the bar is constantly changing and local knowledge is required.

   An **anchorage**, as indicated on the chart, is available for vessels waiting the tide in a depth of 4 m, 8 cables ESE of Alnmouth Church on the alignment (198°) of Birling Carrs (5.139) with Warkworth Castle.

Alnmouth

Aln Harbour (5.163)

(Original dated 2000)

(Photograph - Air Images)

Coquet Road
Chart 1627 plan of Warkworth Harbour
5.164

1   **General information.** Coquet Road (55°20′N, 1°33′W) lies between Coquet Island and Coquet Flat, which extends 6 cables N of the island and the spit with Pan Bush at its N extremity. Both Pan Bush and Coquet Flat are covered by a red sectors of Coquet Light (5.137), which is on the SE side of the island. Coquet Road is sheltered from the SE, through S to NW, but is otherwise exposed and should only be used in an emergency. In particular a dangerous sea builds up over Pan Bush and the shoals to its N.

2   **Tidal streams.** In Coquet Road and Channel the S-going stream commences at –0515 HW Tyne and the N-going stream at +0045 HW Tyne. The stream is not strong in the road, but the S-going stream runs strongly across North Steel, a drying rocky ledge extending 2½ cables N of Coquet Island. In the channel the streams run strongly, in SE-NW direction when the rocks off Hauxley Point are dry, but more N-S when the rocks are covered.

3   **Directions.** From a position N of Coquet Road the alignment (179°) of Hauxley Point (55°19′N, 1°33′W) with the point 6 cables S of it leads between Pan Bush (5.156) and Coquet Flat into Coquet Road.

Small craft

Chart 156
Beadnell Harbour
5.165

1   Beadnell Harbour (55°33′N, 1°38′W), which lies on the SW side of Beadnell Point is a small harbour formed by two piers with an entrance between the piers 8 m wide. Local knowledge is required. There are depths of 2 m in the harbour at HW springs, bottom silt over rock except in the elbow of South Pier where sand accumulates. Beadnell Point affords good protection and there is little sea in the harbour other than in SE gales.

Newton Haven
5.166

1   Newton Haven (55°31′N, 1°37′W) is an opening in the rocks abreast the village of Low Newton-by-the-Sea. The haven is formed by Fills (5.139) and Emblestone, a drying rocky ledge, on its E and S sides with depths of 3·5 m. It is exposed to heavy seas during strong winds between N and ENE and should only be used with local knowledge.

Boulmer Haven
5.167
1 **General information.** Boulmer Haven (55°25′N, 1°35′W) is a clear area with depths of 1 m to 2 m among the rocks within the N part of Marmouth Scars, a rocky ledge off Seaton Point (5.139). The entrance, named The Marmouth, is 37 m wide and has depths of 2·1 m in it.

2 **Directions.** The alignment of the leading beacons close S of Boulmer village leads through The Marmouth to the Haven:

> Front beacon (red and white, white triangular topmark, 10 m in height) (55°24′·9N, 1°34′·9W).
>
> Rear beacon (red and white, topmark two red triangles points together, 11 m in height) (55 m W of front beacon).

Local knowledge is required by those using the harbour.

Fluke Hole
5.168
1 **General information.** Fluke Hole (55°24′N, 1°35′W) is a small bay between the S end of Marmouth Scars, off Seaton Point (5.139) and Marden Rocks which dry. Local knowledge is required.

An **anchorage** is available in depths of 6 m 5 cables SSE of Seaton Point. This anchorage is used by coasters on a temporary basis during N winds.

Other names

Charts 156, 1627 plan of Warkworth Harbour
5.169
1
> Boulmer Bush (55°25′·2N, 1°33′·7W), a rock.
> Cullernose Point (55°28′N, 1°35′W).
> Houghton Stile (55°25′·9N, 1°34′·2W), a ledge.
> Jenny Bell's Carr (55°30′·4N, 1°36′·4W), a drying rock.
> Out Carr (55°30′·6N, 1°36′·1W), a drying rock.

COQUET ISLAND TO BLYTH

General information

Chart 156
Route
5.170
1 From a position ENE of Coquet Island (55°20′N, 1°32′W) the route leads 14 miles SSE to a position SE of Blyth.

Topography
5.171
1 Hauxley Point, which is on the mainland 1 mile SW of Coquet Island, and its vicinity is fronted by drying rocky ledges extending up to 6 cables offshore. Bondicarr Bush, the extremity of the ledges and rocks, is 5 miles N of Snab Point. Druridge Bay, which lies between the two, has a low, sandy coast backed by moderately high land. From Snab Point to Newbiggin Point (5.178), 3 miles SSE, the coast is low and sandy and fronted by occasional rocky ledges. Between Newbiggin Point and Link End (5.178) at the entrance to Blyth Harbour, lies Cambois Bay. The bay is rocky as far as the River Wansbeck, at its mid-point, thence sandy for its S half. Two outfalls, the S of which is unmarked, extend into the bay as shown on the chart.

Measured distances
5.172
1 A measured distance is charted off Newbiggin Point (55°11′N, 1°30′W), marked by two pairs of prominent beacons (framework towers, front tower single black plate, rear tower two black plates, each tower two white projector lights for use at night or low visibility) each pair aligned 258°.

2 Running track 168°/348°: Distance 1852 m.

Use of the measured distance should be requested from the custodians, North East Coast Institute of Engineers and Shipbuilders, Bolbec Hall, Newcastle upon Tyne, NE1 1TB.
5.173
1 Between Coquet Lighthouse (55°20′N, 1°32′W) and Saint Mary's Lighthouse (5.209) the exact distance is 29 749 m on a running track of 169°/349°.

Rescue
5.174
1 There are Coastguard Rescue Teams at Newbiggin and Blyth; see 1.53.

An all-weather lifeboat is stationed at Blyth; inshore lifeboats are stationed at Blyth and Newbiggin. See 1.61 and 1.62 for details of lifeboats.

Tidal stream
5.175
1 Tidal streams run in the direction of the coast and are of no great strength except off salient points where there may be eddies. They are shown on the chart and in the *Admiralty Tidal Stream Atlas: North Sea, Northwestern Part*.

Principal marks
5.176
1 **Landmarks:**
> Coquet Lighthouse (55°20′N, 1°32′W) (5.137).
> Chimney (red obstruction lights) (55°12′N, 1°31′W) at an aluminium smelting plant.
2
> Four chimneys (red obstruction lights) (55°09′N, 1°32′W) at a power station.
> East Pier Lighthouse (white tower, 14 m in height) (55°07′N, 1°29′W) at Blyth.
> Nine wind generators (55°07′N, 1°29′W) on Blyth East Pier.
3 **Major lights:**
> Coquet Light (above).
> East Pier Light (above).

Other navigational aids
5.177
1 **DGPS:**
> Girdle Ness Light (57°08′N, 2°03′W).
> Flamborough Head Light (54°07′N, 0°05′W).

Directions
(continued from 5.142)
5.178
1 From a position ENE of Coquet Island the coastal route runs SSE to a position off Blyth, passing (with positions from Beacon Point (55°12′N, 1°30′W)):
> ENE of Hauxley Head (7½ miles NNW), the E extremity of the drying ledges off Hauxley Point (5.171). Open cast mines are visible S of the Hauxley Point. Thence:
2
> ENE of Bondicarr Bush (7 miles NNW) (5.171), thence:
> ENE of Northern Hill (6 miles N), a rocky patch off the N end of Druridge Bay, thence:

ENE of Cresswell Skeres (3 miles N), two offshore rocky patches, thence:

ENE of Snab Point (2 miles NNW) (5.171), thence:

3 ENE of Newbiggin Ness (7 cables SSE), a shoal 4 cables E of Newbiggin Point. Between the point, which is 12 m high, and Beacon Point to the N, the coast is fringed by drying reefs and rocks up to 4 cables offshore. A light-buoy (special) marks the seaward end of a sewer outfall 1 mile SSE of Newbiggin Point, and a diffuser with a least depth of 12·2 m lies 2 miles S of Newbiggin Ness, at the seaward end of an outfall extending 1½ miles from the shore. Thence:

4 To a position ENE of Link End (4 miles S) and East Pier Lighthouse, which lies at the head of East Pier, 8 cables SSE of the SE extremity of Link End. Link End is low, rounded and sandy and fronted by drying rocks up to 3 cables to seaward. These dangers are further extended by North Spit and South Spit, two shoals, respectively 5 cables NE and 5 cables E of Link End.

5.179

1 **Clearing bearing.** The line of bearing 165° of Tynemouth Head Castle buildings (55°01′N, 1°25′W) open their own width clear of Saint Mary's Island (55°04′N, 1°27′W) (5.211), passes E of the dangers E of Link End and East Pier.

Useful marks
5.180

1 Shirlaw Pike (55°20′N, 1°51′W) (Chart 1192).
Cresswell Hall (cupola) (55°14′N, 1°33′W).
Newbiggin Church (spire) (55°11′N, 1°30′W).
(Directions continue for coastal passage S at 5.211; directions for Blyth are given at 5.197)

Anchorages and Landing
5.181

1 An **anchorage** may be obtained in Druridge Bay (5.171) in depths of 9 m to 11 m about 2½ miles N of Snab Point (5.171).

An **anchorage** may be obtained in the S part of Newbiggin Bay, which lies between Newbiggin Point (55°11′N, 1°30′W) (5.178) and Spital Point (8 cables SW), in depths between 5 m and 9 m. The anchorage is sheltered from N winds.

2 **Landing** may be made by small boats in Hauxley Haven (55°19′N, 1°33′W), a small opening in the rocks close S of Hauxley Point (5.171).

Other names

Charts 156, 1626
5.182

1 Blackdyke (55°12′N, 1°29′W), a shoal.
Brig Head (55°14′N, 1°31′W), a ledge.
Crab Law Rocks (55°07′·8N, 1°29′·6W).
Hadston Carrs (55°18′N, 1°33′W), a ledge.
Horsbridge Head (55°10′N, 1°31′W), drying boulders.
The Knot (55°07′·2N, 1°28′·7W), a spit.
2 The Pigs (55°07′·6N, 1°29′·4W), a ledge.
The Rockers (55°08′·5N, 1°30′·5W), a ledge.
The Scars (55°14′N, 1°32′W), a ledge.
Seal Skears (55°14′N, 1°31′W), a ledge.
Seaton Sea Rocks (55°07′·2N, 1°29′·2W).
The Sow (55°07′·5N, 1°29′·0W), a rock.
White Bank (55°18′N, 1°32′W).

BLYTH

General information

Chart 1626
Position
5.183

1 Blyth Harbour (55°07′N, 1°29′W) lies at the mouth of the River Blyth.

Function
5.184

1 It is a commercial port handling alumina, paper products, grain, stone, general cargoes and coal exports. The population in 1991 was 35 327.

Port limits
5.185

1 The port limits extend up to 1·2 miles from the entrance, covering the port and the immediate approaches, and are shown on the chart.

Traffic
5.186

1 In 1999, 272 vessels totalling 1 599 011 dwt entered the port.

Port authority
5.187

1 Blyth Harbour Commission, 79 Bridge Street, Blyth NE24 2AW.

Limiting conditions
5.188

1 **Controlling depths.** The approach channel from the Fairway Light-buoy to the heads of the breakwaters, which is about 1 cable wide, is dredged to 8·5 m. Within the entrance the inner channel is dredged to depth of 7·6 m over a width of 85 m.

Caution. The channel is subject to shoaling, particularly after E gales, and these depths cannot be guaranteed. The Harbour Master should be consulted for the latest information on depths.

2 **Deepest and longest berth** is the Alcan Bulk Terminal (5.199).

Tidal levels: see *Admiralty Tide Tables.* Mean spring range about 4·3 m; mean neap range about 2·1 m.

Tidal heights are increased by strong N winds and decreased by strong S winds.

5.189

1 **Maximum size of vessel.** Vessels up to 175 m in length and draught of 9 m can use the Alcan Bulk Terminal berth. With the approval of the Harbour Master, larger ships may be accommodated if sufficient notice is given for extra dredging to be arranged.

Arrival information

Notice of ETA
5.190

1 24 hours' notice of entry is required.

Anchorage
5.191

1 An anchorage can be obtained in a position about 1 mile E of East Pierhead in depths of 17 m.

Pilots and tugs
5.192

1 **Pilotage** is not compulsory, but recommended; requests for pilotage should be made at least 1 hour, and at night

2 hours, in advance. The pilot normally boards within 2 miles of the harbour entrance, but in bad weather he boards in the vicinity of the pierheads.

Tugs can be ordered on request from the Tyne. A small harbour pushing tug of 600 hp is available. There is a boat service for running lines.

Harbour

Layout
5.193

1   The harbour, which is artificial and formed from the course of the River Blyth, is about 2 miles long running NNW/SSE. It is protected from the E by Link End which culminates in East Pier extending a further 8 cables to the SSE.

2   Most of the berths lie along the river. South Harbour is close W of the harbour entrance and there is a tidal basin at the N end of the harbour. Lights are exhibited from the extremities of most jetties, piers and berths.

Natural conditions
5.194

1   **Tidal streams** in the dredged areas in the approaches to Blyth might set across the line of the leading lights.

In the harbour the streams are of no great strength and run as follows:

Time from HW	Remarks
–0006 Tyne	In-going stream commences
–0015 Tyne	Out-going stream commences

2   Details of the streams to seaward are shown on the chart and in the *Admiralty Tidal Stream Atlas: North Sea, Northwestern Part.*
5.195

1   **Local weather.** During strong SSE winds the scend in the harbour is considerable due to the conducting effect of the piers. Vessels lying on the SW side of the harbour should take precautions accordingly. Two wave traps inside East Pier ensure that there is no effect on the NE side of the harbour; South Harbour is not affected.

Principal marks
5.196

1   **Landmarks:**
    Chimneys (55°08'·6N, 1°31'·5W) (5.176).
    East Pier Lighthouse (55°07'·0N, 1°25'·8W) (5.176).
    Tower (charted as spire on Chart 1626) (55°06'·3N, 1°29'·8W) at a cemetery.
    Nine wind generators positioned along East Pier (5.176).

2   **Major Light:**
    East Pier Light (above).

Power station

Blyth (5.193)

(Original dated 2000)

(Photograph - Air Images)

Directions

5.197

1   **Outer Leading Lights:**

Front light (orange diamond on framework tower) (55°07′·4N, 1°29′·8W).

Rear light (orange diamond on framework tower) (180 m NW of front light).

2   From a position about 2 cables SE of the harbour entrance the alignment (324°) of the Blyth Outer Leading Lights leads through the approach channel and harbour entrance to a position 3 cables inside the entrance, passing (with positions from the entrance):

SW of Fairway Light-buoy (starboard hand) (5½ cables SE).

3   Through the harbour entrance, which is 1 cable wide facing SSE and lies between East Pierhead on which stands the lighthouse (5.176) and West Pierhead on which stands a light (white tower, 4 m in height).

4   **Caution.** Dredging operations are carried out, usually by day, in the vicinity of the entrance. The signals shown by the dredgers conform to the *International Regulations for Preventing Collisions at Sea.*

5.198

1   **Link End Inner Leading Lights:**

Front light (white 6-sided tower, 5 m in height) (55°07′·7N, 1°29′·8W).

Rear light (white triangle on mast, 11 m in height) (87 m NNW of front light).

The alignment (338°) of the Link End Inner Leading Lights leads through the south part of the harbour.

Basins and berths

5.199

1   **South Harbour.** There are 2 general cargo berths of which North Quay (152 m long, depth alongside 8·5 m) is the largest berth. There is a Ro-Ro pontoon terminal at the S end of West Quay.

River berths E side. There are 7 berths, including 5 waiting berths, and the Alcan Bulk Terminal which has a berth 152 m long, and a depth alongside of 9 m (1997). Battleship Wharf lies 5½ cables NW of Alcan Terminal and has depths alongside of 8·5 m and 5·5 m.

2   **River berths W side.** There are 6 berths of which Dun Cow Quay Berth, 220 m long, depth alongside 8·5 m, is the largest. There is a Ro-Ro berth at the NW end of Wimborne Quay. Bates Wharf, a bulk loading terminal, has a depth alongside of 7·6 m.

Tidal basin There is a berth with a depth alongside of 8·5 m.

A **turning basin**, the W limits of which are marked by beacons, lies to the W of Battleship Wharf.

Port services

5.200

1   **Repairs:** deck and engine repairs can be carried out.

5.201

1   **Facilities:** refuse disposal; deratting; hospitals.

5.202

1   **Supplies:** water at all loading and discharging berths; fuel at Commissioners Quay; provisions.

Small craft

5.203

1   Visiting small craft are normally accommodated at the Royal Northumberland Yacht Club marina in South Harbour. Water and electricity are available to visiting craft at a floating pontoon.

BLYTH TO TYNEMOUTH

General information

Chart 156

Route

5.204

1   From a position E of the entrance to Blyth Harbour (55°07′N, 1°29′W) the route leads 6½ miles SSE to a position E of the Tynemouth.

Topography

5.205

1   Initially the coast is low and sandy, to Seaton Sluice, 2 miles SSE. Thence there is a rocky cliff, fringed by ledges extending up to 3 cables offshore, to the vicinity of Saint Mary's Island (5.211) a further 1½ miles SSE. The island is connected by a causeway to Curry Point, 1 cable SW. The coast then has a sandy foreshore backed by a bank to Brown Point which is low and fringed by rocky ledges and lies 2¼ miles SSE of the island. The final stretch of 1½ miles to Tynemouth is fronted by rocks and ledges.

Measured distance

5.206

1   See 5.173.

Rescue

5.207

1   The Maritime Rescue Sub-Centre for the Tyne Tees coastguard District is situated at North Shields; see 1.53. A VHF/DF station, for emergency use only, is situated at Tynemouth.

An all-weather lifeboat and an inshore lifeboat are stationed at Tynemouth; an inshore lifeboat is stationed at Cullercoats. See 1.61 and 1.62 for details of lifeboats.

Tidal streams

5.208

1   Tidal streams are given on the chart and in the *Admiralty Tidal Stream Atlas: North Sea, Northwestern Part.*

Principal marks

5.209

1   **Landmarks:**

East Pier Lighthouse (55°07′N, 1°29′W) (5.176).

Saint Mary's Island Lighthouse (white tower, 37 m in height, now disused) (55°04′N, 1°27′W).

White building (55°03′·4N, 1°27′·3W).

White dome (55°02′·9N, 1°26′·7W).

Saint George's Church (spire) (55°01′·8N, 1°25′·8W).

Congregational Church (spire) (55°01′·0N, 1°25′·4W).

2   **Major lights:**

East Pier Light (above).

North Pierhead Light (Tynemouth) (grey round masonry tower, white lantern, 23 m in height) (55°00′·9N, 1°24′·1W).

Other navigational aids

5.210

1   **DGPS:**

Girdle Ness Light (57°08′N, 2°03′W).

Flamborough Head Light (54°07′N, 0°05′W).

Directions

(continued from 5.180)

5.211

1   From a position ENE of Blyth Harbour (55°07′N, 1°29′W) the coastal route leads 6½ miles SSE to a position ENE of Tynemouth, passing (with positions from Tynemouth entrance):

Clear, depending on draught, of a wreck with a depth of 9·1 m over it (5½ miles NNW), thence:

2   ENE of Saint Mary's Island (4 miles NNW) on which stands a disused lighthouse (5.209). The island lies towards the seaward extremity of rocky ledges and off-lying rocks which encumber the coast in that vicinity. Thence:

Clear of the light-buoy (special) (3¼ miles N) which is the local reference point for the disposal of explosive ordnance. Vessels should avoid anchoring in its close vicinity. Thence:

3   ENE of Bellhues Rocks (1 mile N) which lie 8 cables ESE of Brown Point (5.205) and within the green sector (161°–179°) of Tynemouth South Pier Light (5.237). Whitley Bay lies between Brown Point and Saint Mary's Island. Thence:

To a position ENE of Tynemouth entrance.

5.212

1   **Clearing bearing.** The line of bearing 165° of Tynemouth Castle building (5.236) open their own length E of Saint Mary's Island passes E of the dangers N of the island.

(Directions continue for coastal passage S at 6.14 and for Port of Tyne at 5.237)

Small craft

Cullercoats

5.213

1   A boat harbour (55°02′N, 1°26′W) lies between Brown Point (5.205) and George Point, 2½ cables S of Brown Point. The harbour is approached through a gap in the ledges.

2   **Leading lights.** The alignment (256°) of Cullercoats Leading Lights leads into the boat harbour:

Front light (post, 3 m in height) (55°02′·1N, 1°25′·8W).

Rear light (column, 4 m in height) (38 m WSW of front light).

Local knowledge is required.

Other names

5.214

1   Brierdean Bushes (55°03′N, 1°26′W), a shoal.
Colville Rock (55°05′·0N, 1°27′·7W).
Crag Point (55°04′·7N, 1°27′·7W).
Inner Bell Rock (55°04′·8N, 1°27′·4W).
Mile Hill (55°05′·6N, 1°29′·2W).
Outer Bell Rock (55°04′·6N, 1°26′·9W).
Sharpness Point (55°01′·4N, 1°25′·1W).
Whitley Shad (55°02′·8N, 1°25′·6W).

PORT OF TYNE

General information

Charts 156, 1934

Position

5.215

1   The Port of Tyne lies along both banks of the River Tyne which enters the sea at Tynemouth (55°01′N, 1°25′W). From the entrance at Tynemouth the river is navigable as far as Lemington, 15 miles up river, but depths (5.220) are only maintained as far as Newcastle Swing Bridge (5.240), 10 miles up river. The river banks are heavily industrialised, with numerous works and ship berths.

2   Tynemouth lies on the N bank of the river, as do North Shields, Wallsend, the city of Newcastle upon Tyne, Scotswood and Lemington. The towns of South Shields, Jarrow, Hebburn, Gateshead and Blaydon lie on the S bank.

Tynemouth (5.215)

(Original dated 2000)

(Photograph - Air Images)

Function
5.216

1   The Port of Tyne is a busy port, with a diverse trade ranging from grain, coal, timber, oil and chemicals to scrap metal and sea dredged aggregates. Vehicle and passenger ferries use the port, and there are container handling facilities.

2   Ship conversion and repair are also significant activities. Modules for North Sea oilfields have been constructed within the port.

North Shields is an important fishing port.

In 1996 the population of Tyneside was 840 200 and that of Newcastle upon Tyne was 285 300.

Port limits
5.217

1   The seaward limit of the port is bounded by an arc, radius 1 mile, drawn from the entrance between the breakwaters. The Port of Tyne Authority has certain powers outside its seaward limit.

Traffic
5.218

1   In 1999 the total trade was over 2¼ million tonnes of general cargo, and over 600 000 passengers used the International Ferry Terminal. The port cleared 1856 vessels, totalling 8 796 315 dwt.

Port authority
5.219

1   The Port of Tyne Authority, Maritime House, Tyne Dock, South Shields NE34 9PT. The Harbour Master's Office is at Neville House, Bell Street, North Shields NE30 1LJ.

Limiting conditions

Controlling depths
5.220

1   Maintained depths are as follows:

Tyne Piers (entrance) to Jarrow Quay Corner 8·6 m (1°28'·1W)

Jarrow Quay Corner to Jarrow Staith W end 6·0 m (1°30'·6W)

Jarrow Staith W end to Newcastle Swing Bridge 5·2 m (1°36'·4W)

2   West of the Swing Bridge depths are not maintained.

Silting is liable to occur and the Harbour Master or the Port Operations and Information Service (5.226) should be consulted for the latest information on depths.

Vertical clearances
5.221

1   An overhead power cable, safe vertical clearance 65 m, crosses the River Tyne at Jarrow (1°28'·3W).

Six bridges span the River Tyne at Newcastle. The minimum clearance of these bridges is 24·7 m. See 5.240 for details of bridges.

Deepest and longest berth
5.222

1   Riverside Quay (S bank, 1°27'W) (5.244).

Mean tidal levels
5.223

1   See *Admiralty Tide Tables.*

2   North Shields (55°00'W, 1°26'W): mean spring range about 4·3 m; mean neap range about 2·1 m.

Newcastle upon Tyne (54°58'N, 1°36'W): mean spring range about 4·5 m; mean neap range about 2·2 m.

Maximum size of vessel handled
5.224

1   There are no length or beam restrictions at the harbour entrance. Such restrictions depend on the berth to be used, see 5.242 to 5.245.

Local weather
5.225

1   The heaviest seas in the entrance are caused during NE gales when the out-going stream is running strongly. In such conditions it is preferable therefore to enter while the in-going stream is still running, noting that at this time it also sets across the entrance. At other times there should be no difficulty in entering the port.

2   In N gales vessels should keep close under the lee of North Pier and in S gales, especially when the out-going stream is running, close under the lee of South Pier.

Arrival information

Port operations
5.226

1   **Port Operations and Information Service** scheme is in operation for the control of shipping, for details see the relevant *Admiralty List of Radio Signals.* Positions of reporting points are shown on the chart.

The control station is situated at the Harbour Master's office at North Shields (55°00'·4N, 1°26'·3W).

Notice of ETA
5.227

1   The ETA of a vessel should be sent to the Port Operations and Information Service 24 hours in advance, or on sailing from the previous port if within 24 hours steaming. ETA should be confirmed by VHF approximately 2 hours in advance. See the relevant *Admiralty List of Radio Signals.*

Outer anchorage
5.228

1   An outer anchorage, whose full limits are shown on chart 156, lies 1½ miles NE of North Pier head. Care should be taken not to anchor in the SE corner of the anchorage as this lies close to the approach to the harbour entrance.

Several wrecks lie in the N part of the anchorage, as shown on the chart.

Pilotage and tugs
5.229

1   **Pilotage.** The Port of Tyne Authority Pilotage District includes the port and its seaward approaches, within a radius of three nautical miles from each of the roundheads of the North and South Piers, contained within an area E of a line South Pier Lighthouse bearing 179° and to the N of a line South Pier Lighthouse bearing 288°.

2   Pilotage is compulsory for all vessels of 50 m or more in length overall with the following exceptions:

Vessels being moved within the harbour outside the main navigable channel.

Vessels transiting the seaward approaches.

Vessels anchoring in that part of the outer anchorage which lies within the pilotage area.

Vessels exempt by law.

3   The pilot boarding point is about 1¼ miles ENE of the harbour entrance as shown on the chart or any other position within the pilotage area by arrangement with the Port Authority. The pilot cutter may identify herself by sounding 4 short blasts on her siren. In bad weather the pilot vessel waits within the harbour entrance and will lead a vessel into the harbour where the pilot will board. The pilot vessel is fitted with VHF and has a black hull, white wheelhouse and "HARBOUR MASTER" painted on both sides.

4   The following sound signals should be sounded by whistle if no other means of communication is available:

Signal	Meaning
1 blast	Head tug lay on starboard bow
2 blasts	Head tug lay on port bow
3 blasts, 1 blast	Stern tug to lay on starboard quarter
3 blasts, 2 blasts	Stern tug to lay on port quarter
Series of rapid blasts	Cease towing

5   The Port of Tyne Authority exercises pilotage jurisdiction as the Competent Harbour Authority. Requests for pilots should be made through Port Operations and Information Service 24 hours in advance and amended or confirmed 2 hours before arrival. Pilotage requirements for departure or harbour movements should be made at least 2 hours in advance.

Tugs are available.

Regulations concerning entry
5.230

1   There is a speed limit of 6 knots in the river.

Special sound signal. In accordance with the Merchant Shipping (Distress Signals and Prevention of Collisions) Regulations 1996, a vessel nearing a bend in the river, when another vessel approaching cannot be seen, should give one prolonged blast when within 5 cables of the bend (Rule 34 (e)).

2   Vessels are to keep southward of mid-channel when proceeding to sea and northward of mid-channel when entering, so as to pass each other port side to port side.

Vessels crossing the river or turning, are responsible for ensuring that they do not interfere with passing traffic.

When one vessel is overtaken by another, she shall give the overtaking vessel room to pass.

3   Wrecks and obstructions are marked in accordance with the IALA Maritime Buoyage System (Region A). A yellow flag illuminated by night, is placed on the shore immediately adjacent to any obstruction.

Harbour

Layout
5.231

1   The majority of berths are riverside. The major berths extend up river to Newcastle, but there are minor berths as far as Lemington 5 miles above Newcastle Swing Bridge. There is one enclosed dock, Tyne Dock.

For details see 5.242 to 5.245.

Dock and bridge signals
5.232

1   Signals with respect to Tyne Dock (5.243) are as follows:

Sound signal by ship	Meaning
3 prolonged blasts	Request to enter dock

Light signal by dock

3 red lights	Vessels may not proceed
3 green lights	Vessels may proceed

2   Light signals are shown on the E side of the lock (54°59′·10N, 1°26′·93W) and at the E end of Riverside Quay (5.244) (54°59′·17N, 1°26′·98W).

5.233

1   Signals with respect to Newcastle Swing Bridge (5.240) are as follows:

Signal	Meaning
3 long blasts by ship	Request to open bridge
Amber light above passage in use	Bridge about to swing
Green disc (day) or green light (night) shown horizontally on side of tower	Vessel to pass this side
Green light (night) from the end of central pier	Vessel to pass this side of central pier

2   The bridge is normally closed to river traffic Monday to Friday, 0800–0930 and 1600–1800 but may be opened in these periods if the closure coincides with LW for vessels bound up-river or the closure coincides with HW for vessels bound down-river. To open the bridge at least 24 hours' notice should be given to the Port Operations and Information Service.

Tidal streams
5.234

1   The in-going stream sets SSE across the harbour entrance about 4 hours before HW Tyne, with spring rates in excess of 1 kn. The tidal stream reverses to a NNW direction 2 hours after HW Tyne. Details of the tidal stream to seaward of the harbour entrance are given on chart 156.

The tidal streams run in the direction of the channel, but set towards the outer bank at the bends in the river. The spring rate in each direction is 2½ kn.

2   Due to the elevations of its sources in Cumberland and the borders of Scotland, the River Tyne is subject to sudden and heavy freshets, when an immense body of water is discharged. In these conditions both the duration and rate of the out-going stream are increased, and the in-going stream correspondingly reduced.

3   The streams set as follows:

Position	In-going begins from HW Tyne	Out-going begins from HW Tyne
River entrance	–0530	+0040
Whitehill Point	–0540	+0020
Newcastle Quay	–0540	+0010

Principal marks
5.235

1   **Landmarks** (Approaches):
       Saint George's Church (spire) (55°01′·8N, 1°25′·8W).
       Congregational Church (spire) (55°01′·0N, 1°25′·4W).
       North Pier Lighthouse (55°00′·9N, 1°24′·1W) (5.209).
       Water Tower (54°58′N, 1°24′W) (Chart 152) at
       Cleadon Waterworks.

2   **Major lights:**
       North Pier Light (above).

Herd Groyne Directional Light (red pile structure, red and white lantern) (55°00'·5N, 1°25'·3W).

5.236

1 Landmarks (River passage):
Tynemouth Head and castle buildings (55°01'N, 1°25'W).
South Shields Town Hall (cupola) (54°59'·7N, 1°25'·7W).
Left hand edge of Western Quay (55°00'·4N, 1°26'·4W).
North Shields Gasworks (55°00'·2N, 1°27'·2W).
Pylon (54°59'·1N, 1°28'·3W) on Jarrow Quay.

Directions
(continued from 5.212)

Approaches
5.237

1 From a position about 2 miles ENE of the harbour entrance the white sector (246½°–251½°) of Herd Groyne Directional Light (5.235), shown throughout 24 hours, leads through the harbour entrance which is 366 m wide and lies between North Pier Lighthouse (5.209) and South Pier Lighthouse (grey round stone tower, red and white lantern, 12 m in height).

Harbour Entrance to the Narrows
5.238

1 From a position in the centre of the harbour entrance, when the white sector of Herd Groyne Directional Light should be disregarded, the route lies WSW in the dredged channel which is marked by light-buoys, passing (with positions from North Pier Lighthouse):

2 NNW of Herd Groyne (8 cables WSW), marked by a light (5.235) at its E extremity, thence:
To a position SSE of Fish Quay (1 mile WSW), which is 1 cable W of No 1 Groyne. No 1 Groyne is marked by a light (green metal beacon, 4 m in height). The Narrows lie between Fish Quay and The Lawe on the S bank of the river.

Narrows to Newcastle upon Tyne
5.239

1 From the Narrows to Newcastle upon Tyne the river consists of a series of dredged reaches. There are few navigational marks although lights are exhibited from most piers, jetties and berths. Vessels proceeding up-river should keep in mid-channel, taking note of the tidal streams.

2 In sequence from seaward these reaches are:
Shields Harbour Reach, (1½ miles in length). The entrances to Royal Quays Marina (5.250) and Tyne Dock lie within this reach. A ferry runs between North and South Shields as shown on the chart.

3 Long Reach, (2½ miles in length). Swinging area of about 360 m in diameter is situated at the E end of the reach. An overhead power cable (5.221) spans the river 3 cables W of the swinging area.
Bill Reach, (1½ miles in length). A light-beacon stands at the S end of the reach on Bill Point.

4 Saint Anthony's Reach, (5 cables in length). The turn at Saint Anthony's Point at the SE end of the reach is marked by a light-beacon (green structure, 10 m in height) close SE of the point, and on the S bank by a light-beacon (red metal framework tower, 5 m in height) 2 cables E of the point and two fixed vertical lights on a red column 1 cable SE of the point.

5 Felling Reach, (7 cables in length). Friar's Goose Light-beacon (red pile structure on platform, 7 m in height) stands on the S bank, 3·7 cables WNW of Saint Anthony's Point and Saint Peter's Light-beacon (green pile structure on platform, 10 m in height) stands on the N bank 1 cable NW of the point.

6 Saint Peter's Reach, (8 cables in length). The Newcastle Bridges (5.240) are 6 cables W of the NW end of the reach.

Newcastle bridges
5.240

1 In order from the E the six Newcastle bridges spanning the River Tyne are:
Tyne Bridge (54°58'N, 1°36'W) a single span road bridge with a width of 114 m and a vertical clearance of 24 m.

2 Newcastle Swing Bridge ¾ cable above Tyne Bridge with four spans of which the centre two swing on a central pier providing a channel 31 m wide on the N side and 29 m wide on the S side. When closed there is a vertical clearance of 4·6 m. The central pier, which extends upstream to the next bridge, is marked by lights at its corners. Staging on the S side of the river is also marked by lights (see 5.233 for traffic signals and opening times).

3 Newcastle High Level Bridge ¼ cable above the swing bridge. The swing bridge central span projects under the bridge dividing the channel, giving a N channel 27 m wide and one S of 30 m. The vertical clearance is 24·7 m.
Queen Elizabeth II Bridge 2¼ cables above the High Level Bridge. The vertical clearance is 25 m.

4 King Edward Bridge 1 cable above the Queen Elizabeth II Bridge. The vertical clearance is 25 m. There are two channels each 89 m wide, up-river traffic use the N channel and down-river traffic the S channel.
Redheugh Bridge 1 cable above King Edward Bridge. The vertical clearance is 29 m. Lights are shown from each side of the main span defining the N and S edges of the channel.

5 **Note.** A new footbridge is under construction (2000) 500 m downstream of Tyne Bridge. The single arch bridge will have a clear channel width of 30 m and a vertical clearance of 25 m.

River Tyne above Newcastle
5.241

1 The river is navigable as far as the Stella Power Station at Lemington, which is 5 miles above Newcastle Swing Bridge. The depth is not maintained in the channel above the Newcastle Bridges and vessels requiring to navigate in this stretch of the river should consult the Harbour Master to ascertain that sufficient water is available.

2 The river is crossed by several bridges and power cables between Newcastle and Lemington. Scotswood Rail Bridge is the lowest, with a vertical clearance of 6·4 m.

Basins and berths

Shields Harbour Reach
5.242

1 Fish Quay and Western Quay at the N end of the reach are used by fishing vessels.

2 Tyne Commission Quay, length 335 m and depth 7·1 m, is the largest berth in the reach and lies on the river wall

Newcastle Harbour from NE (5.239)

(Original dated 2000)

(Photograph - Air Images)

forming Royal Quays Marina. To the S of Tyne Commission Quay lie No 3 and No 4 Ro-Ro berths at the International Ferry Terminal, and Whitehill Point Jetty.

5.243

1   **Tyne Dock** (54°59'·1N, 1°26'·9W) is entered through an outer basin and a tidal entrance 21·3 m wide and is fitted with gates. A one way system operates in the entrance. There is a depth in the entrance of 8 m and within the dock of between 8·2 m and 7·0 m. There are two quays in the dock, total length 440 m.

2   Vessels up to a length of 122 m, beam 19 m and draught 7·6 m can use the dock at HW springs.

Long Reach

5.244

1   Riverside Quay at the E end of Long Reach and close W of Tyne Dock is the largest berth in the Port of Tyne with a length of 514 m and a depth alongside of 11 m. Tyne Bulk Terminal, depth alongside 11 m, is close W of Riverside Quay with Tyne Car Terminal, consisting of three jetties having depths alongside between 7·0 and 9·5 m, close W again. On the N bank of the river there are two tanker berths and a tanker cleaning berth. To the W of these berths is a sludge jetty and W again Howden Jetty used for the discharge of aggregates. Northumberland Dock, largely reclaimed except for a small tidal basin, lies between the tanker berths and the sludge jetty. Jarrow

Staith, a wooden lay-by berth not presently in use but formerly dredged to 7·1 m, lies at the W end of the reach.

Newcastle

5.245

1   Newcastle Quays (54°58'N, 1°36'W) lie on the N bank and run E from Tyne Bridge for a distance of 900 m. Spiller's Grain Berth is close E of the quays and the largest berth in the complex, length 237 m, depth alongside 6·0 m.

Port services

5.246

1   **Repairs** of all kinds can be carried out. There are a number of dry docks, the largest is 259 m long, breadth 44 m. There are also slipways available.

5.247

1   **Other facilities:** hospitals at North and South Shields, Wallsend and Newcastle; deratting available and certificates issued; customs office at North Shields; small craft fuelling points at W end of Fish Quay and at Royal Quays Marina. Facilities for reception of oily waste and for disposal of garbage vary depending upon the berth concerned. Tyne Harbour Radio should be contacted before arrival.

5.248

1   **Supplies:** all types of fuel oil; fresh water at most berths or by water boat.

5.249

1   **Communications.** There are regular ferry services to Scandinavian, Baltic and North European ports. There is an airport at Newcastle serving UK and European cities, and both main line and cross country rail services depart from Newcastle Central Station.

Small craft
5.250

1   Royal Quays Marina, situated in the former Albert Edward Dock (54°59'·7N, 1°27'·0W), has 170 pontoon berths and a range of shoreside facilities, including fuel, a boat lift and secure storage. Access from the river is through a lock and is available at all states of the tide.

Further development, which will increase berthing capacity to 400, is planned (2000).

Royal Quays Marina (5.250.1)

(Original dated 2000)

(Photograph - Air Images)

2   Moorings and berths are also available at Saint Peter's Marina, on the N bank at the E end of Saint Peter's Reach,

where the depth over the sill is 5 m at HWS and 4 m at HWN; minimum maintained depth inside the marina is 2·5 m and craft up to 33 m length can be accommodated. Petrol and diesel are available and contact can be made on VHF.

Saint Peter's Marina (5.250.2)

(Original dated 2000)

(Photograph - Air Images)

Other names
5.251

1   Collingwood's Monument (55°00'·9N, 1°25'·1W).
Dunston Staiths (closed) (54°57'·5N, 1°37'·9W), tidal basin.
Elswick Reach (54°57'·6N, 1°38'·5W).
Freestone Point (55°00'·9N, 1°24'·9W).
Jarrow Slake (54°59'·0N, 1°27'·8W).

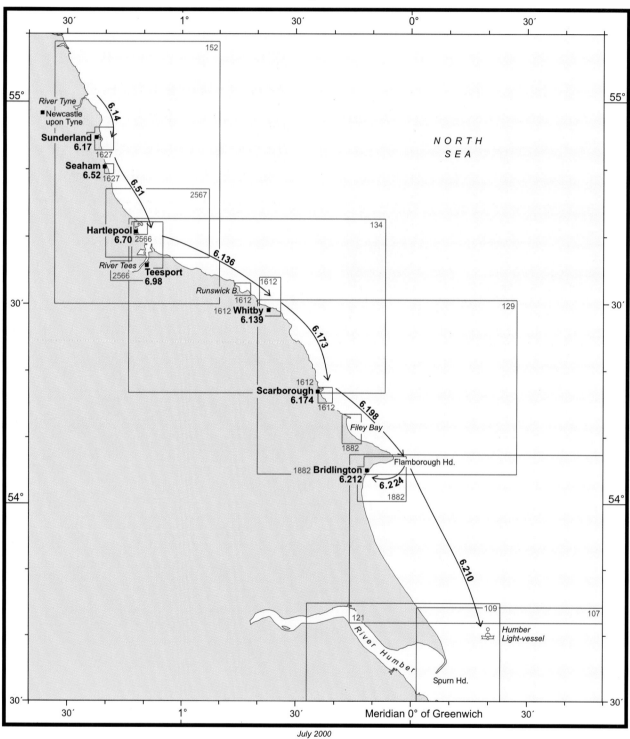

July 2000

CHAPTER 6

RIVER TYNE TO RIVER HUMBER

GENERAL INFORMATION

Charts 1190, 1191
Synopsis
6.1

1   In this chapter the coastal passage from the entrance to the River Tyne (55°01′N, 1°25′W) to the entrance to the River Humber, 105 miles to the SE, is described, together with the ports of Sunderland (6.17), Seaham (6.52), Hartlepool (6.70), Teesport (6.98), Whitby (6.139), Scarborough (6.174) and Bridlington (6.212).

Topography
6.2

1   River Tees (54°39′N, 1°08′W) lies 25 miles SSE of the River Tyne along a relatively straight run of the coast. Thence the coast runs ESE, gradually curving to the SSE as its approaches the most prominent physical feature on this stretch of coast, Flamborough Head (54°07′N, 0°05′W), which juts out 5 miles from the general run of the coast. S of the head the coast runs S to the entrance to the River Humber. The shoreline is generally cliffy, fronted by rocky ledges, except for Tees Bay, Filey Bay and to the S of Flamborough Head, where it is low lying and sandy.

2   The 30 m depth contour runs parallel to the coast up to 3 miles off as far as Flamborough Head where it runs close to the head. Thereafter it broadens out to about 10 miles off as far as the entrance to the River Humber. Other than charted wrecks there are no dangers outside this depth contour. Within the 30 m depth contour dangers are either marked by light-buoys or covered by sector lights.

North Sea gas fields
6.3

1   The main concentration of North Sea gasfields lies S of the latitude of Flamborough Head. Platforms and rigs associated with the recovery of the gas can be encountered within 20 miles of the coast although most of the activity is further to seaward. For a full description see 2.17.

Dumping grounds
6.4

1   See 2.4 for details.

Visibility
6.5

1   Visibility may be affected by industrial smoke haze between the River Tyne and the River Tees.

Tidal streams
6.6

1   Offshore the tidal streams are weak with spring rates not exceeding 1½ kn, except off Flamborough Head where the rates increase to about 3 kn.

    For details see charts and *Admiralty Tidal Stream Atlases: North Sea, Northwestern Part* and *North Sea, Southern Part*.

RIVER TYNE TO SUNDERLAND

General information

Chart 152
Route
6.7

1   From a position ENE of the entrance to Tynemouth (55°01′N, 1°25′W) the route leads 3 miles SSE thence a further 3 miles S to a position E of the entrance to Sunderland.

Topography
6.8

1   Initially the coast is sandy, backed by sandhills, but gives way to a series of rocky points fringed by ledges, which include Lizard Point and Souter Point, 3½ miles SSE of Tynemouth, where the trend of the coast alters from SSE to S. The ledges continue for a further 1 mile to Whitburn Bay, which is sandy with off-lying ledges and a shoal bank, with depths of less than 5 m extending up to 5½ cables offshore. The bay terminates at Roker Cliff, close N of the entrance to Sunderland.

2   Sunderland lies at the mouth of the River Wear, a rapid narrow stream about 65 miles long, mainly confined between banks of limestone rock. It drains a considerable amount of hilly country.

Exercise area
6.9

1   Whitburn Rifle Range lies close W of Souter Point from which red flags or lights are exhibited when firing is taking place. The NE and SE range safety limits are marked by two light-buoys (special) moored, respectively, 1¼ miles NE and 1½ miles SE of Souter Point.

Rescue
6.10

1   There is a coastguard station 6 cables N of the entrance to Sunderland harbour. A Coastguard Rescue Team is maintained; see 1.53.

    An all-weather lifeboat and an inshore lifeboat are stationed at Sunderland. See 1.61 and 1.62 for details of lifeboats.

Tidal streams
6.11

1   Tidal streams in the area are weak. For details see the chart and *Admiralty Tidal Stream Atlas: North Sea, Northwestern Part*.

Principal marks
6.12

1   **Landmarks:**

    Souter Lighthouse (white round tower, orange band and lantern, 23 m in height) (54°58′·2N, 1°21′·7W), disused.

    Water tower (54°58′N, 1°24′W) on Cleadon Hill.

    Lighthouse (disused) (54°56′N, 1°22′W).

2   Roker Pier Lighthouse (54°55′·3N, 1°21′·0W) (white round tower, three red bands and cupola, 23 m in height).

    Block of flats (54°55′N, 1°22′W). Four similar blocks of flats lie SW over a distance of 2½ cables.

    Block of flats (54°54′N, 1°22′W). Two similar blocks of flats lie NW over a distance of 1¼ cables.

3   **Major lights:**
　　East Pier Light (55°07′N, 1°29′W) (5.176).
　　Tynemouth North Pierhead Light (55°00′·9N, 1°24′·1W) (5.209).
　　Roker Pier Light (above).

Other navigational aids
6.13
1   DGPS:
　　Girdle Ness Light (57°08′N, 2°03′W).
　　Flamborough Head Light (54°07′N, 0°05′W).

Directions
(continued from 5.212)
6.14
1   From a position (55°01′N, 1°22′W) ENE of Tynemouth, the route leads 3 miles SSE, thence a further 3 miles S to a position E of Sunderland Harbour entrance, passing (with positions from the entrance (54°55′N, 1°21′W)):
　　ENE of Marsden Point (4 miles NNW), which is fringed by rocky reefs. Man Haven, a small inlet in the rocks lies close NW of the point, thence:
2　　ENE of Lizard Point (3 miles N), noting the two light-buoys (special) ENE and SE of the point which mark the range safety limits (6.9). Souter Lighthouse (6.12) stands 1 cable inshore of the point.
　　Marsden Bay backed by a limestone bank, 15 m to 18 m high, lies between Lizard and Marsden Point. Several detached rocks lie in the bay. Thence:
3　　E of Souter Point (2¼ miles N), which is easily distinguished from the N and S, thence:
　　E of Mill Rock (1¾ miles NNE), thence:
　　E of a buoy (special, conical) (1½ miles NNE) marking the seaward end of an outfall, thence:
　　E of a buoy (port hand) (1 mile N) marking a wreck which dries. Whitburn Steel, a rock, is 1 cable NW of the wreck, thence:
　　ENE of the entrance to Sunderland Harbour.

Useful mark
6.15
1   Lift shaft faced with light grey bricks (54°58′·6N, 1°22′·5W). There is a marine grotto in front of the lift shaft.

(Directions continue for coastal passage S at 6.51 and for Sunderland at 6.36)

Other name
6.16
1   Trow Point (54°59′·6N, 1°24′·0W) (Chart 1934).

SUNDERLAND

General information

Chart 1627 plan of Sunderland Harbour
Position
6.17
1   **Sunderland Harbour** (54°55′N, 1°22′W) lies at the mouth of the River Wear (6.8).

Function
6.18
1   Sunderland, population 292 300 (1998), is an important port which handles steel, forest products, dry and liquid bulk cargoes, non-ferrous metals and general cargo.

Approach and entry
6.19
1   The harbour is approached from the ENE through the mouth of the River Wear, which is protected by breakwaters.

Traffic
6.20
1   In 1999 the port handled 395 vessels and 1 101 760 tonnes of cargo.

Port authority
6.21
1   Port of Sunderland, Quayside House, Wylam Wharf, Low Street, Sunderland, SR1 2BU.

Limiting conditions
6.22
1   **Controlling depths.** The entrance channel within the Outer Harbour is dredged to 7·8 m. A dredged depth of 7·6 m is maintained from the entrance to the Inner Harbour for a distance of 5 cables. Thence a depth of 5·7 m is maintained as far as Wearmouth Bridge (6.23).
2   **Caution.** Because of silting and possible obstructions depths should be checked with the Harbour Master and reliance not placed solely on published data. Local charts showing depths and temporary obstructions can be obtained from the port authority.
　　Deepest and longest berth. Corporation Quay (6.39).
　　Tidal levels: see *Admiralty Tide Tables*. Mean spring range about 4·4 m; mean neap range about 2·2 m.
6.23
1   **Bridges.** The river is spanned by Wearmouth Bridge, 1 mile from the entrance, and close W by Sunderland Railway Bridge. This is the lower bridge, with a vertical clearance of 25 m, and there are gauges either side of the bridge indicating the vertical clearance and tide gauges indicating height of tide above LAT. Queen Alexandra Bridge is 1¼ miles above the rail bridge and also has a greater headroom than the rail bridge.
6.24
1   **Maximum size of vessel.** Riverside berths 183 m loa and 8·2 m draught; South Docks 141·8 m loa and 8 m draught at MHWS (7·16 m at MHWN).
6.25
1   **Local weather.** Gales from the ENE and ESE send a heavy sea into the Outer Harbour. Souter Point (6.14) affords some protection to the entrance to the harbour during gales from the N.
　　Winds between WNW and NNE increase the height of sea level, and winds between SSW and SSE have the opposite effect.

Arrival information

Port operations
6.26
1   **Danger signal.** By day or night, when there is a danger in the harbour, three red flashing lights disposed vertically are exhibited from a framework tower on the Old North Pier (54°55′·1N, 1°21′·7W). This signal indicates vessels must not leave or enter harbour.

Notice of ETA
6.27
1   Twelve hours' notice of ETA, including draught, is required with amendments at least 2 hours in advance. Vessels carrying dangerous substances are required to give 24 hours' notice.

Sunderland Harbour (6.31)

(Original dated 2000)

(Photograph - Air Images)

Outer anchorage

6.28

1 There is an anchorage 1 mile E of Roker Pier Lighthouse (6.12), good holding ground, in depths of 12 m to 14 m. Care must be taken to avoid wrecks in the vicinity.

Pilots and tugs

6.29

1 **Pilotage** is compulsory within the South Docks complex, upriver of the W end of Corporation Quay and for vessels carrying dangerous substances, under tow or with any mechanical or navigational defect.

2 The pilot usually boards within a 1·5 mile radius of Roker Pier Lighthouse from an MFV type vessel painted black with red boot topping and the word "Pilots" forward on the wheelhouse. There is also a black pilot launch.

In poor visibility a vessel requiring a pilot should sound letter G morse code.

Tugs are available.

Regulations concerning entry

6.30

1 **Tanker distinguishing signals** are required to be shown when nearing or in the harbour. By day the signal is a red flag and by night a red light at the masthead or where it can best be seen, in addition to other lights required by law.

Harbour

Layout

6.31

1 **The port** consists of an Outer and Inner Harbour. The Outer Harbour is formed by Roker Pier to the N which curves 4½ cables ESE, and New South Pier which curves 4 cables NNE, respectively, from either side of the mouth of the River Wear. Rocky ledges extend up to 3½ cables offshore N and S of the two piers.

2 Inner Harbour is entered between Old North Pier and Old South Pier which lie close to the entrance. There are a number of riverside berths and South Docks consisting of two enclosed docks, Hudson Dock and Hendon Dock, running S from the S bank of the river.

Dock signals

6.32

1 South Docks control signals are displayed from the framework tower (6.26) and from a tower at No 3 Gateway at the N end of Hudson Dock when the docks are open for traffic, as follows:

Signal	Meaning
Three green lights on both towers	Vessel may enter docks
Three green lights on No 3 gateway and three red lights on Pilot Station	Vessel may leave docks
No signals exhibited	Dock closed for traffic

2 Lights are displayed vertically at both positions.

6.33

1 **Swing Bridge.** When the swing bridge is across the entrance to Hudson Dock, and the dock gates are open, two red lights disposed vertically are exhibited at the entrance to the dock. No signal is exhibited when the lock gates are shut.

A vessel may indicate that she wishes to enter or leave the dock by sounding a succession of "K"s in morse code.

Tidal streams

6.34

1 Tidal streams to seaward of the harbour entrance are given on the chart. In the River Wear, which is subject to freshets, the streams in the vicinity of Sunderland run as follows:

Time from HW Tyne	Remarks
−0605	In-going stream commences
−0005	Out-going stream commences

Principal marks
6.35

1   **Landmarks:**
Roker Pier Lighthouse (54°55′·3N, 1°21′·0W) (6.12).
Lighthouse (disused, white tower) (54°55′·9N, 1°21′·9W).
Blocks of Flats (54°55′·0N, 1°22′·1W) (6.12).
Blocks of Flats (54°54′·2N, 1°22′·1W) (6.12).
Chimney (54°53′·2N, 1°21′·7W) at Hendon Paper Works.

2   **Major light:**
Roker Pier Light (above).

Directions
(continued from 6.15)

Approach and entry
6.36

1   From a position ENE of the harbour entrance the line of bearing 251° of Old North Pierhead (54°55′·1N, 1°21′·5W), on which stands a light (yellow metal tower, 8 m in height), leads through the Outer Harbour entrance whence the track alters WSW for the Inner Harbour entrance, passing (with positions from Old North Pier Light):

SSE of the wreckage (6 cables ENE), least depth 6m, thence:

2   To the Outer Harbour entrance (3 cables ENE), 200 m in width, lying between Roker Pierhead, on which stands Roker Pier Lighthouse (6.12), and an obstruction marked by a buoy (port hand) 40 m N of New South Pierhead. A light (white metal tower, 10 m in height) stands close to the pierhead. Thence:

3   To the Inner Harbour entrance which is 100 m wide lying between Old North Pier and Old South Pier, from which a light (red can on red metal framework tower) is exhibited.

Once clear of the entrance a direct approach can be made to the riverside berths and Half Tide Basin which leads to the enclosed docks.

Enclosed docks
6.37

1   The enclosed docks are entered at their N end through Half Tide Basin, which has a tidal swinging basin to its N. Half Tide Basin is entered through No 1 Gate which is 21·3 m wide with a depth over the sill of 9·6 m at MHWS.

2   Hudson Dock is entered from Half Tide Basin through No 3 Gate, which is 19·2 m wide between fenders and has a depth of 9·0 m over the sill at MHWS. The gates are normally open from 2 hours before to 30 minutes after HW, but vessels may lock in at any time provided notice is given by the previous HW and subject to the vessel's draught. South Outlet, from Hudson Dock to the sea, is closed.

3   Hendon Dock is entered through a waterway at the S end of Hudson Dock which is 27 m wide and 62 m long with a depth of 9·4 m at MHWS.

Depths in the docks are not uniform and may be less than the depth over the entrance sill. See caution 6.22.

Useful mark
6.38

1   Saint Andrew's Church (tower) (54°55′·6N, 1°22′·1W).

Basins and berths
6.39

1   **Riverside berths:**
Corporation Quay, 323 m long, depth alongside 8·8 m.
Fish Quay.
One other quay.
South Docks:
Hudson Dock, 1490 m of quays, depths 6 m to 9 m.
Hendon Dock, 700 m of quays, depth 9 m when newly dredged.
North Dock is now occupied by a small craft marina.

Port services
6.40

1   **Repairs.** All kinds of repairs can be undertaken.
There is a dry dock in Half Tide basin; length 115·3 m; breadth 16·6 m.
6.41

1   **Other facilities:** hospital with helicopter landing site; deratting and issue of exemption certificates; facilities for the reception of oily waste; diving services.
6.42

1   **Supplies:** furnace fuel oil at Corporation Quay and oiling berths at S end of Hendon Dock; other fuel oils by road tanker; fresh water; provisions.

Small craft
6.43

1   Sunderland Marina is situated in North Dock (6.39). There are berths for 88 vessels at pontoons and a further 110 at moorings. Vessels up to 12 m in length can be accommodated at all states of the tide.

SUNDERLAND TO TEES BAY

General information

Charts 152, 2567
Route
6.44

1   From a position ENE of Sunderland (54°55′N, 1°22′W) the route leads 15 miles SSE to a position ESE of The Heugh, the E extremity of Hartlepool peninsula, which is the N entrance point to Tees Bay.

Topography
6.45

1   Initially the coast S of Sunderland is heavily industrialised, but this gives way to a grassy bank fringed by rocky ledges and shoals up to 4 cables offshore, as far as Seaham 5 miles SSE of Sunderland. From Seaham to The Heugh, 10 miles SSE, the coast is backed by cliffs between 20 and 30 m high. The coast itself is fronted by rocky ledges as far as Moorstack and Dogger Rocks which lie 3½ miles SSE of Seaham, thence it is composed of gravel and sand with the occasional rocky ledge as far as The Heugh which is low and rocky. The whole length of the coast from Sunderland to The Heugh is intersected by ravines known locally as denes. Castle Eden Denes, in the vicinity of Moorstack Rocks is a nature reserve, with access limited to definite footpaths.

Submarine cable
6.46

1   An isolated submarine cable (experimental length 5 cables) lies 2¼ miles NE of Black Halls Point (6.51).

Rescue
6.47

1   There are Coastguard Rescue Teams at Seaham and Hartlepool. See 1.53.

All-weather lifeboats are stationed at Teesmouth and Hartlepool, and an inshore lifeboat at Hartlepool. See 1.61 and 1.62 for details of lifeboats.

Tidal streams
6.48

1   Tidal streams off the coast are weak. For details see charts and *Admiralty Tidal Stream Atlas: North Sea, Northwestern Part.*

Principal marks
6.49

1   **Landmarks:**
For marks in Sunderland see 6.35.
Ryehope Pumping Station (charted as water tower) (54°51'·8N, 1°22'·7W) with a pronounced collar at the top.
Steetly Magnesite Works Chimney (54°42'·5N, 1°12'·7W).

2   **Major Lights:**
Tynemouth North Pierhead Light (55°00'·9N, 1°24'·1W) (5.209).
Roker Pier Light (54°55'·3N, 1°21'·0W) (6.12).
The Heugh Light (white metal tower, 13 m in height) (54°41'·8N, 1°10'·5W).

Other navigational aids
6.50

1   **Racon:**
Tees Fairway Light-buoy (54°41'N, 1°06'W).
DGPS:
Girdle Ness Light (57°08'N, 2°03'W).
Flamborough Head Light (54°07'N, 0°05'W).

Directions
(continued from 6.15)
6.51

1   From a position ENE of Sunderland the route leads 15 miles SSE to a position ESE of The Heugh, passing (with positions from the entrance to Seaham Harbour (54°50'N, 1°19'W)):
ENE of Hendon Rock (4 miles N); two wrecks lie 4 cables NE and the seaward end of an outfall lies 1 cable SSE. White Stones, a group of rocky shoals, lie 6 cables S of Hendon Rock. Thence:

2   ENE of Salterfen Rocks (2¾ miles NNW), extending 3 cables offshore, with Pincushion Rock 9 cables S, thence:
ENE of Louis Rocky Patch, (6 cables E), thence:
ENE of a light-buoy (port hand) (1¾ miles SE), marking the seaward end of an outfall, thence:
ENE of Beacon Point (2¼ miles S) with Beacon Hill close W, thence:

3   ENE of Black Halls Point (6 miles SSE) fronted by Black Halls Rocks, thence:
To a position ESE of The Heugh (10 miles SSE) the E extremity of Hartlepool Peninsula on which stands a lighthouse (6.49). Two jetties, the larger of which is marked by a light-beacon, lie 1½ miles NW of The Heugh and there are several outfalls marked by beacons along this length of coast.

4   Tees Fairway Light-buoy (safe water) in the centre of Tees Bay, is 2½ miles ESE of The Heugh.
(Directions continue for Hartlepool at 6.90, for Tees Bay and the River Tees at 6.120 and for passage S at 6.136)

Seaham

Chart 1627 plan of Seaham Harbour
General information
6.52

1   **Position.** The artificial harbour (54°50'N, 1°19'W) lies 5 miles S of Sunderland.
6.53

1   **Function.** Seaham, population 22 130 (1991), is a commercial port handling bulk, semi-bulk and unitised cargoes.
6.54

1   **Topography.** The town lies in a break in the limestone cliffs, which are about 15 to 18 m high, and run to the N and S of the port. There are rocky ledges and detached rocks extending up to 3 cables offshore on either side of the breakwaters protecting the harbour.
6.55

1   **Traffic.** In 1999 the port handled 270 vessels and 650 000 tonnes of cargo.
6.56

1   **Port authority.** The Seaham Harbour Dock Company, Seaham House, North Terrace, Seaham, County Durham, SR7 7EU.

Limiting conditions
6.57

1   **Controlling depths.** There is a depth of 2·1 m in the harbour entrance and a least depth of 1·4 m in the channel leading to South Dock (6.67). A rocky patch, charted depth of 1·9 m, lies 1 cable ESE of the harbour entrance and close NNE of the approach. Depths are liable to change after gales.
Deepest and longest berth in South Dock (6.67).

2   **Tidal levels:** see *Admiralty Tide Tables.* Mean spring range about 5·8 m; mean neap range about 3·5 m.
Maximum size of vessel handled. Length 120 m, beam about 18 m, draught 5·5 to 6·7 m dependent upon height of tide.
Local weather. ESE gales cause the heaviest seas in the approach; in these conditions Port Control should be contacted before attempting entry.

Arrival information
6.58

1   **Port radio service** is maintained from 2½ hours before HW to 1½ hours after HW and during office hours. See the relevant *Admiralty List of Radio Signals.*
6.59

1   **An anchorage** may be obtained to the ENE of North Breakwater from 3 cables to 1 mile off in depths between 8 and 16 m, sand, fairly clear of rocks. There is no protection except in offshore winds.
Caution. The bottom is foul to the S of a line of bearing 070° from the head of North Breakwater.
6.60

1   **Pilotage** is not compulsory, but is recommended for strangers. The pilot cutters are equipped with VHF radio and are on station over the HW period when a vessel is expected.

2   In poor visibility vessels requiring a pilot should sound numeral one, morse code. The pilot vessel sounds the same signal.

3   **Tugs** are available. Vessels requiring a tug show an ensign at the mainmast by day and a white light at the yardarm by night.

Seaham Harbour (6.63)

(Original dated 2000)

(Photograph - Air Images)

6.61

1   **Local knowledge.** Depths on the approach to the harbour are extremely irregular within the 5 m depth contour and strangers are advised not to approach the harbour at night.

6.62

1   **Regulations.** Byelaws are in force. The speed limit in the harbour is 5 kn.

Harbour

6.63

1   **Layout.** The harbour consists of an outer tidal harbour and an enclosed dock, South Dock. The entrance lies between two breakwaters which curve ESE and NE 3½ cables from the shore and protect the outer harbour. Within the outer harbour there are wave screens protecting the entrance to South Dock.

2   On the NW side of the harbour there is a small tidal basin leading to North Dock, which is tidal, dries and is used only by fishing boats.

6.64

1   **Dock traffic signals** are displayed from the roof of the Port Control building at the N side of the entrance to South Dock, as follows:

Signal	Meaning
Single red light	Vessels may enter dock.
Single green light	Vessels may leave dock.

2   Vessels should also contact Port Control on VHF.

Other than vessels entering and leaving, no vessel movements may take place within South Dock when the traffic signals are displayed.

Directions

6.65

1   From a position 1 mile ESE of the harbour entrance the route leads WNW to the entrance, passing (with positions from the harbour entrance, (54°50′·2N, 1°19′·2W)):

SSW of Louis Rocky Patch (6 cables E), thence:

NNE of North Scar, a rock, (2 cables SE) the E point of Liddle Scars, thence:

2   Close SSW of a rock (6.57) (1 cable E) the S point of North East Bush, a rocky patch, thence:

To the harbour entrance between the breakwaters, which faces ESE and is 85 m wide. The breakwater heads both exhibit lights (6.66), thence:

3   To the dock entrance passing through the wave screen which exhibits three red lights in a triangle (red metal column, 4 m in height) on its S side. The docks gates are 19·8 m wide and operated from 2½ hours before HW to 1½ hours after HW. They cannot be operated during SE gales due to scend. There is a depth over the sill of 6·7 m at MHWS.

Useful mark

6.66

1   North Breakwater Head Light (white metal column, black bands, 10 m in height) (54°50′·3N, 1°19′·2W).

South Breakwater Head Light (red metal column, 7 m in height).

Berths

6.67

1   **South Dock** has 900 m of quays available giving 8 berths. A depth of at least 6·1 m is maintained in the dock.

Port services

6.68

1   **Repairs.** Limited repairs can be undertaken. Small craft can be lifted by crane out of South Dock.

Hospital available at Sunderland (6.41).

Other facilities. Reception of oily waste.

Supplies: all types of fuel oil; fresh water at the quays; provisions.

Other names

Chart 152
6.69

Horden Point (54°47′N, 1°18′W).
Maiden Paps (54°53′N, 1°23′W), the twin summits of Tunstall Hills.
Warden Law (54°51′N, 1°25′W).

HARTLEPOOL

General information

Chart 2566 plans of Hartlepool Bay and Tees Bay
Position
6.70

Hartlepool Harbour (54°42′N, 1°12′W) lies on the N side of Hartlepool Bay, 3 miles NNW of the entrance to the River Tees.

Function
6.71

The town, population 87 310 in 1991, has a medium size commercial port handling a wide range of goods, in particular forestry products. There are facilities for container, Ro-Ro, ore and bulk carrying vessels. There is also a modern cool store facility at the Deep Water Berth.

Platforms and pipelines for North Sea oilfields are constructed at Hartlepool.

Topography
6.72

The Heugh (6.51), which is the E extremity of Hartlepool Peninsula, lies to the E and N of the port. Its cliffs suffer from erosion and are protected by a sea wall. The seaward side of the peninsula as a whole is fronted by rocky ledges running 1 mile NW from The Heugh and extending up to 2 cables offshore.

Port limits
6.73

See 6.101.

Approach and entry
6.74

Hartlepool is approached from the E through Tees Bay, thence Hartlepool Bay at the N end of Tees Bay and finally through a dredged channel to the port.

Traffic
6.75

In 1999 the port handled 309 vessels totalling 1 279 666 dwt.

Port authority
6.76

Tees and Hartlepool Port Authority Limited, Queens Square, Middlesbrough TS2 1AH.

Limiting conditions
6.77

Controlling depths. There is a nominal depth in the approach channel of 5·7 m. The channel is subject to silting and the Harbour Master should be consulted for the latest information.

Deepest and longest berth is Irvine's Quay 380 m long, 9·5 m depth (6.93).

Tidal levels: see *Admiralty Tide Tables.* Mean spring range about 4·6 m; mean neap range about 2·4 m.

Visibility. Industrial smoke from Teeside may obscure the land.
6.78

Maximum size of vessel. Vessels up to length 190 m, beam 33 m and draught 4·5 m plus height of tide can be handled. Vessels approaching the maximum dimensions must consult the Harbour Master in advance.

Arrival information

Port operations
6.79

Port Operations and Information Service scheme, with full radar surveillance, is maintained for the control of shipping in Tees Bay, the approaches to Hartlepool and seawards for 12 miles. See the relevant *Admiralty List of Radio Signals.*

Traffic signals
6.80

Entry/exit signal. A single fixed amber light, day and night, exhibited from a mast on the NE side of the entrance to Victoria Harbour and visible to seaward and from the docks, indicates that vessels may enter but not leave the port. When no such light is exhibited, vessels may leave but not enter the port.

Notice of ETA
6.81

Vessels carrying dangerous cargoes should notify the Tees Harbour Master of their ETA at least 24 hours in advance. Other vessels over 20 m in length should advise the Tees Harbour Master 6 hours in advance.

Outer anchorage
6.82

See 6.111.

Pilots and tugs
6.83

Pilotage is compulsory for all vessels greater than 95 m in length, navigating in Victoria Harbour inwards of Middleton Beacon (54°41′·6N, 1°11′·2W), except for vessels exempt by law and vessels greater than 85 m in length entering the North Basin. Pilotage is also compulsory for vessels greater than 20 m in length carrying dangerous cargoes or vessels requiring the services of a tug.

2 Pilots board either 2 miles NNE or 1 mile E of Tees Fairway Light-buoy (6.51), as shown on the chart.

Tugs are available.

Local knowledge
6.84

Entry into Hartlepool should not be attempted without local knowledge.

Regulations concerning entry
6.85

Vessels entering or leaving Hartlepool, or crossing Tees Bay, should not hamper the safe navigation of a vessel using the Tees approach channel.

Vessels over 20 m in length entering Hartlepool must contact the Harbour Master on VHF R/T and confirm that:
The vessel is seaworthy in every respect.

2 All secondary power or mechanical systems are in operation and are immediately available in the event of failure of any primary system, and all main propulsion units, including thrusters, have been tested in both directions.

Hartlepool Harbour (6.86)

(Original dated 2000)

(Photograph - Air Images)

3 The steering is under direct manual control. and not by any device or equipment designed to function in place of the steersman.

Anchors are cleared away ready for use.

All vessels carrying dangerous or polluting goods, as defined in the Merchant Shipping (Reporting Requirements for Ships carrying Dangerous or Polluting Goods) Regulations 1995 must comply with the requirements of these Regulations. See 1.40.

Harbour

Layout
6.86

1 Hartlepool is entered through Outer Harbour, which dries, except for a dredged channel leading to Victoria Harbour, a tidal basin. There is also an enclosed basin, North Basin, in the NW corner of Victoria Harbour.

Dock signals
6.87

1

Signal	Meaning
Exhibited to seaward	
One fixed green light	Vessel may enter North Basin
One fixed red light	Vessel must not approach the lock to the North Basin.
Exhibited to docks	
Two fixed green lights disposed vertically	Vessels may proceed out of the North Basin.
One fixed red light	Vessels must not approach the lock

2 The green lights exhibited to seaward indicate to vessels in Victoria Dock that inward traffic is moving.

Tidal streams
6.88

1 Tidal streams off the entrance to Hartlepool are shown on the chart. Tidal streams for Tees Bay are at 6.117.

There are eddies off the entrance to Outer Harbour.

Principal marks
6.89

1 **Landmarks:**

Steetly Magnesite Works Chimney (54°42′·5N, 1°12′·7W) (Chart 2567).

Major light:

The Heugh Light (54°41′·8N, 1°10′·5W) (6.49).

South Gare Breakwater Light (54°38′·8N, 1°08′·1W) (6.118).

Directions
(continued from 6.51)

Outer approaches
6.90

1 From a position 1½ miles ESE of The Heugh (54°42′N, 1°11′W), the track leads 1 mile W to a position 8 cables SE of the harbour entrance within the white sector of the directional light indicating the dredged channel (6.91), passing (with positions from the harbour entrance (54°41′·6N, 1°11′·1W)):

2 N of a rocky shoal (1 mile SE), marked by Longscar Light-buoy (E cardinal) which lies close E of the shoal. The NE extremity (1 mile SSE) of Long Scar, a detached ledge of rock which dries, is 3½ cables SW of the shoal. Long Scar runs 4 cables SW from its extremity, with several

146

smaller detached patches on either side. Longscar Light-buoy and two isolated rock pinnacles close SW are covered by the white sector (317°–325°) of Old Pier Light (6.91).

Inner approaches
6.91

1 The white sector (324°·4–325°·4) of the light exhibited from a light-tower (54°42'·0N, 1°11'·6W), leads through the dredged channel, marked by light-buoys and buoys, to the harbour entrance, passing (with positions from the harbour entrance):

2 WSW of the head of a breakwater (4 cables ESE) which is made of sand and cement, and runs 2 cables SSE from the shore close SSE of The Heugh. The Stones, detached rocks, lie close NE of the breakwater head. Thence:

WSW of a beacon (pole, 7 m high) (1½ cables SE) which stands on Inscar Point, thence:

3 To the harbour entrance, which is 80 m wide and lies between Old Pier on the NE side, on which stands a light (white wooden framework tower, red bands, 12 m in height) and Middleton Light-beacon (metal tower) standing on the head of Middleton Breakwater, which extends SE from the shore.

4 The dredged channel continues through Outer Harbour into Victoria Harbour (6.93) from where direct approach can be made to the entrance to North Basin, fitted with lock gates, 21·3 m wide and a depth over the sill 8·1 m at MHWS. The lock is operated from 3 hours before HW to 1 hour after HW.

Both the in-going and out-going streams set across the approach.

Useful mark
6.92

1 Saint Hilda's Church (tower) (54°41'·7N, 1°10'·8W).

Basins and berths
6.93

1 **Victoria Harbour:** Deep Water Berth, 290 m long, depth alongside 9·5 m, with a floating pontoon and a link span bridge providing a Ro-Ro berth at the NE corner of the berth; Victoria Quay, 140 m long, depth alongside 9·5 m; Irvine's Quay, 380 m long, depth alongside 9·5 m; Fish Quay.

North Basin: 494 m of quays, depth 7·9 m at MHWS, Ro-Ro berths NE and SW corners.

Port services
6.94

1 **Repairs** of a limited nature can be carried out.
6.95

1 **Other facilities:** deratting and exemption certificates issued; 4 hospitals; Ro-Ro berths see 6.93.
6.96

1 **Supplies:** heavy and diesel oil; water at the quays; provisions.

Small craft
6.97

1 Union Dock, Jackson Dock and Coal Dock have been separated from the commercial docks to form Hartlepool Marina. Approach is via a channel, dredged to 0·8 m, through West Harbour (4 cables SW of the harbour entrance) which otherwise dries, thence through a lock on the E side of the marina. Access to the lock is limited to 5 hours either side of HW. Vessels wishing to use the lock should contact the marina on VHF 15 minutes before arrival; see the relevant *Admiralty List of Radio Signals* for details. There are 260 berths and most of the usual facilities are available. Maximum craft length is 48·7 m and the maximum draught is 5 m.

2 Other berths for small craft are in West Harbour and in the E arm of Victoria Dock. Small craft can be launched from slips at local yacht clubs.

Hartlepool Marina (6.97)

(Original dated 2000)

(Photograph - Air Images)

TEES BAY AND RIVER TEES

General information

Charts 2567, 2566 plans of Tees Bay and River Tees
Position
6.98

1 Tees Bay is 6 miles across and lies between The Heugh (6.51) and Salt Scar (6.136) off Redcar. Hartlepool (6.70) lies close W of The Heugh and Hartlepool Bay forms the NW corner of Tees Bay. The mouth of the River Tees is 3½ miles WNW of Salt Scar.

Function
6.99

1 Teesport is the centre of a major petro-chemical complex encompassing Redcar, Middlesbrough, Billingham, South Bank, Stockton and Thornaby. There are also facilities for handling ore and other bulk cargoes and for container and Ro-Ro traffic, as well as general cargo at Tees Dock.

The population of the area in 1991 was 369 609.

Topography
6.100

1 The coast either side of the mouth of the River Tees is generally sandy and backed by low sandhills. Long Scar (6.90) and Little Scar 4 cables to its S are off-lying ledges in the N of Tees Bay, with West Scar (6.136) which runs E into Salt Scar (6.136) at the SE end of the bay. The entrance to the River Tees is 2 miles SSE of Long Scar and is formed between two breakwaters, North and South Gare. Shoals lying either side of the entrance extend up to 1 mile offshore.

Port limits
6.101

1 Tees Bay and Hartlepool Bay are within the jurisdiction of the Tees and Hartlepool Port Authority Limited. The seaward limits of the authority, which lie between Black Halls Point and West Scar and 2 to 4 miles offshore, are shown on the chart.

South Gare Breakwater   *North Gare Breakwater*

Entrance to River Tees (6.98)

(Original dated 2000)

(Photograph - Air Images)

Approach and entry
6.102
1   The River Tees is approached from the NE from Tees Bay through a deep water dredged channel.

Fishing
6.103
1   An important prawn fishing area lies offshore. See 1.18.

Traffic
6.104
1   In 1999 the port handled 5122 vessels totalling 71 445 643 dwt, and over 52 million tonnes of cargo.

Port authority
6.105
1   Tees and Hartlepool Port Authority Limited, Queen's Square, Middlesbrough. TS2 1AH. The Harbour Master's office is at Tees Dock (6.123).

Limiting conditions
6.106
1   **Controlling depths.** The approach channel has a dredged depth of 15·4 m from Tees Fairway Light-buoy (6.51) to the entrance where it reduces to 14·1 m. Thereafter the maintained depth is progressively reduced to 4·5 m at Billingham, 7 miles from the entrance. The maintained depths are shown on the chart. Above Billingham the channel is not dredged.

2   **The deepest and longest berths** are in the Phillips Petroleum UK Ltd Terminal (6.123) and in the Redcar Ore Terminal (6.123).

    Caution. All depths are subject to siltation. For the latest information the Harbour Master should be consulted.

3   **Vertical clearances.** The overhead power cable between Teesport Terminal and North Tees Terminal has a safe vertical clearance of 61·9 m. There is a clearance of 48·8 m below the transporter bridge (54°35'·1N, 1°13'·6W) at Middlesbrough. Tees (Newport) Bridge (54°34'·3N, 1°15'·6W) at the S end of Billingham Reach is permanently in the down position and has a vertical clearance of 6·4 m.

4   **Mean tidal levels.**
        See *Admiralty Tide Tables.*
        River Tees Entrance: mean spring range about 4·6 m; mean neap range about 2·3 m.
        Middlehaven: mean spring range about 4·8 m; mean neap range about 2·4 m.

5   *Note.* The River Tees Barrage at Blue House Point (54°33'·9N, 1°17'·1W) came into operation in December 1994 thereby impounding the upper river. Mariners are advised that this operation has the effect of truncating the salt water wedge in the vicinity of the Barrage, thus causing a change in the normal tidal flow of the lower river (i.e. that part of the river between the barrage and the sea).

6   It is possible that the effect of this might be experienced a number of miles downstream of the Barrage, where the combination of fluvial and tidal flows might cause flows which are opposite to those which Mariners would normally expect.

6.107
1   **Maximum size of vessel handled.** The quoted dimensions are length 305 m, beam 48·0 m and draught 17·0 m, but these figures depend on the prevailing conditions. Vessels in excess of 16·15 m draught should consult the Harbour Master prior to entry.

Arrival information

Port operations
6.108

1 **Port Operations and Information Service** scheme with full radar surveillance is maintained for the control of shipping, covering Tees Bay and extending 12 miles to seaward, Tees River to tidal limits, and Hartlepool. See the relevant *Admiralty List of Radio Signals.*

Traffic signals
6.109

1 **River Tees.** The following signals, associated with Traffic Control (6.113), require vessels to obtain the specific authority of the Harbour Master to enter the approach channel from seaward or from up river of the main channel below the overhead power cables (54°36′N, 1°10′W) 4 cables SW of Tees Dock;

2 From a mast at South Gare (54°38′·8N, 1°08′·2W)

By day: White light flashing once every second.

By night: Three red lights disposed vertically.

In fog: Two blasts of 6 seconds duration every 30 seconds.

From the radar tower (54°36′·2N, 1°09′·6W) at Tees Dock

By day: White light flashing once every second.

Notice of ETA
6.110

1 Vessels over 20 m in length are required to give 6 hours' notice of their ETA and ETD and movements within the port. This early notice is necessary as some vessel movements may invoke the use of Traffic Control (6.113).

Outer anchorage
6.111

1 There is an anchorage in Tees Bay to seaward of the prohibited areas listed below and to the E of Fairway Light-buoy, but anchoring in N or E gales is not recommended.

Anchoring is prohibited as follows:

Within 6 cables of the Tees Fairway Light-buoy (54°41′·0N, 1°06′·3W).

In the approach channel leading from the Fairway Light-buoy to the harbour entrance.

2 Within 2½ cables of the Ekofisk pipeline which runs from the shore 1 mile NW of the River Tees entrance to the NE, passing 6 cables NW of Fairway Light-buoy.

Within 2½ cables of the Everest gas pipeline which runs from the shore 1·8 miles SE of the South Gare Breakwater.

Pilots and tugs
6.112

1 Pilotage is compulsory for all vessels greater than 95 m in length, navigating in the seaward approach channel and River Tees as far as No 27 Light-buoy (54°35′·05N, 1°11′·78W) except for vessels exempt by law; and for vessels greater than 80 m in length navigating in the River Tees between No 27 Light-buoy and Newport Bridge. Pilotage is also compulsory for vessels greater than 20 m in length carrying dangerous cargoes or vessels requiring the services of a tug.

2 The pilot boards either 2 miles NNE or 1 mile E of Fairway Light-buoy. It should be noted that the tidal stream sets at right angles to the channel (see 6.117 for further information) and care is required embarking the pilot.

Tugs are available, but outside working hours 6 hours' notice is normally required if tugs are needed after 1800.

Regulations concerning entry
6.113

1 Vessels over 20 m in length entering River Tees Channel or leaving the berth must confirm to the Harbour Master that:

The vessel is seaworthy in every respect.

All secondary power or mechanical systems are in operation and are immediately available in the event of any failure of a primary system, and all main propulsion units, including thrusters, have been tested in both directions.

2 The steering is under direct manual control and not by any device or equipment designed to function in place of the steersman.

Anchors are cleared away ready for use.

Traffic control is operated when a vessel over 200 m in length is underway within the river limits to allow the vessel to negotiate the channel without embarrassment from other traffic. Such vessels can only enter the channel when an "all clear" route is available.

3 Restricted transit control is operated for vessels carrying certain dangerous cargoes to ensure a clear passage or carefully controlled limited passing of other traffic, the latter being controlled by the Harbour Master.

No vessel may navigate in the approach channel or River Tees in visibility of less than 1000 m, except with the permission of the Harbour Master.

4 Except with the permission of the Harbour Master all vessels over 20 m in length must enter the approach channel N of a line joining Tees North Light-buoy and Tees South Light-buoy (54°40′·2N, 1°06′·9W).

All vessels carrying dangerous or polluting goods, as defined in the Merchant Shipping (Reporting Requirements for Ships carrying Dangerous or Polluting Goods) Regulations 1995 must comply with the requirements of these Regulations. See 1.40.

Harbour

Layout
6.114

1 There are riverside berths from Corus Redcar Ore Terminal, 1½ miles inside the entrance, to Billingham, 7 miles from the entrance. The larger and deeper berths are to be found in the 2 mile stretch of river between Redcar and Teesport. Tees Dock, which is tidal, is on the SE bank of the river at Teesport. Middlehaven (6.122), 2½ miles up river from Teesport, is in use on a limited basis by smaller vessels.

2 Seaton-on-Tees Channel, which leads off W from the river 1 mile inside the entrance is marked by light-buoys (lateral). The intakes of a nuclear power station situated on the N bank of the channel are marked by beacons.

Dredging
6.115

1 Port authority vessels are engaged in dredging and hydrographic survey work on a continuing basis and they, as well as any other vessels contracted for such work in the River Tees, comply in all respects with the *International Regulations for Preventing Collisions at Sea 1972.*

Tees Dock   *North Tees Terminal*

Container Terminal

Teesport from NE (6.114)

(Original dated 2000)

(Photograph - Air Images)

Dock signals
6.116

1   **Tees Dock.** The following signals, exhibited from a tower on the SW side of the dock entrance, control movements in and out of Tees Dock;

Signal	*Meaning*
White light occulting every 10 seconds	Vessel may enter dock
White light group flashing 3 every 10 seconds	Vessel may leave dock

Tidal streams
6.117

1   **Tees Bay.** See chart 2567 and *Admiralty Tidal Stream Atlas: North Sea, Northwestern Part.*
   Off River Tees Entrance the tidal streams run as follows:

Time from HW Tees	*Remarks*
–0305	SE-going stream commences
+0310	NW-going stream commences

2   The spring rate in each direction has been reported to reach 2 kn.
   There may be turbulence during the out-going stream from the river, especially with E and NE gales.
   In River Tees Entrance the tidal streams run as follows:

Time from HW Tees	*Remarks*
–0520	In-going stream commences
–0040	Out-going stream commences

3   The spring rate in each direction is 2 to 3 kn.
   The streams run in the direction of the channel, but set towards the outer banks at bends. There is turbulence during the out-going stream off the entrance to the oil terminal (6.123), about 1½ miles SW of South Gare Lighthouse, where the Tees River stream is met by that of Seaton-on-Tees Channel.

4   With freshets the duration and rate of the out-going stream is increased and the in-going stream correspondingly reduced.

Principal marks
6.118

1   **Landmarks:**
   There are numerous tanks and chimneys on either bank of the river shown on the chart both individually and in groups. At night the glare from the flares and blast furnaces is visible a long way to seaward.

2   **Major lights:**
   The Heugh Light (54°41′·8N, 1°10′·5W) (6.49).
   South Gare Breakwater Light (white round tower, 13 m in height, on breakwater head) (54°38′·8N, 1°08′·1W).

Other navigational aids
6.119

1   **Racon:**
   Tees Fairway Light-buoy (54°41′N, 1°06′W).
   DGPS:
   Flamborough Head Light (54°07′N, 0°05′W).

Directions
(continued from 6.51)

Tees Bay to River Tees entrance
6.120

1 **River Tees Leading Lights:**

Front light (Red metal framework tower, white bands) (54°37'·2N, 1°10'·1W).

Rear light (Metal framework tower) (560 m SSW of front light).

The alignment (210°) of these lights leads through the approach channel to the harbour entrance, passing (with positions from front light):

2 Through the prohibited anchorage area (6.111) centred on Tees Fairway Light-buoy (safe water) (4¼ miles NNE). The buoy should invariably be passed on the vessel's port hand guarding against the cross set. Thence:

3 Between Tees North Light-buoy (starboard hand) and Tees South Light-buoy (port hand) (3½ miles NNE) which mark the start of the dredged channel (6.106). The channel is 244 m wide and marked by light-buoys on both sides. A wreck with a depth of 12·2 m over it lies 3 cables NW of Tees North Light-buoy. Thence:

4 WNW of South Gare Breakwater (2 miles NNE) with a lighthouse (6.118) at its head. The breakwater extends 5 cables N from the NW extremity of Tod Point. Traffic signals (6.109) are exhibited from a mast on a brick building 60 m S of the lighthouse and a radar tower stands close S of this building. Thence:

5 To a position ESE of North Gare Breakwater (1·7 miles N) which extends only to the LW line and lies 4½ cables W of the channel.

Caution. In bad weather the River Tees might be entered from half flood to HW. During NE, E and especially SE gales, care is necessary. A ground swell builds up in the area in NE gales.

River Tees Entrance to Teesport
6.121

1 From a position about 7½ cables within the entrance on the centreline of the channel the track follows the River Tees, which is dredged (6.106) and marked on both sides by light-buoys, and runs in a generally SSW direction for 2½ miles, passing (with positions from front leading light):

2 ESE of the entrance to Seaton-on-Tees Channel (6.114) (7 cables NNE). There is a turning circle off the entrance to the channel, and a half tide training wall runs along the E side of the River Tees. At this point the river curves to the S away from the alignment of the leading lights, but an arm of the river continues on this alignment towards berths 3 to 8 at the Phillips Petroleum UK Ltd Oil Terminal (6.123). Thence:

3 NW of Tees Dock (6.123) (1 mile SSE). Teesport Container Terminal is close SW of the dock, with the Huntsman (ICI) North Tees Terminal on the opposite bank. An overhead power cable, safe vertical clearance 61·9 m, crosses the river between the two terminals. There is a turning circle off the entrance to Tees Dock.

River Tees above Teesport
6.122

1 Above Teesport the track follows the river, passing (with positions from Tees Bridge (54°34'·3N, 1°15'·6W)):

NW of Tees Dockyard and Tees Offshore Base (2·8 miles ENE), thence:

2 NNE of Middlehaven, (1·4 miles ENE), which is an impounded dock. Above the dock there are several wharfs and jetties, which can be seen on the chart. Thence:

Below a transporter bridge (1·4 miles NE) (6.106). Dredged depths only continue for 1·8 miles beyond this bridge to Simon Riverside Jetty, thence:

3 To Tees (Newport) Bridge (6.106). Above Tees (Newport) Bridge there is a road bridge, vertical clearance 18 m, and 1·1 miles above Tees (Newport) Bridge the Tees Barrage has a lock system for small vessels which require passage up to Stockton. Prior to entering the channel and lock system Mariners must contact Tees Barrage Radio on VHF. See the relevant *Admiralty List of Radio Signals* for details.

Basins and berths
6.123

1 There are numerous berths along the length of the River Tees on both banks. The major berths lie close to the river entrance as far as Teesport. They are;

West bank:

Phillips Petroleum UK Ltd Oil Terminal, 8 berths of which 4 are 295 m long, depth 18·2 m.

Teesport – Phillips Petroleum berths (6.123)

(Original dated 2000)

(Photograph - Air Images)

2 Seal Sands Storage, 2 berths handling chemicals.

Vopak, 3 tanker berths, largest berth 179 m long, depth 11 m.

BASF, 2 berths handling chemicals.

North Tees Terminal, 4 berths handling oil and chemicals, largest berth 271 m long, depth 12·7 m.

3 **East bank:**

Corus Redcar Ore Terminal, one berth, 306 m long, depth 17·3 m.

Northumbrian Water RSTC Berth.

Riverside Ro-Ro Terminal, depth 10·4 m.

Teesport Container Terminal, depth 8·5 m.

4 Tees Dock, 9 berths handling general cargo, steel and potash and includes two Ro-Ro berths. Longest berth 190 m, depth 10·9 m, Ro-Ro berths 8·8 m.

Teesport Terminal, 3 tanker berths, largest 198 m long, depth 10·9 m.

Port services
6.124

1   **Repairs.** Repairs of all kinds can be carried out. There is one repair yard with three dry docks, and a small shipyard with a slipway capable of handling vessels up to 1000 dwt.

Largest dry dock: length 175·26 m; breadth 22·25 m; depth at sill 2·5 m (LAT).
6.125

1   **Other facilities:** deratting and exemption certificates issued; reception of oily waste; customs; hospitals at Middlesbrough.
6.126

1   **Supplies:** all types of oil fuel at Teesport or by barge; fresh water at quays or by water boat; provisions and stores.
6.127

1   **Communications.** The nearest airport is at Teeside (54°30′N, 1°25′W), 14 miles distant.

Harbour regulations
6.128

1   Vessels on the River Tees must comply with the Tees and Hartlepool Harbour Byelaws 1977 and the Tees and Hartlepool Port Authority General Directions.

Copies of these regulations are supplied to all vessels over 20 m in length which visit the River Tees.

Small craft
6.129

1   Facilities for small craft are limited.

RIVER TEES TO WHITBY

General information

Chart 134
Route
6.130

1   From a position in the vicinity of Tees Fairway Light-buoy (54°41′N, 1°06′W) the route leads 21 miles ESE to a position NNE of Whitby.

Topography
6.131

1   Except for the rocky ledges off Redcar (54°37′N, 1°04′W) the coast is fronted by sandy beaches as far as Saltburn, 5 miles ESE. Thence the coast is an almost continuous line of cliffs, varying in height between 30 and 180 m, to Sandsend Ness, 10 miles ESE. These cliffs are cut away by alum works, now discontinued, and broken by deep ravines at Skinningrove, 6½ miles ESE of Redcar, Staithes 4 miles further ESE and Runswick, a further 2 miles ESE. This stretch of coast is subject to heavy landslips and fringed by an irregular ledge of rocks which dry out for about 3 cables. Whitby lies 2 miles ESE of Sandsend Ness and there is a broad sandy beach between the two.

Rescue
6.132

1   There are Coastguard Rescue Teams at Redcar (54°37′N, 1°05′W), Skinningrove (54°34′N, 0°54′W), Staithes (54°33′N, 0°47′W), Kettle Ness (54°32′N, 0°43′W) and Whitby. There is a VHF/DF station for emergency use only at Whitby, which is remotely controlled from Humber (Bridlington) Maritime Rescue Sub-Centre. See 1.53.

2   An all-weather lifeboat is stationed at Whitby. Inshore lifeboats are stationed at Whitby, Redcar (two boats) and Runswick Bay (6.163). See 1.61 and 1.62 for details of lifeboats.

Tidal streams
6.133

1   The tidal streams generally follow the coastal direction and rates up to 1½ kn can be experienced. Tidal streams are given on the chart and in *Admiralty Tidal Stream Atlas: North Sea, Northwestern Part.*

Principal marks
6.134

1   **Landmarks:**

For marks in the Tees and Hartlepool area see 6.89 and 6.118.

Coatham Church (spire) (54°37′N, 1°05′W).

Chimneys (54°34′N, 0°54′W) close N of Skinningrove village.

Radio mast (red obstruction lights) (54°34′N, 0°50′W).

Pair of chimneys (54°33′N, 0°49′W) at Boulby.

Hotel (54°29′N, 0°37′W) at Whitby.

2   **Major lights:**

The Heugh Light (54°41′·8N, 1°10′·5W) (6.49).

South Gare Breakwater Light (54°38′·8N, 1°08′·1W) (6.118).

Whitby High Light (white 8-sided tower and dwellings, 13 m in height) (54°28′·6N, 0°34′·0W).

Other navigational aids
6.135

1   **Racon:**

Tees Fairway Light-buoy (54°41′N, 1°06′W).

DGPS:

Flamborough Head Light (54°07′N, 0°05′W).

Directions
(continued from 6.51)
6.136

1   From a position in the vicinity of Tees Fairway Light-buoy (54°41′N, 1°06′W) the route leads ESE to a position NNE of Whitby, passing (with positions from Redcliff (54°34′N, 0°50′W)):

2   NNE of Saltscar Light-buoy (N cardinal) (6½ miles WNW), which is moored 1½ miles ENE of Salt Scar and West Scar, two detached rocky ledges lying up to 8 cables offshore. Other ledges lie to the S and SW of Salt Scar. Thence:

3   NNE of The High (6½ miles WNW), a rocky shoal. A light-buoy (special) marking the seaward end of an outfall is moored at the S end of The High. A submarine cable runs NE from the shore close N of the landward end of this outfall. Thence:

4   NNE of Hunt Cliff (3 miles WNW), which is dark red and nearly perpendicular. A ridge extends SSW to Warsett Hill lying close SW of the cliff. Saltburn Scar, which marks the change from a sandy coast to one fronted by rocky ledges is immediately W of Hunt Cliff. Thence:

5   NNE of Redcliff, which is dark red and one of the boldest features on the coast and lies under Easington Heights, thence:

NNE of a light-buoy (special) (1½ miles ENE) marking the seaward end of an outfall off Boulby, thence:

6 NNE of Cowbar Nab (1¾ miles ESE), a prominent point. Old Nab, a low black cliff with a flagstaff is 6 cables E of Cowbar Nab, thence:

NNE of Kettle Ness (5½ miles ESE), a precipitous reddish point, excavated by an alum works. A cone shaped hill is close by, thence:

7 NNE of Sandsend Ness (7 miles ESE), an abrupt point with a disused alum works and fringed by rocky ledges. Kelder Steel, a rocky ledge to the NW of Sandsend Ness extends 4 cables offshore, thence:

NNE of Whitby Light-buoy (N cardinal) (9 miles ESE) 7 cables off the entrance to Whitby Harbour. A number of dangerous wrecks lie within the 20 m depth contour between Kettle Ness and Whitby.

8 **Caution.** Because of the irregularity of the coast between Hunt Cliff and Whitby, vessels should not approach within the 20 m depth contour.

6.137

1 **Clearing bearings:**

The line of bearing 295° of The Heugh Light (6.49) passes 8 cables NE of Salt Scar Light-buoy.

The line of bearing 285° of Hunt Cliff, just open N of Cowbar Nab, passes NE of Kettle Ness and Kelder Steel.

2 The line of bearing 145° of North Cheek (54°27′N, 0°31′W) (6.173) and open E of Whitby High Lighthouse passes NE of Whitby Light-buoy and Whitby Rock (6.153). At night the line of bearing 150° or more of Whitby High Lighthouse, which is within the white sector of the light, also passes NE of Whitby Light-buoy.

6.138

1 **Useful Marks:**

Redcar Church (tower) (54°37′N, 1°03′W).

Eston Nab radio masts (54°33′N, 1°07′W).

Saint Mark's Church (tower) (54°36′N, 1°01′W), Marske-by-the-Sea.

2 Church (tower) (54°35′N, 0°59′W), Saltburn-by-the-Sea.

Captain Cook's Monument (322 m) (54°29′N, 1°05′W) on Easby Moor (Chart 1191).

Lythe Church (spire) (54°30′N, 0°41′W).

(Directions continue for coastal passage S at 6.173)

Whitby

Chart 1612 plan of Whitby Harbour
General information
6.139

1 **Position.** Whitby Harbour (54°29′N, 0°37′W) stands on the mouth of the River Esk.

6.140

1 **Function.** Whitby, population 13 640 in 1991, is a small commercial and fishing port and also a centre for recreational craft.

6.141

1 **Topography.** To the W of Whitby the coast is sandy, while to the E it is formed by a rocky ledge fronted by rocks, both covered by kelp. The coast is backed by a steep bank.

The River Esk rises about 16 miles above Whitby and drains hilly country. In wet weather the river is subject to sudden and heavy freshets which scour the harbour, but in dry weather the stream is hardly perceptible.

6.142

1 **Traffic.** In 1999 the port handled 41 vessels with a total tonnage of 61 665 dwt.

6.143

1 **Port authority.** Scarborough Borough Council (6.177); the port is operated by Whitby Port Services Ltd. Correspondence should be addressed to the Harbour Master, Pier Road, Whitby, Yorkshire YO21 3PU.

Limiting conditions
6.144

1 **Controlling depths.** Across the bar, a flat ledge of shale, there is a depth of 1·4 m, with depths of 1·5 m between the outer pierheads and 1·4 m between the inner pierheads. These latter depths are maintained by continual dredging.

2 **Deepest and longest berth** is Endeavour Wharf (6.156).

Tidal levels: see *Admiralty Tide Tables.* Mean spring range about 4·6 m; mean neap range about 3·5 m.

Maximum size of vessel handled is length 85 m, beam 14 m and draught 4·5–6·0 m depending on tide.

6.145

1 **Local weather.** No attempt should be made to enter Whitby Harbour in gales from the N to NE, when the sea breaks a long way offshore and renders the approach dangerous.

In N gales Lower Harbour is unusable and Upper Harbour (6.149) acts as a place of refuge.

Arrival information
6.146

1 **Port radio station** is situated at the Harbour Office. ETA and requests for pilots, at least 30 minutes in advance, should be sent to this office during working hours, otherwise to the Bridge (6.150). See the relevant *Admiralty List of Radio Signals.*

6.147

1 An **anchorage** may be obtained in Whitby Road (6.153), about 7 cables NNW of the harbour entrance. Holding is good, but in W or SW gales the anchorage is reported to be uncomfortable.

6.148

1 **Pilotage** is compulsory for vessels over 37 m in length and fishing vessels over 45·5 m in length. The pilot boards in the vicinity of Whitby Light-buoy, weather permitting.

A green light is exhibited from the lighthouse standing on West Inner Pierhead (6.153) when a piloted vessel is entering harbour at night.

Harbour
6.149

1 **Layout.** The harbour is divided into Upper and Lower Harbours, which are separated by a passage, 21 m wide, spanned by a swing bridge. As far as possible a channel 27 m wide with a depth of 1 m is maintained from the inner pierheads through the swing bridge to Upper Harbour.

2 There are several riverside berths, mainly on the W bank (6.156), which require ships to take the ground at LW. The bottom of both harbours is gravel, mud and shale.

There is a marina at the S end of Upper Harbour. Close S of the marina a concrete covered power cable, which dries, forms a weir across the river.

6.150

1 **Bridge signals.** A vessel requiring the swing bridge to be opened sounds three long blasts. Green lights exhibited from the bridge indicate it is open and red lights that it is closed. Bridge control, which is equipped with VHF R/T, keeps watch from 2 hours before HW to 2 hours after HW.

Abbey   *Marina*

Whitby Harbour (6.149)

(Original dated 2000)

(Photograph - Air Images)

6.151

1   **Tidal streams** are weak in Whitby Road, but the SE-going stream (flood) during the 2 hours before HW and the NW-going stream (ebb) run strongly across the harbour entrance. It is reported that, with W or SW gales the SE-going stream reaches 3 kn in Whitby Road and 5 kn in the vicinity of Whitby Light-buoy; the NW-going stream is negligible.

2   With freshets in the river the out-going stream may reach 5 kn in the entrance.

6.152

1   **Principal marks:**
    Disused lighthouse (yellow round stone tower, 22 m in height, standing on West Inner Pierhead) (54°29'·6N, 0°36'·7W).
    Metropole Hotel (54°29'·4N, 0°37'·4W).

2   Sneaton Castle (flagstaff) (54°29'·0N, 0°38'·4W).
    Saint Mary's Church (tower and flagstaff) (54°29'·3N, 0°36'·5W).
    Whitby Abbey (ruins) (54°29'·3N, 0°36'·3W).
    TV mast (54°29'·4N, 0°36'·2W).
Major light:
    Whitby High Light (54°28'·6N, 0°34'·0W) (6.134).

Directions
6.153

1   **Whitby Harbour Outer Leading Marks and Light:**
    Front mark (black and white pole, white triangular topmark) (54°29'·4N, 0°36'·6W).
    Rear mark (white disc, black stripe) (20 m S of front mark).
    Light (close W of Saint Mary's Church) (105 m S of front mark).

Abbey

TV Mast

Whitby Abbey (6.152)

(Original dated 2000)

(Photograph - Air Images)

2   The alignment (169°) of the two marks and the light (at night the line of bearing 169° of the leading light seen between the two lights situated on the outer pierheads (below)) leads through Whitby Road to the harbour entrance, passing (with positions from the harbour entrance):

3   W of Whitby Light-buoy (N cardinal) (7 cables N). From the SE passing NE of the buoy, thence:
    E of Upgang Rocks (1 mile WNW), an area of foul ground inside the 5 m depth contour over which

4 W of Whitby Rock (3½ cables NE). The Scar, a rocky ledge, lies inshore of the rock and both are covered in kelp. The rocks dry in places and the swell breaks heavily over them, thence:

5 To the harbour entrance, which lies between West Outer Pierhead, from which a light (green wooden tower, 7 m in height) is occasionally exhibited, and East Outer Pierhead marked by a light (red wooden tower, 7 m in height), thence:

6 Between the inner pierheads (¾ cable S). A disused lighthouse (6.152) stands on West Inner Pierhead and a second similar lighthouse (13 m in height) stands on East Inner Pierhead.

6.154

1 **Whitby Harbour Inner Leading Light-beacons.** The alignment (029°) astern of leading lights, which stand on the elbow of East Inner Pier close S of the disused lighthouse, leads from the alignment of the Outer Leading Marks through Outer Harbour to Fish Quay (6.156):

2 Front light (white triangle, standing on pier coping) (54°29′·5N, 0°36′·6W).
Rear light (white disc, black stripe) (close NE of front beacon).

6.155

1 **Clearing bearings**
The alignment (147°) of the light structure on West Outer Pierhead with the E extremity of Whitby Abbey ruins passes 2 cables NE of the 5 m depth contour containing Upgang Rocks.

2 The alignment (176°) of the disused lighthouse on East Pier with the Mortuary Chapel Spire, which stands above trees in Esk Vale, and the W extremity of a prominent house in the town passes W of Whitby Rock and The Scar, as shown on the chart.

Berths

6.156

1 **Lower Harbour:** Fish Quay, 213 m long, least depth 0·3 m; Tate Hill Pier: Fish Pier.
Upper Harbour: Endeavour Wharf, 213 m long, least depth 2·0 m; Eskside Wharf.

Port services

6.157

1 **Repairs:** repairs can be undertaken; floating dock with lifting capacity of 500 tonnes; small shipyard.
Other facilities: hospital with helicopter landing site (54°29′N, 0°37′W); customs.
Supplies: marine diesel by road tanker; fresh water at quays; provisions and limited stores.

Small craft

6.158

1 There is a marina in Upper Harbour and three boatyards. There are three public and one private slipway for launching small craft. Whitby Yacht Club is situated at the N end of Fish Quay.

Anchorages and minor harbours

Chart 2567
Redcar
6.159

1 **General information.** Redcar (54°37′N, 1°04′W), used by fishing vessels, is situated 3 miles SE of South Gare

Breakwater (6.120). Coatham adjoins the NW side of Redcar.
Landmarks:
Coatham Church (spire) (54°37′N, 1°05′W).
Redcar Church (tower) (54°37′N, 1°03′W).

2 **Directions.** Lade Way Leading Lights:
Front Light (metal column, 5 m in height on promenade) (54°37′·1N, 1°03′·8W).
Rear Light (Brick building, 8 m in height) (43 m WSW of front light).
The alignment (247°) of these leading lights leads to Redcar Sands, passing between the rocky ledges of High Stone and Sandy Batt. The remains of a boiler lie on this line, SW of High Stone.

3 Luff Way Leading Lights:
Front Light (metal column, 5 m in height on esplanade) (54°37′·1N, 1°03′·6W).
Rear Light (metal column, 8 m in height) (115 m S of front light).
The alignment (197°) of these leading lights leads to Redcar Sands

Chart 134
Skinningrove Wick
6.160

1 An **anchorage** can be obtained for small vessels in Skinningrove Wick (54°35′N, 0°53′W) in depths of 9 to 11 m, clay. The position is indicated on the chart.

Staithes Harbour
6.161

1 Staithes (54°33′N, 0°48′W) is a small fishing village close to Cowbar Nab (6.136). The harbour, which dries, is formed by two breakwaters; the E breakwater head is marked by a beacon (diamond topmark). The entrance, 61 m wide, faces NE and has depths of 4·6 m at HW springs.

Port Mulgrave
6.162

1 Port Mulgrave (54°33′N, 0°46′W), which dries, is formed by two breakwaters and has a depth of 5·2 m alongside at HW springs.

Chart 1612 plan of Runswick Bay
6.163

1 **General information.** Runswick Bay (54°32′N, 0°44′W) lies between Kettle Ness (6.136) and a point 1 mile W. The village of Runswick is on the W side of the bay and there is usually a good landing close S of the village.
The bay is encumbered by drying rocky ledges. In onshore winds a sea breaks across the entrance, where depths are slightly less than in the centre of the bay.

2 An **anchorage** for small vessels can be obtained 5½ cables NE of the lifeboat house with the deep ravine at the head of the bay bearing 229°. The anchorage is indicated on the chart.

Chart 134
Sandsend Road
6.164

1 An **anchorage** can be obtained in Sandsend Road (54°30′N, 0°39′W) in depths of 11 m, sand over clay, between Sandsend Ness (6.136) and Upgang Rocks (6.153).

Other name

6.165

1 Cattersty Sands (54°34′N, 0°54′W).

WHITBY TO SCARBOROUGH

General information

Chart 129, 134
Route
6.166

1　From a position NE of Whitby (54°29′N, 0°37′W) the coastal route runs 4 miles SE thence SSE 12 miles to a position ENE of Scarborough.

Topography
6.167

1　The coast between Whitby and Scarborough is cliffy, fringed by rocky ledges and relatively steep-to.

Depths
6.168

1　Depths in an area shown on the chart, extending up to 2 miles off the coast between South Cheek (6.173) and Scarborough, are from old leadline surveys. Uncharted shoals and other hazards may exist in this area.

Rescue
6.169

1　There are Coastguard Rescue Teams at Robin Hood's Bay (54°26′N, 0°32′W), Ravenscar (54°24′N, 0°29′W), Burniston (54°20′N, 0°25′W) and Scarborough; see 1.53.

　An all-weather lifeboat and an inshore lifeboat are stationed at Scarborough. See 1.61 and 1.62 for details of lifeboats.

Tidal streams
6.170

1　Tidal streams are given on the chart and in the *Admiralty Tidal Stream Atlas: North Sea, Northwestern Part.*

Principal marks
6.171

1　**Landmarks:**
　For marks in Whitby see 6.152.
　Radio mast (54°24′N, 0°31′W).
　Scarborough Castle (ruined keep) (54°17′·2N, 0°23′·3W).

2　**Major lights:**
　Flamborough Head Light (54°07′N, 0°05′W) (6.196).
　Whitby High Light (54°28′·6N, 0°34′·0W) (6.134).

Other navigational aid
6.172

1　**DGPS:**
　Flamborough Head Light (54°07′N, 0°05′W).

Directions
(continued from 6.138)
6.173

1　From a position NE of Whitby the route leads 4 miles SE thence 12 miles SSE to a position ENE of Scarborough, passing (with positions from South Cheek (54°24′N, 0°29′W)):

　NE of Saltwick Nab (6 miles NNW), a dark rocky promontory owned by the National Trust. Black Nab, a dark rocky islet, lies 5 cables SE, thence:

2　NE of Whitby High Light (5 miles NNW) (6.134), thence:

　NE of North Cheek (2¼ miles NNW), a bold headland, in an area of high, dark cliffs with occasional red tinges, thence:

3　ENE of South Cheek with the village of Ravenscar close SW. Robin Hood's Bay lies between North and South Cheek. The coast is formed by a cliff and grassy bank, broken by the occasional deep gully, backed by cultivated ground rising like an amphitheatre. The shore of the bay is encumbered by ledges up to 5 cables offshore. Thence:

4　ENE of Hayburn Wyke (3½ miles SSE), an indentation at the mouth of a wooded valley where the coast decreases in elevation. Cloughton Wyke, a similar feature, is 1¼ miles further SSE. Thence:

　ENE of Hundale Point (5 miles SSE) with Long Nab a further 5 cables SSE, thence:

5　ENE of Scalby Ness (7 miles SSE), which is encumbered by rocks. An outfall, marked by a light-buoy (port hand), runs 8 cables ENE from Scalby Ness, thence:

　To a position ENE of Scarborough Rock (8 miles SSE), a headland at the N entry point to Scarborough Bay (6.176). The town of Scarborough encompasses the point but lies mainly to its SW.

(Directions continue at 6.198)

Scarborough

Chart 1612 plans of Scarborough Bay and Scarborough Harbour
General information
6.174

1　**Position.** Scarborough (54°17′N, 0°23′W) is situated at the NW corner of Scarborough Bay.
6.175

1　**Function.** There is a small harbour in which vessels take the ground at LW. It is also a fishing and yachting centre and an important seaside resort.

　The population of Scarborough was 53 600 in 1991.
6.176

1　**Topography.** Scarborough Bay lies between Scarborough Rock and White Nab, a cliffy point, 1 mile S. The bottom of the bay is smooth and depths are regular. The town at the N end of the bay rises in the form of an amphitheatre and is fronted by South Sands; the S part of the bay is bordered by grassy slopes fronted by rocky ledges.
6.177

1　**Port authority.** Scarborough Borough Council, Harbour Department, 18 West Pier, Scarborough YO11 1PD.

Limiting conditions
6.178

1　**Controlling depths.** Old Harbour, which is dredged in its W part to chart datum, is entered through a channel 10 m wide with a least charted depth of 0·1 m. Both East Harbour and its entrance channel dry. The harbours are subject to silting and the Harbour Master should be consulted for the latest information on depths.

　Tidal levels: see *Admiralty Tide Tables.* Mean spring range about 4·8 m; mean neap range about 2·3 m.

2　**Maximum size of vessel handled.** Length 80 m; draught 4·66 m at HW springs.

　Caution. The bottom of both harbours is mud, sand and clay with stones and boulders. Tidal scour and dredging may expose these stones such that they are dangerous to vessels. Vessels using the harbour should be capable of taking ground on a hard bottom.
6.179

1　**Local weather.** Scarborough Bay is open to the E and the harbour should not be attempted in strong NE to SSE winds when the entrance channel can be affected by silting (6.178), nor should the approach be made across broken water in Scarborough Bay in bad weather. Strong NNW winds also send a heavy swell into the bay.

Arrival information
6.180
1   An **anchorage**, indicated on the chart, may be obtained 5 cables SE of Vincent's Pier Lighthouse (54°16′·9N, 0°23′·3W) in 8 m, sand over blue clay. Anchoring is prohibited in the fairway leading to the harbour entrance.
6.181
1   **Pilotage** is compulsory for vessels over 37 m in length, and for fishing vessels over 45·5 m in length. The pilot normally boards 1 mile E of Vincent's Pier Lighthouse (6.185).
   Tugs. Local fishing vessels will assist by arrangement.

Harbour
6.182
1   **Layout.** The harbour is formed by four piers which divide it into two independent harbours, Old Harbour, the larger of the two, and East Harbour.
6.183
1   **Tidal signals** are exhibited when there is more than 3·7 m of water at the bar as follows:

Position	Signal
West Pierhead (watch hut)	2 fixed red lights
Vincent's Pier Lighthouse	Fixed yellow light
Vincent's Pier SW corner	2 fixed green vertical lights
Vincent's Pier at bridge	2 fixed green vertical lights

6.184
1   **Tidal streams** are barely perceptible in Scarborough Bay. Off East Pier the N-going stream runs with some

strength from 1 hour before HW to 2 hours after LW; during SE winds it sets constantly past the harbour entrance.
6.185
1   **Principal marks:**
   Scarborough Castle (54°17′·2N, 0°23′·3W) (6.171).
   Saint Mary's Church (tower and flagstaff) (54°17′·2N, 0°23′·5W).
   Vincent's Pier Lighthouse (white round tower, 15 m in height) (54°16′·9N, 0°23′·3W).
   War Memorial (54°16′·1N, 0°24′·2W) on N slope of Oliver's Mount.

Directions
6.186
1   From a position E of Scarborough, the alignment (273°) of the two N towers of the Grand Hotel (54°16′·8N, 0°23′·8W) leads to a position S of the harbour (54°16′·9N, 0°23′·3W), from whence either entrance may be approached, passing:
   N of Ramsdale Scar (2 cables SSW of the entrance), a foul rocky area, thence:
2   To East Harbour entrance, 8 m wide and lying between Vincent's Pier head and East Pier on which stands a light (mast, 4 m in height) or;
   To the channel close W of Vincent's Pier which leads to Old Harbour entrance, 29 m wide and lying between Old Pier and West Pier. Tidal signals (6.183) are displayed from both pierheads.
3   **Caution.** Navigation close to East Pier and Scarborough Rock should be avoided if a heavy swell is running from N or E.
   The harbour should be entered between half-flood and first quarter ebb taking into account the tidal signals.
   In the three winter months the entrance to East Harbour is closed by a boom. Access to East Harbour is then

Castle   *Scarborough Rock*

Lighthouse

Scarborough Harbour (6.182)

(Original dated 2000)

(Photograph - Air Images)

between Vincent's Pier and Old Pier at the site of the drawbridge.

Berths
6.187

1   **Old Harbour:**
 North Wharf, 152 m long.
 West Pier, used by fishing vessels.
  East Harbour:
 East Harbour, which dries 2 to 5 m, is used as a small craft haven.

Port services
6.188

1   **Repairs** to engine and deck; grid for vessels up to 43 m in length.
  Facilities: hospital; helicopter landing site at the hospital (54°17′N, 0°27′W); customs.
  Supplies: marine diesel at SE end of West Pier; fresh water at quays; provisions.

Small craft
6.189

1   **Berths** are allocated permanently to small craft in East Harbour. There are drying pontoon berths for visiting small craft, with additional berths available on the E side of Vincent's Pier, but visitors should consult the Harbour Master first. Small craft are only allowed into Old Harbour in an emergency.

2   **Boat landing** is on the W side of Vincent's Pier in depths of 0·1 to 1·0 m alongside.
  There are boat slips in both harbours.

Other names
6.190

1   Dickenson's Point (54°16′·3N, 0°23′·5W).
 Dovehole Scar (54°16′·4N, 0°23′·2W).
 Perilous Rocks (54°15′·7N, 0°22′·1W).
 South Steel (54°′ 17·1N, 0°22′·9W).

SCARBOROUGH TO FLAMBOROUGH HEAD

General information

Chart 129
Route
6.191

1   From a position ENE of Scarborough the coastal route leads 15 miles SE to a position E of Flamborough Head.

Topography
6.192

1   From White Nab (6.176), the S entrance point to Scarborough Bay, to Old Horse Rocks, 3 miles SE, the coast is fronted by foul ground extending up to 5 cables offshore. Thence the coast is steep-to as far as Filey Brigg, which juts out 1 mile to seaward and lies 2 miles further SE. Filey Bay is S of Filey Brigg and curves from S to SE for 3½ miles to King and Queen Rocks. The shore of the bay is cliffy, backed by a steep grassy bank and fronted by a broad sandy beach. Between King and Queen Rocks and Flamborough Head, 6 miles ESE, the coast consists of precipitous cliffs.

Exercise area
6.193

1   Submarines exercise in an area NE of Flamborough Head, which is shown on the chart together with a cautionary notice.

Rescue
6.194

1   There are Coastguard Rescue Teams at Filey, Speeton (54°10′N, 0°14′W) and Flamborough Head; see 1.53.
  There is a VHF D/F station at Flamborough Head remotely controlled by Humber Maritime Rescue Sub-Centre. See 1.59.

2   An all-weather lifeboat is stationed at Filey. Inshore lifeboats are stationed at Filey and at North Landing, Flamborough (6.201). See 1.61 and 1.62 for details of lifeboats.

Tidal stream
6.195

1   Within Filey Bay the tidal streams are barely perceptible, but the NW-going stream runs in an E direction along the S side of Filey Brigg at a rate of ½ kn. Between Brigg End and Filey Brigg Light-buoy (6.198) there might be turbulence; the spring rate is 1¾ kn.

2   In the vicinity of Flamborough Head the streams are stronger closer inshore and although the stream is rectilinear, there is no slack water. There might be turbulence close inshore off Flamborough Head and eddies occur both sides of the head.
  Tidal streams are given on the chart and in the *Admiralty Tidal Stream Atlas: North Sea, Northwestern Part.*

Principal marks
6.196

1   **Landmarks:**
 Scarborough Castle (54°17′·2N, 0°23′·3W) (6.171).
 War Memorial (54°16′·1N, 0°24′·2W) (6.185).
 Radio mast (54°11′N, 0°26′W).
 Flamborough Head Lighthouse (white round tower, 27 m in height) (54°07′·0N, 0°04′·8W) near the summit of the head.
 Disused Lighthouse (2½ cables NW of Flamborough Head Lighthouse).

2   **Major light:**
 Flamborough Head Light (above).

Other navigational aid
6.197

1   **DGPS:**
 Flamborough Head Light (54°07′N, 0°05′W).

Directions
(continued from 6.173)
6.198

1   From a position ENE of Scarborough the coastal route leads 15 miles SE to a position E of Flamborough Head, passing (with positions from Filey Brigg (54°13′N, 0°15′W)):

2   NE of a light-buoy (special, can) (4½ miles NW) marking a diffuser at the seaward end of an outfall extending 1 mile NE from White Nab (6.176), thence:
  NE of Yons Nab (3¼ miles NW). Cayton Bay lies between Yons and White Nab. Two submarine cables run NE from the bay, thence:

3   NE of Filey Brigg, a chain of ill-defined rocky ledges extending 4½ cables ESE of Carr Nase, a well

Disused Lighthouse   *Light*   *Selwicks Bay*

Flamborough Head from S (6.198)

(Original dated 2000)

(Photograph - Air Images)

defined point. High Brigg, the central ledge, is 2 m high and Brigg End is the E extremity of the brigg. Filey Light-buoy (E cardinal) is moored 4½ cables ESE of Brigg End. Thence:

4   NE of King and Queen Rocks (3½ miles SSE). Filey Bay (6.200) with the town of Filey, a seaside resort, at its NW end lies between the rocks and Brigg End. Carr Nase affords shelter to the bay from the N, thence:

5   To a position E of Flamborough Head (8½ miles SE) which is a perpendicular cliff of white chalk. Flamborough Steel, a rocky ledge extends 2 cables SE of the head. Flamborough Head is bold and well lit and is a common point of landfall and departure. The N side of the head is a breeding place for seabirds, especially gulls, which are far more common to the N than the S of the head.

6   **Cautions.** Flamborough Head Light might be obscured up to 8 miles to the N, within 1½ miles of the coast and in the N part of Bridlington Bay (6.204). The exact distance at which the cliffs screen the light depends on the state of the tide and height of eye of the observer.

The area of coast between King and Queen Rocks and North Landing, 1¼ miles NW of Flamborough Head has not been surveyed.

Useful marks
6.199

1   Saint Oswald's Church (tower) (54°13′N, 0°17′W) in Filey.
Radio mast (54°09′N, 0°15′W).
Radio mast (54°08′N, 0°19′W).
(Directions continue for coastal passage S at 6.210)

Anchorage and boat landings

Chart 1882 plan of Filey Bay
Filey Bay
6.200

1   An anchorage can be obtained 7 cables E of Filey in depths of 5 m, clay covered with sand. The anchorage in Filey Bay affords fair protection with winds as far E as

NNE. Submarine cables run SE from the shore to the S of the anchorage and the Feshes, a stony patch, lies to the N.

Chart 129
Boat landings
6.201

1   **North Landing**, 1¼ miles NW of Flamborough Head, is a small inlet which is sometimes used as a landing place by small fishing vessels.

Selwicks Bay, close N of Flamborough Head Lighthouse, can be used at HW as a landing in offshore winds.

Other names

Chart 129
6.202

1   Bempton Cliffs (54°08′N, 0°09′W), a bird reserve.
Buckton Cliffs (54°09′N, 0°11′W).
North Cliffs (54°08′N, 0°06′W).

FLAMBOROUGH HEAD TO RIVER HUMBER

General information

Charts 121, 107
Route
6.203

1   From a position E of Flamborough Head (54°07′N, 0°04′W) the route leads 33 miles SSE to the vicinity of Humber Light-vessel (safe water) (53°39′N, 0°20′E).

Topography
6.204

1   From Flamborough Head the coast runs W then curves round to the SSE forming Bridlington Bay. The bay is 8 miles across with the town of Bridlington at its head. S of the bay the coast continues to run SSE for 30 miles, terminating at Spurn Head (7.22), the N entrance point of the River Humber.

2   Initially the coast is formed of rocky cliffs but these soon give way to clay. These dark clay cliffs then extend as far as Kilnsea (53°37′N, 0°08′E), 2½ miles N of Spurn Head and then become sandhills as the coast curves SW to

Spurn Head. The background to the coast is low and there are few identifiable features.

3   The 20 m depth contour, which is close E of Flamborough Head, passes 1 mile E of Smithic Shoal (54°04′N, 0°07′W), thence 5 miles offshore as far as Withernsea (53°43′N, 0°02′E) where it trends to the SE. Apart from a few charted wrecks, there are no dangers outside this depth contour.

4   The coast S of Bridlington is being eroded at an estimated rate of 1·7 m a year. This amounts to about 1 mile in the last 1000 years, sweeping away villages, churches and landmarks.

Firing range
6.205

1   There is a firing danger area 1½ miles SE of Hornsea (53°55′N, 0°10′W), as shown on the chart.

Rescue
6.206

1   There are Coastguard Rescue Teams at Bridlington, which is the Maritime Rescue Sub-Centre (MRSC) for the Humber District, Hornsea, Withernsea (53°44′N, 0°02′E) and Easington (53°37′N, 0°11′W). See 1.53.

2   The MRSC operates a VHF direction finding service based on remotely controlled sites at Whitby, Flamborough and Easington. See 1.59.

An all-weather lifeboat is stationed at Bridlington. Inshore lifeboats are stationed at Bridlington and Withernsea. See 1.61 and 1.62 for details of lifeboats.

Tidal streams
6.207

1   The tidal stream near the shore from close S of Bridlington to Spurn Head runs parallel to the coast. The spring rate in each direction increases from about 1 kn near Bridlington to 2 to 3 kn off Spurn Head. There are ripples or overfalls over the rough bottom 5 miles NNE of Spurn Head. There is little change further to seaward where the stream is more or less rotary anti-clockwise, with a spring rate in each direction of 1½ kn.

2   Tidal streams are given on the charts and in *Admiralty Tidal Stream Atlas: North Sea, Southern Part.*

Principal marks
6.208

1   **Landmarks:**
    Flamborough Head Lighthouse (54°07′·0N, 0°04′·8W) (6.196).
    Priory Church (tower) (54°05′·7N, 0°12′·0W).
    Holy Trinity Church (spire) (54°05′·2N, 0°11′·0W).
    Block of flats (54°04′·9N, 0°11′·5W).

2   Lighthouse (disused, white octagonal tower, 39 m in height) (53°44′N, 0°02′E).
    Radio mast (53°39′N, 0°06′E).
    Spurn Head Lighthouse (disused) (53°35′N, 0°07′E) (black round tower, white band, 39 m in height), a second disused lighthouse is close W.

3   **Major light:**
    Flamborough Head Light (above).

Other navigational aids
6.209

1   **Racon:**
    Humber Light-vessel (53°39′N, 0°20′E).
    DGPS:
    Flamborough Head Light (54°07′N, 0°05′W).

Directions
(continued from 6.199)
6.210

1   From a position E of Flamborough Head (54°07′N, 0°04′W) the coastal route leads SSE to the vicinity of Humber Light-vessel, passing:

2   ENE of North Smithic Shoal and South Smithic Shoal, (centre 54°05′N, 0°06′W), which run SW into one another and extend from North Smithic Light-buoy (N cardinal) 5 miles SW to SW Smithic Light-buoy (W cardinal). The two shoals lie on the approach to Bridlington Bay (6.214). Thence:

3   ENE of Hornsea Gap (53°54′N, 0°10′W), a break in the coastal cliffs which are 9 to 12 m high. The coast in this vicinity is being eroded; thence:

4   ENE of a foul area (centre 53°52′N, 0°03′W), thence:
        Clear of Rough Gas Field (53°50′N, 0°28′E). See also 1.23.

The route continues SSE, passing (with positions from Withernsea (53°44′N, 0°02′E)):

        ENE of Withernsea, a gap in the cliffs marked by a disused lighthouse (6.208), thence:

5   ENE of Dimlington High Land (4 miles SSE), where the cliffs rise to an elevation of 40 m. A wreck, least depth 1·4 m and marked by a light-buoy (E cardinal), lies 2 miles NNE of Dimlington High Land. A number of gas pipelines (1.23), shown on the chart, runs from the coast in an ENE direction to offshore gas fields. Thence:

6   To the vicinity of Humber Light-vessel (safe water) (53°39′N, 0°20′E), which lies 9 miles ENE of Spurn Head.

Useful marks
6.211

1   Ulrome Church (tower) (54°00′N, 0°14′W) standing amid trees.
    Skipsea Church (tower) (53°59′N, 0°13′W) standing amid trees.
    Mappleton Church (spire) (53°53′N, 0°08′W).

2   Hilston Tower (53°47′N, 0°03′W) of red bricks.
    Tunstall Church (spire) (53°46′N, 0°01′W).
    Withernsea Church (tower) (53°44′N, 0°02′E).
    Easington Church (tower) (53°39′N, 0°07′E).
    Kilnsea Church (53°37′N, 0°08′E) tower.
    (Directions continue for River Humber at 7.19 and for coastal passage SE at 8.16)

Bridlington
Chart 1882 plans of Bridlington Bay and Bridlington
General Information
6.212

1   **Position.** Bridlington (54°05′N, 0°12′W) lies at the head of Bridlington Bay.
6.213

1   **Function.** The small harbour is only used by fishing boats and recreational craft. The town is a holiday resort, with a population of 31 334 in 1991.
6.214

1   **Topography.** Bridlington Bay is a roadstead which lies SW of Flamborough Head with North Smithic Shoal and South Smithic Shoal (6.210) across its approaches. The two shoals are limestone with a surface covering of sand. Depths within the bay are regular but it is too shallow for deep draught vessels.

2   Initially the coast is composed of cliffs fronted by rocky ledges, but about 3½ miles W of the head the cliffs change

from rock to clay and reduce in elevation. Bridlington and the coast to the S of it are fronted by broad sands.

6.215

1   **Approach and entry.** Bridlington is approached from Bridlington Bay passing to the N of North Smithic Shoal or SW of South Smithic Shoal (6.210) as appropriate.

6.216

1   **Port authority.** Bridlington Piers and Harbour Commissioners, Gummers Wharf, West End, Bridlington, East Yorkshire YO15 3AN.

Limiting conditions

6.217

1   **Controlling depths.** Both the harbour and the near approach dry. There is a dredged depth of 4·3 m alongside South Pier (6.220) at HW springs.

Tidal levels: see *Admiralty Tide Tables*. Mean spring range about 5 m; mean neap range about 2·4 m.

Maximum size of vessel handled is length 45 m and draught 3·9 m.

Arrival information

6.218

1   **Port radio.** Vessels approaching the harbour may call the duty watchkeeper on VHF. For details, see the relevant *Admiralty List of Radio Signals*.

2   **Anchorage** may be obtained in any part of Bridlington Bay between South Smithic Shoal and the coast. A recommended anchorage, in 10 m, is shown on the chart

1¾ miles SW of Flamborough Lighthouse. This anchorage is protected from the NNE, but vessels should not remain in the bay in E winds unless well provided with ground tackle when some protection is obtained from North Smithic Shoal and South Smithic Shoal.

3   A temporary anchorage for small vessels in good holding ground may be found 4½ cables ESE of Bridlington North Pierhead.

Caution. In N gales a heavy steep sea may be experienced over North Smithic Shoal until well within the lee of Flamborough Head. In these circumstances a vessel seeking shelter in Bridlington Bay should not attempt to pass S of North Smithic Light-buoy (6.224).

6.219

1   **Pilotage**, which is not compulsory, is undertaken by local fishermen. Vessels requiring a pilot should approach within 2½ cables flying flag G. The pilot boards 1 hour before berthing time.

Harbour

6.220

1   **Layout.** The harbour is enclosed by two piers, North Pier which runs 1 cable S from the shore and South Pier extending 2 cables E from the shore. The harbour bottom is clay covered with sand and silt.

Within the harbour there are berths for about 40 trawlers and accommodation for recreational craft.

Block of Flats

North Pier

Bridlington Harbour (6.220)

(Original dated 2000)

(Photograph - Air Images)

6.221

1 **Tidal signals** are exhibited by day from the E end of Fish Quay, close to South Pierhead, as follows:

Signal	Meaning
Red flag	Depth of 2·7 m or more in entrance
White flag, black circle below red flag	Entrance obstructed

2 At night, tidal signals are exhibited from the North Pierhead Light (6.224) as follows:

Signal	Meaning
Fixed red light	Depth of 2·7 or more in entrance. Harbour clear
Fixed green light	Depth less than 2·7 m in the entrance

6.222

1 **Tidal streams** off the entrance are given on the chart. The streams in this vicinity appear to be affected by eddies and begin about 1½ hours earlier than the streams S of Bridlington.

6.223

1 **Principal marks:**
Flamborough Head Lighthouse (54°07'·0N, 0°04'·8W) (6.196).
Priory Church (tower) (54°05'·7N, 0°12'·0W).
IIoly Trinity Church (spire) (54°05'·2N, 0°11'·0W).
Block of flats (54°04'·9N, 0°11'·5W).
Major light:
Flamborough Head Light (above).

Directions

6.224

1 **North-east approach.** From a position E of Flamborough Head (54°07'N, 0°04'W) the route leads 6 miles WSW then N to the harbour entrance, passing (with positions from South Landing (54°06'N, 0°07'W)):
NNW of North Smithic Light-buoy (N cardinal) (2 miles E), thence:
SSE of Flamborough Head (6.198) (1½ miles ENE), thence:

2 NNW of North Smithic Shoal (6.210) (1½ miles ESE), thence:
SSE of South Landing and close to the anchorage (6.218). South Landing is a break in the cliffs used by fishermen during N winds. There is a prominent road down a ravine from the cliffs above. Thence:
NNW of South Smithic Shoal (6.210) (2½ miles S), thence:

3 SSE of the harbour entrance (2¾ miles WSW), thence:

NNW of the Light-buoy (special) (3 miles SW), marking the seaward end of an outfall extending 9 cables from the coast, thence:
To the harbour entrance, which is 27 m wide and faces S. It lies between North Pierhead, on which there is a light (column, 9 m in height), and South Pierhead.

4 When entering the harbour the entrance should be opened up well to the S to avoid The Canch, a sandspit which dries ¾ cable S of North Pierhead.
A number of yacht racing marks (special) are laid between South Smithic Shoal and the shore during the summer months.

6.225

1 **South-east approach.** From a position SSE of South West Smithic Light-buoy the alignment (331°) of Christ Church (spire) (54°05'·1N, 0°11'·5W) with Priory Church (tower) (6.223) leads to the harbour entrance, passing (with positions from the harbour entrance):

2 Close WSW of S W Smithic Light-buoy (W cardinal) (2½ miles SSE), which lies on this alignment, thence:
ENE of the Light-buoy (special) (6.224) (9 cables SSE), thence:
To the harbour entrance (6.224).
These marks may be difficult to distinguish from the SE.

6.226

1 **Clearing bearings:**
The line of bearing 241° of four white square houses at Wilsthorpe (54°03'·5N, 0°12'·8W), which are prominent from seaward, passes SE of Flamborough Steel (6.198) and close NW of North Smithic Light-buoy and leads through the N channel.
The line of bearing 325° of Flamborough Head Lighthouse passes NE of North Smithic Shoal.

6.227

1 **Useful marks:**
Sewerby Hall (54°06'N, 0°09'W), standing amid trees.
New Spa Theatre (54°04'·8N, 0°11'·7W).

Port services
6.228

1 **Repairs** can be effected on craft up to 50 tonnes. There are two slipways and a boat hoist.
Other facilities: hospital; helicopter landing site.
Supplies: marine diesel at South Pier; fresh water; provisions.

Small craft
6.229

1 Yachts and small craft berth in the harbour. There is a chandlery.

Other name
6.230

1 Hamilton Hill (54°01'·5N, 0°13'·4W).

NOTES

Chapter 7 - River Humber

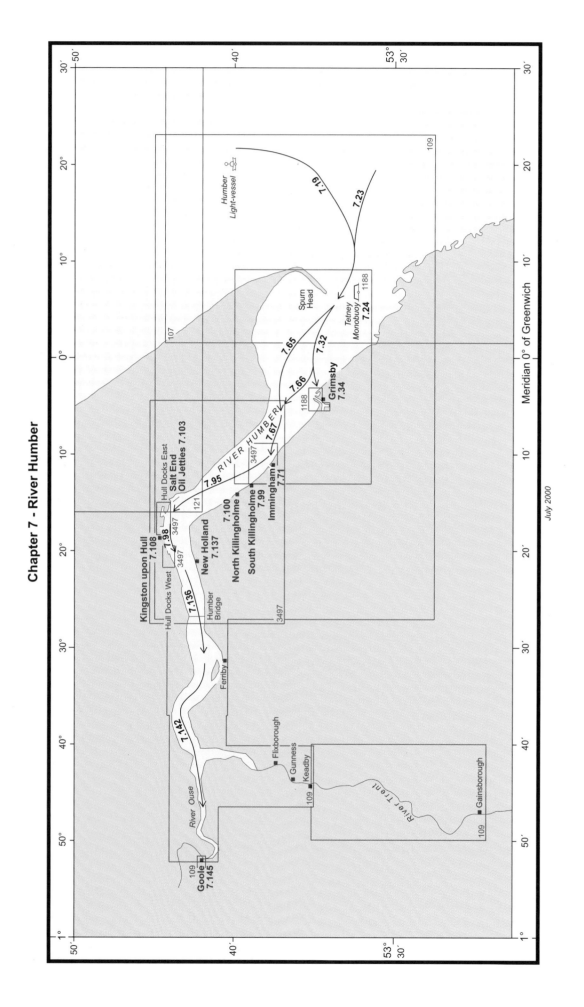

July 2000

CHAPTER 7

RIVER HUMBER

GENERAL INFORMATION

Chart 109
Description
7.1

1   The River Humber is formed by the junction of the Rivers Ouse and Trent, 34 miles from the sea. It also acts as the common outlet for numerous other streams which drain the greater part of Yorkshire and the Midlands. At its head the river is 5 cables wide but increases to 6 miles at its entrance point between Spurn Head and Donna Nook (53°29′N, 0°10′E), a low point on the S side of the estuary. Both sides of the estuary are bordered by extensive flats which dry up to 2 miles in places. The navigable channels are narrowed by numerous shoals.

2   The River Humber is mainly confined between low embanked lands, from which water has been progressively excluded by the process of silting or "warping" as it is known locally.

3   The important ports on the River Humber, all operated by Associated British Ports, are Kingston upon Hull or simply Hull (7.108), Grimsby (7.34), Immingham (7.71) and Goole (7.145). There are oil terminals at Immingham, Killingholme (7.102), Salt End (7.103) and Tetney (offshore) (7.24).

Pilotage
7.2

1   Spurn Pilot Station, equipped with radar, is situated on Spurn Head 3½ cables SW of the lighthouse. The Humber Pilotage limits coincide with the port limits, shown on the chart, and encompass the approaches to the River Humber from just seaward of Humber Light-vessel (53°39′N, 0°20′E) to Goole on the River Ouse and Gainsborough on the River Trent.

Pilotage is compulsory for vessels over 60 m in length and all vessels carrying dangerous substances in bulk.

2   Vessels requiring a pilot should give at least 12 hours' notice, confirming 2 hours in advance and giving ETA, length overall, draught, destination, agent and cargo. The pilot boards 1½ miles ENE of the Humber Light-vessel or in the deep water anchorage (below) for vessels exceeding 40 000 dwt or over 11 m draught, and for smaller vessels in the vicinity of the Spurn Light-float (53°34′N, 0°14′E) or in Hull Roads at Riverside Quay, Albert Dock (53°44′·1N, 0°20′·5W).

3   Large vessels awaiting a pilot should anchor in the deep water anchorage centred 3½ miles SE of Humber Light-vessel. The limits of the anchorage, which contains 3 designated anchor berths, are marked by 4 light-buoys (cardinal), as shown on the charts. Local experience indicates that on occasions the actual tidal stream considerably exceeds the predicted rate (see 1.89 Storm Surges). Vessels anchoring in this area on occasions when there are fast tidal streams should keep well clear of other anchored vessels and of the buoys. It is inadvisable for these vessels to embark a pilot closer to shore due to the strong tidal streams, and they might not find a suitable anchorage if they are unable to proceed direct to their final berth.

4   **Caution.** Vessels anchored in this area have been known to drag anchor in a N direction at a rate of 2 kn towards and over the gas pipelines which are situated about 4 miles N (see 1.37).

In bad weather VTS Humber will advise on boarding points.

5   Vessels claiming exemption from compulsory pilotage must advise Spurn Pilots of their intentions, who will give advice on available anchorage space. For details see the relevant *Admiralty List of Radio Signals.*

VHF R/T communications should not be attempted at long range as this may cause unnecessary interference on the circuit.

Local knowledge
7.3

1   The low flat shores offer few marks. In clear weather, due to good marking, navigation should not be too difficult. However the channel is constantly changing and buoys are moved accordingly. Above Kingston upon Hull the changes are so frequent that only local charts published by Associated British Ports are available. Local knowledge is essential.

Port operations
7.4

1   **Vessel Traffic Service** scheme, with full radar surveillance from the approaches to the river to the Humber Bridge (7.130), is maintained for the control of shipping in the Rivers Humber, Ouse and Trent. Subsidiary port radio stations, which are used to pass berthing information, are maintained by the ports, oil terminals and jetties within the scheme.

2   Vessels are required to report their ETA at Spurn Light-float (53°34′N, 0°14′E) not less than 24 hours in advance or one hour after departure from their last port of call, whichever is the later, giving the name of ship and call sign and nationality, length overall, grt and net tonnage, draught (and air draught, if the air draught exceeds 30 m for ships proceeding beyond the Humber Bridge), destination, agent's name, nature of cargo or ballast, if a pilot is required and boarding place, last port of call, any defects in the vessel's hull, machinery, navigation equipment or anchors and windlass. Amendments to ETA must be reported.

3   The above procedures are mandatory for all vessels over 50 grt and those carrying dangerous substances.

Vessels within the Humber VTS area are required to maintain VHF watch.

4   A booklet, **Humber Passage Plan,** has been prepared by Associated British Ports in order to facilitate the safe movement of large vessels bound to and from the Tetney Monobuoy (7.24), the various terminals at Immingham and Killingholme, and Salt End Jetties (7.103). The Passage Plan applies to vessels of 40 000 dwt and over, vessels with a draught of 11 m and over, and gas carriers of 20 000 m³ capacity and over.

5   For details see the relevant *Admiralty List of Radio Signals.*

Regulations affecting entry
7.5

1   The Humber Navigational Byelaws 1990 apply from Spurn Light-float throughout the River Humber, the River Trent to Gainsborough and the River Ouse to Goole.

Masters are to ensure that the vessel does not cross the fairway in such a manner as to cause inconvenience or danger to other vessels.

2   Vessels not confined to the fairway by reason of their draught shall not impede other vessels confined to the fairway.

Vessels turning shall give four short blasts on the whistle followed by one short blast if turning to starboard or two short blasts if turning to port.

3   Vessels are cautioned to prevent their wash causing damage to other vessels moored at riverside jetty or terminal.

Masters should report at the earliest possible time any incident in which their vessel is involved with a wreck, in grounding or fouling a light-vessel, light-float or buoy. The initial report should be made to VTS Humber.

4   The Humber Serious Marine Emergency Plan lays down the action to be taken in the event of such an emergency, which includes pollution, whether the vessel is underway or alongside. The Master of a vessel involved in an incident is required to inform VTS Humber passing on all the relevant information available to him. In the event of a pollution incident, this plan activates the Humber oil spill contingency plan "Humber Clean". For details see the relevant *Admiralty List of Radio Signals*.

5   Masters are advised that under the Humber Navigation Byelaws 1990, a vessel sheltering, anchoring or moving within the River Humber should not transfer fuel, goods, spares, materials or personnel between vessels without first informing VTS Humber and obtaining the permission of the Harbour Master, Humber.

6   All sea-going vessels carrying a dangerous substance in bulk, or in ballast and not gas-free, are prohibited from entry into or exit from the Humber in visibility of 5 cables or less without the express permission of the Harbour Master, Humber.

Dangerous substances
7.6

1   The Dangerous Substances in Harbour Areas Regulations require vessels carrying Dangerous Substances into the Humber harbour area to:

Give 24 hours' notice of the entry of Dangerous Substances into the harbour area, but when this is not possible notice must be given before the vessel navigates the Humber.

2   Display a red flag (day) or an all round red light (night), which requires that other vessels keep a safe distance.

Maintain VHF watch.

Be in a state of readiness to be moved at any time, tidal conditions permitting.

Possess the appropriate and valid certificate of fitness.

3   Report untoward incidents immediately.

These regulations apply equally to vessels sailing from any berth within the Humber Harbour Area.

VTS Humber should be given notice of cargoes of Dangerous Substances at the time of ordering a pilot and at 2 hours to the estimated time of departure.

4   Masters are reminded that communication with Humber Pilots Ltd is not to be construed as communication with VTS Humber. VTS Humber must be contacted directly; see the relevant *Admiralty List of Radio Signals*.

See also 1.40.

Outer anchorages
7.7

1   Bull Anchorage, 1¼ miles S of Spurn Head, used by outbound vessels and those awaiting berths.

Haile Anchorage, adjoining the SW corner of Bull Anchorage, is for the use of vessels carrying explosives and, subject to the agreement of the Harbour Master, Humber, may be used for tank washing and gas-freeing. No 2C light-buoy (port hand) marks the SW corner of Bull Anchorage and the S corner of Haile Anchorage.

2   Hawke Anchorage 2 miles WNW of Spurn Head for vessels awaiting a berth or for tidal reasons.

These anchorages are shown on the chart.

Masters are reminded to report their positions, when anchored, to VTS Humber.

See also 7.2 for larger vessels.

Advice on anchoring for vessels arriving off the Humber can be obtained from VTS Humber, see the relevant *Admiralty List of Radio Signals*.

Rescue
7.8

1   The Humber area Maritime Rescue Sub-Centre is at Bridlington (6.212). Within the Humber there are Coastguard Rescue Teams at Hull, Cleethorpes (53°33′N, 0°01′W) and Donna Nook (53°28′N, 0°09′E). See 1.53.

An all-weather lifeboat is stationed at Spurn Head and an inshore lifeboat at Cleethorpes. See 1.61 and 1.62 for details of lifeboats.

Tidal streams
7.9

1   The tidal streams 10 miles to the E of Spurn Head are not affected by the river streams and are given on the chart and in the *Admiralty Tidal Stream Atlas: North Sea, Northwestern Part*. As the entrance to the River Humber is approached the direction of the S-going stream becomes more W and that of the N-going stream more E. The in-going spring rate is 2½ kn and the out-going 3½ kn at a position 4 miles E of Spurn Head.

2   At the entrance to the river the streams run very strongly across Chequer Shoal (7.20) in the direction of the channel, and still following the direction of the channel, around Spurn Head; they are weaker on the S side of the channel.

Within the river the tidal streams are rapid and irregular. In some instances the tidal stream at springs sets in a different direction from the tidal stream at neaps.

3   **Caution.** Mariners are advised that the flood stream sets strongly to the N in the Bull Channel (7.32) which can carry vessels out of the fairway. It is reported (1994) that vessels have frequently tended to collide with No 5 Gate Buoy which marks the N side of the channel.

4   During and after periods of heavy rain both the duration and rates of the out-going streams are increased and the in-going correspondingly reduced; these changes are small at the river entrance but increase further upstream. Off Immingham the out-going stream may continue to run for an hour after the time at which the in-going stream would normally begin. It is also reported that off Immingham the streams begin earlier with N winds and later with S winds.

5   Details of the tidal streams in the estuary and the river are given on the charts.

7.10

1   **Fresh water and salt water streams.** The quantity of fresh water increases as the river is ascended. On the surface the out-going stream is observed to be considerably stronger and of longer duration than the in-going stream. It

seems probable therefore that the fresh water runs out mostly on the surface, while the salt water enters below the surface. If the in-going stream of salt water below the surface is stronger and of longer duration than the in-going surface stream, and the converse holds for the out-going stream, then deeper draught vessels will be affected accordingly.

Local weather
7.11

1   NW gales coincident with in-going tidal streams cause the highest sea at the entrance to the River Humber.

APPROACHES TO RIVER HUMBER

General information

Chart 109
Route
7.12

1   From the vicinity of the Humber Light-vessel (53°39′N, 0°20′E) the route leads 2 miles S, then 5½ miles SW, thence 2 miles WSW and finally 2½ miles WNW to a position S of Spurn Head.

Topography
7.13

1   The shores of the River Humber are low-lying and fronted by extensive sands. The main approach channel is through New Sand Hole, which runs 4½ miles SW from a position 2 miles S of the Humber Light-vessel to the Spurn Light-float. New Sand Hole is a deep and narrow depression with depths ranging from 18 to 44 m. At its NE end it broadens into a basin with depths in excess of 20 m. This feature, lying several miles inside the general run of the 20 m depth contour, is a useful identification feature in low visibility.

Controlling depths
7.14

1   The shoalest depth on the approach from the N is to be found close WSW of Spurn Light-float (53°33′·5N, 0°14′·3E).

The shoalest depth on the approach from the E and SE is to be found about 3 miles ESE of Spurn Light-float.

Depths are constantly changing and the charts and the Harbour Authority should be consulted for the latest information.

Pilotage
7.15

1   See 7.2. Depths in the channels are subject to change as well as strong tidal streams (7.9) and therefore exempted strangers are recommended to take a pilot.

Traffic regulations
7.16

1   See 7.5.

Principal marks
7.17

1   **Landmarks:**
        Radio masts (red lights) (53°39′N, 0°07′E).
        Spurn Head Lighthouse (53°35′N, 0°07′E) (6.208).
        Hydraulic tower (53°35′N, 0°04′W) at Grimsby.

Other navigational aids
7.18

1   **Racon:**
        Humber Light-vessel (53°39′N, 0°20′E).
        Spurn Light-float (53°34′N, 0°14′E).
      DGPS:
        Flamborough Head Light (54°07′N, 0°05′W).

Directions
(continued from 6.211)

Approach from the north
7.19

1   **Caution.** Depths offshore are irregular, and shoals, particularly those outside the main channel, are subject to change. Only those channels which are buoyed should be used.

Humber Light-vessel to Spurn Light-float. From a position E of Humber Light-vessel (53°39′N, 0°20′E) the track initially leads S, passing:

2   W of North New Sand Light-buoy (N cardinal) (53°38′·5N, 0°22′·0E), marking the NW limit of the deep water anchorage (7.2), thence:
        E of Outer Binks Light-buoy (starboard hand) (53°37′·3N, 0°20′·2E).

Thence the track leads 5½ miles SW through New Sand Hole, which is buoyed, to a position close S of Spurn Light-float, passing:

3   NW of Mid New Sand Light-buoy (W cardinal) (53°36′·7N, 0°21′·3E) at the W limit of the deep water anchorage. An obstruction and two wrecks lie within 1 mile SW of the buoy. Thence:
        NW of the NE extremity of a coastal bank (53°35′N, 0°19′E) extending NE from Donna Nook (7.1), marked by North and South Haile Light-buoys (port hand).

4   Thence the route continues SW, passing (with positions from Spurn Head (53°34′N, 0°07′W):
        SE of a series of shoals (centre 5 miles E) stretching 3½ miles NE of Spurn Light-float, marked on their SE side by N and S Binks Light-buoys (starboard hand) and:
        SE of Outer Binks (centre 4 miles E), an extensive shoal, thence:

5   To a position close S of Spurn Light-float (E cardinal, black hull, yellow light-tower, black top, 12 m in height) (4½ miles ESE), moored 2 cables SE of shoals extending SSE of Outer Binks. Spurn Light-float moorings vary between 110 and 250 m depending on the weather. When they exceed 110 m in length VTS Humber broadcasts the fact every 2 hours.

7.20

1   **Spurn Light-float to Chequer No 3 Light-buoy.** From a position close S of Spurn Light-float the line of bearing 260° of Haile Sand Fort (53°32′·1N, 0°02′·2E), surmounted by a mast 6 m in height, leads through the channel for 2 miles to a position S of Chequer No 3 Light-buoy, passing:

2   NNW of Haile Sand Flat (4½ miles SE), which extends 4 miles NNE of Donna Nook and is marked at its NE extremity by Haile Sand Light-buoy (port hand), and:

3   SSE and S of Chequer Shoal (3 miles ESE), a patch of stony ground marked at its E extremity by SE Chequer Light-float (S cardinal) and its S extremity by Chequer No 3 Light-buoy (S cardinal).

Disused Lighthouse

Pilot Jetty   *Operations Centre*   *The Binks*

Spurn Head from SW (7.22)

(Original dated 2000)

(Photograph - Air Images)

7.21

1   **Clearing bearing.** The alignment (285°) of Bull Sand Fort (53°33'·7N, 0°04'·2E) (7.32) with the Hydraulic tower at Grimsby (7.17) passes S of Chequer Shoal and N of Haile Sand Flat.

7.22

1   **Chequer No 3 Light-buoy to Spurn Head.** From a position S of Chequer No 3 Light-buoy the track leads 3 miles WNW to a position SW of Spurn Head (53°34'N, 0°07'E), passing:

SSW of The Binks (2 miles E), an irregular shoal running E from Spurn Head, and:

NE of Bull Anchorage (7.7) (1¼ miles S). Tetney Monobuoy (7.24) lies S of the anchorage, thence:

2   To a position about 3½ cables SW of Spurn Head and. Spurn Head consists of sandhills 6 m to 9 m high and terminates in Spurn Point, an indeterminate feature from which a light (green cone on metal tripod) is exhibited. Spurn Head Lighthouse (6.208) stands 5 cables NE of the head.

Spurn Point is a National Nature Reserve; see 1.48.

(Directions continue for Grimsby at 7.32 and R Humber at 7.65)

Approach from east and south east
7.23

1   From the vicinity of 53°32'N, 0°23'E the alignment (286°) of Spurn Light-float (7.19) with Spurn Head Lighthouse (6.208) leads to the main channel in a least charted depth of 8·4 m, passing (with positions from Donna Nook (53°29'N, 0°09'W)):

2   NNE of the NE extremity of a detached shoal (4½ miles ENE), lying to the NE of Rosse Spit, which extends 4¼ miles from the shore. Rosse Spit Light-buoy (port hand) is moored NE of the shoal. There is a firing range off Donna Nook marked by buoys and beacons, see 8.8. Thence:

3   Into the main channel S of Spurn Light-float, thence as for approach from the N at 7.20.

Caution. Deep draught vessels from the E or SE should not attempt this route but pass E and N of Humber deep water anchorage (7.2) and follow directions for approach from the N at 7.19.

Tetney Monobuoy
7.24

1   **Tetney Monobuoy** (53°32'·3N, 0°06'·8E), a lighted mooring buoy with moorings extending 2½ cables, lies in an open roadstead. It is used by large tankers drawing up to 15·5 m for discharging oil. Vessels berth and sail at HW. A submarine pipeline runs 3 miles SW from the buoy to the shore at Tetney Haven Oil Terminal. The inner end of the pipeline is marked by beacons. When the buoy is not in use a floating hose, marked by quick flashing lights, extends up to 290 m from the buoy.

2   Other vessels should give a wide berth to tankers secured to the buoy or manoeuvring in its vicinity.

The terminal has a port radio station; see the relevant *Admiralty List of Radio Signals*.

Small craft
7.25

1   **Tetney Haven** (53°31'N, 0°03'E) can be entered by craft drawing 1·5 m within 2 hours of HW, through a channel marked by beacons, which runs from a point 5 cables NW of Haile Sand Fort (7.20) to the Haven. There is a yacht club at Tetney Haven.

7.26

1   **Spurn Head.** Small craft can shelter in an inlet 5 cables NW of the head.

SPURN HEAD TO GRIMSBY

General information

Chart 1188
Route
7.27

1   From a position about 3½ cables SW of Spurn Head (53°34'N, 0°07'E) the route leads 2¾ miles WNW through the Bull Channel, thence 1 mile W to the approaches to Grimsby.

Pilotage
7.28

1 See 7.2.

Traffic regulations
7.29

1 See 7.5.

Tidal streams
7.30

1 At the entrance to the River Humber the tidal streams run in the direction of the fairway on both sides of Bull Sand (7.32). They are generally stronger in the fairway than over the banks at both sides.

See table on chart for details.

Principal marks
7.31

1 Landmarks:
Spurn Head Lighthouse (53°35′N, 0°07′E) (6.208).
Water tower (53°34′N, 0°02′W) at Cleethorpes.
Building (53°34′·6N, 0°03′·5W) at Grimsby.
Hydraulic tower (53°35′N, 0°04′W) at Grimsby.
Three chimneys (53°35′N, 0°06′W).

Directions
(continued from 7.22)
7.32

1 From a position about 3½ cables SW of Spurn Head (53°34′N, 0°07′W) the track leads WNW through the channel, which is marked by buoys, thence W to the approaches to Grimsby, passing (with positions from Spurn Head):

2 SSW of the entrance to Hawke Channel (7.65) (4 cables W), marked by Hawke Light-float (E cardinal). Middle Shoal divides the Hawke and Sunk Channels to the N from Bull Channel and Grimsby Road (7.66) to the S. The shoal runs 5½ miles to the WNW and is subject to great change. Hawke Anchorage (7.33) lies along the SW side of Middle Shoal. Thence:

3 NNE of Bull Light-float (N cardinal) (1¼ miles SW), thence:
NNE of Bull Sand Fort (1½ miles WSW), standing centrally on Bull Sand and marked by light-buoys (N and S cardinal). The depths and configuration of the sand change continuously. Haile Channel, which is buoyed, separates Bull Sand from Haile Sand. The latter fronts the coast from Cleethorpes to Donna Nook (Chart 109) 8 miles SE. Thence:

4 NNE of Clee Ness Sand (3½ miles W), an extensive flat running NW from Haile Sand. The NE limit of the flat is marked by No 4A Clee Ness Light-float (port hand). Clee Ness Sand fronts Cleethorpes and extends up to 2½ miles offshore, drying on its inner half. A light (red beacon) is exhibited from an iron pier at Cleethorpes.

5 Thence the line of bearing 265° of the hydraulic tower (7.48) leads to a position in the channel (53°35′·2N, 0°00′·2E) between Grimsby Middle and Clee Ness Sand from which a direct approach to Grimsby can be made. South Shoal Light-buoy (S cardinal) is moored on the SE corner of Grimsby Middle and 3 cables N of No 4B Light-buoy (port hand) on the S side of the channel.

6 An alternative track from the one described above leads, from a position between Bull Light-float and No 2C Light-buoy, which marks the S extremity of Haile Anchorage (7.7) at the entrance to Haile Channel, NW and NNW through the channel to pass NNE of Clee Ness Sand, passing (with positions from Spurn Head):

7 SSW of Bull Sand Fort (1½ miles WSW), thence:
E and NE of No 4 Light-buoy (port hand) (2¼ miles WSW), marking the W side of the channel, thence:
NNE of Clee Ness Sand, thence follow the directions as described above.
(Directions continue for Grimsby at 7.49)

Anchorage
7.33

1 **Hawke Anchorage**, centre 53°36′N, 0°02′E, shown on the chart is a general anchorage for smaller vessels on the SW side of Middle Shoal (7.32). Depths vary between 4 and over 10 m, and are generally in excess of 7 m. Vessels using the anchorage must keep clear of the channel.

GRIMSBY

General information

Chart 1188
Position
7.34

1 **Grimsby** Harbour (53°35′N, 0°04′W) lies on the SW side of the River Humber, 6 miles W of Spurn Head.

Function
7.35

1 It is a large fishing and commercial port. The population was 90 703 in 1991.

Approach and entry
7.36

1 Grimsby is approached through the Bull Channel (7.32) leading to the E end of the approach fairway lying to the SE of Grimsby Road (7.66) and entered through one of two entrance locks, depending on the vessel's berth.

Traffic
7.37

1 In In 1999 870 vessels totalling 2 238 608 dwt used the port, and over one million tonnes of cargo were handled. In addition, about 6 000 tonnes of fish were landed at the fish docks.

Port authority
7.38

1 Associated British Ports, Port Office, Cleethorpe Road, Grimsby, DN31 3LL.

Limiting conditions
7.39

1 **Controlling depth** for the fairway was 1·4 m in 1999. There is a charted depth of 1·3 m in the fairway, 1 cable N of the centreline.
Deepest and longest berth. Royal Dock (7.50).
Tidal levels: see *Admiralty Tide Tables.* Mean spring range about 6 m; mean neap range about 3 m.
7.40

1 **Maximum size of vessel handled.** The commercial docks can accommodate vessels up to 145 m in length, 20·5 m beam and 6·4 m draught (spring tides), 5·8 m draught (neap tides). Vessels over 81·7 m in length have to canal through the entrance lock.

Fish Docks   *Marina*   *Royal Dock*

Hydraulic Tower

Grimsby Harbour (7.46)

(Original dated 2000)

(Photograph - Air Images)

2   The Fish Docks can accommodate vessels up to 73 m in length, 12·8 m beam and 5·5 m draught. Larger vessels have to canal through the entrance lock.

7.41

1   **Local weather.** Winds from the NNE cause the highest tides at Grimsby and those from the NNW the most sea, but the swell seldom prevents the lock gates being open.

    Approaching the locks can be difficult in strong E or W winds.

Arrival information

Port operations

7.42

1   See 7.4. A local port radio service is maintained. See the relevant *Admiralty List of Radio Signals.*

Traffic signals

7.43

1   **Royal Dock.** Main signals No 2 and No 4 of the International Port Traffic Signals, given in *The Mariner's Handbook*, are exhibited from a mast close W of the entrance lock to Royal Dock.

    Fish Dock. Main signals No 2 and No 4 are exhibited from a mast on the W side of the entrance lock to Fish Dock.

Outer anchorage

7.44

1   Hawke Anchorage (7.33).

    Vessels of light draught can obtain an anchorage in Grimsby Road (7.66). Anchoring is prohibited in the fairway approaching Grimsby, as shown on the chart.

Pilots and tugs

7.45

1   For pilotage in the River Humber see 7.2. Pilotage within the docks is undertaken by private pilots.

    Tugs are available, but require 24 hours' notice.

Harbour

Layout

7.46

1   The harbour consists of two enclosed dock complexes, Fish Docks on the E side and on the W side Royal Dock which leads to Alexandra Dock through Union Dock.

Tidal streams

7.47

1   Both the in-going and out-going streams circulate round Royal Dock Tidal Basin (7.49) and, except at HW neaps, run SE across Royal Dock lock entrance.

Principal marks

7.48

1   **Landmarks:**

      Water tower (53°34′N, 0°02′W) at Cleethorpes.

      Hydraulic tower (53°35′N, 0°04′W) at the entrance to Royal Dock.

      Three chimneys (53°35′N, 0°06′W).

Directions
(continued from 7.32)

7.49

1   From a position (53°35′·2N, 0°00′·1E) in the channel S of Grimsby Middle (7.66), the route leads W for 2½ miles through the fairway, which is about 3½ cables wide and is shown on the chart, to the harbour entrance, passing (with positions from the harbour entrance):

2   S of Lower Burcom Light-float (port hand) (1½ miles ENE), marking the SW side of the channel to Immingham, thence:

    To the harbour entrance.

3   **Royal Dock entrance** lock (1½ cables SSW) is approached through the Tidal Basin. The entrance to the basin is 76 m wide and lies between W Pierhead on which stands a light (brown metal column, 7 m in height) and a dolphin from which a light is also exhibited. The alignment (221°) of two beacons (cross topmark) situated on the W side of Royal Dock entrance lock indicates the extent of

170

the shoal water on the W side of the Tidal Basin. The entrance lock is 85 m long and 21·3 m wide and has a depth over the sill of 8·2 m at MHWS and 6·8 m at MHWN. The lock normally operates from 1½ hours to 30 minutes before HW depending on draught.

4　**Fish Dock entrance** lock (1½ cables S) is approached to the E of the dolphin (above), thence between Fish Dock East Pierhead (brown metal column, 7 m in height) and Middle Pierhead (brown wooden mast, 7 m in height), to the lock which is 21·4 m long and 13·0 m wide and has a depth over the sill of 8·2 m MHWS and 6·8 m at MHWN.

Berths

7.50

1　**Commercial docks:**

Royal Dock; 1219 m of quayage; maintained depth 6·8 m; Ro-Ro berth.

Union Dock.

Alexandra Dock; two Ro-Ro berths.

2　**Fish Docks** are divided into No 1, No 2 and No 3 Fish Docks. The maintained depth is generally 6·8 m, but there is only 5·7 m alongside at a number of berths.

Depths within the docks are liable to change and the Dock Master should be consulted for the latest information.

A fish market complex is situated in the NW part of Fish Dock No 1, and a small craft marina occupies part of Fish Dock No 2.

Port services

7.51

1　**Repairs.** There are two slipways; the largest can handle vessels up to 1200 tonnes.

7.52

1　**Other facilities:**

Facilities available for the reception of oily waste, noxious and harmful substances.

Deratting and exemption certificates issued.

Hospital with helicopter landing site.

Divers available.

7.53

1　**Supplies:** marine diesel in Fish Docks; furnace fuel oil from Hull; water at the quays; provisions and stores.

7.54

1　**Harbour regulations.** At least 2 hours' notice must be given to the Dock Master's Office prior to a vessel moving in or sailing from the port.

For regulations concerning Dangerous Substances see 7.6.

Small craft

7.55

1　Grimsby and Cleethorpes Yacht Club is located on the E side of the entrance to Alexandra Dock and to the N of the motorway bridge.

Fish Dock Marina with 400 berths has been established in Fish Dock No 2. Access is via the lock into the Fish Docks. Comprehensive services for small craft are available. See chart for details.

SPURN HEAD TO IMMINGHAM

General information

Chart 1188

Route

7.56

1　From a position about 3½ cables SW of Spurn Head (53°34′N, 0°07′E) there are two routes to Immingham, one N and the other S of Middle Shoal. The N route, which is the deeper, leads WNW firstly through Hawke Channel and then W through Sunk Channel for a total distance of 7½ miles. The S route leads 2¾ miles WNW through Bull Channel then 1 mile W to the fairway off Grimsby, thence WNW 3½ miles to the S of Grimsby Middle and Middle Shoal. The two routes join W of Middle Shoal and the combined route then leads 3½ miles WNW to a position off the entrance lock at Immingham.

2　An alternative route to the S route leads S of Bull Sand through Haile Channel for 1½ miles NW and 1½ miles NNW, to join the S route, mentioned above, NW of Bull Sand.

Controlling depths

7.57

1　On the N route Sunk Channel is regularly dredged to a depth of 8·8 m. The Least Available Depth (LAD) in the Sunk Channel is given by VTS Humber in their regular river broadcasts. See also the relevant *Admiralty List of Radio Signals.*

On the S route depths are generally in excess of 6 m; the latest information should be obtained from the Port Authority.

Pilotage

7.58

1　See 7.2.

Traffic regulations

7.59

1　See 7.5.

When on passage S of Grimsby Middle inward-bound vessels must keep strictly to the N side of the channel and outward-bound vessels strictly to the S side.

7.60

1　**Caution.** Mariners are warned against the dangers of overtaking off Immingham Oil Terminal (7.52). The main channel is very narrow at this point, and the wash from overtaking vessels which pass close to tankers moored at the Terminal may endanger the security of their cargo handling operations.

7.61

1　**Prohibited anchorages** are established in the approach channel to Grimsby and in the channel NE of Burcom Sand (53°36′N, 0°04′W) between No 6 Lower Burcom Light-float and No 8 Middle Burcom Light-buoy. Anchoring is also prohibited within 200 m of the three outfalls extending 1½ miles NE from the coast between Grimsby and Stallingborough Flat (7.67).

2　These prohibited areas are shown on the chart.

Measured distance

7.62

1　A measured distance for use of small vessels is charted close W of Hawkin's Point (53°38′N, 0°03′W), marked by three pairs of beacons (black pole, black circular topmark, 12 m in height).

Running track 112°/292°.

Distance 1854·1 m between each pair of beacons.

Tidal streams

7.63

1   The tidal streams run strongly in the Hawke and Sunk Channels and are liable to sudden change in the Hawke Channel.

For S route see 7.30.

Off Immingham the in-going stream sets strongly across Holme Ridge (7.67) to the channel W of Foul Holme Spit. See tables on the chart for details.

Principal marks

7.64

1   **Landmarks:**

See 7.48 for marks at Grimsby.

Two chimneys (53°37′N, 0°11′W) at Immingham.

Flare (53°38′·8N, 0°15′·3W).

Directions

(continued from 7.22)

North of Middle Shoal

7.65

1   **Hawke and Sunk Channels.** Hawke Channel leads into Sunk Channel. The latter is dredged and 213 m wide. From a position between Spurn Head (53°34′N, 0°07′E) and Hawke Light-float (E cardinal) (5 cables WNW of Spurn Head) at the E end of Hawke Channel, the route leads WNW through the Hawke Channel, thence W through the Sunk Channel, being guided by the numbered light-buoys that mark each side of both channels, to a position in mid-channel 5 cables W of the W end of Sunk Channel. Hawkin's Point (53°38′N, 0°03′W) is the S point of Sunk Island and lies 6¾ miles WNW of Spurn Head. Between the two is a bay, which lies to the N of the Hawke and Sunk Channels. The whole bay dries, with Trinity Sand to the E and Sunk Sand to the W.

7.66

1   **Bull Channel and Grimsby Road.** For directions from Spurn Head to the approach to Grimsby see 7.32. From a position (53°35′·2N, 0°02′·2E) in mid-channel between Grimsby Middle and Clee Ness Sand (7.32), the route leads WNW through a buoyed channel to a position 5 cables W of the W end of Sunk Channel, passing (with positions from Grimsby Harbour entrance (53°35′·7N, 0°04′·0W)):

2   NNE of entrance of the fairway (1¾ miles E) to Grimsby, thence:

SSW of Grimsby Middle (2¼ miles NE), marked at its W extremity by Middle No 7 Light-float (S cardinal), thence:

3   NNE of Burcom Shoal (2 miles WNW) which fronts the coast for 3 miles to the NW of Grimsby. Burcom Sand, which dries, lies at its SE end. The light-buoys (special) which mark the seaward end of two of the outfalls (7.61), lie either side of Middle Burcom No 8 Light-buoy (port hand) on the SW side of the channel. Thence:

4   To a position in the channel 5 cables W of the W end of Sunk Channel.

Middle Shoal to Immingham

7.67

1   From a position in mid-channel W of Middle Shoal the route leads 3½ miles WNW through the channel, which is buoyed, to a position NE of the entrance lock to Immingham Dock, passing (with positions from the lock entrance):

SSW of the measured distance (7.62) (3 miles E), thence:

2   NNE of a light-beacon (port hand) (2½ miles SE) marking the end of the outfall (7.61) E of Stallingborough Flat, thence:

SSW of Holme Ridge (1 mile NE), and:

NNE of Immingham Oil Terminal (7.83) (7 cables E), thence:

To a position NE of the entrance lock to Immingham Dock (7.84).

Useful mark

7.68

1   Lights in line Killingholme:

Front light (white tower, 14 m in height) (53°38′·8N, 0°12′·9W).

Rear light (red tower, 24 m in height) (189 m WNW of front light).

These lights in line (292°) afford useful guidance to vessels approaching and manoeuvring off Immingham.

(Directions continue for Immingham at 7.82 and Kingston Upon Hull at 7.95)

Small craft

7.69

1   Stone Creek (53°39′N, 0°08′W), with moorings and jetties for yachts, lies on the coast of Sunk Island opposite Immingham. Recommended routes for the approach are shown on the chart. The entrance is marked on each side by a beacon and posts mark the E side of a channel leading to the Boat Club jetty.

Other names

7.70

1   Pyewipe Flats (53°36′N, 0°07′W).

Stallingborough Haven (53°37′N, 0°10′W).

Sunk Spit (53°37′N, 0°04′W).

IMMINGHAM

General information

Chart 3497 plan of Immingham

Position

7.71

1   **Immingham Dock and Jetties** (53°38′N, 0°11′W) lie on the SW bank of the River Humber 5½ miles NW of Grimsby.

Function

7.72

1   Immingham, population 12 278 (1991), is the centre of the Humberside chemical and oil refineries. The port mainly handles dry and liquid bulk commodities but also has a substantial general cargo/unit load trade.

Traffic

7.73

1   In 1999 Immingham handled 5306 vessels totalling over 76 million dwt, and about 46 million tonnes of cargo.

Port authority

7.74

1   Associated British Ports, Port Office, Cleethorpe Road, Grimsby, DN31 3LL.

Limiting conditions

7.75

1   **Controlling depths.** See 7.57.

Deepest and longest berths. Riverside berths: deepest Humber International Terminal (7.86), longest Immingham Oil Terminal; Immingham Dock (7.84).

Tidal levels: see *Admiralty Tide Tables*. Mean spring range about 6·4 m; mean neap range about 3·2 m.

7.76

1   **Maximum size of vessel handled:**

	Length	Draught	Remarks
Immingham Dock	198 m	10·36 m	26·1 m breadth
Eastern and Western Jetties	213 m	10·36 m	30 000 dwt
Immingham Oil Terminal	366 m	13·1 m	290 000 dwt, part laden
Immingham Bulk Terminal	303 m	14·0 m	200 000 dwt, part laden
Humber International Terminal	265 m	14·2 m	100 000 dwt
Immingham Gas Terminal	280 m	11·0 m	50 000 dwt

(row marked "2" at Immingham Bulk Terminal)

Arrival information

7.77

1   For Port operations see 7.4; for outer anchorages see 7.7, 7.33 and 7.44; for pilotage see 7.2.

    Tugs are available at Immingham.

Traffic signals

7.78

1   **Vessels manoeuvring.** Synchronised traffic lights are exhibited, day and night, from Tower A, a signal tower at the entrance to Immingham Dock, and Tower B, a signal mast at the head of the approach arm to the Oil Terminal, as follows:

Signal	Meaning
White light, 2 flashes, each 2 seconds duration, every 10 seconds	A vessel is arriving at or leaving Immingham Dock, East Jetty or West Jetty or manoeuvring at the Bulk terminal
White light 1 flash of 6 seconds every 15 seconds	Vessel manoeuvring off Immingham Oil Terminal Jetty

(row marked "2" at first signal)

3   **Entrance lock.** Main signals 2 and 5 of the International Port Traffic Signals as given in the *Mariner's Handbook* are shown from Tower A to regulate traffic entering or leaving Immingham Dock. Instructions for approaching the lock or berthing at Eastern or Western Jetties are given on VHF radio.

Harbour

Layout

7.79

1   There are a number of jetties and terminals at Immingham, which run for 2 miles along the SW bank of the River Humber, as well as an enclosed dock. From SE to NW they are the Immingham Oil Terminal (7.83), Eastern and Western Jetties (7.84) which lie either side of the entrance lock to the enclosed dock, Immingham Bulk Terminal (7.85), Humber International Terminal (7.86) and finally Immingham Gas Terminal (7.87).

Tidal streams

7.80

1   The spring rate for the in-going stream is 3 kn and for the out-going stream 3½ to 5 kn. The rates off the jetties are similar but in some instances may reach 4 kn and 7 kn respectively.

2   Between the elbows of Eastern and Western Jetties the stream is much weaker than off the jetties and the line of this division is often indicated by ripples. The line is usually nearer the lock entrance at HW than at LW, and there may be a NW-going eddy on the lock entrance side between +0100 and +0520 HW Immingham.

3   The division between the weak streams in the vicinity of the jetties and the entirely slack water at the lock entrance occurs on the line between the outer masonry piers and the pile jetties.

4   When entering with a strong tidal stream running, the stern of the vessel is swung down tide as its bows enter the slack water. If entry speed is high then collision with the opposite jetty is possible. Nevertheless speed must be sufficient to maintain good steerage. In these conditions vessels are advised to proceed at low speed close in to Western Jetty during the in-going stream and Eastern Jetty during the out-going stream.

5   Vessels entering without tug assistance should do so at slack water if possible.

    Details of the tidal streams in the channel off Immingham Dock entrance are given on the chart.

Principal marks

7.81

1   **Landmarks:**
    Two chimneys (53°37′N, 0°11′W).
    Coke silo (53°37′·6N, 0°11′·7W).
    Flare (53°38′·8N, 0°15′·3W).

Directions
(continued from 7.68)

7.82

1   There is direct access to the riverside berths from the River Humber.

2   From the River Humber the access to Immingham Dock is through an entrance lock, which is approached between Eastern and Western Jetties (7.84). The entrance lock has a length of 256 m, width 27·4 m and there is a depth over the inner sill of 11·3 m at MHWS and 9·9 m at MHWN. The lock has three pairs of gates, which can divide it into an outer part 96 m long and an inner part 160 m long. The lock can be entered at any state of the tide.

3   Depths in the entrance to Immingham Dock vary. The Dock Master should be consulted for the latest information.

Basin and berths

Immingham Oil Terminal

7.83

1   Immingham Oil Terminal Jetty lies 7 cables E of the entrance to Immingham Dock. The shore arm of the jetty extends 5 cables NE with three T-headed tanker berths and associated dolphins and mooring dolphins running WNW and ESE. The berths and dolphins exhibit lights at their extremities. There is a barge passage through the shore arm, marked by lights, 2½ cables from the shore.

Immingham Dock and Jetties

7.84

1   Immingham Dock has 1700 m of quays providing a number of berths, the majority of which have 11 m depth

Immingham Oil Terminal (7.83)

(Original dated 2000)

(Photograph - Air Images)

alongside. There are four Ro-Ro berths in each Arm of the dock.

Eastern and Western Jetties, which lie either side of the approach to the entrance lock and run parallel to the shore, provide 3 tanker berths. The berths are marked by lights at their extremities.

Eastern Jetty   *Western Jetty*

Immingham Dock (7.84)

(Original dated 2000)

(Photograph - Air Images)

Immingham Bulk Terminal
7.85

1   Immingham Bulk Terminal, an L-shaped jetty lying 2 cables offshore and 6 cables NW of the entrance to Immingham Dock, has a seaward face 518 m in length marked by lights at either end, with depths alongside of over 14 m. The terminal handles coal and iron ore, with 2 appliances each rated at 2000 tph.

Humber International Terminal
7.86

1   Humber International Terminal lies adjacent to the NW end of Immingham Bulk Terminal, 8 cables NW of Immingham Dock. The terminal, consisting of a concrete

deck on tubular steel piles, is 300 m in length and has a depth alongside of 14·7 m. A light is exhibited from the NW end of the berth.

Immingham Gas Terminal
7.87

1   Immingham Gas Terminal, an L-shaped jetty lying 2 cables offshore and 1 mile NW of the entrance to Immingham Dock, has a seaward face of 80 m and associated mooring dolphins, all marked by lights, with a dredged depth alongside of 12 m.

Gas Terminal   *Oil Jetty*

Immingham Gas Terminal (7.87) &
South Killingholme Oil Jetty (7.99)

(Original dated 2000)

(Photograph - Air Images)

Port services
7.88

1   **Repairs.** All types of repair can be undertaken.
Other facilities:
        Facilities available for the reception of oily waste, noxious and harmful substances.
2   Deratting and exemption certificates issued.
        Customs.
        Hospital (at Grimsby).
        Divers available.

Bulk Terminal   Humber International Terminal
                                  (under construction)

Immingham Bulk Terminal (7.85)

(Original dated 2000)

(Photograph - Air Images)

Supplies: all types of fuel oil; water at the quays; stores and provisions.

IMMINGHAM TO KINGSTON UPON HULL

General information

Chart 3497
Route
7.89

1 From a position in mid-channel off the entrance to Immingham Dock (53°38′N, 0°11′W), the route leads 7 miles NNW to a position off the entrance to King George Docks at Hull thence 2 miles W to a position off the entrance to Albert Dock at the W end of Hull.

Controlling depths
7.90

1 The controlling depth in the buoyed channel between Immingham and Hull is 6·2 m (1999), as shown on the chart, 1¾ to 2 miles NNW of the entrance lock to Immingham Dock. However depths are subject to frequent change and the buoyage moved as necessary. The Harbour Master Humber should be consulted for the latest information.

Pilotage
7.91

1 See 7.2.
 Masters without local knowledge, and not subject to compulsory pilotage, are advised to obtain the services of a pilot.

Traffic regulations
7.92

1 **Regulations affecting entry.** See 7.5.

Prohibited anchorage areas:
 The fairway.
 Either side of the pipelines, indicated by pairs of beacons (red diamond topmarks) on each shore, which cross the river in the vicinity of Thorngumbald Clough (53°42′·5N, 0°13′·5W).
2 Off Salt End (7.103).
 Off Albert Dock (7.98).
These areas are shown on the chart.

Tidal streams
7.93

1 The tidal streams run generally in the direction of the channel, but there is likely to be a set towards the outer side of the bend N of Skitter Sand (7.96).
 Off Hull, in the vicinity of Albert Dock, the in-going stream is of shorter duration but stronger than the out-going stream and can reach 5 kn. The out-going stream reaches 4 kn. Details of the tidal streams are given on the chart.

Principal marks
7.94

1 **Landmarks:**
 For marks at Immingham see 7.81.
 Cooling towers (53°44′N, 0°14′W).
 Grain silo (53°44′·6N, 0°16′·5W).
 Barrier towers (53°44′·4N, 0°19′·7W), Old Harbour.
 Holy Trinity Church (tower) (53°44′·5N, 0°19′·9W).

Directions
(continued from 7.68)

Immingham to Salt End
7.95

1 From a position off Immingham (53°38′N, 0°11′W) the buoyed channel leads 6 miles NNW to Salt End, passing (with positions from the entrance to Immingham Dock):
 WSW of Clay Huts (1 mile NE) composed of stiff clay and marked on its SW side by No 11A

2 Light-buoy (starboard hand). Clay Huts Light-float (safe water) is moored in mid-channel SW of Clay Huts, thence:

ENE of South Killingholme Oil Jetty (1¼ miles NW) (7.99), which lies 2 cables NW of Immingham Gas Terminal (7.87), thence:

WSW of Foul Holme Spit (2 miles NNW), which forms the NE side of the channel to the NNW of Clay Huts. The spit is composed of white sand and subject to great and frequent changes. Thence:

3 ENE of Humber Sea Terminal (2¾ miles NW) (7.101), which is approached through Whitebooth Road leading NW off the main channel. Outfall pipes lie 4 and 5 cables SE of the jetty. The seaward ends are each marked by a light-buoy (port hand) and the landward ends by poles (yellow cross) in transit.

4 The channel continues NNW, passing (with positions from Salt End (53°43′·8N, 0°14′·5W)):

ENE of Halton Flat (3 miles S), as defined by the 5 m depth contour. Halton Flat is a sandbank extending along the SW shore for 3½ miles and up to 1 mile offshore, which lies on the SW side of the channel. Thence:

5 WSW of Paull Sand (2½ miles SSE), which fronts the NE shore to the NNW of Foul Holme Spit and lies on the NE side of the channel, thence:

WSW of Thorngumbald Clough (1¼ miles SSE) a prominent point on which lights (7.97) are sited, thence:

To a position in mid-channel SSW of Salt End Jetties (7.103).

Salt End to King George Dock
7.96

1 From Thorngumbald Clough to Hull the channel is curved and narrow. The tidal streams (7.93) are strong and the in-going stream sets on to The Hebbles. Additionally the shoals mentioned below are subject to frequent change. This stretch of the River Humber therefore is the most critical part of the navigation.

2 From a position in mid-channel off Salt End Jetties (53°43′·6N, 0°14′·8W), the route leads 1¾ miles NW through the buoyed channel to a position off King George Dock, passing (with positions from King George Dock):

NE of Skitter Sand (1¼ miles SSW), which fronts the S shore lying either side of Skitter Ness, a low rounded point, thence:

3 SW of The Hebbles (8 cables SE), a shoal which dries in parts. The shoal fronts the NE shore between Salt End and the entrance to King George Dock, thence:

NW of Hull Middle (6 cables SSW), a shoal of mud and sand which dries, thence:

4 To a position off the entrance to King George Dock, which lies at the E end of Kingston upon Hull.

Useful mark
7.97

1 **Lights in line Thorngumbald Clough:**

Front light (white tower, 10 m in height) (53°42′·5N, 0°13′·5W).

Rear light (red tower on metal framework tower, 15 m in height) (113 m SE of front light).

The lights are synchronised and visible between the bearings of 130° and 140°.

Hull Road
7.98

1 The buoyed channel leads 2 miles W from King George Dock entrance (53°44′·5N, 0°16′·0W) through Hull Road, which runs along the shore immediately S of Kingston upon Hull, to the entrance to Albert Dock, passing (with positions from Albert Dock entrance):

2 N of Hull Middle (centre 1½ miles ESE) (7.96) on the S side of Hull Road, thence:

S of Alexandra Dock (1½ miles E), thence:

S of the junction with the River Hull (3 cables E). Old Harbour lies at the mouth of the River Hull. Thence:

To a position (2·3 miles W) off the entrance to Albert Dock.

(Directions continue for Hull Docks at 7.118, and for River Humber above Hull at 7.136)

Berths
7.99

1 **South Killingholme** Oil Jetty (53°38′·8N, 0°12′·6W) extends 488 m NE from the SE shore. The L-shaped head, which has a seaward face of 85 m and associated mooring dolphins, all marked by lights, extends SE with depths of 10 m alongside. The jetty can accept ships up to 213 m in length. Power cables, suspended 2 m above water level at lowest point, are strung from the dolphins to the jetty.

7.100

1 **North Killingholme Haven** (53°39′·8N, 0°14′·0W), is a cargo terminal providing three berths. Vessels up to 5000 dwt, 140 m loa and maximum draught 4·5 m (N side) and 6·5 m (S side) can be accommodated. The white sector of North Killingholme Haven Light leads into the harbour, as shown on the chart.

7.101

1 **Humber Sea Terminal** (53°40′·0N, 0°13′·8W) is an L-shaped jetty extending 2 cables NE from the SE shore. The jetty, which provides 2 Ro-Ro berths, has a depth of 9·3 m alongside; the approach channel from Whitebooth Road is dredged (2000) to 7·2 m.

7.102

1 **North Killingholme** Oil Jetty (53°40′·0N, 0°13′·9W) lies close inshore of Humber Sea Terminal. The T-shaped jetty, with a lighted dolphin at either end, has depths alongside of 10·1 m and can accept ships up to 177 m in length.

There are two boat passages marked by lights under the approach arm of the jetty.

7.103

1 **Salt End** Jetties (53°43′·6N, 0°14′·8W) are two T-shaped oil jetties connected by a common approach to the shore at Salt End, lying close E of Kingston upon Hull. In 1999 the terminal handled 613 vessels totalling 3 393 508 dwt.

2 The depth alongside both jetties is 9·8 m. No 3 Jetty (the SE jetty) is 121 m in length and No 1 Jetty 79 m in length. There are dolphins between the two jetties and one to the SE of No 3 Jetty as well as a dolphin and two mooring buoys to the NW of No 1 Jetty. The extremities of the jetties and the dolphins are marked by lights. The maximum size of vessel that can be accepted is length 214 m, draught 10·4 m and 40 000 dwt.

3 There is a dredged approach to the jetties whose limits (104° N limit; 000° S limit) are marked by two pairs of similar lighted beacons in line (yellow cross). The N limit beacons stand on W end of No 1 Jetty Head and the S limit beacons stand on E end of No 3 Jetty Head. The lights of each pair of beacons are synchronised and only exhibited when vessels are berthing at Salt End.

Salt End Jetties (7.103)

(Original dated 2000)

(Photograph - Air Images)

Anchorages
7.104
1   An anchorage may be obtained in Hull Road (7.98) in depths of between 6 and 9 m, N of Skitter Sand (7.96) and Hull Middle (7.96). There is foul ground 2 and 4 cables E and SE of the Old Harbour (7.98). Vessels should not anchor too close to The Hebbles (7.96) although the tidal streams are weaker there.

2   Larger vessels are advised not to remain at anchor in Hull Road at LW springs as depths are liable to vary from those shown on the chart and grounding is possible.

Whitebooth Road (7.95) affords an anchorage in depths between 5 m and 9 m.

Small craft
7.105
1   **East Halton Skitter** (53°41′·5N, 0°15′·7W) is a creek on the SW side of the river providing shelter for craft drawing up to 1·5 m which can enter within 2 to 2½ hours of HW.
7.106
1   **Hedon Haven** (53°43′·6N, 0°13′·9W) is approached by a channel indicated on the chart. The haven is used by fishermen and can take craft drawing 1 5 m within 2 hours of HW.

Other names
7.107
1   East Marsh (53°42′N, 0°17′W).
Foul Holme Sand (53°41′N, 0°11′W).
Halton Marshes (53°41′N, 0°16′W).

KINGSTON UPON HULL

General information

Chart 3497 plans of Hull Docks
Position
7.108
1   Kingston upon Hull (53°45′N, 0°18′W), usually known simply as Hull, stands on low-lying ground at the junction of the Rivers Hull and Humber, 20 miles above Spurn Head.

Function
7.109
1   The port handles general cargo and passenger vessels, mainly trading with West Europe and Scandinavia. It is also an important fish processing and distribution centre, although no longer a major fishing port.

The population was 310 636 in 1991.

Traffic
7.110
1   In 1999 the port handled 2232 vessels totalling 9 978 756 dwt.

Port authority
7.111
1   Associated British Ports, PO Box No 1, Port House, Corporation Road, Kingston upon Hull, HU9 5PQ.

Limiting conditions
7.112
1   **Controlling depths.** See 7.90.
Deepest and longest berth is in King George Dock (7.121).
Tidal levels: see *Admiralty Tide Tables.* Mean spring range about 6·8 m; mean neap range about 3·4 m.
7.113
1   **Maximum size of vessel** handled in the enclosed docks is length 196 m, beam 25·5 m and draught 10·4 m (MHWS), 9·4 m (MHWN).

Arrival information
7.114
1   For Port operations see 7.4; for anchorages see 7.7 and 7.104; for pilotage see 7.2.
Tugs are available at Hull.

Harbour

Layout
7.115
1   The main berthing facilities are the three enclosed docks. King George Dock together with Queen Elizabeth Dock, the largest complex, and Alexandra Dock lie to the E of the port. Albert Dock, which leads into William Wright Dock, lies to the W. The latter docks are used by the fishing fleet.

River Terminal 1, the first of three planned Ro-Ro berths, lies close W of the entrance to King George Dock. Nos 2 and 3 will lie close E.

2   Old Harbour, which extends about 5 cables upstream in the River Hull from its junction with the Humber, is the original harbour and still used by commercial vessels up to 500 grt. There is a tidal surge barrier 1 cable upstream of the entrance to the River Hull.

Hull Marina occupies the old Humber and Princes Docks.

Dock signals
7.116
1   **King George, Albert and Alexandra Docks.** Main signals 2 and 5 of the International Port Traffic Signals, given in *The Mariner's Handbook* control traffic using the entrance locks. These signals are exhibited from grey lattice masts situated close to the entrances of their particular dock.

2   A high intensity quick flashing light is exhibited from the S side of the entrance to Albert Dock to warn other traffic that vessels are leaving the lock.

A red light exhibited from a steel mast at the inner end of the Alexandra entrance lock indicates that entry to the lock from the dock itself is prohibited.

3 **River Terminal 1.** A slow occulting yellow light is exhibited, close to the right of the docking signals on the W side of the entrance lock to King George Dock, when a vessel is berthing or unberthing at the terminal.

4 **Marina.** Main signals 2 and 4 of the International Port Traffic Signals, exhibited from the W side of Humber Dock Basin, control access to the basin. In addition access through the lock gate is controlled by a fixed red or green light exhibited from the W side of the outer end and the E side of the inner end of the lock gates.

5 **Tidal surge barrier.** Two pairs of yellow quick flashing lights, disposed vertically, on both sides of the entrance to the River Hull are exhibited when the river is closed to traffic. A fog signal is sounded in conjunction with the lights during periods of reduced visibility.

Principal marks
7.117
1 **Landmarks:**
> Cooling towers (53°44′N, 0°14′W).
> Grain silo (53°44′·6N, 0°16′·5W).
> Barrier Towers (53°44′·4N, 0°19′·7W) in Old Harbour.
> Holy Trinity Church (Tower) (53°44′·5N, 0°19′·9W).

Directions
(continued from 7.98)

Entry into King George Dock
7.118
1 The following light-beacon in line (001½°) with the signal mast indicates the E limit of the dredged approach area to the entrance lock (53°44′·5N, 0°16′·4W):

> Front beacon (yellow post, white triangle topmark) (110 m S of signal mast).
> Signal mast (grey lattice, 27 m in height) (53°44′·5N, 0°16′·4W), close to the Dock Master's office.

2 The W limit of the dredged approach area is indicated by the following light-beacons in line (057°):
> Front beacon (yellow triangular topmark) (3·3 cables W of the signal mast).
> Rear beacon (yellow triangular topmark) (close NE of the front beacon). Both these beacons are situated on the new (1993) River Terminal 1 Ro-Ro jetty head (7.122).

3 The entrance lock to King George Dock is 228 m in length, 25·7 m in width with a depth over the sill of 13·1 m at MHWS and 11·5 m at MHWN. Vessels can be accepted over the full 24 hour period for entry into King George Dock. Larger vessels restricted by the tide are usually accepted from 3 hours before HW to HW.

Entry into Alexandra Dock
7.119
1 The following light-beacons in line (327°) indicate the E limit of the dredged approach area to the entrance lock:
> Front light-beacon (post, yellow triangle topmark) (53°44′·6N, 0°17′·7W).
> Rear light-beacon (post, yellow triangle topmark) (33 m NNW of front light-beacon).
The entrance lock to Alexandra Dock is 167·8 m long, 25·7 m wide with a depth over the sill of 10·4 m at MHWS.

Entry into Albert Dock
7.120
1 Entry is from the river through a lock at the E end of the dock, which is 97 m in length, 24·3 m in width, with a depth over the sill of 8·6 m at MHWS. Vessels enter and leave Albert Dock from 2½ hours before HW to 1½ hours after HW. Entry is frequently made stern first.

Grain Silo

King George & Queen Elizabeth Docks — Hull (7.121.1)

(Original dated 2000)

(Photograph - Air Images)

Alexandra River Pier

Alexandra Dock — Hull (7.121.2)

(Original dated 2000)

(Photograph - Air Images)

Basins and berths

Enclosed docks
7.121

1 There are 5068 m of operational quays and a depth of 10·7 m available at most berths in the King George and Queen Elizabeth Docks, capable of taking vessels up to 196 m length, 25·5 m beam, 10·4 m draught and about 34 000 dwt. There are seven Ro-Ro terminals in the two docks, with two additional terminals to be completed in Queen Elizabeth Dock. A steel terminal with a fully enclosed handling facility is situated in a former dry dock at the SE end of King George Dock. The covered berth can accept vessels up to 127 m in length, 20·1 m beam, 7 m draught and 13·5 m air draught.

2 There are 3453 m of operational quays and a depth of 6·5 m available in Albert and William Wright Docks, capable of taking vessels up to 122 m length about 5000 dwt.

There are 4082 m of quays and a depth of 8·3 m available in Alexandra Dock, capable of taking vessels up to 153 m length, 23·7 m beam, 7·9 m draught and about 9000 dwt. A Ro-Ro berth lies in the SW corner of the dock.

Other berths
7.122

Riverside Quay off Albert Dock; Old Harbour (7.115).

River Terminal 1, capable of taking vessels with 6·5 m draught, lies 3 cables W of the entrance to King George Dock. Light-beacons in line and a light beacon in line with the signal tower (7.118) mark the W and E limits of the dredged approach area. Two more Ro-Ro berths are planned to be built on the river E of the entrance to King George Dock.

Port services
7.123

1 **Repairs.** All kinds of repairs can be carried out. There are two dry docks in Alexandra Dock and one in William Wright Dock, as well as four further dry docks in private shipyards.

The largest dry dock has a length of 176 m, width at entrance of 18·6 m and a depth at the sill of 6·1 m (MHWS) to 4·6 m (MHWN).

7.124

1 **Other facilities:**
Hospital with helicopter landing site.
Deratting and exemption certificates issued.
Customs.
Salvage and diving services.
Facilities available for the reception of oily waste, noxious and harmful substances.

7.125

1 **Supplies:** all types of oil fuel; fresh water at the quays; stores and provisions.

7.126

1 **Communications.** The Rivers Hull, Derwent, Ouse and Trent connect the Humber with the internal navigation to the W and with the River Thames. The port also has good road and rail communications.

Small craft
7.127

1   Hull Marina (53°44′N, 0°20′W), operated by Hull City Council, has pontoon berths for 330 small craft up to a length of 22·8 m. The marina has a depth of 2·5 m. The marina is entered through Humber Dock Basin which is close E of Albert Dock entrance and thence through lock gates which operate 3 hours either side of HW. The usual facilities are available. See 7.118 for dock signals.

Humber Dock

Humber Dock Basin

Hull Marina (7.127)

(Original dated 2000)

(Photograph - Air Images)

RIVER HUMBER ABOVE KINGSTON UPON HULL

General information

Charts 3497, 109
Route
7.128

1   From Kingston upon Hull (53°45′N, 0°18′W) the River Humber leads in a generally W direction, 14 miles, to its head at the junction of the Rivers Ouse and Trent.

Controlling depths
7.129

1   Above Kingston upon Hull there is usually a depth of 1 m at MLWS in the River Humber, but the river is subject to constant change and no controlling depth can be given.

Humber Bridge
7.130

1   Humber Bridge (53°42′N, 0°27′W) a single span suspension bridge, crosses the river between Barton upon Humber and Hessle (7.139). The main span is marked by lights and lies between two conspicuous towers (7.135). The span is 1410 m long with a vertical clearance of 30 m.

Masters of vessels with an air draught exceeding 30 m shall not navigate under the bridge without the prior approval of the Harbour Master.

Pilotage
7.131

1   See 7.2.

Local knowledge
7.132

1   Due to the constant changes in the channel in the River Humber above Kingston upon Hull, local knowledge is necessary. Vessels proceeding above Kingston upon Hull therefore should have a qualified pilot on board.

Bird sanctuary
7.133

1   A refuge for the protection of pink-footed geese lies on the N bank of the river from the village of Brough (53°44′N, 0°33′W) to the junction of the rivers (4¼ miles ENE). Landing by boat is not permitted between 1 September and 20 February.

Tidal streams
7.134

1   The tidal streams in the River Humber above Kingston upon Hull normally run at a rate of 3 kn to 4 kn, but on occasions may exceed 6 kn.

Principal marks
7.135

1   **Landmarks:**
        See 7.117 for marks in Kingston upon Hull.
        Chimney (53°41′·8N, 0°25′·7W).
        Spire (53°43′·4N, 0°26′·1W) at Hessle.
        Humber Bridge support towers (N side 53°42′·8N, 0°26′·9W, S side 53°42′·1N, 0°26′·9W).
        Chimneys (53°40′·6N, 0°31′·6W) at Ferriby Sluice.

Directions
(continued from 7.98)
7.136

1   From a position off the entrance to Albert Dock (7.98), the channel above Hull leads WSW then generally W to the head of the River Humber. The channel leads N of Hull Middle (7.96) and is marked by light-floats and light-buoys. No further directions can be given as the navigation marks are moved when the occasion requires to conform with the changes in the channel.

Minor Harbour

New Holland
7.137

1   **General information.** New Holland (53°42′N, 0°21′W) lies on the S bank of the River Humber, 2½ miles W of Skitter Ness (7.96). In 1999 the port handled 400 vessels totalling 951 071 dwt. The main berths are operated by New Holland Bulk Services Ltd, PO Box 1, Barrow-on-Humber, DN19 7SD.

    Caution. Passing vessels should reduce speed to avoid damage to those alongside New Holland Pier.

2   **Berths.** New Holland Pier is a T-shaped pier extending 2¼ cables NNW from the shore with a pontoon at the E end of the T-head. The extremities of the pier are lit, as is a dolphin close off the W end. The pier provides 4 berths the largest of which can accommodate vessels of length 114 m and up to 5000 dwt. The small tidal dock close E of the pier has two berths. The dock can be entered by craft drawing 1·5 m at HW neaps or within 2 hours of HW at springs.

3   **Facilities.** There is a shipyard and slipway 3 cables ENE of the pier.

     Supplies. Fuel oil by barge or road tanker; water at the quays; provisions.

Small craft

7.138

1   **Barrow Haven** (53°42′N, 0°24′W) which has a jetty, can be entered by craft drawing 1·5 m about 2 hours either side of HW. There is a recommended approach route shown on Chart 3497.

7.139

1   **Hessle Haven** (53°43′N, 0°26′W) can be entered by craft drawing 1·5 m at HW neaps or 2 hours either side of HW springs. There is a recommended approach route shown on Chart 3497.

7.140

1   **Barton Haven** (53°42′N, 0°27′W) fronted by Barton Ness Sand has a pier and can be entered by craft drawing 1·5 m at HW neaps.

7.141

1   **Winteringham Haven** (53°42′N, 0°35′W), 5 miles W of Humber Bridge, can be entered by craft drawing 1·5 m 1½ hours either side of HW. The alignment (276°) of white leading posts leads to the entrance.

RIVER OUSE TO GOOLE AND SELBY

General information

Chart 109 plan of Whitton Ness to Goole and Keadby

River Ouse, Faxfleet to Goole

7.142

1   Blacktoft Channel leads through the River Ouse from its junction with the River Trent at Faxfleet, towards Goole. The channel is marked by shore lights and beacons as far as Goole, which is 7 miles up river from the junction.

     Pilotage is compulsory to Goole (see 7.2). River pilots are available.

2   Due to the changing nature of the channel, local knowledge is essential.

     Tidal streams in the river normally run at a rate of 3 to 4 kn but may exceed 6 kn.

River Ouse, Goole to Selby

7.143

1   The river is navigable to Selby (7.159) 16 miles above Goole and marked by navigation lights as far as Long Drax (7.158), 8 miles above Goole.

     Pilotage is not compulsory above Goole but is advisable, particularly if passing through the river bridges at Selby (7.144). River pilots are available. They board and land at Victoria Pier at Goole. The chart does not go above Goole.

7.144

1   **Bridges** cross the River Ouse at the following points:
     Skelton Railway Bridge (1 mile above Goole) a swing bridge. Bridge control can be contacted on VHF. When vessels approach the bridge they sound 1 long blast followed by 6 short blasts. Inbound vessels are recommended to use Eastern Channel and outbound vessels Western Channel.

2   Boothferry Bridge (4 miles above Goole) a road swing bridge at Booth. The same signal as for Skelton Railway Bridge is sounded to request opening. The bridge control can be contacted on VHF.

3   Motorway bridge, also at Booth, has four piers marked by lights on both the upstream and downstream sides. A light shown from the bridge indicates the main channel in use.

4   Selby road and rail bridges, both swing bridges. The same signal as for Skelton Railway Bridge is sounded to request their opening. Both bridge controls can be contacted on VHF. Selby Road Bridge must be navigated with caution as its navigational span is only 10·7 m wide and the channel 9·9 m wide. Vessels exceeding 38 m in length and 8 m beam must pass the bridge in daylight at slack water, or against the stream and attended by a tug. Vessels with a beam greater than 9·5 m must obtain prior consent of the trustees.

Goole

Chart 109 plan of Goole

General information

7.145

1   **Position.** The Port of Goole (53°42′N, 0°52′W) lies on the W bank of the River Ouse close N of its junction with the Dutch River.

     Function. Goole is a small commercial port, trading principally with European ports and the Baltic. The population was 18 284 in 1991.

2   **Traffic.** In 1999 the port handled 1369 vessels and about 2·7 million tonnes of cargo.

     Port authority. Associated British Ports, Port Office, East Parade, Goole DN14 5RB.

Limiting conditions

7.146

1   **Controlling depths.** Due to the changing nature of the channel there is no set controlling depth, but vessels drawing up to 5·5 m can reach Goole on ordinary spring tides and up to 4·6 m at ordinary neap tides. Within the docks the water is maintained at a constant level to allow vessels drawing 5·5 m to enter subject to tidal restrictions.

2   **Largest dock** is West Dock (7.153).

     Tidal levels: see *Admiralty Tide Tables*. Mean spring range about 5·4 m; mean neap range about 3 m.

7.147

1   **Maximum size of vessel** handled is length 100 m, beam 24 m, draught 5·5 m and 4500 dwt. Larger and deeper draught vessels may be accepted after consultation with the Dock Master.

Arrival information

7.148

1   For Port Operations see 7.4; for pilotage see 7.2.

     Tugs are available between Hull and Goole and small tugs are available within the docks.

Harbour

7.149

1   **Layout.** Goole Docks consist of a number of interconnected docks which can be entered from either the River Ouse or the Inland Navigation (7.167).

7.150

1   **Dock signals** are shown from a signal mast at the entrance to Ocean Lock as follows:

24 hour Signals	*Meaning*
High intensity flashing white light	A vessel is leaving the lock and entering the tideway.

Victoria Lock

Goole Docks from NE (7.149)

(Original dated 2000)

(Photograph - Air Images)

2 | Three red lights vertically disposed | Vessels may not proceed into the lock. (May also mean that the lock is being prepared for vessels to enter).

| Three lights vertically disposed (green above white above green) | Vessels may proceed into the lock according to instructions.

3   When a signal indicates that a vessel is leaving the Ocean Lock and entering the tideway, no other vessel shall pass into the area bounded on the N by an imaginary line drawn 090° from the Signal Mast, and on the S by an imaginary line drawn 270° from Upper East Goole light beacon No 29 on the E bank of Goole Reach.

4   A red flag, by night a red light, exhibited from the SE end of Victoria Lock, indicates that vessels may not enter that lock. The entry signal is a green flag, by night a green light. The flags are exhibited from a flagstaff and the lights from a lamp standard.

7.151

1   **Tidal signals** are shown from a signal mast on the N side of all lock entrances from HW to 45 minutes after HW as follows:

| *By day* | Black square flag |
| *By night* | Fixed white light |

Directions
7.152

1   Goole Docks are entered from the River Ouse via two locks of the following dimensions:
Ocean Lock: length 104 m; width 24·4 m; depth over sill at MHWN 6·1 m.
Victoria Lock: constructed in two sections, total length 145 m; width 14·2 m; depth over sill at MHWN 6·0 m.

2   The locks are operated from approximately 2½ hours before HW to 1½ hours after HW at Goole. Ocean Lock is manned throughout 24 hours and can be operated for small craft and barge traffic at any time; an additional charge is made for this service.

Basins and berths
7.153

1   The nine interconnected docks provide about 3 miles of quays. The largest dock is West Dock which has a length varying between 280 m and 320 m, width varying between 78 m and 88 m, and 740 m of quays.

7.154

1   **Submarine cable.** A high voltage submarine cable crosses the Gutway between Ship Dock and Railway Dock. Mariners are advised against dropping or dredging anchors in the vicinity.

Port services
7.155

1   **Repairs.** Limited repairs can be carried out. There are two dry docks, the larger is 91·7 m in length, 15 m wide at the entrance, and depth 4·5 m at the sill.
Other facilities:
Facilities for the reception of oily waste, noxious and harmful substances.

2   One Ro-Ro ramp capable of loads up to 450 tonnes. Hospitals.
Supplies: all types of fuel oil by road tanker or barge; fresh water; stores and provisions.
Communications. The Aire and Calder Navigation (7.167) is entered from South Dock at Goole.

Small craft
7.156

1   There are no facilities or berths for small craft within the commercial docks, but berthing facilities for small craft

are available in the Aire and Calder Navigation. There is a slipway for small craft.

Minor ports

7.157

1   **Howden Dyke** (53°45′N, 0°52′W), 2½ miles upstream from Goole on the River Ouse, provides 4 berths on jetties with a total length of 186 m. Vessels up to 3000 dwt, length 88 m, beam 14 m and draught 5·0 m at spring tides to 3·0 m at neap tides can be accommodated. Vessel take the bottom at low water, which is soft mud. Fresh water and fuel (by road tanker) available.

7.158

1   **Long Drax**, 8 miles upstream from Goole, has a lay-by berth. Obstructions, least depth 1·8 m, extend 40 m into the river off the upper end of the berth.

7.159

1   **Selby** (53°47′N, 1°04′W), population 15 292 (1991), is a small commercial port. There is a quay, length 74 m, and the port has accommodated vessels up 74 m length and draught 6·0 m but vessels over 61 m should consult the Port Authority prior to entry. Oily waste reception facilities available.

RIVER TRENT TO GAINSBOROUGH

Chart 109 plans of Whitton Ness to Goole and Keadby and Keadby to Gainsborough

General information

7.160

1   **Route.** From Trent Falls (53°42′N, 0°42′W) close S of the junction of the Rivers Trent and Ouse, which then form the River Humber, the route follows the River Trent in a generally S direction for 21 miles to Gainsborough. The river is tidal as far as Gainsborough.

7.161

1   **Pilotage** is compulsory, see 7.2.

7.162

1   **Local knowledge** of the changes in channels is necessary and vessels taking passage in the river should have a qualified pilot on board.

7.163

1   **Tidal streams** run at a rate of 3 to 4 kn in the lower reaches of the river but may exceed 6 kn. A bore occurs in the River Trent at equinoctial spring tides.

Directions

7.164

1   As far as Keadby, 7 miles above Trent Falls the river is marked by navigation lights and beacons, but owing to the constant changes in the channel no directions can be given. See 7.136.

Trent Ports and wharves

7.165

1   There are a number of wharves along the banks of the river as far as Keadby. Although small these busy wharves are capable of handling vessels between 90 and 100 m in length, draught up to 5·5 m at springs and 3·1 m at neaps and up to 3000 dwt. In 1999 they received 1146 vessels totalling 2 459 531 dwt. From N to S these wharves are:

2   King's Ferry Wharf (53°39′N, 0°42′W), one berth.
Flixborough Wharf (53°37′N, 0°42′W), two berths.
Neap House Wharves (53°36′N, 0°42′W), three berths.

3   Grove Wharf (53°36′N, 0°43′W), nine berths on a quay length 360 m.
Keadby Wharf (53°35′N, 0°44′W), one berth.
Gunness Wharves (53°35′N, 0°43′W), three berths either side of Keadby Bridge.

Gainsborough

7.166

1   The inland port of Gainsborough (53°24′N, 0°47′W) is 62 miles from the sea. The port has six berths and is capable of taking vessels up to 58 m in length and a draught of 4 m depending on the tide. Vessels bound for Gainsborough have to pass under Keadby Bridge with a vertical clearance of 5 m. Fuel is available from barge or road tanker, water is supplied at the quays.

INLAND WATERWAYS

General information

7.167

1   There is access to the Inland Waterways from the River Ouse at Goole and Selby and the River Trent at Keadby (7.164). The two major waterways concerned, which have both been modernised, are the Aire and Calder Navigation, entered at Goole, and the South Yorkshire Navigation, entered at Keadby lying 7 miles upstream from Trent Falls (7.160). The two waterways are linked by New Junction Canal and give access to Leeds, Castleford, Wakefield, Doncaster, Rotherham and Mexborough as well as a number of wharfs along the banks of the River Trent and the waterways. The Aire and Calder navigation carries about 2½ million tonnes of cargo a year, mainly coal and some grain.

2   The governing dimensions in metres for vessels entering the waterways at Goole are:

Port	Length	Beam	Draught	Headroom
Aire and Calder				
Leeds	62·5	6·1	2·5	3·7
Wakefield	42·6	5·4	1·98	3·7
South Yorkshire Navigation				
Mexborough	71·0	6·1	2·5	3·7
Rotherham	61·0	6·0	2·5	3·7

Chapter 8 - River Humber to Cromer, including The Wash

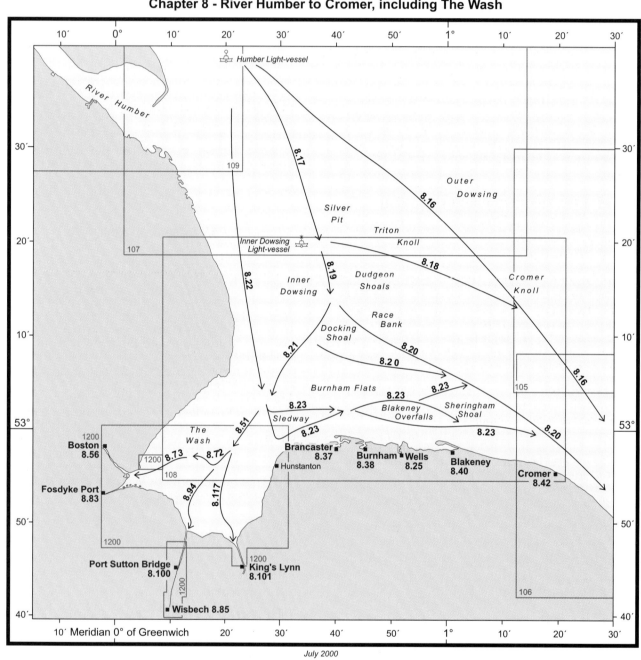

July 2000

RIVER HUMBER TO CROMER INCLUDING THE WASH

GENERAL INFORMATION

Charts 1190, 1503

Synopsis

8.1

1   In this chapter, the coastal and inshore passages from the Humber Light-vessel (53°39′N, 0°20′E) SE to Cromer (8.42) and from Humber Light-vessel to The Wash are described together with The Wash (8.44), the ports of Boston (8.56) and King's Lynn (8.101) and the other minor ports bordering The Wash.

Topography

8.2

1   The deep bight between the entrance to the River Humber and Cromer (52°56′N, 1°18′E), about 53 miles SE, is for the most part encumbered with numerous and dangerous sands; some fringe the coast but others lie a considerable distance offshore. The Wash (8.44) roughly square in shape, is the upper part of this bight and lies to the SW of a line between Gibraltar Point (53°06′N, 0°20′E) (8.44) and Gore Point (8.44) 10 miles SE.

2   From Donna Nook (53°29′N, 0°10′E), the S entrance point of the River Humber, to Gibraltar Point, 23 miles SSE, the coast is composed of sandhills. The flat which fronts this part of the coast, apart from some shoals, shelves gradually to the 10 m depth contour, which lies 8 miles E of Donna Nook. At its S end the flat merges with the shoals forming the bar to Boston Deep (8.74).

3   From Gore Point to Wells (8.25), 12 miles E, the coast is again composed of sandhills, thence it is embanked and fronted by marshes but towards Cromer (8.42) it begins to rise and form cliffs of a moderate height.

Local conditions

8.3

1   The tidal streams are strong and the spring range of the tide is up to 6 m. The weather is frequently misty. The sands and shoals in The Wash, which form an almost continuous chain within the 5 m depth contour, are subject to constant change. These conditions, associated with a low featureless coastline, render navigation difficult and care is necessary. Sounding is important and the state of the tide should always be considered.

Routes

8.4

1   There are a number of routes both for vessels bound from the Humber or Flamborough Head passing E of Cromer thence through The Would (9.24), and for vessels bound for The Wash and its ports. These routes are indicated on the Index Diagram (above) and detailed in the Directions (8.16 to 8.23).

HUMBER TO CROMER

General information

Charts 107, 108

Routes

8.5

1   From the vicinity of the Humber Light-vessel (53°39′N, 0°20′E) to Cromer, 53 miles SE, the principal through route is via the Outer Dowsing Channel. This route and the alternatives, all of which eventually join it, are described below.

2   There is also an inshore route for vessels of light draught which leads S from the Humber to the entrance to The Wash thence E to Cromer. This route, which has several alternatives, together with the small harbours on the Norfolk coast are also described.

Controlling depths

8.6

1   Depending on the precise route taken a minimum depth of 12·8 m can be maintained in the Outer Dowsing Channel. However a depth of 10·1 m is charted in position 53°25′·6N, 1°00′·0E, close W of the channel, and a group of shoaler patches (3 miles S) lie to the W of the central part of the channel.

      The other routes are of shallower depths and the charts should be consulted for the latest information.

Hazards

8.7

1   **Oil and Gas Fields.** A number of production platforms and wells, whose positions are best seen on the chart, lie close to some of these routes. Gas pipelines, also shown on the chart, cross some routes.

      Caution. See 1.37 regarding the hazard from gas pipelines.

8.8

1   A **firing practice and exercise area** is situated between Haile Sand (53°30′N, 0°08′E) and Saltfleet Overfalls, 7 miles SE. The area, which is marked by DZ light-buoys (special) and beacons (port hand), extends 6 miles to seaward. A floating target (yellow) is moored 1½ miles E of Donna Nook (53°29′N, 0°10′E).

8.9

1   **Wrecks.** There are numerous wrecks throughout the area which are shown on the charts. These are not mentioned in the directions but care may be necessary to avoid them, depending on draught.

8.10

1   **Fishing vessels** operate in large numbers in the vicinity of the banks described below.

Harbours

8.11

1   Along the Norfolk coast between Gore Point (52°59′N, 0°33′E) and Cromer, 28 miles to the E, there are a number of small harbours. During strong onshore winds from the E through N to W their harbour entrances become a mass of broken water and the marks difficult to see. The situation worsens when the SE or out-going stream begins or if there is a swell following a previous onshore gale. In these conditions the harbours are not accessible.

Rescue

8.12

1   There are Coastguard Rescue Teams at Mablethorpe (53°20′N, 0°15′E), Chapel Saint Leonards (53°13′N, 0°20′E), Skegness (53°08′N, 0°20′E), Wrangle (53°00′N, 0°06′E), Sutton Bridge (52°46′N, 0°12′E), Wells (52°58′N, 0°51′E), Cley next the Sea (52°58′N, 1°03′E), Sheringham (52°57′N, 1°13′E) and Cromer (52°56′N, 1°18′E); see 1.53.

2   All-weather lifeboats are stationed at Skegness, Wells, and Cromer. Inshore lifeboats are stationed at Mablethorpe,

Skegness, Wells, Sheringham and Cromer; see 1.61 and 1.62 for details of lifeboats.

Tidal streams
8.13

1   Tidal streams are given in the *Admiralty Tidal Stream Atlas: North Sea, Southern Part* and in the tables on the charts. Throughout the area the streams change their direction quickly when they are weak, but only at 10°–15° per hour from two hours before until two hours after the times of their greatest strength.

2   Closer inshore spring rates reach 3 kn and there might be ripples or overfalls near the shoals off the coast.

Principal marks
8.14

1   **Landmarks:**

 See 7.17 for marks in the approaches to the River Humber.

 Building (53°20′N, 0°16′E) at Mablethorpe.

Conspicuous building, Mablethorpe (8.14)

(Original dated 2000)

(Photograph - Air Images)

 Radio mast 1·5 miles SSW of building above.
 Building (pyramid) (53°11′N, 0°21′E).
 Gasometer (53°08′N, 0°20′E) at Skegness.

2   Blakeney Church (tower) (52°57′N, 1°02′E), a turret on NE angle, 33 m in height.
 Cromer Church (tower) (52°56′N, 1°18′E) with battlements.
 Two radio masts (52°55′N, 1°21′E).

3   **Major lights:**

 Inner Dowsing Light-vessel (red hull, light-tower amidships) (53°19′·5N, 0°34′·0E).
 B1D Dowsing (Amethyst lighted offshore platform) (53°34′N, 0°53′E).
 Dudgeon Light-buoy (W cardinal) (53°16′·6N, 1°17′·0E).
 Cromer Light (white octagonal tower, 18 m in height) (52°55′N, 1°19′E).

Other navigational aids
8.15

1   **Racon:**

 Humber Light-vessel (53°39′N, 0°20′E).
 B1D Dowsing platform (53°34′N, 0°53′E).
 Inner Dowsing Light-vessel (53°20′N, 0°34′E).
 Dudgeon Light-buoy (53°17′N, 1°17′E).
 Cromer Light (52°55′N, 1°19′E).

2   **DGPS:**

 Flamborough Head Light (54°07′N, 0°05′W).

Directions
(continued from 6.211)

Outer Dowsing Channel
8.16

1   From a position N of the Humber Light-vessel (53°39′N, 0°20′E), the route leads 20 miles SE to the NW end of the Outer Dowsing Channel, thence 23 miles SSE through the channel to a position N of Cromer, passing:

 S of the Amethyst Gas Field (53°37′N, 0°44′E), thence:

2   Across the N end of Silver Pit (53°36′N, 0°44′E), a deep submarine valley lying N/S across the approach to the River Humber. At its edges the depths change rapidly, though this change is less marked at its N and S extremities. The edge of the deep is usually marked by tide ripplings and these and the change in depths are useful guides. Thence:

3   Clear of B1D Dowsing (53°34′N, 0°53′E) (8.14) to the NW end of the Outer Dowsing Channel.

The route then leads generally SSE through the channel, passing:

 WSW of Outer Dowsing Shoal, which extends 13½ miles SSE from its NW extremity. N Outer Dowsing Light-buoy (N cardinal) (53°33′N, 1°00′E) and Mid Outer Dowsing Light-buoy (starboard hand) mark the NW extremity and SW side of the shoal respectively. Thence:

4   ENE of a group of detached patches (53°22′N, 1°02′E) which lie 2 miles to 4 miles W of the Outer Dowsing Channel and at the E end of Triton Knoll (53°24′N, 0°53′E) (8.18). Thence:

 ENE of East Dudgeon Shoals (53°18′N, 0°59′E) marked on their NE side by E Dudgeon Light-buoy (E cardinal), thence:

5   WSW of Cromer Knoll (53°18′N, 1°18′E), a shoal which extends 4 miles NNW. Dudgeon Light-buoy (8.14) lies 5 cables W of the S extremity of the shoal. Thence:

 ENE of Sheringham Shoal (53°03′N, 1°11′E), a thin isolated shoal running 5 miles E/W. It is marked at its E extremity by E Sheringham Light-buoy (E cardinal) and at its W extremity by W Sheringham Light-buoy (W cardinal). Thence:

6   To a position N of Cromer (52°56′N, 1°18′E).

(Directions continue for coastal route SE at 9.14)

Between Triton Shoal and Dudgeon Shoal
8.17

1   **Humber to Inner Dowsing Light-vessel.** From a position N of the Humber Light-vessel (53°39′N, 0°20′E), the route initially leads 9 miles SE, passing NE of the Humber deep water anchorage (7.2). Thence the track leads 17 miles S to a position ENE of Inner Dowsing Light-vessel (8.14), passing (with positions from Inner Dowsing Light-vessel):

2   Clear of a dangerous wreck, approximate position 1·9 miles S of Humber Light-buoy, thence:

 E of Protector Overfalls (7 miles NW). Protector Light-buoy (port hand) is moored to the E of the N part of Protector Overfalls, thence:

 E of several detached patches (4 miles NNW) which lie E of Protector Overfalls, thence:

 To a position ENE of Inner Dowsing Light-vessel.
8.18

1   **Inner Dowsing Light-vessel to Cromer.** From a position ENE of Inner Dowsing Light-vessel (53°19′·5N,

0°34′E) the route leads ESE 20 miles to a position W of Dudgeon Light-buoy (W cardinal) (8.14) thence SSE to a position N of Cromer, passing:

2   NNE of North Ridge (53°24′N, 0°49′E) and Dudgeon Shoal (53°17′N, 0°55′E). North Ridge is marked at its W extremity by W Ridge Light-buoy (W cardinal) and extends 9 miles ESE into Dudgeon Shoal. At low water there are conspicuous overfalls when there is a strong tidal stream running across the ridge. Thence:

3   SSW of Triton Knoll (53°24′N, 0°53′E), consisting of many detached patches extending 7 miles WNW/ESE. The knoll is indicated by tide rips, thence:

4   NNE of East Dudgeon Shoals (53°18′N, 0°59′E), marked on its NE side by E Dudgeon Light-buoy (E cardinal), thence:

     SSW of the detached patches (53°22′N, 1°02′E) extending ESE from Triton Shoal, thence:

5   To a position W of Dudgeon Light-buoy at the S end of Outer Dowsing Channel where the route rejoins that through Outer Dowsing Channel (8.16).

Under certain tidal conditions this route might be preferable to the route described in 8.16. The *Admiralty Tidal Stream Atlas: North Sea, Southern Part* and the tables on chart 1190 should be consulted.

Between Docking Shoal and Race Bank
8.19

1   **Inner Dowsing Light-vessel to Docking Shoal.** From a position ENE of Inner Dowsing Light-vessel (53°19′·5N, 0°34′E), the route runs 7 miles S to a position NW of Docking Shoal, passing (with positions from Inner Dowsing Light-vessel):

2   E of Inner Dowsing (4 miles SSW), a narrow ridge of sand running 7 miles N/S and marked at its S extremity by S Inner Dowsing light-buoy (S cardinal).

     W of North Ridge (8 miles E) with W Ridge Light-buoy (W cardinal) at its extremity, thence:

     To a position NW of Docking Shoal (7 miles SE) (8.20).

8.20

1   **Channel between Docking Shoal and Race Bank.** From the vicinity of 53°15′N, 0°42′E at the NW end of the channel between Docking Shoal and Race Bank, the route leads ESE for 26 miles to a position N of Cromer Lighthouse, passing:

2   NE of Docking Shoal (53°10′N, 0°44′E), an extensive triangular shaped shoal spreading to the S and SE, which is marked at its N point by N Docking Light-buoy (N cardinal) and its SE point by E Docking Light-buoy (port hand), and:

3   SW of Race Bank (53°13′N, 0°51′E), a thin shoal stretching 10½ miles SSE which is marked at its NW extremity by N Race Light-buoy (starboard hand) and its SE extremity by S Race Light-buoy (S cardinal).

The route continues SSE, passing (with positions from Blakeney Point (52°59′N, 0°59′E)):

4   NNE of Blakeney Overfalls (4 miles NNW), a shoal lying parallel to the shore and marked at its E extremity by Blakeney Overfalls Light-buoy (port hand), thence:

     Clear of Sheringham Shoal (8 miles NE), marked by light-buoys (E and W cardinal) (8.16), thence:

5   To a position N of Cromer (11 miles ESE), where the route joins that through the Outer Dowsing Channel (8.16).

   Side channel. A channel whose W end is in position 53°09′N, 0°38′E, lies between Docking Shoal to the N and Burnham Flats (8.21) to the S. It leads 12 miles ESE and E before joining the route described above, SSE of Race Bank. Local knowledge is required.

Docking Shoal to The Wash
8.21

1   From a position NW of Docking Shoal the route leads 5 miles S to a position E of Scott Patch thence SSW 10 miles to Lynn Knock at the entrance to The Wash, passing (with positions from Gibraltar Point (53°06′N, 0°20′E)):

2   E of Docking Shoal (centre 53°10′N, 0°44′E) and N Docking Light-buoy (N cardinal) (8.20), thence:

     E and SE of Scott Patch (11½ miles NE). Scott Patch Light-buoy (E cardinal) is moored at the S end of Scott Patch. The light-buoy is 2 miles NW of the entrance to the side channel (8.20) between Docking Shoal and Burnham Flats. Thence:

3   WNW of Burnham Flats (12 miles E), an extensive shoal extending 6 miles S and 9 miles ESE. Burnham Ridge, consisting of a number of sand waves, fronts Burnham Flats to the W and lies S of the Burnham Flats Light-buoy (W cardinal) which is moored off the N extremity of the flats. There might be less water than charted on the ridge. Thence:

4   ESE of Lynn Knock (4½ miles ESE), which consists of unstable sandwaves and is subject to heavy overfalls during spring tides. The E side of Lynn Knock is marked by Lynn Knock Light-buoy (starboard hand). Thence:

5   WNW of Woolpack (10 miles ESE) (8.23). Woolpack Light-buoy (port hand) is moored WSW of Woolpack and at the W end of Sledway (8.23). Three shoals lie in the channel to the W and SW of Sledway. These shoals are formed of sandwaves and are liable to change. Thence:

6   To the vicinity of North Well Light-buoy (safe water) (5½ miles SE) which is moored at the NE end of The Well, a deep extending into The Wash. *(Directions continue for The Wash at 8.51)*

Humber to The Wash, inshore route
8.22

1   **Local knowledge** is required.

Vessels of a suitable draught may use the inshore route which leads 34 miles S from the vicinity of Mid New Sand Light-buoy (53°36′·7N, 0°21′·3E) (7.19) to North Well Light-buoy at the entrance to The Wash, passing:

2   Clear of a dangerous wreck, approximate position 1·9 miles S of Mid New Sand Light-buoy, thence:

     E of Rosse Spit (53°30′N, 0°17′E), marked at its NE extremity by Rosse Spit Light-buoy (port hand), thence:

3   Clear of the firing and exercise area (centre 53°28′N, 0°15′E) (8.8). Saltfleet, Theddlethorpe and Trusthorpe Overfalls, forming practically one shoal, lie to the S of the area in a line 7 miles long running parallel to the coast. Trusthorpe Overfalls lie to seaward of Mablethorpe, a seaside resort, made conspicuous by the building (8.14). Thence:

4   Clear of Protector Overfalls (53°25′N, 0°25′E) (8.17).

The route continues S, passing (with positions from Ingoldmells Point (53°11′N, 0°21′E)):

E of Boygrift Light-tower (isolated danger) standing close offshore 6·2 miles N. Thence:

5   W of Inner Dowsing Overfalls (8½ miles NE), a group of detached patches lying SW of Inner Dowsing Light-vessel (8.14) and to the W of Inner Dowsing (8.19). There are considerable overfalls on these patches. Thence:

6   Clear of an offshore anemometry mast (lattice mast, 50 m in height) (3 miles ENE), from which a light is exhibited; thence:

E of Ingoldmells Point, which stands at the end of a long run of sand hills and coast protected by groynes. A buoy (special), marking an outfall, lies 1½ miles E of the point. Thence:

7   E of Skegness Middle (4 miles S), which lies off Skegness. The shoal, through which a buoyed channel leads SSW to Wainfleet Road, see 8.73, lies to the N of a group of shoals which dry and run roughly parallel to the coast off Gibraltar Point. These shoals from E to W are Outer Dogs Head, Outer Knock and Inner Knock. Between Inner Knock and the shore the passage formed by Wainfleet Road and Wainfleet Swatchway leads to Boston Deep, see 8.73. Thence:

8   E of Lynn Knock (4½ miles ESE) (8.21) and Lynn Knock Light-buoy (starboard hand) to the vicinity of North Well Light-buoy (safe water).

(Directions continue for The Wash at 8.51)

The Wash to Cromer, inshore route
8.23

1   **Local knowledge** is required.

Vessels of a suitable draught can use the inshore route which leads 29 miles ESE from the vicinity of North Well Light-buoy (53°03′N, 0°28′E) through Sledway to a position N of Cromer, passing (with positions from Scolt Head (52°59′N, 0°42′E)):

2   S of Woolpack (5 miles NW), a shoal patch which dries, to the N of Sledway. Woolpack Light-buoy (port hand) is moored 1½ miles WSW of Woolpack and also marks the W end of Sledway. Thence:

3   N of Middle Bank (6 miles E), which extends E into Gore Middle, both of which dry and lie to the S of Sledway, thence:

NNE of Scolt Head, a remarkable long sandhill and the N point on this coast, thence:

4   NNE of Bridgirdle (2½ miles NE) a spit which dries with Stiffkey Overfalls, a tongue of shoal water, to its E. Bridgirdle Buoy (port hand) is moored N of Bridgirdle and on the NW edge of Stiffkey Overfalls, thence:

5   N of Wells Harbour (6 miles E) (8.25). Wells Fairway light-buoy (safe water) is moored to the N of the harbour entrance. The coast between Wells and the entrance to Burnham Harbour (3½ miles W) is lined by sandhills covered with coarse grass known as Holkham Meals, thence:

6   Clear of Knock (8 miles ENE) and Blakeney Overfalls (10 miles ENE) (8.20).

The route continues ESE, passing (with positions from Cromer (52°56′N, 1°18′E)):

7   NNE of Blakeney Point (12 miles WNW), with Blakeney Harbour (8.40) to the S. The coast between Blakeney and Wells is embanked and

fronted by marshes with The High Sand and West Sand extending 1¼ miles offshore. The background is well wooded. Thence:

8   Clear of Pollard (7½ miles WNW), an isolated shoal, thence:

Clear of Sheringham Shoal (8 miles NW) (8.16), thence:

9   N of a light-buoy (port hand) (2½ miles NW) marking the N extremity of a foul area containing the remains of a collapsed rig, thence:

To a position N of Cromer (8.42).

10   **Side channel.** As an alternative to Sledway, vessels of suitable draught may use The Bays (52°59′N, 0°32′E), a narrow, shallow and uneven passage lying between Gore Middle and Middle Bank to the N and the sandbanks off Gore Point to the S. Once clear SE of Gore Middle, the route leads 6 miles ENE passing WNW of Bridgirdle before rejoining the route above.

(Directions continue for coastal passage ESE at 9.24)

Useful marks
8.24

1   Saint Clement's Church (tower) (53°24′N, 0°12′E).
Tower (53°23′N, 0°13′E) black, 8 m in height.
Ingoldmells Church (tower) (53°12′N, 0°20′E).
Addlethorpe Church (tower) (53°12′N, 0°19′E).
Thornham Church (tower) (52°58′N, 0°35′E) in ruins.
Titchwell Church (spire) (52°58′N, 0°37′E) among trees.

2   Brancaster Church (52°58′N, 0°38′E), a square tower among trees.
Brancaster Harbour Light (on club house) (52°58′N, 0°38′E).
Lifeboat house (white, red roof) (52°58′N, 0°51′E).
Wells Church (52°57′N, 0°51′E) with a square tower.
Stiffkey Church (tower) (52°57′N, 0°56′E).

3   Morston Church (tower) (52°57′N, 0°59′E).
Salthouse Church (tower) (52°57′N, 1°05′E).
Mast (52°57′N, 1°08′E).
Weybourne Church (tower) (52°57′N, 1°09′E) with 3 water towers close W.

Four masts (red obstruction lights visible 5 miles but masked within 1½ miles of the coast) (52°54′N, 1°11′E).

Wells Harbour

Chart 108
General information
8.25

1   **Position.** Wells Harbour (52°58′N, 0°51′E) is on the Norfolk coast, 1 mile SE of High Cape.

Function. It is a small commercial port. The population of Wells-next-the-Sea, which lies just S of the port, was 2400 in 1991.

2   **Approach and entry.** Wells Harbour is approached from the N through The Run, a channel between the banks of sand and shingle fronting the coast. The channel is subject to frequent change.

Port authority. Wells Harbour Commissioners, Harbour Office, The Old Lifeboat House, West Quay, Wells-next-the-Sea, NR23 1AT.

Limiting conditions
8.26

1   **Controlling depths.** The channel dries up to 1·2 m.
Berth: 225 m long, depth alongside at LW 0·3 m.
Tidal levels: see *Admiralty Tide Tables*.

The Bar (52°59′N, 0°49′E): MHWS about 6·0 m; MHWN about 4·8 m.

Wells Harbour (52°57′N, 0°51′E): MHWS about 3·5 m; MHWN about 2·0 m.

2   See *Admiralty Tide Tables* for details of low water stand.

Maximum size of vessel handled. Vessels drawing 3 m can enter the harbour at HW springs; vessels drawing 1·8 m can enter the harbour at HW neaps. Craft drawing up to 1·5 m can enter the channel 2 hours either side of HW.

Local weather and sea state. North winds cause the highest seas at the bar.

Arrival information

8.27

1   **Port radio** is manned most of the time during daylight hours, and from 3 hours before HW when vessels are expected. See the relevant *Admiralty List of Radio Signals*.

Notice of ETA. Commercial shipping must give notice of ETA to the Harbour Master at least 8 hours in advance.

2   An **anchorage** can be obtained in depths of 8 m, clay, N of the harbour entrance on the line of bearing 207° of Holkham Church (52°57′N, 0°48′E) which stands on a mound among trees.

Pilotage is not available. Any vessel wishing to enter the harbour should contact Wells Harbour radio for advice on entry. If requested, the Harbour Master or his deputy can meet vessels at the harbour entrance in the harbour launch and lead in through the channel to the berth.

3   **Local knowledge** is required to enter harbour at night, especially during onshore winds.

Harbour

8.28

1   **Layout.** There is one berth, The Quay, which runs E/W and curves round N/S fronting the town. Visiting craft use W end of the berth. A number of creeks run into the marshes N of the channel, opposite the town.

8.29

1   **Tidal stream** at the bar is as follows:

Time from HW Immingham	Remarks
–0545	In-going stream begins
+0020	Out-going stream begins

8.30

1
   Principal marks:
Lifeboat house (52°58′N, 0°51′E) (8.24).
Wells Church (52°57′N, 0°51′E) (8.24).

Directions

8.31

1   Wells Fairway Light-buoy (safe water) (52°59′·9N, 0°49′·6E) is moored 8 cables NW of the entrance to the approach channel called The Run. It lies between Bob Hall's Sand to the E and West Sands to the W. The outer part of the channel is marked by light-buoys, which are moved as necessary and should not be relied upon; temporary pellet buoys may be laid to show changes in the channel.

2   The inner part of the channel lies between the sands off High Cape and those off The Bink, 1½ miles E. High Cape and The Bink are sand ridges. The channel is marked by buoys (port and starboard hand), some of which are lighted, and beacons (port hand).

3   The lifeboat house (8.24) stands on the coast at the N end of a straight embankment constructed for the reclamation of Holkham Marshes, and which runs S from the sandhills to the town. At the S end of the embankment the channel turns E for The Quay.

Port services

8.32

1   **Facilities:** hospital; health centre.

Supplies: marine diesel on the quay; water points on main quay; slipway trolley for vessels up to 12 m (40 ft) in length; car parking on quay; refuse disposal at bulk bins on quay; chandlery; boat builders/repairers; salvage pumping; marine engineers; moorings available; stores and provisions.

Small craft

8.33

1   There are numerous small craft moorings in the harbour, a slipway for small craft, ample drying berths and a sailing club.

Anchorages and minor harbours

Chart 107
Saltfleet
8.34

1   Saltfleet village (53°25′N, 0°11′E), 4 miles SSE of Donna Nook, may be identified by the many trees in the neighbourhood and a disused windmill. A narrow channel runs into Saltfleet which can be used by craft drawing up to 1·5 m on HW.

Chart 108
The Bays
8.35

1   An anchorage for small vessels might occasionally be obtained in The Bays (8.23) (52°59′N, 0°32′E), which is protected from N winds by Middle Bank.

Thornham Harbour

8.36

1   Thornham Harbour (52°58′N, 0°35′E), 1 mile E of Gore Point, is formed by a creek. The approach channel which crosses a broad sandy foreshore, changes constantly in depth and direction and requires local knowledge for its use. Thornham Staith, 1 mile above the entrance can be reached by vessels drawing 2·7 m at HW springs and 1·4 m at HW neaps. The ruined tower of Thornham Church (52°58′N, 0°35′E) is a useful mark.

Brancaster Harbour

8.37

1   **General information.** Brancaster Harbour (52°58′N, 0°41′E), 1 mile S of Scolt Head (8.23), a nature reserve with restricted access during the nesting season, is approached from the W through a channel between sandbanks. A wreck, marked by a beacon (isolated danger), lies 5 cables W of Scolt Head. The channel changes constantly in depth and direction and requires local knowledge for its use. It is marked by about 12 buoys which are difficult to see in broken water when the entrance should not be attempted. Brancaster Staithe, where there is a boatyard, can be reached by vessels drawing 1·5 m at HW springs.

2   **Supplies:** fuel; water; provisions.

Useful marks:
Brancaster Church (52°58′N, 0°38′E) (8.24).
Titchwell Church (52°58′N, 0°37′E) (8.24).
Brancaster Harbour Light (52°58′N, 0°38′E) (8.24).

3   An **anchorage** can be obtained in Brancaster Road, 1 mile N of Scolt Head, in depths of 5 m to 7 m, stiff clay and sand. Depths decrease to the N of the road to the order of 1 m. Well anchored vessels ride well in Brancaster Road as the sea is broken by the shallower ground to the N.

Burnham Harbour
8.38

1 **General information.** Burnham Harbour (52°59′N, 0°45′E), 2¼ miles E of Scolt Point, consists of a tidal creek leading to Burnham Overy Staithe which can be reached by vessels drawing 1·8 m at HW springs. The approach is through a channel between sandy coastal banks and requires local knowledge for its use. The entrance should not be attempted in strong onshore winds because of broken water, nor during the out-going tide or in a swell. A red float marks the outer channel. The inner channel is marked by red and green floats.

2 **Pilotage** is available if required.

An **anchorage** for small craft is available in depths of 2 to 3 m, sand and gravel, W of Gun Hill.

Holkham Bay
8.39

1 An anchorage can be obtained in Holkham Bay (52°59′N, 0°48′E) which lies between Burnham Harbour (8.38) and High Cape (8.31). It has good holding ground, bottom clay.

Blakeney Harbour
8.40

1 **General information.** Blakeney (52°57′N, 1°02′E) has a small harbour formed by a creek. The harbour lies 2 miles SE of Blakeney Point, a National Trust bird sanctuary, which is the W extremity of a narrow strip of land running WNW from the general line of the coast. There are mussel lays off the point standing 0·6 m above the sand. They are protected by a fishery order. The state and direction of the entrance channel are greatly affected by the prevailing winds.

2 **Pilotage** is available by prior arrangement. The pilots board at the bar within 1 hour of HW. Local knowledge is required.

Limiting conditions. Vessels drawing up to 1·5 m can use the harbour, providing they can take the ground at LW. Vessels can enter the harbour 2 hours either side of HW at springs and 1½ hours either side at neaps. The entrance channel should not be attempted in strong onshore winds.

3 **Tidal levels:** see *Admiralty Tide Tables.* Blakeney Bar (52°59′N, 0°59′E), MHWS about 5·7 m, MHWN about 4·5 m; Blakeney (52°57′N, 1°01′E), MHWS about 3·4 m, MHWN about 2·0 m.

Tidal streams off Blakeney Bar begin 10 minutes later than at Wells (8.25) and are strongest when the sandbanks are covered. The in-going stream might set strongly to the E across the channel during the last two hours of the rising tide.

4 **Principal mark:**

Blakeney Church (52°57′N, 1°02′E) (8.14).

Directions. The alignment (170°) of the following beacons on the dunes at Blakeney leads to the E of Bar Buoy (special) and into the approach channel:

Front beacon (orange, triangle topmark).

Rear beacon (orange, square topmark).

The beacons are moved without notice as required by changes in the channel and are therefore not charted.

5 A buoy (port hand) marks a dangerous wreck on the N side of the channel. Two stranded wrecks lie about 1 mile SW of the dangerous wreck. Within the channel Nos 1 to 10 Buoys (black barrels, summer only) mark the W side of the channel as it curves round Blakeney Point and should be kept on the starboard hand when entering. The entrance to the channel lies between No 1 buoy and the stranded

wreck and vessels should keep at least 1 cable offshore when rounding the wreck. The channel runs 1 mile SSW before turning abruptly ESE and is marked by the occasional buoy and stake. Cley Channel, leading to Cley next the Sea, joins the Blakeney Channel on its N side about 5 cables from Blakeney.

6 **Supplies:** marine diesel (heavy and light); petrol; water; stores.

Sheringham
8.41

1 Sheringham (52°57′N, 1°13′E) lies in a hollow between easily distinguished hills and is used by fishing vessels. A light is exhibited from a post (red, 2 m in height) until 2030 each evening.

Charts 106, 108
Cromer
8.42

1 The seaside town of Cromer stands on a cliff NW of the lighthouse (52°56′N, 1°18′E). Either side of Cromer the cliffs rise steeply and the country behind is bold and well-wooded. The cliffs in the vicinity of Cromer are being eroded and there are extensive barriers and groynes fronting the town. A pier with a slipway extends seaward 1 cable abreast the town.

2 An **anchorage** can be obtained 1¾ miles NNW of Cromer Lighthouse, bottom chalk, with particles of sand, shell and stones. The anchorage is protected from the SSE to the WSW. Lobster pots are laid in the area by local fishermen.

Church

Pier

Cromer (8.42)

(Original dated 2000)

(Photograph – Air Images)

THE WASH
General information

Charts 108, 1200
Routes
8.43

1 From North Well Light-buoy (8.21), the route leads 6 miles SE to Roaring Middle Light-float (52°58′·6N, 0°21′·2E) (8.51) situated in the centre of The Wash. From the light-float the route divides, leading, from W to E, to Boston (8.56), Fosdyke Port (8.83), Spalding (8.84) and King's Lynn (8.101).

2　　There is also an alternative route to Boston through Boston Deep (8.74). These ports and the routes leading to them are described in this section.

　　Caution. As a consequence of the movement of banks (8.3) buoys are altered, sometimes without notice.

Topography
8.44

1　　The Wash is formed by the estuary of several rivers, the principal of which are the Rivers Witham (8.77), Welland (8.83), Nene (8.96) and Great Ouse (8.122), which give access to the ports of The Wash. The rivers find their way through the sands to their outlets in The Wash at LW.

2　　Gibraltar Point (53°06′N, 0°20′E) which is low and ill-defined is the W entry point of The Wash. From the point to New Cut (8.75) at the mouth of River Witham, 13 miles SW, the coast is marshy and embanked and fronted by wide drying flats extending up to 3 miles offshore. The villages are situated about 2 miles inland and apart from the Range Control Tower (8.45) there are no distinguishing marks.

3　　Welland Cut (8.83) runs 5 miles SSW from New Cut between drying sandbanks to the mouth of the River Welland. Thence the coast trends ESE for 14 miles, intersected by Wisbech Cut (8.96) the embanked entrance to River Nene, to Lynn Cut (8.122). It is backed by marshy low-lying ground and fronted by extensive drying sands.

4　　At Lynn Cut the coast turns to the NNE and is again marshy and embanked as far as Snettisham Scalp, 4 miles NNE, which is a bird reserve with restricted access. To the N for 4½ miles as far as Hunstanton there is a shingle beach fronted by drying sands. Saint Edmund's Point at Hunstanton is a cliff of marl, and grey and red chalk, remarkable both for its variety of colour and as the only cliff in the vicinity. It lies 2 miles SW of Gore Point, the SE entrance point to The Wash. The point is composed of small sandhills with marshland within it.

Firing practice and exercise areas
8.45

1　　The whole of Wainfleet Sand (53°05′N, 0°18′E) and most of Friskney Flats, an area fronting the coast from close SW of Gibraltar Point to 6 miles SW of the point and extending seaward 2½ miles to 3 miles, is used as a live bombing range. There are numerous targets, beacons and warning buoys shown on the chart.

2　　The Firing Range Control Tower (53°04′N, 0°14′E) is 4 miles SW of Gibraltar Point. Two other range towers (huts on piles) are 2 miles NE and SW of the main tower respectively.

　　When the range is in use the towers display a red flag by day and fixed red lights at night. Mariners should avoid the area, calling "Boston Dock" on VHF in case of an emergency.

8.46

1　　Holbeach Firing Danger Area fronts the SW coast from Lawyer's Creek (52°53′N, 0°06′E) 4 miles E to Wisbech Channel (8.95). Its limits are marked by RAF beacons and buoys (special), some lighted, and RAF No 4 Light-buoy (E cardinal) on the W side of Wisbech Channel. When the range is in use red flags or lights are shown from the two flagstaffs on the shore limits of the range. When the warning signals are shown vessels may transit the area in the ordinary course of navigation, but may not linger or engage in fishing.

Rescue
8.47

1　　There is a Coastguard Rescue Team at Hunstanton (52°57′N, 0°30′E); see 1.53.

　　An inshore lifeboat is stationed at Hunstanton; for details of lifeboat see 1.62.

Tidal streams
8.48

1　　Tidal streams in The Wash run regularly inwards and outwards. They are given in the *Admiralty Tidal Stream Atlas: North Sea, Southern Part* and in the tables on the charts.

2　　The spring rate in each direction is about 2 kn. The in-going stream is usually a little stronger, but shorter in duration than the out-going stream. The streams set in the direction of the principal channels, but across subsidiary channels, which differ in direction from the principal channels on the W side of the head of the estuary.

3　　In Boston Deep (53°00′N, 0°15′E) (8.74), the streams run mainly in the direction of the channel with a spring rate in each direction of 2½ kn.

　　In Freeman Channel (52°58′N, 0°13′E) (8.72), the tidal streams run SSW/NNE across the channel when the sandbanks either side are covered. Otherwise the streams are weak in the channel but their direction may be irregular.

4　　Strong and continued NE winds cause an in-going current, which increases both the rate and duration of the in-going tidal streams correspondingly reducing the out-going tidal streams, and which can also increase sea level height at the head of the estuary by up to 0·6 m. Strong and continued SW winds have the opposite effect. These changes are not constant, with NE winds a back pressure develops at the head of the estuary, setting up a circulation with, probably, an in-going stream in mid-estuary and an out-going stream at the sides. Once the wind ceases the excess water at the head of the estuary runs seaward as an out-going current until sea level is normal.

5　　The tidal streams in the rivers are much affected by meteorological and astronomical conditions, and little reliable information regarding them is available. Generally the out-going stream in the rivers begins soon after local HW and is of longer duration than the in-going stream. Heavy rain increases the rate and duration of the out-going stream and correspondingly reduces those of the in-going stream. Rates of the resulting freshets in excess of 6 kn to 8 kn might be experienced.

Principal marks
8.49

1　　**Landmarks:**
　　　　Gasholder (53°08′N, 0°20′E) at Skegness.
　　　　Firing Range Control Tower (53°04′N, 0°14′E).
　　　　Saint Botolph's Church (tower) (52°58′·7N, 0°01′·4W) known as The Boston Stump.
　　　　Windmill (55 m in height) (52°57′N, 0°32′E).
　　　　Water Tower (52°55′·8N, 0°29′·9E).
　　　　Snettisham Church (spire) (52°52′·7N, 0°30′·7E).

Other navigational aids
8.50

1　　**Racon:**
　　　　North Well Light-buoy (53°03′N, 0°28′E).
　　DGPS:
　　　　Flamborough Head Light (54°07′N, 0°05′W).

Directions
(continued from 8.21 and 8.22)

North Well Light-buoy to Roaring Middle Light-float
8.51

1 From the vicinity of North Well Light-buoy (53°03′N, 0°28′E) the route leads 6 miles SW through The Well and the extension SW, Lynn Deeps, to the vicinity of Roaring Middle Light-float, passing (with positions from Gore Point (52°58′N, 0°32′E)):

2 SE of Inner Dogs Head (7 miles NW), a sandy isolated shoal, thence:

NW of Sunk Sand (2½ miles W), a drying shoal which lies 1½ miles off Saint Edmund's Point (8.44) and 2½ miles W of Gore Point, thence:

3 SE of Long Sand (9 miles W), a drying shoal which runs 6 miles NE/SW, and:

NW of South Sunk Sand (4 miles SW), the NW extension of the coastal drying bank which fronts the E coast of The Wash, thence:

To the vicinity of Roaring Middle Light-float (N cardinal) (7 miles W).

Useful marks
8.52

1 Holme Church (Tower) (52°58′N, 0°32′E).
Old Lighthouse (white, round tower) (52°57′N, 0°30′E) disused; standing on Saint Edmund's Point.
(Directions continue for Boston at 8.72, for Wisbech at 8.94 and for King's Lynn at 8.117)

Small craft channels and harbour

Parlour Channel
8.53

1 Boston Deep can be entered from The Well (8.51) through Parlour Channel (53°02′N, 0°22′E), which is buoyed. There might be less depth than charted at its W end and it is not in general use. Tidal streams follow the channel when the Inner Dogs Head and Long Sand (8.51), the drying banks either side of it, are exposed, but once they are covered the tidal stream sets across the channel (see 8.48).

The Bays to The Wash
8.54

1 An unmarked channel leads SW from The Bays (53°00′N, 0°32′E) between Sunk Sand and the coast, then rounds the S extremity of Sunk Sand running between it and South Sunk Sand. It is only suitable for small craft.
Local knowledge is required.

Wainfleet
8.55

1 The small harbour of Wainfleet (53°06′N, 0°19′E) lies 5 cables W of Gibraltar Point and is formed by the outlet of the River Steeping into Wainfleet Swatchway (8.73). The approach channel, which is liable to change, is entered about 8 cables SSE of Gibraltar Point and is marked by perches. Craft drawing 1·5 m can enter 2 hours either side of HW. An overhead power cable with a vertical clearance of 11 m spans the river 3 cables inside the entrance.

2 Local knowledge is required.

BOSTON AND APPROACHES

General information

Charts 108, 1200
Position
8.56

1 Boston (52°58′N, 0°01′W) is situated on both banks of the River Witham, 4 miles from the mouth of the river which lies in the SW corner of The Wash.

Function
8.57

1 There is a small commercial port on the N bank of the River Witham. The population of Boston (1991) was 36 600.

Port limits
8.58

1 The limits of the Port of Boston Authority include the NW part of The Wash from Skegness (53°10′N, 0°20′E) to a point on the SW coast of The Wash 6 miles SE of the Welland Cut (8.83). The S part of these limits is shown on the chart.

Approach and entry
8.59

1 Boston may be approached either through Freeman Channel (8.72) or from Boston Deep (8.74). Both routes merge in Lower Road which leads to New Cut and the River Witham.

Traffic
8.60

1 In 1999 the port handled 630 vessels totalling 1 521 184 dwt.

Port authority
8.61

1 Port of Boston Limited, Dock Office, Boston, Lincolnshire PE21 6BN.

Limiting conditions
8.62

1 **Controlling depths.** The approach channel dries 0·6 m close S of Clay Hole (52°57′N, 0°08′W). There is a depth over the sill of the entrance lock to Boston Dock of 7·5 m at MHWS and 5·4 m at MHWN. The lock is normally operated from 2½ hours before HW to 1½ hours after HW. A sill clearance of 1·5 m is usually required for vessels entering the lock.

2 **Overhead power cables** with a safe vertical clearance of 45 m span the River Witham close E of the entrance to Boston Dock.

Deepest berth. Boston Dock (8.79). The riverside berths (8.79) can accommodate larger vessels than the Dock, but they have to take the bottom.

Tidal levels: see *Admiralty Tide Tables.* Mean spring range about 6·4 m; mean neap range about 3·1 m.
8.63

1 **Maximum size of vessel handled.** Vessels up to 119 m in length, beam 13·6 m and draught 5·5 m (HW springs) can reach Boston. The maximum dimensions of vessels using the entrance lock is 86 m in length, beam 13·6 m and draught 5·5 m (HW springs). Larger vessels may be accepted at the Harbour Master's discretion.

Arrival information

Port operations
8.64

1   **Vessel Traffic Service** scheme is in operation for the control of shipping. For positions of reporting points and other details see the relevant *Admiralty List of Radio Signals*.

Notice of ETA
8.65

1   Twelve hours' notice of ETA at Clay Hole (52°57′N, 0°08E) is required if possible before 1700. Vessels are required to give 24 hours' notice of their arrival, or as soon as possible for shorter voyages. If dangerous goods are to be loaded or discharged, the nature and quantity of such goods is to be stated.

Outer anchorages
8.66

1   Outer anchorages are available as follows:

        SW end of Lynn Deeps (52°58′N, 0°19′E) (8.51) at a position shown on the chart.

        Lower Road (8.75), between Bar Sand and Butterwick Low (52°58′N, 0°09′E) in depths of 9 m, bottom black mud and fine sand.

2   SW end of Boston Deep (8.74), SW of Scullridge (53°00′N, 0°14′E) at a position shown on the chart. The bottom is sand and loose stones.

        For smaller vessels in Clay Hole (52°57′N, 0°08′E) (8.75) at a position shown on the chart.

3   **Caution.** During NE gales there is a considerable sea in Boston Deep from the half flood to the half ebb, but generally there is less sea at the SW end. In N gales vessels ride more securely in Boston Deep than in the more exposed Lynn Deeps.

Pilots and tugs
8.67

1   **Pilotage** is compulsory S of Lower Road at the SW end of Boston Deep (8.74). Pilots board to the E of Freeman Channel at Boston Roads Light-buoy (8.72) or in the vicinity of No 9 Light-buoy (52°57′·5N, 0°08′·5E) in Lower Road.

2   In fog, a vessel requiring a pilot should sound "G" in Morse code, which is also sounded by the pilot vessel on station.

    A tug is available at Boston.

Local knowledge
8.68

1   Boston Deep is entered at its N end through Wainfleet Road and Wainfleet Swatchway (8.73). The shoal banks around the channel are constantly changing and the buoys might not mark the channel; nor is it easy to identify objects ashore. Local knowledge is required to use this channel.

Harbour

Layout
8.69

1   The Port of Boston consists of an enclosed dock on the N side of the River Witham and riverside berths mainly on the N bank of the river between the dock entrance and the swing bridge upstream.

Boston Dock from E (8.69)

(Original dated 2000)

(Photograph – Air Images)

Tidal streams
8.70

1 Tidal streams in New Cut and in the River Witham off Boston are as follows:

Time from HW Immingham	Remarks
–0430	In-going stream begins in New Cut
–0300	In-going stream begins off Boston
+0100	Out-going stream begins in New Cut
+0115	Out-going stream begins off Boston

2 The streams are fairly strong. Off Boston the in-going stream is reported to run at a spring rate of 4 kn, during the first half of the tide, after which it decreases.

Principal mark
8.71

1 Saint Botolph's Church (52°59′N, 0°01′W) (8.49).

Directions
(continued from 8.52)

Roaring Middle Light-float to Lower Road
8.72

1 From the vicinity of Roaring Middle Light-float (52°58′·6N, 0°21′·2E), the route leads 3½ miles WSW to the E entrance point to Freeman Channel, the main approach channel to Boston, thence in a generally WNW direction 2½ miles through the channel to a position at the NE end of Lower Road, passing:

Clear of Boston Roads Light-buoy (safe water) (52°57′·7N, 0°16′·2E), thence:

2 To the E entrance point of Freeman Channel (52°58′N, 0°15′E), which is marked by Boston No 1 Light-buoy (starboard hand) and Alpha Light-buoy (port hand), thence following the channel which is buoyed. The channel is 1¼ cables wide at its narrowest part and lies between The Ants, a detached drying sandbank close W of the SW end of Long Sand (8.51) and Roger Sand which dries and is attached to the coastal bank by Toft Sand and Hook Hill at its SW extremity. Thence:

3 To the W end of Freeman Channel (52°58′N, 0°11′E), marked by Freeman Inner Light-buoy (W cardinal) and Delta Light-buoy (port hand) and which lies at the NE end of Lower Road.

Approaches to Boston Deep
8.73

1 Boston Deep might be approached through Wainfleet Road and Wainfleet Swatchway or through Parlour Channel (8.53). The deep can also be approached from the NE between Inner Dogs Head and Outer Dogs Head (8.22), crossing the bar that joins the two shoals. There are no navigation marks and this approach is not recommended.

2 **Wainfleet Road and Wainfleet Swatchway** lie between Inner Knock (8.22) and the coastal bank. Wainfleet Road (53°06′N, 0°22′E) is approached via the buoyed channel through Skegness Middle (8.22), and leads SSW to Wainfleet Swatchway (2 miles SSW). Wainfleet Roads Buoy (port hand; not charted) is at the S end of the Road and Wainfleet Swatchway is marked by perches. Inner Knock Buoy (port hand; not charted) marks the W side of

Inner Knock and Swatchway Buoy (starboard hand) the S entrance point to the Swatchway (53°03′N, 0°20′E).

3 **Caution.** Considerable depth changes occur in the approach to Wainfleet Road and the charted depths should not be relied upon. Buoyage is altered in accordance with the depth changes.

Boston Deep to Lower Road
8.74

1 From its NE extremity Boston Deep (53°04′N, 0°21′E) runs in a generally SW direction for 8½ miles to Lower Road at its SW end. It is marked by buoys. The Deep lies between the coastal bank formed by Wainfleet Sand, Friskney Flats and Wrangle Flats which dry and extend up to 3 miles offshore and the offshore banks of Inner Dogs Head, Long Sand (8.51) and The Ants (8.72). See 8.45 for details of firing area.

2 **Caution.** The buoys marking the channel are small and difficult to see. They might be moved without notice and should not be relied on implicitly.

Lower Road to New Cut
8.75

1 From a position at the NE end of Lower Road (52°58′N, 0°11′E), the route leads 2 miles SW, thence a further 2 miles WSW, through the main entrance channel leading to New Cut, passing (with positions from Tabs Head Light-beacon (52°56′·0N, 0°05′·0E)):

2 Through Lower Road (3½ miles NE), which is buoyed and lies between Butterwick Low, a drying flat 2 miles wide fronting the shore, and the offshore shoals of Roger Sand, Bar Sand and Toft Sand, thence:

3 S of Clay Hole (2 miles NE) which lies at the SW end of Lower Road, thence:

Across the drying portion of the main channel (1¾ miles ENE) (8.62), thence:

NW of Black Buoy Light-buoy (port hand), thence through the channel which is marked by light-buoys (starboard hand). Thence:

4 N of Welland Light-beacon (port hand) (2½ cables ENE), which marks the seaward end of Welland Cut half-tide training wall (8.83), thence:

Between Tabs Head Light-beacon (port hand) and Dolly Peg Light-beacon (black triangular topmark), which mark the entrance to New Cut. A light-beacon (tide gauge, conical topmark) stands on the N bank 1¼ cables W of Tabs Head Light-beacon.

8.76

1 The entrance to the former main channel, marked by Golf Light-buoy (port hand), lies 4 cables SSE of Clay Hole. This channel is buoyed, but the section of the channel E of Welland Beacon dries 0·6 to 1·3 m and it is now little used.

Caution. the channels at the S end of Lower Road continually alter and buoyage is frequently changed, often without warning.

New Cut and River Witham
8.77

1 From Tabs Head Light-beacon, New Cut curves 2 miles WNW to the entrance of the River Witham; Boston Dock is situated a further 2½ miles NW above the river entrance. The track is marked by a series of paired white leading lights, Nos 1 and 1a to 9 and 9a, and by red lights on the southerly bank and green lights on the northerly bank.

Details of the leading lights and other lights are given on the chart.

Gat Channel
8.78

1   Gat Sand, the NE extremity of the coastal bank, and Roger Sand are separated by Gat Channel (52°56′N, 0°12′E). The channel is closed at its W end by Hook Hill (8.72) and is only used by local fishing boats.

Basins and berths
8.79

1   **Boston Dock.** 730 m of quay providing 8 berths in depths of 7·6 m at springs and 5·4 m at neaps; Ro-Ro berth and two ramps at E end.

Riverside berths. Riverside Quay which dries out, bottom soft mud, extends 700 m upstream of the dock entrance providing 7 berths.

Witham Wharf cement berth on S bank.

Port services
8.80

1   **Repairs.** Minor engine repairs only.

Other facilities: hospital with helicopter landing site adjacent; deratting exemption certificates only can be issued; customs.

Supplies: fuel oils by road tanker; fresh water; stores and provisions.

Small craft

River Witham Navigation
8.81

1   The River Witham Navigation is entered through Grand Sluice Lock 1 mile upstream of Boston Dock. The lock is 22·7 m in length and 4·6 m in width; craft of 1·4 m draught with a height of no more than 2·3 m can use the Navigation. The sluice is the upper limit of the tidal river and, in dry weather, silting may occur below the sluice.
8.82

1   There are no facilities within the port for small craft, but there is a marina close upstream of Grand Sluice Lock.

Fosdyke Port
8.83

1   **General information.** Fosdyke Port (52°52′N, 0°02′W) is situated close NE of Fosdyke Bridge and is 3 miles SW of the entrance of the River Welland. The port handled 18 vessels totalling 26 019 dwt in 1999.

Port authority. Port of Fosdyke Ltd, Fosdyke Bridge, Boston PE20 2DB.

Pilotage is compulsory and available in conjunction with the Port of Boston. See 8.67.

2   **Directions.** Fosdyke Port is approached through the Welland Cut lying in Fosdyke Wash, which leads to the River Welland. Welland Cut, which is embanked, runs 4 miles SW between two drying sandbanks, Herring Hill and The Scalp. It is entered close W of Welland Light-beacon (52°56′·1N, 0°05′·4E) (8.75) thence the channel is marked by a series of light-beacons (red lights on the SE training wall and green lights on the NW training wall) as well as a number of radar reflectors which stand at 5 cable intervals on the SE training wall. An overhead power cable, safe vertical clearance 24 m, spans the river ¾ mile NE of the bridge.

3   **Local knowledge** is essential for passage through the cut.

Within Fosdyke Wash the in-going stream begins at −0345 HW Immingham and the out-going stream at +0100 HW Immingham.

Berth. A wharf, 69 m in length, lies on the N side of the river. Vessels up to 96 m in length and draught 5 m (spring tides), 3 m (neap tides), can be accommodated.

Spalding
Chart 1190
8.84

1   **General information.** Spalding lies on the River Welland 6 miles above Fosdyke Bridge (52°52′N, 0°02′W), which is built on piles. At Fulney, 1 mile below Spalding there is a lock 33·5 m long and 9 m wide. The river has a least width of 18 m to Spalding and vessels of draught 2·1 m can reach the town at springs.

WISBECH AND APPROACHES

General information
Chart 1200
Position
8.85

1   Wisbech (52°41′N, 0°10′E) stands on both banks of the River Nene.

Function
8.86

1   It is a small commercial port. The population of the town was 24 981 in 1991.

Port limits
8.87

1   The limits of the port include Wisbech Channel as far as Bar Flat (8.94) and are shown on the chart.

Traffic
8.88

1   The port handled 67 vessels totalling 110 772 dwt in 1999.

Port authority
8.89

1   Fenland District Council, Port of Wisbech Authority. Harbour Master's Office, West Bank, Sutton Bridge, Lincs. PE12 9QR. The statutory functions of the Port Authority are met by the Harbour Master, Port Sutton Bridge (8.100).

Limiting conditions
8.90

1   **Controlling depths.** Wisbech Channel dries 0·3 m in position 52°51′·6N, 0°14′·4E. However the channel is tortuous and both the line and depths are liable to change.

The depths alongside the berths within the harbour at LW are between 0·3 m and 1·5 m and vessels take the bottom, soft mud.

2   **Tidal levels:** see *Admiralty Tide Tables*. Wisbech Cut, (52°48′N, 0°13′E) mean spring range not available; mean neap range about 2·9 m.

Largest vessel. The port is capable of accommodating vessels up to 83 m long, beam 11·5 m and 2000 dwt. Maximum draught is 4·9 m at HW springs; at HW neaps it is 2 m less than predicted height of tide.

Arrival information
8.91

1   **Bridge signals:** Cross Keys Bridge (52°46′·0N, 0°11′·8E) at Sutton Bridge is a revolving iron structure with an opening 18 m wide. The following signals, exhibited in both directions control river traffic:

Signal	Meaning
Red light	Bridge closed
Amber light	Preparatory signal for opening bridge
Green light	Bridge open

2   The E and W dolphins of the bridge are marked by lights. Vessels requiring the bridge to be opened should sound Morse Code "B" (-···), or call on VHF. Prior notice should be given when possible.

Anchorage is available in the SW end of Lynn Deeps (52°58'N, 0°19'E) at a position shown on the chart, and in the vicinity of Bar Flat Light-buoy (52°55'·2N, 0°16'·8E).

3   **Pilotage** is compulsory. Pilots board in the vicinity of Bar Flat Light-buoy, or in bad weather S of RAF No 4 Light-buoy (52°52'·5N, 0°13'·2E) from a cutter marked "Pilots". The cutter is on station from 2½ hours before HW when vessels are expected. See the relevant *Admiralty List of Radio Signals*.

Harbour

Tidal streams
8.92

1   Tidal streams in Wisbech Cut, at Sutton Bridge and at Wisbech are as follows:

Time from HW Immingham	Remarks
Wisbech Cut	
−0400	In-going stream begins
HW	Out-going stream begins

2

Sutton Bridge	
−0300	In-going stream begins
+0030	Out-going stream begins
Wisbech	
−0200	In-going stream begins
+0130	Out-going stream begins

3   The streams are reported to be strong at springs, but at neaps, with freshets in the river, the in-going stream does not reach Wisbech. The in-going stream normally runs for 4 hours at Sutton Bridge and at springs, for 3 hours at Wisbech. It should be noted that fresh to strong S winds cause tidal heights to be lower than predicted.

Principal marks
8.93

1   **Landmarks:**
   Trial Bank (52°50'·5N, 0°15'·3E), an artificial island, elevation 10 m, light-beacon 3 m in height.
   Mound (52°49'·1N, 0°17'·3E) 8 m in elevation, causeway to shore.

Directions
(continued from 8.52)

Roaring Middle Light-float to Wisbech Channel
8.94

1   From the vicinity of Roaring Middle Light-float (N cardinal) (52°58'·6N, 0°21'·2E), the track leads 5½ miles SW to the entrance to Wisbech Channel, passing (with

Trial Bank (8.93)

(Original dated 2000)

(Photograph - Air Images)

positions from Wisbech Channel entrance (52°54'N, 0°16'E)):
   SE of Freeman Channel entrance (4 miles N) (8.72) and Roger Sand (8.72) to the S of the channel, thence:

2   NW of Roaring Middle (1½ miles NE), a shoal which dries, marked on its W side by Nos 2 and 4 Buoys (port hand), thence:
   Clear of Bar Flat Light-buoy (E cardinal) (1½ miles NNE), which is moored NW of Roaring Middle, thence:
   SE of Gat Channel entrance (8.78) (2 miles N), lying between Roger Sand and Gat Sand, thence:

3   To the entrance to Wisbech Channel, lying close SW of Bar Flat.

Wisbech Channel
8.95

1   Wisbech Channel is entered from the NE and then runs in a generally S direction 4½ miles between the extensive drying sands which front the coast. The sand to the W of the channel is Old South and, to the E, Outer Westmark Knock and Inner Westmark Knock.

2   The channel is marked by light-buoys and beacons which include some of the marks indicating the E limit of the danger area (8.46). The S part of the channel is marked by light-beacons and buoys. Those painted green and exhibiting white or green lights should be left to starboard and those red and with red lights left to port.

Frequent changes occur in the channel and navigation marks are liable to be moved without prior notice.

River Nene and Wisbech Cut
8.96

1   From its entrance, formed by Wisbech Cut, and marked by Big Tom Light-beacon (red, 10 m in height) (52°49'·6N, 0°13'·2E) on the E side and West End Light-beacon (black, 7 m in height) 2 cables SW and on the W side, the River Nene leads 9 miles S to Wisbech. The river banks are marked by light-beacons or lights mounted on stakes, similar to those in Wisbech Channel (8.95). The stakes are moved as necessary when bank erosion takes place.

2   Overhead power cables span the river between 1 and 2 miles S of Sutton Bridge with a lowest safe vertical clearance of 31 m.

Berths
8.97

1   Quays are situated on both sides of the river and total 800 m providing 6 principal berths.

Port services
8.98

1   **Repairs.** Minor engine repairs only.

Other facilities: hospital with helicopter landing site; facilities for disposal of galley waste; deratting can be carried out and exemption certificates issued.

Supplies: fuel by road tanker; fresh water; stores and provisions.

Communications. Wisbech is connected by the River Nene and canals to Peterborough and Northampton and thence to the Grand Union Canal.

Small craft
8.99

1   Wisbech Yacht Harbour consists of pontoon moorings for small craft on the E bank of the River Nene close S of the commercial quays. There are plans (2000) to increase the number of berths.

Port Sutton Bridge
8.100

1   **General information.** Port Sutton Bridge (52°46′N, 0°12′E) is 3 miles from the entrance to the River Nene. The recently constructed wharf is capable of receiving vessels up to 120 m in length, draught of 6·3 m and 5000 dwt. In 1999 463 vessels totalling 881 949 dwt used the port.

2   **Port authority.** Port Sutton Bridge, West Bank, Sutton Bridge, Spalding, Lincolnshire, PE12 9QR.

Pilotage is compulsory.

Directions. See 8.94 to 8.96.

Berths. The wharf is 350 m in length, providing 4 berths. Depths alongside are 9·3 m at HW springs, 5·25 m at HW neaps and 2·9 m at LW springs. A small swinging basin lies 1½ cables SSW of the wharf.

3   **Other facilities:** facilities for disposal of galley waste.

Supplies: fuel by road tanker; fresh water; provisions.

KING'S LYNN AND APPROACHES

General information

Chart 1200
Position
8.101

1   King's Lynn (52°45′N, 0°24′E) lies 2 miles SSE of the entrance to Lynn Cut, which is the artificially straightened mouth of the River Great Ouse with embankments up to 3·5 m high.

Function
8.102

1   There is a small commercial port at King's Lynn which handles steel, timber, fuel and agricultural products. The population was 41 281 in 1997.

Topography
8.103

1   The town lies on flat ground but fine wooded country rises behind it.

Port limits
8.104

1   The port limits, which are shown on the chart, extend over the SE half of The Wash, adjoining those of Wisbech (8.87) and Boston (8.58).

Approach and entry
8.105

1   King's Lynn is approached from The Wash through Teetotal Channel (8.118) which leads to Lynn Cut. There are a number of alternative channels, but these are suitable only for small craft and local knowledge is required.

Traffic
8.106

1   In 1999 the port handled 599 vessels, with imports of 555 593 tonnes and exports of 388 955 tonnes.

Port authority
8.107

1   Harbour authority: King's Lynn Conservancy Board, Harbour Office, Common Staith, King's Lynn PE30 1LL.

Dock authority: Associated British Ports, Dock Office, St Ann's Fort, King's Lynn PE30 2EU.

Limiting conditions
8.108

1   **Controlling Depths.** The approach to King's Lynn is navigable by sea-going vessels only around HW. Lynn Cut carries sufficient water to ensure it does not dry, but in places the bed level is 1·0 m above chart datum. Depths of water are subject to change and the Harbour Master should be consulted for the latest information.

2   Within the harbour there is sufficient water to ensure it does not dry, but in places the bed level is 1·6 m above chart datum. The depth in the two docks, Alexandra and Bentinck, is maintained at a minimum of 5·3 m.

Overhead power cables with a safe vertical clearance of 46 m cross the river 1 mile N of the town.

3   **Deepest and longest berths:** Riverside and South Quay (8.124) are the longest berths and Boal Quay (8.124), the deepest berth, although the latter is not normally used by commercial vessels. Enclosed docks, Alexandra and Bentinck Docks (8.124).

Tidal levels: see *Admiralty Tide Tables*. Mean spring range about 5·8 m; mean neap range about 3·2 m.
8.109

1   **Maximum size of vessel.** The port can accommodate vessels up to 140 m in length, 20 m beam and draught 5·5 m (spring tides), 3·4 m (neap tides), taking the ground on the riverside berths. For vessels underway, allowances over vessel's maximum draught against predicted height of tide above local datum (i.e. 0·7 m below chart datum) are required, depending upon the size of the vessel. These allowances are subject to rapid change; the Harbour Master should be consulted for the latest information.

2   Vessels over 100 m in length might be considered suitable to transit on daylight tides only.

All vessels over 80 m in length or near the upper limits of beam or draught should consult the Harbour Master prior to entry.

Arrival information

Port operations
8.110

1   **Dock signals** are shown from a flagstaff on the S side of Alexandra Dock as follows:

Signal day/night	Meaning
Square blue flag/ Red light	Vessel may enter dock.

Square red flag/ Vessels leaving dock. Vessels in
Green light harbour keep clear.

No flag or light Lock closed.

Notice of ETA
8.111

1 Notice of 24 hours' is required with amendments up to 6 hours in advance.

Outer anchorage
8.112

1 There is an anchorage area, shown on the chart (52°57′N, 0°22′E), to the S of Roaring Middle Light-float.

Pilots and tugs
8.113

1 Pilotage is compulsory for vessels over 35 m in length. There are two pilot cutters, each painted blue with white superstructure and orange wheelhouse tops. The pilot cutter will be on station to the NE of No 1 Light-buoy (52°56′·0N, 0°20′·0E) when vessels are expected from 2 hours before HW until it is too late for the vessel concerned to reach King's Lynn.

2 Tugs are available. The attendance of a tug is compulsory for tankers over 73 m in length and other vessels over that length not fitted with bow thrusters.

Harbour

Layout
8.114

1 There are two enclosed docks, Alexandra Dock entered through a lock on the E bank of the river and Bentinck Dock, entered from Alexandra Dock. Fisher Fleet, a tidal basin used mainly by fishing vessels, lies 1½ cables N of Alexandra Dock. Riverside berths lie on the E bank and extend 1½ cables N and 6½ cables S of Alexandra Dock entrance.

Tidal streams
8.115

1 In the approaches the tidal streams follow channels which lie in a SSW/NNE direction, but set across other channels especially when the sandbanks are covered, see tables on the chart. Off King's Lynn the streams set as follows:

Time from HW Immingham	Remarks
–0300	In-going stream begins
+0130	Out-going stream begins

2 The tidal streams off King's Lynn are fairly strong.
The times of HW are uncertain and subject to the influence of the wind.

Principal marks
8.116

1 **Landmarks:**
Trial Bank (52°50′·5N, 0°15′·3E) (8.93).
Mound (52°49′·1N, 0°17′·3E) (8.93).
Pylons (52°46′·4N, 0°23′·0E) for an overhead power cable spanning the river (8.108).

Directions
(*continued from 8.52*)

Roaring Middle Light-float to Lynn Cut
8.117

1 **Roaring Middle Light-float to Teetotal Channel.** From the vicinity of Roaring Middle Light-float (52°58′·6N, 0°21′·2E) the route leads 4 miles SSW to Teetotal Channel,

Bentinck Dock   Silo

Alexandra Dock

King's Lynn (8.114)

(*Original dated 2000*)

(Photograph - Air Images)

the main approach channel to Lynn Cut, passing (with positions from Snettisham Scalp (52°52'·4N, 0°26'·8E)):

SW of Sunk Sand (5 miles N) and South Sunk Sand (4 miles N) (8.51). Sunk Light-buoy (W cardinal) is moored W of South Sunk Sand. Thence:

2   E of Roaring Middle (6 miles NW), the N point of the drying sands which lie up to 6½ miles N of the S coast of The Wash. No 1 Light-buoy (N cardinal) is moored NE of Roaring Middle and marks the N side of the approach to Teetotal Channel. Thence:

3   To Teetotal Channel entrance (5 miles NW) marked by Nos 2 and 3 Light-buoys (port and starboard hand).

8.118

1   **Teetotal Channel to Lynn Cut.** From Teetotal Channel entrance (52°54'·9N, 0°19'·7E), the route leads 7 miles in a generally S and SE direction to the entrance to Lynn Cut. The E side of the channel lies along the drying line of the coastal bank consisting of Seal Sand and Daseley's Sand and the W side along the drying line of Thief Sand, a detached shoal, and Hull Sand, the coastal bank. The channel leading S to Lynn Cut is marked by light-buoys which are subject to frequent change as the channel itself changes.

2   For the final 2½ miles of the channel a training wall, marked at its N end by West Stones Light-beacon (N cardinal) and at its S end by West Bank Light-beacon (yellow pile, tide gauge, 10 m in height) (52°47'·4N, 0°22'·1E), lies to the W of the channel. It should be noted that this training wall, which is marked by beacons and light-beacons, does not necessarily mark the edge of the channel. There is a shorter training wall extending 1 mile NNW on the E side of the channel, marked at its N end by East Stones Light-beacon (port hand). Both training walls dry.

Alternative approach channels to Lynn Cut
8.119

1   **Old Lynn Channel** is entered between Roaring Middle (52°55'N, 0°18'E) and Bar Flat (8.94), 1 mile W. It leads 2½ miles SSW and splits either side of Whiting Shoal. Old Lynn Road runs SSE terminating in Scotsman's Sled and lies to the W of Whiting Middle. The E arm of Old Lynn Channel lies to the E of Whiting Shoal and joins the main approach channel.

2   Old Lynn Channel is only suitable for small craft, and local knowledge is required.

8.120

1   **Daseley's Sled**, the old approach channel to Lynn Cut, lying 1½ miles E of Teetotal Channel (8.118), is no longer used.

8.121

1   **Cork Hole** lies 3 miles E of Teetotal Channel and runs S between the coastal bank and Stylemans Middle, a detached shoal, and Pandora Sand, before joining the main approach channel close N of West Stones Light-beacon.

Lynn Cut and River Great Ouse to King's Lynn
8.122

1   From the S end of the approach channel the channel continues SSE through Lynn Cut and the River Great Ouse to King's Lynn. At its outer end Lynn Cut is 161 m wide at HW reducing to 111 m wide at LW; at its inner end the cut is 148 m wide at HW and 140 m wide at LW. The entrance to Alexandra Dock is 2 miles SSE of West Bank Light-beacon. The entrance lock is 15·2 m wide and has a depth over the sill at HW springs of 7·6 m, and 5·4 m at HW neaps. The lock is open from 1 hour before HW and closed shortly after HW. Bentinck Dock is entered from Alexandra Dock through a passage 96 m long and 15·2 m wide, which is spanned by two swing bridges.

2   **Caution.** A small passenger ferry crosses the river 1½ cables S of the entrance to Alexandra Dock.

Useful marks
8.123

1   Silo (52°45'·7N, 0°23'·9E).
    Saint Nicholas Church (Spire) (52°45'·4N, 0°23'·9E).
    Saint Margaret's Church (tower and flagstaff) (52°45'·1N, 0°23'·8E) with two towers.

Basins and berths
8.124

1   **Riverside berths.**
    Riverside Quay, 220 m long (approx.); depth 2·5 m (1997) but subject to change.
    South Quay, 396 m long, dries at LW; Boal Quay, 122 m long, dries at LW.

2   **Fisher Fleet.**
    Fish Landing Stage, 120 m long; dries at LW.
    Enclosed docks.
    Alexandra Dock, 350 m quay, Ro-Ro berth;
    Bentinck Dock, 800 m quay. Both docks maintain a minimum depth of 5·3 m.

Port services
8.125

1   **Repairs.** Limited repairs to both hull and engine can be carried out.
    Other facilities:
    Facilities available for the reception of oily waste.
    Hospital with helicopter landing site.
    Deratting can be carried out and exemption certificates issued.
    Customs.

2   **Supplies:** fuel by road tanker; fresh water; stores and provisions.
    Communications. King's Lynn is connected by river and canal to Cambridge.

Small craft
8.126

1   There are no special facilities for visiting small craft. Some swinging moorings are normally available for visitors upstream of Boal Quay, on prior application to the Harbour Master. There is a tidal grid, a public hard and a boat slipway.

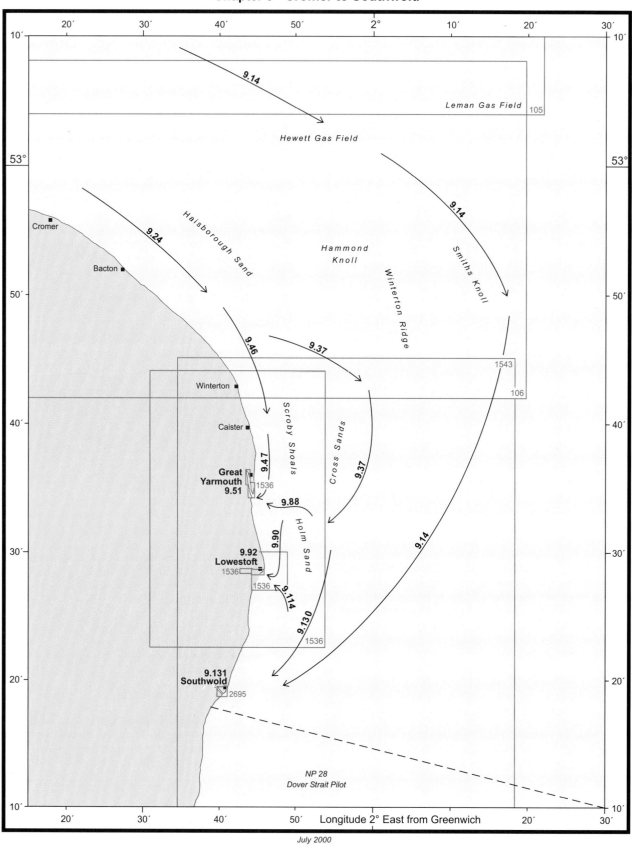

CHAPTER 9

CROMER TO SOUTHWOLD

GENERAL INFORMATION

Charts 1503, 1504
Synopsis
9.1

1   In this chapter the continuation of the offshore passage from Outer Dowsing Channel SSE between Hewett Ridges and Leman Bank thence E of Smith's Knoll and finally SSW to Southwold (9.131) is described at 9.14 together with the coastal passage SE from Cromer through The Would (9.24) and Haisborough Gat (9.30).

The chapter describes the ports of Great Yarmouth (9.51) and Lowestoft (9.92) and their approaches.

Topography
9.2

1   From Cromer (52°56′N, 1°18′E) the coast curves gently to the SE, thence S and finally SSW from Lowestoft to Southwold, which is 43 miles from Cromer following the line of the coast.

2   The coastal and offshore waters are generally shallow with depths of less than 40 m. Between Winterton Ness, 17 miles SE of Cromer, and Lowestoft, 15 miles further S, shallow banks front the coast. There are also off-lying banks, some with depths of less than 3 m over them. These off-lying banks are described in Chapter 2.

Transfer of cargo
9.3

1   Transfer of liquid cargo between tankers takes place occasionally about 11 miles ESE of Southwold. Vessels engaged in such transfers might be at anchor or otherwise unable to manoeuvre and should be given a wide berth.

Tidal streams
9.4

1   In coastal waters the streams follow the line of the coast and of the channels between the banks. Offshore the streams are more or less rotary, but when strongest they follow the line of the channel.

Details of the tidal streams are given on the charts and in *Admiralty Tidal Stream Atlas: North Sea, Southern Part.*

Gasfields and pipelines
9.5

1   A number of gasfields, most of them connected to the shore by pipelines, lie within the area described in this chapter. For a description of the platforms and pipelines associated with the gasfields see 1.23, 1.36 and 1.37.

Oil and gasfields within the limits of this volume are listed at 2.17.

Dumping grounds
9.6

1   Underwater explosives may still remain in former dumping grounds off East Anglia in the vicinity of 52°25′N, 2°21′E and in the area bounded by:

      52°30′N, 2°25′E
      53°00′N, 2°35′E
      53°00′N, 3°15′E
      52°30′N, 3°02′E.

CROMER TO SOUTHWOLD OFFSHORE ROUTE

General information

Charts 1503, 106, 1543
Route
9.7

1   From a position about 15 miles N of Cromer (52°56′N, 1°19′E), the offshore route leads 25 miles SSE passing between Leman Bank and Hewett Ridges to the N end of Smith's Knoll, and thence 40 miles S passing E of Smith's Knoll to a position E of Southwold.

There are channels leading between the shoals W of Smith's Knoll (9.14) and E of Haisborough Sand (9.24), but they are not well marked and should only be attempted with local knowledge.

Least charted depths
9.8

1   Depths along this route are greater than 20 m.

Gas pipelines
9.9

1   A number of gas pipelines, shown on the chart, run from Bacton Gas Terminal (52°52′N, 1°28′E) NNE and E across The Would (9.24) thence to offshore production platforms. Vessels should not anchor or trawl near these pipelines, see 1.37.

Rescue
9.10

1   See 9.20.

Tidal streams
9.11

1   The spring rate in each direction is about 2½ kn. Details of the tidal streams are given on the charts and in the *Admiralty Tidal Stream Atlas: North Sea, Southern Part.*

Principal marks
9.12

1   **Major lights:**
    Cromer Light (52°56′N, 1°19′E) (8.14).
    Smith's Knoll Light-buoy (S cardinal) (52°44′N, 2°18′E).
    Lowestoft Light (white round tower, 16 m in height) (52°29′·2N, 1°45′·5E).
    Southwold Light (white round tower standing in the middle of the town, 31 m in height) (52°19′·6N, 1°41′·0E).

Other navigational aids
9.13

1   **Racon:**
    Cromer Light (52°55′N, 1°19′E).
    N Haisbro' Light-buoy (53°00′N, 1°32′E).
    Smith's Knoll Light-buoy (52°44′N, 2°18′E).
    DGPS:
    Flamborough Head Light (54°07′N, 0°05′W).
    North Foreland (51°22′N, 1°27′E) (*Dover Strait Pilot*).

Directions
(continued from 8.16)

Cromer to Southwold, offshore route
9.14

1 From a position about 15 miles N of Cromer (52°56′N, 1°19′E), the route leads 33 miles ESE to a position E of the N end of Smith's Knoll, thence 17 miles SSE passing E of Smith's Knoll, when the route leads SSW to converge with the coastal route E of Cross Sand (9.37), passing:

2 SSW of Inner Cromer Knoll (53°13′N, 1°26′E), which is 5½ miles SE of Cromer Knoll (8.16), thence:

SSW of Haddock Bank (53°17′N, 1°35′E), which runs NW/SE over a distance of 15 miles, thence:

3 SSW of Leman Bank (53°08′N, 1°56′E), a thin bank stretching 23 miles NW/SE along the N side of the channel. Lying parallel to Leman Bank and to its NE there are a number of similar banks (2.15). Thence:

4 Clear of North Hewett Gas Field (53°06′N, 1°46′E), Hewett Gas Field (5 miles S) and Della Gas Field (5 miles ESE). See 1.23 for information on platforms. Thence:

NNE of Hewett Ridges (52°57′N, 2°04′E), consisting of two banks. The N bank extends along the S side of the channel, thence:

5 NNE and ENE of Smith's Knoll (52°53′N, 2°13′E). The channel narrows to 3 miles between the N end of Smith's Knoll and the SE end of Leman Bank. The knoll is a narrow ridge 16 miles long which parallels the Norfolk coast. Thence:

6 Clear of Camelot Gas Field (52°57′N, 2°09′E), situated close to the N end of Smith's Knoll, and S of Leman Gas Field (6 miles N), one of the larger gas fields, which lies E of Leman Bank and N of Smith's Knoll. Thence:

7 ENE of Smith's Knoll Light-buoy (52°44′N, 2°18′E) (9.12), which is moored 2 miles SE of the S end of Smith's Knoll. Thence:

To a position E of Southwold (9.131) converging with the route at 9.130.

(Directions for passage S to the Thames Estuary and the Dover Strait are given in the Dover Strait Pilot)

Useful marks
9.15

1 Gas production platforms, the positions of which can best be seen on the chart.

CROMER TO WINTERTON NESS

General information

Chart 106
Route
9.16

1 From a position about 8 miles N of Cromer (52°56′N, 1°19′E), the inshore route leads 24 miles SE through The Would to a position NE of Winterton Ness.

Topography
9.17

1 The coast between Cromer and Winterton Ness, 18 miles SE, is subject to extensive landslips and fringed by a submarine forest. The coast is composed of cliffs as far as Happisburgh, 10 miles SE of Cromer, where it changes to sandhills which run to Winterton Ness. Initially the sandhills have an elevation of 9 to 12 m but they gradually decline to the SE.

2 Between Hempstead and Waxham (5½ miles and 3½ miles NW of Winterton Ness) coast defences, consisting of large artificial reefs of stone positioned about 1½ cables offshore, have been constructed. They have a height of about 1·7 m above MHWS and are marked by lit and unlit beacons. Leading lights have been established for the Happisburgh Lifeboat Station, which is located at Sea Palling (52°47′·35N, 1°36′·28E).

3 Between Waxham and Winterton Ness the coast is protected by a number of groynes marked by beacons (black conical topmarks) at their heads.

Least charted depths
9.18

1 At the NW end of The Would there are charted depths of 16 m. Thereafter depending on the precise track followed depths in excess of 20 m can be maintained in The Would.

Gas pipelines
9.19

1 See 9.9.

Rescue
9.20

1 There are Coastguard Rescue Teams at Mundesley (52°53′N, 1°27′E), Happisburgh (52°49′N, 1°32′E) and Winterton-on-Sea; see 1.53.

An inshore lifeboat is stationed at Happisburgh. See 1.62 for details of lifeboat.

Tidal streams
9.21

1 The spring rate in each direction is about 2½ kn. Details of the tidal streams are given on the charts and in the *Admiralty Tidal Stream Atlas: North Sea, Southern Part.*

Principal marks
9.22

1 **Landmarks:**
Cromer Church (tower) (52°56′N, 1°18′E).
Radio masts (52°55′N, 1°21′E).
Radome (52°54′N, 1°24′E) at Trimingham.

Radome at Trimingham (9.22)

(Original dated 2000)

(Photograph – Air Images)

Water tower (52°53′N, 1°26′E) at Mundesley.
Two radio masts (red obstruction lights) (52°51′N, 1°28′E).
Happisburgh Church (tower) (52°49′N, 1°32′E).

2   Winterton Church (tower) (52°43′N, 1°41′E), visible above sandhills.

Several wind generators (52°43′N, 1°40′E) in two rows of 5 each aligned N/S.

Major light:

Cromer Light (52°56′N, 1°19′E) (8.14).

Other navigational aids
9.23
1   **Racon:**

Winterton Old Lighthouse (52°43′N, 1°42′E).

DGPS:

North Foreland (51°22′N, 1°27′E) (*Dover Strait Pilot*).

Directions
(continued from 8.23)

Cromer to Winterton Ness
9.24
1   The Would, a channel about 7 miles wide, lies between the Norfolk coast and Haisborough Sand.

2   From a position NE of Cromer (52°56′N, 1°19′E) (8.42), the route leads 21 miles SE through The Would to a position NE of Winterton Ness, passing (with positions from Happisburgh Lighthouse (white tower, three red bands, 26 m in height) (52°49′N, 1°32′E)):

3   SW of Haisborough Sand (8½ miles NE), which is 10 miles long and 1 mile wide lying parallel to the Norfolk coast. It is marked to the NW by N Haisbro' Light-buoy (N cardinal), to the SE by S Haisbro' Light-buoy (S cardinal) and to the W by Mid Haisbro' Light-buoy (starboard hand). The shoal has three drying patches (1995) close NE, E and ESE of the Mid Haisbro' Light-buoy. Except at slack water their positions are indicated by tidal eddies and even a slight sea or moderate swell breaks on the shallower parts of the shoal. There are a number of foul patches on the S part of the shoal. There are strong eddies on and around the bank, especially to the NW (52°59′·5N 1°34′·5E).

4   Thence:

NE of Bacton Gas Terminal (3¾ miles NW). The buildings of the Gas Terminal, which are brightly illuminated at night, stand 5 cables NW of the prominent church in Bacton. Thence:

5   To a position NE of Winterton Ness (7½ miles SE). Winterton-on-Sea, situated behind sandhills and close to a nature reserve, is 1¼ miles SSE of the ness. Winterton Old Lighthouse (white round tower, black band near top), which is disused, stands on a hill 3½ cables SE of Winterton Church (9.22).

Useful marks
9.25
1   Newarp Light-vessel (red hull, light tower amidships, Newarp in white) (52°48′·3N, 1°55′·8E).

The churches and church towers listed below are relatively close to one another and liable to be confused.

Trimingham Church (square tower) (52°54′N, 1°23′E).

Stow Hill Mill (52°52′N, 1°26′E).

Trunch Church (tower) (52°52′N, 1°24′E).

2   Knapton Church (tower) (52°51′N, 1°26′E).

Hempstead Church (52°48′N, 1°34′E) surrounded by trees.

Lessingham Church (52°48′N, 1°33′E).

Ingham Church (52°47′N, 1°33′E).

Sea Palling Church (square tower) (52°47′N, 1°36′E).

Waxham Church (square tower) (52°47′N, 1°37′E).

(Directions continue for coastal passage ESE at 9.37)

Anchorage and landing
9.26
1   **Overstrand** (52°55′N, 1°21′E), which stands back from the cliff with a wooded background, has a long tarmac ramp used by fishing boats.

9.27
1   **The Would** offers an anchorage in offshore winds, off the coast between Bacton (52°52′N, 1°28′E) and Winterton Ness (11 miles SE), avoiding the numerous wrecks, pipelines and cables shown on the chart. Haisborough Sand offers some protection from E winds; N and NW winds cause the greatest sea.

Other name
9.28
1   Sidestrand village (52°55′N, 1°22′E).

WINTERTON NESS TO THE SEAWARD APPROACHES OF GREAT YARMOUTH AND LOWESTOFT

General information

Charts 106, 1543

Route
9.29
1   From a position NE of Winterton Ness (52°44′N, 1°41′E) the route leads 12 miles ESE through Haisborough Gat and thence 15 miles SSW to a position E of Holm Channel, the principal approach from seaward to the ports of Great Yarmouth and Lowestoft.

Topography
9.30
1   Haisborough Gat is 2 miles wide and the continuation SE of The Would (9.24). It lies between a series of banks, principally Hammond Knoll (9.37) and Winterton Ridge (9.37) to the NE and Newarp Banks (9.37) to the SW. Once clear of the Gat, the route lies to seaward of the coastal shoals and banks.

For a description of the coast S of Winterton Ness see 9.40.

Least charted depths
9.31
1   Depending on the precise track followed, depths in excess of 20 m can be maintained in Haisborough Gat and to its SSW.

Submarine cables
9.32
1   Cables run NE and E from Winterton-on-Sea, 1 mile SE of Winterton Ness, across Haisborough Gat. The S pair of cables are no longer in use.

Rescue
9.33
1   See 9.42.

Tidal streams
9.34
1   The spring rate in each direction is about 2½ kn, although rates close to banks may be higher. Details of the tidal streams are given on the charts and in *Admiralty Tidal Stream Atlas: North Sea, Southern Part*.

Principal marks
9.35

1 **Landmarks:**

Winterton Church (tower) (52°43′N, 1°41′W) (9.22).
Water tower at Caister (52°39′N, 1°43′E), of stone;
taller radio mast close NW.

Water Tower and Radio Mast at Caister (9.35)

(Original dated 1996)

(Photograph - Naval Party 1016)

Major lights:

Smith's Knoll Light-buoy (52°44′N, 2°18′E) (9.12).
Lowestoft Light (52°29′·2N, 1°45′·5E) (9.12).

Other navigational aids
9.36

1 **Racon:**

Winterton Old Lighthouse (52°43′N, 1°42′E).
Newarp Light-vessel (52°48′N, 1°56′E).
Cross Sand Light-buoy (52°37′N, 1°59′E).

DGPS:

North Foreland (51°22′N, 1°27′E) (*Dover Strait
Pilot*).

Directions
(continued from 9.25)

9.37

1 From a position NE of Winterton Ness (52°44′N,
1°41′E) the route leads 8 miles ESE through Haisborough
Gat thence 15 miles SSW to a position E of Holm Channel,
passing:

SSW of S Haisbro Light-buoy (S cardinal) (52°51′N,
1°48′E), marking the S extremity of Haisborough
Sand (9.24), thence:

2 SSW of Haisborough Tail (52°53′N, 1°51′E), which is
2½ miles E of Haisborough Sand and parallel to
the latter's SE end. Depths between the two shoals
are uneven. Thence:

NNE of Winterton Shoal (52°46′N, 1°47′E), marked
by tidal eddies, and:

3 SSW of Hammond Knoll (52°53′N, 1°55′E) parallel
to and 2 miles E of Haisborough Tail. Hammond
Knoll Light-buoy (W cardinal) is moored 1¾ miles
SE of the shoal and E Hammond Light-buoy (E
cardinal) is moored 2 miles E of the shoal and
1 mile NNW of Winterton Ridge (below). Thence:

4 Clear of Newarp Light-vessel (52°48′N, 1°56′E)
(9.25). Normally S-bound vessels pass SW and
N-bound vessels NE of the light-vessel. Thence:

NNE and E of Newarp Banks (52°46′N, 1°55′E), a
series of shoals running NW/SE for over 4 miles,
thence:

5 SSW of Winterton Ridge (52°49′N, 2°02′E), which
extends over 4 miles NNW/SSE. S Winterton

Ridge Light-buoy (S cardinal) marks the SE end of
the shoal. Thence:

W of Hearty Knoll (52°46′N, 2°08′E), which runs
NNW/SSE along the NE side of the Gat at its SE
end, thence:

6 E of Cross Sand, which as defined by the 20 m depth
contour extends 12 miles S from Newarp Banks to
merge with the SE extremity of Corton Sand
(9.47). It has three shallow areas, respectively
North Cross Sand (52°43′N, 1°53′E), Middle Cross
Sand (52°40′N, 1°53′E) and South Cross Sand
(52°37′N, 1°51′E), which are indicated by tide
rips. There are sandwave formations on North
Cross Sand. NE Cross Sand Light-buoy (E
cardinal) is moored SE of North Cross Sand, E
Cross Sand Light-buoy (port hand) to the E of
Middle Cross Sand and S Corton Light-buoy (S
cardinal) to the S of South Cross Sand.

7 The sands are continually altering and should not be
approached on their unmarked sides without local
knowledge. Thence:

Clear of Cross Sand Light-buoy (safe water)
(52°37′N, 1°59′E), 4 miles E of the S end of
Middle Cross Sand, thence:

8 To a position NE of Holm Sand (52°30′N, 1°48′E).
The sea breaks over the shoal in all but the
calmest weather and it has an extensive drying
area. Holm Channel (9.88), the principal approach
channel to Great Yarmouth and Lowestoft, is
entered NE of Holm Sand. Stanford Channel
(9.114) is entered S of Holm Sand. Corton
Light-buoy (E cardinal) is moored SE of the
entrance to Holm Channel.

9 **Caution.** Considerable dredging activity takes place in
an area, indicated on Chart 1543, extending about 11 miles
E of Corton Light-buoy and 6 miles NNE and 10 miles S
of Cross Sand Light-buoy. The dredgers move slowly and
might reverse their course suddenly.

*(Directions continue for the approaches to Great
Yarmouth and Lowestoft at 9.88 and coastal passage S
at 9.130)*

Other name
9.38

1 Middle Ground (52°50′N, 2°08′E).

WINTERTON NESS TO GREAT YARMOUTH

General information

Charts 106, 1536
Routes
9.39

1 The approach to Great Yarmouth from the N through
Cockle Gatway which leads S to Caister Road and
Yarmouth Road is described below. The main approach
from the S and E through Holm Channel to Gorleston
Road is given at 9.88.

2 **Caution.** Changes in the sandbanks and channels are
frequent. No channel should be used unless it is buoyed,
even if the charted depths appear sufficient; experience has
shown that changes in channels which are not buoyed are
more frequent than elsewhere.

Due to these rapid changes, buoyage might be altered
before the relevant Notice to Mariners has been published.

Topography
9.40

1   From Winterton Ness (52°44′N, 1°41′E) the coast runs 5½ miles SSE to Caister Point. The coast is sandy and backed by sandhills and sandy cliffs, up to 17 m in height. South of Caister Point the coast runs 4½ miles S to the entrance to Great Yarmouth. This stretch of coast is low and sandy.

2   A chain of sandbanks, lying up to 5 miles offshore, extend 15 miles S from a position 3½ miles NE of Caister Point (52°39′N, 1°44′E). These banks protect the channel formed by the various roads which lead to Great Yarmouth and Lowestoft. The depths over these natural breakwaters are usually less than 5 m and in places they dry up to 1·5 m. They are also subject to great changes, the shoaler parts disappear and the deeper parts become shoals themselves.

Controlling depths
9.41

1   The approach from the N passes over Cockle Shoal, where depths are of the order of 3 to 5 m but are constantly changing, and the charts and Yarmouth Pilots should be consulted for the latest information.

Rescue
9.42

1   The Maritime Rescue Co-ordination Centre for the Yarmouth Region and District (constant watch) is situated close NE of Haven Bridge (52°36′·5N, 1°43′·5E) within Yarmouth Harbour.

Coastguard Rescue Teams are based at Winterton and Gorleston; see 1.53.

2   An all-weather lifeboat and an inshore lifeboat are stationed at Great Yarmouth. See 1.61 and 1.62 for details of RNLI lifeboats.

Caister Volunteer Rescue Service maintains an all-weather lifeboat and an inshore lifeboat at Caister.

Tidal streams
9.43

1   Off the coast between Winterton Ness and Great Yarmouth the S-going tidal stream is strong at local HW and the N-going stream at local LW. Ripples or overfalls form when the streams cross shoals or other bottom inequalities and are more pronounced at LW when the strong N-going stream is running. When N gales oppose the N-going stream the sea breaks heavily over the shoals.

2   The tidal streams generally run in the direction of the coast and through channels aligned with the coast. They set across the shoals and channels not so aligned, the S-going stream setting towards the shoals on the SW side of the channels and the N-going stream towards the shoals on the NE sides. In particular the S-going stream sets onto the Scroby Shoals (9.47) and the N-going stream onto the Caister and Cockle Shoals (9.46).

3   For details see tables on the charts and the *Admiralty Tidal Stream Atlas: North Sea, Southern Part.*

Principal marks
9.44

1   **Landmarks:**
   Winterton Church (tower) (52°43′N, 1°41′E).
   Several wind generators, (52°42′·5N, 1°40′·3E), 60 m in height.
   Water Tower (52°39′N, 1°43′E) (9.35).

2   Tower in Great Yarmouth (52°36′·25N, 1°44′·25E) close SW of Britannia Pier.

Tower, Great Yarmouth (9.44)

(Original dated 2000)

(Photograph - Great Yarmouth Port Authority)

   Nelson's Monument (52°35′·3N, 1°44′·1W).
   Chimney, at power station (52°35′·0N, 1°44′·1E).
   Offshore mark:
   Wind monitoring mast (52°40′·2N, 1°47′·3E), 50 m in height, marked by a red obstruction light. A light is exhibited from the mast.

3   **Major light:**
   Lowestoft Light (52°29′·2N, 1°45′·5E) (9.12).

Other navigational aids
9.45

1   **Racon:**
   Winterton Old Lighthouse (52°43′N, 1°42′E).
   Cross Sand Light buoy (52°37′N, 1°59′E).
   DGPS:
   North Foreland (51°22′N, 1°27′E) (*Dover Strait Pilot*).

Directions
(continued from 9.24)

Winterton Ness to Great Yarmouth
9.46

1   **The Would to Cockle Gatway.** From the vicinity of 52°50′N, 1°45′E at the SE end of The Would and NE of Winterton Ness, the route leads 8 miles S to Cockle Shoal at the S end of Cockle Gatway, passing (with positions from Winterton Ness (52°44′N, 1°41′E)):
   W of Winterton Shoal (4½ miles NE) (9.37), thence:

2   Between Winterton Ness (9.24) and Winterton Overfalls (3½ miles E) at the N end of Cockle Gatway. A spit extends 1 mile E of Winterton Ness and is marked at its extremity by Cockle Light-buoy (E cardinal). Winterton Overfalls extend 2 miles NNE/SSW and are usually indicated

3 Over Cockle Shoal (3 miles SE) which lies at the S end of Cockle Gatway, marked at its N end by N Scroby Light-buoy (N cardinal) and at its mid point by Hemsby Light-buoy (port hand). Cockle Shoal joins the N ends of Caister Shoal and North Scroby Shoal.

4 There are usually heavy tide rips over Cockle Shoal and a sandwave field (1.82) in depths of about 10 m, which can produce shoals of 5 m or less. See 9.41 for controlling depths.

9.47

1 **Caister Road to Great Yarmouth.** From the N end of Caister Road (52°41·5′N, 1°45·3′E), the route leads 8 miles S through Caister and Yarmouth Road to a position E of the entrance to Great Yarmouth, passing (with positions from Caister Point (52°39′N, 1°44′E)):

2 E of Caister Shoal (1½ miles NNE), which runs N/S over a distance of 4½ miles and forms the W side of Caister Road. The sea breaks heavily over the shoal which is marked on its E side by N Caister Light-buoy (port hand) and Mid Caister Light-buoy (port hand), and:

3 W of the Scroby Shoals, which lie parallel to the coast and stretch 7 miles from Cockle Shoal in the N to abreast the entrance to Great Yarmouth. They consist of North (2½ miles NE), Middle (2½ miles ESE) and South Scroby (4 miles SSE) and form the E side of Caister Road and Yarmouth Road. The sea breaks heavily over both North and Middle Scroby and the latter has extensive drying patches. There are tide rips over South Scroby. The shoals are marked by light-buoys to their N and W. Scroby Shoals are continually altering and should not be approached on their unmarked sides without local knowledge. Thence:

4 E of Yarmouth Outfall Light-buoy (port hand) (1¼ miles SSE), marking the seaward extremity of an outfall, thence:

Britannia Pier from NE (9.47)

(Original dated 2000)

(Photograph - Great Yarmouth Port Authority)

5 E of Britannia Pier (2¼ miles S), which is on the seafront at Great Yarmouth. It has a large pavilion and there is a depth of 2 m alongside its head, from which a light is exhibited. The Jetty and Wellington Pier, the latter with a large pavilion, lie 4 and 6 cables S of Britannia Pier. Lights are exhibited from both their heads. Thence:

6 W of Corton Sand (5 miles SSE) to a position off the entrance to Great Yarmouth. The sand is joined at its N end to South Scroby Sand and runs 3 miles

to the S to form the NE side of Holm Channel (9.88). The sea breaks over the centre of the shoal.

Side channels
9.48

1 **Hemsby Hole** leads from Cockle Gatway in the N to Yarmouth Road, and lies between Cockle and Caister Shoals and the coast. Depths of over 10 m can be maintained in the greater part of the channel but at the S end as it enters Yarmouth Road it passes over a ridge where depths are less than 3 m and constantly changing. Hemsby Hole is not marked by buoys and should not be attempted without local knowledge.

9.49

1 **Barley Picle**, which is not buoyed, lies between Scroby Shoals (9.47) and Cross Sand (9.37). It provided an approach to Great Yarmouth through a channel between Scroby Shoals and Corton Sand (9.47), but this channel has silted and Barley Picle is effectively closed to the W by these shoals.

Anchorages
9.50

1 An anchorage can be obtained in any part of Caister and Yarmouth Roads (9.47), depth 10 to 24 m, sand, shells, stones and shingle, but clear of the spoil ground and other charted obstructions.

2 The roads are exposed to E winds which cause a short choppy sea, in some respects worse than that outside the sandbanks. In these conditions it is best to anchor off the shallower parts of the off-lying sandbanks, indicated by the heavier breakers, in particular close W of the S part of Scroby Shoals. In the latter position no direct sea is experienced but some swell finds its way round the ends of the bank.

3 At night an anchorage off the coast between Britannia Pier (9.47) and the haven entrance is used.

Gorleston Road (9.89), SE of the haven entrance, provides a good anchorage, depth 10 to 20 m, sand. It is partially sheltered by South Scroby and Corton Sand.

4 Small craft will find the best anchorage W of Caister Shoal.

Masters should ensure that they do not anchor in the approaches to the port entrance.

GREAT YARMOUTH

General information

Chart 1536 plans of Great Yarmouth Haven
Position
9.51

1 Great Yarmouth (52°36′N, 1°44′E) stands on a narrow strip of land between the E bank of the River Yare and the sea. Two lifting bridges at the N end of Great Yarmouth Haven connect the town with the suburbs of Cobholm and Southtown on the W bank and thence with Gorleston-on-Sea to the W and S of the river mouth.

Function
9.52

1 The medium sized commercial and ferry port, known as Great Yarmouth Haven, is situated on the lower reaches of the River Yare. It is also an important base for vessels employed on North Sea oil and gas fields. Fishing was of importance but has now declined.

The population of Great Yarmouth Borough was 89 100 in 1999.

Topography
9.53

1   The coast is low and sandy to the N of the haven entrance, which is formed by the mouth of the River Yare. To the S of the entrance there are low cliffs (9.80).

Traffic
9.54

1   In 1998 the port handled 3104 vessels totalling 4 043 190 grt.

Port authority
9.55

1   Great Yarmouth Port Authority, 20–21 South Quay, Great Yarmouth NR30 2RE.

Limiting conditions
9.56

1   **Controlling depth** in the approach and entrance is 5·0 m, but depths are subject to constant change. Temporary shoaling can occur after strong E winds when depths may be 1 m less than expected.

The haven (9.64) has a least depth in the fairway of 5·0 m.

2   **Deepest and longest berth.** All the major berths have similar depths alongside. The longest single berth is at East Quay (9.73).

Tidal levels: see *Admiralty Tide Tables*. Mean spring range about 1·9 m; mean neap range about 1 m.

9.57

1   **Maximum size of vessel handled.** Vessels using the harbour are normally restricted to a length of 123 m and draught 5·7 m, although vessels 138 m in length have entered the haven.

9.58

1   **Local conditions.** Entry should be delayed when there are heavy seas in the entrance, particularly with strong SE winds over an out-going stream. Otherwise light-draught vessels may enter at most times, but high or low slack water is recommended, see 9.67.

Arrival information

Port operations
9.59

1   **Vessel Traffic Service** scheme is in operation for the control of shipping, for details see the relevant *Admiralty List of Radio Signals*. Reporting positions are shown on the chart.

9.60

1   **Notice of ETA** is 8 hours if a pilot is required otherwise 1 hour. ETA in the former case should be confirmed 2 hours prior to arrival. The message should also include length overall, draught, grt, last port of call, cargo and berth.

Traffic signals
9.61

1   Main signals 1, 2, 3 and 5 of the International Port Traffic Signals, given in *The Mariner's Handbook*, are exhibited from the red brick building with white base on the E end of South Pier to control inbound traffic. Should these lights fail at night then the Brush Light, the leading and South Piers lights (all 9.70) will be extinguished or vessels will be informed by Yarmouth Port Radio.

2   Vessels proceeding down river shall not pass S of the lifeboat house, 400 m N of Brush Bend (9.70), when main signal 2 of the International Port Traffic Signals is

exhibited from the W side of the Port Control office at the root of South Pier. Should these lights fail then vessels will be informed by Yarmouth Port Radio.

Anchorages
9.62

1   See 9.50.

Pilots and tugs
9.63

1   Pilotage is compulsory for all vessels over 40 m in length, except warships, vessels exempt by law and vessels changing berth within the River Yare. The services of a pilot are recommended not only for navigation but also for changing berth and swinging ship as the river is only just wide enough for these purposes.

2   Pilots board the Great Yarmouth/Lowestoft Outer Boarding Ground, 5 cables SW of Corton Light-buoy (52°31'·1N, 1°51'·5E) or not less than 5 cables from the haven entrance. The pilot boats have a black hull and orange superstructure.

3   One tug is available.

Harbour

Layout
9.64

1   The entrance to Great Yarmouth Haven is formed by the mouth of the River Yare. From the entrance the river leads 2½ cables W, then turns abruptly N at Brush Lighthouse opening up the haven itself. There are riverside berths on either bank of the River Yare from close N of the lighthouse for 2 miles N to Haven Bridge.

Bridge traffic signals
9.65

1   Three red lights disposed vertically, exhibited from Haven Bridge (9.71) and visible downstream or upstream as appropriate, prohibit traffic passing through the bridge from that direction. These lights are switched on five minutes before the bridge is due to open.

Tidal streams
9.66

1   One mile ENE of the haven entrance tidal streams set as follows:

Time from HW Dover	Remarks
+0600	S-going stream begins.
−0020	N-going stream begins. Spring rate in each direction 2½ kn.

2   Off Brush Quay the tidal streams set as follows:

Time from HW Dover		Remarks
+0545	(Local LW +2 hours)	In-going stream begins. It rarely exceeds 2 kn except at Haven Bridge where it can reach 3 kn.
−0030	(Local HW +1½ hours)	Out-going stream begins, normal rate 4 kn, but can reach 6 kn.

3   The streams begin later upriver.

9.67

1   The S-going stream outside the harbour entrance runs past North Pier and turns NW passing South Pier as the in-going stream. The main part of the stream runs W to Brush Bend but a part forms an eddy current running E along North Pier. In these conditions inbound vessels must

Great Yarmouth Harbour Enrance (9.64)

(Original dated 2000)

(Photograph - Air Images)

take care to avoid being set onto North Pier, as the NW-going eddy current acts strongly on the port bow deflecting the vessels towards North Pier.

2   The out-going stream runs past North Pier and turns N with the N-going stream. The latter does not set so sharply across the entrance as the eddy on the in-going stream. However at South Pier part of the stream sets SE before joining the N-going stream. Inbound vessels may then round South Pier stemming this stream. In mid-channel inbound vessels may find the bow deflected to port towards South Pier by this set.

3   During and after heavy rain the duration and rate of the out-going stream is increased and the in-going stream correspondingly reduced. Under these circumstances the out-going stream may attain 6 kn off Brush Quay and there may be a continuous out-going stream for 18 hours.

4   Slack water normally occurs at local HW+1½ and LW+2 hours. Prolonged strong winds or heavy rainfall may cause these times to vary and also alter the tidal range by more than 1 m. The following can be expected:

	HW slack	LW slack	Tidal height
N wind	later	earlier	increased
S wind	earlier	later	decreased
Heavy rain	Earlier	later	increased

9.68

1   **Tidal signal.** When the in-going stream is running between the pierheads a quick flashing amber light is exhibited from the red brick building with white base on the E end of South Pier. This light can only be seen from seaward between the bearings of 235° and 295°; its intensity is such that it can overpower other navigation lights in the vicinity.

Principal marks
9.69

1   **Landmarks:**
      Nelson's Monument (52°35'·3N, 1°44'·1E).
      Chimney (52°35'·0N, 1°44'·1E) (9.44).

Nelson's Mounment (9.69)

(Original dated 2000)

(Photograph - Great Yarmouth Port Authority)

Directions
(continued from 9.47 and 9.89)

Haven entrance to Brush Quay
9.70

1   **Brush Quay leading lights:**
      Front light (white column) (52°34'·3N, 1°44'·1E) on E edge of Brush Quay.
      Rear light situated in Brush Lighthouse (red round brick tower, 21 m in height) (35 m W of front light) which also exhibits a main light.

South Denes Power Station (9.69)

(Original dated 2000)

(Photograph - Great Yarmouth Port Authority)

2   The alignment (264°) of these lights leads through the haven entrance, which is 61 m wide, passing (with positions from Brush Lighthouse):

    S of North Pier (2½ cables E) which projects 150 m E from the coast and exhibits a light (green metal column, ladder, 7 m in height) from its head, thence:

3   N of South Pierhead (2 cables E) which extends from the coast at Gorleston-on-Sea, and lies 140 m SW of North Pierhead. A main light is exhibited from the Equipment Building (red brick building close W of pierhead). The lower half of the building is painted white and illuminated to assist mariners in low visibility and at night. Seven sets of lights are also exhibited from the coping of the pier. Thence:

4   S of the training wall (1½ cables E) which lies parallel to and 40 m S of the embanked N side of the haven entrance. Five sets of lights are exhibited from the training wall. Thence:

5   N of South Pier (1 cable E) which is embanked. At the inner end of South Pier the embankment curves sharply to the N to form Brush Quay or The Brush. Lights are exhibited from South Pier and Brush Bend. A buoyed anchor should be ready to assist the turn if necessary at the bend. Tugs may also assist the turn. On completion of the turn there is direct approach to the various riverside berths lying to the N.

River Yare and Great Yarmouth Haven
9.71

1   From a position E of Brush Lighthouse, the River Yare runs 2 miles N to Haven Bridge. This part of the river forms the haven, which has a generally uniform width of about 80 m. A gas pipeline (see 1.36) crosses the haven at its S end. Warning notices (diamond shaped, yellow, black letters) indicate its landing places.

2   Haven Bridge is a lifting bridge with a vertical clearance of 2·3 m when closed and a width of 26·8 m when open.

Brush Lighthouse and Front leading light (9.70)

(Original dated 1998)

(Photograph - Naval Party 1016)

Lights mark the navigation span. Advance application is required for the bridge to be opened.

Useful marks
9.72

1   Church (tower) (52°36'·1N, 1°43'·9E).
    Church (tower) (52°34'·7N, 1°43'·6E).

Berths
9.73

1   Apart from the berths used in support of offshore activities the main berths from the S are:

    E bank: East Quay, length 260 m, depth alongside 5 m; Ocean Terminal, length 140 m, depth alongside 5·5 m; Atlas Quay length 460 m with Ro-Ro berth; South Quay, length 470 m, depth alongside 5 m.

    W bank: Bollard Quay, length 300 m, depth alongside 4·5 m.

Port services
9.74
1   **Repairs** of all types can be carried out.
9.75
1   **Other facilities:** ship domestic waste disposal; deratting; customs; hospitals, one with helicopter landing site. Oily waste reception available.
9.76
1   **Supplies:** all types of fuel from facilities on either bank; water at most berths; stores and provisions.
9.77
1   **Communications.** The River Yare is joined by the River Bure close N of Haven Bridge (9.71). Thence it runs 3½ miles WSW under Breydon Bridge and through Breydon Water to be joined by the River Waveney. The three rivers provide over 120 miles of inland navigation and access to Norwich, Coltishall and Beccles and to the Lowestoft and Norwich Navigation (9.121).

Small craft
9.78
1   There are limited berthing facilities for small craft at Town Hall Quay.

The opening span of Breydon Bridge (9.77) is 23 m. When closed the fixed spans provide the greater vertical clearance of 4·5 m. Vessels should use the fixed span on the starboard side of the channel.

SOUTH APPROACH TO GREAT YARMOUTH TO NORTH APPROACH TO LOWESTOFT

General information

Chart 1536
Routes
9.79
1   In addition to the inshore route from the N (9.46-9.47), Great Yarmouth can be approached from the E through Holm Channel, thence from the S through Gorleston Road.

Lowestoft can be approached from the E through Holm Channel thence from the N through Corton Road and Lowestoft North Road.

2   These routes are described below.

Lowestoft can also be approached from the S through Stanford Channel. This route is described at 9.114.

Caution. Changes in the sandbanks and channels are frequent. No channel should be used unless it is buoyed, even if the charted depths appear sufficient; experience has shown that changes in channels which are not buoyed are more frequent than elsewhere.

3   Due to these rapid changes, buoyage may be altered before the relevant Notice to Mariners has been published.

Topography
9.80
1   From the entrance to Great Yarmouth Haven (52°34′N, 1°44′E), the coast runs 5½ miles SSE to Lowestoft Ness, the E most point of England. The entrance to Lowestoft Harbour is 6 cables SSW of Lowestoft Ness. The coast as far as Corton village, 3½ miles S of Great Yarmouth Haven, consists of cliffs up to 17 m high composed of sand gravel and red loam. To the S of Corton the coast is low-lying and sandy.

2   The 5 m depth contour lies close to the coast between Lowestoft Ness and Great Yarmouth Haven.

Offshore the chain of sandbanks (9.40) continues to the S, protecting the seaward side of the various roads which lead to Great Yarmouth and Lowestoft.

Controlling depths
9.81
1   Depths in Holm Channel are of the order of 6·5 to 8 m, but are constantly changing and the charts and Yarmouth Pilots should be consulted for the latest information.

Depths are greater than 10 m in Gorleston Road, Corton Road and North Lowestoft Road to a position 1½ miles NE of the entrance to Lowestoft Harbour.

Movement reporting
9.82
1   Vessels on passage which pass close to Lowestoft are recommended to obtain details of vessel traffic movements from the Port Operations Service. See the relevant *Admiralty List of Radio Signals.*

Rescue
9.83
1   There is a Coastguard Rescue Team at Lowestoft; see 1.53.

An all-weather lifeboat is stationed in the Outer Harbour at Lowestoft. See 1.61 for details of lifeboat.

Tidal streams
9.84
1   In Corton Road and North Lowestoft Road the tidal streams probably run in the direction of the coast. East of Holm and Newcome Sands the tidal streams appear to be deflected E by the shoals in the vicinity. For details see information on the chart.

2   For tidal streams off and in the entrance to Lowestoft see 9.108.

Principal marks
9.85
1   **Landmarks:**
     For marks at Great Yarmouth see 9.69.
     Corton Church (tower) (52°31′N, 1°45′E).
     Building (St Peter Court Flats) (52°29′N, 1°45′E).
     Silo (52°28′N, 1°45′E).
   Major light:
     Lowestoft Light (52°29′·2N, 1°45′·5E) (9.12).

Useful Mark
9.86
1   Hotel   Tower   (52°33′·7N,   1°43′·9E)   at Gorleston-on-Sea.

Other navigational aids
9.87
1   **Racon:**
     Cross Sand Light-buoy (52°37′N, 1°59′E).
   DGPS:
     North Foreland (51°22′N, 1°27′E) (*Dover Strait Pilot*).

Directions
(continued from 9.37)

Holm Channel
9.88
1   From the vicinity of Corton Light-buoy (E cardinal) (52°31′N, 1°52′E), the route leads 3 miles NW through Holm Channel to the junction between Gorleston Road to the N and Corton Road to the S. Holm Channel is buoyed and lies between Corton Sand (9.47) and Holm Sand (9.37). See caution 9.79.

St. Margaret's Church spire

Lowestoft Light   *Monument*

Landmarks at Lowestoft (9.85)

(Original dated 2000)

(Photograph - Air Images)

Corton Church (9.85)

(Original dated 2000)

(Photograph - Air Images)

Gorleston Road to Great Yarmouth
9.89

1   From the S end of Gorleston Road, the route leads 2 miles N through the Road to position E of the entrance to Great Yarmouth Haven (52°34′N, 1°44′E), passing (with positions from the Haven entrance):

2   W of Corton Sand (2 miles E) (9.47), marked on its W side by W Corton Light-buoy (W cardinal), which also marks the E side of the fairway, thence:
          To a position E of the haven entrance.
          (Directions continue for Great Yarmouth at 9.70)

Corton Road to Lowestoft
9.90

1   From the N end of Corton Road the route leads 4 miles S through the Road and thence Lowestoft North Road to a position NE of the entrance to Lowestoft, passing (with positions from Corton Church (52°31′N, 1°45′E)):

2   W of Holm Sand (3 miles SE) (9.37) which extends 3½ miles S to a position E of the entrance to Lowestoft. Holm Sand is marked on its W side by NW Holm, W Holm and SW Holm Light-buoys (all starboard hand). These buoys also mark the E side of the fairway through Corton Road and Lowestoft North Road. Thence:

3   To a position E of Lowestoft Ness (2¾ miles SSE) (9.80) and NE of the entrance to Lowestoft. An obstruction marked by light-buoys (N side-E cardinal, S side-S cardinal) lies 3 cables E of the Ness.

4   **Caution.** There are numerous groynes, most marked by beacons (triangular topmarks, but can-shaped close to Lowestoft) along the coast, which are a danger to craft close inshore.

(Directions continue for Lowestoft at 9.112)

Anchorages
9.91

1   **Corton Road** affords a good anchorage between Corton Sand (9.47) and the coast, blue clay and mud, in depths of 8·4 to 12·9 m.

2   **Lowestoft North Road** affords an anchorage between Holm Sand (9.37) and the coast, sand and gravel, in depths of 6·2 to 16 m. This anchorage is exposed to E winds which cause a short, choppy sea in some respects worse than the sea outside the sandbanks. A number of submarine cables running in an E direction from Lowestoft Ness cross the S part of Lowestoft North Road.

LOWESTOFT AND SOUTH APPROACH

General information

Chart 1536 plans of Approaches to Lowestoft and Lowestoft Harbour
Position
9.92

1   Lowestoft (52°28′N, 1°45′E) stands on the summit and slopes of a steep bank with many trees on it. The town shows up well from seaward.

Function
9.93

1 Lowestoft is an important fishing and commercial port, with a modern fish market and processing facilities and the ability to handle a wide range of bulk, container and general cargoes. It is also a major centre for servicing the offshore oil and gas industry, and a large fleet of supply and safety vessels operates from the port. Rig structures and modules are fabricated, and there are extensive ship repair facilities.

2 The population of Lowestoft was 67 000 in 1999.

Traffic
9.94

1 In 1999 the port was used by 1251 commercial vessels and 3442 fishing vessels.

Port authority
9.95

1 Associated British Ports, Port House, Lowestoft NR32 1BG.

Limiting conditions
9.96

1 **Controlling depths.** A maintained channel, depth 4·7 m, leads from the harbour entrance to a position 6½ cables W of the lifting bridge (9.115). The channel is liable to silting, but this is soon cleared by dredgers. Further W the channel progressively reduces in depth to 1·8 m at the W end of Lake Lothing (9.107). There are tide gauges in Bridge Channel.

2 **Deepest and longest berth.** Cargo Terminal (9.117).

Tidal levels: see *Admiralty Tide Tables*. Mean spring range about 1·9; mean neap range about 1 m.

9.97

1 **Sea levels.** Winds from the ENE through S to SW depress the sea level, while winds from the other directions raise it. A wind from the ESE force 3 to 4 can depress the sea level by about 0·1 m and a NW wind force 3 to 4 can raise it by a similar amount. It is reported that strong winds and gales can raise or depress sea levels by as much as 1·2 m.

2 Such changes in sea level have several consequences. At neaps sea level may rise continuously during the normal period of the falling tide or at springs the normal in-going and out-going streams may be nearly cancelled. There may also be seiches of considerable range. During strong N gales the rising tide may be interrupted frequently by falls and the falling tide by rises.

3 In these circumstances the tidal streams at the entrance and in the harbour are equally affected and may change from in-going to out-going and the reverse, at frequent intervals, attaining a rate of up to 4 kn at the bridge in extreme conditions. See also Tidal streams 9.108.

9.98

1 **Maximum size of vessel handled.** The port can accept vessels up to 125 m in length and draught 6·0 m at MHWS.

Arrival information

Port operations
9.99

1 **Port radio.** Lowestoft Harbour Control maintains constant watch on VHF; for details see the relevant *Admiralty List of Radio Signals*.

Traffic signals
9.100

1 International port traffic signals (see *The Mariner's Handbook*) are in force for the control of shipping. They are shown from the light-tower on South Pier, as follows:

Signal	Meaning
Three vertical red lights exhibited vertically	Vessels shall not proceed.
Green, white, green lights exhibited vertically	A vessel may proceed only when it has received specific orders to do so.

2 The above signals are also shown from the E arm of the Yacht Basin entrance, and are used to control exit from the basin. These signal lights are only visible from inside the basin; there are no signal lights for vessels entering the Yacht Basin. Vessels should therefore proceed with caution when entering and leaving the basin.

3 **Note.** In the interests of safety, all vessels must observe these international port signals and navigate with the understanding that the Port Control, and departing vessels in the Outer Harbour, have extremely limited vision to the N of the entrance piers.

4 Small craft without VHF may consider the green, white, green signal in favour of proceeding with extreme caution and navigational courtesy.

9.101

1 The Lowestoft Harbour Bridge (9.115) will be opened only on demand for commercial shipping. Shipping is discouraged from passage during the periods 0815–0900, 1230–1300, and 1700–1730 daily. Small craft and yachts may use the bridge opening for commercial traffic if prior arrangement has been made with Lowestoft Harbour Control. In addition, and subject to prior notification of 20 minutes, small craft and yachts might be given a bridge opening at the following times:

2 Monday-Friday 0700, 0930, 1100, 1600, 1900 and 2100.

Saturday, Sunday and public holidays 0745, 0930, 1100, 1400, 1730, 1900 and 2100.

3 Navigation in the bridge channel is controlled by VHF, see the relevant *Admiralty List of Radio Signals,* with additional amber and green "traffic lights" when the bridge is operated. Large vessels may not approach within 137 m of the bridge unless so directed.

Notice of ETA
9.102

1 Twenty-four hours' notice of ETA is required. Vessels should confirm ETA 3 hours and 1 hour before arrival, stating preferred pilot boarding position. See the relevant *Admiralty List of Radio Signals* for details.

Outer anchorages
9.103

1 A recommended anchorage in depths of 15 to 21 m, shown on the chart, lies 4 miles SSE of the harbour entrance. For anchorages N of Lowestoft see 9.50 and 9.91.

Pilots and tugs
9.104

1 Pilotage is compulsory for all vessels carrying dangerous cargo and other vessels over 60 m in length, except those exempt by law and those on passage through the area of compulsory jurisdiction.

2 Lowestoft pilots are able to provide pilotage through Holm Channel for Lowestoft bound vessels, see 9.63. Otherwise pilots board vessels approaching from the N in

Trawl Dock   *Waveney Dock*   *Hamilton Dock*

Yacht Basin

Lowestoft Outer Harbour from S (9.107)

(Original dated 2000)

(Photograph - Air Images)

the vicinity of W Holm Light-buoy (52°30′N, 1°47′E) at the Lowestoft Inner Boarding Ground and for vessels from the S at the Lowestoft South Boarding Ground, 7 cables ENE of Newcome Sand Light-buoy (port hand) (52°26′N, 1°47′E), which marks the S limit of the Stanford Channel (9.114). During bad weather pilots will only embark and disembark at the Lowestoft Inner Boarding Ground.

3   Vessels waiting for a pilot should not approach closer than these limits. The pilot vessel keeps watch when a vessel is expected and has a dark hull, orange upperworks with "PILOT" painted on each side. See the relevant *Admiralty List of Radio Signals*.

Tugs are available.

Local knowledge
9.105

1   In view of the continually changing nature of the shoals in the approaches to Lowestoft, especially from the S, local knowledge is essential. For first time visitors the services of a pilot are recommended. See caution 9.79.

Speed
9.106

1   The maximum speed for vessels, except HM Ships, is 4 kn. Because the harbour is narrow vessels are required to proceed at the minimum safe speed to avoid interaction with moored vessels and pontoons. This applies especially to large displacement vessels underway at LW.

Harbour

Layout
9.107

1   The harbour is entirely artificial and consists of Outer and Inner Harbours. Outer Harbour, mainly used by fishing vessels and vessels connected with North Sea oil and gas

fields, comprises Trawl, Waveney and Hamilton Docks to the N and Yacht Basin to the S.

2   North Pier, which forms the seaward side of Waveney Dock, is the site for oil platform module fabrication. Platforms under construction can be conspicuous.

3   Inner Harbour formed by Lake Lothing, is used by general commercial, offshore supply and large safety vessels. It is approached through the Outer Harbour and Bridge Channel which is spanned by a double leaf bascule bridge (9.115). There are a number of berths along the banks of the lake.

Tidal streams
9.108

1   In the entrance to Lowestoft Harbour the tidal streams are strong and complex. See also Sea levels 9.97.

The tidal streams set as follows:

Time from Remarks
HW Dover

Outside the entrance

−0610	S-going stream begins
+0010	N-going stream begins. Spring rate in each direction 2½ kn.

2   Across the entrance

+0555	S-going stream begins.
HW	N-going stream begins. However within 90 m of the entrance the S-going stream runs strongly for 3 hours, then is much reduced or even forms a N-going eddy advancing the start of the N-going stream to between −0415 and −0315 Dover.

3   In the entrance

+0430   In-going stream begins.

–0145   Out-going stream begins. At springs the in-going rate is 2 kn for 3 hours, after which it is much weaker; the out-going rate is 1 kn. At neaps both rates are ½ kn.

9.109

1   After HW Lowestoft, the N-going stream produces a strong N set across the harbour entrance, which is met by the out-going stream. Together these run NE along North Pier extension. In these conditions a vessel entering will have the out-going stream on her starboard bow, while the N-going stream is on her port quarter, resulting in a tendency to sheer towards South Pier as the entrance is approached.

2   When the S-going stream and in-going streams are running, a SW stream results along North Pier extension and into the harbour or across South Pier, and a vessel will tend to be swept onto South Pier as the entrance is approached.

Principal marks
9.110

1   **Landmarks:**
Building (St Peter Court Flats) (52°29′N, 1°45′E).
Water tower (52°27′N, 1°44′E).
Silo (52°28′N, 1°45′E).
St Margaret's Church Spire (52°29′·2N, 1°44′·6E).
Kessingland Church (tower) (52°25N, 1°43E).
Major light:
Lowestoft Light (52°29′·2N, 1°45′·5E) (9.12).

Other navigational aid
9.111

1   **DGPS:**
North Foreland (51°22′N, 1°27′E) (*Dover Strait Pilot*).

Directions
(continued from 9.90)

General
9.112

1   To minimise the effects of the tidal streams at the harbour entrance (9.108) it is recommended that vessels enter harbour on the in-going stream and depart on the out-going stream. The optimum time to enter Lowestoft is 1 hour before local HW, when the tidal streams across the entrance should be weak. Whether approaching from the N or S, the approach should be made as slowly as possible until about 100 m off the entrance when speed should be increased and the appropriate wheel applied to maintain the centreline of the entrance.

2   Entry is feasible during E gales just after LW as the offshore sandbanks make an excellent breakwater. Entry is not advisable for large or low powered vessels during SE gales.

Entry from the North
9.113

1   From a position about 1 mile NE of the harbour entrance the line of bearing 226° of the head of Claremont Pier (5 cables SSW of the harbour entrance) leads to a position 1 cable ESE of the harbour entrance whence direct approach to the entrance can be made, passing (with positions from the harbour entrance):

2   ESE of a pair of light-buoys (E and S cardinal), marking an obstruction with 4·7 m over it (7½ cables NE), thence:
Over The Ridge (5 cables NE), a shingle bank with depths of 4·2 to 5·2 m over it.Thence:
NW of N Newcome Light-buoy (port hand), marking the NE extremity of Newcome Sand (9.114) (5½ cables E), thence:

3   NW of Lowestoft Bank (4½ cables ESE), which connects to the N part of Newcome Sand (9.114) and to the W with the coastal bank which extends from the shore close S of the harbour entrance. Lowestoft Bank has depths of approximately 2 m over it. Thence:

4   To the harbour entrance which is 45 m wide and lies between North and South Piers. North Pier and its extension runs 3 cables SW from the NE corner of the harbour. South Pier extends 2 cables E from the shore along the S side of the harbour. Similar lights (white tower on small pavilion, 9 m in height, floodlit) are exhibited from the pierheads.

5   **Caution.** A wall on North Pier, 3 m high, partially prevents small boats leaving Waveney Dock from seeing or being seen.

Stanford Channel
9.114

1   Stanford Channel, marked by light-buoys, lies between Holm Sand (9.37) and Newcome Sand, a series of shoal patches running ENE/WSW. The N part of the shoal, 1 mile SSE of the harbour entrance, is the most significant feature with depths of less than 1 m.

2   From a position ENE of Newcome Sand Light-buoy (9.104) the route leads 1½ miles NNW following the Stanford Channel to a position E of The Ridge (9.113) to join the route from the N as described in 9.113 above. S Holm Light-buoy (S cardinal) marks the S extremity of Holm Sand.
See caution 9.79.

Harbour entrance to Inner Harbour
9.115

1   From the harbour entrance the route follows the dredged channel, which is 40 m wide, in a generally WNW direction 2½ cables through Outer Harbour to the bascule bridge thence into Inner Harbour, passing (with positions from the bridge):
SSW of the entrance to Waveney Dock (2 cables E) which leads to Hamilton Dock, thence:
S of the entrance to Trawl Dock (1 cable E), thence:

2   To Bridge Channel which is 22·7 m wide and lies between Inner N and Inner S Piers and leads to the Inner Harbour. The Lowestoft Harbour (Bascule) Bridge is only opened on demand for commercial shipping, see 9.101. When closed, the bridge has a clearance of 2·2 m at MHWS (approximately 2·4 m on the tide gauge) with a reduction of 0·5 m for the arch sides.

Useful marks
9.116

1   Saint Margaret's Church Spire (52°29′·2N, 1°44′·6E).
Water tower (52°27′·2N, 1°43′·8E).
Pakefield Church (tower) (52°27′·2N, 1°44′·2E).
Water tower (52°26′·8N, 1°43′·6E).

Basins and berths

9.117

1   **Outer Harbour.** There are 1400 m of quays available with depths alongside of 3 to 5 m.

Inner Harbour. There are about 2000 m of quays mainly on the N side of Lake Lothing. Cargo Terminal, about 6½ cables W of the bridge, has a length of 150 m and depth alongside of 4·7 m. CEFAS Quay, 2 cables W of the bridge has been dredged to 6 m below chart datum, but silts to normal channel depth.

Port services

9.118

1   **Repairs.** The local shipyards can undertake repairs of all types. There are several slipways and the largest is capable of taking vessels up to 55 m in length and 800 dwt.

There is a dry dock, length 76 m, width 14·5 m and depths below chart datum of 2·2 m at the blocks at the entrance and 1·8 m at the head.

9.119

1   **Other facilities:**

Limited salvage capability.

Hospital.

Facilities available for the reception of oily waste, noxious and harmful substances.

Helicopter landing by arrangement with the port authority.

9.120

1   **Supplies:** Fuel is available at Hamilton Quay in Hamilton Dock, and by road tanker at other berths; ice is available at Waveney Dock; fresh water at the quays; stores and provisions available locally.

9.121

1   **Communications.** The Lowestoft and Norwich Navigation, which passes through Lake Lothing to Oulton Broad and Oulton Dyke, provides access for small craft via the Rivers Waveney and Yare to Norwich.

Small craft

9.122

1   There are pontoon moorings for small craft in the Yacht Basin; the Royal Norfolk and Suffolk Yacht Club should be consulted. Lowestoft Cruising Club has established a marina on the N shore of Lake Lothing 2 cables E of Mutford Bridge Lock, which connects the lake to Oulton Broad. There are other moorings for small craft at Oulton Broad Yacht Station, managed by Waveney District Council. These moorings lie in Oulton Broad close SW of Mutford Bridge Lock.

2   Small craft may pass through the bascule bridge (9.115) with larger vessels provided prior arrangement has been made with Lowestoft Harbour Control, see 9.101.

Mutford Lock and bridges.

9.123

1   The lock, with safe usable dimensions of 22 m in length and 6·5 m in width, has a depth of 2 m plus tidal variations and should be used by craft suitable for the depth of Oulton Broad. Visiting craft with a draught exceeding 1·7 m should seek advice from Mutford Lock staff and consider Oulton Broad tide which is approximately 3 hours after Lowestoft with a mean range of 0·7 m.

2   Mutford Road Bridge, adjacent to the lock, has a clearance of 2·1 m at MHWS (approximately 2·4 m on the Lowestoft tide gauge) and it is therefore essential for all craft requiring an opening to make an advance booking and to be prepared to wait. Such bookings will automatically

include Carlton Road Bridge located close E. VHF is occasionally monitored by Mutford Bridge Control. See the relevant *Admiralty List of Radio Signals*.

3   Craft entering with a fixed air draught of more than 7·3 m are confined to the River Waveney by fixed bridges.

There is a measured distance (920 m) for small craft in the River Waveney above Oulton Broad. It is controlled by the local authority.

LOWESTOFT APPROACHES TO SOUTHWOLD

General information

Chart 1543

Route

9.124

1   From a position NE of Holm Sand (52°30′N, 1°48′E) the coastal route leads 15 miles SSW to a position ESE of Southwold.

Topography

9.125

1   South of Lowestoft the offshore banks merge with the coastal bank and close the shore in the vicinity of Benacre Ness (9.130), 5 miles S of Lowestoft. Thence the 5 m depth contour lies 3 to 4 cables to seaward and parallel to the shore.

2   The coast generally consists of low cliffs interspersed with beaches. For about 2 miles to the S of Benacre Ness the coast is eroding and after HW springs or storms debris such as tree trunks may be encountered offshore.

Rescue

9.126

1   There is a Coastguard Rescue Team at Southwold. See 1.53.

An inshore lifeboat is stationed at Southwold. For details of lifeboat see 1.62.

Tidal streams

9.127

1   Details of the tidal streams are given on the charts.

Principal marks

9.128

1   **Landmarks:**

For marks at Lowestoft see 9.110.

Kessingland Church (tower) (52°25′N, 1°43′E).

Covehithe Church (tower) (52°23′N, 1°42′E).

Southwold Church (tower) (52°20′N, 1°41′E).

Water tower (3 cables W of Church tower) at Southwold.

2   **Major light:**

Lowestoft Light (52°29′·2N, 1°45′·5E) (9.12).

Southwold Light (52°19′·6N, 1°41′·0E) (9.12).

Other navigational aid

9.129

1   **DGPS:**

North Foreland (51°22′N, 1°27′E) (*Dover Strait Pilot*).

Directions
(continued from 9.37)

9.130

1   From a position NE of Holm Sand (52°30′N, 1°38′E), the route leads 15 miles SSW to a position ESE of Southwold, passing (with positions from Benacre Ness (52°24′N, 1°44′E)):

Southwold Harbour (9.134)

(Original dated 2000)

(Photograph - Air Images)

ESE of Holm Sand (6 miles NNE) (9.37) and E of E Newcome port hand light-buoy (5·8 miles NNE) thence:

2 ESE of Newcome Sand (3½ miles NNE) (9.114), thence:

ESE of Barnard (1 mile NNE), an irregular shoal which is steep-to on its seaward side and is marked on its E side by E Barnard Light-buoy (E cardinal), thence:

3 ESE of Benacre Ness, a low indefinite point, with a well wooded and slightly undulating background. Thence:

To a position ESE of Southwold.

(Directions for passage S to the Thames Estuary and the Dover Strait are given in the Dover Strait Pilot.)

Southwold

Chart 2695 plan of Southwold Harbour
General information
9.131

1 Southwold (52°20′N, 1°41′E), a seaside resort, stands on a hill and is almost surrounded at HW by the River Blyth, Buss Creek and the sea. The harbour is used mainly by small fishing boats and recreational craft; in addition, 12 commercial vessels totalling 114 596 dwt used the port in 1999. Southwold Harbour is administered by Waveney District Council, Town Hall, Lowestoft.

The population was 3905 in 1991.

Limiting conditions
9.132

1 **Controlling depths.** The harbour is approached over a bar which has varying depths, usually between 0·5 and 2 m. Because of the changing nature of the bar the Harbour Master should be consulted before attempting to enter the harbour. Within the harbour there is a minimum depth in the channel of 1·4 m.

2 **Tidal levels:** see *Admiralty Tide Tables*. Mean spring range about 2·1 m; mean neap range about 1·3 m.

Local conditions. There is a confused sea in the entrance with an onshore wind and an out-going stream. If the wind is strong onshore then it is dangerous to cross the bar. Entry at LW with a strong out-going stream is also very difficult.

Arrival information
9.133

1 **Port radio** service on VHF is operated. For details see the relevant *Admiralty List of Radio Signals*.

Traffic signals. Three flashing red lights, disposed vertically, indicate that conditions are unsuitable for entering harbour and the port is closed. At other times three flashing green lights indicate that the port is open. These signals are exhibited from N pierhead.

2 An **anchorage**, shown on chart 1543, is available 7 cables ESE of the entrance to Southwold Harbour.

ETA should be sent 24 hours in advance if possible and confirmed 2 hours before arrival.

Pilotage. No pilot boat exists at Southwold, however remote pilotage on VHF is available on request. See the relevant *Admiralty List of Radio Signals*.

Harbour
9.134

1 **Layout.** The harbour is up to 64 m wide between The Quay on the N side and S pier. The Quay, which is in a poor state of repair and exposed to any swell, has a least depth alongside of 0·5 m. Most craft berth at upstream pontoons and jetties near the Harbour Master's office at Blackshore Quay.

2 **Tidal streams** are slack for a short period in the harbour entrance about 30 minutes after local HW. The spring out-going stream can attain a rate of 4 to 5 kn. The

stream scours the N bank of the harbour in the vicinity of The Quay displacing the channel to that side.

9.135

1 **Principal marks.**
Landmarks:
Southwold Church (52°19′·7N, 1°40′·8E) (chart 1543).
Water tower (52°19′·6N, 1°40′·4E) (chart 1543).
Major light:
Southwold Light (52°19′·6N, 1°40′·0E) (9.12) (chart 1543).

Directions

9.136

1 From a position SE of the harbour entrance the route is NW to the entrance crossing the bar, composed of sand and shingle, which varies with the season and the effect of wind and sea. The entrance is formed by two piers and is 46 m wide decreasing to 35 m within the pierheads. Lights (metal column, 3 m in height) are exhibited from each pierhead. Within the entrance the route follows the channel formed initially by the piers and then by the River Blyth. A recommended time to enter the harbour is 2 to 3 hours after the commencement of the in-going stream.

Port services

9.137

1 **Facilities:** hospital; helicopter landing site Southwold Common.

Supplies: marine diesel by road tanker; water at the quays; provisions and stores.

Small craft

9.138

1 There is a boatyard and boat slipway. Repairs to small craft can be made. There are berthing facilities for visiting small craft by prior arrangement with the Harbour Master.

The River Blyth is navigable by small craft for up to 5 miles to Blythburgh. A bridge, vertical clearance 2 m, spans the river 8½ cables above the harbour entrance. There is a barrage across Buss Creek at its junction with the River Blyth.

APPENDIX I

The Dockyard Port of Rosyth Order 1975

(As amended by **The Dockyard Port of Rosyth (Amendment) Order 1980**)

Made	*22nd October 1975*
Laid before Parliament	*29th October 1975*
Coming into Operation	*24th November 1975*

At the Court at Buckingham Palace, the 22nd day of October 1975

Present,

The Queen's Most Excellent Majesty in Council

Her Majesty, in pursuance of sections 3 and 5 of the Dockyard Ports Regulation Act 1865, of section 6 of that Act as amended by section 92(2) of, and Part II of Schedule 3 to, the Criminal Justice Act 1967, of Section 7 of that Act, and of all other powers enabling Her in that behalf, and, in so far as section 7 of the Act is concerned, on the joint recommendation of the Secretary of State for Defence and the Secretary of State for Trade, is pleased, by and with the advice of Her Privy Council, to order, and it is hereby ordered, as follows:

Commencement and Citation

1. This Order shall come into operation on the 24th day of November 1975 and may be cited as the Dockyard Port of Rosyth Order 1975.

Interpretation

2.-(1) The Interpretation Act 1889, shall apply to the interpretation of this Order as it applies to the interpretation of an Act of Parliament.

(2) In this Order the following expressions shall, unless the context otherwise requires, have the meanings respectively assigned to them, namely:–

"the Act" means the Dockyard Ports Regulation Act 1865;

"Collision Regulations" has the meaning assigned to that expression by section 418 of the Merchant Shipping Act 1894;

"the Dockyard Port" means the Dockyard Port of Rosyth as it is described in Article 3 hereof;

"master" means the person having command or charge of a vessel for the time being;

"power driven vessel" includes any vessel propelled by machinery;

"prolonged blast" means a blast of from four to six seconds duration;

"Queen's Harbour Master" means the person for the time being appointed under the Act to be Queen's Harbour Master for Rosyth and any person having authority to act as Queen's Harbour Master;

"short blast" means a blast of about one second's duration;

"under way" — a vessel is "under way" when she is not at anchor or made fast to the shore or aground;

"vessel" includes every description of water craft including non-displacement craft used or capable of being used as a means of transportation on water; battle-practice targets and other floating naval targets; and any of Her Majesty's ships and vessels in charge of Her Majesty's officers except where otherwise provided;

"whistle" means any vessel's whistle or siren.

Description of Limits

3. For the purposes of the Act and of this Order the limits of the Dockyard Port shall be as follows:–

All the Waters of the Firth of Forth and River Forth including all the bays, creeks, lakes, pools and rivers as far as the tide flows, excepting the Harbours of Charlestown, Inverkeithing, Port Edgar and South Queensferry, lying between the following meridians:–

3°15′ 20″ West and 3°33′ 48″ West.

Delineation of Limits

4. On the Chart Annexed to this Order are marked the limits of the Dockyard Port.

Regulations and Rules

5. The Regulations contained in the First Schedule hereto and the Rules contained in the Second Schedule hereto shall operate as therein provided within the limits (as described in Article 3 hereof) of the Dockyard Port, and if any inconsistency shall arise between the said Rules and any regulations at any time in force for preventing collisions at sea, the said Rules shall prevail.

Penalties

6.-(1) The master of every merchant or other private vessel shall observe and cause to be observed the Regulations contained in the First Schedule hereto, so far as they relate to his vessel, and any other master or other person who infringes any provision of the said Regulations or who fails to cause the same to be observed or who fails to observe any direction given thereunder or who fails to comply with any condition attached to a licence granted thereunder, shall commit an offence against this Order and shall for every such offence be liable to a penalty not exceeding the sum of £50.

(2) The master of every merchant or other private vessel shall comply with the Rules contained in the Second Schedule hereto and any such master, who by his wilful default infringes any of the said Rules, shall in respect of each offence by guilty of a misdemeanour.

Revocation

7. On the coming into operation of this Order the Orders in Council relating to the Dockyard Port dated the 30th day of July 1958, the 29th day of October 1965. the 20th day of December 1967, the 25th day of February 1970, and the 30th day of September 1970 are hereby revoked, without prejudice, however, to the validity of anything done thereunder or to any liability incurred in respect of any act or omission before the date of the coming into operation of this Order, and any licence or direction given or made thereunder, being a licence or direction which could be given or made under this Order, shall continue to have effect as if it were so given or made.

N.E. Leigh

FIRST SCHEDULE

Regulations

Moorings for Her Majesty's ships, etc.

1. Moorings for Her Majesty's vessels, buoys, light, marks, mark buoys and other aids to navigation, and such other buoys as may be required for any purpose in connection with naval, military or air force operations, may be placed by the Queen's Harbour Master in such positions as may be considered necessary for the requirements of Her Majesty's service.

Private Moorings

2. No person shall lay moorings for private vessels, hulks, rafts, pontoons, bathing stages, house boats, timber or any floating structures in the Dockyard Port, except with the licence in writing of the Queen's Harbour Master and in accordance with any conditions attached thereto, and all such moorings shall be in such positions as the Queen's Harbour Master shall deem fit, and shall be removed forthwith on the order of the Queen's Harbour Master.

Clearing anchors and moorings

3. If at any time the anchor of any merchant or other private vessel hooks any Crown moorings, or any electric cables, or moorings of buoys, or any pipe, the master of such vessel shall not proceed to unhook the same, but shall forthwith give notice thereto to the Queen's Harbour Master, in order that aid may be given for clearing such moorings or cables or pipe without doing damage to the same.

Shipkeepers

4. No merchant or other private vessel of above five metric tonnes, compelled or allowed to anchor in or near any of the navigable channels of the Dockyard Port, shall be left at any time without a shipkeeper.

Fishing

5.-(1) Any person fishing in the Dockyard Port may be required to comply with directions given to him by the Queen's Harbour Master.

(2) No fishing from boats or fishing by persons swimming under the water shall be carried on within 150 metres from the walls, slipways, roadways or boundaries of Her Majesty's naval establishments, or from any naval moorings, floating docks or dolphins or ships of Her Majesty save with the licence in writing of the Queen's Harbour Master and in accordance with any conditions attached thereto.

(3) No fishing may take place—
    (a) in the Protected Channel between Oxcars and Beamer Rock as defined in Rule 3(5) in the Second Schedule to this Order, and
    (b) in the approach channel for Beamer Rock to Her Majesty's Dockyard, Rosyth, bounded by a line joining the following positions:–
        (i) South Arm Light
        (ii) No. 6 buoy
        (iii) No. 4 buoy
        (iv) 56°00′20″North 03°24′47″West
        (v) 56°00′31″North 03°24′34″West
        (vi) No. 3 buoy
        (vii) "B" light-beacon
        (viii) "A" light-beacon except when the channel in which it is proposed to fish is clear of shipping.

Swimming and diving

6. No person shall swim or dive within 150 metres from the walls, slipways, roadways or boundaries of any of Her Majesty's naval establishments, or from any naval moorings, floating docks, dolphins or ships of Her Majesty, save with the licence in writing of the Queen's Harbour Master and in accordance with any conditions attached thereto.

Dumping of Rubbish, etc.

7. No person shall unload, cast or allow to fall—
    (a) into the waters of the Dockyard Port, except with the consent of the Queen's Harbour Master and in such places as he may appoint, or
    (b) upon the banks or any portion of the shores of the Dockyard Port where the same may be liable to be washed into the waters of the Dockyard Port by rain, tide or otherwise any ballast, stones, earth, clay, refuse, rubbish or any other substance or object which is or might become a hazard to navigation.

Use of whistles

8. A whistle shall not be used within the limits of the Dockyard Port except—
    (a) as a signal of distress; or
    (b) to prevent collisions; or
    (c) in fog, mist, falling snow, heavy rainstorms or any other conditions similarly affecting visibility; or
    (d) in accordance with the Rules contained in Schedule 2 to this Order and for the control of tugs; or
    (e) to test the whistle.

Reserved areas — marking, etc.

9. Whenever it may be necessary for mining or gunnery operations or experiments, dredging operations, or other naval, military or air force purposes, to reserve any area for such operations, experiments or purposes, the area will be marked by buoys or posts coloured yellow with topmarks or lights, where necessary, as laid down for special marks in the International Association of Lighthouse Authorities Maritime Buoyage System (Region "A"), and after twenty-one days' warning notice has been issued by the Ministry of Defence (Navy) and published in the Edinburgh Gazette, no vessel shall anchor within or pass through the area so marked, unless compelled to do so by stress of weather or to avoid an accident; nor when such area is uncovered or nearly uncovered at low water shall any person pass through or remain in it nor permit any vessel,

animal or thing to remain therein except in accordance with permission granted by the Queen's Harbour Master.

Anchorage.

10. All merchant and other private vessels within the limits of the Dockyard Port shall comply with any directions given by the Queen's Harbour Master with a view to the proper protection of Her Majesty's vessels and property.

11. No merchant or other private vessel shall make fast to, or lie at, any of the buoys marking the channels or shoals in the Dockyard Port.

12. Save with the licence in writing of the Queen's Harbour Master and in accordance with conditions attached thereto, no merchant or other private vessel shall be moored or fastened to any Crown moorings, buoys, breakwaters, boom defences, dolphins, jetties, piles or vessels in the Dockyard Port.

13. No merchant or other private vessel shall anchor or fish on the line of any electric cable or pipe laid down in the Dockyard Port, when such line is indicated by posts or other discernible marks on the shore or is shown on current Admiralty Charts, or within any area shown on current Admiralty Charts as an area in which anchorage is prohibited.

14. Save with the licence in writing of the Queen's Harbour Master and in accordance with any conditions attached thereto, no merchant or other private vessel shall be moored or anchored in the Dockyard Port within 180 metres from the centre of any of Her Majesty's moorings or from any of Her Majesty's docks, dockyards, arsenals, wharves, vessels, hulks, or powder magazines, or be moored, anchored or placed in the Dockyard Port, so as to give a foul berth to any vessel already at anchor or at moorings, or to obstruct the passage or entrance into the Dockyard or Dockyard Port.

15. No merchant or other private vessel shall lie or be moored so as to impede the free approach to any pier in the Dockyard Port used for purposes of regular passenger traffic, and when buoys are placed by the Queen's Harbour Master to mark an approach to such pier, no vessel shall lie within the space so marked.

Navigational marks.

16. No person shall trespass on, damage or without authority interfere with any light, beacon, sea-mark, tideboard, or buoy of any description in the Dockyard Port. This Regulation and Regulation 17 shall apply without prejudice to any right or jurisdiction of the Northern Lighthouse Board.

17. No person shall display any mark, light or beacon which, being visible from the waters of the Dockyard Port, is in the opinion of the Queen's Harbour Master liable to be confused with a navigational aid.

SECOND SCHEDULE

Rules

Observance of Regulations for preventing collisions at sea

1. All vessels when within the limits of the Dockyard Port shall, except as is otherwise provided in this Schedule, carry and use such lights and signals as are prescribed by the Collision Regulations and all vessels shall observe the steering and sailing rules set forth in such Regulations, except in so far as they are inconsistent with the Rules hereinafter contained.

2. (Deleted by Amending Order 1980).

3.-(1) On any occasion when it becomes necessary to ensure a clear passage within the Protected Channel, the Queen's Harbour Master will arrange with Forth Navigation Service to control movement of vessels accordingly. In addition, Ministry of Defence Police craft, exhibiting an all round blue flashing light, will patrol this vicinity to ensure compliance from small craft.

(2) Whenever such controls are in force, no vessel shall enter the Protected Channel or anchor or moor therein, and any vessel already within the Protected Channel shall forthwith leave that Channel and keep clear of it, except—

    (i)   the vessel in whose favour the signal is displayed;

    (ii) any tug or tugs attendant on her;

    (iii) any vessel secured alongside Hound Point Oil Terminal;

    (iv) any vessel specifically authorised by the Queen's Harbour Master or his representatives.

(3) (Deleted by Amending Order 1995)

(4) Whenever such controls are in force, the rules in paragraph 3(2) above are deemed to apply to the Protected Channel eastward of the Forth Railway Bridge only. Vessels intending to proceed eastward through the Forth Railway Bridge by way of the Protected Channel shall not approach the aforesaid bridge within a distance of half a nautical mile so long as the controls apply, unless they are permitted to do so by Rule 3(2)(iv).

(5) For the purposes of this Rule and Rule 5 the aforesaid Protected Channel comprises an area of water encompassed by a line joining the following positions, and as shown on the chart annexed to this Order:–

    (i)   56°01′ 46″ North 03°16′ 57″ West

    (ii)   56°00′ 43″ North 03°22′ 23″ West

    (iii)   56°00′ 16″ North 03°23′ 21″ West

    (iv)   56°00′ 14″ North 03°24′ 10″ West

    (v)   56°00′ 31″ North 03°24′ 34″ West

    (vi)   56°00′ 09″ North 03°25′ 00″ West

    (vii) 56°00′ 02″ North 03°24′ 10″ West

    (viii) 56°00′ 10″ North 03°23′ 18″ West

    (ix)   56°00′ 10″ North 03°22′ 02″ West

    (x)   56°01′ 31″ North 03°16′ 49″ West

and thence to (i) above.

(6) Whenever such controls are in force in favour of any vessel, that vessel shall exhibit the signal (shapes and lights) prescribed in the Collision Regulations for a vessel, restricted in her ability to manoeuvre. When by nature of her construction, a vessel is unable to display the prescribed signal, that signal is to be exhibited by the tug or tugs in attendance.

Passage through the Bridges at Queensferry

4. No vessel may pass another under the Forth Railway Bridge; subject to Rule 5, outgoing power driven vessels shall have priority through the aforesaid bridge over incoming power driven vessels, and incoming power driven vessels shall not approach the Forth Railway Bridge within

a distance of half a nautical mile until it shall have been ascertained that no vessel is coming out.

5.-(1) When the controls described in Rule 3(1) are in force, it shall be the duty of all vessels including those specifically authorised to enter or remain in the Protected Channel (as defined in Rule 3(5) above), to keep out of the way of the favoured vessel (as signified by the signals prescribed in Rule 3(6) above) in the vicinity of the Forth Railway Bridge, and not to approach the bridge until the Main Traffic Warning Light has been extinguished.

(2) In conditions where visibility is less than half a nautical mile (hereinafter referred to as conditions of poor visibility) no vessel may enter the Protected Channel in the area bounded by the Forth Railway Bridge to the east and by the meridian through the Beamer Rock Light to the west unless she has obtained clearance to do so from the Forth Navigation Service operated by the Forth Ports PLC. Vessels that are already within the said area at the time when conditions of poor visibility become applicable may proceed providing they do so with the utmost caution and comply with conditions hereinafter provided as to priority of passage. Subject to Rule 5(1) outgoing vessels shall have priory of passage over incoming vessels in the specified range.

Vessels crossing the River

6. Every vessel crossing from one side of the River towards the other side shall do so at a proper time having regard to vessels navigating up and down the River, and shall be navigated so as not to cause obstruction, injury or damage to any other vessel.

Vessel turning round

7. When a power driven vessel under way (including a tug with a tow) is about to turn round by night or by day, she shall signify the same by four short blasts on the whistle in rapid succession, followed after a short interval, if turning with her head to starboard, by one short blast, and if with her head to port, by two short blasts, and whilst turning shall repeat such signal to any approaching vessel. These sound signals and those prescribed by the following Rule are only to be used by vessels in sight of one another.

Signal directing vessels and boats to keep out of the way

8. When a power-driven vessel underway by day or by night is for any reason unable to manoeuvre as required by the Collision Regulations and these Rules, she shall signify the same to any approaching vessel in sight by sounding at intervals of not more than 2 minutes, three blasts of the whistle in succession, namely one prolonged blast followed by two short blasts.

9. (Deleted by Amending Order 1980).

Speed of vessels navigating the Dockyard Port

10. Without prejudice to any other obligation to navigate with due care and at a moderate speed, all power driven vessels when navigating the waters of the Dockyard Port shall (except for such purpose and subject to such conditions as may be specified in a licence in writing given by the Queen's Harbour Master) observe the following speed restrictions:–
   (a) When East of the Forth Railway Bridge:
      (i)   vessels exceeding 100 metres in length — 12 knots over the ground;
      (ii) vessels less than 100 metres in length — 15 knots over the ground.
   (b) When West of the Forth Railway Bridge: All vessels — 12 knots over the ground.
   (c) All vessels regardless of length shall not exceed a speed of 10 knots over the ground when within 5 cables of a vessel lying alongside Crombie Jetty or Hound Point Terminal or when within 5 cables of a vessel at anchor or at a buoy.

Marking wrecks and submerged obstructions

11. Should any vessel sink, be stranded, or become a wreck in any part of the Dockyard Port so that an obstruction is caused, or is likely to be caused, the master or owner of such vessel shall immediately notify the Queen's Harbour Master. If in his opinion it is necessary, the Queen's Harbour Master may arrange to mark any wreck or obstruction by the appropriate New Danger buoy as laid down in the International Association of Lighthouse Authorities Maritime Buoyage System (Region "A").

EXPLANATORY NOTES

(These Notes are not part of the Order)

1. This Order is made under the Dockyard Ports Regulation Act 1865, which provides for defining the limits of a dockyard port, the appointment of a Queen's Harbour Master for the port, the making of regulations to govern the mooring or anchoring of vessels and the making of rules concerning the lights or signals to be carried or used and the steps for avoiding collision by vessels navigating the waters of the port.

2. The Order supersedes the Dockyard Port of Rosyth Order 1958 and subsequent amending Orders. Apart from minor amendments such as metrication changes, the Order—
   (a) defines the limit of the dockyard port more accurately;
   (b) redefines the area of the Protected Channel in which HM vessels have priority when passing through the Dockyard Port and provides for such priority to be extended to certain other vessels;
   (c) redefines the area within which fishing restrictions apply so as to align it with the Protected Channel;
   (d) makes minor amendments to the Rules governing the navigation of vessels through the Forth Railway Bridge.

3. *The Dockyard Port of Rosyth (Amendment) Order 1980* amends the Dockyard Port of Rosyth Order 1975 by altering the Rules contained in that Order regarding passage through the bridges at Queensferry.

4. The Order makes provision for:
   (a) The introduction of the International Association of Lighthouse Authorities Maritime Buoyage System (Region "A");
   (b) The introduction of the International Regulations for Preventing Collisions at Sea 1972;
   (c) The exclusion of the Harbour of Port Edgar from the limits of the Dockyard Port.

APPENDIX II

Extracts from Forth Byelaws and General Directions for Navigation.

Part II — Lights, Daymarks and Signals

Deep-draughted vessels

15. A vessel having a draught in excess of 10 metres and navigating in the fairway west of the Fairway Buoy, may exhibit the lights or signals for vessels constrained by their draught in Rule 28 of the International Regulations for Preventing Collisions at Sea, 1972 as amended by Resolution A 464 (xii) of the International Maritime Organisation.

Vessel entering a fairway

16. A power-driven vessel about to enter a fairway from a dock, lock, basin, wharf, jetty or anchorage shall sound one prolonged blast.

Forth Railway Bridge

17. When the North Queensferry Signal Station Traffic Light is in operation no vessel shall pass under the north or south arch of the Forth Railway Bridge.

Kincardine-on-Forth Road Bridge

18. A vessel intending to pass under the Bridge shall give one prolonged blast of the whistle.

Part III — Navigation

Notice of arrival, departure or movement

19. Without prejudice to any directions issued by the Forth Navigation Service, the master of every vessel which trades to sea shall, whenever practicable, give prior notice to the harbour master of that vessel's arrival, departure or movement.

Working anchorages and mooring buoys

20. Vessels (other than vessels or boats engaged in rescue work) must keep clear and reduce speed when passing close to vessels and barges at the following anchorages and mooring buoys lying to the south of Burntisland.

Anchorage B (2) 56°02'·70 North, 03°12'·85 West.
Anchorage B (4) 56°02'·88 North, 03°13'·65 West.
Anchorage B (5) 56°02'·73 North, 03°14'·17 West.

Master or competent person to remain on bridge

21. The master of every power-driven vessel underway shall either be on the bridge or control position of the vessel himself or ensure that there is on the bridge or control position a member of the crew who is capable of taking command of the vessel and, when the pilot is on board, is capable of understanding the pilot's directions.

Notice to be given of incidents

25. The Master of a vessel which has been in collision or on fire, or has sustained damage or which has caused damage to other vessels or property shall give immediate notice of the incident to the harbour master and where the damage to the vessel is such that it affects or is likely to affect her seaworthiness the master thereof shall not move the vessel, other than to clear the fairway or moor or anchor in safety, except with the permission of the harbour master and in accordance with his directions.

Notice to be given of damaged vessels

26. The master of a vessel:–
(a) which has sustained damage outside the area of the Authority which affects or is likely to affect her seaworthiness, or

(b) from which oil or some dangerous or flammable substance is escaping or is likely to escape;
shall give notice thereof to the harbour master and the vessel shall not proceed west of Fairway Buoy 56°03'·50 North, 03°00'·00 West except with the permission of the harbour master and in accordance with his directions.

Vessels not to obstruct fairways

27. A vessel whether under power or sail which is not confined to a fairway shall not make use of a fairway so as to cause an obstruction to other vessels which can navigate only within such fairway and shall give such vessels a clear course and as wide a berth as safe navigation requires.

Vessels entering or crossing a fairway

28. Notwithstanding the Collision Regulations, no vessel shall enter or cross a fairway except when the fairway in the vicinity of the vessel is clear and only in such a manner as not to impede or endanger other vessels navigating in the fairway.

Hound Point Marine Terminal

34.(a) Vessels must reduce speed if necessary and must not approach within 100 metres when passing vessels berthed at Hound Point Marine Terminal.

Kincardine-on-Forth Road Bridge

35.(a) Only one vessel at a time shall approach the Bridge with the intention of passing under the Bridge.
(b) In the event of vessels approaching the Bridge from opposite directions, the vessel or vessels from seaward shall have precedence. A vessel or vessels outward bound from Alloa shall not pass a line 1000 metres from the Bridge until it is evident that no vessel is attempting inward passage.
(c) In the event of two or more vessels abreast or nearly abreast approaching the Bridge from the same direction the vessel to starboard shall have precedence and this precedence is to be given in sequence from starboard to port.
(d) There is to be a distance of at least 600 metres between vessels when about to pass under the Bridge.
(e) Vessels are to approach the Bridge at reduced speed which must not exceed 10 knots over the ground.
(f) No vessel is to anchor in the fairway within 1000 metres of the Bridge.
(g) All other vessels are to keep out of the way of any vessel approaching the Bridge and intending to pass under the Bridge.

Forth Road Bridge

36. Vessels must not approach within 100 metres of the main piers of the Forth Road Bridge.

Braefoot Marine Terminal

37.(a) No vessel shall enter Mortimer's Deep without the express permission of the harbour master unless the vessel is destined for Braefoot Marine Terminal.
(b) No vessel shall enter Mortimer's Deep when a vessel is berthed at the Braefoot Marine Terminal or when any vessel is bound for such Terminal or manoeuvring in the vicinity of Mortimer's Deep. This byelaw shall not apply to a second vessel or harbour craft bound for such Terminal except that the second vessel or harbour craft shall not enter Mortimer's

Deep until the first vessel is securely berthed at such Terminal.

Part IV — Anchoring and mooring

Master to apply for an anchorage etc

38.(a) On arrival of a vessel in the Forth, the master shall forthwith apply to the harbour master for an anchorage, mooring or berth and shall not change such without his approval.

Vessels not to anchor in a fairway

46. Except in an emergency, no vessel shall anchor in a fairway or in any other area which has been designated a prohibited anchorage as shown on the largest scale Admiralty Chart published for the area.

Immobilisation of vessels

47. No vessel shall be immobilised for any purpose except with the permission of the harbour master and subject to any conditions he may reasonably impose.

Part V — Miscellaneous

Rubbish not to be thrown into the Forth or on the shore

59. No person shall cast, deposit or throw or cause or procure to be cast, deposited or thrown any dirt, rubbish, soil, ashes, plastic or other matter or put or cause or procure or allow to fall or flow any offensive or injurious matter or thing whether solid or liquid into the Forth or upon the shores of any part thereof. The provisions of this Byelaw shall not apply to the discharge or escape of any substance the discharge or escape of which is subject to the provisions of or exempted in terms of an Act of Parliament.

General Directions for Navigation in the Forth

Clearance of outward or shifting vessels

4. This direction applies to every vessel which is berthed or anchored within the port and which proposes to navigate any part of the port whether for the purpose of departing from or shifting within the said limits.

(a) **Condition of Navigating Equipment** Before navigating within the port, the master of every vessel (other than pleasure craft having an overall length of less than 12 metres and which are not used wholly or mainly for the carriage of passengers for reward) shall ensure that the equipment for navigating is in order. In the case of a vessel carrying Dangerous or Polluting Goods or a tanker with uncleaned tanks which last carried petroleum, gas or chemical products, the master thereof shall confirm to the Harbour Master (Grangemouth) or (Leith) as appropriate, or in the case of departure from any other Forth harbour or terminal, to the Forth Navigation Service that such equipment is in full working order before commencing navigation

(b) **Notification of Departure** The master of the vessel shall inform the Forth Navigation Service of his intention to navigate at least sixty minutes prior to intended departure.

(c) The master of the vessel which proposes to commence navigating must:

(1) give at least ten minutes notification to the Forth Navigation Service of his intention to do so; and

(2) obtain a clearance from the Duty Officer of the Forth Navigation Service before the vessel commences to navigate.

(d) **Clearance to navigate** A clearance for a vessel shall cease to have effect 15 minutes after the time for which it was given. Accordingly, where a vessel has obtained a clearance but has not started to navigate the port in time before the clearance has ceased to have effect, the master must obtain a further clearance before the vessel starts to navigate.

Clearance of inward vessels

5. This direction applies to every inward-bound vessel which proposes to enter and navigate in the Forth.

(a) **Estimated Time of Arrival** The Master of a vessel shall advise the Forth Navigation Service not less than 24 hours in advance of the estimated time of arrival of the vessel at the Authority's Eastern limit or as soon as possible after departure from last port if less than 24 hour passage. Any adjustment to the ETA of two or more hours shall be reported in a like manner.

(b) **Vessels Carrying Dangerous or Polluting Goods** Whilst also complying with Statutory Instrument 2498, (The Merchant Shipping (Reporting Requirements for Ships carrying Dangerous or Polluting Goods) Regulations 1995), Masters of vessels carrying such cargoes (as defined by the International Maritime Dangerous Goods Code) shall also provide the following information in their pre-arrival report (sub-section (a) above) to Forth Navigation Service:

(1) Name of Vessel

(2) Summer Deadweight Tonnage

(3) Country of Registry

(4) Maximum Draught

(5) Cargo Type

(6) Last Port

(7) Destination Port

(8) ETA at Authority's Eastern limit, or anchorage

(9) Any defects, including defects and capability of vessel and/or personnel which may affect the safe navigation of the vessel.

(10) Confirmation that both anchors will be cleared and available for immediate use at all times when in the Firth of Forth.

(11) Confirmation that a pilotage passage plan has been prepared which will be discussed and agreed with the pilot on boarding.

(c) **Clearance to Navigate** The master of a vessel shall:

(1) On reaching the Authority's Eastern limit, contact Forth Navigation Service on VHF Channel 71, advising of vessel's estimated time of arrival at the pilot boarding position, or anchorage.

(2) Supply any further information as may be required by Forth Navigation Service. Masters are advised that Forth Navigation Service may seek verbal (tape-recorded) confirmation of any of the information previously given under sub-section (b) (1)–(10) of this Direction.

(3) Obtain clearance from Forth Navigation Service to proceed inwards towards pilot boarding position, designated anchorage area or other destination as agreed with Forth Navigation Service.

Use of South Channel

7. This direction applies to commercial and naval vessels having a gross tonnage of 50 tonnes or more and includes such vessels navigating between Leith and Granton to ports eastward in the Forth and vice versa. It does not apply to such vessels bound from Leith or Granton to Burntisland

and/or ports westward in the Forth and vice versa; nor does it apply to tugs, pilot vessels, lighthouse vessels, fishery protection and research vessels, dredgers and other small craft navigating in the Forth in the course of their normal duties.

When a vessel to which this direction applies is navigating in the Forth and is bound to or from the ports of Leith or Granton, it is recommended that the vessel should, when conditions are suitable, use the fairway which passes south of Inchkeith Island as shown on Admiralty Charts and designated South Channel.

Passage under the Forth Railway Bridge

8. This direction applies to vessels intending to pass under the Forth Railway Bridge.

(a) **Passing** No vessel may pass another vessel under the Forth Railway Bridge whether in conditions of good visibility or not. In the event of vessels approaching the Bridge from opposite directions, the outward bound vessel shall have priority of passage under the Bridge and the inbound vessel shall keep clear.

(b) **Reduced Visibility** In conditions where visibility is less than half a nautical mile, an inward bound vessel shall not, under any circumstances, pass number 19 Buoy, unless she has obtained clearance to do so from the Forth Navigation Service.

Movements of tankers of 50,000 deadweight tonnes or over

9. When a tanker having a deadweight tonnage of 50,000 tonnes or more is navigating the fairway between the Fairway Buoy and the vicinity of Hound Point, the following directions will apply:–

(a) **Priority** The outward bound tanker from Hound Point shall have right of way over any inward bound tanker for Hound Point.

(b) Passing:
  (1) No two tankers each having a deadweight tonnage of 50,000 tonnes or more shall pass each other when navigating the fairway west of No 7 buoy.
  (2) If either of the above tankers has a deadweight tonnage of 120,000 tonnes or more, then neither shall pass the other in the fairway west of Inchkeith.

(c) **Tug Escort:**
  (1) A tanker having a deadweight tonnage of 50,000 tonnes or more when sailing from Hound Point shall continue to be escorted by a tug until such tanker has reached No 5 buoy.
  (2) A tanker which is inward bound for Hound Point shall be escorted by a tug on reaching No 7 buoy.

(d) **Approach** Every tanker destined for Hound Point shall regulate its approach thereto so as not to arrive off the terminal before the agreed berthing time.
  (**Note:** *Movement of very large crude carriers ("VLCCs"). When an inward or outward bound VLCC is navigating the fairway between Fairway Buoy and the vicinity of Hound Point, it may be necessary to hold or slow down other vessels. Such regulation of movements shall usually be after liaison with Masters, Commanding Officers, or the pilots concerned but, in the event of disputes, the duty officer of the Forth Navigation Service will make the final decision.*)

Movements of all tankers destined for Braefoot Marine Terminal

10.(a) Movements of Liquefied Gas Carriers, Natural Gasoline Tankers, Bunker Fuel Vessels and other Tankers in the Forth which are bound to or from Braefoot Marine Terminal.

(1) Every tanker destined for Braefoot Marine Terminal shall regulate its approach thereto so as not to arrive off its berth before the agreed berthing time.

(2) When a tanker is entering or leaving the Forth Deep Water Channel via the Western approach to Mortimer's Deep, no other vessel shall approach within that section of the fairway lying between No 13 fairway buoy and an imaginary line drawn on the Admiralty Chart and joining Hound Point to Hopeward Point.

(3) When a tanker is entering or leaving the Forth Deep Water Channel via the Eastern approach to Mortimer's Deep, no other vessel shall approach within that section of the fairway lying between No 7 and No 11 fairway buoys.

(b) Movements of Liquefied Gas Carriers in excess of 145 metres in length (approximately 12 000 cubic metres capacity) when departing in loaded condition from Braefoot Marine Terminal.

(1) When such a tanker is departing through the Western approach to Mortimer's Deep, no other vessel shall pass in the opposite direction or overtake and pass or approach within one nautical mile of the tanker whilst she is in any estuary waters lying between an imaginary line drawn on the Admiralty Chart joining Hound Point to Hopeward Point and No 3 fairway buoy.

(2) When such a tanker is departing via the Eastern approach to Mortimer's Deep, no other vessel shall pass in the opposite direction or overtake and pass or approach within one nautical mile of the tanker whilst she is in any estuary waters lying between No 11 and No 3 fairway buoys.

(c) Movements of other vessels in the estuary.

(1) When tankers, either bound to or from Braefoot Marine Terminal, are navigating within or outwith the fairway between an imaginary line drawn on the Admiralty Chart and joining Hound Point to Hopeward Point and No 3 fairway buoy, it may be necessary to hold or slow down other vessels. In the event of inbound traffic being delayed, Forth Navigation Service may, at their discretion, direct vessels to a holding position not less than one mile North of No 3 fairway buoy until the outbound tanker is past and clear. Such regulation of movements shall usually be after liaison with the Masters, Commanding Officers or Pilots concerned but the Duty Officer at the Forth Navigation Service will make the final decision.

(2) Pleasure craft not exceeding 12 metres in length overall shall be exempt from directions 10(b) and 10(c) (1) of this Direction. Pleasure craft not exceeding 22 metres in length and carrying passengers for reward may, subject to the express approval of the Duty Officer at the Forth Navigation Service, be exempt from direction 10(b) of this Direction provided such craft are equipped with VHF radio capable of making contact with Forth Navigation Service and provided that they shall only enter, depart or navigate within Mortimer's Deep after obtaining prior clearance from Forth Navigation Service.

Movement of Selected Vessels bound to or from Grangemouth Docks

11.(a) **Hen & Chickens Buoy** Vessels shall not navigate within the fairway west of the Hen & Chickens Buoy, Longitude 03°38′·00 West without the express permission of the harbour master and when such a vessel is underway in the fairway no other vessel shall proceed in the opposite direction to the said vessel within that section of the fairway.

(b) Vessels are prohibited, except in the case of emergencies, from anchoring in the fairway west of Hen & Chickens Buoy.

(c) **Docking** Vessels will normally be locked into and out of the docks singly unless expressly permitted otherwise by the harbour master.

(d) When a vessel is manoeuvring in the docks, no other vessel shall proceed underway within the docks without the express permission of the harbour master.

(**Note:** *For the purposes of the Direction, a selected vessel is a vessel of more than 80 metres LOA which carries, in bulk, goods classified in the IMDG Code as being of Classes 2, 3.1, or 3.2. A vessel of more than 80 metres LOA which has residues in empty tanks or cargo holds which have been used for the carriage of such Classes (as above) and have not been cleaned, purged, gas freed or ventilated as appropriate, is also a selected vessel).*

Anchorages

13. The master of any vessel intending to anchor within the port shall inform the Forth Navigation Service of his intention to anchor and shall, if required by the Duty Officer, anchor his vessel in one of the anchorages detailed in the Appendix hereto and shall not move from such anchorage unless clearance to do so has been given by the Duty Officer.

(This note is not part of the Forth Byelaws.)

The Appendix to the Byelaws is not included in this volume; the anchorages are shown on the charts and mentioned in the text where appropriate. There are also a number of areas where anchoring is prohibited, which are also shown on the charts and mentioned in the text.

APPENDIX III

The Territorial Waters Order in Council 1964

AT THE COURT AT BUCKINGHAM PALACE

The 25th day of September 1964

Present,

THE QUEEN'S MOST EXCELLENT MAJESTY IN COUNCIL

Her Majesty, by virtue and in exercise of all the powers enabling Her in that behalf, is pleased, by and with the advice of Her Privy Council, to order, and it is hereby ordered, as follows:

1. This Order may be cited as the Territorial Waters Order in Council 1964 and shall come into operation on 30th September 1964.

2.-(1) Except as otherwise provided in Articles 3 and 4 of this Order, the baseline from which the breadth of the territorial sea adjacent to the United Kingdom, the Channel Islands and the Isle of Man is measured shall be the low-water line along the coast, including the coast of all islands comprised in those territories.

(2) For the purpose of this Article a low-tide elevation which lies wholly or partly within the breadth of sea which would be territorial sea if all low-tide elevations were disregarded for the purpose of the measurement of the breadth thereof and if Article 3 of this Order were omitted shall be treated as an island.

3.-(1) The baseline from which the breadth of the territorial sea is measured between Cape Wrath and the Mull of Kintyre shall consist of the series of straight lines drawn so as to join successively, in the order in which they are there set out, the points identified by the co-ordinates of latitude and longitude in the first column of the Schedule to this Order, each being a point situate on the low-water line and on or adjacent to the feature, if any, named in the second column of that Schedule opposite to the co-ordinates of latitude and longitude of the point in the first column.

(2) The provisions of paragraph (1) of this Article shall be without prejudice to the operation of Article 2 of this Order in relation to any island or low-tide elevation which for the purpose of that Article is treated as if it were an island, being an island or low-tide elevation which lies to seaward of the baseline specified in paragraph (1) of this Article.

4. In the case of the sea adjacent to a bay, the baseline from which the breadth of the territorial sea is measured shall, subject to the provisions of Article 3 of this Order—

    (a) if the bay has only one mouth and the distance between the low-water lines of the natural entrance points of the bay does not exceed 24 miles, be a straight line joining the said low-water lines;

    (b) if, because of the presence of islands, the bay has more than one mouth and the distances between the low-water lines of the natural entrance points of each mouth added together do not exceed 24 miles, be a series of straight lines across each of the mouths drawn so as to join the said low-water lines;

    (c) If neither paragraph (a) nor (b) of this Article applies, be a straight line 24 miles in length drawn from low-water line to low-water line within the bay in such a manner as to enclose the maximum area of water that is possible with a line of that length.

5.-(1) In this Order—

    the expression "bay" means an indentation of the coast such that its area is not less than that of the semi-circle whose diameter is a line drawn across the mouth of the indentation, and for the purposes of this definition the area of an indentation shall be taken to be the area bounded by the low-water line around the shore of the indentation and the straight line joining the low-water lines of its natural entrance points, and where, because of the presence of islands, an indentation has more than one mouth the length of the diameter of the semi-circle referred to shall be the sum of the lengths of the straight lines drawn across each of the mouths, and in calculating the area of an indentation the area of any islands lying within it shall be treated as part of the area of the indentation;

    the expression "island" means a naturally formed area of land surrounded by water which is above water at mean high-water spring tides; and

    the expression "low-tide elevation" means a naturally formed area of drying land surrounded by water which is below water at mean high-water spring tides.

(2) For the purpose of this Order, permanent harbour works which form an integral part of a harbour system shall be treated as forming part of the coast.

(3) The Interpretation Act 1889(a) shall apply to the interpretation of this Order as it applies to the interpretation of an Act of Parliament.

6. This Order shall be published in the *London Gazette*, the *Edinburgh Gazette* and the *Belfast Gazette*.

W.G. AGNEW

(a) 52 & 53 Vict.c.63.

EXPLANATORY NOTE

(This Note is not part of the Order, but it is intended to indicate its general purport).

This Order establishes the baseline from which the breadth of the territorial sea adjacent to the United Kingdom, the Channel Islands and the Isle of Man is measured. This, generally, is the low-water line round the coast, including the coast of all islands, but between Cape Wrath and the Mull of Kintyre a series of straight lines joining specified points lying generally on the seaward side of the islands lying off the coast are used, and where there are well defined bays elsewhere lines not exceeding 24 miles in length drawn across the bays are used.

TERRITORIAL SEA (AMENDMENT) ORDER 1998

For the schedule to the Territorial Waters Order in Council 1964 (a) there shall be substituted the schedule set out below:

SCHEDULE

POINTS BETWEEN CAPE WRATH AND LAGGAN JOINED BY GEODESICS TO FORM BASELINES

	Latitude North			Longitude West			Name of Feature
	°	′	″	°	′	″	
1.	58	37	40	5	00	13	Cape Wrath
2.	58	31	12	6	15	41	Lith-Sgeir
3.	58	30	44	6	16	55	Gealltuig
4.	58	29	09	6	20	17	Dell Rock
5.	58	18	28	6	47	45	Tiumpan Head
6.	58	17	36	6	52	43	Màs Sgeir
7.	58	17	09	6	55	20	Old Hill
8.	58	14	30	7	02	06	Gallan Head
9.	58	14	01	7	02	57	Islet SW of Gallan Head
10.	58	10	39	7	06	54	Eilean Molach
11.	57	59	08	7	17	42	Gasker
12.	57	41	19	7	43	13	Haskeir Eagach
13.	57	32	22	7	43	58	Huskeiran
14.	57	14	33	7	27	44	Rubha Ardvule
15.	57	00	50	7	31	42	Greuab Head
16.	56	58	07	7	33	24	Doirlinn Head
17.	56	56	57	7	34	17	Aird a' Chaolais
18.	56	56	05	7	34	55	Biruaslum
19.	56	49	21	7	39	32	Guarsay Mor
20.	56	48	00	7	39	57	Sron an Duin
21.	56	47	07	7	39	36	Skate Point
22.	56	19	17	7	07	02	Skerryvore
23.	56	07	58	6	38	00	Dubh Artach
24.	55	41	36	6	32	02	Frenchman's Rocks
25.	55	40	24	6	30	59	Orsay Island
26.	55	35	24	6	20	18	Mull of Oa
27.	55	17	57	5	47	54	Mull of Kintyre
28.	54	58	29	5	11	07	Laggan

The positions of points 1 to 28 are defined by co-ordinates of latitude and longitude on the Ordnance Survey of Great Britain (1936) Datum (OSGB 36).

The Territorial Waters (Amendment) Order 1996 (b) is hereby revoked.

N. H. Nicholls
Clerk of the Privy Council

EXPLANATORY NOTE

(This note is not part of the Order)

The Order amends the Schedule to the Territorial Waters Order in Council 1964 by adding a new baseline between Mull of Kintyre and Laggan, as well as making minor changes to points 5, 9 and 22, which result from the publication of a new, larger scale chart of the area.

(a) 1965 III, p.6452A; revised Schedules were substituted by the Territorial Waters (Amendment) Order in Council 1979 and the Territorial Sea (Amendment) Order 1996.

(b) SI 1996/1628

TERRITORIAL SEA ACT 1987

Be it enacted by the Queen's Most Excellent Majesty, by and with the advice and consent of the Lords Spiritual and Temporal, and Commons, in this present Parliament assembled, and by the authority of the same, as follows:

1.-(1) Subject to the provisions of this Act—

    (a) the breadth of the territorial sea adjacent to the United Kingdom for all purposes be 12 nautical miles; and

    (b) the baselines from which the breadth of that territorial sea is to be measured shall for all purposes be those established by Her Majesty by Order in Council.

(2) Her Majesty may, for the purpose of implementing any international agreement or otherwise, by Order in Council provide that any part of the territorial sea adjacent to the United Kingdom shall extend to such line other than that provided for by subsection (1) above as may be specified in the Order.

(3) In any legal proceedings a certificate issued by or under the authority of the Secretary of State stating the location of any baseline established under subsection (1) above shall be conclusive of what is stated in the certificate.

(4) As from the coming into force of this section the Territorial Waters Order in Council 1964 and the Territorial Waters (Amendment) Order in Council 1979 shall have effect for all purposes as if they were Orders in Council made by virtue of subsection (1)(b) above: and subsection (5) below shall apply to those Orders as it applies to any other instrument.

(5) Subject to the provisions of this Act, any enactment or instrument which (whether passed or made before or after the coming into force of this section) contains a reference (however worded) to the territorial sea adjacent to, or to any part of, the United Kingdom shall be construed in accordance with this section and with any provision made, or having effect as if made, under this section.

(6) Without prejudice to the operation of subsection (5) above in relation to a reference to the baselines from which the breadth of the territorial sea adjacent to the United Kingdom is measured, nothing in that subsection shall require any reference in any enactment or instrument to a specified distance to be construed as a reference to a distance equal to the breadth of that territorial sea.

(7) In this section "nautical miles" means international nautical miles of 1,852 metres.

2.-(1) Except in so far as Her Majesty may by Order of Council otherwise provide, nothing in section 1 above shall affect the operation of any enactment contained in a local Act passed before the date on which that section comes into force.

(2) Nothing in section 1 above, or in any Order in Council under that section or subsection (1) above, shall affect the operation of so much of any enactment passed or instrument made before the date on which that section comes into force as for the time being settles the limits within which any harbour authority or port health authority has jurisdiction or is able to exercise any power.

(3) Where any area which is not part of the territorial sea adjacent to the United Kingdom becomes part of that sea by virtue of section 1 above or an Order in Council under that section, subsection (2) of section 1 of the Continental Shelf Act 1964 (vesting and exercise of rights with respect to coal) shall continue, on and after the date on which section 1 above of that Order comes into force, to have effect with respect to coal in that area as if the area were not part of the territorial sea.

(4) Nothing in section 1 above, or in any Order in Council under that section, shall affect—

    (a) any regulations made under section 6 of the Petroleum (Production) Act 1934 before the date on which that section or Order comes into force; or

    (b) any licences granted under the said Act of 1934 before that date or granted on or after that date in pursuance of regulations made under that section before that date.

(5) In this section—

"coal" has the same meaning as in the Coal Industry Nationalisation Act 1946; "harbour authority" means a harbour authority within the meaning of the Harbours Act 1964 or the Harbours Act (Northern Ireland) 1970; and "port health authority" means a port health authority for the purposes of the Public Health (Control of Disease) Act 1984.

3.-(1) The enactments mentioned in Schedule 1 to this Act shall have effect with the amendments there specified (being minor amendments and amendments consequential on the provisions of this Act).

(2) Her Majesty may by Order in Council—

    (a) make, in relation to any enactment passed or instrument made before the date on which section 1 above comes into force, any amendment corresponding to any of those made by Schedule 1 to this Act;

    (b) amend subsection (1) of section 36 of the Wildlife and Countryside Act 1981 (marine nature reserves) so as to include such other parts of the territorial sea adjacent to Great Britain as may be specified in the Order in the waters and parts of the sea which, by virtue of paragraph 6 of Schedule 1 to this Act, may be designated under that section;

    (c) amend paragraph 1 of Article 20 of the Nature Conservation and Amenity Lands (North Ireland) Order 1985 (marine nature reserves) so as to include such other parts of the territorial sea adjacent to Northern Ireland as may be specified in the Order in the waters and parts of the sea which, by virtue of paragraph 9 of Schedule 1 to this Act, may be designated under that Article.

(3) Her Majesty may by Order in Council make such modifications of the effect of any Order in Council under section 1(7) of the Continental Shelf Act 1964 (designated areas) as appear to Her to be necessary or expedient in consequence of any provision made by or under this Act.

(4) The enactments mentioned in Schedule 2 to this Act are hereby repealed to the extent specified in the third column of that Schedule.

4.-(1) This Act may be cited as the Territorial Sea Act 1987.

(2) This Act shall come into force on such day as Her Majesty may by Order in Council appoint, and different days may be so appointed for different provisions and for different purposes.

(3) This Act extends to Northern Ireland.

(4) Her Majesty may by Order in Council direct that any of the provisions of this Act shall extend, with such exceptions, adaptations and modifications (if any) as may be specified in the Order, to any of the Channel Islands or to the Isle of Man.

INDEX

Abercorn Point	4.223	
Aberdeen	3.57	
Albert Basin	3.71	
Victoria Dock	3.71	
Aberdeen Bank	2.11	
Aberdeen Bay	3.60	
Aberdour	4.131	
Aberlady Bay	4.22	
Abertay Sands	3.193	
Abertay Spit	3.197	
Addlethorpe	8.24	
Aire and Calder Navigation	7.167	
Alloa	4.262	
Alloa Inch	4.264	
Almond, River	4.134	
Aln Harbour	5.163	
Alnmouth	5.163	
Alnmouth Bay	5.139	
Altarstones	3.261	
Amble	5.144	
Annachie Water	3.17	
Annat Bank	3.144	
Anstruther	3.258	
Anstruther Easter	3.254	
Anstruther Wester	3.254	
Anticyclones	1.105	
Ants, The	8.72	
Arbroath	3.162	
Arthur's Seat	4.54	
Auchmithie Bay	3.180	
B1D Dowsing	8.14	
Babbet Ness	3.245	
Bacton Gas Terminal	9.24	
Balcomie Brigs	3.245	
Balcomie Tower	3.235	
Bamburgh Castle	5.92	
Bar Flat	8.94	
Bar Sand	8.75	
Barley Picle	9.49	
Barnhill Bay	4.135	
Barns Ness	5.12	
Barns Ness Light	5.12	
Barnyard	5.139	
Barrow Haven	7.138	
Barry Sands	3.197	
Barton Haven	7.140	
Barton upon Humber	7.130	
Bass Rock	5.12	
Bass Rock Light	5.12	
Battery Point	4.189	
Bays, The	8.23	
Beacon Hill	6.51	
Beacon Point	5.178	
Beacon Point, Easington	6.51	
Beacon Rock	3.197	
Beadnell Bay	5.139	
Beadnell Harbour	5.165	
Beadnell Point	5.139	
Beal Point	5.88	
Beamer Rock	4.223	
Beamer Rock Light	4.208	
Beanstack	5.131	
Belhaven Bay	5.12	
Bell Rock	3.159	
Bell Rock Light	3.157	
Bellhouse Point	4.135	
Bellhues Rocks	5.211	
Bellman's Head	3.108	
Bempton Cliffs	6.202	
Benacre Ness	9.130	

Bervie Bay	3.122	
Bervie Brow	3.122	
Bervie Water	3.125	
Berwick Bay	5.88	
Berwick Lighthouse	5.39	
Berwick-upon-Tweed	5.59	
Big Bush	4.135	
Big Harcar	5.131	
Big Tom Light-beacon	8.96	
Bill Reach	5.239	
Billingham Oil Jetty	6.122	
Billow Ness	3.262	
Bink, The	8.31	
Binks, The	7.22	
Binn of Burntisland, The	4.106	
Binn's Tower	4.222	
Birkhill Bank	3.225	
Birling Carrs	5.139	
Black Devon	4.264	
Black Halls Point	6.51	
Black Halls Rocks	6.51	
Black Law	5.114	
Black Nab	6.173	
Black Ness	4.223	
Black Rocks	4.105	
Black Rocks Point	5.88	
Black Rocks Point Light	5.92	
Blackdog Rock	3.46	
Blackdyke	5.182	
Blackness	4.232	
Blackness Castle	4.222	
Blacktoft Channel	7.142	
Blae Rock	4.103	
Blakeney	8.40	
Blakeney Overfalls	8.20	
Blakeney Point	8.23	
Blaydon	5.215	
Blindman Rock	3.51	
Blue Caps	5.131	
Blyth	5.183	
East Pier Light	5.176	
Blyth, River: Blyth	5.183	
Blyth, River: Southwold	9.138	
Bo'ness	4.223	
Bo'ness Anchorage	4.231	
Bob Hall's Sand	8.31	
Boddin Point	3.159	
Bondicarr Bush	5.171	
Booth	7.144	
Borewell Chimney	5.42	
Boston	8.56	
Boston Deep	8.74	
Botney Cut	2.13	
Boulby	6.136	
Boulmer Bush	5.169	
Boulmer Haven	5.167	
Boulmer Stile	5.139	
Brachans	3.115	
Brada	5.131	
Braefoot Marine Terminal	4.136	
Braefoot Point	4.153	
Brancaster	8.37	
Brancaster Road	8.37	
Breydon Water	9.77	
Bridgeness Tower	4.222	
Bridgirdle	8.23	
Bridlington	6.212	
Bridlington Bay	6.204	
Brierdean Bushes	5.214	
Brig Head	5.182	
Brigg End	6.198	
Briggs	4.67	

Brimmond Hill	3.49	
Broken Bank	2.15	
Brothock Water	3.164	
Brough	7.133	
Broughty Castle	3.190	
Broughty Ferry	3.181	
Brown Point	5.205	
Brucehaven	4.225	
Brush Lighthouse	9.70	
Bruxie Hill	3.120	
Buchan Deep	3.3	
Buchan Ness	3.14	
Buchan Ness Light	3.12	
Buchanhaven	3.16	
Buchans, The	4.135	
Buckhaven	4.22	
Buckton Cliffs	6.202	
Buddo Ness	3.245	
Buddon Ness	3.192	
Budle Bay	5.88	
Budle Point	5.88	
Bull Anchorage	7.7	
Bull Channel	7.32	
Bull Light-float	7.32	
Bull Sand	7.32	
Bull Sand Fort	7.32	
Bullars of Buchan	3.56	
Burcom Sand	7.66	
Burcom Shoal	7.66	
Bure, River	9.77	
Burnham	8.38	
Burnham Flats	8.21	
Burnham Overy	8.38	
Burnham Ridge	8.21	
Burnmouth	5.83	
Burntisland	4.106	
Burrow Hole	5.114	
Bush	5.102	
Bush of Blackstanes	5.34	
Buss Creek	9.138	
Butterwick Low	8.75	
Caiplie	3.254	
Caiplie Rock	3.254	
Cairn-mon-earn	3.90	
Cairnie Pier	3.225	
Caister Road	9.47	
Caister Shoal	9.47	
Callers	5.94	
Calot Shad	5.75	
Cambo Ness	3.245	
Cambois Bay	5.171	
Cambuskenneth	4.254	
Camus Stone Law	3.197	
Canch, The	6.224	
Capernaum Point	4.225	
Captain Cook's Monument	6.138	
Car Craig	4.103	
Cargill Rock	5.34	
Carnoustie	3.159	
Carr End	5.125	
Carr Nase	6.198	
Carron	4.130	
Carron, River: Grangemouth	4.236	
Carron, River: Stonehaven	3.96	
Castle Eden Denes	6.45	
Castle Haven	3.152	
Castle Point: Dunstanburgh	5.139	
Castle Point: Holy Island	5.105	
Castlefoot Rock	5.24	
Castleford	7.167	
Castlehead Rocks	5.131	

Catterline 3.125
Cattersty Sands 6.165
Cayton Bay 6.198
Cellardyke 3.254
Chapel Ness 4.22
Chapel Rock 3.174
Charlestown 4.227
Charlestown Road Anchorage 4.230
Charts, charting 1.25
Cheek Bush 3.174
Chequer Shoal 7.20
Cheswick 5.88
Cheviot, The 5.96
Clachnaben 3.90
Clackmannan Tower 4.260
Clay Hole 8.75
Clay Huts 7.95
Cleadon Hill 6.12
Clee Ness Sand 7.32
Cleethorpes 7.32
Cley next the Sea 8.40
Climate and weather 1.101
Climatic tables 1.129
Closure of ports 1.42
Cloud 1.118
Cloughton Wyke 6.173
Coal Pit 2.14
Coastal conditions 1.2
Coatham 6.159
Cockenzie 4.47
Cockenzie Roads 4.47
Cockle Gatway 9.46
Cockle Shoal 9.46
Coldingham Bay 5.84
Collieston 3.54
Collingwood's Monument 5.251
Colville Rock 5.214
Coquet Flat 5.164
Coquet Island 5.139
Coquet Light 5.137
Coquet, River 5.143
Coquet Road 5.164
Cork Hole 8.121
Corsik Rock 4.47
Corton 9.85
Corton Road 9.90
Corton Sand 9.47
Cove 5.31
Cove Bay 3.92
Covehithe 9.128
Coves, The 3.254
Cow and Calves 4.94
Cowbar Nab 6.136
Cowie 3.115
Crab Law Rocks 5.182
Crabwater Rock 5.74
Crafords Gut 5.131
Crag Point 5.214
Craig David 3.122
Craig Ewan 3.17
Craig Harbour 3.230
Craig Heugh 4.20
Craig Waugh 4.66
Craigdimas 4.152
Craigielaw Point 4.22
Craigleith 5.12
Craigmaroinn 3.115
Craigmore Rocks 4.223
Crail 3.257
Cramond 4.134
Craster Harbour 5.162
Craster Skeres 5.3
Crawton Ness 3.122
Cresswell Hall 5.180
Cresswell Skeres 5.178

Crombie 4.223
Crombie Point 4.233
Cromer 8.42
Cromer Knoll 8.16
Cromer Light 8.14
Cross Keys Bridge 8.91
Cross Law 5.12
Cross Sand 9.37
Cruden, Bay of 3.45
Crumstone 5.94
Cullercoats 5.213
Cullernose Point 5.169
Culross 4.223
Currents 1.83
Curry Point 5.205
Customs 1.45

Dalgety Bay 4.153
Daseley's Sand 8.118
Daseley's Sled 8.120
Dee, River 3.57
Deil's Heid, The 3.159
Depressions 1.107
Devil's Hole 2.11
Dhu Craig 4.223
Dickenson's Point 6.190
Dickmont's Den 3.180
Dickmontlaw 3.157
Dicky Shad 5.3
Dimlington High Land 6.210
Distress and rescue
    General 1.51
    Lifeboats 1.60
Docking Shoal 8.20
Dods Bank 4.223
Dog Rock 4.223
Dogger Bank 2.13
Dogger Rocks 6.45
Doig Rock 4.189
Dolly Peg Light-beacon 8.75
Don, River 3.51
Doncaster 7.167
Donibristle Bay 4.193
Donna Nook 7.1
Doolie Ness 3.152
Doon Hill 5.14
Doonie Point 3.115
Dour Burn 4.131
Dovehole Scar 6.190
Downie Point 3.92
Downing Point 4.153
Drum Flat 4.171
Drum Sand 4.171
Drumcarrow Craig 3.241
Druridge Bay 5.171
Dudgeon Light-buoy 8.14
Dudgeon Shoal 8.18
Dunbar 5.15
    Old Harbour 5.23
    Victoria Harbour 5.16
Dunbar Roads 5.22
Dunbuy Rock 3.56
Dundee 3.198
    Camperdown Dock 3.211
    Victoria Dock 3.211
Dundee Law 3.190
Dunglass Mansion 5.31
Dunnottar Castle 3.107
Dunston Staiths 5.251
Dunstanburgh Castle 5.139
Dysart 4.45

Earn, River 3.230
Easby Moor 6.138

Easington Heights 6.136
East Dudgeon Shoals 8.16
East Halton Skitter 7.105
East Haven 3.180
East Lomond 3.252
East Marsh 7.107
East Stones Light-beacon 8.118
East Vows 4.22
East Wideopen 5.102
Eastermost Rough 2.13
Ebb Carrs 5.86
Eden, River 3.232
Edinburgh 4.52
Edinburgh Castle 4.101
Elbow: (55°38′N, 1°40′W) 5.131
Elbow: Buddon Ness 3.192
Elie Bay 4.50
Elie Ness 3.254
Elie Ness Light 3.252
Elliot Horses 3.159
Elliot Water 3.159
Elswick Reach 5.251
Emblestone 5.166
Embleton Bay 5.139
Emmanuel Head 5.94
Esk, River: Musselburgh 4.48
Esk, River: Whitby 6.141
Esk Vale 6.155
Eston Nab 6.138
Ethie Haven 3.179
Examination Service 1.44
Exercises 1.20
Eye, River 5.43
Eyebroughy 4.22
Eyemouth 5.43

Faggot 5.139
Falls, The 5.94
False Emmanuel Head 5.131
Familars Rocks 4.135
Fang 5.102
Farne Deeps 5.3
Farne Island 5.99
Farne Island Light 5.92
Farne Islands 5.88
Farne Sound 5.88
Fast Castle 5.12
Fast Castle Head 5.12
Faxfleet 7.142
Felling Reach 5.239
Fenham Flats 5.88
Ferny Ness 4.51
Feshes 6.200
Fidra 4.22
Fidra Light 4.20
Fife Ness 3.237
Fife Ness Light 3.235
Filey 6.200
Filey Bay 6.200
Filey Brigg 6.198
Fills 5.139
Findon 3.92
Findon Ness 3.92
Firth of Forth 4.1
    Forth Ports PLC 4.2
    Forth Railway Bridge 4.172
    Forth Road Bridge 4.172
    Pilotage 4.4
Fisherrow 4.48
Fisherrow Sand 4.48
Fishery limits 1.67
Fishing 1.10
Flamborough Head 6.198
    Lighthouse 6.196
Flamborough Steel 6.198
Flisk Point 3.230

Flixborough 7.165
Fluke Hole 5.168
Fog and Visibility 1.123
Forvie, Sands of 3.54
Fosdyke Bridge 8.83
Fosdyke Port 8.83
Fosdyke Wash 8.83
Foul Holme Sand 7.107
Foul Holme Spit 7.95
Freeman Channel 8.72
Freestone Point 5.251
Friarton Road Bridge 3.225
Friskney Flats 8.74
Fronts 1.109
Fulney 8.84

Gaa Sand 3.192
Gaa Spit 3.192
Gainsborough 7.166
Gales 1.115
Garron Point 3.92
Garron Rock 3.92
Garvock, Hill of 3.120
Gat Channel 8.78
Gat Sand 8.78
Gateshead 5.215
Gellet Rock 4.233
George Point 5.213
Gibraltar Point 8.44
Gin Head 5.34
Girdle Ness 3.92
Girdle Ness Light 3.49
Girdle Wears, The 3.14
Girdlestone 3.92
Glenury Viaduct 3.107
Glororum 5.129
Glororum Shad 5.102
Goldstone 5.94
Goldstone Channel 5.100
Goole 7.145
Gore Middle 8.23
Gore Point 8.44
Gorleston Road 9.89
Gorleston-on-Sea 9.51
Gosford House 4.23
Goswick Bay 5.131
Goswick Links 5.92
Goswick Sands 5.88
Gourdon 3.126
Granary Point 5.130
Grangemouth 4.234
    Eastern Channel 4.248
    Grange Dock 4.248
Granton 4.74
Great Car 5.12
Great Carr 5.162
Great Ouse, River 8.122
Great Yarmouth 9.51
Great Yarmouth Haven 9.52
Green Scalp 3.193
Greenheugh Point 5.34
Greg Ness 3.92
Grey Mare 3.56
Grim Brigs 3.92
Grimsby 7.34
    Fish Dock 7.49
    Royal Dock 7.49
Grimsby Middle 7.66
Grimsby Road 7.66
Grimstone 5.94
Grove 7.165
Guardbridge 3.239
Guardy 5.34
Guile Point 5.105
Gullane House 4.20

Gullane Point 4.22
Gun Hill 8.38
Gun Rocks 5.102
Gunness 7.165
Gunnet Ledge 4.103
Gunsgreen Point 5.41
Guzzard 5.97

Hackley Head 3.51
Haddock Bank 9.14
Hadston Carrs 5.182
Haile Anchorage 7.7
Haile Channel 7.32
Haile Sand 7.32
Haile Sand Flat 7.20
Haile Sand Fort 7.20
Haisborough Gat 9.30
Haisborough Sand 9.24
Haisborough Tail 9.37
Half Ebb Rock 5.25
Halidon Hill 5.36
Hallgreen Castle 3.124
Halton Marshes 7.107
Halton Middle 7.95
Hamilton Hill 6.230
Hammond Knoll 9.37
Happisburgh 9.17
Happisburgh Lighthouse 9.24
Hare Law 3.197
Hare Ness 3.115
Hare Point 5.36
Harkness Rocks 5.131
Hartlepool 6.70
    Victoria Harbour 6.93
Hartlepool Bay 6.74
Hartlepool Peninsula 6.51
Hasman Rock 3.92
Hauxley Haven 5.181
Hauxley Head 5.178
Hauxley Point 5.171
Hawes Pier 4.191
Hawkcraig Point 4.152
Hawke Anchorage 7.33
Hawke Channel 7.65
Hawkin's Point 7.65
Hayburn Wyke 6.173
Haystack 4.153
Hearty Knoll 9.37
Hebbles, The 7.96
Hebburn 5.215
Heckles, The 4.51
Hedon Haven 7.106
Heiferlaw 5.137
Hempstead 9.17
Hemsby Hole 9.48
Hen and Chickens 4.223
Hendon Rock 6.51
Hepburn Hill 5.137
Herd Groyne 5.238
    Light 5.235
Herring Hill 8.83
Herwit 4.66
Hessle Haven 7.139
Hettle Scar 5.55
Heuchboy 4.103
Heugh Beacon 5.114
Heugh Hill 5.114
Heugh, The 6.51
    Light 6.49
Heughs of St Cyrus 3.122
Hewett Ridges 9.14
High Brigg 6.198
High Cape 8.31
High Sand, The 8.23
High Stone 6.159

High, The 6.136
Hill of Auchlee 3.90
Hills, The 2.13
Hilston Tower 6.211
Hinkar 5.54
Holbeach Firing Danger Area 8.46
Hole Mouth 5.108
Holkham Bay 8.39
Holkham Marshes 8.31
Holm Channel 9.88
Holm Sand 9.37
Holme 8.52
Holme Ridge 7.67
Holy Island 5.88
    Harbour 5.103
Holy Island Castle 5.92
Holy Island Sands 5.88
Hook Hill 8.72
Hopetoun Monument 4.20
Horden Point 6.69
Hornsea Gap 6.210
Horsbridge Head 5.182
Horse Shoe 3.193
Houghton Stile 5.169
Hound Point 4.171
Hound Point Marine Terminal 4.174
Howden Dyke 7.157
Hull 7.108
    King George Dock 7.121
    Old Harbour 7.115
    Queen Elizabeth Dock 7.121
Hull Middle 7.96
Hull, River 7.98
Hull Road 7.98
Hull Sand 8.118
Humber Bridge 7.130
Humber Light-buoy 7.19
Humber, River 7.1
    Pilotage 7.2
    Tidal streams 7.9
    VTS 7.4
Humber Sea Terminal 7.101
Humidity 1.128
Hummel Rocks 4.135
Hundale Point 6.173
Hunstanton 8.44
Hunt Cliff 6.136
Hurkars 5.54
Hurst 3.254

Ice 1.7
Ice Carr 5.139
Immingham 7.71
    Bulk Terminal 7.85
    Dock 7.84
    Gas Terminal 7.87
    Humber International Terminal 7.60
    Oil Terminal 7.83
Inch Brake 4.259
Inch Garvie 4.172
Inchcolm 4.103
Inchcolm Light 4.105
Inchkeith 4.128
Inchkeith Light 4.20
Inchmickery 4.103
Incinerator vessels 1.9
Indefatigable Banks 2.15
Ingham 9.25
Ingoldmells Point 8.22
Inlandpasture Chimney 5.42
Inner Bank 2.15
Inner Bell Rock 5.214
Inner Buss 5.54
Inner Cromer Knoll 9.14
Inner Dogs Head 8.51
Inner Dowsing 8.19

Inner Dowsing Light-vessel 8.14
Inner Dowsing Overfalls 8.22
Inner Hirst 5.131
Inner Knock 8.22
Inner Sound 5.99
Inner Westmark Knock 8.95
Inscar Point 6.91
Inverbervie 3.122
Inverkeithing 4.189
Iron Craig 4.135
Isle of May 3.247
Isle of May Light 3.252
Islestone 5.99
Islestone Shad 5.102

Jarrow 5.215
Jarrow Slake 5.251
Jenny Bell's Carr 5.169
Jim Howe Bank 2.15
Job's Craig 3.152
Jock's Hole 3.230
Johnshaven 3.127
Johnston, Tower of 3.120

Keadby 7.164
Keith Inch 3.20
  Leading Light 3.35
Kelder Steel 6.136
Kellie Law 3.252
Keptie Hill 3.173
Kessingland 9.128
Kettle Ness 6.136
Kettle, The 5.129
Kiel Burn 4.43
Killingholme, North 7.102
Killingholme, South 7.99
Kilminning Craig 3.255
Kilnsea 6.211
Kincardine 4.261
Kincardine Bridge 4.259
Kincraig Point 4.22
Kiness Burn 3.240
King and Queen Rocks 6.198
King's Ferry 7.165
King's Lynn 8.101
Kinghorn Ness 4.103
Kingsbarn 3.238
Kingston upon Hull 7.108
Kinkell Ness 3.235
Kirk Haven 3.261
Kirkcaldy 4.42
Kirktown of Slains 3.54
Kirktown Spire 3.33
Kirton Head 3.14
Knapton 9.25
Knivestone 5.90
Knock 8.23
Knocks Reef 5.102
Knot, The 5.182
Knuckle Rock 3.174

Lade Way 6.159
Lady Ground 5.12
Lady Shoal 3.193
Lady's Folly 3.262
Lamb 5.12
Lamberton Hill 5.36
Lammerlaws Point 4.103
Largo 4.43
Largo Bay 4.22
Largo Law 3.252
Larick Scalp 3.193
Lathallan School 3.124
Lawe, The 5.238
Lawyer's Creek 8.46
Leeds 7.167
Leith 4.52
  Docks 4.70
  Outer Harbour 4.69
  Western Harbour 4.69
Leith Road 4.67
Leith Sands 4.67
Leithies, The 5.34
Leman Bank 9.14
Lemington 5.215
Lessingham 9.25
Leven 4.44
Leven, River 4.44
Liddle Scars 6.65
Limekiln Rock 4.135
Limekilns 4.226
Limits of the Book 1.1
Link End 5.178
Little Carr 5.162
Little Craigs 4.135
Little Harcar 5.131
Little Herwit 4.66
Little Scar 6.100
Lizard Point 6.14
Long Batt 5.131
Long Craig: (56°01′N, 3°08′W) 4.135
Long Craig: (56°41′N, 2°27′W) 3.180
Long Drax 7.158
Long Forties 2.11
Long Nab 6.173
Long Reach 5.239
Long Sand 8.51
Long Scar 6.90
Longannet Point 4.259
Longhoughton Steel 5.139
Longstone 5.94
Longstone Lighthouse 5.92
Lothing, Lake 9.107
Louis Rocky Patch 6.51
Low Newton-by-the-Sea 5.166
Low Torry 4.223
Lower Road 8.75
Lowestoft 9.92
Lowestoft and Norwich Navigation . 9.121
Lowestoft Bank 9.113
Lowestoft Light 9.12
Lowestoft Ness 9.80
Lowestoft North Road 9.90
Lucky Scalp 3.193
Luff Hard Rock 5.54
Luff Way 6.159
Lunan Bay 3.179
Lundin, Pier of 4.43
Lundin, Standing Stones of 4.51
Lynn Cut 8.122
Lynn Deeps 8.51
Lynn Knock 8.21
Lythe 6.138

Mablethorpe 8.22
Macduff's Castle 4.101
Maiden Paps 6.69
Maidenfoot, The 5.30
Man Haven 6.14
Mappleton 6.211
Marden Rocks 5.168
Marine exploitation 1.21
Marischal College 3.73
Maritime topography 1.82
Marmouth Scars 5.167
Marmouth, The 5.167
Marr Bank 2.11
Marsden Bay 6.14
Marsden Point 6.14
Marsden Rock 6.14
Marshall Meadows Bay 5.85
Maw Carr 5.82
Meadulse Rocks 4.103
Megstone 5.97
Methil 4.24
Mexborough 7.167
Middens 4.135
Middle Bank: Forth 4.103
Middle Bank: Wash 8.23
Middle Cross Sand 9.37
Middle Ground 9.38
Middle Shoal 7.32
Middlehaven 6.122
Middleton Breakwater 6.91
Mile Hill 5.214
Mill Rock 6.14
Milsey Bay 5.34
Milton Ness 3.122
Minscore 5.131
Monifieth 3.197
Monifieth Sands 3.197
Montrose 3.128
Montrose Basin 3.141
Moorstack 6.45
Mormond Hill 3.12
Morrison's Haven 4.51
Morston 8.24
Mortimer's Deep 4.138
Mossmorran 4.137
Muchalls 3.92
Mugdrum Island 3.217
Mundesley 9.22
Musselburgh 4.48
Musselburgh Road 4.48
Musselburgh Sand 4.48
Mutton Rock 3.92
My Lord's Bank 3.225

Narrow Deep 4.66
Narrows, The 5.238
Neap House 7.165
Nelson's Monument 4.65
Nene, River 8.96
New Cut 8.75
New Holland 7.137
New S Pier 6.31
New Sand Hole 7.13
Newark Castle 3.255
Newarp Banks 9.37
Newarp Light-vessel 9.25
Newbiggin Bay 5.181
Newbiggin Ness 5.178
Newbiggin Point 5.178
Newburgh: (56°21′N, 3°41′W) 3.230
Newburgh: (57°19′N, 2°00′W) 3.55
Newcastle 5.245
  Bridges 5.240
Newcome Sand 9.114
Newcome Shoal 3.194
Newhaven Harbour 4.92
Newport-on-Tay 3.223
Newton Haven 5.166
Newton Hill 5.95
Newton Skere 5.3
Newtonhill 3.92
Nick Cove 5.34
Nigg Bay 3.95
Nob 5.107
North Beanstack 5.131
North Berwick 5.30
North Berwick Law 5.10
North Carr Rock 3.237
North Channel 4.103
North Cheek 6.173
North Cliffs 6.202

North Craig 4.66
North Cross Sand 9.37
North East Bush 5.139
North East Bush, Seaham 6.65
North Gare Breakwater 6.120
North Head 3.14
North Head Rock 3.14
North Landing 6.201
North Queensferry 4.190
North Ridge 8.18
North Scar 6.65
North Sea: Oil and Gas fields 2.17
North Shields 5.215
North Smithic Shoal 6.210
North Sunderland 5.116
North Sunderland Lighthouse 5.97
North Tours 5.131
North Wamses 5.102
Northern Hares 5.131
Northern Hill 5.178

Old Horse Rocks 6.192
Old Law 5.105
    East Beacon 5.113
    West Beacon 5.113
Old Lynn Channel 8.119
Old Lynn Road 8.119
Old Nab 6.136
Old Slains Castle 3.51
Old South Sand 8.95
Oulton Broad 9.121
Ouse, River 7.142
    Bridges 7.144
Out Carr 5.169
Out Head 3.245
Outer Bell Rock 5.214
Outer Binks 7.19
Outer Dogs Head 8.22
Outer Dowsing Channel 8.16
Outer Dowsing Shoal 8.16
Outer Knock 8.22
Outer Silver Pit 2.13
Outer Tours 5.94
Outer Well Bank 2.13
Outer Westmark Knock 8.95
Outer Wingate 5.100
Overstrand 9.26
Ower Bank 2.15
Ox Rock 3.262
Oxcars 4.103
Oxcars Bank 4.103
Oxcars Light 4.105
Oxscar 5.98

Pakefield 9.116
Pan Bush 5.156
Pan Point 5.157
Pan Rocks 5.157
Pandora Sand 8.121
Park Dyke 5.94
Parlour Channel 8.53
Parton Stiel 5.113
Pathead Bay 4.101
Paull Sand 7.95
Pease Bay 5.12
Peat, The 3.230
Peffer Burn 4.50
Peffer Sands 5.12
Perilous Rocks 6.190
Perth 3.226
Peterhead 3.18
    Harbour 3.31
Peterhead Bay 3.20
    Harbour 3.31

Pettico Wick 5.33
Pettycur 4.129
Pigs, The 5.182
Pilotage, General 1.28
Pincushion Rock 6.51
Pinnacles 5.102
Pitscur Buss 3.56
Pittenweem 3.259
Plough Rock 5.100
Plough Seat Reef 5.100
Podler Ware Spit 5.141
Podlie Craig 5.34
Pollard 8.23
Pollution of the sea 1.39
Port Edgar 4.192
Port Erroll 3.53
Port Mulgrave 6.162
Port Services summary 1.76
Port Seton 4.46
Port Sutton Bridge 8.100
Portlethen 3.92
Portobello 4.48
Position fixing systems 1.32
Precipitation 1.119
Pressure 1.103
Prestonhill Quarry Terminal 4.189
Principal Ports 1.75
Protection of wildlife 1.48
Protector Overfalls 8.17
Pyewipe Flats 7.70

Quarantine 1.45
Queen Alexandra Bridge 6.23
Queen's Road 3.230
Queensferry 4.191

Race Bank 8.20
Ramsdale Scar 6.186
Rath Grounds 5.34
Rattray Bay 3.14
Rattray Briggs 3.17
Rattray Hard 3.14
Rattray Head 3.14
Rattray Head Light 3.12
Ravenscar 6.173
Ravenscraig Castle 4.101
Red Brae 5.139
Red Castle 3.161
Red Head 3.159
Redcar 6.159
Redcar Sands 6.159
Redcliff 6.136
Redheugh 5.33
Ridge End 5.100
Ridge, The 9.113
Roaring Middle 8.94
Roaring Middle Light-float 8.51
Robin Hood's Bay 6.173
Rockers, The 5.182
Rockheads 4.42
Rodgers, The 5.34
Roger Sand 8.72
Roker Cliff 6.8
Roker Pier 6.31
Roker Pier Lighthouse 6.12
Ron, The 3.12
Roome Bight 3.254
Roome Ness 3.254
Ross Carrs 5.41
Ross Links 5.88
Ross Low 5.131
Ross Point 4.135
Rosse Spit 7.23
Rost Bank 4.103

Rosyth 4.195
    Anchorage 4.229
    Dockyard Port 4.10
    Main Basin 4.211
    Main Channel 4.209
    Tidal berths 4.211
Rosyth Castle 4.208
Rotherham 7.167
Ruddon's Point 4.23
Ruddystone 5.12
Run, The 8.31
Runswick Bay 6.163
Ryehope Pumping Station 6.49

Safe harbours 1.6
Saint Abb's Boat Harbour 5.82
Saint Abb's Head 5.12
Saint Abb's Head Light 5.10
Saint Anthony's Bush 4.135
Saint Anthony's Reach 5.239
Saint Colm's Abbey 4.105
Saint Cuthbert's Islet 5.112
Saint Cuthbert's Tower 5.129
Saint Cyrus 3.124
Saint David's 4.188
    Direction Light 4.189
Saint Edmund's Point 8.44
Saint Mary's Island 5.211
Saint Nicholas Rock 5.94
Saint Peter's Reach 5.239
Salisbury Craigs 4.65
Salt End 7.103
Salt Scar 6.136
Saltburn 6.131
Saltburn Scar 6.136
Salterfen Rocks 6.51
Saltfleet 8.34
Saltfleet Overfalls 8.22
Salthouse 8.24
Salthouse Head 3.20
Saltwick Nab 6.173
Sand Ridge 5.88
Sandford Bay 3.34
Sandsend Ness 6.136
Sandsend Road 6.164
Sandstell Point 5.61
Sandy Batt 6.159
Satan Bush 5.12
Scalby Ness 6.173
Scalp Bank 3.4
Scalp, The 8.83
Scar, The 6.153
Scarborough 6.174
Scarborough Bay 6.176
Scarborough Castle 6.171
Scarborough Rock 6.173
Scars, The 5.182
Scart Rock 5.24
Scaup, The 3.141
Scolt Head 8.23
Scotsman's Sled 8.119
Scotstown Hard 3.14
Scotstown Head 3.14
Scotswood 5.215
Scott Patch 8.21
Scoughall Road 5.32
Scroby Shoals 9.47
Scurdie Ness 3.122
Scurdie Ness Light 3.120
Scurdie Rocks 3.122
Sea conditions 1.95
Sea level 1.88
Sea Palling 9.17
Sea water characteristics 1.97
Seafield Vows 4.135
Seaham 6.52

Seahouses 5.116
Seal Carr: Berwick 5.41
Seal Carr: Forth 4.135
Seal Craig 3.92
Seal Sand 8.118
Seal Skears 5.182
Seal Spit 5.114
Seaton Point 5.139
Seaton Sea Rocks 5.182
Seaton Shad 5.139
Seaton Sluice 5.205
Seaton-on-Tees 6.114
Seggieden 3.230
Selby 7.159
Selwicks Bay 6.201
Sewerby Hall 6.227
Shaper's Head 5.41
Sharpness Point 5.214
Sheringham 8.41
Sheringham Shoal 8.16
Shield Rock 3.254
Shields Harbour Reach 5.239
Shieldhill 3.122
Shirlaw Pike 5.180
Shoreston Outcars 5.99
Sicar 5.12
Siccar Point 5.34
Sidestrand 9.28
Sillo Craig 3.180
Silver Pit 8.16
Silversands Bay 4.135
Skares, The 3.51
Skate Hole 2.13
Skate Road 5.108
Skateraw 5.12
Skatie Shore 3.92
Skegness 8.22
Skegness Middle 8.22
Skellies, The 3.240
Skelly Rock 3.56
Skerry, The 3.14
Skinfast Haven 3.262
Skinningrove 6.131
Skinningrove Wick 6.160
Skipsea 6.211
Skitter Ness 7.96
Skitter Sand 7.96
Slains Lodge 3.51
Sledway 8.23
Smiths Knoll 9.14
Smiths Knoll Light-buoy 9.12
Snab Point 5.171
Sneaton Castle 6.152
Snettisham 8.49
Snettisham Scalp 8.44
Snipe Point 5.88
Snook 5.94
Snook Point 5.139
Snook, The 5.88
Society Bank 4.223
Sole Pit 2.14
Souter Lighthouse 6.12
Souter Point 6.14
South Carr 5.41
South Carr Beacon 5.12
South Channel 4.66
South Cheek 6.173
South Cross Sand 9.37
South Esk, River 3.128
South Gare Breakwater 6.120
  Light 6.118
South Goldstone 5.98
South Head 3.14
South Landing 6.224
South Low 5.131

South Shields 5.215
South Smithic Shoal 6.210
South Steel 6.190
South Sunk Sand 8.51
South Wamses 5.102
South West Patch 2.13
South West Spit 2.13
South Yorkshire Navigation 7.167
Southend Rock 5.125
Southwold 9.131
Southwold Light 9.12
Sow, The 5.182
Spalding 8.84
Spital Point 5.181
Spittal 5.59
Spittal Hirst 5.3
Spittal Point 5.61
Spurn Head 7.22
  Lighthouse 6.208
Spurn Light-float 7.19
St Andrew's 3.240
St Andrew's Bay 3.232
St Monance; see St Monans 3.260
St Monans 3.260
Staithes 6.161
Stallingborough Flat 7.67
Stallingborough Haven 7.70
Stanford Channel 9.114
Staple Island 5.102
Staple Sound 5.102
Stanford Channel 9.114
Steel Bush 5.139
Steeping, River 8.55
Steeples, The 5.25
Steetly Magnesite Works 6.49
Stiel Reef 5.94
Stiffkey 8.24
Stiffkey Overfalls 8.23
Stirling 4.263
Stirling Hill 3.52
Stone Creek 7.69
Stone Ridge 5.114
Stonehaven 3.96
Stonehaven Bay 3.92
Stones, The 6.91
Stow Hill 9.25
Strabathie, Hill of 3.49
Strathlethan Bay 3.122
Stubb Rock 5.13
Stylemans Middle 8.121
Submarine pipelines 1.36
Submarine cables 1.38
Sunderland 6.17
  Harbour 6.31
  Hendon Dock 6.39
  Hudson Dock 6.39
  Railway Bridge 6.23
Sunk Channel 7.65
Sunk Island 7.65
Sunk Sand: Humber 7.65
Sunk Sand: Wash 8.51
Sunk Spit 7.70
Sutton Bridge 8.100
Swallow Craig 4.135
Swarte Bank 2.15
Swedman 5.98

Tabs Head Light-beacon 8.75
Tancred Bank 4.223
Tantallon Castle 5.14
Tay Railway Bridge 3.224
Tay, River 3.181
Tay Road Bridge 3.222
Tayport Harbour 3.195
Tayport High Direction Light 3.190

Tees Bay 6.98
Tees Bridge 6.106, 6.122
Tees, River 6.100
Tees, River Barrage 6.106
Teesport 6.100
  Berths 6.123
Teetotal Channel 8.118
Temperature 1.125
Tentsmuir Point 3.193
Tentsmuir Sands 3.232
Territorial waters 1.66
Tetney Haven 7.25
Tetney Haven Oil Terminal 7.24
Tetney Monobuoy 7.24
Thank Rock 4.194
Theddlethorpe Overfalls 8.22
Thief Sand 8.118
Thill Rock 4.22
Thorngumbald Clough 7.95
Thornham 8.36
Tidal streams 1.85
Tides 1.91
Titchwell 8.24
Tod Head 3.122
Tod Point 6.120
Todhead Point 3.122
Todhead Point Light 3.120
Toft Sand 8.72
Torness Point 5.12
Torry Bay 4.223
Totties 3.115
Tours 5.94
Traprain Law 5.10
Tree o'the House 5.97
Trent Falls 7.160
Trent, River 7.160
Trial Bank 8.93
Trimingham 9.22
Trinity Sand 7.65
Triton Knoll 8.18
Triton Shoal 5.113
Trow Point 6.16
Trunch 9.25
Trusthorpe Overfalls 8.22
Tullibody Inch 4.264
Tunstall 6.211
Turbot Bank 2.11
Tweed, River 5.61
Tweedmouth 5.59
Tyne, Port of 5.215
Tyne, River 5.215
Tyne Sands 5.12
Tynemouth 5.215
  North Pierhead Light 5.209
  Riverside Quay 5.222
Tynemouth Head 5.236

Ugie, River 3.16
Ulrome 6.211
Upgang Rocks 6.153
Upper Taylorton 4.254
Usan Ness 3.159

Vault Point 4.152
Vaultness 5.34
Vessel traffic 1.8
Vincent's Pier 6.185

Wainfleet 8.55
Wainfleet Road 8.73
Wainfleet Sand 8.74
Wainfleet Swatchway 8.73
Wakefield 7.167
Wallace's Head 5.25
Wallsend 5.215

Wansbeck, River 5.171
Ward Point 3.51
Warden Law 6.69
Warkworth 5.143
  Harbour 5.153
Warkworth Castle 5.137
Warnham Bar 5.130
Warnham Flats 5.88
Warren Burn 5.130
Warren Mill 5.130
Warsett Hill 6.136
Wash, The 8.44
Water of Leith 4.52
Waveney, River 9.77
Waxham 9.17
Wear, River 6.8
Wearmouth Bridge 6.23
Wee Bankie 3.5
Well Bank 2.15
Well Hole 2.14
Well, The 8.51
Welland Cut 8.83
Welland Light-beacon 8.75
Welland, River 8.83
Wells 8.25
Wemyss Castle 4.101
West Bank Light-beacon 8.118
West End Light-beacon 8.96

West Haven 3.180
West Lomond 3.252
West Ness 3.254
West Sand 8.23
West Sands 8.31
West Scar 6.136
West Stones Light-beacon 8.118
West Vows 4.22
West Wideopen 5.102
Weybourne 8.24
Whale Back 4.223
Wheel Shoal 5.114
Whirl Rocks 5.94
Whitberry Point 5.12
Whitburn Bay 6.8
Whitburn Rifle Range 6.9
Whitburn Steel 6.14
Whitby 6.139
Whitby High Light 6.134
Whitby Road 6.153
Whitby Rock 6.153
White Bank 5.182
White Nab 6.176
White Stones 6.51
Whitebooth Road 7.95
Whitehouse Point 4.187
Whiting Middle 8.119
Whiting Ness 3.154

Whiting Shoal 8.119
Whitley Bay 5.211
Whitley Shad 5.214
Wildfire Rocks 5.34
Winds 1.110
Windylaw Cove 5.34
Wingate 5.100
Winteringham Haven 7.141
Winterton Ness 9.24
Winterton Overfalls 9.46
Winterton Ridge 9.37
Winterton Shoal 9.37
Winterton-on-Sea 9.24
Wisbech 8.85
Wisbech Channel 8.95
Wisbech Cut 8.96
Witham, River 8.77
  Navigation 8.81
Withernsea 6.210
Woolpack 8.23
Would, The 9.24
Wrangle Flats 8.74

Yare, River 9.71
Yarmouth Road 9.47
Yellow Craig 5.86
Yons Nab 6.198
Ythan, River 3.55

NOTES

NOTES

NOTES

NOTES

NOTES

PUBLICATIONS OF THE
UNITED KINGDOM HYDROGRAPHIC OFFICE

A complete list of Sailing Directions, Charts and other works published by the Hydrographer of the Navy, together with a list of Agents for their sale, is contained in the "Catalogue of Admiralty Charts and Publications", published annually. The list of Admiralty Distributors is also promulgated in Admiralty Notice to Mariners No 2 of each year, or it can be obtained from:

The United Kingdom Hydrographic Office,
Admiralty Way,
Taunton, Somerset
TA1 2DN

Produced in the United Kingdom
for UKHO by Pindar plc